HANDEL AND THE ENGLI

Handel and the English Chapel Royal

DONALD BURROWS

OXFORD
UNIVERSITY PRESS

OXFORD

UNIVERSITY PRESS

Great Clarendon Street, Oxford OX2 6DP

Oxford University Press is a department of the University of Oxford.
It furthers the University's objective of excellence in research, scholarship,
and education by publishing worldwide in

Oxford New York

Auckland Cape Town Dar es Salaam Hong Kong Karachi Kuala Lumpur
Madrid Melbourne Mexico City Nairobi New Delhi Shanghai Taipei Toronto

With offices in

Argentina Austria Brazil Chile Czech Republic France Greece
Guatemala Hungary Italy Japan Poland Portugal Singapore
South Korea Switzerland Thailand Turkey Ukraine Vietnam

Published in the United States
by Oxford University Press Inc., New York

British Library Cataloguing in Publication Data

Data available

Library of Congress Cataloging in Publication Data

Data available

ISBN 978-0-19-955096-8

1 3 5 7 9 10 8 6 4 2

Typeset by SPI Publisher Services, Pondicherry, India
Printed in Great Britain
on acid-free paper by
CPI Antony Rowe, Chippenham, Wiltshire

EDITOR'S FOREWORD

This series is designed to explore the vast and varied territory of church music, as a consistently important part of British musical history that has tended to be neglected or underrated in recent writings. This volume, the sixth in the series, is unlike the others in an important way, for it explores the interaction of the English cathedral tradition with one of the greatest composers in European history. So, in addition to being a contribution to our understanding of British church music, it is destined to take a prominent place in modern Handel scholarship. Donald Burrows comes to the series as one of a small group of leading Handel scholars who also has extensive knowledge and experience of church music.

In a sense Handel was marginal to the story of English cathedral music. He composed nothing for the daily cathedral service. But his music for the public religious celebration of royal and national events not only drew on the established English idiom of anthem and service setting, but was influential on later church music; and some of it found a permanent place in the canon. Professor Burrows describes exactly how Handel tailored his German and Italian musical upbringing to the particular requirements of successive British sovereigns: Anne, George I, and George II.

The study is of particular value to the student of 'cathedral' music, even if Handel was not in the mainstream. His stature has ensured the preservation, and the scholarly examination over nearly three centuries, of far more documentary evidence than can be assembled for lesser contemporaries such as Croft or Greene. The background to each piece, and the process of composition, can be examined in luxuriant detail, and the music scrutinized within a context of several generations of accumulated understanding and criticism. These opportunities have been carried out by Professor Burrows with extraordinary skill, and with a comprehensive knowledge of both Handel's life and output and the politics and organizational structure of the Chapel Royal and the court in general. He has also brought this knowledge to bear on some of Handel's English predecessors, notably Purcell and Croft.

Within the world of Handel scholarship, the emphasis is different. Handelians of the twentieth century duly corrected the Victorian image of Handel as a primarily religious composer and moralist. But in carrying out this necessary operation, and rescuing the operas and dramatic oratorios from neglect or misunderstanding, Winton Dean and others have too heavily played down the religious elements in Handel's music, including the oratorios. Handel may not have equalled Bach in personal religious conviction. But he could use his powers to express spiritual devotion as well as any other human feeling; and his unmatched mastery of ceremonial music found a natural home in coronation anthems and victory celebrations. By devoting a full-length book to this part of Handel's output Burrows is restoring due balance. Perhaps his book will enable twenty-first-century readers to attain, at last, a truly proportionate view of Handel's many-sided genius.

NICHOLAS TEMPERLEY

Urbana, Illinois,
January 2004

PREFACE AND
ACKNOWLEDGEMENTS

Almost exactly thirty years before the completion of this book my first published article on a musical topic appeared in the *Musical Times*, to accompany the first performance of my reconstruction of Handel's Anthem on the Peace, a work that had not been heard since 1749. My interest in the anthem had begun in a rather casual way during preparations for a performance of *Messiah* that I conducted in 1972, but over the following year it developed into a fascination with Handel and his music that has had consequences on a scale that I could not have imagined. More specifically and immediately, it awakened my interest in Handel's English church music—the musical repertory to which the Peace Anthem belonged—and the contexts for this repertory in Handel's relationships to the British court, the contemporary political background, and the broader history of English church music. Around 1970 Handel's Cannons anthems (then known as 'Chandos anthems') were becoming more widely known through a series of recordings by the choir of King's College, Cambridge, who also recorded an outstanding performance of Handel's Coronation Anthems. Two different areas of Handel's music were represented by these pieces: while the Cannons anthems form a compact group written during a short and concentrated period for the chamber-scale musical ensemble of a noble patron, the Coronation Anthems are part of a diverse repertory of occasional church music that he composed for occasions involving the British royal court over a period of nearly forty years. The unifying factor in the latter repertory was the participation of the musicians employed in the court establishments of the Chapel Royal and the Royal Musicians.

My exploration of the repertory beyond the Peace Anthem led me to a concert in 1975 at which I conducted the first modern performances of some works from Handel's Chapel Royal music, and indeed further concerts followed of other related music by Handel and by William Croft, the leading English composer of church music at the time of his arrival in London; I also became involved in due course with performances of Chapel Royal works that were directed by Charles Farncombe, Christopher Hogwood, and Simon Preston. As I proceeded further, I investigated the musical sources and the documentary background to Handel's original performances, finding that these were mutually illuminating. The topic of Handel and the English Chapel Royal eventually developed into a thesis that I completed with The Open University in 1981: this was the first doctoral thesis from the Music Department, and for me it began a long-term association with the University that I also could not have forseen a decade earlier.

For the thesis it had been necessary to limit the scope of the topic to Handel's association with the Chapel Royal during the reigns of Queen Anne and King George I, but I was aware that there was a more comprehensive story to be told, and also one that deserved wider public exposure. In the decade that followed I really intended to do something about it, but other matters intervened on account of my involvement with a burgeoning series of Handel projects in Britain, Germany, and America, which took me towards involvement with his operas and oratorios at the expense of the church music. I eventually returned to the idea of the present book, a proposal for which was accepted by Oxford University Press in 1991. Other projects had to be completed first, however. 1994 saw the publication of my biography of Handel, and of a co-authored catalogue of Handel's autographs. After that I settled back to the Chapel Royal task in earnest, and had even begun to arrange permissions for the illustrations, when there was an unforeseen and unavoidable interruption: the Earl of Malmesbury deposited the papers of his ancestor James Harris at the Hampshire Record Office, and I was diverted as a matter of urgency onto a book that presented all of the references to music and theatre from the Harris papers, which are a rich resource of first-hand material about Handel's career, among other things. The book came to publication in 2002, and it was time for the serious attempt to deal with Handel and the Chapel Royal before something else blocked the road.

My thesis provided a working basis for much of the present book, and during in the intervening two decades I had prepared music editions of several items from Handel's Chapel Royal music, as well as continuing to investigate the documentary background, but nevertheless considerable new labour has been involved in bringing the book to completion. Inevitably both the style and the content of the thesis material have required considerable revision, and much of the post-1726 material has taken me into virgin territory: I have been surprised, for example, by the extent of the relevant references from the London newspapers that eluded Otto Erich Deutsch in his *Documentary Biography* of Handel. In the process of recasting material from the thesis I have taken account of subsequent scholarship, concerning matters relating directly to Handel and to the British court, but also other areas of relevance, such as Purcell's church music, and the eighteenth-century makers and players of organs and trumpets. A considerable part of the thesis had been devoted to surveys of the early musical sources for individual works in Handel's English church music, which are now redundant on account of the information that can be found in the commentaries to published music editions. Here I refer only to the most directly relevant aspects of Handel's autographs, and

occasionally to other musical sources that contribute significantly to an understanding of the musical text or the manner of its performance. Reference to the
thesis has provided a convenient way of indicating supporting evidence or
tabular material for some statements and conclusions that are given in summary
form in the present book: I have, however, included an updated version of my
list of the members of the London choirs as Appendix B, on account of its
possible general usefulness for reference.

In one important respect I have repeated and expanded the pattern of my
thesis, by dealing in approximately equal measure with the musical pieces as a
series of individual (and remarkable) artefacts, and with the historical circumstances of the pieces in relation to Handel's biography and British political
history. I have endeavoured to make the more specialized areas comprehen-
sible to interest groups for both 'music' and 'history', but it is inevitable that
matters of detail concerning the music require concrete reference to specific
places in musical scores. Underlying the book is a belief, derived from my own
practical experience, that it deals with a musical repertory that is engaging in
itself, but also of significance in relation to Handel's compositional practice and
the history of church music in the Baroque period, in London and beyond.

Handel's personal and creative career in London is conventionally described
principally in terms of his activity in the genres of opera and oratorio. Measured by minutes of music, or by the duration of the composer's involvement in
any one year, the dominance of these genres is not open to challenge. Yet there
is also a strand in Handel's London career that involves English church music,
and which covers, through a number of different phases and through a series of
particular occasions, nearly all of his active years as a composer in London. To
that extent this book presents a creative biography in terms of his compositions, but also a personal biography in terms of his relationship with members
of the British royal family, a professional biography in terms of his relationships
with some of London's leading musicians, and a political biography in terms of
his relationship to developments in British and international affairs. It also
attempts to describe a creative repertory that is a worthy companion to his
operas and oratorios.

One area in which the Chapel Royal music provides particularly interesting
insights into Handel's compositional practice concerns his reuse and recomposition of the same music from one work to another. Some aspects of his
recompositions are attributable to time and circumstance, arising from the
musical character of the Chapel Royal singers, as soloists and as an ensemble.
Yet practical and aesthetic issues cannot be separated: a musical movement may
be shortened in order to suit a particular singer or a particular occasion, but the
decision on *how* to shorten is an aesthetic one, involving matters of proportion,
tonal organization, and compositional technique. In the matter of Handel's

reworking of music from other composers it would be foolish for me to make any claims of comprehensive coverage: no doubt there are as yet unknown instances, and although I describe borrowings that seem to me to be of particular interest and significance I may not have covered all the examples that have yet been discovered. This is an area with large and dangerous pitfalls for the commentator: for example, the chorus 'Lo, thus shall the man be blessed that feareth the Lord' from the wedding anthem *Sing unto God* is arguably an example of Graun's compositional style rather than Handel's. Yet the way that the movement functions within the anthem is indeed Handel's, and this level of description has been my principal concern. I have found that, once brought into the light of performance, Handel's Chapel Royal music is well able to stand up for itself. Indeed, the subject of Handel and the Chapel Royal has a dual attraction: it is possible, given a little historical imagination, to achieve some level of creative contact with the original circumstances for the composition and performance of the works, and yet the musical pieces are also an experience that is worth repeating in the different circumstances of the twenty-first century. Handel's Chapel Royal music deserves its place of canonic honour in the creative landscape of English church music, and of European music in the eighteenth century.

The surviving musical, documentary, and iconographic material relating to Handel and the Chapel Royal is diverse and interesting, and I am especially grateful for the cooperation that I have received from the owners and keepers of my source documents, and of the items that I have used for illustrations, in granting permission for quotation and reproduction. Plate II, and Figs. 8.1, 10.1, 10.2, and 16.1 are reproduced by gracious permission of Her Majesty the Queen. Plate III, and Figs. 7.1 and 18.2 are Crown Copyright. Other images are reproduced by courtesy of: the Guildhall Library, Corporation of London (Pl. I and V, Figs. 4.3, 12.2), Westminster City Archives (Pl. IV), the British Library Board (Figs. 3.1, 4.1, 5.1, 8.2, 9.1, 10.3, 11.1, 13.1, 14.1, 14.2, and 19.1), the Staats- und Universitätsbibliothek Carl von Ossietzky, Hamburg (Fig. 12.1), and the Dean and Chapter of Westminster (Fig. 13.2). I record my thanks to the staff of the Lord Chamberlain's Office and of the institutions named for their unstinting assistance.

I am grateful to three people who read and commented on the text of the book at various draft stages: Nicholas Temperley, the editor of Oxford Studies in British Church Music, and two long-standing colleagues in both music and scholarship, Graydon Beeks and Bruce Wood. From the present Chapel Royal, I have received welcome assistance and encouragement from David Baldwin, the Serjeant of the Vestry. On various points of fact and interpretation I am indebted to information from Kerry Downes, John Greenacombe, Dominic Gwynn, Trevor Herbert, Anthony Hicks, Peter Holman, David Hunter, Neil

Jenkins, H. Diack Johnstone, Annette Landgraf, Tom McGeary, John H. Roberts, Ruth Smith, Tony Trowles, Elaine Moohan, Jonathan Wainwright, and John Wolffe. The preparation of the book has necessitated the persistent and often fiddly pursuit of precious details: I thank the librarians and archivists of the collections that have been essential to my task for their patience and assistance, often well beyond the call of duty. I also record my thanks to Mike Levers (The Open University) for photographic work, to Blaise Compton (The Open University) for processing the music examples, and to Malcolm Dickson for providing Fig. 18.1.

Bruce Phillips promoted the initial proposal for this book at Oxford University Press; I thank the successive editors at the Press who have seen the project through and Bonnie Blackburn for copy-editing. I consider myself fortunate that this, in company with three of my previous books, has been produced from the City of Oxford, and regret that, in this respect, it will be among the last of such music books. Rosemary Kingdon, then Secretary to the Music Department at The Open University, typed the initial draft of the book: I also regret the discontinuance of this essential institutional resource. I am grateful to the Arts Faculty of The Open University for support that has enabled me to undertake the new research for this book and has facilitated its presentation.

In the longer time-scale for the preparation of the book I am conscious of my debt to three particular sources of interest and encouragement: the late Colin Scull, former Serjeant of the Vestry of Her Majesty's Chapel Royal, Anthony Caesar, former Sub-Dean of the Chapel Royal (and incidentally one of my predecessors as conductor of the Abingdon and District Musical Society, with which I gave the first performance of the Peace Anthem), and Gerald Hendrie, formerly Professor of Music at The Open University and editor of several relevant volumes of Handel's church music for the *Hallische Händel-Ausgabe*. Nor can I forget my profound gratitude to the fellow-conspirators who have, over the years, joined me in the performances of Handel's Chapel Royal music, in particular Dana Marsh, Philip Cave, Ashley Stafford, and Michael Morton, worthy modern successors to the artistry of Messrs Elford, Gethin, Hughes, and Weely.

D.B.

Milton Keynes
December 2003/November 2004

CONTENTS

Appendices

LIST OF ILLUSTRATIONS

LIST OF TABLES

ABBREVIATIONS AND CONVENTIONS

Music Editions

HG
: *G. F. Händel's Werke: Ausgabe der Deutschen Händelgesellschaft*, ed. Friedrich W. Chrysander and Max Seiffert, 1–48, 50–96 (Leipzig and Bergedorf bei Hamburg, 1858–94, 1902); also 6 supplementary vols. (1888–1902) of related works by other composers, including Francesco Antonio Urio, Te Deum (Band 2) and Alessandro Stradella, Serenata *Qual prodigio e ch'io miri?* (Band 3)

HHA
: *Hallische Händel-Ausgabe im Auftrage der Georg-Friedrich-Händel Gesellschaft*, Serie I–V and Suppl. vols. (Leipzig and Kassel, 1955–)

MB
: *Musica Britannica: A National Collection of Music* (London, 1951–)

NHE
: *Novello Handel Edition*, Watkins Shaw, Donald Burrows (gen. eds.), (Sevenoaks and London, 1978–)

PS
: *The Works of Henry Purcell*, 32 vols. (Purcell Society; London, 1878–1965, rev. 1974–)

Manuscript Documentary Sources

NCB
: Chapel Royal, New Cheque Book (see Bibliography)

OCB
: Chapel Royal, Old Cheque Book (see Bibliography)

WA1
: Westminster Abbey, WAM 60200. Manuscript account book and commonplace book, with entries 1721–77. Originally an account book kept by John Church (d. 1740/1) recording income for the Choir from Rents, Tombs Money, Funerals, etc. Continued after his death, partly by Anselm Bayly, as a record of admissions and deaths of members of the Choir

WA2
: Westminster Abbey, WAM 61228B. Precentor's Book. Manuscript choir register and commonplace book, with entries 1724–1802 and signatures. Begun by George Carleton, who became Chanter of the Abbey in 1728

Literature and Journals

Boyer, *Anne* (*Annals*)	Abel Boyer, *The History of the Life of Queen Anne Digested into Annals*, vols. 1–11 for 1702–12 (London, 1703–13)
Ashbee and Harley	*The Cheque Books of the Chapel Royal*, ed. Andrew Ashbee and John Harley, 2 vols. (Aldershot, 2000)
Burrows, *Dissertation*	Donald Burrows, 'Handel and the English Chapel Royal during the Reigns of Queen Anne and King George I' (Ph.D. diss., The Open University, 1981)
BUXWV	Identification of Buxtehude's compositions by the numbers in G. Karstädt (ed.), *Thematisch-systematisches Verzeichnis der musikalischen Werke von Dietrich Buxtehude: Buxtehude-Werke-Verzeichnis*, 2nd edn. (Wiesbaden, 1985)
GSJ	*The Galpin Society Journal*
HHB	*Walter Eisen and Margret Eisen, Händel-Handbuch, herausgegeben vom Kuratorium der Georg-Friedrich-Händel-Stiftung*, suppl. to *HHA*, 4 vols. (Leipzig 1978–85). Vols. i–iii contain the *Thematisch-systematisches Verzeichnis* to Handel's works prepared by Bernd Baselt, which lists Handel's works by *HWV* numbers and gives musical incipits for individual movements, as well as information about instrumentation, sources, musical borrowings, and secondary literature for each work; a short form of the catalogue, without musical incipits, is published as Bernd Baselt, *Verzeichnis der Werke Georg Friedrich Händels: Kleine Ausgabe* (Leipzig, 1986). Vol. iv of *HHB*, *Dokumente zu Leben und Schaffen*, is a revised and supplemented version of Deutsch, *Handel: A Documentary Biography*.
HWV	Identification of Handel's compositions by the numbers in Baselt's thematic catalogue (see *HHB*, above)
ML	*Music & Letters*
MQ	*The Musical Quarterly*
MT	*The Musical Times*
NG	*The New Grove Dictionary of Music and Musicians*, ed. Stanley Sadie, 20 vols. (London, 1980)
NG II	*The New Grove Dictionary of Music and Musicians*, 2nd edn., ed. Stanley Sadie and John Tyrrell, 20 vols. (London, 2001)
RMARC	*Royal Musical Association Research Chronicle*

Libraries and Archives

The codes, based on RISM sigla, are used for references to documentary
materials as well as musical sources.

Germany

D-Hs	Hamburg, Staats- und Universitätsbibliothek Carl von Ossietzky

Great Britain

GB-Bu	Birmingham, University Library (Barber Music Library)
GB-Cfm	Cambridge, Fitzwilliam Museum
GB-Ckc	Cambridge, King's College
GB-Ep	Edinburgh, Public Library
GB-Lbl	London, British Library
GB-Lcm	London, Royal College of Music
GB-LEc	Leeds, Central Library (Taphouse Collection)
GB-Lg	London, Guildhall Library
GB-Llp	London, Lambeth Palace Library
GB-Lpro	London (Kew), Public Record Office (The National Archives)
GB-Lsp	London, St Paul's Cathedral Library
GB-Lwa	London, Westminster Abbey Muniment Room and Library
GB-Mp	Manchester Public Library (Henry Watson Music Library)
GB-Oas	Oxford, All Souls College
GB-Ob	Oxford, Bodleian Library
GB-WRch	Windsor, St George's Chapel Library

United States of America

US-AUS	University of Texas at Austin, Harry Ransom Humanities Research Center
US-Cu	University of Chicago, Joseph Regenstein Library
US-NBu	New Brunswick, Rutgers University Library
US-NYp	New York, Public Library at Lincoln Center, Music Division
US-SM	San Marino, California, Henry E. Huntington Library
US-STu	Stanford University, Music Library
US-Wc	Washington, DC, Library of Congress

Newspapers

References to eighteenth-century newspapers and journals follow the abbreviations in Michael Tilmouth, 'A Calendar of References to Music in Newspapers published in London and the Provinces (1660–1719)', *RMARC* I, with additions in similar style. Some newspapers were published at different periods with variant titles: the following list does not include all subtitles, but will enable individual newspapers to be identified from the collections at GB-Lbl, GB-Ob, and US-Wc.

AOWJ	*Applebee's Original Weekly-Journal*
BBEP	*B. Berington's Evening Post*
BJ	*The British Journal: or, The Censor*
BM	*The British Mercury*
BWM	*The British Weekly Mercury*
CJ	*The Country Journal: or, The Craftsman*
CS	*Common Sense: or, The Englishman's Journal*
DA	*The Daily Advertiser*
Dawks	*Dawks's News-Letter*
DC	*The Daily Courant*
DG	*The Daily Gazetteer*
DJ	*The Daily Journal*
DP	*The Daily Post*
DPB	*The Daily Post-Boy*
EP	*The Evening Post*
FP	*The Flying-Post: or, Post-Master*
GA	*The General Advertiser*
GEP	*The General Evening Post (London)*
GJ	*The Gentleman's Journal*
GM	*The Gentleman's Magazine*
LDP	*The London Daily Post, and General Advertiser*
LEP	*The London Evening-Post*
LG	*The London Gazette*
LJ	*The London Journal*
NorG	*The Norwich Gazette*
OW	*The Old Whig*
OWJ	*The Original Weekly Journal*
PA	*The Public Advertiser*
PB	*The Post-Boy*

PLP	*The Penny London Post*
PM	*The Post Man, and The Historical Account, &c.*
PPP	*Parker's Penny Post*
RWJ	*Read's Weekly Journal; or, British Gazetteer*
SJ	*The Salisbury Journal*
SJEP	*The St. James's Evening Post*
SJP	*St. James's Post*
Supp	*The Supplement*
UJ	*The Universal Journal*
US	*The Universal Spectator, and Weekly Journal*
WEP	*The White-hall Evening-Post*
WJ	*The Weekly Journal, With Fresh Advices Foreign and Domestick*
WJBG	*The Weekly Journal: or, British Gazetteer*
WJSP	*The Weekly Journal, or Saturday's-Post*
WM	*The Weekly Medley, or Gentleman's Recreation*
WO	*The Weekly Oracle; or, Universal Library*
WP	*The Weekly Packet*
WR	*Weekly Remarks*

Voices, Instruments, Keys

These apply to the music examples, to the tables in Chapters 3–5, 9, and 14 referring to an anthem by Croft and canticle settings by Purcell, Croft, and Handel, and also to Appendix A.

Voices and Vocal Parts

S	Soprano/Treble
A	Alto
T	Tenor
B	Bass

Solo voices are indicated by capital letters, chorus parts by lower case.

Instruments and Instrumental Parts

fl.	flute
rec.	recorder
ob.	oboe
bn.	bassoon

tpt.	trumpet
timp.	timpani
vn.	violin (vns. for Violins 1 and 2)
va	viola
vc	cello
d.b.	double bass
str.	strings (4-part strings including violas)
b.c.	basso continuo
org.	organ
unacc.	unaccompanied (otherwise, b.c. and orchestral bassi, as appropriate, are included in the accompaniment for all movements in the tables)
orch.	orchestra

Time Signatures and Keys

T/s	time signature

Major keys are represented in tables by capital letters, minor keys by lower case.

Pitch Designations

The Helmholz system is used: *c* for tenor C, *c′* for middle C, etc.

Dates

The Julian (Old Style) calendar was used in Britain until September 1752: the civil new year began on 25 March (though New Year's Day was celebrated at court on 1 January), and the dates were eleven days behind those of the Gregorian (New Style) calendar that was current in most other European countries. To avoid any ambiguity, for dates between 1 January and 24 March the year date is given as (for example) 1714/15. In tables, dates are given in abbreviated form, as for example 11–3–1714/15 (i.e. 11 March 1715 in modern style).

Currency

British currency was in pounds, shillings, and pence (£. s. d., as in £20.8.11): there were 20 shillings to the pound and 12 pence to the shilling. A guinea was 21 shillings, or £1.1.0.

Spelling and Punctuation

Quotations from eighteenth-century documents follow the styles of the originals, but with regularization or modernization of punctuation, and the expansion of abbreviated word forms. Texts set by Handel are given in modern spellings (e.g. 'magnify' rather than 'magnifie'), as they are found in current musical editions.

References to Handel's Music

For most of Handel's anthems, bar references are unambiguous in relation to the published music editions listed in the Bibliography. However, editions of some works differ in the numbering of movements, and thus also in the bar numbering, where short sections occur that can be regarded either as independent movements or as components of larger movements. This is particularly the case with settings of the Te Deum. In the text I have tried to describe the music in ways that can be interpreted from any music edition, but inevitably there are occasional references to movement/bar numbers, especially in the notes. For Handel's Caroline, A Major, and Dettingen settings of the Te Deum, the movement numbers that I have used are incorporated into Tables 5.1, 9.2, and 14.1; similarly, *This is the day* is covered in Table 12.2. I have not been able to find a tidy solution to the particularly problematic cases of the Utrecht Te Deum and the Funeral Anthem for Queen Caroline: where numbered movement citations are unavoidable, I provide references to *HHA* and *NHE* editions. *HG* volumes do not have movement or bar numbers, and any necessary references are located by page number.

Music Examples

Texts and music are given in the most convenient modern forms, except for those examples that represent features of the original sources and require reproduction of the original clefs and score layout. Instrumental bass staves are unlabelled, unless the musical source provides some specific and relevant indication: in many movements with orchestral accompaniment, a single un-labelled stave in Handel's scores served for the orchestral bass line (cellos, double basses, bassoons) and also for the basso continuo, which included the organ.

Biblical References

These follow the numbering of chapters and verses from the Authorized (King James) Version of the English Bible, and from the Psalms as included in the Book of Common Prayer.

I

Introduction

THE subject of this book is Handel's relationship with the English Chapel Royal—the institution and its individual musical performers—and the musical repertory that he composed in the context of that relationship. Historically the topic is of importance because of Handel's involvement in the celebration of political and domestic events relating to the British court: his music for the Peace Thanksgivings in 1713 and 1749, for the Coronation in 1727, and even for the return of King George I from his visits to Hanover in 1724–6, contributed to strengthening the image of the court, and brought the composer into prominence as a public figure. Concerning the music itself, Handel effected a major change in the course of English church music, not only through the grand manner of his orchestrally accompanied chorus movements but also through the introduction of a more modern melodic and harmonic style that is apparent in his music for soloists. In relation to Handel's biography, his activity in English church music forms a parallel strand in his career to that in the London theatres where, over a span of nearly fifty years, he was responsible for performances of three-act Italian operas, and then English oratorios on a comparable musical scale. His creative life covered about forty of those years, from his arrival in London towards the end of 1710 until the onset of blindness, which effectively terminated his work as a composer by the spring of 1753. As a performer he made his debut with the London public with the harpsichord obbligato to an aria in *Rinaldo*, his first London opera, and at the end of his life he continued to perform occasionally, even during his years of blindness, in organ concertos that featured in the oratorio performances. While his own performances in the theatre were subsidiary to his functions in composing, rehearsing, and directing the performances of his operas and oratorios, nevertheless the presence of his forceful personality seems to have been fundamental to their success, and it was probably as a figure at the harpsichord or organ in the theatre that he was principally recognized as a musician.

Handel's English church music involved him with a different network of professional, social, and political relationships from that relating to the theatre companies, though sometimes the two interacted: Chapel Royal singers performed in Handel's oratorios, and the theatre orchestra provided a pool of additional instrumentalists for the Chapel Royal music. Handel's career as a composer and director of performances of church music, though not as extensive as his work in the theatre, spanned nearly all of his creative life in London: his first English anthem was probably written towards the end of 1712, and his last in the spring of 1749, with further revisions that may have been made as late as 1751. In contrast to the regular repertory performances of his theatre seasons, the occasions for which he composed English church music were relatively infrequent, but nevertheless his activity falls into a number of phases, in which different circumstances involved him in the composition of works for particular occasions or types of occasions. His most concentrated period of composition in English church music arose from his association with James Brydges (subsequently the Duke of Chandos) in 1717–18, when he wrote a dozen substantial pieces. Although both the music and the performers for these works have some relevance to the present topic, the circumstances of the Cannons anthems were unusual and relate to the relatively short-lived 'consort' that performed them at the church of St Lawrence adjoining Brydges's estate at Cannons Park, about ten miles north-west of the Cities of London and Westminster. The remainder of Handel's English church music was performed in central London, and is unified by its association with singers from the English Chapel Royal, who formed the core of the performers even on large-scale occasions when their numbers were considerably augmented.

The musicians of the Chapel Royal—singers, organists, and composers—constituted a professional circuit that in some respects represented an English counterpoise to the 'foreign' musicians of the opera house; indeed, some of the most talented Chapel Royal singers seem to have gravitated towards the Chapel when their hopes of careers as singers in the London theatres were curtailed by the rising popularity and success of Italian opera, at the expense of English theatrical genres involving music, during the first decade of the eighteenth century. The singers in London's principal ecclesiastical choirs formed a fairly close community, interconnected by their service in several choirs simultaneously, and doubtless they experienced both the pressures and the benefits that developed as a result of daily professional contact in musical performances at church services over a number of years. Although these musicians never attracted the level of attention or controversy associated with the opera stars or with the more renowned actor-singers in the English theatre companies, nevertheless their activities were reported in the London newspapers. Sometimes they were named as soloists in reports of church services, court performances, or public concerts; nearly always their deaths were recorded, since their offices were income-bearing 'places' and were thus regarded as having a public interest. Chapel Royal staff were part of the British court establishment under the Lord Chamberlain, though the Chapel was a relatively minor area in that department, and one that had in some respects unusual independence because appointments were made through the clerical Dean and Sub-Dean of the Chapel. Nevertheless, the Chapel Royal was the only permanent group of singers employed by the British court during the eighteenth century.

The parallel institutional group of instrumentalists for the court was the Royal Musicians—Queen's Musicians under Queen Anne, and King's Musicians thereafter—under the direction of the Master of the Queen's/King's Music. The Royal Musicians were 'in waiting' to serve the Court as needed but, unlike the Chapel Royal whose functions were almost continuous throughout the year in order to maintain the daily services with a rota of singers, the Musicians seem to have had only occasional functions, such as providing music for the court balls at St James's Palace and for the infrequent installations of Knights of the Garter at Windsor. Twice a year the Royal Musicians and at least some members of the Chapel Royal performed together in the court odes for the New Year and the monarch's birthday: these were given in London before the court, including the royal family, following a tradition that had been consolidated during the last two decades of the seventeenth century. Also available for various court functions were the Royal Trumpeters under the management of the Serjeant Trumpeter. The Trumpeters were also an establishment within the Lord Chamberlain's department, but they do not seem to have had as close a connection with the other court musicians as that which existed between the Chapel Royal and the Royal Musicians: while there were some state occasions for which the Trumpeters had a duty of attendance, many other 'orchestral' events required a special arrangement for the participation of a couple of the best players. Since the Royal Musicians were constituted as a group of string players, the involvement of oboes or bassoons similarly required the employment of extra players, this time from outside the major court establishments, though (particularly from the second quarter of the eighteenth century onwards) individual players might also have positions in the bands of the Guards. The Royal Musicians apparently did not include players for the double bass, and these too had to be bought in for special performances. The various musical establishments of the court are described in more detail in Chapters 16–17. The combined forces of the Chapel Royal and the Royal Musicians provided a substantial musical resource, certainly the largest one that was available in Britain for church music; when this was supplemented by additional singers from the other permanent London choirs and players from London's considerable pool of professional instrumentalists, Handel probably had command of the largest combined performing group of choir and orchestra in Europe.

Nearly all of the services for which Handel wrote church music involving the Chapel Royal were related to major political or national events, or to occasions that directly concerned members of the royal family. The political circumstances surrounding the 'Utrecht' celebrations in 1713 had a significant effect on the permanent establishment of his career in London, severing him from his post in Hanover and attracting his first royal pension. Handel's participation in the Utrecht thanksgiving service, the 1727 coronation service, and the 1737 funeral service for Queen Caroline brought him to the attention of a larger and more diverse audience than that of London's opera-goers: with these events Handel became a more accessible public figure, establishing a wider reputation in London. The Music for the Royal Fireworks in 1749 was probably the only other public performance at which a substantial body of Londoners had the opportunity to hear Handel's music directed by the composer.[1] By 1749, furthermore, Handel's Chapel Royal music had already begun to spread to wider audiences through performances in which the composer was not directly involved—at church services for the Festival of the Sons of the Clergy in London, and then through events associated with local charities and music festivals in Britain's provincial cities. The Utrecht Te Deum and Jubilate were published in full score during the 1730s, followed in the 1740s by the Coronation Anthems, the Funeral Anthem for Queen Caroline, and the Dettingen Te Deum.

The Chapel Royal performances with which Handel was involved had a particular political aspect in relation to the Hanoverian royal family. Handel pursued a career that maintained at least the appearance of independent artistic status, and he seems to have been skilful in navigating the various factional currents among London's politicians so that he remained on good terms with different interest groups. Nevertheless, his close association with the Court, reinforced by his musical contribution to events that were personal to the royal family, gave him both the benefits and the disadvantages of identification with the Hanoverian establishment. His second royal pension, commencing in 1723, was granted to provide recognition of his services to the court as 'Composer for the Chapel Royal'. This gave him a total annual pension income of £400 per year, and in addition from about the same time he received another £200 as Music Master to the royal princesses. This very substantial annual income of £600 provided Handel with personal financial security: indeed in eighteenth-century terms it represented considerable wealth. On the other hand, he was liable to be identified with the 'German' interest at court at times when this was politically controversial, particularly

---

[1] In the case of the *Water Music* in 1717 any 'audience' would have overheard the musical entertainment from a private and unadvertised Royal late-night open-air party.

during George I's reign, and satirists coupled his name with that of Robert Walpole, who was perceived as the court's minister, at the time of the unpopular Excise Bill in 1733. Handel's identification with the court must from time to time have produced pressures on his London career and reputation, and affected the attitudes of those with whom he had to deal in his professional and private life, however cunningly he avoided identification with any particular party alignments. His association with Chapel Royal services in the 1720s, and with the 1727 Coronation, seem to have been the consequence of specific Royal favour towards the composer, and Handel may well have levered himself into these events in order to advance and secure his own London career. If he did indeed solicit court favour, it has left no documentary trace, but that may be a reflection of the subtlety of Handel's approach, and of the possibility that he had direct access to informal lines of influence. Certainly we may suppose that he recognized that a memorable contribution to a royal event, whether in church or in the theatre, was a means towards influencing the more powerful and aristocratic elements in British society. The Utrecht music made its mark with musical connoisseurs early in Handel's London career: thirty years later Handel devoted his energies to the composition of some particularly powerful music in anticipation of a thanksgiving for the Dettingen victory, partly in order to restore his reputation at a time when one group of influential patrons was angered by his refusal to write for the current opera company.

Since the more powerful patrons of the successive opera companies would also have been present at some of the church services at which Handel's music was performed, there was some interaction between the two parts of Handel's career. Furthermore, although the professional worlds of the theatre singers and the Chapel Royal singers were independent of each other, the situation changed when Handel introduced and developed his own genre of English theatre oratorio in the 1730s. Not only did the choral music in his oratorios owe something—sometimes even specific movements—to his previous English church music, but he employed some of the Chapel Royal singers as performers for his oratorios. The initial stage in the development of the oratorios was not without controversy for, if Charles Burney's famous account is to be believed, the original plan to transfer a private production of *Esther* by the Chapel Royal choristers to the London stage in 1732 was thwarted by a ban from the Bishop of London in his role as Dean of the Chapel. Yet there is no doubt that the boys and men of the Chapel eventually provided some of the chorus singers for Handel's theatre oratorio performances. Most of the oratorio soloists that Handel named simply as 'the Boy' probably came from the Chapel; although only one Gentleman was a principal oratorio soloist for Handel while holding his Chapel Royal post, Handel's leading tenor John

Beard had received his musical education as a Chapel chorister under Bernard Gates.

Contemporary reports of Chapel Royal events, particularly from the London newspapers, along with documentary institutional records for the Chapel and for the court, provide material for understanding Handel's musical scores in terms of important areas of performance practice—numbers of performers, the groupings of voices and instruments, and venues. In the matter of venues our circumstances are particularly fortunate. While none of the London theatres in which Handel performed has survived in any form that he would have recognized, the stone edifices that saw the performances of his church music remain intact, and the changes to their internal layout and furnishings can largely be identified. While we cannot now perform Handel's music from the galleries that he used at Westminster Abbey and St Paul's Cathedral, the basic structures of the buildings remain. As for the Chapels Royal themselves, the extent of the principal Chapel at St James's Palace during Handel's time is clear within the present building's interior, and the Queen's Chapel in Marlborough Gate remains essentially the same building as the one that was taken over and refurnished for the wedding of Princess Anne in 1734. Above all, the surviving venues provide a first-hand reminder of the basic acoustic differences between the large and small buildings for which Handel composed various items in the repertory.

This book will be concerned with Handel's Chapel Royal music in its historical context, but with no intention to play down the religious significance of the composer's work. The eighteenth-century Church of England subsequently received a bad image from churchmen with a different ecclesiastical outlook, though the picture has been at least partly modified by modern historical and contextual studies.[2] The 1730s saw the beginning of John Wesley's reform activity as well as Bishop Gibson's intervention over oratorio performances, but the serious institutional consequences of the polarization produced by 'enthusiasm' lay beyond Handel's lifetime. Not surprisingly, the clergy who were responsible for the church services with which the Chapel Royal was associated were not only among the most secure and affluent, but also necessarily the closest to the political establishments. However, they seem to have taken their religious duties seriously, and they included some of the best-educated clergy who would have taken an active interest in the latest developments in biblical scholarship. (The 1730s also saw the publication of Alexander Cruden's *Complete Concordance to the Holy Scriptures*, including the Apocrypha, dedicated to Queen Caroline.) Their routine duties included the administration of the sacraments, but their prime functions on public occasions

---

[2] See Walsh, Haydon, and Taylor, *The Church of England*.

were to preach and to pray, mainly within the liturgical structure of the Order for Morning Prayer from the Book of Common Prayer. This liturgy, and the parallel one for Evening Prayer, provided the principal religious experience, and probably the preferred one, in eighteenth-century England. When speaking from the pulpit at the various events that were dignified with official celebration, the clergy naturally looked for appropriate biblical support. Although there are occasional comparisons, in contemporary literature as well as in sermons, between the British nation and the Israelites of the Old Testament as people favoured (or indeed 'chosen') by God, there is little evidence that this was perceived as a continuous identification. If a text was needed for a sermon on an occasion celebrating a military victory, the New Testament provided little material: there was a similar problem for sermons dealing with the subject of the contribution of music to church services.

While Handel's composition of music for the Chapel Royal may have served to consolidate and advance his own reputation and career, this need not lead us to suppose that he approached the task in a cynically calculating spirit, without any concern for the content of the texts that he was setting. As far as we know he was fully supportive of the events that were commemorated by his music and, although we lack any confessional documents on the subject, it seems that he undertook his compositions from the situation of a Christian believer.[3] He apparently had no serious reservations about the framework of Lutheran religious belief in which he had been brought up and, like the Hanoverian monarchs, he found little difficulty in adapting to Anglican culture. According to Charles Burney, when Handel was sent the texts of the anthems for the 1727 coronation by the bishops, 'he murmured, and took offence, as he thought it implied his ignorance of the Holy Scriptures: "I have read my Bible very well, and shall chuse for myself"'.[4] Many of the texts that he set, such as that of the Te Deum, were defined by the liturgy; others, such as that for the Funeral Anthem for Queen Caroline, were assembled and adapted by the clerical equivalent of an opera or oratorio librettist. For many of the anthems based on psalm texts we do not know the extent of any consultation that may have been involved in their selection, or the identity of the people that Handel may have consulted. What seems certain, however, is that he had his own ideas about the materials that would result in an effective musical setting, and that he had a good working knowledge of biblical texts. In addition to the experiences from his schooling and early church posts in Halle, we must assume considerable early influence on Handel from the Lutheran pastors on his mother's side

---

[3] See Hawkins, *A General History*, ii. 910–11. Handel's will commenced with the conventional formula 'In the Name of God Amen' (Deutsch, *Handel*, 691).

[4] Burney, *An Account*, Sketch, 34.

of his family, which may have become even more significant in the period following his father's death. Long before he came to London, therefore, he probably knew well not only his Bible, but also the outlook and behaviour of professional clergy.

Although English church music had a tradition that was in many respects independent of those in continental Europe, some attention must be given to Handel's experience before coming to London. No examples survive of his earliest church music, which we may assume he composed under the guidance of his teacher Friedrich Wilhelm Zachow at the Marktkirche in Halle.[5] In Zachow's church cantatas the Italian-derived operatic forms of aria and accompanied recitative are mixed with indigenous German forms based on the chorale, and his attraction to the current Italian style marks him out as one of the more progressive organist-composers of his period.[6] The instrumental ritornellos to some cantata arias show that Zachow had grasped the principle of melodic extension upon which the Italian style was based:[7] the supporting harmonic drive of the Italian style is also in evidence, with firm directional control over passages of chromatic harmony.[8] His handling of larger instrumental forces was based on the 'concertato' principle, employing contrasted blocks of sound from groups of voices and instruments.[9] Although Zachow's church music is related more closely to J. S. Bach's cantatas than to Handel's English church music, some techniques that we normally associate with Handel's music can be found in them. There are, for example, broad affirmative strokes of the type employed by Handel in the Coronation Anthems,[10] and examples of an arioso-type texture that was employed by Handel for 'We believe that thou shalt come' in the Utrecht Te Deum, and also in several solo movements in the Chapel Royal music (see Ex. 1.1). Some features of Zachow's cantatas display parallels with contemporary developments in English music. His use of trumpets with strings is reminiscent of the scoring of Purcell's odes,[11] and some of his ostinato bass figures are remarkably similar to Purcell's favourite ground-bass types.[12] Many an English verse anthem, furthermore, moves with the short phrases and close imitations of Ex. 1.2.

---

[5] One surviving work, the first setting of *Laudate pueri Dominum* (HWV 236), may have been composed in Germany, but after Handel had left Halle. The date and authorship of the *Gloria* attributed to Handel in 2000 remain uncertain.

[6] Most of Zachow's cantatas were probably composed before 1701: see Günter Thomas, 'Zachow, Friedrich Wilhelm', in *NG II*.

[7] See e.g. the opening of 'Mein Jesu, habe Dank' in Zachow, *Gesammelte Werke*, 189.

[8] 'Ach und weh', ibid. 56.

[9] See the instrumental prelude to *Lobe den Herrn*, ibid. 145.

[10] See 'Der Herr hat Grosses an uns getan', ibid. 175.

[11] See ibid. 50.

[12] 'Zu Bethlehem, in David's Stadt', ibid. 96.

Ex. 1.1. Zachow, *Lobe den Herrn, meine Seele*, No. 5 (*Gesammelte Werke*, p. 164)

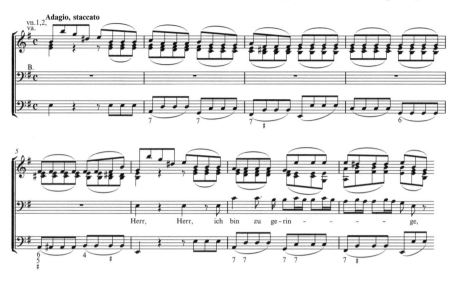

Ex. 1.2. Zachow, *Lobe den Herrn, meine Seele*, No. 3 (*Gesammelte Werke*, p. 159)

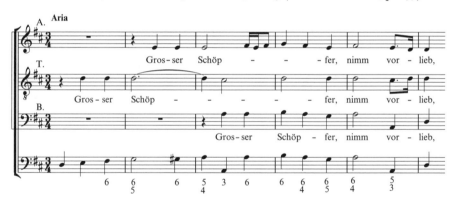

Although individual elements in Zachow's music may have influenced Handel, his style nevertheless remains that of a late seventeenth-century composer, and his student was quickly to develop a broader musical manner. When Handel left Halle for Hamburg in 1703 his musical activity shifted away from church music to the opera house and the composition of keyboard music, but it seems likely that he took some interest in the musical life of the Hamburg churches, and in particular the city's performances of Passion music.[13] Three

---

[13] Keiser's setting of *Der blutige und sterbende Jesus* was performed in Hamburg in 1704 (Smallman, *The Background of Passion Music*, 32), and the *St John Passion*, formerly attributed to

years later he moved to Italy, and there his creative opportunities included the composition of Latin church music, in which he displayed a musical style far removed from the world of Zachow.

Handel's surviving church music from his Italian years falls into two groups of works: cantata-type motets and antiphons, mainly for a soprano-register soloist with string accompaniment, and larger concerted pieces. The latter, comprising the psalm settings *Dixit Dominus*, *Laudate pueri Dominum* and *Nisi Dominus* (HWV 232, 237, 238), are of particular relevance as a background to his subsequent English church music. All were composed at Rome in 1707, *Laudate pueri Dominum* and *Nisi Dominus* in July, probably for a service of Vespers under Cardinal Colonna's patronage,[14] and *Dixit Dominus* the previous April. Although the circumstances of the performances are not well documented, it seems that the ensemble movements were sung with more than one voice to each part: surviving original-performance part-books for *Laudate pueri Dominum* have material for 'Canto primo', 'Soprano secondo concertato', and 'Soprano secondo Ripieno', and continuo organ parts for 'Primo choro' and 'Secondo Choro', even though no movement has more than five independent vocal lines.[15] The score of *Dixit Dominus* includes 'solo' and 'tutti' indications against the voice parts, which suggest the use of more than one singer to a part elsewhere,[16] and one chorus entry is marked 'Tutti Capella'.[17]

Handel's Latin psalm settings present us with the sudden appearance of a fully formed concerted style, combined with a complementary skill in achieving an appropriate balance between solo and ensemble material. Each work includes some music for solo voices, either as separate movements or in passages where one voice alternates with the full ensemble of four or five parts. His contact at first hand with contemporary Italian music, of which the music of Antonio Caldara with its smooth, purposeful harmony may be taken as representative,[18] moulded Handel's own musical technique towards providing a stronger harmonic thrust and larger phrase spans: the extent of his

---

Handel but possibly by Keiser, may have been performed there during Handel's period of residence.

[14] See Shaw and Dixon, 'Handel's Vesper Music'.

[15] The distribution of the performers may have been established by the double-choir 'Gloria Patri' to *Nisi Dominus*.

[16] *HG* 38, pp. 85–9; see also *Nisi Dominus*, ibid. 128.

[17] Ibid. 104. From the autograph (GB-Lbl RM 20.f.1, fo. 66ᵛ) it appears that Handel wrote 'Capella' first and added 'tutti' as an afterthought.

[18] Caldara held office at the Mantuan court until 1707, and became Prince Ruspoli's *maestro di cappella* at Rome in Mar. 1709, at the end of Handel's period of association with Ruspoli. Although Caldara may have been influenced by Handel, his style was formed earlier, largely under the influence of Legrenzi. See Kirkendale, *Caldara* and, for the music, Caldara, *Kirchenwerke*.

development can be seen in a movement such as 'Sit nomen Domini' from *Laudate pueri Dominum*,[19] where he uses chains of sevenths, a directional bass line, and overlapping phrases between voice and oboe to impel the music forward. The result is thoroughly 'modern', closer to the style of later works such as Vivaldi's famous D major *Gloria* than to the German works that Handel had left behind.

The chorus movements in his Latin psalms include only a limited amount of extended imitative writing: the final sections of the doxologies in *Dixit Dominus*[20] and *Nisi Dominus*[21] could be described as fugal, and apart from these there are a few short exposition-like passages elsewhere in *Dixit Dominus*.[22] More characteristic of Handel's technique is the contrapuntal working of two or more themes presented simultaneously.[23] Sometimes this is effectively combined with the contrast between a single voice and the full chorus, with the solo part establishing one of the themes before it is integrated into the larger texture.[24] Once the music is under way, the contrast between a single part and the full ensemble remains an important resource. It is used with striking effect in *Dixit Dominus* both as a way of extending the musical interest[25] and as a means of introducing new material within a movement. A remarkable example of the latter use occurs in the first movement, where a cantus firmus theme, introduced in the treble part, is answered and complemented by shorter phrases, themselves in blocks of alternating rhythmic imitation, from the rest of the chorus and orchestra: see Ex. 1.3. The techniques used here may be related to those practised in Germany in the treatment of chorale melodies, but the forceful simplicity of Handel's presentation is far from the ruminative style of most chorale preludes. One texture that became a favourite of Handel's was based on similar principles, the solo line having division-type passage-work against staccato choral chords: see Ex. 1.4.

The most remarkable sign of Handel's technical assurance in the choral writing of the Latin psalms is the effective balance between homophonic and contrapuntal elements. The polyphonic density is skilfully varied and, above all, Handel knows exactly when to slip from a chordal opening into imitative phrase extension, and when to pull the threads together again into a concerted homophonic passage to round off a section. The Latin psalms show that Handel was a master of the techniques required for church music as early as 1707, and these techniques were carried forward to his English choral music. It only needs a change of words, for example, to turn Ex. 1.3 into a minor-key

---

[19] *HG* 38, pp. 28–9.   [20] Ibid. 114 and seq.
[21] The 'Gloria Patri' to this work is not in *HG*; see Handel, *Nisi Dominus*, ed. Shaw.
[22] *HG* 38, pp. 58, 93.   [23] Ibid. 79, for example.
[24] Ibid. 29, 55.   [25] Ibid. 77.

Ex. 1.3. Handel, *Dixit Dominus*, No. 1

'Hallelujah' chorus. The Latin works provided him with experience in dealing with psalm texts, and also with a mine of thematic material on which he drew for his later English works, including his anthems for the Chapel Royal and for Cannons.

The English Chapel Royal was an institution with its own traditions, formed long before Handel arrived in London. Handel's activity modified the musical life of London, including that part of its life which found expression in instrumentally accompanied church music, but he was also influenced

Ex. 1.4. Handel, *Laudate pueri Dominum* (HWV 237), No. 8

by the musical traditions that were represented by the Chapel and its leading performers. It is not surprising that the Chapel's history in the later seventeenth century has received attention on account of its significance to Henry Purcell's biography: Purcell grew up as a chorister among the musical traditions of the Chapel, which continued to provide the context for one important strand of his subsequent career. For the present purpose it is necessary to consider the Chapel's history from a rather different perspective, paying particular attention in Chapter 2 to the fifteen years that separated Purcell's death from Handel's arrival in London. A brief (and thus necessarily superficial) summary of the relevant events affecting the chapel in the fifty years preceding Handel's arrival, and a reminder of the longer-term background, may nevertheless be useful at this point. From the time of the English Reformation in the 1530s political and religious issues were interconnected, though people might also have strong convictions on individual aspects of religious allegiance. Furthermore, while there were possible political options from time to time in England between Anglican, Roman Catholic, and Puritan institutions, there were also factions within the Church of England that supported different views on issues of theology, ritual, and religious practice. Roman Catholicism was a factor in European political alliances as well as in matters of religious observance: the Revocation of the Edict of Nantes in 1685 brought renewed attention to issues about individual liberty and religious toleration as well. In the seventeenth century British mistrust of France coloured the image of Roman Catholicism, yet the dynastic reality was that Roman Catholic courts in Europe provided the brides for three Stuart kings—Charles I, Charles II, and James II.

The Restoration of the monarchy with the return of King Charles II to London in 1660 marked the end of the Commonwealth period that had followed the Civil War, though it did not resolve many of the underlying religious and political issues that had generated the conflict. The Act of Uniformity in 1662 defined the nature of the religious settlement for the Church of England, and in so doing it forced the ejection of many clergy from the Church, leading to the establishment of English Nonconformity. The Act was accompanied by the publication of a new Book of Common Prayer, in a recognizable succession from those of the previous century, which regulated the church's liturgy and ritual. Charles II was attracted to Roman Catholicism but maintained Anglican observance in the Chapel Royal. However, upon his death in 1685 his brother, who succeeded as King James II, set up a personal Roman Catholic chapel for himself and his consort, initially using the Queen's Chapel at St James's but then converting a room at Whitehall Palace into a Chapel Royal. The Roman Catholic Chapel had a separate musical and clerical establishment, but the Anglican Chapel Royal continued to function in the original Chapel at Whitehall, where Protestant services were maintained for Princess Anne, James's younger daughter. James had two surviving daughters by his first (Protestant) wife, and in 1688 his second (Roman Catholic) wife gave birth to a son. After a period of increasing political tension and turmoil, James fled to France in December 1688. Early the next year Parliament declared the throne vacant and James's daughter Mary was made joint sovereign (as Queen Mary II) with her husband William of Orange (King William III): they were both grandchildren of Charles I. The events of 1688–9 are sometimes referred to as the 'English Revolution'. Following Mary's death in December 1695 William remained as sole monarch, and in 1701 the Act of Settlement defined the terms of the succession upon his death: the crown would pass to his sister-in-law Anne and then, in default of any surviving children of hers, to the nearest Protestant line, currently represented by Charles II's cousin Sophia, widow of Ernst August, Elector of Hanover. By the Act, Roman Catholics were debarred from the succession, thus excluding the descendants of James II by his second wife. Their son (also James) was in any case the subject of a rumour that he was a child of other parents, and had been smuggled into the birth-chamber at the Palace in a warming-pan. The succession proceeded as planned following the deaths of William in March 1702 and of Anne in August 1714. Sophia of Hanover had died shortly before Anne, so the crown passed to her son, as George I: he succeeded as the first King of Great Britain, following the Act of Union that had incorporated Scotland in 1707. During the first half of the eighteenth century there remained a

substantial body of opinion in Britain that was uneasy about the Act of
Settlement. Some supported the restoration of the line through James II's
son (Jacobites); others, while not wishing to see the consequent establishment
of a Roman Catholic Church, would not take the oath of allegiance to the
Hanoverian line (non-jurors). James II's son and grandson were referred to by
Jacobites as 'King James III' and 'King Charles III', respectively: to others, they
were the Old Pretender and the Young Pretender.

Mention has been made of the simultaneous existence of two Chapels Royal
during the 1680s, and some clarification is needed. The term 'Chapel Royal' is
still used, as it was in Handel's day, with two separate meanings: to denote an
establishment of priests, musicians, and other staff, and secondly to denote a
particular building.[26] Strictly, it has a yet wider application in both usages. In
the eighteenth century the British Court also had lesser permanent establishments of French, Dutch, and Lutheran Chapels Royal, serving various com-
munities of Protestants that had entered Court life through association with
King William III, Prince George of Denmark (Queen Anne's husband), and
the Hanoverian family.[27] The various buildings occupied by these establishments were Chapels Royal, but this description could cover any rooms used as
chapels within any royal palace; furthermore, in probably the most authentic
usage, any building in which the king or queen attended a service as monarch
was, as the Sub-Dean described St Paul's Cathedral in 1715, 'the King's
Chappell upon this Occasion'.[28] In this book 'Chapel Royal' will be used for
the monarch's principal Chapel establishment, and for the room at St James's
Palace that has been the principal home of that establishment for more than
two centuries. Eighteenth-century references to the 'Chapel Royal, St James's
Palace' are normally to this Chapel. The two meanings are usually easily
distinguished in context: in some possible cases of ambiguity buildings will
be referred to as 'Royal Chapels'.

[26] A third possible usage, to denote a regular congregation in addition to the staff, was not
current in the eighteenth century.
[27] See Burrows, 'German Chorales and English Hymns'. There was also a small residual
Scottish Chapel Royal in Edinburgh, with no musicians.
[28] *OCB*, fo. 54ᵛ; Ashbee and Harley, i. 139.

PART I

History and Repertory

2

The Chapel Royal before Handel's Arrival in England: Symphony Anthems and Thanksgivings

The Early History of the Chapel Royal

THE English Chapel Royal or household chapel began in Anglo-Saxon times as a body of priests and servants who ministered to the spiritual needs of the sovereign and travelled with the court.[1] The first evidence for the office of Dean as head of the Chapel appears about 1350; in 1483 King Edward IV reorganized the Chapel's constitution and formally introduced the office of Sub-Dean. From the mid-thirteenth century at least, the Chapel employed professional singers and these were gradually formed into a recognizable musical establishment. The earliest recorded appointment of a Master of the Children dates from the 1440s: from that time we can be sure of the existence of a permanent institution consisting of children and clerks. From 1483 the clerks, some of them singers and some in priests' orders, were called Gentlemen. In the Eltham Palace Ordinances of 1526 King Henry VIII reduced the travelling component of the Chapel, which had the compensatory effect of tying the full permanent establishment to the principal London palace. From 1603 the Dean was regularly selected from the ranks of the Bishops and, even though the Chapel had by that date become less nomadic than in medieval times and bishops were not inevitably tied to their diocesan seats, the divided duties of the Dean inevitably resulted in the gradual shifting of responsibility for the routine running of the Chapel onto the Sub-Dean.

At the time of the English Reformation the Chapel Royal became critical to the course of church history in both liturgical and musical matters. New vernacular liturgical experiments were apparently first tried out at the Chapel Royal, whose practice was regarded by 1548 as the approved reformed model in Lord Protector Somerset's command to the University of Cambridge, that 'you in your colleges, chapels or other churches use one uniform order, rite

---

[1] For a fuller account of the Chapel's history, see Baldwin, *The Chapel Royal*.

and ceremonies in the mass, matins and even-song and all divine service in the same to be said or sung, such as is presently used in the king's majesty's chapel, and none other.'² The origins and development of these liturgies at court affected the content and the style of the eventual official liturgical manual for the Church of England—the Book of Common Prayer, first published in 1549. It is significant that the earliest official English-language liturgy was the Litany of 1544, generated at a critical stage during the war with France, when the need was felt special for prayers at a time of national crisis.³ Its content is reflected in the Litany published in the second, 1552, Prayer Book;⁴ the occasional prayers at the end of that service, and the prayers for the king in the 1549 Prayer Book Communion Service, are texts specifically concerned with the nation's well-being, and were created by clergy who worked close to the court. The Chapel Royal was henceforth at the centre of a national church where religion and politics were intertwined, and the religious as well as institutional life of the Chapel came to reflect this.

Theological interest inevitably centred around the interpretation of the Mass that was found in the early Prayer Books, but the distinctive flavour of the new Anglicanism which the Chapel represented is to be found in other liturgies than the Communion Service. Although Henry VIII destroyed the monasteries he also set in train the process by which Thomas Cranmer developed the daily services of Morning and Evening Prayer (Matins and Evensong) based on the monastic hours. Here the Reformers' natural emphasis on the Word took on a characteristic English form, and eventually creative musical activity turned away from musical settings of the Mass towards the provision of anthems (as musical illumination of the Word) and settings of the canticles for Matins and Evensong. The prescribed texts of the canticles included two to be 'said or sung in English' at Morning Prayer, *Te Deum laudamus* ('We praise thee, O God') and *Jubilate Deo* ('O be joyful in the Lord, all ye lands'), that were to receive particular attention from later composers. It was in Morning and Evening Prayer, and not in the Communion Service, that the 1662 Prayer Book made official recognition of the anthem with the rubric 'In Quires and Places where they sing, here followeth the Anthem', legitimizing a long-standing practice of singing an anthem after the third collect.⁵ The anthems,

---

    ² le Huray, *Music and the Reformation*, 11.
    ³ Previous official activity had been concerned with the provision and use of an English Bible (Royal Injunctions of 1536 and 1543), rather than with liturgies.
    ⁴ Harrison, *The First and Second Prayer Books*, 361–7.
    ⁵ Injunctions accompanying the royal visitation in 1559 had authorized the singing of suitable music 'in the beginning, or in the end of common prayers': see le Huray, *Music and the Reformation*, 31–3. The collects were a series of prayers, originally at the end of the liturgies of Morning and Evening Prayer.

settings of sacred texts in English, were initially compositions with simple homophonic texture for full choir, but within thirty years of the Reformation these were supplemented by 'verse' anthems with passages for one or more solo voices. In 1662 the prayers and thanksgivings for special occasions were detached from the Litany so that they could also be used regularly in the course of Matins and Evensong. The period between the 1552 and 1662 Prayer Books had seen enormous swings in the religious and political life at court, including a relatively brief return to Roman Catholicism during the reign of Queen Mary I and a complete hiatus in the Chapel Royal's existence during the Common-wealth period. The Restoration settlement that is represented by the 1662 Prayer Book returned substantially to the outlines that had been developed in the earlier English liturgies.

The Chapel Royal Symphony Anthem 1660–1694—Rise and Eclipse

The Restoration of the monarchy in 1660 saw a resumption of the routine services by the Chapel Royal and indeed a restoration of the choir itself, working in the chapel at Whitehall Palace. In the course of the next few years, probably beginning in 1662, a new musical practice was introduced in the Chapel, memorably described by John Evelyn: 'Instead of the antient grave and solemn wind musique accompanying the *Organ* was introduced a Consort of 24 Violins betweene every pause, after the *French* fantastical light way.'[6] The employment of wind instruments with the organ to accompany the singers in the Chapel had fallen out of use completely by about 1670: henceforward the daily services were accompanied by organ alone, joined occasionally by stringed instruments for specially written anthems.[7] There is no evidence that the new 'symphony anthems' with instrumental ritornellos for a string ensemble were performed anywhere other than by the Chapel Royal during the first twenty years of their development, and the type of vocal writing cultivated in them was intimately related to the particular styles of solo singers from the Chapel. The symphony anthem was therefore a specifically Chapel Royal genre. Its progress during the period 1660–1700 was variable, and depended critically on the influence that successive monarchs had on the music of the Chapel from reign to reign.

Whether or not the introduction of string instruments into the anthems was at King Charles II's personal instigation in the first place, it seems to have met

---

[6] Evelyn, *Diary*, iii. 347 (21 Dec. 1662).
[7] See Holman, *Four and Twenty Fiddlers*, ch. 16.

with his approval. The formation of the 24 'Violins' (in practice, an ensemble of string instruments covering sufficient registers for music in four or five parts) under the Master of the King's Musick, which ensured the availability of the string players, must similarly have received royal encouragement. The establishment of the King's Musicians represented a consolidation of a longer tradition of court string-players into a substantial band, from a previously rather muddled situation in which string-players had functioned in various overlapping ensembles. Other royal ensembles of 'private music' continued through the reigns of Charles II and James II, but then their appointments were phased out under William III, leaving only the 24 Musicians, with the Master and an Instrument Keeper.[8] However, the occasions when all twenty-four players were in simultaneous attendance were probably quite rare: by the eighteenth century there was a regular practice of alternate months of 'waiting', leaving half of that number on call at any time. For the symphony anthems in the Chapel Royal it seems that only a small group of players was involved: from the 1670s there were three groups of five players in alternating rosters.[9] The Chapel Royal and the King's Musicians could be regarded as vehicles for the display of kingship and conspicuous private ownership, but there is no reason to doubt that Charles II's interest in the music of the Chapel Royal was genuine. Symphony anthems seem to have been performed only when the King went to the Chapel, and on some Sundays and special occasions: the surviving repertory is not large enough to have supported regular weekly performances.[10] The new genre complemented the existing repertory of full anthems and verse anthems for the daily services by contemporary and earlier composers: the anthem word-book, *Divine Harmony*, published in 1712, reveals that works by Tallis, Mundy, Byrd, Hooper, Batten, and Orlando Gibbons were still in use.

The King's tastes and the composers' proclivities combined in approving the infusion of the English verse anthem with the French style in the symphony anthem,[11] though the 'French' element in the works of Cooke, Locke, and Pelham Humfrey is more apparent in the instrumental than in the vocal writing. By the time Henry Purcell became Organist of the Chapel Royal in 1682 the French stylistic influence was giving way to a new Italian one,[12] and, although it is difficult to isolate specific stylistic changes, this may account for

[8] See Holman, *Four and Twenty Fiddlers*, esp. chs. 12 and 17.   [9] Ibid. 398.

[10] The strings were used to accompany the anthem at 3.30 Evening Prayers except during Lent. 'On weekdayes i.e. on Wednesdays and Friday's the King being at Sermon are sung two Anthems one after the Litany, the other after the Sermon', presumably without strings: Alford, Manuscript Register, p. 15, dated 16 Oct. 1675; Ashbee and Harley, ii. 284.

[11] Lewis, 'English Church Music', 494–5.

[12] See Purcell's preface to *Sonnata's of III Parts* (1683).

the more solid impression that Purcell's symphony anthems create when compared with the works of the older composers among whom he had grown up in the Chapel. The bulk of Purcell's symphony anthems were composed between 1682 and 1688,[13] after the genre had already seen twenty years of successful life in the Chapel. The years between 1680 and 1685 mark the high point of the Chapel Royal symphony anthem, and the field was not Purcell's alone: John Blow composed twenty-three symphony anthems in the ten years following his appointment as a Gentleman of the Chapel in 1674, in a rare situation of amicable and creative rivalry with the younger man.[14]

The cooperation of the Chapel Royal and the King's Musicians that the performance of symphony anthems entailed was also nourished by the performance of secular court odes for the new year and royal birthdays.[15] The joint ensemble must have grown used to working together, and a cohesive unit of professional musicians seems gradually to have emerged. By 1683 the practical traditions built up in the Chapel Royal and in the performance of court odes moved into the wider circle of London's musical life through the inauguration of the Musical Society for the celebration of St Cecilia's day.[16] Court musicians formed the core of the performers for these events, and it is clear from the lists of stewards that the performers themselves provided part of the management which ensured the success of the Musical Society. At the same time, there was evidently also a growing group of connoisseurs to whom the court ensemble and its style appealed. The publication of Purcell's first set of trio sonatas in 1683 is another pointer to the existence of the same audience, well disposed to the Organist of His Majesty's Chapel Royal. The court's string-players had performed in the London theatres during the 1660s and 1670s, but it was the St Cecilia performances that provided the public platform for the Chapel Royal (along with singers from the related choirs at Westminster Abbey and St Paul's Cathedral) and the King's Musicians as a group. The edifying treatment of the subject of music in the St Cecilia odes was in any case not too far removed from the spirit of the Chapel's normal activity.

Uncertainties about the future may have given a special impetus to the court musicians' involvement with the Cecilian celebrations in November 1683. By then King Charles II was growing old and the Chapel Royal must have doubted whether much support could be expected from his successor. Events confirmed these fears. Although the Coronation of King James II and his queen consort in 1685 included substantial new anthems from Purcell, Blow,

---

[13] See Arkwright, 'Purcell's Church Music', and the work-list for 'Purcell, Henry' in *NG II*.
[14] See Blow's anthems in *MB* 7, 50, 64, and 79, and the Introductions to these vols.
[15] The early history of the court odes is related in detail in McGuinness, *English Court Odes*.
[16] See *NG II*, 'Cecilian Festivals'. St Cecilia's day is 22 November.

and William Turner, and followed the outlines of the traditional English coronation liturgy except in the omission of the Communion Service, the new king transferred his regular religious devotions from the Chapel Royal to a newly formed Roman Catholic establishment (at first nominally the Queen's personal chapel) that functioned initially at the Queen's Chapel, St James's Palace, and subsequently moved to a new Chapel at Whitehall where services were inaugurated with midnight Mass at Christmas 1686.[17] Yet the period following James II's withdrawal from the regular Chapel Royal provides a telling demonstration that the Chapel had evolved a strong and self-supporting tradition. Twenty years previously the formation of a rival royal Roman Catholic Chapel with its own musical establishment had proved to be a dangerously popular alternative to the Chapel Royal, especially when Matthew Locke's energies were diverted to it.[18] This time, however, after an initial period of uncertainty,[19] by mid-1687 the Chapel was again going about its usual business with confidence, maintaining the Anglican services in their regular venue, in parallel with the separate establishment of foreign priests, musicians, and 'Gregorians' that served the Roman Catholic Chapel.[20] James II's sister Princess Anne evidently took the King's place in the Chapel Royal at Whitehall, which is even referred to as 'the Princess's Chappell'.[21] Anne's presence provided some guarantee of a safe Anglican future for the Chapel since she was married to the Protestant Prince George of Denmark, and she seems to have taken an interest in the Chapel's musical traditions, insisting that the 'violins' were in attendance when she was present.[22] In 1687–8 Purcell produced as many symphony anthems per year as he had done in the peak period of 1682–5, composing one of the most elaborate (*Blessed are they that fear the Lord*) for the Thanksgiving for the Queen's pregnancy in 1688,[23] the event which constituted the greatest threat to the future of the Chapel as an Anglican institution. The Chapel Royal survived the turbulent period at court in 1688–9 and arrived intact at the coronation of King William III and Queen Mary II in April 1689, though somewhat depleted in numbers because vacancies occurring during the previous reign had not been filled. The new king and queen

---

[17] See Colvin, *The History of the King's Works*, v. 286–90.

[18] *MB* 38 (le Huray, *Locke*), Preface.

[19] The only orchestrally accompanied anthem from the first part of James II's reign known to me is William Turner's *Preserve me O God*, dated 24 Aug. 1686.

[20] For the Roman Catholic establishment, see the lists in Ashbee, *Records*, v. 84, 86. The leading Chapel Royal musicians apparently showed no interest in participating.

[21] Lafontaine, *The King's Musick*, 386 (8 Mar. 1687/8).

[22] Ashbee, *Records*, ii. 15–16 (21 Oct. 1687).

[23] See Zimmerman, 'Anthems of Purcell'. The anthem, composed for the Thanksgiving in Jan. 1687/8, may have been repeated at the Thanksgiving on 17 June 1688 for the Queen's safe delivery.

restored Henry Compton to his place as Dean of the Chapel, from which he had been removed by James II, and appointed a new Sub-Dean, Ralph Battell, to replace the ageing William Holder. The Chapel no doubt prepared for business as usual.

In the event, it was King William's Calvinism rather than James's Romanism that removed the string-players from the Chapel, and Purcell's few late anthems are accompanied by organ only. The King's orders, relayed through the Dean of the Chapel on 23 February 1688/9, were specific: 'That there shall be no musick [i.e. instruments] in the Chappell, but the Organ'.[24] Purcell's increased attention to the theatre in the last years of his life was in part the result of the diminishing demands of the Chapel tradition in which he had been brought up. He had only limited opportunities for composing music for the court musicians outside the context of the Chapel. Since he never held office as Master of the King's Music, Purcell was not called upon to compose the music for the odes for the New Year or the King's birthday, though he composed eleven works in the similar genre of Welcome Songs between 1680 and 1688: furthermore, the Queen's birthday ode was his task, and his ode for the Duke of Gloucester's sixth birthday in July 1695 suggests that he received continued support from Princess Anne.[25] Other musicians of the Chapel may also have looked to the female members of the royal family for support: circumstantial evidence certainly indicates that they could expect little from the King. A pattern similar to that of 1685–7 can be discerned. The Chapel Royal probably began the reign with considerable uncertainty about the future, but then the ambitions of the Chapel's musicians began to reassert themselves. This time the reassertion was primarily theological, and was initiated in a more public venue than the Chapel itself.

In 1693 the Musical Society introduced a sermon at St Bride's Church, Fleet Street, in addition to the performance of an ode on St Cecilia's day.[26] The sermon, preached by the Sub-Dean of the Chapel Royal himself, is a spirited defence of church music, and its tone suggests that a detailed theological rationale for church music was required as ammunition by the musicians of the day.[27] Presumably King William's austere tastes in the Chapel had become

---

[24] Alford, Manuscript Register, p. 21b; Ashbee and Harley, ii. 287. The same regulations also specified the parts of the service that were to be sung.

[25] The Duke, Anne's longest-surviving child, died in 1700.

[26] Husk, *An Account*, 12, 32. The sermon may have been a separate event or, rather more likely, it originated in a service of Morning Prayer that perhaps also included the performance of an anthem.

[27] Battell, *The Lawfulness and Expediency of Church-Musick*. In addition to being the first known sermon connected with the Cecilian Festivals, this is also the first in a sequence of sermons in defence of church music that goes well into the 18th c. and includes those preached at the early meetings of the Three Choirs Festival: for a list, see Ruth Smith, 'The Argument and

irksome to them and, although it would have been tactless for someone
holding a court position to make a direct attack on current practices, Battell
did venture to attack the Geneva Bible's commentary on the use of instruments
in church.[28] Another sermon, preached at the St Cecilia festival in 1696 by
Samson Estwick,[29] is rather more explicit in suggesting that the musical
traditions of English Church music were under attack. Estwick, though he
was more associated with Oxford than London in earlier years, had been a
Minor Canon at St Paul's Cathedral since 1691 and can be reasonably taken as a
representative of the attitudes of the London church musicians.[30] The more
controversial part of his sermon suggests that the Anglican church music
needed defending against both Roman Catholicism and the Dissenters. If, as
he argues, church music contributes to spiritual improvement, then this 'gives
us just occasion to blame the Practice of the Church of *Rome*, which has fram'd
and contriv'd her Praises more to the Honour of Men than of God; and not
only so, but she has lock'd up the few sound Pieces of Devotion remaining in
their *Breviary*, in a Language not understood by the generality of their
People'.[31] Having suggested that the Church of Rome had abused the opportunities provided by church music, Estwick then attacked the Dissenters for
condemning the music as well as the abuse:

If the Use and Practice of Church-Musick is of such long standing in the House of
God, and Voices and Instruments were appointed by God himself, to promote the
Edification of his People, this shews us the unjust Exceptions the Dissenters takes [*sic*]
against our Way of Worship, making it to be Popish and Superstitious, and what not;
not considering in the meantime, that those excellent Offices of Praise, I mean our
Hymns[,] were practiced long before Popery was in being; and as to the manner of
adorning 'em with good Musick; this I presume is no fault, however I could wish for
the good of their Souls, that they would come to our Churches, and try whether it is a
fault or not.[32]

A substantial part of Battell's 1693 sermon had been taken up with a defence of
the use of orchestral instruments in church, the major feature of Chapel Royal

---

Contexts', 480–1. The subject of music in church had, of course, been raised as a theological
issue at the Reformation period.

   [28] Ibid. 11.

   [29] Estwick, *The Usefulness of Church-Musick*. The sermon was 'Preach'd at Christ-Church'
(perhaps Christ Church, Oxford) and was published in London. The dedication to the 'Stewards
of St. Cecilia's Feast' is to the London society: the Stewards named include Moses Snow, a
Gentleman of the Chapel Royal, and Matteis, the composer of the Cecilian ode for London in
1696. See also Husk, *An Account*, 37.

   [30] Estwick retained a Chaplaincy at Christ Church until 1711, simultaneously with the Minor
Canonry at St Paul's, where he had been a Chorister in his youth. He was a practising clerical
musician, and one of the founders of the Academy of Vocal Music.

   [31] Estwick, *The Usefulness of Church-Musick*, 20.   [32] Ibid. 21.

practice that had suffered under King William III. It is very likely that an attempt was made to return to orchestrally accompanied music in the Chapel the following year. From the 1693 sermon we know that the Sub-Dean, who was the person most closely concerned with day-to-day policy in the Chapel, would have been in favour of this, but some exceptional circumstance was needed to justify the reintroduction of the orchestra for a special celebration. Such an occasion did present itself in 1694, but in order to explain the background to the events in the Chapel Royal it is necessary to return to the matter of special liturgies.

Special Liturgies for National Occasions; the Origin and Influence of Purcell's D major Canticle Settings

As outlined above, the first Prayer Books included prayers in the Litany and the Communion Service that related to the political life of the nation. However, not many years had elapsed after the introduction of the Prayer Book before it was felt that something more specific was required for significant national events, and special liturgies were published by command of the King (or Queen) in Council for use in all churches on specific days; they were prepared under the guidance of the Archbishop of Canterbury or leading prelates acting with his approval.[33] Sometimes they consisted of single occasional prayers to be added to the normal Prayer Book liturgies, or amendments to specific prayers (for example, the prayer for the royal family). More substantial additions were annual liturgies that formed part of the year's calendar of services. These were normally reissued in a revised form from reign to reign, but became sufficiently established to be included in contemporary publications of the Prayer Books. By 1690 the annual liturgies were four in number: Sovereign's Accession Anniversary, Execution of King Charles I (30 January), Restoration Anniversary (29 May), and Deliverance from the Gunpowder Plot (5 November). 30 January was a Fast day, and the others were Thanksgivings. The regular liturgies were, however, supplemented by others, issued in booklet form, for special Fasts and Thanksgivings, and it is the eighteenth-century publications for particular Thanksgivings that are relevant to the present topic. These comprised a special liturgy for Morning Prayer, usually with the Litany and Communion Service, and sometimes with a special form for Evening Prayer as well; in some cases the liturgies did not specify Morning Prayer or Evening Prayer but began with a rubric that applied to both, though the subsequent specified canticles were nevertheless those for Morning Prayer. The earliest of

---

[33] Luttrell, *A Brief Historical Relation*, v. 442; Boyer, *Anne (Annals)*, v. 140.

the special Thanksgiving liturgies come from the reign of Queen Elizabeth I, the first dating from 1587 and presumably celebrating the success of Drake's attack on Cadiz.[34] By 1690 the revisions to Morning and Evening Prayer in the occasional liturgies for the Thanksgivings followed a traditional pattern, and the parts of the service that might have been relevant to musical settings were as follows:

1. The opening sentences, usually short verses of Scripture: there is no evidence that they were sung.

2. A selection of biblical texts, often running to considerable length, replacing the introductory Psalm *Venite exultemus* ('O come, let us sing unto the Lord') at Morning Prayer. Many liturgies published before 1700 include a rubric that the verses were to be said by 'the Clerk and People' alternately: this was reinforced by printing alternate verses in light and heavy type, and the typography was preserved long after the rubric was dropped. The selection of texts was ingenious: verses from different contexts were juxtaposed but the selectors often had a fine sense of fitness to the occasion, and created effective sequences of ideas. Although there are no examples of anthems that were directly derived from these collations of verses, their existence may have influenced the texts of some anthems for Thanksgiving Days, which are often selected from disparate biblical verses with similar imaginative eclecticism.[35]

3. Canticles. These were the regular ones from the Prayer Book services: at Morning Prayer the Thanksgiving liturgies included *Te Deum laudamus* and *Jubilate Deo*, sometimes with *Cantate Domino* as an alternative to the latter.

4. Specified psalms, placed before the reading of the lessons and replacing the daily psalms that were ordered in the Prayer Book calendar. Two or three psalms were chosen as appropriate for each service; the choice varied from one service to another. Only occasionally were the texts of anthems for the Thanksgivings taken from these psalms, and the coincidence is so infrequent as to suggest that the occurrences were accidental.

5. Anthems. Neither anthem texts nor rubrics for the inclusion of anthems appear in any special liturgy.

---

[34] *A Prayer and Thanksgiving fit for this present and to be used in the Time of Common Prayer* (1587). The early liturgies were intended for repeated use: the first single-day Thanksgiving may have been that for the Restoration, celebrated on 28 June 1660.

[35] e.g. Croft's *O Praise the Lord, all ye that fear him*, and the Blow/Clarke/Croft anthem *Behold how good and joyful*: see *Divine Harmony*, 26, 34–5. On the subject of mixed (and adapted) biblical texts for anthems of the period, see Ruth Smith, *Handel's Oratorios*, ch. 3, which also includes (in Table 2) detailed examples from anthems by Blow and Greene.

The special liturgies were commanded to be celebrated throughout the country (see below, Fig. 4.1): no doubt some were delivered with more enthusiasm than others in the nation's parishes, but in London the Thanksgivings were generally kept with due ceremony, and on the days of the annual liturgies it was normal for the national Estates to attend services (usually with a special sermon) at a regular location—the monarch and royal family at the Chapel Royal, the House of Lords at Westminster Abbey, and the House of Commons at St Margaret's church, Westminster. Those at Westminster Abbey and St Margaret's were public events, involving processions from Parliament. For the Chapel Royal the annual liturgies became part of the court calendar and the special Thanksgivings could provide occasions for the performance of more ambitious music than at the routine daily services.

The military campaigns during the reign of William III generated a cycle of special liturgies: in most years there was a Fast in the spring as the campaign began, asking for 'Pardon of Sins, the Preservation of the King's Sacred Person and the Prosperity of his Arms', and in the late autumn there was a Thanksgiving for the 'Preservation of his Majesty's Person, together with his Safe and Happy return to the Kingdom' and any victories that could be celebrated. The campaigns in Ireland during 1690 and 1691 were, from the King's point of view, successful in 'reducing' that country so that he could turn his attention to the Continent. The 1692 Thanksgiving included mention of a victory by the fleet, but there was very little military success to celebrate in the first two Continental campaigns, and it was not until 1694 that the King returned with anything that could be regarded as significant progress.[36]

It was against this background of tempered optimism towards the end of 1694 that Purcell composed his D major settings of the morning canticles. As is well known, these were first performed on St Cecilia's Day 1694, but it seems possible that Purcell originally hoped for a court performance on the Thanksgiving Day. The Te Deum text was widely recognized throughout Europe as the ideal canticle for national rejoicing, whether occasioned by military or diplomatic success, or by the birth of an heir to the throne.[37] Purcell may also have been influenced by the reputation of Lully's orchestrally accompanied Te Deum, which gained its composer some favour with the French King when it was performed at a royal birthday and a royal wedding, in 1677 and 1679 respectively.[38] Purcell may also have taken a hint from Battell's 1693 sermon,

[36] See Clark, *The Later Stuarts*, 162–74.

[37] Only a month before Purcell's Te Deum was composed it was reported from Vienna that 'Te Deum has been sung in our cathedral for the victory obtained over the Turks and Tartars' (Luttrell, *A Brief Historical Relation*, iii. 397).

[38] Lully, *Te Deum Laudamus*, Preface. There were also subsequent comparable settings by Lalande (1684) and Charpentier, the latter probably composed at about the same time as Purcell's; see Charpentier, *Te Deum Laudamus*, Preface.

which included within the same sentence reference to Ambrose's Te Deum text and to his introduction of musical instruments into the services at Milan Cathedral. It is not known where the composition of Purcell's Te Deum fits into the chronology of events in 1694. The King arrived back in London from the Continent on 9 November[39] and two days later Purcell completed the anthem *The Way of God is an undefiled way* to celebrate his return: this anthem does not have orchestral accompaniment, but it is in the correct key to form a partner with the D major canticles and it includes imitations of typical trumpet-and-drum writing.[40] On 21 November a royal proclamation named Sunday 2 December as the Thanksgiving Day: the special liturgy for that day was issued under the imprimatur of the Archbishop of Canterbury on 16 November.[41] On 22 November Purcell's Te Deum and Jubilate received its first performance, at the church service for the annual Cecilian celebrations in St Bride's, Fleet Street. This performance produced a change of emphasis in the St Cecilia Festival by applying the musical performing resources to church music.[42] The significance of the event may have been more far-reaching still, for the Chapel Royal and the Royal Musicians could have regarded the St Cecilia service as a public rehearsal for a forthcoming court performance. The Te Deum and Jubilate were not, in the event, performed at the Chapel Royal on the Thanksgiving Day but a week later: 'Tuesday 11 December 1694. Sunday last was performed before their majesties in the chappel royal the same vocal and instrumental musick as was performed at St. Bride's Church on St. Cecilia's day last.'[43] This appears to have been the only occasion on which King William III heard orchestrally accompanied church music in his Chapel Royal.

Unfortunately the deaths of Queen Mary and Henry Purcell within the following twelve months prevented this innovation from being followed up further within the Chapel. The influence of Purcell's canticle settings on his contemporaries, however, was marked and long-lasting. It was the first English church music of its type to combine trumpets with the strings.[44] In this scoring Purcell followed Lully's model, which is also for two trumpets and strings,

---

[39] Boyer, *The History of King William*, ii. 397.

[40] *PS* 32, especially bars 24–42 (pp. 58–9); for the date of the anthem, see Zimmerman, 'Anthems of Purcell' and Arkwright, 'Purcell's Church Music'.

[41] Luttrell, *A Brief Historical Relation*, iii. 402. Order of service *A Form of Prayer and Thanksgiving to Almighty God, to be used . . . on Sunday the Second Day of December next ensuing* (London, 1694).

[42] It is uncertain whether an ode was performed at the 1694 Festival, but see Husk, *An Account*, 34.

[43] Luttrell, *A Brief Historical Relation*, iii. 410.

[44] Purcell had previously used trumpets with string orchestra in most of his odes for Queen Mary's birthday since 1690.

though Lully's full string orchestra has his characteristic five-part texture instead of Purcell's four-part one.[45] It is not certain whether the influence was direct and that Purcell had access to a copy of Lully's score, but superficially there is some resemblance between the scoring and the sectional treatment of the text in the two settings.[46] However, Purcell's 1694 music does not imitate Lully's grandiloquent style of 1677 and the thrust of his harmonic rhythms reflects more recent Italian influences on the English composer. Purcell's time-scale is less expansive than Lully's: inevitably, since the Te Deum text comprises a large number of short verses, this means that some of Purcell's musical sections are also rather short, though he largely overcame this problem by combining verses into longer sequences of text that were suitable for more extended musical movements, and by arranging that some sections flowed into the following ones. Although the circumstances of the first performances are not known, the style of Purcell's music implies a larger string ensemble than that for the earlier Chapel Royal symphony anthems: perhaps there were a dozen or more string players, and enough singers to constitute a multi-voice chorus. In solidity of construction, the canticles resemble his more recent odes rather than the symphony anthems: overall, there is a good balance between the jubilation of the full ensemble and the more intimate moments of the 'verse' sections.

In 1720 Thomas Tudway distinguished Purcell's Te Deum and Jubilate (in conjunction with the subsequent settings by Croft and Handel) from the regular Anglican musical repertory: 'such like pieces as these, are only proper in the Church, for great occasions of Publick Thanksgivings; &c, These compositions therefore, are not Strictly call'd Church Music, although, they are upon the same divine Subject; I have been the more particular upon them, because, they are the production of this Age only, at least in England.'[47] The combination of a substantial group of singers and players at church services for special occasions in London had some precedents, for example in the music performed at coronations, but Tudway correctly sensed the novelty of Purcell's music. The application of orchestral accompaniment to the canticles for Morning Prayer was new, as also was the application of the grander style that Purcell had adopted in the 1690s in his theatre music from *Dioclesian* onwards.

---

[45] There are no drum parts to Lully's Te Deum, but reports of the 1677 and 1679 performances mention the use of drums ('Les tymbales et les Trompètes n'y furent point oubliés'; see Lully, *Te Deum Laudamus*, Preface.) The possibility of improvised timpani participation in the English works is considered in Ch. 18.

[46] The latter feature of Lully's setting was favourably commented on by *Le Mercure Galant*: 'Ce qu'on y admira particulièrement c'est que chaque couplet estoit de différent musique' (Lully, *Te Deum Laudamus*, Preface).

[47] Preface to GB-Lbl Harl. MS 7442; Spink, *Restoration Cathedral Music*, 447.

Purcell's 1694 music proved to be an important creative stimulant to his successors. For the St Cecilia Festival services in 1695 and 1696 John Blow and William Turner composed settings of the Te Deum and Jubilate that were obviously closely modelled on Purcell's. Equally important, however, seems to have been the effect on morale. Blow and Turner returned to the composition of instrumentally accompanied anthems for special occasions and even perhaps sought occasions for which they could compose them. Turner produced two such anthems in June 1696, probably in connection with the Commencement at Cambridge at which he received his doctorate.[48] In 1697 the King's Continental campaigns came to an end with the Peace of Ryswick; the Thanksgiving service for this event coincided with the period for the completion of the 'Choir' (chancel) of Wren's new St Paul's Cathedral and it was believed that the King would attend the service there: '20. November (1697). His majestie intends on the thanksgiving day to goe to St. Paul's Cathedral, where the doctors of musick, singing men, etc., are to perform all the ceremonies.'[49] In the event, the Lord Mayor and the Aldermen of the City of London went to St Paul's and Blow's symphony anthem *I was glad* was performed, but the King went to the Chapel Royal at Whitehall instead.[50] In 1698 Blow was one of the Stewards of the annual Festival of the Sons of the Clergy, the service for which was also held at St Paul's Cathedral,[51] and it was probably for that occasion that he composed his anthem *Blessed is the man that feareth the Lord*.[52] For both of these large-scale anthems he used an orchestra consisting of trumpets and strings, Purcell's 1694 scoring, and a combination that was now almost becoming a tradition in itself. There is then a gap in the production of instrumentally accompanied anthems until 1701, when Blow provided an anthem with string accompaniment, *O sing unto the Lord*, for one of the edifying and charitable musical performances arranged by Cavendish Weedon at Stationers' Hall.[53] The preface to the programme for this performance, like the St Cecilia Festival sermons, argues in defence of music in church 'by which the Minds of the People are sweetly surpriz'd into Pious Ardour, and Charm'd into Devotion by Delight', though it makes no mention of the wholesomeness of instrumental participation.[54]

---

[48] They were composed too late to have been intended for the important Thanksgiving service of 1696 (Deliverance from a Plot against the King's life). The anthems survive in a copy at GB-Mp MS 130 Hd4 v.235. John Blow and other Gentlemen of the Chapel Royal went to Cambridge to assist in the performance of Turner's doctoral exercise (*FP*, 2 July 1696).

[49] Luttrell, *A Brief Historical Relation*, vi. 307.

[50] Ibid. 313. For the anthem, see *MB* 50 (Wood, *Blow* II), pp. xix, 1–48.

[51] Freeman, *A Compleat List* (1733), *sub* 1698.

[52] *MB* 79 (Wood, *Blow* IV), pp. xxix–xxx, 1–26.

[53] *MB* 50 (Wood, *Blow* II), pp. xix–xx, 93–123.

[54] Weedon, *The Oration, Anthems and Poems . . . January the 31st 1701*, Epistle Dedicatory, [3].

Queen Anne's Reign: Removal of the Chapel Royal to St James's Palace, and the State Thanksgiving Services

After the death of Queen Mary such musical encouragement as there was at court must have come, as in 1685–9, from Princess Anne, who had a group of her own musicians by 1699,[55] and to whom Blow dedicated the published collection of his songs, *Amphion Anglius*, in 1700. The dedicatory preface to *Amphion Anglius* mentions Blow's intention also to publish a volume of his church music, which never came to fruition, and a surprisingly large part of the text is taken up with a defence of church music: evidently even the preface to a volume of secular music was considered a suitable platform for putting forward the view that 'nothing but the perverse sowerness of a Fanatick, would ever drive Divine Musick out of the Church'.[56] Anne is also known to have exerted some patronage on behalf of the singer Richard Elford before he obtained his place at the Chapel Royal.[57] Her influence in the earlier part of William III's reign was small because she had moved away from the court with her husband after a disagreement with the Queen, her elder sister, but the problem was formally resolved after Mary's death and in November 1695 the King invited Prince George and Princess Anne to take up residence at St James's Palace, which they did the next year.[58] This event set the stage for a major change in the routine life of the Chapel Royal early in Queen Anne's reign, when its main centre of operations removed from Whitehall to St James's.

Both St James's Palace and Whitehall Palace had Royal Chapels during William III's reign, and William had used that at St James's during the period between his wife's death and burial.[59] However, this was an exceptional arrangement and the major court chapel, at which the Chapel Royal choir was resident when the court was in London, was at Whitehall Palace. On the night of 4–5 January 1697/8 this Chapel was destroyed in the fire which consumed a large part of the Palace. Orders were given almost immediately for fitting up the Banqueting House in Whitehall, which had survived intact, as a chapel, but in the meantime the existing chapel at St James's Palace was temporarily put into use, though the King lived mainly at Kensington.[60] The new Banqueting House chapel was opened on 9 December 1698 with a

---

[55] Ashbee, *Records*, ii. 65 (23 Oct. 1699): the reference suggests that her players compensated for deficiencies in the ranks of the King's Musicians for the performance of the King's birthday ode.

[56] Blow, *Amphion Anglius*, The Dedication, 5.

[57] See App. C, 'Elford'.

[58] Kenyon, *The Stuarts*, 168; Luttrell, *A Brief Historical Relation*, iii. 351 and iv. 126.

[59] Ibid. iii. 437 and iv. 125.   [60] Ibid. iv. 328–9, 363.

service that included an anthem by Blow, *Lord, remember David* (without orchestral accompaniment) to celebrate the occasion,[61] and the choir moved in: the list of the members of the Chapel Royal establishment at Queen Anne's coronation (23 April 1702) describes them as 'Her Majesty's Chapel at Whitehall'.[62] However, having settled into St James's Palace as Princess, Anne soon made up her mind to remain there as Queen and it was logical to move the Chapel Royal from Whitehall. Accordingly it was reported that 'the Queen intends to convert the banquetting house at Whitehall again into a room of state to receive Ambassadors, etc., and enlarge her chappel at St. James's, turning it into the form of a cathedrall'.[63] The Banqueting House furnishings were not dismantled, but the Chapel Royal establishment removed: 'Tuesday 19. October (1703) The Bishop of Rochester has, by her majesties order, declar'd St. James's Chappel to be the Chappel Royal; and all the singing men and boys belonging to that of Whitehall are to remove to St. James's'.[64]

If the Chapel Royal musicians had anticipated a return to regular symphony anthems in the new reign they were disappointed. Queen Anne did not change the routine of the Chapel significantly, though she appears to have restored the choir to full strength: there had been some depletion in preceding years, caused once again by a dilatoriness in filling vacancies. At the Queen's coronation on 23 April 1702, the only orchestrally accompanied anthem was Blow's *The Lord God is a sun and a shield*, a shortened version of his anthem from the previous coronation in 1689.[65] This perhaps did not provide much encouragement that the Chapel would return to more ambitious music, but in one respect Anne provided new opportunities, extending the public range of the court's religious ceremonies by doing precisely what her predecessor had not done in 1697: she attended services on special Thanksgiving Days at St Paul's Cathedral rather than in her own private chapel. This brought the Chapel Royal choir, accompanied by the Queen's Musicians, before a large metropolitan congregation in a way that had previously only been known at coronations and, to a lesser extent, at royal funerals.[66] The Continental war had

    [61] GB-Lbl Add. MS 31444, fo. 101[r].

    [62] GB-Lpro LC5/153, p. 238.

    [63] Luttrell, *A Brief Historical Relation*, v. 159 (4 Apr. 1702).

    [64] Ibid. 350. The Queen spent most of 1703 at Bath and Windsor. The transference of the Chapel Royal was completed in preparation for her return to St James's Palace at the end of Oct. 1703.

    [65] The anthem printed in *MB* 79, 163–79 gives the 1689 form, as found in the only complete musical source. For the shortened text in 1702, see Planché, *Regal Records*, 138. The short form was performed, along with Blow's setting of the Te Deum, at one of Cavendish Weedon's concerts in May 1702.

    [66] The musical contribution to royal funerals varied in extent, though that at Queen Mary's in Westminster Abbey had been elaborate in 1695. Royal weddings were solemnized in the less public spaces of a Royal Chapel.

resumed and there was a return to the pattern from the 1690s—official Fast Days at the beginning of the annual campaign and Thanksgivings after the victories, which this time Marlborough produced with almost annual regularity.[67] Appendix E summarizes the details, musical and liturgical, of the Thanksgiving services throughout Queen Anne's reign. The first Thanksgiving occurred in 1702 between the coronation and the Chapel Royal's removal to St. James's:

[November 3] The queen hath given orders to the bishop of London to draw up a form of prayer to return God thanks next Sunday in St. Paul's church for the great victory obtained over the French at Vigo, and that she intends to be present. Thurs. Nov. 5 The queen goes to St. Paul's Cathedrall, (the like done in queen Elizabeth's reign) both houses of parliament will also be there.[68]

The reference to 'Queen Elizabeth's reign' was presumably to Elizabeth I's attendance at old St Paul's Cathedral on the Thanksgiving day in November 1588 after the defeat of the Spanish armada.[69] It seems, indeed, that Anne was the first monarch since Elizabeth to attend St Paul's for such a service. The Houses of Parliament accompanied the Queen to St Paul's instead of having their own separate services and sermons; they were joined also by the Mayor and Corporation of the City of London, who had previously also attended separate services of their own. The ceremonial for the Thanksgiving services, unlike that for coronations, did not include the Chapel Royal choir in the processions.[70] The arrangements for the services fell into a regular pattern, described thus in connection with the Thanksgiving on 31 December 1706:

Both houses waited upon the Queen to the thanksgiving at St. Paul's; the commons in their coaches goeing first, then the judges, with the lords spiritual and temporal, in their robes; immediately before her majestie, who was attended by the first troop of guards, and a batallion of foot.... The streets were lined by the train'd bands, and several companies of this city in their livery gowns, and the streets crowded with spectators.

At Temple Bar her majestie was met by the lord mayor, aldermen, and sheriffs on horseback, who conducted her to St. Paul's church, where a fine anthem was sung, and the bishop of Salisbury preacht the sermon.

---

[67] Only the Thanksgivings were celebrated together by the Estates at St Paul's; on Fast days the Queen went to the Chapel Royal.

[68] Luttrell, *A Brief Historical Relation*, v. 232. See also Boyer, *The History of the Life and Reign of Queen Anne*, 35: 'For the greater solemnity on that Day, her Majesty would be pleased to go to St. Paul's Church, as had been accustomed in former Times in this Kingdom.'

[69] Neville Williams, *Elizabeth*, 80.

[70] Sheppard, *Memorials*, i. 232–3. The procession to St Paul's Cathedral usually left St James's Palace at 11 a.m.

After which she returned to St. James's and at night were discharged bonefires and illuminations, and the Tower guns were thrice discharged, viz. at her majesties first setting out, at the anthem, and at her return.[71]

Other reports of the services make it clear that the 'anthem' which was the signal for the second firing of the guns was in fact the Te Deum, and considerable significance seems to have been attached to this feature of the services. The dominance of Purcell's canticles in the early years is striking, especially in view of the existence of an alternative setting by Blow, the senior Chapel Royal Composer during these years. Also remarkable is the fact that the anthems for the services do not have orchestral accompaniment. The possibility that the surviving versions of some of the anthems are transcriptions in which the orchestral symphonies have been removed cannot be ruled out completely, but it would be an unlikely coincidence for every one of the anthems: it seems more likely that it was the normal practice for the orchestra at the Thanksgiving services to accompany the canticles only. The evidence concerning the musical settings is sporadic, but it is probable that orchestrally accompanied canticles were a regular feature at each of the Thanksgiving services. Robert Trevitt's picture of the service on 31 December 1706 (see Pl. I) includes a detailed representation of an orchestra at an occasion for which the documentary and musical sources provide no reference to such participation.[72] The picture also shows that a substantial ensemble of singers and players was involved, rather than the chamber group that had accompanied the Chapel Royal symphony anthems in the 1670s and 1680s.[73]

It is perhaps surprising that the texts set by the composers as anthems for the Thanksgiving services are not usually derived directly from the introductory biblical texts and specified psalms in the official orders of service.[74] This is true even of William Croft's anthem *I will give thanks*, a copy of which was endorsed by the composer as follows: 'The words of this Anthem were chose [*sic*] and given me by Her Most Excellent Majesty Queen Anne, and performed att

---

[71] Luttrell, *A Brief Historical Relation*, vi. 122–3. The occasion differed from previous ones because Prince George of Denmark did not attend, 'being unable to endure the fatigue'; the Duchess of Marlborough had the place of honour in the Queen's coach instead.

[72] Concerning Trevitt's picture, see Ralph Hyde, 'Images of St Paul's'. The picture, which shows Prince George as present, may have been based on sketches made at a previous Thanksgiving service.

[73] Trevitt's picture may reflect a more 'orchestral' practice, ultimately deriving from the 1694 St Cecilia service, that may also have been in operation for Blow's anthems at St Paul's in 1697–8. Blow's anthem for Cavendish Weedon in 1702, however, has a viola-less string scoring more in keeping with earlier Chapel Royal practice.

[74] A partial exception is *Behold how good and joyful* (jointly by Blow, Clarke, and Croft), which begins with verses from one of the set psalms.

St. Pauls upon a Thanksgiving Day'.[75] The text of Croft's anthem does not appear anywhere in the published liturgy for the Thanksgiving on 19 August 1708 with which the anthem is associated, and so it seems likely that the anthems for the Thanksgiving services from the Chapel Royal composers were prepared as an independent addition. The Te Deum, however, was a predictable element in the special liturgies. The Jubilate was included in most, but not all, of the Thanksgiving liturgies: no orchestral settings survive of the Cantate Domino that was sometimes specified instead. Although the special liturgies make no mention of the inclusion of anthems within the services, one organ-accompanied anthem was probably performed as part of the Communion service if this formed part of the scheme. The most detailed documentary report of the music at a Royal Thanksgiving, for the service on 27 June 1706, recorded that two anthems, in addition to Purcell's Te Deum, were sung and that the service ended about 4.15 p.m. after the inclusion of a forty-five minute sermon; it also listed the texts of the anthems, but one of them does not tally with the music attributed to the occasion in other sources.[76]

Change of Venue for the Royal Thanksgivings, and Music for the Festival of the Sons of the Clergy

The series of large public Thanksgiving services continued at St Paul's Cathedral until August 1708, but then there was a return to the old system of separate simultaneous services: the Queen at St James's Palace, the Lords at Westminster Abbey, the Commons at St Margaret's Westminster, and the Lord Mayor and Aldermen at St Paul's.[77] The Chapel Royal lost an important public platform with this change and it is relevant to consider the factors that may have influenced the Queen's decision to celebrate the Thanksgivings more privately.

One important factor was the death of Anne's consort, Prince George of Denmark, on 28 October 1708. The Prince had suffered from ill health since the beginning of the reign and had not been able to take an active part in public life for some time; he had not, for example, attended any of the Thanksgiving services since 1704.[78] After his death the Queen seems to have largely retired

[75] GB-Lbl Add. MS 17847, fo. 5ʳ.

[76] Boyer, *Anne (Annals)*, v. 154.

[77] This is proved by the publication of the separate sermons that were preached on these occasions before the Queen, Lords, Commons, and the City of London.

[78] Prince George's ill health was one of the main reasons for Anne's visits to Bath in 1702 and 1703, on the first of which she seems to have taken Richard Elford as a private musician to entertain the court.

from public appearances except at court occasions within her palaces. The
court mourning for the Prince lasted until Christmas Day 1710.[79] Although
Anne was content to go in state to a thanksgiving in 1702 with the horses still in
their mourning livery for William III, she may have been more sensitive about
the matter when the memory of her own husband was concerned. A second
factor was the Queen's own increasingly bad health. Like her husband, she had
been ill more or less from the beginning of the reign: she had to be carried 'in a
low open chair all the way' in the coronation procession,[80] and one of the
revisions to Blow's anthem *The Lord God is a sun and a shield* for the 1702
Coronation service removed the phrase 'no good thing will he withhold from
them that walk uprightly'. She had to be carried again at the Thanksgiving
service in September 1704,[81] but at other services she is reported to have
walked: her gout, although present in some measure during most of her
reign, possibly had phases of remission. From 1709, however, her condition
seems to have become rather worse. The plans for the royal 'removes' from
one palace to another were first dislocated by the Queen's illness in July 1710,
and from that time onwards Dr John Arbuthnot was more constantly in
attendance as her physician.[82]

The changing political situation also influenced the celebration of the
Thanksgivings. By 1708 war-weariness was becoming apparent, and at court
the Duchess of Marlborough gradually lost the Queen's favour.[83] Behind the
public face of support for the war the Queen's ministers, with the Tories
growing in strength at each successive reshuffle, gradually moved towards
arranging a peace, a shift in policy that reduced the emphasis on the Thanksgivings for military successes. Events during the Sacheverell riots of 1709 called
into question the security situation in London, and the cavalcades associated
with the Thanksgivings might have been regarded as a potential incitement to
discontented parties. Anxiety about security came to the surface in connection
with the service in November 1710 for which, it was rumoured, the Queen
was planning to return to St Paul's.[84] The carelessness of builders who had left
out some of the securing screws in the roof of St Paul's was misinterpreted as a
'screw plot' to harm the Queen and her court on the Thanksgiving day,[85] and
when the Queen eventually went to the Chapel Royal instead the reason was

[79] Boyer, *The Political State*, i. 53.
[80] Boyer, *Anne (Annals)*, i. 25; see also Luttrell, *A Brief Historical Relation*, v. 166, and Stanley, *Historical Memorials*, 80.
[81] Luttrell, *A Brief Historical Relation*, v. 462.
[82] GB-Lpro LC5/155, p. 81.
[83] Marlborough resigned his wife's places in Jan. 1710/11 and was dismissed from his own posts later in 1711.
[84] Luttrell, *A Brief Historical Relation*, vi. 634.
[85] Boyer, *The History of the Life and Reign of Queen Anne*, 480.

reported to be 'to avoid giving the Mob an opportunity to assemble and commit Riots'.[86]

It is even possible that difficulties over the musical arrangements for the services played some part in Queen Anne's move away from St Paul's. The evidence comes from a much later source, a memorandum about the history of the Festival of the Sons of the Clergy that was published in an appendix to the Festival sermon from 1799:

Dr. Godolphin, Dean of St. Paul's, had refused letting Music to be introduced into the Church when Queen Anne went in State to that Cathedral, to a public Thanksgiving, for some of the Duke of Marlborough's Victories; the Year after that Refusal, . . . [the Stewards] being desirous of having Music, in order to increase the Collection, applied to the Dean, who said he could not consent, as he had refused the Queen the Year before. Upon which the Archbishop, the Lord Keeper, and the Lord Mayor were appointed a Committee to wait upon the Queen for her Consent, if the Dean's should be obtained, who graciously answered, She should be very glad if it could be, as she thought it would be a great Means of drawing Company, and increasing the Fund, to which she earnestly wished success; and perhaps the Dean might be prevailed upon to be more obliging to promote a Charity for his own Cloth than he had been to her. Accordingly the Dean did give Leave, and it is said, that either Dr. [Daniel] Purcel, or Dr. Blow, conducted the Music, and that the Rev. Mr. Atterbury, Lecturer of St. Bride's, preached the Sermon. [87]

Francis Atterbury preached the sermon at the Festival of the Sons of the Clergy service on 6 December 1709, which fits in with this chain of events. Henry Godolphin, Dean of St Paul's since 1707,[88] had presumably cooperated in the arrangements for the Thanksgiving service in August 1708 at which Purcell's Te Deum and Jubilate were performed. A critical factor in the situation might have been the death of John Blow on 1 October 1708: perhaps the Dean found it more difficult to work with the younger Chapel Royal composers. Both Blow and Jeremiah Clarke had combined appointments at St Paul's and the Chapel Royal at various times; Richard Brind, the new Organist at St Paul's, did not do so.

Whatever the causes of the change of venue for the services, the actions of the musicians followed the same pattern as that described for the previous reign. As the Chapel Royal returned within the walls of the court, the forms of ceremonial music that had been presented by the Chapel and the Royal Musicians at the Thanksgivings found an outlet elsewhere. This time the

---

[86] Boyer, *Anne (Annals)*, ix. 253.

[87] Moss, *A Sermon*, 19–20; quoted in Pearce, *The Sons of the Clergy*, 208–9, where it is attributed to John Bacon.

[88] Nominated 23 June 1707, elected 14 July 1707.

alternative opportunity was provided by the annual Festival of the Sons of the Clergy rather than the Cecilian performances. The leading Chapel Royal singers, probably in company with Royal Musicians, took an active part in the Sons of the Clergy services, and these services were the means by which they retained their presence in the public musical life of London. The connection between music and charity, later so important to the development of the Three Choirs' Festivals and to Handel's association with the Foundling Hospital, became forged in these services, and in doing so the practice of orchestrally accompanied church music found another plank for its defence. Unfortunately there is little documentary information about the music performed at the Sons of the Clergy services in the decade following 1709, but it seems probable that these occasions took over much of the activity that had previously been devoted to the Cecilian movement and to the Thanksgiving services at St Paul's.[89] They also kept the performance of orchestrally accompanied anthems and canticles before a wider London public. Furthermore, the change of venue for the Queen's service on Thanksgiving days did not attenuate the performance of such music by the court musicians, though this now took place to a much smaller congregation in the Chapel Royal.

The regular performance of orchestrally accompanied settings of the canticles at the Thanksgiving services and the Sons of the Clergy services was the most significant development in English church music in London during the decade preceding Handel's arrival, but the period also saw other important developments. 'Father' Smith and his successor Christopher Shrider built new organs for each of the Royal Chapels and these, together with the organ at St Paul's (completed in 1698; see Ch. 18), provided a new stimulus to the organists and composers of London's choral institutions. The death of John Blow in 1708 severed a link with the past and removed from the scene the most experienced English composer of orchestrally accompanied anthems and canticles; Jeremiah Clarke's suicide the previous year is of less significance in this respect because it occurred before Clarke had had the opportunity to try his hand at large-scale anthems and canticles.[90] Although the death of Blow marked the end of an era, the day-to-day life of the Chapel continued basically unchanged. In 1710 there were still several men in the choir who would have known Henry Purcell. John Gostling, the famous bass singer, was still on the roll and had sung a solo part as recently as the 1706 Thanksgiving service.[91]

---

[89] For the programmes of the Festivals in this period see Burrows, *Dissertation*, ii, App. 4. An orchestrally accompanied Te Deum was reported in 1715; Purcell's setting was performed in 1716, 1719, and 1720; Croft's setting in 1717 and 1718.

[90] See Taylor, *Thematic Catalog*, 13–24. None of Clarke's church music has orchestral accompaniment.

[91] In Croft's anthem *O clap your hands together* (GB-Bu Barber MS 5009).

William Turner, although no longer active as a soloist and composer, still had thirty years of service in the Chapel ahead of him. There was also a new generation of soloists and composers; William Croft became the chief composer after Blow's death.[92]

Croft had already taken on some of the responsibility as a composer for the Chapel during Blow's final years: he had provided anthems for important services since 1704, although he had apparently received no formal reward for his work apart from the honour that the performances bestowed. Blow's death in 1708 came just before that of Prince George and it is possible that Croft's famous setting of the funeral sentences was composed for the Prince's funeral, the first important public ceremony after his appointment.[93] The first Thanksgiving service for which Croft carried musical responsibility was also the first one after the Queen's withdrawal from St Paul's, and he composed a festal Te Deum and Jubilate with orchestral accompaniment for the occasion.[94] The scoring and the layout of this work are clearly in the lineage of Purcell's service, but the harmonic style reveals that Croft had begun to move away from Purcell's world. Charles Burney later said of Croft's orchestrally accompanied anthem *Rejoice in the Lord* that 'it was produced about the middle of Queen Anne's reign, before the arrival of Handel, our great model for Music richly accompanied'.[95] This statement is probably inaccurate: Croft's anthem is more likely, on both stylistic and historical grounds, to have been composed in 1720 (see below, Ch. 6 and App. F). The 1709 Te Deum, with its accompanying Jubilate, was almost certainly the only piece of orchestrally accompanied church music that Croft composed before Handel's arrival. Croft later recast it in the light of his experience of Handel's Utrecht settings, but nevertheless, his own Te Deum is a significant work, showing that he intended to continue the Chapel Royal tradition of 'music richly accompanied' for special occasions and that, as a composer, he had sufficient resource to tackle the task of providing the first new setting of its type since 1696. It is the most important landmark in English church music during the decade preceding Handel's arrival in London in 1710.

[92] John Weldon was Croft's main associate at the Chapel Royal after 1708, but his output for the Chapel was smaller and less varied than Croft's.

[93] Little is known of the history of Croft's famous Burial Service. It was published in Croft, *Musica Sacra*, i (1724), presumably in the version performed at the Duke of Marlborough's funeral in July 1722 (see Ch. 7, p. 180). The music may nevertheless have been composed much earlier.

[94] Date of performance identified from GB-Ob MS Mus.d.30, which, however, has the later, revised, form of the Te Deum.

[95] Burney, *A General History*, ii. 484

3

Handel and the English Verse Anthem: His First Setting of As pants the hart, *c.1712*

Hanover and London, 1710–1712

HANDEL's first English church music was written in London while he was still in the employ of the Hanoverian court. The post of Kapellmeister to which he was appointed in June 1710 must have been, from the first, something of an honorary post: the Hanover opera was in abeyance and the routine music of the Hanover court was in the hands of a Konzertmeister, who was in charge of the court musicians.[1] As Kapellmeister he was probably only expected to provide music for occasional court entertainments and, as far as we know, church music formed no part of his duties. The two surviving letters written by the Electress Sophia that refer to Handel speak mainly of his keyboard playing, which was particularly appreciated by Princess Caroline;[2] in addition to performing and composing keyboard music he may have provided some chamber music, perhaps a concerto or two and some Italian duets. One of the Electress's letters indicates that she was aware of Handel's ambitions as an opera composer, so presumably it was not difficult for him to obtain leave of absence when suitable opportunities arose. Whether or not he had already made some commitment to the London opera company before he accepted the Hanover appointment,[3] his visit to London suited the foreign policy of the Hanoverian court. The Electress and her family were looking towards their forthcoming British inheritance throughout the last years of Queen Anne's reign. A Resident, Christoph Friedrich Kreienberg, was stationed in London from September 1710, and a succession of important Hanoverian diplomats—Grote, Schütz, and Bothmer—served as Envoys Extraordinary: for the Hanover court, an advance party, political or cultural, was obviously desirable in

---

[1] For the Hanover opera, see Hatton, *George I*, 364 n. 53. J. B. Farinelli held the post of Konzertmeister from 1680 to 1713.

[2] See Burrows, *Handel*, 38.

[3] Mainwaring, *Memoirs*, 71–2.

order to prepare the way in London, and to act as a damper on potential Jacobite influence. Queen Anne would not allow any visit, let alone advance residence, by members of the electoral family during her lifetime,[4] and she was conciliatory to Jacobites who were loyal to herself when she found this politically advantageous. Her own title to the British throne was nevertheless based on the exclusion of the Pretender, and her support for the Hanoverian line was firm when she was eventually forced to declare on the matter of the succession; her refusal to countenance Jacobite activity during the last years of her reign was one of the factors that put George Lewis safely on the throne at her death. Visitors and representatives from Hanover were made welcome at the court in London, and Hanoverian court interests encouraged these visitors to make the most of their welcome there.

There is no doubt that Handel himself found favour at Queen Anne's court during his first visit, even before the successful production of *Rinaldo*, his first London opera:

Tuesday, the 6th. of February [1710/11], being the Queen's Birth-day, the same was observed with great Solemnity: the Court was extream numerous and magnificent; the Officers of State, Foreign Ministers, Nobility, and Gentry, and particularly the Ladies, vying with each other, who should most grace the Festival. Between One and Two in the Afternoon, was perform'd a fine Consort, being a Dialogue in *Italian*, in Her Majesty's Praise, set to excellent Musick by the famous Mr. *Hendel*, a Retainer to the Court of *Hanover*, in the Quality of Director of his Electoral Highness's Chapple, and sung by *Cavaliero Nicolini Grimaldi*, and the other Celebrated Voices of the *Italian* Opera: with which Her Majesty was extramly well pleas'd.[5]

This performance probably replaced the court birthday ode that was the traditional task of native English forces, and indeed the Master of the Queen's Music seems to have been displaced from the composition of the royal birthday odes for the rest of the reign. In 1712, when Handel was not in England, the music performed was 'an excellent Consort collected out of several *Italian* Operas, by Signior *Cavaliero Nicolini Grimaldi* and perform'd by him, and the other best voices'.[6] For 1713 Handel composed the birthday ode *Eternal Source of Light Divine*, a work along the lines of the previous English odes and intended for English performers: the background to this work will be described further in Chapter 4.

---

[4] The suggestion that Prince George August (the future King George II) should come to England to take the seat in the House of Lords to which he was entitled as Duke of Cambridge met with a stern answer from Queen Anne, but the Hanoverian request forced Queen Anne to declare against the Pretender (see Hatton, *George I*, 107–8).

[5] Boyer, *Anne (Annals)*, ix. 315; also Boyer, *The Political State*, i. 156.

[6] Boyer, *Anne (Annals)*, x. 344; Boyer, *The Political State*, iii. 67.

From what has been seen in Chapter 2 of Anne's patronage during previous reigns we may assume that the Queen, like Charles II before her, had a genuine interest in the work of the Chapel Royal musicians. Three years into her reign John Vanburgh's new theatre in the Haymarket was opened with the performance of an Italian opera, and from 1708 the programmes of that theatre were devoted solely to opera: it was, indeed, the opportunities at the Queen's Theatre that brought Handel to London. There is no evidence that the Queen herself ever attended performances there and by 1710, in any case, ill health and increasing personal isolation were limiting her social activities. She may nevertheless have taken some pleasure in reading the dedication to the libretto of *Rinaldo*, in which Aaron Hill asserted that 'the Universal Glory of your Majesty's illustrious Name drew hither the most celebrated Masters from every Part of Europe'.[7] Both Hill and Giacomo Rossi drew particular attention to Handel in their prefaces to the libretto, Hill calling him 'Mr. Hendel, whom the World so justly celebrates' and Rossi 'Signor Hendel, Orfeo del nostro Secolo'. If the Queen could not attend the opera, she had at least the satisfaction of having heard the musicians at her own private court performance.

Handel first arrived in London 'in the winter of the year 1710',[8] but it is unlikely that he was there in time for the Thanksgiving Service on 11 November. If he heard any orchestrally accompanied church music at all during his first visit, this might have been at the Sons of the Clergy service at St Paul's Cathedral on 5 December.[9] Croft's anthems for the occasion, *Offer the sacrifice of righteousness* and *O praise the Lord, all ye that fear him*,[10] do not have orchestral accompaniment in the surviving musical sources, but it is probable that an orchestrally accompanied setting of the canticles was performed if such a tradition had been started in the previous year (see Ch. 2), and the most likely music would have been Purcell's. Even if Handel did not hear Purcell's Te Deum and Jubilate performed then, he had ready access to the music through John Walsh's printed edition, which, on the evidence of regular advertisements, remained sufficiently popular for the publisher to keep it in print.[11]

[7] *Rinaldo, Opera* (London, 1711), p. ii: see Harris, *The Librettos*, ii. 1–10.

[8] Mainwaring, *Memoirs*, 74. My interpretation of Handel's itinerary, based on Hanover court documents, is that he left Hanover in mid-October, when the Electoral court set out for the annual hunting party at Göhrde. If, as Mainwaring says, he visited Halle and Düsseldorf before coming to England, he is unlikely to have arrived in London before mid-November at the earliest, but a letter from J. D. Brandshagen to Leibniz dated 21 Oct. 1712 suggests that Handel was then active in the London opera company.

[9] One of Handel's songs was introduced, with an English text, into a performance of *Pirro e Demetrio* at the Haymarket Theatre on 6 Dec. (Deutsch, *Handel*, 30). This may suggest that Handel was in London at the time.

[10] Identified from GB-Llp H. 5133.776(6).

[11] William C. Smith, *A Bibliography 1695–1720*, nos. 108, 248, 276, and 595.

Some London musician who had known Purcell would surely have enlightened the visiting composer from Hanover as to the greatness of England's recent native genius at some time during this first visit. If Handel had any curiosity at all about Purcell's church music, the Te Deum and Jubilate was by far the most easily available work.

The English Verse Anthem: Croft's Music

Whether or not Handel heard any orchestrally accompanied English church music during his first visit, it seems almost certain that he would have heard anthems performed by one or more of the major London choral establishments. As has already been noted, their current repertory, as revealed in the word-book *Divine Harmony* published in 1712, included some music by composers of previous generations, but there was inevitably a bias towards the work of more recent musicians: the leader, represented by thirty-four anthems, was William Croft, the most active contemporary Chapel Royal composer.[12] Croft had been a Child of the Chapel Royal, from which he was formally discharged in April 1699 at the age of 20. He had thus received his musical education from John Blow, though he seems also to have been powerfully influenced by Purcell's music; he may have taken part in performances of Purcell's court odes in 1694–5 and even in the Te Deum and Jubilate in November 1694. One of Croft's anthems composed in 1717 includes a movement directly based on the music of 'Sound the trumpet' from *Come, ye sons of art away*, Purcell's 1694 Birthday Ode for Queen Mary.[13]

Full anthems were performed at the Chapel Royal at weekday morning services, verse anthems at weekday afternoon services, and at both Sunday services.[14] At Westminster Abbey, where Croft was also organist, the proportion of occasions for full anthems was somewhat higher.[15] Nevertheless, full anthems form only a small part of Croft's output: ten full anthems by him survive, against more than sixty verse anthems.[16] Except in their avoidance of lengthy movements for single solo voices the full anthems are not substantially different in style from the verse anthems, and the techniques of choral writing

[12] See Burrows, *Dissertation*, ii, app. 3.
[13] Croft's *Blessed are all they that fear the Lord*: see Burrows, 'Sir John Dolben', 150–1 concerning the date of this anthem. For another example derived from Purcell, see Spink, *Restoration Cathedral Music*, 178–9.
[14] *NCB*, p. 135; Ashbee and Harley, i. 310.
[15] *WA2*, 30.
[16] See Scandrett, 'The Anthems of William Croft', and the work-list for Croft in *NG II*. Concerning Croft's music see also Spink, *Restoration Cathedral Music*, ch. 9.

Ex. 3.1. Croft, *Put me not to rebuke*

employed are common to both types.[17] The opening of *Put me not to rebuke*
(Ex. 3.1) provides a good example of Croft's procedure for building up the
vocal texture in choral movements. He is quite skilful in maintaining
the musical interest in this type of movement by well-timed entries and
suitable modulations, and he normally adopts the traditional motet technique
by beginning each new verbal phrase with a new musical point of imitation.
Most full anthems include a central section for semi-chorus or soloists: this
often forms a complete movement in itself, ending with a full close and
followed by a final imitative choral movement on the same lines as the first
movement. The opening of the central section of *Put me not to rebuke* is given in

[17] Croft himself transferred material between the two types: his most famous full anthem,
God is gone up (text included in *Divine Harmony*, 1712), draws two of its three movements from
his 1706 verse anthem *O clap your hands*.

Ex. 3.2. Croft, *Put me not to rebuke*

Ex. 3.3. Croft, *Try me, O God*

Ex. 3.2. The technique of setting one voice off against the rest, noted in connection with Handel's Latin psalm settings, is also present here: Croft's immediate model was probably Purcell, though the technique itself has a long ancestry.[18] The simultaneous working of two subjects that was noted in

---

[18] One of Purcell's most striking uses of this device occurs in his 1692 St Cecilia Ode, *Hail, bright Cecilia*, at bars 48–9 and 55–9 of the first vocal movement (*PS* 8, no. 2).

Table 3.1. *William Croft's anthem* O praise the Lord, all ye that fear him

Movement	Psalm text	Voices	Key	Time signature and duration
1. O praise the Lord	22: 23	AABB, alternating with satb chorus	D major	$\frac{3}{2}$ 111 bars (48 + 23 + 40)
2. Let them give thanks	107: 2	AT[a]	B minor	c 47 bars
3. We will rejoice	20: 5	AB	D major	c 16 bars
4. Now know I	20: 6	A	D minor	$\frac{3}{2}$ 66 bars
5. Some put their trust	20: 7	satb	D minor	2[b] 39 bars
6. They are brought down	20: 8	B	D major	c 18 bars
7. Save, Lord, *leading to*	20: 9	AAB	B minor	$\frac{3}{2}$ 22 bars
8. Be thou exalted	21: 13	AAB and satb chorus	D major	¢ 43 bars (24 + 19)

Soloists named in GB-Lcm MS 839: Hughs, Elford (Altos); Weely, Gates (Basses)

[a] Written in the tenor clef, but intended for Weely (1st Bass).
[b] i.e. $\frac{3}{2}$.

Handel's early choral technique is also a feature of Croft's, as in the full anthem *Try me, O God* (Ex. 3.3).

For an example of Croft's verse anthems it is appropriate to take one of those that Handel might have heard if he had attended the Sons of the Clergy Festival service in December 1710. *O praise the Lord, all ye that fear him* was composed for the Thanksgiving Service in November 1709 and repeated at the Sons of the Clergy service the following year. The movements and sections for soloists employ the voices in which the Chapel Royal was strongest, altos and basses.[19] The scheme of the anthem is given in Table 3.1. The selection of the text from four different psalms is noteworthy, and two other features are immediately apparent: the planned variety of key and metre, and the rather front-heavy design with no subsequent movement rivalling the first one in length. In its symmetry of key scheme this anthem is more carefully organized than most of Croft's. The opening verse section for the soloists (Ex. 3.4) leads into a chorus based on the same material. The central movement for solo alto, quoted in full, is typical of the music that Croft wrote for the Chapel Royal's leading alto soloist, Richard Elford (Ex. 3.5). The vocal line is generated over a rather stiff, but harmonically well-directed, bass part which harks back to Purcell's ground basses; Croft makes attempts at phrase extension but relies too much on simple repetition. His harmony is smoother than Purcell's and his declamation less angular: these features suggest the influence of the Italian style, but the breadth

[19] When the anthem was printed in the second volume of *Musica Sacra*, Croft presented the opening verse as if for ATBB. It is clear from the clefs used in GB-Lcm MS 839 and from the soloists' names added by Croft to this MS that it was nevertheless intended for AABB. Scandrett, 'The Anthems of William Croft', reproduces the *Musica Sacra* version as Anthem 70.

Ex. 3.4. Croft, *O praise the Lord*, No. 1

Soloists' names from GB-Lcm MS 839

Ex. 3.5. Croft, *O praise the Lord*, No. 4

Ex. 3.5. *Cont'd*

associated with this style is missing.[20] If Croft's music sounds a little more 'modern' than Purcell's, his very fluency of harmony and word-setting can be a drawback as well, producing a static, over-sweet effect which is magnified in large-scale movements by the conservatism of his tonal designs.[21]

The chorus that follows the alto solo movement is of the same type as that illustrated in Ex. 3.1. The subsequent bass solo (Ex. 3.6) is interesting for its use of slow/fast contrast, some word-painting in the Purcellian tradition, and some doubtful word-setting at the end which, had it come from Handel, would have been attributed to his imperfect command of the English language. The final verse and chorus sections of the anthem really form one unit, the end of movement 7 cadencing into the beginning of no. 8 with an effective contrast of key, metre, speed, and texture, the homophony of the first giving place in the second to short imitative phrases with semiquaver figuration.[22] A promising theme combination emerges at the words 'so will we sing and praise thy power' (Ex. 3.7) but this is not developed: Handel would surely have seized upon its possibilities. Croft's anthems are at their best when questions of musical development do not arise, and many of his most successful movements are those on a small scale where the brevity of the half-verses of the psalm is matched by telling, pithy musical phrases.

This anthem is longer than most of Croft's, no doubt on account of the special occasion for which it was composed, but in style it is typical of the anthems that were written for the Chapel Royal at the time of Handel's first London visit. Some of Croft's solo movements tend more towards a recitative style than anything found in this anthem,[23] though they rely on a background of regular harmonic rhythms that suggest affinities with orchestrally accompanied recitative rather than operatic continuo recitative. This may indicate a deliberate demarcation between 'theatre' and 'church' styles, but it may also have been affected by conditions of performance: organ accompaniment, particularly if the organist is at some distance from the singer, limits rhythmic flexibility.[24] One other feature of Croft's anthems that does not happen to be illustrated by *O praise the Lord* is his habit of concluding with an 'Alleluja'

[20] Direct influence is suggested by GB-Lcm MS 1101, a volume of music bearing Croft's signature and the date 1697, which includes music by Bassani, Carissimi, A. Scarlatti, and Stradella, among others.

[21] Harmonic fluency is not accompanied by technical perfection: consecutives are by no means absent from Croft's compositions.

[22] In key, metre, and layout, no. 7 seems indebted to 'O Lord, save thy people' from Purcell's D Major Te Deum.

[23] See e.g. 'My soul fleeth unto the Lord' from *Out of the deep* for a particularly florid example of recitative writing; on the other hand, a simpler movement such as 'Thou hast laid me in the lowest pit' from *O Lord God of my salvation* is closer to contemporary theatrical recitative.

[24] Handel's English church music is also lacking in secco recitative, the only brief examples occurring in his settings of *As pants the hart*. The church music from Handel's Italian period

Ex. 3.6. Croft, *O praise the Lord*, No. 6

chorus, continuing a feature from Purcell's anthems.[25] A surprisingly large number of these are in minor keys and, indeed, it is not at all uncommon to find anthems by Croft with jubilant texts which end with minor-key movements.[26]

divides as we might expect: there is no operatic-type recitative in the large choral works but it may be found in the cantata-type music, such as 'Vestro religiosi principes' from *Cælestis dum spirat aura* (HWV 231).

[25] Scandrett, 'The Anthems of William Croft', counts twenty-one examples.

[26] I have counted eleven examples. Many of them, including *Behold God is my salvation*, *I will lift up mine eyes*, and *The Lord is my strength*, begin with a movement in the major key but end with a minor-key movement.

Ex. 3.7. Croft, *O praise the Lord*, No. 8

In harmonic and melodic aspects of musical style, his music from the period up to 1710 represents a very similar stage of technical and stylistic development to that of Zachow's. If Handel needed a model in order to assimilate the current state of the English anthem genre, then Croft's music would have provided the best examples, and it is very likely indeed that Handel would have heard his music at Chapel Royal services. This does not mean that Handel imitated Croft's musical style, however. His attitude to genre 'models' seems to have been that he used them to find out the sort of thing that was required, and then he fulfilled the external specification in his own style. In the case of church music, his previous experience in Germany and Italy remained relevant, as well as his intention to accommodate in general terms to London's local expectations.[27]

Handel's Return to London, 1712

It is very unlikely that Handel composed any English church music during his first visit in 1710–11, or set any English words to music at all. Having been received at court and by the London opera audience on the strength of his achievements at the Queen's Theatre, he may not have felt anything more than a tourist's curiosity about English music. However, he devoted some time to the study of the English language when he was back in Hanover,[28] which

---

[27] It is thus only in the most general way that Croft's music 'provided Handel with a point of departure' (Spink, *Restoration Cathedral Music*, 185).

[28] See the letter to Andreas Romer, Deutsch, *Handel*, 44.

suggests that he had definite plans for an early return and that, furthermore, he desired closer contact with English cultural and political institutions. It was possible for a successful professional musician working at the London opera house to remain part of a separate Italian/German community if he so wished: many composers and solo singers did not seek any further integration into London's musical life. Handel, on the other hand, seems to have decided that his next visit to London would be on different terms, and it is likely that he planned this visit to be one of longer duration, since for the moment London offered prospects that were at least as attractive as those at the operatic centres in Italy and Germany. Once established in London, it would only be a matter of time before the Hanoverian succession consolidated his position and secured his future. Perhaps he was even confident that the opera house could expect support from the future king. There was therefore every motive for Handel to improve his English in Hanover and to prepare to come to terms with English tastes and culture on his return. From this perspective, English church music may have been of considerable significance to him in 1712. Instrumental music, with its internationally recognized styles, posed no cultural problem for acceptance, nor did theatre music, since the London patrons were currently enthusiastic about Italian opera. It was in the field of church music that the English recognized their own indigenous tradition, and the Chapel Royal was the centre of the resources for this tradition. If he wanted to make his mark as something more than a foreigner on a flying visit, the Chapel Royal was the place to do it. The music that Handel composed during the period 1712–14 suggests that artistic interest and curiosity, as well as self-interest and the desire for advancement at court, played its part in his practical investigation of the musical and creative opportunities that the Chapel Royal provided.

There was probably an element of professional comradeship that drew Handel towards the Chapel Royal's leading musicians. While he was engaged primarily with the opera house and its performers, he probably also sought out and enjoyed the company of members from the circuit of London's ecclesiastical choirs, no doubt relating their work to that of the church musicians among whom he had grown up in Halle. Although some of John Hawkins's anecdotes about Handel, written more than half a century later, may have defects in both veracity and chronology, it is significant that they include tales about the composer's association with London's church musicians during his early years in the capital. According to Hawkins, after playing the organ at St Paul's Cathedral it was Handel's practice 'to adjourn with the principal persons of the choir to the Queen's Arms tavern in St Paul's church-yard, where was a great room, with a harpsichord in it; and oftentimes an evening was there spent in music and musical conversation'.[29] One particular anecdote has Handel at the tavern in the company of Samuel Weely, a bass singer with places in the choirs of both St Paul's Cathedral and the Chapel Royal.[30] It seems very likely that Handel sampled the musical fare at services in both places—St Paul's Cathedral on account of its large organ and the interest of the new building, and the Chapel Royal on account of its association with the court. In the performance of anthems and sung canticles he would have heard some of the same soloists at the Cathedral and the Chapel.

Music that Handel composed for the Chapel Royal during his early years in London can be identified from the inclusion of the name of the alto soloist Richard Elford (d. 1714) on the autographs. Of the five works of English church music from this period, only the composition of the Utrecht Te Deum can be dated with certainty. Composed within about three months of his return to England, the Utrecht Te Deum demonstrates that Handel adapted to specifically 'English' needs with remarkable speed: by then he had discovered the conventional principles of declamation and the formal moulds of English church music, and also the musical strengths of the singers in the Chapel Royal choir. Of the Chapel Royal works from this period, there is only one that, on circumstantial evidence, may have been composed before the Utrecht music: that is, towards the end of 1712. *As pants the hart* (HWV 251a) was almost certainly Handel's first English anthem: since this work relates to the genre of the English verse anthem, and also contains musical references to Handel's German and Italian past, it is a suitable work to bring together the strands that have been described so far.

As pants the hart for cooling streams (HWV 251a)

Background

Divine Harmony, a book of anthem texts based on the Chapel Royal repertory, was advertised for sale in July 1712, shortly before Handel's return to London.[31] This was the first publication of its kind to appear in London since Clifford's *Divine Services and Anthems* of 1663–4 and, because the Chapel Royal repertory had expanded enormously in half a century, it was long overdue. There are good reasons for accepting Thomas Ford's testimony that the book was the work of John Church,[32] one of the leading Gentlemen of the Chapel

---

[29] Hawkins, *A General History*, ii. 859.   [30] Ibid. ii. 852 n.

[31] Advertised in *PB*, 15–17 and 19–22 July 1712 and *DC*, 16 July.

[32] GB-Ob MS Mus.e.17, p. 10. Ford's notebook was probably first compiled about 1710, but he made sporadic additions to it over the following decade. 'Hendel' is among the composers he lists, but without any further amplification.

and Master of the Choristers at Westminster Abbey: the ascription fits with the circumstance that Church was the leading copyist of the part-books from which the Chapel Royal musicians performed at this period,[33] and the tone of the preface to *Divine Harmony* is similar to that found in Church's *Introduction to Psalmody*, published a decade later. *Divine Harmony* includes some texts submitted by provincial organists and was offered on general sale to the public, but it clearly related mainly to the repertory of London's professional choirs and the title page said that it was 'Publish'd with the Approbation of the Sub-Dean of Her Majesty's Chappels Royal'. The Sub-Dean of the time was Ralph Battell, the preacher of the 1693 St Cecilia sermon in defence of church music. At least two of the surviving copies have bindings with Royal insignia and must have been among the books that were provided in the Royal Chapels, presumably to enable the congregation to follow the texts when the anthems were performed.[34]

Divine Harmony would have given Handel an up-to-date picture of the current repertory, and also a chance to relate his newly improved command of the English language to the words of the Chapel's anthems. Most of the texts were chosen from the Prayer Book and from the Authorized Version of the Bible, but, as it happens, the one that seems to have caught Handel's attention was a rather hybrid collection of verses from different versions of Psalm 42, attributed to Dr [John] Arbuthnot, 'Physician in Ordinary to Her Majesty' but also a man of letters, known principally as an essayist.[35] It is unlikely that the similarities between Arbuthnot's text and Handel's (see Table 3.2), particularly in the adaptation of Tate and Brady's metrical version of the first verse of the psalm, were accidental. Unfortunately, the music of Arbuthnot's anthem does not seem to have survived: it may already have vanished or have been withdrawn from circulation by 1717.[36] It is possible that Arbuthnot did not

[33] GB-Lbl RM.27.a.1–14: see Laurie, 'The Chapel Royal Part-Books'. Church was also the person to whom Thomas Tudway turned when he wanted a copy of Croft's Te Deum (see GB-Lbl Harl. MS 3782, fo. 83).

[34] Copies at GB-Lbl and Lcm; the royal insignia on the covers were apparently scored through when the Chapel renewed their stock with later editions of the word-books. The provision of the anthem books for use in the Chapel is recorded in GB-Lpro LC5/156, p. 106 (dated 28 Feb. 1714/15): John Bowack was paid for '272 Anthem Books bound in red and blew turkey leather for Windsor and St. James's, Provided by her late Majesty's command'.

[35] He was a friend of Jonathan Swift, who introduced him to Alexander Pope in 1713, and was associated with Swift, Pope, and John Gay in the Scriblerus Club. See Aitken, *The Life and Works*, 37–8, 56–7.

[36] In July Tudway attempted to obtain 'Dr. Arbuthnot's Anthems which he made for ye Queen's Chappell' (GB-Lbl Harl. MS. 3782, fo. 76), but to judge from his finished collection (Harl. MS 7337–42) he did not succeed. Hawkins's statement (*A General History*, ii. 859) that Arbuthnot's *As pants the hart* 'is to be found in the books of the chapel royal' must refer only to the text in *Divine Harmony*, for the music is not in the Chapel Royal part-books of the period.

Table 3.2. As pants the hart *by Arbuthnot and Handel: sources for the text, from versions of Psalm 42*

Arbuthnot (*Divine Harmony*, p. 102)	Sources	Handel (HWV 251a autograph)	Sources
1. As pants the hart for cooling streams; so longs my soul for thee, O God.	TB (adapted)	As paints the hart for cooling streams, so longs my soul for thee, O Lord.	TB (adapted)
2. My soul is athirst for God, yea, even for the living God: when shall I appear before the presence of God?	PB		
3. Tears are my constant food, while thus they say, where is now thy God?	TB	Tears are my daly food, when thus they say: where is now thy God?	?PB (adapted)
4.	PB	Now, when I think thereupon, I pour out my heart by myself For I went with the multitude and brought them out into the house of God.	PB
5.		In the voice of praise of thanksgiving, among such as keep holy-day.	PB
6. Why so restless thou, O my soul, why so disquieted within me?	?	Why so full of grief, O my soul, why so disquieted within me?	?PB (adapted)
7. Put thy trust in God; for I will praise Him, for all his gracious aid.	?	Put thy trust in God, for I will praise him. Amen	?PB adapted, with 'praise him' from AV
9. One deep calleth unto another at the voice of the water spouts: all thy waves and storms are gone over me.	mixture of PB (v. 9) and AV (v. 7)		

Sources: TB Tate and Brady, *A New Version of the Psalms* (7th edn., with Supplement, 1712)
      PB *The Book of Common Prayer* (1662 version)
      AV *The Holy Bible* (Authorized Version)

Notes:
Verse 1: Both texts use lines 1 and 3 of TB's Verse 1:

> As pants the hart for cooling streams / When heated in the chase;
> So longs my soul, O God, for thee / And thy refreshing grace.

Handel's error 'Paints' also accidentally occurs in the later editions of Playford, *The Whole Book of Psalms* (16th edn., 1722, Medius and Bassus parts, p. 65) but not in the earlier editions up to the 12th edn. (1713).
Verse 3: PB version: My tears have been my food day and night: while they daily say unto me, Where is now thy God?
Verse 4: PB has 'and brought them forth'.
Verse 5: PB has 'praise and thanksgiving'
Verse 6: PB version: Why art thou so full of heaviness, O my soul: and why art thou so disquieted within me?
Verse 7: PB version: Put thy trust in God: for I will yet give him thanks for the help of his countenance.
      AV version: Hope thou in God: for I shall yet praise him for the help of his countenance.

actually compose any music for *As pants the hart* but selected and paraphrased the text for someone else, though the variants are too substantial to support the idea that the text as printed in *Divine Harmony* is one that he selected for Handel in 1710–11. Arbuthnot was a man of wide interests and he may have made some attempt at musical composition to while away the time during slack periods when he was in waiting as the Queen's Physician; as he also had some status at court, it is not unlikely that the Chapel Royal would have agreed to perform his music. He is reported to have had a high opinion of Handel's music,[37] and this may have originated when the composer rearranged and reset his text, doubtless to better effect. There is evidence of a personal friendship between the two men during Handel's first years in London, which carried a political significance whose relevance will be seen in Chapter 4.

Arbuthnot was not the only influential literary figure of the time to take an interest in the subject of the English anthem. In June 1712 *The Spectator* published an essay, usually attributed to Addison, which, after some remarks on the impending departure of Nicolini (the leading soloist of the opera company), turned to the subject of church music:

I would heartily wish there was the same Applications and Endeavours to cultivate and improve our Church-Musick, as have been lately bestowed on that of the Stage. Our Composers have one very great Incitement to it: They are sure to meet with Excellent Words, and at the same time, a wonderful Variety of them. There is no Passion that is not finely expressed in those parts of the inspired Writing, which are proper for divine Songs and Anthems.

There is a certain Coldness and Indifference in the Phrases of our *European* Languages, when they are compared with the Oriental Forms of Speech; and it happens very luckily, that the *Hebrew* idioms run into the *English* tongue with a particular Grace and Beauty. Our Language has received innumerable Elegancies and Improvements, from that Infusion of *Hebraism*, which are derived to it out of the Poetical Passages in Holy Writ. They give a Force and Energy to our Expressions, warm and animate our Language, and convey our Thoughts in more ardent and intense Phrases, than any that are to be met with in our own Tongue. There is something so Pathetick in this kind of Diction, that it often sets the Mind in a Flame, and makes our Hearts burn within us. How cold and dead does a Prayer appear, that is composed in the most elegant and Polite Forms of Speech, which are natural to our Tongue, when it is not heightened by that Solemnity of Phrase, which may be drawn from the Sacred Writings. It has been said by some of the Ancients, that if the Gods were to talk with Men, they would certainly speak in *Plato's* Stile; but I think we may say, with Justice, that when Mortals converse with their Creator, they cannot do it in so proper a Stile as in that of the Holy Scriptures.

---

[37] Mainwaring, *Memoirs*, 93.

If any one wou'd judge of the Beauties of Poetry that are to be met with in the Divine Writings, and examine how kindly the *Hebrew* Manners of Speech mix and incorporate with the *English* Language; after having perused the Book of Psalms, let him read a literal Translation of *Horace* or *Pindar*. He will find in these two last such an Absurdity and Confusion of Stile with such a Comparative Poverty of Imagination, as will make him very sensible of what I have been here advancing.

Since we have therefore such a Treasury of Words, so beautiful in themselves, and so proper for the Airs of Musick, I cannot but wonder that Persons of Distinction should give so little Attention and Encouragement to that kind of Musick which would have its Foundation in Reason, and which would improve our Virtue in proportion as it raised our delight.[38]

Subsequent issues of *The Spectator* included verses of metrical psalm para-phrases, possibly intended to stimulate musical settings, many of which have remained in circulation until the hymnals of the present time: 'The Lord my pasture shall prepare', 'When all thy mercies, O my God', and 'The spacious firmament on high' were originally published in July–August 1712. Arbuth-not's anthem text, which must be earlier than these, is neither metrical nor rhymed. Taking together the evidence of the essay in *The Spectator* and the publication of *Divine Harmony*, it seems that Handel's return to England coincided with a renewed interest in the anthem as a genre. More specifically, Arbuthnot's text, if not also his music, seems to have been Handel's starting point for his own version.

As pants the hart is the only text that Handel composed in the accepted form of English verse anthem without orchestral accompaniment: he made two verse anthem settings, the second of which was completed about ten years later and will be considered in Chapter 8. It is possible that his first setting was intended for a routine service in the Chapel Royal, in which case the lack of any documentary material that would point to a specific date for its perform-ance is not surprising; nor can its date be established with certainty through the style of handwriting or the watermark of the paper in the autograph (see Fig. 3.1). Although evidence from musical borrowings needs to be interpreted with caution, the early date of this anthem may be supported by its stylistic debt to German and Italian works, including one wholesale borrowing from a secular Italian duet (probably composed in Hanover) which sets this anthem apart from the rest of Handel's English church music: Handel's first London opera *Rinaldo* similarly made immediate reuse of music from the operas and cantatas that he had composed in Italy. In terms of musical style, the anthem appears rather primitive next to the Utrecht music, but different genres are involved and this makes direct comparison unreliable. There would have been

---

[38] *The Spectator*, no. 405, 14 June 1712. Reprinted in Gregory Smith, *The Spectator*, iii. 260–1.

Fig. 3.1. The opening of Handel's first English anthem, *As pants the hart*, HWV 251a. British Library, Add. MS 30308, fo. 17ʳ

practical sense in Handel trying out his first essay in English church music through the more straightforward genre of the verse anthem, which would have had good prospects for immediate inclusion in a Chapel Royal service. He thought sufficiently highly of the music that he composed for this anthem to return to it later: indeed, he seems to have returned to *As pants the hart* as a 'starter' when he needed to compose English church music at subsequent periods.

The Anthem

Although the text of the anthem is based on only half of the psalm, it forms a complete unit in itself and has a clear emotional progression. In the opening verses the psalmist expresses his need to find God: his situation is miserable and isolated, surrounded by mocking unbelievers. He remembers, in contrast, the strength he derived from the community of believers (verse 4);[39] the recollection of this wider solidarity shakes the psalmist from his depression, and he resolves to put his trust in God. In addition to contrasts of mood, the text also gives opportunities for throwing the individual (the 'I' of verse 4) into relief against the background of 'the multitude' which, in musical terms, prompted an effective use of the contrast between solo voices and chorus. The text has a literary symmetry, the 'tears' of verse 3 balancing 'Why so full of grief?' in verse 6: Handel set these two verses as the extended movements for solo voices. His overall scheme falls into an arch pattern, the central emotional transition in verses 4 and 5 being framed by an aria and a chorus on each side.

The opening theme of the first movement is rather chorale-like in outline,[40] and may owe something to Handel's youthful German training; furthermore, the movement's second motif (Ex. 3.8) is the kind of contrapuntal tag that Handel may have been taught in his early musical studies under Zachow.[41] There are other possible derivations for the opening theme, however. It is a 'subject' of the traditional ricercar type; it is also remarkably close to the theme of a *Miserere* by Caldara, published in 1715 but possibly composed earlier and known to Handel when he was in Rome during 1707–9; there is even a resemblance to the opening of an anthem composed by John Blow in 1697: see Ex. 3.9. The example by Blow shows that Handel's opening was not seriously distant in style from that of contemporary English anthems; he found it easy enough to adapt his previous experiences to the needs of the English form. He had already explored some of the possibilities of the theme (also in D minor) in the last movement of his secular Italian trio *Quel fior che all'alba ride* (HWV 200), though the musical development of the trio movement relied on the interplay of two subjects rather than the imitative possibilities from the slower one.[42] When composing the anthem, Handel made a couple of false starts at the opening (Ex. 3.10): it is interesting that he began with a free bass similar to

[39] The images used almost certainly refer to the gatherings of Jews at the Temple in Jerusalem for the Passover.

[40] I have not been able to discover any specific chorale melody which Handel might have used as his starting point.

[41] Handel returned to it again *c.*1722 in his Italian duet *Se tu non lasci amore*, HWV 193 (*HG* 32, p. 112, 'Mà con chi parlo').

[42] *HG* 32, pp. 171–5. HWV 200 was probably composed as a companion to the trio HWV 201, written by Handel at Naples in 1708.

Ex. 3.8. Handel, *As pants the hart* (HWV 251a), No. 1

that of the trio but ended up with the simpler imitative treatment typical of
Ex. 3.9 (b–e). The imitative build-up at the opening, and the suspensions both
there and in the subsequent phrase 'so longs my soul' (Ex. 3.8), convey the
spirit of the text admirably. Handel may even have realized the possibilities of
an allusive relationship between text and musical texture at the beginning:
although the line 'when heated in the chase' from the version of Tate and
Brady is omitted, the simile describing the 'longing' of the soul is clear enough
to suggest pursuit (*fuga* = flight) and searching (*ricercare* = searching again).

The movement falls into two parts of almost exactly equal length, with a
central cadence in C major at bar 27. The first half is solely concerned with
elaborating the texture through imitative entries of the opening phrase, beginning with soloists and introducing the chorus with entries of the theme
from bar 16 onwards. In the anthem *O praise the Lord, all ye that fear him*,
described above, Croft also leads from a 'verse' opening for soloists into a
chorus based on the same material, but he does not overlap the verse and
chorus sections to give the cumulative effect that Handel achieves in *As pants
the hart*, nor is the device used in any of Croft's other anthems composed before
1720. Handel's movement was composed for the same combination of adult
soloists (Hughes, Elford, Weely, Gates) as Croft's 1710 anthem, with the
addition of a treble. This was surely no accident: Handel soon identified the
Chapel's best voices, and wrote accordingly. Furthermore he distinguished the
Chapel's 'first' alto and bass voices (Hughes and Weely) from the 'seconds'.[43]

The second half of the movement begins with the soloists taking up the
passage in Ex. 3.8 and returning the music via A minor to the tonic D minor. As
the tonic is reached, the chorus re-enters and the two themes are worked
together (bar 34 onwards): the device of drawing a movement together by
combining two themes that have previously been heard separately is another
feature that has no counterpart in Croft's anthems. Handel uses it to lead towards
a purely homophonic rhetorical conclusion (bars 47–51) which is followed by a

[43] For the singers, see App. C and Ch. 17.

Ex. 3.9. (*a*) Handel, *As pants the hart* (HWV 251a), No. 1; (*b*) Zachow, Choral Prelude 'Ach Gott vom Himmel, sieh darein' (*Gesammelte Werke*, p. 337); (*c*) Kerll, *Ricercata* (DDT 53 and 54, p. 59); (*d*) Caldara, *Miserere mei, Domine* (*Kirchenwerke*, p. 21); (*e*) Blow, *My God, my God, look upon me*

Ex. 3.9. *Cont'd*

Ex. 3.10. Handel, *As pants the hart* (HWV 251a), No. 1 (voice parts shown in keyboard reduction): (*a*) first sketch; (*b*) second sketch

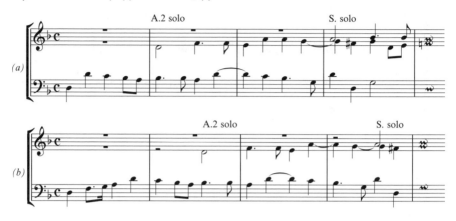

four-bar instrumental ritornello to round the movement off. As will be seen in Chapter 8, Handel was uncertain about the value of this ritornello in his later versions of the movement: he could not decide whether it was best concluded with the choral climax, or whether the memory of it should be given time to subside in an instrumental postlude before the next movement.

This first version of *As pants the hart* is remarkable among Handel's anthems in its concentration of the solo music onto one singer, but it is not surprising that he gave the emotional nub of the anthem to Richard Elford. There is ample evidence for Elford's high reputation as a singer, and for the favoured patronage that he received from the Queen early in her reign (see App. C, 'Elford'). Handel may also have known about Elford's brief attempt at a career on the London stage some ten years previously. The solo music in this anthem is more operatic in form than any to be found in Handel's later church music, which may be another sign that this was Handel's first English anthem and that the composer's previous experience was being pressed into service in a new situation. The movements following the opening chorus are in effect a *scena* for Elford consisting of a short aria, an arioso, and a recitative. The long notes on 'Tears' in the aria and the rhetorical musical phraseology of the recitatives were obviously written to make the most of Elford's expressive vocal talents.

The aria 'Tears are my daily food' is built over an ostinato bass, a technique much cultivated in England by Purcell's successors; examples can be found in solo movements composed for Elford in Croft's anthems and in Eccles's odes.[44]

---

[44] See above, Ex. 3.5, for an example from Croft's anthems. A comparable movement from an ode by Eccles is 'No Albion, thou canst ne'er repay' from *Inspire us, genius of the day* (GB-Lbl Add. MS 31456) from 1702–3, which is built on a bass strikingly similar to Handel's.

It would be a mistake to see the employment of an ostinato bass as an exclusively 'English' feature on Handel's part, since it occurs in continuo-accompanied arias from his earlier Italian period.[45] Nevertheless, contact with almost any of Croft's verse anthems would have revealed that movements of this type were a favoured feature in the English verse anthem. Handel's aria, although it is built upon a bass which is longer, more chromatic, and more sinewy than most of Croft's, is hardly more extensive overall than comparable movements by the English composer. After a central cadence on the dominant at bar 24, a varied repeat of the opening material commences in the dominant key, but this quickly takes a new turn, and close imitation between voice and bass heralds a return to the tonic and the opening bass at bar 41, providing a focus for the text 'where is now thy God?' which is fundamental to the dramatic sequence of the anthem. The Phrygian cadence at the end of the aria, mirroring that at bar 24, leads on (as the words demand) into the next section, an arioso designed on the same lines as Handel's operatic accompanied recitatives (Ex. 3.11). An introductory instrumental ritornello to the arioso provides a little time for reflection, a musical representation of the psalmist 'thinking thereupon', and there is an effective distinction between the lament for the isolation of the individual in the minor-key arioso and the business-like recovery in the succeeding major-key recitative, as the mood of the psalm changes.

The music for the instrumental obbligato part that Handel wrote for 'Now, when I think thereupon' and its preceding ritornello is written in the treble clef; the stave was not labelled by the composer and Chrysander suggested that the part was intended for solo oboe or violin,[46] but it is doubtful that an orchestral melody instrument was brought in just for these seventeen bars. The location of the obbligato part between the voice part and the basso continuo in the autograph at the beginning of the movement also suggests that it was not intended for an orchestral instrument, whose music would normally have been written above the voice part.[47] The obbligato part must therefore be considered in the light of the Chapel Royal's normal practice in the instrumental accompaniment to verse anthems. It was not uncommon for English composers to include brief thematic right-hand parts for organ in verse anthems: see, for example, the opening of Ex. 3.4. If Handel's obbligato part was intended for organ, practical problems arise: the distance between the two

---

[45] See e.g. 'Se la Bellezza' from *Il Trionfo del Tempo* (HG 24, p. 14).

[46] *HG* 34, p. 282. None of the secondary MS copies give an instrumental specification for this obbligato part.

[47] On the autograph (GB-Lbl Add. MS 30308, f. 21ᵛ) Handel wrote 'NB Mr Eilfurt' before the ritornello, and at the beginning of 'For I went with the multitude'. This was probably to direct the copyist to the unusual arrangement of the staves, but it may just possibly indicate a plan to cut the intervening section (to the detriment of the sense of the surrounding text) on account of practical difficulties in performing the ritornello.

Ex. 3.11. Handel, *As pants the hart* (HWV 251a), No. 2a

hands is rather large, it is difficult to arrange an effective transition from background continuo accompaniment to obbligato role and back again, and the melodic span of the obbligato makes it difficult to provide any filling-in of the harmony without obscuring the melodic line.[48] (Such filling-in seems desirable here, in order to clarify the harmonic progressions.) Bernard Smith's instruments of the period did not have the pedals which at a later time would have provided a technical solution.

However, the organist did not have to accompany verse anthems alone at the Chapel Royal: before Handel arrived in England, a Violist and a Lutenist had become established members of the Chapel.[49] A similar disposition of the parts is found in Ex. 3.12, from an anthem by Croft, and it may assume the participation of a viol as well as the organ. Surviving eighteenth-century part-books for the Chapel Royal Violist show that the player's function was to play the bass line,[50] and a bass viol usually blends well with the tone of the pipework from English organs of the period. The use of the viol on the bass

---

[48] The written-out organ accompaniments in the surviving part-books from the sets used by the London choirs at this period display a concern to avoid unplayable textures: see Herissone, ' "To fill" '.

[49] See Ch. 16, 'Other instrumentalists'.

[50] The relevant books from the period are GB-Lbl RM 20.a.10 and 11.

line could therefore have released the organist from literal responsibility in connection with the written bass part, some of which could have been taken an octave higher. The organist's left hand may consequently have been free to provide some harmonic filling-in where necessary, perhaps on a second manual and assisted by the lute, while the obbligato part was played by the organist's right hand and the bass part was provided by the viol. Under this arrangement, it would have been possible for the organist to supply both Handel's obbligato line—not entirely comfortably, though the same is true of obbligato passages in Croft's anthems. It seems most likely that the obbligato was intended for organ. Another possibility, less likely but nevertheless worthy of consideration, is that Handel's obbligato part was intended for lute, to be accompanied by the viol bass, a background of quiet organ chords and such chords on the lute as fell conveniently under the hands. This scoring would have been appropriate to the nature of the text and effective in the small Royal Chapels. The key (A minor) suits the lute well enough, but the notation of the part is not characteristic of lute music. (In practice, the Lutenist's instrument was almost certainly a theorbo.) None of the music in the surviving Chapel Royal part-books for lute includes a similar obbligato part: from these part-books it seems that the lute usually contributed a harmonic role from a figured bass part, so it is more likely that the lute provided the chords to accompany an organ obbligato than vice versa.[51] Nevertheless John Shore, the Chapel's Lutenist, was an inventive lute maker and player, and the possibility that Handel's obbligato part was intended for him cannot be ruled out entirely.

'For I went with the multitude' (Ex. 3.13) is the clearest example of operatic-style continuo-accompanied secco recitative in Handel's English church music. The declamation is correct but rather square, with a hiatus in bar 21 that looks like a weakness, though we have no way of knowing how

Ex. 3.12. Croft, *I waited patiently*, No. 2

Source: GB-Lbl Add. MS 17847. This follows the layout of the original, on 2 staves.
The treble solo was composed for Thomas Gethin, later one of Handel's tenor soloists.

[51] The earliest lute volumes of the Chapel Royal part-books are GB-Lbl RM 27.a.12 and RM.27.c.14: the earliest sections of the former were copied before 1710. Three of Blow's anthems include movements with obbligato lute parts, but the layout and tessitura of these parts do not resemble those of Handel's obbligato line.

Ex. 3.13. Handel, *As pants the hart* (HWV 251a), No. 2a

Original ending:

much liberty Elford (whose strength, according to Croft, lay in giving 'such a due Energy and proper Emphasis to the *Words* of his *Musick*') took with the rhythmic values. The move into more measured rhythms at the Adagio (bar 25) demonstrates Handel's overall sense of dramatic design, since it provides a foil for the high-spirited chorus entry that follows. His choice of 'house' as the word to carry the melisma is not so appropriate, and may be one of the few signs in this anthem of a 'German' outlook on word-setting, especially plausible here because the English and German nouns are so similar at first sight. As shown in Ex. 3.13, Handel at first provided a closing postlude, but then deleted it to give a more direct lead into the ensuing chorus, 'In the voice of praise'. For the chorus itself he may have been indebted, as in the first chorus, to the German keyboard and vocal models from his youth, this time in the use of a typical canzona-type repeated-note subject.[52]

[52] See e.g. Zachow's 'Der Herr is Wahrhaftig auferstanden' (Zachow, *Gesammelte Werke*, 248), and the fugal sections of Buxtehude's Praeludia for organ in G minor and A minor, BUXWV 148 and 153. Some caution is needed concerning Handel's subject, however: if the repeated notes are run together as minims, the theme takes on a rather different appearance, resembling the 'Ut re mi' in Sweelinck's keyboard pieces based on the hexachord.

The theme, with its rather heavy and frequent accents, excellently characterizes the holiday-making crowd. The Jews going to the Passover feast were no more of a disciplined entity than the turba of the crucifixion narratives, and something of their rough jubilation seems to be reflected in Handel's music. The opening subject and its associates generate enough energy for a short binary-form fugue without any further development.

The following duet, 'Why so full of grief?', is based on music from the last movement of Handel's Italian duet *Troppo cruda, troppo fiera* (HWV 198) for soprano and alto with basso continuo, possibly composed in Hanover.[53] It is the only movement from Handel's English church music of this period to be so closely based on a previous composition. Perhaps he was pressed for time in the composition of the anthem, but this need not have been the motive for his use of music from the duet: it is more likely that the text fused with his memory of the music that he had previously composed.[54] The mood of the two duet movements is rather similar: in the anthem, the psalmist is returning towards putting his trust in God, and in the Italian duet the poet concludes that, while there remains hope, the lover can bear the burden of yearning for the beloved. The opportunity for self-borrowing may have influenced Handel towards setting this movement of the anthem as a duet instead of providing another solo movement for Elford: in context, the duet movement preserves the first-person mode of expression (as indeed also happens in the Italian duets), while at the same time shifting the music towards a more generalized presentation that was suitable for the anthem. Handel shortened the Italian duet, adapted the music to English words, and added ritornellos at the beginning and the end. The movement was rewritten in G minor (instead of E minor, as in the duet), and there was a considerable amount of recomposition: Handel did not make his task as easy for himself as he could have done. The musical emphasis on 'Why?' as the music progresses (cunningly adapted from 'sospirar' = 'sigh', in the Italian duet) is effective in its context and, perhaps accidentally, the musical motif for this phrase echoes the rhetorical ending to the first chorus of the anthem. On the whole the adaptation is successful, though perhaps Handel's inexperience of the English language may have deceived him into choosing a minor-key setting of the text on account of the inclusion of the word 'grief', when the sense of the text appears to demand something more cheerful.[55]

---

[53] *HG* 32, pp. 41–4. For the probable period of composition, see Burrows, 'Handel and Hanover', 55–9.

[54] There is an obvious parallel with Handel's use of material from other Italian duets in *Messiah* some thirty-five years later.

[55] In his English church music Handel is rather more modern than Croft in associating major and minor keys with optimistic and sad moods, respectively: for example, he does not write minor-key 'alleluja' movements.

Taking a broader view of the scheme of the anthem as a whole, however, the use of the minor key here is defensible: the duet creates an interlude between two lively major-key choruses, and the movement as it stands forms a splendid foil to the final chorus. That chorus itself is straightforward. Three snippets of tune heard in the opening bars are worked out in imitation and combination through closely related keys, and there is a good stretto conclusion from bar 37. A curious set of consecutives at bars 19–21 escaped Handel's eye even when he revised the anthem later. The plain concluding plagal cadence for 'Amen' provides a final hint of the anthem's early place in the canon: only once later, in the Anthem on the Peace in 1749, did Handel conclude with a simple 'Amen', and then not as a plagal cadence.

If this was indeed Handel's first English anthem, it is an impressive achievement. In spite of its debt to Italian and German influences, an English congregation would have recognized it as being within the conventions of a verse anthem. The theme combination in the first movement and the return of the bass theme in the second movement are features that connoisseurs of the English anthem could have regarded as attractive technical novelties, but nevertheless in the service of the verbal text. The emotional progression of the text is well represented in the musical setting and formal devices are used to good effect. The first aria leads into the arioso meditation: the more down-to-earth secco recitative, beginning in a new but related key centre, changes the mood and leads into the chorus, and so on. The key scheme reinforces the onward movement of the text, and the fact that the anthem does not end in the same key as it began may not have great significance: this feature is shared with many of Handel's Italian duets and cantatas.[56] In these works, as in the anthem, it is the progression from mood to mood, from movement to movement, which is important. Handel's later church music generally ends in the tonic established in the first movement, often because of the use of fixed-key instruments like trumpets, but it may be anachronistic to expect large-scale tonal perspectives in music composed in 1712, though 'tonic' endings are the general rule in Croft's anthems, as indeed also in those of his Chapel Royal predecessors.

Circumstances of Performance

Since there are no documentary records concerning the anthem, we can not be certain where it was performed.[57] The most likely site is the Chapel Royal at

---

[56] See Timms, 'Handel and Steffani', 377.

[57] There is a possibility that the anthem was never performed at all, though Handel's pencilled annotations on the autograph suggest an advanced state of preparation for a specific performance.

St James's Palace, described in Chapter 18. There is also the slight possibility of a performance at St Paul's Cathedral, for the Sons of the Clergy service in December 1712, though the more intimate style of Handel's music suggests the Chapel Royal as the intended venue. When Handel arrived back at London in 1712 the court was at Windsor: the most likely time for the composition and performance of this anthem is during the period between the Queen's return to St James's Palace in December 1712 and her removal to Kensington the following May. In August 1713 the court left Kensington for a short stay at Hampton Court before proceeding to Windsor: the Queen intended to take up residence again at St James's in December, but she was detained by ill health and was still at Windsor when she approved the warrant for Handel's first royal pension on 28 December. It is tempting to suggest than an anthem of Handel's might have been performed at Windsor on Sunday 27 December 1713, but this is improbable;[58] there is no question of a performance then in the presence of the Queen, who was seriously ill at the time. The combination of soloists named by Handel in the first movement is much more likely to have been available when the court was in London. All four adult soloists had commitments in the other London choirs and their periods of 'waiting' were probably intricately timetabled because it was then impossible to fulfil duties at the Chapel Royal and also at Westminster Abbey or St Paul's on the same Sunday morning when the court was away from St James's: the list of travelling charges for 1713 suggests that there were not many days when Weely and Gates were in waiting together at the Chapel Royal (see below, Table 16.1).

Assuming that the anthem was performed at one of the daily services in the Chapel Royal, the singers would have comprised at most a dozen Gentlemen and between six and ten choristers, accompanied by organ, possibly with lute and viol. The five soloists named by Handel would have taken their normal places in the choir stalls and, since they were also part of the 'chorus', there would not have been a dramatic musical distinction between solo and ensemble roles, and the transitions between 'solo' and 'tutti' sections in the first movement would have been subtle. The choir was presumably divided into 'sides' in the Chapel, with Alto 1 and Bass 1 facing Alto 2 and Bass 2 over the central aisle. While it is possible that the four named singers for the first and last movements were the complete complement of the alto and bass voices, Handel's 'chorus' indications to subsequent entries in the first movement imply additional singers. The Lutenist and Violist (and even Elford, as the

---

[58] There may have been no choral service by the Chapel Royal on this date, depending on whether Sundays were reckoned within 'Play Weeks' (see *OCB*, fo. 57ʳ; Ashbee and Harley, i. 144). The proximity of the vacation period, the fact that the court was out of town, and the current severity of the Queen's illness could have provided reasons for excusing the Chapel's attendance. There is no evidence that Handel himself attended the court at Windsor.

principal soloist) may have preformed from the organ gallery. No subsequent performances of the anthem in this version are documented.

Autograph

Handel wrote the anthem (GB-Lbl Add. MS 30308, fos. 17–26) on paper of a type and size which is not found elsewhere in his autographs. As already noted, he named four Chapel Royal soloists in the first and last movements; he also named Elford as the soloist for the central movements, joined by 'the Boy' for the duet. In the central and final chorus movements Handel wrote 'Chorus partout' at the vocal leads. In the autographs of his English church music directions in French occur only on this anthem and the Utrecht music, so this provides a further hint of the anthem's early date. He designated the soloists as 'Mr Hughs', 'Mr Eilfurt', 'Mr Whely', 'Mr Gates', and 'The Boy'. Although 'Eilfurt' (for Elford) is sufficiently unusual to suggest that Handel had not learned the name properly at this stage, no chronological conclusions can be drawn in relation to other autographs. The composer's spellings of singers' names always tended to be idiosyncratic (and phonetic): the autograph of the Utrecht music has less correct forms for Weely and Gates. Handel gave no instrumental specifications against the basso continuo staves.

   Some features of the autograph are also of interest in view of the early place of the anthem in Handel's London career. In the first movement he wrote 'paints' for 'pants' throughout and in the central chorus he wrote 'praise of [instead of 'and'] thanksgiving'. There are a few interesting compositional revisions. As already noted he made two corrections to the opening bass part (see above, Ex. 3.10), the first of which must have been rejected immediately since the barring from bar 4 is incompatible with Ex. 3.10(*a*). The autograph of the duet movement is very fluent, suggesting that the adaptation from the Italian duet was worked out in advance, though there are noticeably more corrections in the recomposed bars 44–6. In the final chorus Handel began with a layout as for the opening chorus (SAATBB voices) but the music quickly reduces to four vocal parts: he may have intended solo entries at the beginning (as in the first movement) but thought better of it later, and this would explain the presence of the soloists' names as well as the chorus indication.

4

Handel's Music for the Peace of Utrecht, 1713

Handel and the Utrecht Thanksgiving Service

HANDEL'S first visit to London had coincided with the establishment of a Tory ministry, buttressed by the Queen's favour and a substantial majority in the 1710 election. The change of government had important consequences for the direction of British foreign policy. During the period of Handel's first visit the secret diplomacy had already begun which led to the signing of the first peace articles between Britain and France in September 1711. While Handel was back in Hanover, momentous events took place in London. Early in 1712 the Duke of Marlborough was dismissed from his post as Captain-General of the armed forces; after nearly a decade of concerted action by British, Imperial, and Dutch forces, the alliance was broken by the 'restraining orders' that were given to the army in May 1712, which effectively left the rest of the allied armies without British support during the campaigns of that year. Such developments could only be regarded with displeasure in Hanover, and the Elector made known his attitude towards Anne's unilateral peace-making in strong terms.[1] In addition to being treacherous to the alliance, the British action put in jeopardy the 1709 agreement that had provided a barrier in the Netherlands against the French, a matter that was of great concern to Hanover.

It is therefore surprising to find a composer who was still in the employment of the Elector of Hanover turning to the composition of music celebrating the forthcoming peace between Britain and France, as Handel did within a few months of his return to England in the autumn of 1712. His association with the celebrations for the Peace of Utrecht eventually terminated his Hanover appointment, in circumstances that are revealed in a letter from the Hanoverian Resident in London on 5/16 June 1713:

---

[1] Hatton, *George I*, 105–6. Although there is no doubt about George's attitude to developments in English foreign policy, he may have seen beyond the immediate crisis: it turned out to his long-term advantage to have the Peace settlement, with its consequent diminution of the Jacobite threat, before he gained the British crown.

A few days ago I wrote to you on the subject of Mr Handel, that since His Highness was determined to dismiss him, Mr Handel submitted to that wish, and that he desired nothing save that the affair be conducted with a good grace and that he should be given a little time here so that he could enter the Queen's service. Moreover, it seems to me from your letters that this was precisely the generous intention of His Highness. But since then Mr de Hattorf has informed Mr Handel via Mr Kilmansegge that his Highness had dismissed him from his service, telling him that he could go wherever he pleased. In other words, he was given notice in a way which he found particularly mortifying. I will admit to you frankly that Mr Handel is nothing to me, but at the same time I must say that if I had been given a free hand for a week or two I could have resolved the whole affair to the satisfaction of both His Highness and Mr Handel, and even to the benefit of the Elector's service. The Queen's doctor, who is an important man and enjoys the Queen's confidence, is his grand patron and friend, and has the composer constantly at his house. Mr Handel could have been extremely useful, as he has been on several occasions, by giving me information of circumstances which have often enlightened me as to the condition of the Queen's health. . . . You must know that our Whigs rarely know anything about the Queen's health. [In return,] since the Queen is more avid for stories about Hanover than for anything else, the Doctor can satisfy her from his own information: you understand the stories to which I am referring. Afterwards they are passed on to some serious ecclesiastical gentlemen, and this has a marvellous effect. . . . I arranged things so that Mr Handel could write to Mr de Kilmansegge to extricate himself gracefully, and I let slip a few words to inform him that, when some day His Highness comes here, he might enter his service.[2]

As late as June 1713, in the word-book for the London opera *Silla*,[3] Handel was still described as 'Sig. Georgio Federico Hendel Maestro di Capella di S.A.E. d'Hannover', but he must have received notice of dismissal from his post by late May 1713, probably while the *Silla* word-book was being prepared.[4] Handel's public contribution to the state Thanksgiving Service for the Peace of Utrecht, which identified him with the British interest, was probably the critical factor that broke his relationship with the Hanover court. News of the forthcoming service may have been relayed to Hanover at the beginning of March,[5] and the Hanoverian representatives in London were presumably

---

[2] Hannover, Niedersächsisches Hauptstaatsarchiv, Dep.103.I.Nr.148. Copy by Jean de Robethon of a newsletter from Kreienberg (Hanoverian Resident in London) to Hanover; original in French. The 'Queen's Doctor' John Arbuthnot was closely associated with the court and with Harley's Tory ministry: see Aitken, *The Life and Works*, 33–5, 38–42, 51, 55, 67–8.

[3] *L. C. Silla, Drama per Musica*, with a dedicatory preface by Giacomo Rossi dated 2 June 1713 (O.S.): see Harris, *The Librettos*, ii. 209–17.

[4] Handel's Hanoverian salary was withheld in 1713. In 1715 he received a retrospective payment for six months' service from St John's Day (Midsummer) 1712. See Burrows, 'Handel and Hanover', 40.

[5] Reports of the rehearsals for the music, naming Handel as the composer, appeared in the London newspapers early in March, though I have not found references to this in any of the extant newsletters sent to Hanover by the London Resident's office.

instructed to make sure that notice of dismissal was served on Handel before the service itself took place.

He must have foreseen this result when he composed the Utrecht Te Deum and Jubilate: he would have been aware of the strength of feeling in Hanover, and the fact that he was willing to risk the Elector's displeasure suggests that he had already decided not to return to Hanover again. It is out of the question that he could have temporarily forgotten the imminence of the Elector's succession to the English throne: the Queen's illness on which he appears to have been so well informed, and the shadow of possible Jacobite intervention, were constant reminders. Presumably Handel's reasoning was that, since a peace agreement between Britain and France was not to be prevented, he might as well turn the situation to his own advantage. Once the immediate furore had died down, the Elector himself might take the same attitude to the peace agreement; in the meantime, the Utrecht music would ingratiate Handel with his London patrons, the British court, and the government.

Contemporary London newspapers have several references to Handel's Utrecht canticles. He completed the Te Deum on 14 January, nearly four months before the Peace was proclaimed. Given the unpredictable timetable of the final stages in the negotiations for the Peace, the date of the composition is not remarkable, since Handel (like many people in London) might have anticipated the possibility of an earlier settlement. In February news of the music reached the papers, though Handel was not named:

We hear that a New Service of Musick is Composing, to be used on the day that the Peace is Proclaimed, when her Majesty is expected at St. Paul's; and that the same will be very suddenly. (*Dawks*, 19 Feb. 1713)[6]

The Guns are mounting on the Tower Walls, which have been repair'd for that End; and an Anthem of Te Deum is composing to be sung on the Day the Peace is proclaim'd, and the Queen's Musick are shortly to practice upon the same. (*EP*, 21–4 Feb. 1713)[7]

---

[6] Subsequent issues of the same paper (24 and 26 Feb.) say that it was expected that the Peace would be proclaimed on 8 Mar. and that the Thanksgiving Service would be on 23 Apr.: both predictions were optimistic by about two months. The *Hamburger Relations-Courier* for 17 Mar. carried a report of the composition of the music, naming Handel, under 'London, 7 März 1713'. If this date is in Modern Style, as most of the Hamburg reports are, this would be equivalent to 24 Feb. Old Style. Since the English papers first begin to mention Handel on about 7 Mar., it seems likely that this reference is in Old Style. See Becker, 'Die frühe Hamburgische Tagespresse', 34.

[7] As noted in Ch. 2, the singing of the Te Deum at St Paul's was usually one of the signals for the firing of cannon at the Tower of London on Thanksgiving Days, but reports of the 1713 Thanksgiving do not mention this happening during the service.

It is not known whether Handel received an invitation from the court to contribute to the Thanksgiving service: if such an invitation had come through the official channels of the Chapel Royal it would have been one of Ralph Battell's last acts as Sub-Dean.[8] Possibly Handel wrote the music speculatively, relying on rumour and reputation to win first public, and later official, acceptance. Similar uncertainty surrounds the generation of his birthday ode for Queen Anne at this time. The items from the newspapers show that a return to a full state Thanksgiving service at St Paul's Cathedral was expected, and that the Queen's Musicians were to be involved in the rehearsal of the Te Deum, which indicates institutional support from the court. Whether or not Handel's music had some official status from the beginning, the public rehearsals were numerous by contemporary standards and they were well reported: Handel, his influential friends, or Tory supporters of the Peace settlement, appear to have made an effort at promotion. There were three rehearsals in March:

A Te Deum, Composed by Mr. Hendel, which is to be perform'd on the Day of Thanksgiving for the Peace at St. Paul's, was Rehearsed there on Thursday [5 March] last, and this Afternoon [7 March], where was present many Persons of Quality of both Sexes; it is much Commended by all that have heard the same, and are competent Judges therein. (*Dawks*, 7 Mar. 1713)

London March 19. This day the Te Deum (to be sung when the Peace is proclaim'd) was rehearsed at the Banqueting House at Whitehall, where abundance of the Nobility and Gentry were present. (*EP*, 17–19 Mar. 1713)[9]

The use of the Banqueting House Chapel indicates that by 19 March Handel's music was officially accepted in court circles. The London correspondent of the Hamburg *Relations-Courier* reported that there was an admission fee of half a guinea to this rehearsal.[10] A further rehearsal at Whitehall followed in May,[11] and there was presumably at least one more last-minute rehearsal nearer to the service itself on 7 July. Newspaper reports of the service give surprisingly little information about the music. Only one source mentions Handel by name, in an incidental reference to 'the singing of Te Deum to excellent Musick, both Vocal and Instrumental, compos'd by the famous Mr. Hendel'.[12] Two other

---

[8] There is at present no authority for Tudway's statement that the settings of the canticles by Croft and Handel were composed 'by the Queen's order' (GB-Lbl Harl. MS 7342, fo. 12^v).

[9] *Dawks*, 19 Mar. added that the music 'gives wonderful Satisfaction, being universally Admird'.

[10] Becker, 'Die frühe Hamburgische Tagespresse', 35.

[11] *BM*, 13 May: 'Te Deum has again been rehears'd at Whitehall, as it is to be perform'd on the Thanksgiving Day.'

[12] Boyer, *The Political State*, vi. 15.

newspapers contain comments to the effect that 'The Church-Musick was as Excellent in its Performance, as it was Exquisite in its Composure'.[13]

The Utrecht canticles served, as *Rinaldo* had done in 1710, to put Handel at the centre of London's musical life. Indeed, the Thanksgiving service and the rehearsals brought him to a wider and more diverse audience than his operas had done. In addition, there were two reasons why the Thanksgiving service itself attracted special attention: it was long delayed, and it was planned as a Royal event. A conclusion to the Peace, with attendant official celebrations, had been expected since September 1712,[14] but the negotiations continued through the first quarter of 1713: by the time the peace was proclaimed on 5 May,[15] Handel's music had already been publicly rehearsed at least three times. On 18 May a proclamation was issued setting the date of the national Thanksgiving at 16 June, which is the date on the published liturgy (see Fig. 4.1). However, this gave too short a time 'for making the Preparations necessary for so great a Solemnity' and the Thanksgiving day was put back to 7 July.[16] There was mounting interest as preparations for the day proceeded: a maypole was set up in the Strand, the Queen's statue was erected outside St Paul's Cathedral, a new state coach was built, and plans were made for a firework display.

There is no doubt that it was the Queen's intention to attend the Thanksgiving service at St Paul's. Commands were issued to the militia to line the streets of the procession route,[17] and on 3 July the Queen sent a message to the House of Commons to the effect that 'for the greater Solemnity of that Day, her Majesty will be pleased to go to St Paul's Church, as has been accustomed in former Times in this Kingdom, to return Thanks to Almighty God for the Blessings of Peace. . . . And that her Majesty hath been pleased to give necessary Orders for providing convenient Places in the said Cathedral for the Members of this House.'[18] For the first time since 1708 it was planned to gather all the Estates together at the Cathedral for one service. The Queen announced at the last minute that she would not be able to attend, but otherwise the arrangements that gave the Thanksgiving a special emphasis remained unchanged:

Monday the 6th of July, Mr. Chancello[r] of the Exchequer, by her Majesty's Command acquainted the Commons, That her Majesty not having entirely recover'd

---

[13] *PB*, 7–9 July; also *Dawks*, 9 July.

[14] *PB*, 30 Aug.–2 Sept., and 11–13 Sept. 1712.

[15] The proclamation was dated 4 May, but read in public the next day.

[16] Boyer, *The Political State*, v. 399.

[17] GB-Lpro LC5/155, p. 224.

[18] Boyer, *The Political State*, vi. 12

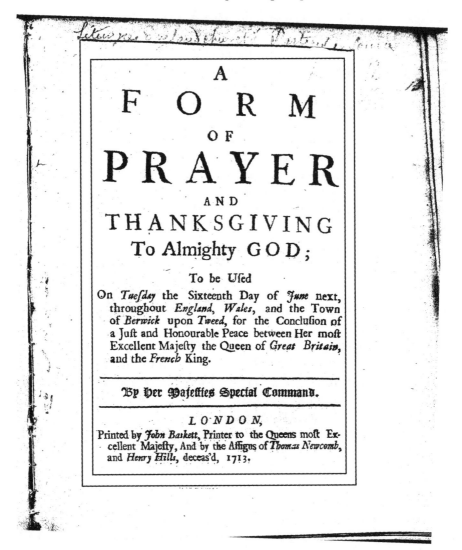

Fig. 4.1. Title page and p. [6] (showing the specified canticles) from the published order of service for the Thanksgiving Day for the Peace of Utrecht. The date given is that originally planned for the Thanksgiving. British Library

her Strength since her last Fit of the Gout, and being apprehensive that the Fatigue of going to St. Paul's Church, as she intended, may be too great, chuses rather to return her Thanks to Almighty God for the Blessings of Peace in her Chapel at St. James's; but desires, that this House will proceed to St. Paul's Church to Morrow with as much Solemnity as if her Majesty was to be in Person there.[19]

[19] Boyer, *The Political State*, vi. 13.

A Form of Prayer

¶ Inſtead of the *Venite*, this Hymn ſhall be uſed.

Pſal. 96.1.   O Sing unto the Lord a new ſong : ſing unto the Lord, all the whole earth.

Ver. 2.   Sing unto the Lord, and praiſe his Name : be telling of his Salvation from day to day.

Ver. 7.   Aſcribe unto the Lord, O ye kindreds of the people : aſcribe unto the Lord worſhip and power.

Pſal. 92. 4.   For thou, Lord, haſt made us glad through thy works : we will rejoyce in giving praiſe for the operations of thy hands.

Pſal.13. 6.   We will ſing of the Lord, becauſe he hath dealt ſo lovingly with us : yea, we will praiſe the Name of the Lord moſt high.

Pſal. 29. 10.   The Lord hath given ſtrength unto his people : the Lord hath given his people the bleſſing of Peace.

Pſal. 107. 21.   O that men would therefore praiſe the Lord for his goodneſs : and declare the wonders that he doth for the children of men!

Ver. 22.   That they would offer unto him the Sacrifice of thankſgiving : and tell out his works with gladneſs!

Ver. 32.   That they would exalt him alſo in the congregation of the people : and praiſe him in the ſeat of the Elders!

Pſ. 117. 2.   For his merciful kindneſs is ever more and more towards us : and the truth of the Lord endureth for ever. Praiſe the Lord.

Glory be to the Father, and to the Son : and to the Holy Ghoſt ;
As it was in the beginning, is now, and ever ſhall be : world without end. Amen.

¶ Proper Pſalms are LXXXV, CXXII, CXLV.

¶ Proper Leſſons.

The Firſt, Micah IV. Firſt five Verſes.
Te Deum.
The Second, S. Matth. V. to Verſe 10.
Jubilate Deo.

¶ Then

Fig. 4.1. *Cont'd*

The occasion turned out to be magnificent, spectacular and popular:

Notwithstanding the Disappointment of the Queen not going to St. Paul's, the Crouds of Spectators, as well in the Houses as Streets, thro' which both Houses of Parliament, Judges and Great Officers of State pass'd in their Way to that Cathedral, were prodigiously great, and, as it generally happens on such Occasions, made the best part of the Shew.[20]

[20] Ibid. 21. This is followed (pp. 22–4) by a description of the elaborate firework displays that were held in the evening following the service.

The crowds lining the streets included 4,000 charity children, singing specially composed hymns in honour of Queen Anne and the Peace.[21] Predictably, some people made a point of staying away:

It was observ'd, that very few Members of the Whig Party, in either House, appear'd at the Solemnity, which is not much to be wonder'd at; since it would have been preposterous, if not a mocking of Religion, for Men to return Almighty God Thanks for a Peace, which they had endeavoured to prevent, and still disapproved.[22]

Lady Cowper was one of those who stayed away, and suspected that the Queen's absence might have been diplomatic. The entry in Lady Cowper's diary contains a backhanded hint of the significance attached to Handel's music:

7 July 1713 This Day, the Church Opera, after many Rehearsals was finish'd at the Cathedral of St. Paul. Why or wherefore the Queen was not present, Whither she cou'd not or wou'd not, is hard to know: for Court secrets are kept better than ever. 'I sat not in the Assembly of the Mockers, nor rejoiced' (Jer. 15.17).[23]

However, an entry in the diary of Sir David Hamilton, one of the Queen's physicians, suggests that the reasons for the monarch's absence were genuinely medical rather than political: 'July 6 1713 I advis'd Her not to go to St. Paul's, least she Suffer'd in her Health, but rather to St. James's, & that would satisfy the people and not injure Her.'[24]

It appears from the resolutions of the members of the House of Commons on 6 July that they expected the service to take place in the morning: they planned to take their seats in the Choir at St Paul's at nine, and the roads would be closed between that time and two in the afternoon.[25] However, the service took place in the afternoon, though it followed the liturgy of Morning Prayer. Some newspaper accounts say that the procession left for St Paul's at 11 a.m., others give the time as noon:[26] it is possible that the procession formed up at eleven and moved off about mid-day. The time of the service's conclusion is given incidentally in the report of the death of the Bishop of London, who 'departed this Life in the 81st Year of his Age, on Tuesday about Six in the Evening, the Time when the Service in Thanksgiving for the Peace was just finish'd in his Lordship's Cathedral.'[27] The procession to the Cathedral followed precedents from the previous Thanksgiving services: the Speaker and

---

[21] The texts of these hymns were printed in *PB*, 11–14 July.
[22] Boyer, *The Political State*, vi. 15.
[23] Hertfordshire County Record Office, Panshanger MS D/EP F35.
[24] Panshanger MS D/EP F207.
[25] Boyer, *The Political State*, vi. 13–14.
[26] Compare e.g. the reports in *EP*, 7–9 July and *Dawks*, 9 July.
[27] *PB*, 5–7 July. The Bishop, Henry Compton, had also been Dean of the Chapel Royal continuously since 1689 and, in earlier years, had been responsible for the education of Princess Anne. He died at his residence in Fulham.

200 Members of Parliament were followed by the Judges, Barons, Bishops, Viscounts, Earls, Marquises, and Dukes, the Lord President, the Lord Treasurer, and the Lord Chancellor, all in their ceremonial robes.[28] In the Cathedral itself the seating arrangements followed the general plan devised for the Thanksgiving services in the previous decade (see Ch. 18).

As with the earlier Thanksgiving services, the printed order of service gives only a limited amount of information that is relevant to the music. The texts of the canticles, Te Deum and Jubilate Deo, come at their usual places next to the 'Proper Lessons' (Micah 4: 1–5; Matthew 5: 1–10) in Morning Prayer. Neither in Morning Prayer nor in the following Communion Service is there a specified place for an anthem. Croft's anthem for the Thanksgiving *This is the day* was presumably performed at St Paul's:[29] its length precludes a performance at St James's Palace as well on the same day. The Chapel Royal may have done double duty on the Thanksgiving day, at St James's before the Queen and then at St Paul's: it was probably on account of the Queen's state of health that the service at St James's was short and included little or no music. As the Queen's intention was that the service at St Paul's Cathedral was to proceed as if she were present, there can be no doubt of the Chapel Royal's participation there. The soloists named by Croft on the score of *This is the day* are the principal Chapel Royal singers of the period: Hughes and Elford (Altos), Freeman and Church (Tenors), Gates, Williams, and Weely (Basses). These names include all of the singers named by Handel for the Utrecht Jubilate. Very soon after the Thanksgiving day, many of the leading musicians travelled to Oxford, where William Croft's 'exercise' as Doctor of Music was performed at the Sheldonian Theatre on 10 July.[30] Croft's ode also celebrated the Peace, and the Queen's role as peacemaker. A newspaper report named the principal singers as Elford, Hughes, Freeman, Gates, and Weely, and noted the participation of 'the best Hands of her Majesty's Musick, and in the Opera House'.[31]

The Utrecht Te Deum

Handel's 1713 canticles must be considered against the background of their English forerunners. Purcell's famous setting of the Te Deum and Jubilate was easily accessible to Handel through the printed edition, and he would probably

---

[28] *PB*, 7–9 July.

[29] GB-Lcm MS 839, a copy of the anthem in the hand of James Kent and with the composer's annotations, is entitled: 'Thanksgiving anthem for the Peace 1713'. The text of the anthem was printed in the appendix to *Divine Harmony* with the note: 'Composed upon the Peace, and Perform'd on the Day of Thanksgiving at St. Paul's July 7th 1713'.

[30] See Johnstone, 'Music and Drama at the Oxford Act of 1713'.

[31] *BM*, 15 July 1713; see Johnstone, 'Music and Drama', 209.

have known of Croft's 1709 setting by reputation even if he did not have easy access to the music. Those by Blow and Turner are less likely to have come his way.[32] It seems very likely that Handel subjected Purcell's version to some study before attempting his own setting of the English texts, but unfortunately the earliest documentary reference linking the two composers is general, and also too late and too tenuous to provide firm evidence on the subject.[33] The principal characteristics of the settings by Purcell, Croft, and Handel are shown in Table 4.1 on pp. 111–13. The similarities between Purcell's and Handel's settings, as regards external features, are obvious. Trumpets are used at the same places in the text (except at 'Thou art the King of Glory', where Handel's tonal scheme takes him away from the keys available to those instruments), and the five-part texture with divided soprano parts imparts a characteristic sonority to the choral movements. Some differences between the two works are equally obvious. Handel's setting takes nearly twice as long to perform as Purcell's: the larger scale of Handel's music is felt both in the melodic and harmonic characteristics of the themes and in the extent of the complete movements. In particular, his substantial chorus movements provide a much more weighty effect: for example, while Purcell disposes of 'All the earth doth worship Thee, the Father everlasting' in eighteen bars, Handel sets the text as a two-subject fugal movement of forty-three bars. Purcell's setting of the Te Deum takes about fifteen minutes, Handel's about twenty-five minutes.[34] With the Utrecht canticles Handel changed the style of orchestrally accompanied English church music, as decisively as Purcell's canticles had done two decades previously in comparison with the preceding symphony anthems. The participation of the woodwind instruments in Handel's setting also adds a new dimension: there are independent oboe parts in the tutti sections and obbligato parts for flute and oboe in vocal solo movements. Handel's extensive employment of the woodwind instruments in the Te Deum was something of a novelty: the four previous English settings were accompanied by Purcell's 'Te Deum scoring' of strings and trumpets, though Croft's version does include one movement with an oboe obbligato.[35]

---

[32] GB-Lbl Add. MS. 31457 (Blow) and GB-Mp MS 130 Hd4 v.235 (Turner). Their individual characteristics are not sufficiently different from Purcell's to justify inclusion in Table 4.1, especially since their influence on Handel's own composition is doubtful.

[33] 'Had every Man the same Value for our *Purcel*, as the wonderful *Hendel* has, I had never set Pen to Paper', *UJ*, 25 July 1724, in a letter defending 'Old Stile' music. Since the identity of the author is not known, we cannot tell the value of this evidence: it may record an opinion expressed by Handel, or it may have been merely an inference from his music.

[34] Timings from recordings conducted by Simon Preston, Archiv 2723 076 (Purcell, 1981) and L'Oiseau-Lyre DSLO 582 (Handel, 1980)

[35] Oboes may have doubled the violins in Purcell's 1692 St Cecilia Ode, but the combination of woodwind and strings in London's secular venues probably did not face the difficulties posed

Presumably Handel was already well acquainted with the verbal content of the Te Deum text before he came to England, either from the Latin original or from one of the German paraphrases.[36] The English text from which both Handel and Purcell worked is that of the 1662 Prayer Book.[37] The Chapel Royal Altar Prayer Book from the period 1710–14 survives today, and the text of the Te Deum from this is reproduced in Fig. 4.2. The 1662 version of the Te Deum was a revision of the text found in the previous prayer books: some words were altered, and colons were inserted in an attempt to make the Latin canticle conform in appearance to the conventions of Hebrew poetry as found in the Psalms.[38] The colons fragment the appearance of the canticle, which is already rather discontinuous with its twenty-nine, generally rather short, verses: composers dealt with this situation by recombining the verses into paragraphs which they could set as continuous, though sometimes episodic, movements. There is general agreement about the paragraphing in the settings by Purcell and Handel:

Purcell: verses 1–2, 3–6, 7–10, 11–13, 14–15, 16–23,   24–5, 26–8, 29
Handel: verses 1–2, 3–6, 7–13,   14–15, 16–17, 18, 19–23, 24–5, 26–8, 29

The clearest difference emerges in verses 16–23. Purcell set 16–21 as a series of short solo movements, largely running on from one another, and 22–3 forms a further extension of the paragraph. Handel breaks this part of the text up with an imitative chorus at verse 18, making up for lost time by running 19–23 as one movement. Verses 22–9, believed by liturgical scholars to be a later addition to the original fourth-century text,[39] are obviously regarded as an integral part of the Te Deum by Purcell and Handel, who set it as one hymn throughout and make a stronger break between verses 23 and 24, incorporating the re-entry of the trumpets, than between verses 21 and 22. Handel goes a stage further than his predecessors in smoothing over the join of verses 21–2 by bringing the chorus in at 22 so that the petition in this verse reinforces that of

by the sharp pitch of Bernard Smith's organs for the Royal Chapels: it was probably only in the 1720s that this problem was resolved with a special 'sharp oboe' (see Ch. 19).

[36] The Te Deum was regularly used in the Lutheran liturgy, and Luther's metrical German version 'Herr Gott, dich loben wir', first published in 1529, would have been well known to Handel, as it was also to J. S. Bach. The chorale melody (adapted from plainsong) that was used for Luther's text does not seem to have had any direct musical influence on Handel's settings of the Te Deum.

[37] For verse 4 Handel followed the Prayer Book form 'Cherubin and Seraphin' in the Utrecht and Caroline Te Deums (1713–14), but wrote 'Cherubim and Seraphim' in his later settings.

[38] The earlier versions are reprinted in Harrison, *The First and Second Prayer Books*, 22–3 and 350–1.

[39] See *NG II*, 'Te Deum Laudamus'.

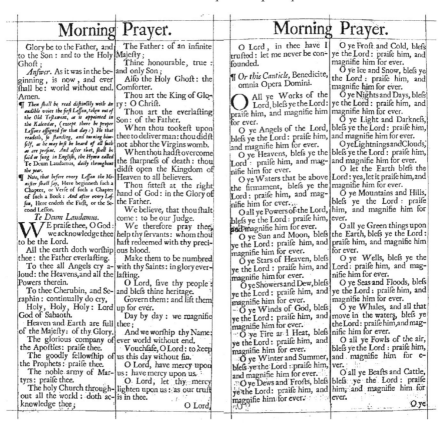

Fig. 4.2. Pages from the large altar copy of *The Book of Common Prayer* that was used by the Chapel Royal, 1710–1714, showing the text of Te Deum laudamus. Private collection

the soloist in the previous one. Elsewhere Handel's use of the chorus closely follows Purcell's: both composers, for example, set verses 2 and 14 as imitative choruses, and use a mixture of contrapuntal and homophonic textures at verses 24–5 and 29. Characteristically, Purcell's imitations are short, close-worked, and full of inversion or augmentation/diminution devices: Handel's are broader, less complicated, and based on longer themes (see Ex. 4.1). Handel tends more towards the employment of two simultaneous subjects, though Purcell also used this device at verse 14 (see Ex. 4.2).

It is interesting to compare the composers' settings for verses 24–5. Purcell treated these verses in one movement: after a compact imitative opening he moves quickly to a more homophonic texture with the theme in the trumpet parts (12 bars), which is then followed by a more extended imitative section for the closing words of verse 25 'ever world without end' (19 bars—see Ex. 4.1).

Ex. 4.1. (*a*) Purcell, Te Deum in D major; (*b*) Handel, Utrecht Te Deum (orchestral parts omitted)

Ex. 4.2. (*a*) Purcell, Te Deum in D major; (*b*) Handel, Utrecht Te Deum (orchestral parts omitted)

Handel, on the other hand, set the two verses as separate movements. For verse 24 he wrote a grand concertato movement with antiphonal blocks of upper and lower voices, each with appropriate orchestral accompaniment, and with independent trumpet parts adding a third layer (32 bars, including the ten-bar trumpet introduction). Verse 25 is composed as a short imitative movement (19 bars), in which Handel's style is at its closest to Purcell's: the trumpet writing also seems to echo Purcell's. Purcell and Handel alike treat verse 25 as the end of a paragraph of the text: Purcell uses augmentation in the bass part to achieve the effect of finality, while Handel resorts to a long dominant pedal.

The first movement shows the contrast between the approach of the two composers at its greatest. Both of them begin with instrumental introductions. Purcell's short prelude is based on the music of the subsequent vocal entries: whether the vocal phrases were moulded by the capacities of the brass instruments or the instrumental material was controlled by the syllabic demands of the vocal parts, there is a clear derivation of one from the other. Handel's vocal and instrumental material is more independent. His Te Deum begins like a

Corelli concerto, with a short arresting Adagio introducing a fugal Allegro movement;[40] the latter eventually becomes the accompaniment to the first chorus entry. The choral and orchestral elements are not thematically related, and the chorus entry therefore adds a new rich contribution to a movement that is already under way, the climactic effect being reinforced by the first entry of the trumpets. All three of Handel's characteristic textures (homophonic, imitative, and one-part-against-the-rest) are represented in the choral section of the movement.[41]

It is significant that Handel, unlike Purcell, Blow, and Turner, chose to give the opening verses to the chorus rather than soloists. The proportion as well as the length of chorus music in Handel's setting is much larger than in those of its predecessors: indeed, the balance has swung sharply the other way, for the amount of solo work in his Te Deum is very slight. There are no really extended solo movements: only the opening of 'When thou tookest upon Thee', an aria-type interlude for alto lasting a mere fourteen bars, approaches this category.[42] Purcell's version of 'Vouchsafe, O Lord' (45 bars) is, in fact, much closer to an aria in spirit and length than anything to be found in the Utrecht Te Deum; Handel's setting of the same text, beginning with an alto duet and then building up through a solo ensemble to the choral conclusion, is both shorter and more weighty in texture than Purcell's.[43] Handel's use of choruses and ensembles where Purcell uses soloists is so consistent that it must represent a definite stylistic choice. Perhaps, if Handel had heard Purcell's setting performed at the Sons of the Clergy service in 1710 or 1712, he decided that Purcell's treatment was not robust enough for the acoustic conditions at St Paul's.[44] Another possible explanation is that Handel wrote the Te Deum before he received official approval for the music, and therefore played for safety until he knew that the best Chapel Royal soloists would be available. Whatever the cause, the emphasis on the chorus gives the Utrecht Te Deum a different character from its predecessors.

The greater use of the chorus is complemented by heavier orchestral participation. Purcell's Te Deum has extensive verse sections with only basso continuo accompaniment: in Handel's setting orchestral accompaniment is almost continuous and its removal becomes a striking effect—at, for example, 'O Lord, have mercy upon us', or the beginning of the chorus 'All the earth

[40] Direct comparison can be made with Corelli's D major Concerto, Op. 6 No. 4.

[41] At bars 17–24, 40–6, and 25–32 respectively.

[42] 'The glorious company of the Apostles' has successive phrases for solo tenor and bass amounting to thirty-four bars, but these are not an independent movement.

[43] The motifs with which Handel began the movement had already been used by him in arias from the Italian cantata *Ero e Leandro* (HWV 150) and from *Rinaldo*.

[44] As indicated in Ch. 2, Purcell's Te Deum and Jubilate were probably not composed with St Paul's in mind, *pace* Tudway's preface to GB-Lbl Harl. MS 7342.

doth worship Thee'. In the latter instance Handel was 'composing out' an idea implicit in Purcell's setting, Purcell's two-bar arpeggio to gather 'all the earth' becoming Handel's fourteen-bar fugal exposition. Handel's musical word-painting of 'everlasting' is another idea developed from Purcell's setting. His withdrawal of all accompaniment (including the basso continuo) at the words 'When Thou hadst overcome the sharpness of death' was a novelty, a dramatic gesture in contrast to the succeeding tutti outburst 'Thou didst open the kingdom of heaven': there is nothing comparable in Purcell's setting and it must have been startling to the 1713 audience. If the effect of this section is rather blunted for modern audiences, this is because of our familiarity with the similar passage at 'Since by man came death' in *Messiah*. It occurs in the course of one of the most successful sequences of the Utrecht setting, for throughout verses 16–23 (beginning at 'When Thou took'st upon thee') Handel links the short sections together convincingly. The autograph shows that he was more than usually anxious to get things right: he discarded two versions of the unaccompanied bars and subjected the preceding alto solo to critical revision, removing a couple of bars of redundant matter.

Handel's Te Deum explores a wider range of keys than Purcell's. In this respect his work comes closer to Croft's setting, which returns to the safety of the D major tonic far less frequently than Purcell's. Croft's version anticipates Handel's plan specifically in its use of B minor (rather than D minor) for 'Vouchsafe, O Lord'. However, the constant return to the tonic is so obvious a weakness of Purcell's plan that Handel may have worked out his own scheme independently: it would not be surprising if he came to some of the same answers as Croft. The movement away from the tonic at verses 3 and 7 in Handel's setting was an extension of features found in the previous settings: none of them, however, went as far from the tonic as Handel did in verses 11–21, although Croft anticipated him slightly with a more adventurous scheme than his predecessors.

Some insight into Handel's attitude to word-setting can be gained from his treatment of verses 3–5. Burney's suggestion that Handel set verse 3 in the minor key because he 'confined the meaning of the word *cry* to a sorrowful sense'[45] seems a little less likely when we remember that all four previous English settings had begun this verse in the minor, though they ended in the major: none of them, however, saw the opportunity that Handel seized upon, of bringing in a chorus entry for 'the heavens and all the powers therein'— tenor and bass voices representing 'powers' in contrast to solo alto 'angels'. The following verse ('To Thee cherubim') as set by Purcell was singled out by Thomas Tudway in 1720 as one of the models of English word-setting, as

---

[45] Burney, *An Account*, First Performance, 29. Burney remarked that Handel's setting, besides being in a minor key, was also 'slow, and plaintive': in fact, Handel added no tempo indication.

such glorious representation, of the Heavenly Choirs of Cherubins, & Seraphins, falling down before the Throne & Singing Holy, Holy, Holy &c As hath not been Equall'd, by any Foreigner, or Other; He makes the representation thus; He brings in the treble voices, or Choristers, singing, To thee Cherubins, & Seraphins, continually do cry; and then the Great Organ, Trumpets, the Choirs, & at least thirty or forty instruments besides, all Join in most excellent Harmony, & Accord; The Choirs singing only the word Holy; Then all Pause, and the Choristers repeat again, continually do cry; Then the whole Copia Sonorum, of voices and instruments, Joine again, & sing Holy; this is done 3 times upon the word Holy only, changeing every time the Key, & Accords; then they proceed altogether in Chorus, with Heav'n & Earth are full of the Majesty of thy glory; This most beautifull and sublime representation, I dare challenge, all the Orators, Poets, Painters & of any Age whatsoever, to form so lively an Idea, of Choirs of Angels Singing, and paying their Adorations.[46]

Blow and Turner followed Purcell's model closely at this point, but Croft anticipated Handel by rejecting the repetition of 'continually do cry' in favour of bringing the 'accords' on the repetitions of the word 'Holy' next to each other. There the similarity between Croft and Handel ends, for Croft goes on to set verse 6 as a separate movement for alto solo (a novel treatment of this text), while Handel regards 'Holy, holy, holy' as introductory matter to verse 6 and proceeds in a continuous choral sequence.[47] Handel preserves Purcell's representation of the Cherubin and Seraphin by two treble parts (Croft had cast them as tenors) and his deleted sketch for bar 22 suggests that his original idea was melodically not unlike Purcell's (see Ex. 4.3).

Handel follows Purcell's plan at the opening of the next movement with short florid sections for solo voices culminating in the chorus entry at 'The holy Church'. His treatment of the chorus at verse 10 itself is more extended than Purcell's and the linking of verses 10–11 is a special feature of Handel's setting. It seems that he understood the text here better than his English predecessors: the list of the persons of the Trinity in verses 11–13 is a statement of what the holy Church of verse 10 is acknowledging. The rest of the movement follows Purcell's model, but with the chorus used on a much grander scale. Handel set verse 15 imitatively where Purcell treated it briefly in simple homophony. The dramatic Adagio interruption at 'O Christ', which suddenly takes the music out of key with a new dominant seventh and then a diminished seventh chord, was an afterthought, the four bars being interpolated in the autograph. (The previous two choral statements, at bars 133–5, had originally been to the words 'O Christ': Handel altered them to repeat 'of

[46] GB-Lbl Harl. MS 7342, fo. 12ᵛ. Tudway's description is not entirely accurate: the setting of 'Heaven and earth' is divided between solo and chorus voices.
[47] Handel followed exactly the same treatment in his subsequent settings of the Te Deum, running verse 6 on from verse 5.

Ex. 4.3. (*a*) Handel, Utrecht Te Deum, Handel's sketch fo. 12ᵛ; (*b*) Purcell, Te Deum in D major

glory'.) The revision is not wholly a happy one: this is one of the few places where Handel seems to be striving for effect rather than making an effective response to the text. He may have been prompted by a purely musical consideration: although the movement originally ended on the dominant chord of F major and the subsequent fughetta for 'Thou art the everlasting Son' is in that key, the subject itself begins on the dominant note and there was therefore no strong cadential effect to the first beat.

One further movement, beginning 'We believe that thou shalt come', calls for comment since it provides a compendium of some of the characteristic features of Handel's setting. The instrumental prelude, with flute obbligato against quaver string accompaniment, owes something Handel's previous experience with arioso-style movements and something to Zachow.[48] In the movement Handel grouped verses 19–23 in a logical way, and one that had not been tried by his English predecessors. He saw the opportunity for a threefold alternation of solo and chorus voices, skilfully progressing through various

---

[48] See e.g. 'Tu del ciel ministro eletto' from *Il trionfo del Tempo* (HG 24, p. 95) and, for Zachow, Ex. 3.1 above.

tonal centres while preserving an overall G minor tonic. Each time the chorus enters it heightens the effect of the preceding solo sections, giving dramatic support without interrupting the flow.

Handel's Te Deum has been described here in terms of its relationship to the possible models from Purcell and Croft. In the course of the eighteenth century the settings by Purcell and Handel became established repertory pieces in Britain, accessible through the published editions and seeing continued performance at church services associated with civic or charitable events. In 1771 Anselm Bayly, then Sub-Dean of the Chapel Royal but formerly one of the Chapel's leading alto soloists, devoted a substantial section of his treatise *The Sacred Singer* (republished almost immediately in the same year in an expanded form as *A Practical Treatise on Singing and Playing*) to these works. Bayly had probably been the original alto soloist for Handel's Dettingen Te Deum in 1743 and he would have heard, or performed in, Purcell's setting of the canticles and Handel's Utrecht version at the services for the Festival of the Sons of the Clergy (and probably elsewhere). Bayly considered the text of the Te Deum as 'consisting of three paragraphs to be stopped and divided into cadences and periods' beginning at 1, 14, and 26, and he observed that 'In the Te Deum to animate the musician's imagination there are three great ideas, namely, praise, adoration and petition, varied and heightened by names and epithets of dignity and mercy'.[49] His specific observations on Purcell's setting and Handel's 'first' (i.e. Utrecht) are as follows:

The strain and harmony should be plain and modest, opening with one, or two voices, as in *Purcel*'s grand *Te Deum* and Handel's first. . . .

The movement to the first words should be very simple, that it may stand in contrast to the next, 'All the earth', that is, the whole world christian and unchristian doth worship thee under the universal revelation of the father everlasting, the being of all mankind; where it is impossible to be too full and solemn, the notes plain and in unison rather than in harmony, particularly on *all* and *everlasting*. *Purcel* hath sublimely expressed the word *all* by the single voices taking it one after another, and then joining; nor is *everlasting* ill expressed by a division instead of holding notes, except that it runs on the syllable *e* instead of *la*. Handel less simple and less expressive than *Purcel*, in his first *Te Deum* runs away in a fugue with too long and too gay a division on the solemn word *worship*. . . .

The Hebrew word *sa-ba-oth* of three syllables, signifying hosts, particularly those hosts of heaven, the sun, moon, stars and winds, is by modern composers mistaken for sabbath, and so printed in *Purcel*'s and *Handel*'s *Te Deum*, but the singers should correct it. . . .

'Thine honourable, true and only Son; also the holy Ghost the comforter' standing in opposition to the father everlasting should be near as possible in the same movement,

---

[49] Bayly, *A Practical Treatise*, 76, 81; the punctuation of the quotations has been regularized.

ending with a full cadence on comforter, not on Christ; where the first composer was guilty of a fault in making a pause, and almost every succeeding writer hath implicitly followed the same erroneous track: *Purcel* indeed without stopping proceedeth immediately with the next words. . . .

Handel is superior even to himself in his first *Te Deum*, [in setting the verse] 'Thou didst not abhor' . . . 'We believe that thou shalt come to be our judge'—this passage is usually set with too grave ideas of honor and despair, as if in the mouth of the wicked ready to be condemned, instead of true believers to be saved; who stand before their judge with reverential awe indeed, but with certain hope and uplift countenances, as finely expressed by *Handel* in his first *Te Deum*.[50]

The Utrecht Jubilate

The Jubilate Deo, Psalm 100, has a much more straightforward text for the composer than the Te Deum. Both Purcell and Handel adopted the obvious plan of setting each verse as a separate movement: more extended arias or duets therefore alternate with choruses as discrete movements, without the shorter transitions that characterize the Te Deum settings. As in the Te Deum, Handel's timescale is larger, choral participation is increased, and his key scheme is more adventurous in comparison with the previous settings. In the opening movement Handel followed Purcell by using the well-tried English combination of alto voice and solo trumpet;[51] his manner of leading into the chorus entry also echoes Purcell's. The principal motifs of the movement were reworked by Handel from the opening movement of his own D major *Laudate pueri*, written in Italy in 1707,[52] the principal one generating a florid alto line, interspersed by long notes that provided Elford with the same expressive opportunities as his aria in *As pants the hart*. Unlike his English predecessors, Handel set the second half of verse 1 as a separate chorus movement, the concerto-like first movement giving place to one of contrapuntal interest. The opening theme of the second movement, setting the first clause of the verse, is worked in a fugal exposition and then the theme goes into the orchestra as an accompaniment to a new long-note theme carrying the second clause, after

[50] Bayly, *A Practical Treatise*, 76, 81; the punctuation of the quotations has been regularized.
[51] 'Well-tried' in odes rather than church music, since trumpets participated more regularly in the court odes; *Eternal source of light divine*, Handel's own ode, begins with the alto/trumpet combination. Some of Croft's anthems composed before 1712, for example *O clap your hands* and *Blessed be the Lord my strength*, contain alto solo movements with organ accompaniment including a right-hand part for the trumpet stop. While Handel followed Purcell in beginning the Jubilate with the alto/trumpet combination, Blow, Turner, and Croft began with a three-voice verse combination and confined the use of the trumpets to the introduction and the choral sections.
[52] *HG* 38, pp. 19–27.

Ex. 4.4. Handel, Utrecht Jubilate (orchestral parts omitted)

which the two themes are then worked together (see Ex. 4.4). Although this treatment has links with Handel's previous German and Italian experience, the effect is not far removed from Purcell's combination of a theme with its own augmentation at Ex. 4.1(*a*).

In the duet 'Be ye sure that the Lord, he is God' Handel gave himself the first real opportunity in the canticles for extended solo writing. For the first time the names of soloists appear on his music: Hughes and Weely, a regular Chapel Royal combination for whom he also provided a duet in the birthday ode *Eternal source of Light divine*. It is interesting that he had found out that Hughes, and not Elford, was Weely's regular duet partner: the Chapel's practice seems to have been to match 'first' basses with 'first' altos. Handel's movement has a straightforward binary structure with a central ritornello. A certain angularity about the end of bar 1 in the oboe part suggests that the music may have been reworked from an earlier composition, possibly from the Hamburg period.[53] The long and somewhat archaic choral movement that follows may also have been worked up from previous material. The first half is a free fugue based on the alternation and combination of themes that are first heard independently in chorus and orchestra;[54] the second part of the movement, beginning at bar 93, introduces a new theme for the verse's second clause, which also quickly acquires a complementary contrasted subject.[55] The subjects both here and at the beginning of the movement are introduced immediately in stretto, yet even so Handel contrives to make the stretto over the pedal notes in the last bars of the movement sound more final than the music that has gone before. At 162 bars, this chorus movement was probably the longest of its type yet composed in England. The trio movement for verse 4 is rather more Purcellian than the duet, in its melodic contours and also in its adherence to the tonic. The fragmented bass line at the opening is in a style that might have been composed by Croft, though it is unlikely that he would have thought of using the chromatic scale from bar 4 to generate the broadening out of the movement that Handel achieves from bar 30 onwards.

The final choruses form a free prelude and fugue in Handel's most spacious manner: he had already coupled contrasted choruses three times previously in the canticles, though involving less extensive movements. The eight-part vocal writing in the first movement is used to give a spread to sustained chords in combination with oboes and trumpets, heightened by contrast with the orchestral interludes for upper strings only: the closest comparable movement, 'Day by day' in the Te Deum, had made its mark by dividing the chorus voices into contrasted groups, rather than concentrating them in this way. It is impossible for the modern listener to avoid hearing pre-echoes of *Messiah* in this chorus, and the similarity in the music may have been generated by the

---

[53] The non-rising leading note on beat 4 suggests a slight affinity with the 'Almira cadence' noted by Terence Best and Anthony Hicks (see Hicks, 'Handel's Early Musical Development', 86). Compare also the beginning of Handel's Italian duet *A miravi io son intento*, HG 32, p. 68, possibly composed at Hanover.

[54] Chorus theme at bar 1, orchestral theme at bar 15. Handel's way of working up this material anticipates the big choruses of *Israel in Egypt*, composed a quarter of a century later.

[55] First heard in the orchestra at bar 109.

similarity of the texts. In *Messiah* the words are 'Glory to God in the highest', in the Jubilate they are 'Glory to the Father': in each case they drew from Handel a choral outburst with a halo of string echoes.[56] It is interesting that he did not attempt to reintroduce music from the first movement at the words 'As it was in the beginning', in view of the fact that he used this device in the Gloria Patri of each of his three large-scale Latin psalm settings. Instead, themes are combined and textures are contrasted in the last movement of the Jubilate in a manner and on a scale that must have seemed totally new to the London public:[57] the massive rhetorical ending with its pauses and long final stretto is a fitting culmination to Handel's first English essay in 'his grandest and most magnificent style'.[58] Anselm Bayly, who criticized Purcell and Handel alike for some aspects of their word-setting in the Jubilate, and commented that Handel 'enters into the courts of the Lord in a fugue with too little solemnity', nevertheless acknowledged the power of the conclusion: 'The *gloria patri* is set with great ideas of exaltation and praise by both these eminent composers in style, which differ as much as their character, *Purcell* proceeding *per arsin and thesin* delighteth with noble simplicity; *Handel* surpriseth with fullness and grandeur.'[59]

Subsequent Performances

It is uncertain whether Handel ever performed the Utrecht music again after the Thanksgiving Service of July 1713, though he revived the Jubilate in a rewritten version with reduced scoring at Cannons. John Eccles, the Master of the Queen's Music, was paid travelling charges for the attendance of himself and twenty-two of the Queen's Musicians, 'being commanded to perform the Te Deum at Windsor on the 19 of November 1713',[60] so perhaps a performance took place there before the Queen: the Chapel Royal was, of course, in attendance at the time, and presumably Handel would have directed any performance himself. There is also the possibility of a performance in the Chapel Royal in September 1714, to be noted in Chapter 5. Handel may also have been responsible for a performance of the Te Deum and Jubilate on 8 July 1733, during his visit to Oxford.[61] However, neither the autograph nor any

[56] A similar passage occurs in the Te Deum, 'The glorious company', bars 134–7. As it happens, the text as it now stands also ends with the word 'glory', but Handel's original version ended 'O Christ'.

[57] The music was reworked from a keyboard Capriccio (based on a German chorale melody) by Nikolaus Adam Strungk: see Roberts, 'German Chorales', 89.

[58] Burney, *An Account*, First Performance, 35.

[59] Bayly, *A Practical Treatise*, 87–8.

[60] Ashbee, *Records*, ii. 50. See also Beeks, 'Handel and Queen Anne'.

[61] See Deutsch, *Handel*, 327–9. The reports of the service do not mention who directed the music, though the singers named (Powell, Waltz, and Rowe) were part of Handel's company for

early manuscript copies bear any of Handel's characteristic annotations that would suggest a revival under his direction. He composed three further settings of the Te Deum for the Chapel Royal, none of which has an accompanying Jubilate: the possibility that Handel performed the Utrecht Jubilate separately at some stage to complement one of these Te Deums cannot be discounted, though there is no evidence of this from documentary or musical sources. Certainly the Dettingen Te Deum and the Utrecht Jubilate were coupled in later performances for which other people than the composer were responsible.[62]

The Utrecht canticles were within the resources of many performing groups in London and the provinces: they became a popular alternative to Purcell's service, though not immediately. Only one performance apart from the composer's original one is documented before the 1730s, at Bristol on St Cecilia's Day 1727.[63] Nathanial Priest, who was responsible for this performance, had been a former Chapel Royal chorister and presumably obtained the music through Chapel connections.[64] Bernard Gates was responsible for a performance of the canticles at the Academy of Vocal Music in January 1730/1, in circumstances that will be considered in Chapter 10. The fortunes of the Utrecht music underwent a major revolution in the 1730s. The success of the performance at the Sons of the Clergy Festival service on 25 February 1730/1[65] was almost certainly a major factor in persuading John Walsh to print a score of the Te Deum and Jubilate.[66] To judge from the frequency of Walsh's advertisements, his score of Purcell's D major canticles had enjoyed a regular long-term demand, and Handel's setting now took its place alongside: the two works together became the foundation of the repertory for festival services as the expansion of provincial music meetings took place. Handel's canticles featured in the early programmes for the Salisbury St Cecilia Festival

the Oxford oratorio performances. The strongest evidence suggesting that Handel was responsible for the performance is circumstantial: at the 1713 Oxford Act the Professor of Music and Organist of the University Church was paid for a similar performance, but there is no payment in 1733. (Oxford University Vice-Chancellor's Accounts, Ob W.P.B. 21(6), 1697–1735). See also Ch. 11, p. 304.

[62] See the MS organ scores GB-Lbl RM 19.a.14 and Add. MS 27745, both of which associate the Dettingen Te Deum with the Utrecht Jubilate. Announcements of 'Mr. Handel's New Te Deum and Jubilate' for the Sons of the Clergy festivals from 1744 onwards presumably refer to the same combination.

[63] Deutsch, *Handel*, 217.

[64] See App. B, B15.

[65] There is no evidence for a performance of the Utrecht music at the Sons of the Clergy Festival before 1731: the oft-repeated statement (derived from Hawkins, *A General History*, ii. 745–6, and relayed via W. H. Cummings to Pearce, *Sons of the Clergy*) that Handel's setting superseded Purcell's at the Festivals from 1713 onwards is not supported by the evidence.

[66] Walsh's title page describes the Te Deum as that 'Perform'd before the Sons of the Clergy'; see William C. Smith, *Handel*, 157.

(1742) and for the Dublin charity performances in aid of Mercer's Hospital (1736).[67]

Just as Purcell's canticles were joined by Handel's Utrecht settings, so the latter in their turn had eventually to share their place with Handel's own Dettingen Te Deum. In advertisements or reports of provincial programmes it is often impossible to tell which of Handel's settings was performed from the 1740s onwards unless the music is identified as Handel's 'Old' or 'New' Te Deum. In spite of the competition, however, there is no doubt that the Utrecht setting remained fairly constantly in favour throughout the eighteenth century, and the printed edition was maintained by Walsh and his successors. Handel's music, originally a success with the influential and the cognoscenti of the metropolis in 1713, later became equally successful with performers and audiences in provincial cities as well as in London.

Conditions of Performance

Robert Trevitt's engraving of the state Thanksgiving Service on 31 December 1706 (Pl. I) is an important source of information for the arrangement of the musical performers at such services in St Paul's Cathedral.[68] It was part of a series of high-quality views of the Cathedral, and was no doubt produced in response to interest in the novelty of both the building and the Thanksgiving Services.[69] The complete picture is large and elaborate, giving a panoramic view of the Choir of the Cathedral viewed from the north side. Figure 4.3 is a detail showing the gallery area around the organ, a part of the scene which is described thus in the caption to the picture: 'The Choir and other Musitians filled the Organ Gallery and ye Returns of the Galleries adjacent on either Side'. The copy from which Pl. I is reproduced has been coloured:[70] priests in the stalls below are shown in black and white, and the musical gallery includes some 'priestly' singers, as we would expect of the Chapel Royal. Some instrumentalists are dressed in red, which may be a representation of the scarlet livery of the Royal Musicians. Reading from the right, the following musicians are shown in the gallery, dressed in the named colours: six singers (2 red, 2 blue, 2 unclear); violin (red); oboe (yellow), with one unidentifiable (?singer)

---

[67] For these performances see *RMARC* 5, p. 52, and 8, p. 24 (Salisbury); Brian Boydell, *A Dublin Musical Calendar*, 60–1, and Deutsch, *Handel*, 401–3 (Dublin).

[68] 'A Prospect of the Choir of the Cathedral Church of St. Paul on the General Thanksgiving the 31st. of Decembr. 1706. Her Majesty and both Houses of Parliament present / Robt Trevitt Fecit'; original *c.* 64 × 105 cm.

[69] See Ralph Hyde, 'Images of St Paul's', 321. The full picture is reproduced in Keene, Burns, and Saint, *St. Paul's*, Fig. 154.

[70] Lg q8020396. The authenticity of the colouring is unknown, but obvious elements (such as the colours of the dress for the Lords and priests) are correct.

behind; two singers (blue), ?one of them a chorister; lute (red); violin (blue); [organ case]; violin (red); cello (red); priest (black); two singers (blue); large lute/theorbo (blue); priest (black); oboe (red); violin (yellow), with three singers (?1 of whom blue) behind. This gives twenty-five performers in all, sixteen of them probably singers. More musicians are probably hidden by the organ cases and the picture naturally does not show those in the north return of the gallery. On the basis of what is shown in the picture, the total number of musicians would have been in the region of thirty-five to forty. The surviving plans of the organ screen are of the ground floor and do not show the exact arrangement of the staircases above, but it is likely that space in the gallery was limited by two stairwells to the rear.[71]

The visual reporting on Trevitt's picture is detailed and apparently accurate: for example, in the stalls to the east of the organ screen, he correctly shows two rows of people in the 'boxes' and three rows in the gallery above.[72] Although it is possible that the artist may have skimped on his representation of the musicians, this seems unlikely: in the age before photography, this sort of commemorative picture probably erred on the side of making the occasion appear grander than it really was, rather than the opposite. Where Trevitt shows the musicians two to three deep and crowded together at the front of the gallery, this was probably in accordance with the facts. A greater depth in the performing group would have increased the ensemble problems, and it is doubtful whether the gallery provided room for more. No timpani are shown: the scores for Te Deum settings performed at St Paul's before the 1730s did not include these instruments, and their size would probably have made them unwelcome in the gallery. Oboes are shown, but no trumpets, though the latter were essential to the Te Deum performances.[73] The orchestra includes two lute players: Shore's appointment as the Chapel Royal's Lutenist dated from 1 April 1706, and he may be the player represented with the large lute, in which case he probably took the role of Lutenist at the Thanksgivings at the Thanksgivings of 1706–8 (and possibly later), rather than fulfilling the functions that followed from his posts with the Queen's Musicians and the Trumpeters..

Trevitt's picture provides a guide to the arrangements for the 1713 'Utrecht' service, which followed the precedents from the earlier Thanksgivings (see Ch. 18). As in 1706, the musicians would have performed from the gallery

[71] See Plumley and Niland, *A History of the Organs*, pl. 15, 16.

[72] One curious inaccuracy is the depiction of too many panels to the sashes on the organ case: see Plumley and Niland, *A History of the Organs*, 9, 26–7; this has the effect of making the central section of the case look wider than it was.

[73] The trumpets were perhaps placed in the return of the north gallery, which is not shown in the picture.

Fig. 4.3. The musicians in the gallery at St Paul's Cathedral at the Thanksgiving service, 31 December 1706. Detail from Plate I

around the organ. The first occasion on which musicians came down to floor level for a performance of orchestrally accompanied church music at St Paul's was at the Sons of the Clergy service in 1735:[74] in any case the demands on space below in the Choir for political and ecclesiastical participants would have kept the musicians up above for state Thanksgiving services on this scale. Two things are remarkable about Trevitt's representation of the musicians: the performers are not disposed in sections, so that singers and players are inter-mixed, and the ensemble appears a little old-fashioned even for 1706.[75] We must take account of one very important development in London's musical life between 1706 and 1713, the creation of the orchestra for the opera house, as an ensemble that was recognizably more modern in composition and style than anything that Purcell would have known. By the time of Handel's arrival in London the opera orchestra had attracted excellent players, for stringed and woodwind instruments, from the Continent, and it included Saggione, London's first well-documented orchestral double bass player. The extent to which Handel was able to bring in extra players for the 1713 Thanksgiving is

[74] *SJEP*, 11–13 Feb. 1735.
[75] In view of the inclusion of Prince George of Denmark, who did not attend the Thanksgiving in Dec. 1706, it is possible that Trevitt's picture was based on sketches made at previous Thanksgivings in 1705–6: see ch. 2, p. 36.

uncertain because, unlike subsequent events involving court musicians, there are no entries for payments to additional musicians in the public records. Given the crucial importance of the Utrecht service in Handel's London career, however, it seems highly probable that he found some way of introducing, and financing, the participation of some of the best players that were available from the opera orchestra. It is not known how the problem of the likely pitch difference between the oboes (in particular) and the Cathedral organ was resolved: perhaps, as in some of Handel's Italian church music, the oboe parts were transposed and the other players somehow matched the sharp pitch of the organ,[76] or perhaps the organ continuo was transposed a tone lower.

Queen Anne's message to Parliament on the day before the Utrecht Thanksgiving Service expressed her clear intention that the service should proceed as if she were present, and in consequence we can assume the attendance of the Court's musicians. Taking the inference of a total of about forty performers from Fig. 4.3 as a starting point, this seems to suggest that only those court musicians who were currently in waiting (i.e. half of the total force) participated,[77] which might have given the following figures:

Singers: Chapel Royal—5 Priests, 8 Gentlemen, 1 Organist, *c*.6 Children, Lutenist, and Violist
Orchestra: 12 Royal Musicians (string players)

To these we can probably add a few more string players: a double bass or two, and some extra violins to fill out Handel's threefold division of the violin section. Handel's score also required two trumpeters (presumably the best players from the state trumpeters) and additional woodwind players: flute, two oboes, and at least one bassoon. There is no mention of a lute in Handel's scores: Shore may have played another, orchestral, instrument.

In addition to the Chapel Royal singers, the St Paul's Cathedral choir may also have contributed some voices, but this would not have made a significant alteration to the numbers. (It perhaps added a few singers with dual member-ship who were formally 'out of waiting' at the Chapel.) Of the Vicars Choral at St Paul's only Richard Brind, the cathedral organist, was not also a member of the Chapel Royal. Some of the St Paul's choristers might have been useful additions and presumably Charles King, the Master of the Choristers, was also available as an adult voice. The caption to the 1706 picture makes no mention of the St Paul's choir, but does say that 'The Residentiaries & Prebendaries were seated on Chairs within the Rails of the Alter [*sic*], except such as

---

[76] See Shaw, 'Some Original Performing Material', 229.
[77] But see the payment to twenty-two musicians above, for Nov. 1713.

officiated in reading Prayers.' Some of the more musical Prebendaries, such as Samson Estwick and Charles Badham, may have elected to join the musicians in the gallery. The caption suggests that the conduct of the service was the responsibility of the Cathedral, but a note in the Cheque Book concerning a Thanksgiving in 1714/15 reveals that the Chapel Royal claimed this duty: if the monarch was present, the building was the 'King's Chappell upon this occasion', wherever it happened to be.[78] In the 1706 picture the officiating clergy are shown in the normal position halfway along the stalls: if they were from the Chapel Royal, it reduced the number of priests available for musical duties above. The Sub-Dean of the Chapel would certainly have been among those below, probably in one of the stalls immediately behind the Queen.

Handel's forces in 1713 for the Utrecht music are more likely to have been in line with the hypothetical figures for the 1706 Thanksgiving than with the innovatory large forces that he gathered for the 1727 Coronation. Expanding slightly on the 1706 figures, but taking into account the practical limitations of the gallery at St Paul's, a total maximum performing strength of about fifty seems likely.

Autograph

Two general features of the manuscript (GB-Lbl RM 20.g.5) are of interest: the use of directions in French, presumably intended for a copyist, and the old-fashioned use of the flat sign as an alternative to the natural, to denote the correction of a sharp by a semitone. The naturals that are now in the autograph may be later additions: there have certainly been some additions to the word underlay, mainly by a copyist (or copyists) trying to clarify word-setting in the choruses. Some alterations in the autograph suggest that Handel was working from pre-existing sketches, the clearest example occurring at bars 4–5 in the Gloria to the Jubilate. Here a little compositional surgery was needed to rectify an omitted half-bar: since the rest of the movement is barred correctly, the original one-bar version must be a mistake.

The Te Deum is signed and dated at the end 'S. D. G. [i.e. Soli Deo Gloria] G. F. H. Londres de 14 de Janv. V[ieux]. st[yle]. a 1712'. The last page of the Jubilate has been cropped by a binder, probably in the late eighteenth century, and all that is visible now is 'S. D. G. G. F. Hendel . . . 1713'. If the second date is to be taken in old style as well, the composition of the Jubilate was not completed until after 25 March 1712/13. The fact that newspaper notices of the rehearsals make no specific mention of the Jubilate is not conclusive

---

[78] *OCB*, fo. 54ʳ; Ashbee and Harley, i. 139; see also Ch. 6.

evidence that it did not exist before 5 March, since 'Te Deum' seems to have been used to cover the canticles as a whole and the Jubilate is hardly ever referred to separately in reports of previous Thanksgiving services. The autograph of the Jubilate shares identical paper types with the Te Deum, thus indicating that its composition was commenced very soon afterwards. There is, however, a clear break within the autograph of the Jubilate which suggests that Handel suspended work on it for a time, and so the completion of the Jubilate may have been delayed.[79] It seems that Handel stopped after writing a first draft of the duet 'Be ye sure', and recomposed the movement when he returned to the work. It is at this point that the names of soloists suddenly begin to appear in the autograph: hitherto Handel had written 'Solo' (or, more usually, 'Sol') against the voice parts, as if he were not sure who would be available. The leading Chapel Royal soloists—Hughes, Elford, Weely, and Gates—are named for the duet and the trio of the Jubilate. Handel probably rewrote the duet on a more extended scale to make use of the Chapel Royal singers to best advantage; the fragment of the original setting that survives on fo. 73 ends without a closing instrumental ritornello.[80] Perhaps, by the time he returned to the composition, Handel's participation in the Utrecht service had become official, and he was therefore able to count on, and write for, the best Chapel Royal soloists. Handel's spellings of the soloists' names show no improvement over the autograph of *As pants the hart*: 'Mr Hughs' and 'Mr Whale' on the duet, 'Mr Eilfurth', 'Mr Hughs', and 'Mr Gaitz' (replacing 'Mr Wahle') on the trio. In the trio Handel wrote the part for Elford, although of lower tessitura, on the stave above that for Hughes.[81]

At some stage, probably before the performance, Handel altered the word-setting of the Gloria to the Jubilate, an emendation that was conveyed with various degrees of coherence in early manuscript copies.[82] Certain other variations in the copies also hint at the possibility that there may have been a lost performing score on which Handel made further alterations. In the absence of any evidence, we are left to imagine whether Handel directed from the organ or conducted the performance more independently: in common with all of his Chapel Royal music, the organ is the only keyboard continuo instrument that is specified in the autograph. The Utrecht music was the only work of Handel's to be included in Thomas Tudway's grand manuscript anthology of English church music for Edward, Lord Harley,

---

[79] For details see Burrows, *Dissertation*, i. 131–2.

[80] See *HHA* III/3, p. 152.

[81] Handel seems to have had some initial confusion (or indecision) about the voices: he wrote the music on the opening system for Hughes in tenor clef, and Hughes's name is written over 'Gaitz'.

[82] See Burrows, *Dissertation*, i. 134, and *HHA* III/3, pp. xvi–xvii, 178.

completed in 1720.[83] Walsh's printed edition from the 1730s, although hand-somely engraved, had a number of serious errors, including the final chord of the Te Deum, which repeats the previous G major chord instead of closing the plagal cadence with a chord of D: this mistake was transmitted unaltered to Arnold's edition (*c.*1788) and even escaped Chrysander's eyes in 1869.

Handel's Ode for Queen Anne's Birthday

There are two reasons for including Handel's court ode *Eternal source of light divine* in the present study: it involved the personnel of the Chapel Royal, and its composition seems to be closely linked with that of the Utrecht canticles. The ode demonstrates even more clearly than the canticles the extent of Handel's insinuation into the life of the British court during his early years in London. From the Hanoverian point of view, the ode would have been even more difficult to condone than the canticles in 1713, for by setting the ode Handel was giving unambiguous support to the peace settlement referred to in the text.

Just as the Utrecht canticles must be seen against the background of previous Thanksgiving Services, so Handel's ode must be related to the preceding history of the English court ode. By 1700 the performance of celebratory odes on New Year's Day and the monarch's birthday had become a part of the court's annual programme.[84] The composition of the odes, to texts supplied by the Poet Laureate, was one of the main tasks of the Master of the Queen's/King's Musick. Regular payments were made to John Eccles throughout the early years of Queen Anne's reign for 'pricking and fair writing' the odes, usually at the rate of about £11 per ode. The Royal Musicians, or that part of them which was currently in waiting, had to perform the odes as one of their regular duties and the Chapel Royal provided most of the voices, soloists as well as chorus, though it seems that only the leading Children and Gentleman (rather than the full force of those currently in waiting) were usually involved. For some occasions the names of the Chapel Royal performers are known: at New Year 1718/19, for example, the soloists were Hughes and Gates, and the newspaper reports even give the name of the treble soloist, Thomas Ellis.[85] On the days of the court odes and balls, Evening Prayer in the Chapel was cancelled, 'it being difficult for the Gentlemen and Officers of the Chapel to come to the Gate of

---

[83] See Hogwood, 'Thomas Tudway's History of Music'. Handel's music is included in Tudway's last volume, now GB–Lbl Harl. MS 7342.

[84] For the history of the development of the court odes, see McGuinness, *English Court Odes*.

[85] *SJEP*, 30 Dec. 1718–1 Jan. 1718/19. Although Old Style was used in England until 1752, the New Year was celebrated at Court on 1 Jan. For Ellis, see App. B, B39.

the Court by reason of the great Concourse of People on those Publick Days'.[86]
Specific payments to additional performers for the odes do not appear in the
records of the Lord Chamberlain's department during Eccles's period as Master
of the Musick,[87] so perhaps a part of the payments to him for 'pricking and fair
writing' the odes, or even part of his salary, was allocated to this expense. There
is no doubt that the regular court musicians were supplemented from time to
time by performers from elsewhere. For Eccles's Birthday Ode, *Inspire us, genius
of the day* (1702–3),[88] for example, an oboe player was required and the named
vocal soloists included Cook and Robert as well as Chapel Royal Gentlemen
Damascene, Elford, and Williams.[89]

There is a complete set of payments to Eccles for the court odes up to the
year 1708;[90] in 1709 court mourning for Prince George of Denmark probably
cancelled the festivities. No payment is recorded for 1710 and the next
payment, dated 7 March 1710/11, covers the New Year and birthday odes
for 1711.[91] No payment at all is recorded for the remaining years of Queen
Anne's reign, but the series begins again with the first ode of George I's reign,
New Year 1715.[92] A literary text for Eccles's 1711 birthday ode is extant,[93] but
it has already been seen in Chapter 3 that an Italian entertainment under
Handel's direction was produced at court on that occasion. Either two separate
musical performances took place on the Queen's birthday in 1711, or Eccles
was paid for an ode that he had composed but which was never performed, or
the 1710/11 payment is an inaccurately recorded retrospective payment for
1710 odes. The absence of payments to Eccles for 1712–14 shows that something interrupted the regular Court tradition: perhaps the Queen preferred
Italian entertainments, or the change in the ministry put Eccles on the wrong
side of the Whig/Tory divide.[94] He may have composed odes that did not

---

[86] *NCB*, 133; Ashbee and Harley, i. 308. Entered in 1742/3, but apparently recording a time-
honoured practice.

[87] Eccles held the office until his death in 1734/5.

[88] GB-Lbl Add. MS 31456. This ode was apparently composed for King William III's
birthday, probably for Nov. 1702, but William's name has been replaced by Anne's throughout
the MS. The chronology of the table in McGuinness, *English Court Odes*, p. (24), appears to be at
fault over this ode: Eccles's Ode cannot have been performed on Anne's birthday in Feb. 1702/3
as William did not die until 8 Mar. The Ode might have been used for the 1704/5 birthday. The
singers' names on the music seem an integral set intended for one performance, whether in 1703
or 1705.

[89] Cook and Robert are known from various London concert advertisements calendared in
RMARC 1; see also Highfill et al., *A Biographical Dictionary*, iii. 442–3 and xiii. 1–2.

[90] Recorded in GB-Lpro LC5/152–154.

[91] Lpro LC5/155, p. 81; Ashbee, *Records*, ii. 106 (as 'fo. 59ʳ'), and see also 148.

[92] Lpro LC5/156, p. 137.

[93] See McGuinness, *English Court Odes*, p. (27).

[94] Nothing definite seems known about Eccles's politics, though in May 1713 his benefit
concert was advertised as being for the 'Entertainment of . . . the Duke d'Aumont, Embassador

reach performance in the intervening years: a newspaper advertisement refers to 'Mr. John Eccles' Musick for the Birthday 1714 for violins and hautboys'.[95] To sum up, the situation seems to be that Eccles provided the odes until 1711, but not between 1712 and 1714. Handel and Nicolini performed, possibly in place of the ode, on the 1710/11 birthday; Nicolini, in Handel's absence, was responsible for a similar court performance in 1711/12. Contemporary documentary sources tell us nothing about the music performed at the 1712/13 and 1713/14 birthdays, or indeed at the New Year. Queen Anne's birthday was on 6 February. In 1712/13 the Queen, at St James's Palace, was suffering severely from gout on that day: she did not appear at the normal gathering of the court, though she was carried into the Great Presence Chamber in the evening, where she played cards for an hour while 'a sort of ball took place in the adjoining room'.[96] In 1714 the Queen, at Windsor, received the foreign ministers at 2 p.m. on her birthday, and in the evening there was a ball and a 'splendid entertainment',[97] but there is no report of the performance of a court ode.[98]

Handel's ode *Eternal source of light divine* was clearly intended for performance on the Queen's birthday: the text by Ambrose Philips[99] refers to 'the Day that gave great Anna birth' and is a paean in praise of Anne as a peacemaker. This points to 1713 as the year of origin, and the composition of the ode may account for the suggested interruption to Handel's work on the Utrecht Jubilate. A plausible timetable of events might have been as follows: Handel finishes the Utrecht Te Deum on 14 January and proceeds to the composition of the Jubilate. He then receives the text of the ode, lays aside the Jubilate for the moment, and has ten to fifteen days to compose the ode and arrange rehearsals. Following the birthday celebrations on 6 February, Handel then returns to work on the Jubilate. Although the performance of a birthday ode on 6 February was not reported in the newspapers, there is evidence that one took place. John Eccles, although he did not receive the usual payment for the composition and music-copying, was nevertheless paid travelling charges to

extraordinary from France' (*RMARC* I, p. 85), which seems to rule out the possibility that Eccles was specifically opposed to the Peace settlement. D'Aumont was also the dedicatee of Handel's opera *Silla* a month later.

[95] Walsh and Hare advertisement, *EP*, 10 Apr. 1714. This is not calendared in *RMARC* I, nor does the music appear to be known to William C. Smith, *A Bibliography 1695–1720*.

[96] Boyer, *The Political State*, v. 89.

[97] Ibid. vii. 184.

[98] Croft's birthday ode *Prepare ye sons of Art*, in four short movements, may have been composed for performance in 1713 or 1714: soloists named on GB-Lbl RM 24.d.5 are Elford, Weely, and Gates. It is possible that Croft's Oxford doctoral exercise *With noise of Cannon* was also originally planned as a birthday ode, in view of the text's direct references to the Queen.

[99] Authorship identified from Charles Jennens's annotations to his copy of Mainwaring, *Memoirs*: see Dean, 'Charles Jennens's Marginalia', 162.

Windsor for himself and the Queen's Musicians for 'attendance there on Her said Majesties Birthday Febr[uar]y the 6, 1713'.[100]

Handel's score requires trumpets and oboes in addition to the strings, and a distinct group of chorus voices in addition to the soloists. The latter were named by Handel as a combination of Chapel Royal men (Elford, Hughes, and Weely) with two theatre singers, Anastasia Robinson and Jane Barbier. Barbier was already a member of the opera company but Robinson did not make her first appearance on the London stage as a singer until 9 June 1713, and she first performed with the Italian opera company at the Queen's Theatre in January 1713/14.[101] Women had been regularly employed as soloists in the court odes in the 1690s, and this probably continued in the next decade, for which the documentation is rather sporadic. By 1720, however, the vocal performers for the odes seem to have come entirely from the Chapel Royal, and this pattern continued through the following decades, with the incorporation of a few additional (male) singers such as John Beard who had some association with the Chapel.[102] In its inclusion of the women Handel's ode clearly related to previous performing traditions, as well as providing a hearing for one of his opera singers. For the aria 'Let flocks and herds' Handel decided to reallocate the solo part from Mrs Barbier to Elford, and this was probably done at a late stage before the performance: instead of recomposing the music he wrote out another version of the voice part alone, adjusting the vocal range but leaving the substance of the music intact so that it still fitted the original orchestral accompaniment.[103] The only work in Handel's English church music for which he adopted a similar procedure was the 1734 wedding anthem, *This is the day*, where the copyist reproduced the orchestral parts of movements transferred from *Athalia* and Handel filled in the revised voice parts.[104]

The composition of the ode seems to have come easily: there is hardly a hesitation in the autograph and the gatherings are completely regular. Due credit must be given to Philips's text, which provided the composer with eminently settable verses and attractive pastoral imagery. *Eternal source of light divine* contains some of the best music composed by Handel for Chapel Royal soloists during his early years in London, largely because the ode provided more opportunities than anthems and canticles for extended aria writing. Elford's first accompanied recitative is one of the most striking opening

[100] Ashbee, *Records*, ii. 150. This records a combined payment with the travelling charges referred to in n. 60.

[101] See the biographies of these singers in *The New Grove Dictionary of Opera*, ed. Stanley Sadie.

[102] The change of practice may have taken place at the beginning of George I's reign.

[103] The revised vocal part is now fo. 15 of the autograph.

[104] Conducting score, D-Hs M C/266.

movements in any of Handel's works, comparable to the arioso or accompanied recitative movements with which he sometimes began operatic acts.[105]
The interplay between alto voice and solo trumpet in this movement has an
obvious Purcellian ancestry, though it was now carried to an ambitious length
in sustained lyrical phrases: there is no obvious precedent for the style of
Handel's movement. Later in the ode Elford received rather short measure
in the arias, which may be why one was reallocated to him. The three other
Chapel Royal soloists received substantial movements: Gates's piece is not far
distant in style from the operatic 'rage' aria, while the duet for Hughes and
Weely is built over an ostinato bass.

One of the most successful features of the Utrecht Te Deum is Handel's
linking of solo and chorus material, so that the chorus reinforces the effect of
the solo sections. The linking of soloists and chorus in the ode is characterized
by ingenuity rather than drama. To conclude each solo movement the chorus
enters with the motto text 'The day that gave great Anna birth, Who fix'd a
lasting peace on earth': since the words are accommodated to the music of the
preceding aria, this text receives a different musical treatment each time.
Handel also cunningly varied the musical function of the concluding chorus
sections. In the second movement the chorus takes up Elford's exuberant solo,
including the florid divisions, and extends the music to greater length than the
solo itself. In 'Let rolling streams' the chorus provides a tonic completion to the
duet, and in 'Let envy then conceal her head' it fulfils the function of the
reprise section of a da capo aria. In the final movement the Purcellian device of
an echo chorus (probably using the chorus voices to answer four soloists)
illustrates 'to distant climes the sound convey'. The choral element in the
ode is used with resource, and also with a lightness of touch when compared
with the choruses of the Utrecht Te Deum, though the problems and opportunities provided by the texts of the two works are so different that this
comparison is rather unfair.

It is almost inconceivable that Handel could have written *Eternal source of
light divine* without some knowledge of Purcell's odes.[106] At the same time, the
solo movements are not far removed from Handel's musical experience in the
opera house. He revived three movements from the ode, with new texts but
only minor alterations to the music, for his English theatre performances in the
1730s (in *Esther*, *Acis and Galatea*, and *Deborah*), where they proved very
successful in their new contexts. The Hughes/Weely duet 'Let rolling streams'

[105] As e.g. the openings to Act I of *Rodelinda*, Act II of *Arianna* and Act I of *Serse*.

[106] Purcell's work would probably have been more accessible to him than Eccles's more
recent odes. The possibility of some independent influence on Handel from Eccles's work
cannot be ruled out, however: one thematic resemblance has been pointed out in Ch. 3 (n. 44)
with reference to Handel's *As pants the hart*.

also formed the basis for an aria in the 1732 version of *Esther*: it is interesting that the theatrical version is less ornate than the original music for the Chapel Royal singers in the ode.

Autograph

As usual at this period, Handel's spellings of singers' names are rather phonetic, though more accurate than in some other scores: 'Eilfurt', 'Hughs', 'Whaly', and 'Gates' for the Chapel Royal men, 'Mrs Robison' and 'Mrs Barbier' for the ladies (GB-Lbl RM 20.g.2). On the revised setting of 'Let flocks and herds' he came one stage closer, with 'Mr Eilfort'. The autograph is undated and ends with a cue instructing the repeat of the chorus from the second movement. Handel wrote 'Tromba' at the beginning of the first movement, but used the (nearly) English form 'Trompets' at the chorus entry in the last movement. During the 1730s he marked two movements with adaptations for use in other works, inserting alterations that do not apply to the ode.

Table 4.1. *Orchestral settings of the Te Deum and Jubilate by Purcell, Croft, and Handel*

Verse	PURCELL (1694) Key	T/s	Voices	Orch.	CROFT (1709) Key	T/s	Voices	Orch.	HANDEL (Utrecht, 1713) Key	T/s	Voices	Orch.
TE DEUM												
Prelude/Symphony[a]	D	c		full	D	¢		full	D	c		obs. & str.
1. We praise thee	D	¢	ATB	b.c.	D	¢	ATB	b.c.			satb	full
2. All the earth			satb	full	D, b	3/2	satb	full				
(the Father everlasting)					D	¢(²/₂)						
3. To thee all angels	a, d	c	AAB	b.c.	b, D	c	ATB	b.c.	b, f♯	c	AAtb	str.
4. To thee the Cherubin	D		SS		b, D		TT	2vns.	A	C	SS	b.c.
5. Holy, holy			+ssatb	full	D, b	2(²/₂)	satb	full	D		ssatb	full
6. Heaven and earth			ATB, satb	b.c., full	D	c	A	2vns.				
7. The glorious company	b	c	A	2vns.	D, f♯	3/2	B	2vns.	a	3/4	T	2obs.
8. The goodly fellowship	f♯		T		D				e		B	+str.
9. The noble army	D		B						C, d		SS	str.
10. The holy Church	G, D		satb	full	D	¢(4/4)	satb	full	a		ssatb	+obs.
11. The Father	D	3/2	AA	2vns.	d	c	AAAA	str.	F	c	satb	
12. Thine honourable	A		SS		a, F							
13. Also the Holy Ghost	b, D		AA		d				d			
14–15. Thou art the King	D	¢	ssatb	full	D	¢(²/₂)	satb	full	F	c	ssatb	

Cont'd

Table 4.1. *Orchestral settings of the Te Deum and Jubilate by Purcell, Croft, and Handel (Cont'd)*

Verse	PURCELL (1694)				CROFT (1709)				HANDEL (Utrecht, 1713)			
	Key	T/s	Voices	Orch.	Key	T/s	Voices	Orch.	Key	T/s	Voices	Orch.
16. When thou tookest	D	¢	AB	b.c.	d	¢(4/4)	A	2vns.	d, F	¢	A	ob. & vns.
17. When thou hadst (thou didst open)	f♯, b								a		SATB	unacc.
	D								C		ssatb	obs. & str.
18. Thou sittest	D	3/2	SS	b.c.	g	3/2	ATB	b.c.	C	3/4	ssatb	obs. & str.
19. We believe	a	¢	ATB	b.c.	c	3/2	ATB	2vns.	g	¢	AB	fl. & str.
20. We therefore pray (help thy servants)											SATB	
											ssatb	
21. Make them	D	3/2	SS		g	3/2	ATB	b.c.	B♭		AT	
22. O Lord, save	b		AAB		B♭	¢(4/4)	A	ob.			ssatb	str.
23. Govern them	b, D				g, B♭				d, g		SAT,	+fl.
											ssatb	
24. Day by day	D	¢	satb	full	D	2(¢/2)	ATB, satb	b.c., full	D	¢	sst & aatb	full
25. And we worship (ever world)					d		satb	str.		¢	ssatb	
					D	2(¢/2)	ssatb					
26. Vouchsafe, O Lord	d	¢	A	2vns.	b	¢	A	2vns.	b	¢	AA	str.
27. O Lord, have mercy	F, d				f♯, b				f♯		SSTB	b.c.
28. O Lord, let thy									b		ssaatb	obs, str.
29. O Lord, in thee	D	¢	satb	full	D	2(¢/2)	satb	full	D	¢	ssatb	full

JUBILATE

	Purcell				Croft				Handel			
	key	time	voices	scoring	key	time	voices	scoring	key	time	voices	scoring
1. O be joyful [a]	D	3/2	A, satb	tpt, full	D	3/4	ATB, satb	tpt&str, full	D, A	C	A, satb	tpt, full
(serve the Lord)											ssatb	full
2. Be ye sure	a	¢	SA	b.c.	d	3/2	B	2vns.	a	C	AB	ob.&vn. [b]
3. O go your way	D	2(¢)	satb	str.	?[c]		A	?	F	¢	satb	str. (?+obs.)
4. For the Lord	d	C	AB	b.c.	d	3/2	ATB	b.c.	g	C	AAB	obs. & str.
5. Glory be to the Father	D	¢	ssatb	full	D	2(¢)	satb	full	D	C	ssaatbb	full
(as it was)										C	satb	

[a] Purcell's Prelude is based on the same music as the following vocal section, though with a different time signature in the source; Croft's Symphony is a separate orchestral movement. Handel's setting commences with two movements (Adagio, Allegro) in D major, the second introducing the chorus after 13 bars.

[b] ob. & vn. solo; ritornello for obs. & str.

[c] Lost.

Note: The table shows key centres, time signatures (but not tempo indications), and scorings. All items remain in force until superseded by the next entry below. Key centres record the beginning of each section, and the ending if different, but not intermediate modulations. C and ¢ indicate a bar length totalling four crotchets or two minims unless indicated to the contrary; the use of these signatures by Purcell and Croft sometimes appears inconsistent. In the columns relating to voices and instruments, commas indicate successive scorings within a verse, and additions to previous scorings are shown by +. 'Full' orchestra is 2tpts. and str. (Purcell and Croft), or 2tpts., 2obs, bns., and str. (Handel); 'str.' indicates 4-part strings, '2vns.' strings without violas, 'vns.' unison violins with bassi.

Lines show the divisions into musical movements; dotted lines indicate movements or sections that are linked. The sections can be grouped into movements in various ways: the indicators used here are new time signatures and clear final (usually tonic) cadences.

Sources:

Purcell: In the absence of the composer's autograph, an early manuscript copy (US-STu).

Croft: For the Te Deum, the original state of the composer's autograph (GB-Lcm MS 840), discounting subsequent revisions from 1714/15; for the Jubilate, the 1714/15 copyist's score (GB-Bu Barber MS 5007), interpreted in the light of revisions to the original performing parts, GB-Lbl Add. MS 17845.

5

Other Chapel Royal Music from the First Period, 1712–1714

The Accession of King George I

QUEEN Anne granted Handel a pension of £200 per annum on 28 December 1713.[1] This sum was identical to the salary of the Master of the Queen's Musick, and roughly comparable to the 1,000 Thaler carried by Handel's former post as Kapellmeister at Hanover. By the end of 1713 Handel had, in fact, achieved the object of entering the Queen's service that was reported as his intention in Kreienberg's letter quoted at the beginning of the previous chapter.[2] The English payment had to be made as a pension, since Handel was an alien and therefore ineligible for a court appointment, and from Handel's point of view this arrangement had the advantage that it apparently did not carry any specific regular duties at Court. No doubt the Utrecht music and the birthday ode played a critical role in securing the pension, particularly if the former had received a further command performance before the Queen at Windsor on 19 November 1713. Perhaps it was anticipated that Handel would contribute an ode for the Queen's birthday in 1714, but by the beginning of that year the state of the Queen's health had probably cast doubt on the possibility of any lengthy musical entertainments at court.

By the time Handel's pension was granted, Britian's political future appeared much more stable than had been the case when he first arrived in London. It did not take great political acumen to appreciate that the Pretender's political loyalty to Roman Catholicism had in effect secured the Hanoverian succession, and that this succession could not be far distant. When the Queen eventually died, on 1 August 1714, the governments in London and Hanover were well prepared, and prompt action in London prevented a Jacobite uprising: George had already supplied the list of regents who were to govern

---

[1] Copy of warrant, GB-Lpro T52/25, p. 380. See also Ch. 3, in connection with possible performance dates for HWV 251a.

[2] Kreienberg's letter applies a correction to Mainwaring's comment on the pension: 'This act of the royal bounty was the more extraordinary, as his foreign engagements were not unknown' (Mainwaring, *Memoirs*, 89).

the country until his arrival from Hanover.[3] Eventually all royal appointments came in for review, as also did the pension list. The general principle of maintaining the establishments from the previous reign was followed for non-political positions, although ways were naturally sought of rewarding those who had supported the Hanoverian cause. If the new king had harboured any personal animosity towards Handel as the result of the composer's earlier decision to commit himself to Britain rather than Hanover, he could have taken his revenge by discontinuing the pension. All of the evidence points the other way. King George I apparently accepted that Handel was loyal to the country that had become the inheritance of the Electors, and Kreienberg had half-promised Handel a favourable reception 'when some day His Highness comes here'. Handel's pension was continued as before,[4] and the first Sunday service that the King attended at the Chapel Royal included a performance of music by Handel.

There was a delay of several weeks between Queen Anne's death and the arrival of the new king. Communications were slow, the North Sea crossing was dependent on favourable winds, and in any case the affairs of the Electorate had to be put into some sort of order before George could leave Hanover. Furthermore, domestic arrangements had to be made for other members of the royal family who would now make their home in England. The King and his son George Augustus[5] arrived at Greenwich on Saturday 18 September and made their ceremonial entry into London two days later,[6] so their first Sunday morning service at the Chapel Royal, St James's Palace, was on 26 September:

On Sunday Morning last, his Majesty went to his Royal Chapel at St. James's, and the Right Hon. the Earl of Stamford carried the sword of state; *Te Deum* was sung, compos'd by Mr. Hendel, and a very fine Anthem was also sung; and the Reverend Mr. Moor, Brother to the Rt. Hon. the Earl of Drogheda, preach'd before his Majesty. (*EP*, 25–8 Sept. 1714)[7]

The King was therefore received at the Chapel Royal with a performance of a Te Deum: the same canticle (though of course not in English, nor in

---

[3] See Hatton, *George I*, 108–9, 120.

[4] The pension payments recorded in the Treasury Papers can be followed through William A. Shaw, *Calendar 1669–1718*, pp. xxviii–xxxii. In common with most of those on the pension list, Handel's first payment in the new reign took some time to be cleared: he did not receive anything until 12 Aug. 1715 (ibid. p. xxiv, 675).

[5] George Augustus was not created Prince of Wales until 27 Sept.

[6] Beattie, *The English Court*, 257. The newspaper reports (for example in *PB*, 18–21 Sept.) say that the King made his entry into the City of London 'towards noon'; this is in conflict with the commonly received story that the entry took place after dark.

[7] Similar reports appeared in *PB*, 25–8 Sept. (partly quoted in Deutsch, *Handel*, 63), *Dawks*, 28 Sept., and *BM*, 22–9 Sept.: these three spelt the composer's name 'Handel'.

Handel's setting) had been sung in Hanover to celebrate the news of his accession.[8]

The newspaper reports are typically tantalizing in their half-reporting of the Chapel Royal music: although they tell us that a Te Deum by Handel was sung, they do not make it clear who was responsible for the anthem. One newspaper report is more specific about the Te Deum:

Mr. Handel's *Te Deum*, that was set to Musick, and sung at St. Paul's on the Thanksgiving Day for the Peace, was very excellently perform'd there, as was also a very fine Anthem, followed by an incomparable sermon preached by the Hon and Reverend Mr. Moor, Brother to the Earl of Drogheda. (*WP*, 25 Sept.–2 Oct.)

Unfortunately this cannot be regarded as conclusive. The rather gushing style of reporting in *The Weekly Packet* suggests a concern for effect rather than accuracy, and the issue including this item also carried an apology for some inaccurate reporting in the previous number of the paper. A correspondent given to embroidering the facts would probably jump to the conclusion that the Te Deum by Handel with instrumental accompaniment performed at the Chapel Royal was the well-known one: more innocently, there may have been an intention to support the mention of the composer by reference to the only other item of his church music that had received journalistic attention.

Caroline, the Princess of Wales, arrived with her two eldest daughters[9] nearly a month after her husband and father-in-law, landing at Margate on Monday 11 October and arriving at St James's on the afternoon of the 13th.[10] There are two rather diverse snippets of documentary evidence that her arrival was also celebrated with special music at the Chapel Royal. The first comes from Boyer's *The Political State of Great Britain* for October 1714:

Oct. 13 On *Wednesday* Morning [13 October] the King caused *Te Deum* to be sung in the Royal Chappel at *St. James's*, for the safe Arrival of Her Royal Highness, who having rested the night before at *Rochester*, with her Princely Consort, came with him to *St. James's* Palace, about Four a Clock in the Afternoon.[11]

---

[8] See *BM*, 11–18 Aug. Boyer (*The Political State*, viii. 107) reports the same event in a slightly different way which, if accurate, reveals that the Te Deum held a comparable position in England and Germany as the hymn for official celebrations: 'On Sunday, the 19th of August N. S. his Majesty caus'd Te Deum to be sung in all the churches of the Electorate to return the Almighty solemn thanks for having vouchsafed to advance him to the *British* Throne; and Prayers to be made for the Prosperity of his Reign.'

[9] Her son Frederick remained in Hanover as the Elector's representative; her youngest daughter, Caroline, followed her family to England when she was judged old enough to travel.

[10] According to *EP*, 12–14 Oct., they arrived at St. James's at 5 o'clock; *PB* reported 4 o'clock. In view of what follows concerning the origins of the Caroline Te Deum, it is worth noting that this timetable precludes the attendance of the Princess at the Chapel Royal service on the evening of 13 Oct.

[11] Boyer, *The Political State*, viii. 343.

There is no mention of Handel here, and none of any instrumental participation; furthermore, the weekday morning service in the Chapel clearly preceded Caroline's arrival at St James's. It is probable, however, that the King had in fact commanded a special Te Deum setting for performance at the more important Chapel Royal service on the following Sunday, 17 October. Information on that service comes from a Hamburg newspaper:

On Sunday [17 Oct.] the Prince and Princess of Wales accompanied the King to the Chapel Royal, St James's Palace, where Te Deum, with another excellent thanksgiving piece with music composed by the famous musico Mr. Händel, was sung on account of the joyful arrival of the Princess of Wales and the young Princesses.[12]

The service was not reported at all in the London newspapers: this is surprising, but at the time they were too taken up with the arrangements for the forthcoming Coronation on 20 October to give much space to other domestic news.[13]

There are therefore two possible dates for performances of Handel's church music at the Chapel Royal in the autumn of 1714: 26 September and 17 October. On the first occasion the Utrecht Te Deum may or may not have been performed. Handel's shorter D major Caroline Te Deum was almost certainly performed at one or both of the services, and there are good reasons for coupling the remaining piece of his English church music in which Elford is named as a soloist, the anthem *O sing unto the Lord* (HWV 249a), with this Te Deum.[14] If the Utrecht Te Deum was indeed performed on 26 September, Handel might have discovered then that the work composed for St Paul's was not quite appropriate for the more intimate conditions of the Chapel Royal. It may also have happened that the King specifically asked him to compose a new Te Deum for the arrival of Princess Caroline. Alternatively, perhaps Handel composed the new Te Deum for the King's arrival—he would have had nearly two months during which to compose and rehearse it—and repeated it, possibly at the King's request and possibly with the addition of a new anthem, three weeks later. As noted in Chapter 4, there are no annotations or emendations on the autograph of the Utrecht Te Deum and Jubilate relating to a second performance.[15] Some of Handel's annotations on the autograph of the

[12] From the *Hamburger Relations-Courier*, reprinted Becker, 'Die frühe Hamburgische Tagespresse', 35; original in German. The report is dated 'London, 30. October 1714', i.e. 19 Oct. O.S.

[13] It is possible that the Hamburg news item was based on a report in some London newspaper for which no copy survives.

[14] The evidence for linking the two works is described in more detail later in this chapter, in connection with HWV 249a.

[15] However, as also noted in Ch. 4, there is the possibility of a lost conducting score which contained later markings by the composer.

Caroline Te Deum, which will be described later in the chapter, might relate to two performances in 1714.

Documents in the Public Records do not provide any further enlightenment. In contrast to the situation regarding Chapel Royal services in the 1720s, there are no payments for additional performers or music copying; neither are there any records of orders for special music at the Chapel services. Routine government paperwork may have fallen behind at the beginning of the new reign,[16] but there is no reason to suppose that any entries were accidentally omitted: since there are no recorded payments to additional musicians for the Thanksgiving Services of Queen Anne's reign either, the silence of the sources in September/October 1714 is not unexpected. Any payments, apart from the routine salaries of the Royal Musicians and the Chapel Royal, and Handel's own pension, must have been arranged privately: they have left no trace in the Lord Chamberlain's records or in the surviving records of the King's personal payments, which are now at Hanover. Unlike the Utrecht music there are no reports of public rehearsals in the autumn of 1714 at which alternative financial income for the performers might have been raised.

The 'Caroline' Te Deum

Handel's autograph is untitled, but the paper characteristics and the presence of Elford's name are sufficient evidence of the work's origin in 1712–14. The earliest authority for the 'Caroline' association appears to be from Charles Jennens, who inscribed the flyleaf of his own copy of the work 'Te Deum, perform'd on the Arrival of the Princess, the late Q. Caroline'.[17] Jennens was close enough to the composer for his statements to be treated as authoritative, though if he obtained the information from Handel himself it would probably have been c.1740 when his score was copied: his reference to 'the late Q. Caroline' shows in any case that the annotation was made after December 1737. It may be noted that Jennens said that the music was *performed* on the Princess's arrival in 1714, and not that it was *composed* for the occasion, though it may well have been.

---

[16] Evidence for this lies in the delay in the Pension List (see above, n. 4), the delay in making good Chapel Royal appointments that is reflected in *OCB* entries dated 8 Aug. 1715 (see Ch. 16), and the delay in swearing in the Chapel Royal Gentlemen for the new reign that is revealed in GB-Lpro LC3/63.

[17] GB-Mp MS 130 Hd4 v.326. Jennens's annotation was almost certainly the source for the similar statement on the front cover of a score derived from his copy, now GB-Lcm MS 889.

Unfortunately, information about the association with Caroline became corrupted later in the eighteenth century. In 1785 Burney listed the Te Deum as 'composed on the Arrival of Queen Caroline',[18] but when Samuel Arnold published the music for the first time three years later he confounded the Te Deum, as described in Burney's list, with Handel's 1737 Funeral Anthem for Queen Caroline, *The ways of Zion do mourn*: the result is a ludicrous title, 'A Short Te Deum in Score Composed for her late Majesty Queen Caroline in the Year 1737'.[19] Handel certainly revived the Te Deum in later years, but 1737 cannot have been among them. No Te Deum was performed at the 1737 funeral, and the Chapel Royal Te Deum celebrating King George II's return to England earlier in that year was composed by Maurice Greene.[20] Attempts to 'interpret' Arnold's mistake by looking for a 1737 performance of Handel's Caroline Te Deum are misdirected.

The possibility must be considered that, although performed by Handel in the autumn of 1714, the Caroline Te Deum might have been composed earlier. In scale it is closer to Purcell's D major setting than to Handel's own Utrecht Te Deum: was it composed even before the Utrecht setting, possibly at the end of 1712?

Some features of the autograph seem to support 1712, others 1714, as the date of composition.[21] The watermark of the paper suggests 1714 rather than 1712: it does not appear in any of the early London opera autographs, but is first encountered in a fragment from *Amadigi* (1715).[22] The large style of Handel's music-writing on the early pages of the Te Deum suggests 1712, but succeeding pages are much more similar in appearance to his later autographs. The earliest singers' names on the autograph of the Caroline Te Deum appear to be more accurately spelt than those on *As pants the hart* or on the Utrecht Jubilate. These names may have been added in 1714 to a pre-existing autograph but, taken at face value, they support the later date of composition;

---

[18] Burney, *An Account*, Sketch, 45. This part of Burney's list was derived from the Aylesford Collection volumes, and thus from Jennens's annotation.

[19] Fascicle 13 of Arnold's collected edition of Handel's works (1788): see William C. Smith, *Handel*, 159.

[20] From the descriptions of the 1737 funeral it is clear that no Te Deum was performed. Concerning Greene's 1737 Te Deum, see Appendix H. Modern confusion over the non-existent 1737 performance of the Caroline Te Deum can be traced to Chrysander, *G. F. Händel*, 401. *In spite of Chrysander's disclaimer fourteen years later in the preface to HG 37*, the list of Caroline Te Deum soloists (with deviations) was reproduced as performers at the 1737 funeral in Deutsch, *Handel*, 443.

[21] For more detailed information, see Burrows, *Dissertation*, i. 159–60.

[22] The stave rulings in the autograph match one page of the anthem HWV 249a, but there is no comparable folio combining the same rastra and watermark in any dated (or dateable) Handel autograph from the period 1710–14.

as already noted, Handel's spelling of the names of English singers was somewhat erratic throughout his life.[23] The appearance of Thomas Baker's name, apparently among the earliest group soloists, must date from 1714. His Chapel Royal appointment was not confirmed until 1715, but he was appointed to a place as a 'supernumerary Gentleman' from 1 January 1713/14.[24] He was also appointed Sub-preceptor to the young Princesses soon after their arrival in 1714, and it can be assumed from this that he had established himself in London during that year, while still retaining his Chaplaincy at Christ Church, Oxford. The flute part in the third movement is labelled 'Traversiere'.[25] This French form is unusual in Handel's early autographs, and the only comparable appearance of this form of the word is on his autograph of *Il Pastor fido*, dated 24 October 1712 on completion.[26] If the composition of the anthem HWV 249a was contemporary with the Te Deum, the presence of German transposition directions on the autograph of the anthem might suggest that it (and, by implication, the Te Deum) was written soon after Handel's arrival from Germany.

There is no documentary evidence for any special service at the Chapel Royal, St Paul's Cathedral, or Westminster Abbey during the period between September 1712 and August 1714 that might have required or prompted a special Te Deum setting, except for the Utrecht Thanksgiving and the Sons of the Clergy Festivals. The music for the Sons of the Clergy Festival Service on 4 December 1712 was not specified in the newspaper announcements and reports, and cannot at present be identified from any other source, but it is unlikely that Handel composed the Te Deum for that service. The most reliable and specific evidence from the autograph of the Caroline Te Deum, the inclusion of Baker's name, seems to point to composition in 1714 rather than 1712. The affinities of the Te Deum with Purcell's setting rather than the Utrecht Te Deum probably result from Handel's desire to write music that matched the building and the occasion, and they do not provide conclusive indicators to the chronological sequence of the three versions. The Utrecht music was composed for a leisurely ceremony in the expanses of St Paul's Cathedral: the Caroline Te Deum was performed during a regular Sunday service in more intimate surroundings at the Chapel Royal, St James's Palace.

---

[23] On the autograph of *Alexander's Feast* (GB-Lbl RM. 20.d.4, written in 1736), for example, the tenor soloist's name is rendered as both 'Bird' and 'Beard'.

[24] Ashbee, *Records*, v. 103; see Ch. 16 on the subject of Chapel Royal appointments at this period.

[25] GB-Lbl RM 20.g.4, fo. 49[r].

[26] See RM 20.b.12, fo. 6[r]. Other early forms used by Handel are 'Traversiera', *La Resurrezione* (Rome, Mar. 1708), RM 20.f.5, fo. 37[v]; 'Traversa', *Teseo* (London, Dec. 1712/Jan. 1713), early copies; 'Travers', Utrecht Te Deum (London, Jan. 1712/13), RM 20.g.5, fo. 28[v].

In function, and in the circumstances surrounding its performance, the Caroline Te Deum therefore stands closer to Purcell's than to Handel's own setting, so it is not surprising that it is closer in externals to the Purcellian model. The Caroline setting is, for example, of comparable length to Purcell's, and it is scored for the same orchestra of trumpets and strings, but with the addition of a solo flute in one movement. In later revivals Handel may have doubled the violin parts with oboes, but this feature was apparently not included in his original scoring. Handel departs from Purcell's SSATB arrangement of the chorus voices in favour of SAATB, but there is not much division in the alto parts and this arrangement is mainly used to distinguish the part for the alto soloist when it leads into a chorus. There are, nevertheless, a couple of passages where the two independent alto parts are vital to the spacing of choral sonorities,[27] and these pose certain problems regarding the balance between soloists and chorus: it is plausible that Handel envisaged that all of the 'chorus' work in the alto voice would be taken by the two soloists without further choral support.

In his treatment of the text (see Table 5.1) Handel grouped the verses together more compactly than in the Utrecht Te Deum. Indeed, in this respect he outdoes all the previous English settings. Most of the extra economy is achieved by the accommodation of verses 7–23 in the second and third movements. In both movements Handel uses the chorus to complete a solo movement, constructing his timescale and key scheme to work towards those parts of the text where an appropriate chorus entry could be made.[28] In the Utrecht setting he had used this plan in only one movement, 'Vouchsafe, O Lord'. Its unifying effect in the Caroline Te Deum is remarkable: the rapid alternations of soloists and chorus that were characteristic of the earlier English settings are replaced by more stable extended movements.

The third movement, the most innovatory part of Handel's scheme, calls for special comment. None of the previous settings had run verses 16–23 as one movement: Purcell's treatment was in no fewer than five short sections. As a feat of composition, Handel's movement is remarkable for the way that he weaves the short half-verses into a continuous aria, maintaining the musical interest throughout. The opening section, which functions as a musical exposition, moves only slowly away from G minor: when it eventually reaches D minor at bar 26, the succeeding ritornello returns again to the tonic. As the movement progresses, the rate of modulation becomes faster. Excursions to C

---

[27] See e.g. No. 1, bars 72–6 and No. 4, bars 7–8: the first is shown below at Ex. 5.1.

[28] With regard to No. 2, this refers to the plan of the main part of the movement: the bass solo is an addition to a movement that would otherwise have been complete, were it not for the modulation away from A minor in the choral section.

Table 5.1. *The Caroline Te Deum, HWV 280*

Verse		No.	Key	T/s	Voices	Orch.
[Symphony]		I	D	¢		full
1.	We praise thee				ATB	b.c.
2.	All the earth				saatb	full
3.	To thee all angels		b, G		A, saatb	b.c., full
4.	To thee Cherubin		D, f♯		A	b.c.
5–6.	Holy, holy		D		saatb	full
7.	The glorious company	2	a, C	¢	A	str.
8.	The goodly fellowship		e			
9.	The noble army		d, C			
10–13.	The holy Church		a, G		saatb	
14–15.	Thou art the King		C	¾	B	
16–21.	When thou tookest	3	g	¾	A	fl. & str.
22–3.	O Lord, save				saatb	
24.	Day by day	4	D	¢	saatb	tpt., full
25.	And we worship				A, saatb	
26–8.	Vouchsafe, O Lord[a]	5	b, f♯	¢	A	str.
29.	O Lord, in thee	6	D	¢	saatb	full
[a] Handel's later setting:		5B	b	¢	A	fl. & vns.

The orchestral introduction to No. 1 is not a separate movement.
full = 2 tpts. & str.

minor, B flat major, and F major are followed by a beautifully contrived return to the tonic at bar 50; eight bars later the music sets off again, this time to D minor and C minor before returning towards the tonic in preparation for the chorus entry. The skill with which Handel carries the vocal line over the successive perfect cadences in the bass line, by timing the cadences in mid-phrase verbally or musically, is so comparable to Purcell's skill in dealing with the cadences of ground basses that it is difficult not to draw the conclusion that Handel had studied some examples of this aspect of Purcell's music. The instrumental accompaniment provides a further layer of interest, and one which helps to impel the music onwards by supplying overlapping links between the soloist's phrases. The withdrawal of various elements of the accompaniment provides variation in the texture and opportunities for inter-esting re-entries. During the singer's first phrase, for example, the basso continuo part is phased out, leaving the upper parts floating over a harmonic bass provided by the violins. The withdrawal of violins and flute together at bars 44–7 is equally striking, and was probably intended to give the singer a chance to render 'Thou sittest at the right hand of God' with a more expansive delivery. It may be that Handel associated the dotted-rhythm accompaniment figure in the strings with the more petitionary aspects of the text: it is absent for this phrase of the text, but returns for the subsequent pleadings that follow from recognition of the judgement to come. The fundamental textural contrast between held notes for the wind instruments (voice and flute) and staccato strings, on which most of the movement is built, is itself a striking effect, and rather theatrical:[29] the pose could have been transferred successfully to a suitably anguished operatic aria.

This movement is, in every sense, the centrepiece of the Te Deum. To it Handel brought his experience from the composition of operatic arias, modified to suit the world of English church music. It is doubtful that any better music was ever composed for Elford. The shorter solo movements are hardly less interesting as dual revelations of Handel's theatrical experience and his assimilation of the English church music style. The first section of the second movement is a brilliant Italianate aria of modest length, displaying the more athletic aspects of Elford's vocal skills: the choral completion proves to be an introductory link to a second aria in the best Purcellian style. Not only is the latter couched in Purcell's archetypal 'French' manner, with a strong triple-time swing and dance-rhythm dotted-quaver groups, but it is moreover for a bass soloist, albeit not one of Gostling's profundity. 'Vouchsafe, O Lord' is, in its original setting, a straightforward accompanied recitative, operatic enough in presentation: yet it was also ideally suited to the technique, delivery, and range of the Chapel Royal alto Francis Hughes.

The remaining movements stand more directly in the tradition of the earlier English Te Deum settings. The alternation of 'Verse' and 'Chorus' sections (so designated by Handel) in the first movement is much closer to the Anglican tradition than to the big choruses that open the Utrecht Te Deum, and indeed the Caroline Te Deum even begins with the traditional Anglican 'verse' combination of solo alto, tenor, and bass voices. Furthermore, Handel's linking of the instrumental introduction with the theme of the opening vocal phrases in the first movement seems to provide a deliberate reference point to Purcell's setting which is lacking in the Utrecht version. The short duet for alto soloist and trumpet in the course of 'Day by day' is another echo of Purcell, though in general rather than specific terms.

One remarkable feature of the Caroline Te Deum when compared with all previous settings is the lack of imitative choral writing. There is some lively counterpoint in the last movement, but the rest of the chorus music is almost

---

[29] In the autograph it is clear that 'staccato' applies to the string parts, and not to the flute or voice.

completely homophonic. As already noted, Handel's arrangement of the text in the first three movements was designed with a view to leading the chorus in as a climax to the solo sections; the chorus therefore fulfils the role of 'all the earth', the 'cherubin and seraphin', and 'the holy church' in the first two movements, and rounds off the third with 'O Lord, save thy people'. Similar opportunities had been taken in earlier English settings, but in none of them is the structure so clearly focused and the contrast between individual and collective utterance so clearly conveyed. The alternations between 'verse' and 'chorus' in the previous settings are so frequent that the chorus only takes on a collective role in some of the entries: in Handel's Te Deum the chorus, used more sparingly, fulfils a single type of dramatic function.

The fact that the Caroline Te Deum is a less expansive work than the Utrecht setting did not lead Handel to eschew rhetorical or dramatic effects. Indeed, the smaller scale makes these effects all the more powerful, and the choral contribution is accordingly relatively more significant. The treatment of verses 5–6 provides an excellent example. As already noted, Handel ran these two verses more closely together in the Utrecht setting than his English predecessors had done. In the Caroline Te Deum he went a stage further, breaking up the threefold repetition of 'Holy' with pauses and then treating verse 6 as the verbal and musical consequence (see Ex. 5.1). Furthermore, although the passage ends with a tonic perfect cadence, its effect is to lead on into the second movement, the lively beginning of which becomes a spin-off from the energy generated by this choral outburst. In the second movement itself the chorus entry has an opposite function: it begins full of energy, but bars 45–7 constitute a musical relaxation, achieved by rhythmic and harmonic means, in preparation for the introduction of a new burst of activity in the bass solo that follows. A similar sequence of consequence-by-reaction links the last three movements.

Bearing in mind the rather fragmentary and mosaic-like nature of the canticle text, there is a good case for regarding the Caroline setting as the most successful version in the repertory described so far. In it Handel achieved a flow that had been imperfectly realized in the previous settings, now sustained by musical technique as well as by grouping of the verses into more substantial movements. As far as musical style can be an indicator, it seems to confirm the probability that the Caroline Te Deum was composed later than the Utrecht setting. The solo movements are better developed and the choral writing, although on a smaller scale, is used to better structural effect than in the Utrecht Te Deum, which places rather too much reliance on short

Ex. 5.1. Handel, Caroline Te Deum, No. 1

and rather disconnected imitative expositions.[30] Melodies and harmonic rhythms are also rather more directional than in the larger work, and Handel's employment of modest forces does not involve a diminution in musical effect. He was not mistaken in his preference for reviving this work in later years when occasion demanded a short Te Deum.

Handel's Performances

The autograph has many annotations that relate to later revivals, which in itself makes it almost certain that no separate performing score was prepared. The plethora of singers' names added by the composer to the autograph (see Fig. 5.1) refer to the use of the music in at least three separate performances. A full list of these names is transcribed below, under 'Autograph', but their interpretation is fundamental to the present section. The combination of the singers Bayly, Mence, and Wass must refer to the Chapel Royal service in May 1749, on the Thanksgiving Day for the Peace of Aix-la-Chapelle,[31] and the name 'Leigh' post-dates these; the 1749 revival will be considered in Chapter 14. The earlier groups of names on the autograph are more difficult to disentangle. If some sense is to be made of the sequence of entries, it is necessary to establish the number of performances, or planned performances, to which they might refer. One, or possibly two, performances have already been identified in September/October 1714. Elford died on 29 October 1714, about ten days after the second (and more likely) of these dates. According to his obituary he died of a 'fever', but the information is insufficient to establish whether he might have been fit to sing on 17 October. It is possible that Handel had to reallocate his solo music at the last moment: this could explain, for example, the replacement of Elford's name by Hughes at the start of the third movement. However, the possibility of an intermediate performance between 1714 and 1749 must also be considered, for this also could account for some of the entries.

Evidence for such a performance is provided by Handel's second version of 'Vouchsafe, O Lord'. This movement, originally an accompanied recitative for alto with strings, was reset as an aria for alto, flute, and strings. Handel's autograph of the second version is on a separate sheet, now in the collection at the Fitzwilliam Museum, Cambridge.[32] This leaf was never part of the main autograph of the Te Deum, which contains instead an inserted copy of the new movement in the hand of J. C. Smith senior. The reason for this particular

<del>---</del>

[30] The same is true of Purcell's setting: promising chorus movements are called to a halt just as they are under way.
[31] See Burrows, 'Handel's Peace Anthem'.
[32] GB-Cfm MU MS 262, pp. 7–8.

Fig. 5.1. The vocal entries at the beginning of Handel's autograph of the Caroline Te Deum. The singers' names added by Handel relate to successive performances between 1714 and 1749. British Library, RM 20.g.4, fo. 38ᵛ

arrangement of the sources seems to be connected with the use of the autograph as a performing score: the new version could not be bound tidily into the main autograph, so Smith copied it in a more suitable format and this copy was attached over the autograph of the first setting, obliterating the original movement. Smith did not come to England until *c.*1718,[33] so the copy cannot have been made in 1714; Hughes is named as the soloist, so the new movement must

---

[33] See Dean, 'Handel's Early London Copyists', 19–21.

have been composed before 1744.[34] Smith might have copied a 1714 autograph for Handel in 1749 and absent-mindedly included the obsolete name of a soloist, but this seems rather unlikely. The style of Handel's handwriting on the autograph of the second setting is as unhelpful as that on the main autograph for dating purposes: it might have been written in 1714 or later.

The period of composition can, however, be established from the watermark of the autograph of the revised movement, which is of a type that is found in the autographs of the operas *Giulio Cesare* (1723–4) and *Lotario* (1729).[35] The second version of 'Vouchsafe, O Lord' in the Caroline Te Deum must therefore have been composed in the 1720s. Reference to Smith's copy that is inserted in the autograph confirms that it originated at this period, because the paper type of the copy was in use during the 1720s and the note form for the semiquaver ($\wp$) is characteristic of Smith's hand in the 1720s.[36] The chronology of the Chapel Royal performances of Handel's music during the 1720s will be examined in Chapter 7: for the moment, it is necessary only to note that the composition of the revised movement points to a revival of the Te Deum during that decade. The musical characteristics of the movement are the province of Chapter 9.

The singers' names on the autograph must now be reviewed with the knowledge that Handel revived the Te Deum in the 1720s as well as in 1749. My analysis of the names is given in Table 5.2. I have ascribed Gates's name on No. 3 to the 1720s, rather than to a second performance in 1714, on account of the greater accuracy of Handel's spelling. More doubt attaches to the period of the pencil entries shown in Table 5.2: were they written *c.*1714 or a decade later? 1714 seems more probable, for two reasons. There was no need for the correction to the soloist's name on the third movement in the 1720s, when Hughes appears to have been the only alto soloist and therefore took over all of Elford's previous music as well as his own. In 1714, on the other hand, Handel would have been altering the distribution of the music between his current alto soloists by adding this name. Secondly, the alteration to the singers' names in the third movement is linked with another pencilled alteration, showing the replacement of the flute by an oboe. If the inclusion of the flute had been impracticable in the 1720s, Handel would hardly have proceeded to compose the revised version of 'Vouchsafe, O Lord', which inserts an obbligato flute part into the score where there had been none originally.[37] Assuming that the pencil entries were made in 1714, it is fairly easy to find a reason for them.

---

[34] Although Hughes died in 1744, he does not seem to have been active as a soloist after 1733/4.

[35] Burrows and Ronish, *A Catalogue*, watermark type B80.

[36] Smith changed the form of his semiquaver to $\wp$ *c.*1730.

[37] The designation of the obbligato part for flute in No. 5B is not cancelled or amended in the autograph or in Smith's copy.

Table 5.2. *Singers' names added by Handel to the autograph of the Caroline Te Deum*

		1714	Pencil	1720s	1749	1749 or later
No. 1	Alto 1	Eilfort			Bayly	Leigh
		Hughs				
	Tenor				Menz	
	Bass	Gaiz			Wase	
		Beker				
		Whely				
No. 2	Alto	Eilfort			Menz	
	Bass	Beker		Gates		
No. 3	Alto	Eilfort	Hughs		Menz	
					Bayly	
No. 4	Alto		Hughs		Menz	Leigh
No. 5A	Alto	Hughs				
No. 5B	Alto			Hughs		

Pencil amendments were made subsequent to the original group of names, written in ink.
No. 5A is the original recitative setting of 'Vouchsafe, O Lord', No. 5B the later aria version.

Handel may have had to lighten Elford's part, or he may have decided on a more equal division between the two soloists; although he had provided solos for both men in the original scheme, Hughes's share has been rather meagre. The replacement of the flute by the oboe at this 'pencil' stage is probably related to the practical problems over the inclusion of the flute that are also apparent in the accompanying anthem *O sing unto the Lord* (see below).

The semi-chorus arrangement revealed by the names at the first vocal entry in the Te Deum (Fig. 5.1) is interesting and has parallels in earlier music by English composers.[38] The absence of a name from 1712–14 against the solo tenor part is no less revealing: alto and bass soloists were prominent at the Chapel Royal, but tenors were not. It is remarkable that both Hughes and Elford are named against the Alto 1 part throughout the first movement, in view of the overwhelming evidence that they were 'first' and 'second' altos respectively. Handel had recognized this distinction in *As pants the hart* and in the Utrecht Jubilate, but he seems to have applied it rather spasmodically in the Caroline setting. In the second movement Elford's solo part runs onto the Alto 1 stave at the chorus entry, but in the following movement it runs onto the Alto 2 stave.

There is no documentary evidence for any performances of the work, apart from Handel's own, during the composer's lifetime. John Alcock may have

[38] See e.g. the 'Double Voices' specified on Croft's anthem *I will lift up mine eyes* (1713, GB-Lcm MS 839), and the directions for 4 Trebles/2 Counter Tenors/2 Tenors/2 Basses in the first chorus of Purcell's 1692 St Cecilia Ode (early copy, GB-Ob MS Mus.c.26).

arranged a performance at Reading or Lichfield from the manuscript score that he owned by 1746.[39] By the 1770s the Oxford Music Club owned three Te Deums by Handel, the Utrecht, Dettingen, and Cannons versions:[40] in this they reflected a general pattern of availability that seems to have excluded the Caroline setting. There are fewer surviving copies of the Caroline Te Deum than of Handel's later A major Chapel Royal setting: of all Handel's settings of the canticle, the Caroline seems to have remained almost a private matter between Handel and the Chapel Royal. As will be seen in the next chapter, he drew on some of its music for use in one of the Cannons anthems.

Autographs

The various annotations in the main autograph are as follows.[41] The symbol ★ indicates an item that was subsequently deleted; all items are in Handel's hand and in ink, unless otherwise noted.

No. 1, bar 7:   Mr. Eilfort★, Hughs★, Mr Bayly★ (all deleted in ink), Leigh (Alto 1); Mr. Menz (Tenor); Mr. Gaitz★, Beker★, Whely★ (all deleted in ink), Mr. Wase (Bass)
                 bar 36: Mr. Eilfort★, Mr Menz★ (both deleted in ink), Mr. Leigh (Alto 1)
                 bar 60: Hughs★, Mr Bayly★ (both deleted in ink), Mr. Leigh (Alto 1)
No. 2, bar 1:   Mr. Eilfort, Mr. Menz (Alto); bar 55: Mr. Beker, Gates (Bass)
No. 3, bar 1:   Mr Eilfort★ (deleted in pencil), Hughs★ (in pencil), Menz★ (deleted in ink), Mr Baily (Alto). Above the upper instrumental stave: 'Traversiere', deleted in pencil and 'Hautb' added in pencil; the last deleted in ink later.
No. 4, bar 1:   Mr Hughs★ (in pencil) (Alto 1) bar 13: Mr Menz★ (deleted in ink), Mr Leigh (Alto 1)
No. 5A: [M]r. (Hu)ghs (Alto)
No. 5B: [Mr Hughs—in Smith's hand as part of the original copy], Mr Bayly (added by Handel) (Alto) [On the autograph of No. 5B Handel wrote 'Mr Hughs']

The beginnings of Nos. 3 and 5B also have some pencilled additions in the hand of a copyist (possibly S5 or S6) referring to instrumentalists.[42] Both movements are headed 'Teede and Richter' (woodwind players); next to the basso continuo part of No. 5B is written: 'Bass part for Deidrich and Gillier of this movement'. The instrumentalists named were active *c*.1750: three of them appear on the first surviving account list for Handel's performances of *Messiah* at the Foundling Hospital in 1754. Their names were added in 1749 or later, and they cannot have taken part in the earlier performances. The flute/oboe

---

[39] Now GB-Ep, W.MA.14.C.

[40] Mee, *The Oldest Music Room*, 60. The list is undated, but Mee believed it to have been published in the 1770s (p. 44). On the basis of its contents, it may record the library of the Club as it existed *c*.1760.

[41] Autographs: GB-Lbl RM 20.g.4, fos. 38–61; GB-Cfm MU MS 262, pp. 7–8 (No. 5B).

[42] For these copyists, see Larsen, *Handel's 'Messiah'*.

player William Teede was also the copyist S6: he may have taken part in Handel's performances of the Te Deum in 1749 or later, and copied some of the performing material as well.

The autograph is unusual in that it principally comprises large bundles of folios: ten-leaf gatherings, rather than the more usual four-leaf gatherings. Handel's use of the English forms 'Verse', 'Loud', and 'Slow' throughout the autograph is noteworthy. In No. 6, bars 1 and 4 have annotations by Handel next to the Violin 1 stave, 'Violin' and 'tutti' respectively. These are clearly intended as cues for oboe parts, 'Violin' indicating the omission of the oboes, who could not, in any case, play the low *a* in bar 2. Handel also headed the second movement 'tutti', which may be another oboe cue. However, oboes were not explicitly specified anywhere in the original state of the autograph, though early secondary manuscript copies generally interpret Handel's un-labelled violin staves as 'Violin e Haut. 1/Violin e Haut. 2'. His original intention seems to have been to use an orchestra consisting of strings, trumpets, and solo flute, but an oboe may have been added to the violins in the tutti sections early on, and (as already noted) at some stage the flute in the third movement was replaced by an oboe. Whether or not an oboe (or oboes) participated in 1714, one was certainly available for the performance in the 1720s, and two in 1749. The cues in the last movement, although in Handel's hand, are in a different ink from the music to which they refer and may have been added in 1734 when he reused the movement for the wedding anthem *This is the day* (see Ch. 12). The cues appear in the conducting score of the wedding anthem, interpreted by Smith as 'Senza H.' and 'Tutti V e H'. Another possibility is that the oboe cues in this movement and at the start of No. 2 were added *c.*1717 when Handel was drawing on the music for the Cannons Anthem HWV 252.

O sing unto the Lord (HWV 249a)

This anthem may well have been the 'other excellent thanksgiving piece' performed on 17 October 1714: there are certainly good reasons for coupling it with the Caroline Te Deum. Both works include a flute in the orchestra and Baker among the vocal soloists. The characteristic spelling 'Traversiere' for the flutes, noted in the Caroline Te Deum, recurs here; furthermore, the anthem autograph includes one folio of a paper type matching the autograph of the Te Deum. It is probable that the anthem was composed after the Te Deum: in the meantime, the orchestra had gained an oboe.

Just as *As pants the hart* (HWV 251a) was probably Handel's first English anthem, so *O sing unto the Lord* was his first independent English anthem with orchestral accompaniment. These works share the common characteristic that they do not end in the key of the first movement. Perhaps it is anachronistic to expect overall tonic organization in 1714, when Handel may have planned the relationships from movement to movement without any tonic imperative. The framing key relationships in the present anthem (G major–D major) are more closely related than in HWV 251a (D minor–B flat major), but this may be rather accidental: the key of the last movement in HWV 249a was defined by the use of trumpets in D. There is nevertheless a case for seeing a closer tonal organization in the plan of this anthem when compared with HWV 251a, for it is basically a G major/minor work with a D major conclusion:

1	2	3	4	5	6
G major	E minor	C major–E minor	C major	G minor	D major

The adherence to the tonic area, with a move to the minor towards the end, is closer to the plan of Croft's anthems. This is in striking contrast to Handel's canticle settings, which are notable for a greater tonal range than their English counterparts.

Handel made two alterations to his original scheme for the anthem. He replaced the second half of the duet (No. 5) with a chorus. The result is an improvement both to the movement itself and to the progression of the closing movements, and it involved no alteration to the overall key scheme. The other alteration was less happy, and may have been forced upon Handel by the limitations of the flute, probably an incompatibility of pitch and temperament with the organ (see Ch. 19). The autograph bears Handel's direction for the transposition of the second movement down a tone (see below, Fig. 19.1), but this does not seem to have achieved the desired effect, for the movement was then deleted, apparently taking the next movement with it. The deletion, if it is to be taken literally, wrecks both the tonal scheme and the musical contrasts within the anthem. It also removes one of the anthem's most attractive movements.[43]

The text of the anthem is from Psalm 96, verses from which had previously been set by English composers: Purcell and Blow had composed versions with orchestral accompaniment and Weldon had written a more modest verse anthem. Perhaps Handel knew Purcell's setting.[44] If so, he would doubtless have approved of the chorus entry at 'Glory and Worship are before him' (Verse 6), interpolated with fine effect after the movement 'Declare his honour' (Verse 3) for solo bass—a rousing homophonic choral outburst very

---

[43] It is possible that the deleted movements were replaced with some substituted music that has not survived.

[44] Purcell's anthem is included in *PS* 17.

much in the style cultivated by Handel himself. The text of Weldon's anthem was printed in *Divine Harmony*,[45] where the choice of verses (1, 2, 3, 4, 6, 9, and 10) is almost identical to Handel's.[46] Handel, or whoever was responsible for advising him, may have started from Weldon's text and then, looking at the psalm, may have seen a musical opportunity arising from the replacement of verse 10 by verse 11, so that 'Let the whole earth stand in awe of him' could lead into 'Let the heavens rejoice'.[47] This arrangement makes for an effective transition both verbally and musically. Subsequently, Handel did justice to the omitted verse 10 in his other anthems.

The first movement has the same plan as the opening of the Utrecht Jubilate: a verse for solo alto with instrumental obbligato, leading into a choral restatement of the same text. The solo instrument this time is the oboe,[48] and the introductory ritornello is interesting for its ornamented version of the theme, including three-note 'slides' written as grace notes.[49] Some of the movement's musical motifs are reminiscent of 'We believe that thou shalt come' in the Utrecht Jubilate, and Handel's setting of the opening text is, if anything, more true to English stresses then Purcell's (see Ex. 5.2). The first two verses of the psalm are similar in mood and content: Handel, like Purcell, sought contrast by setting the second verse in a minor key. Purcell's version is a contrapuntal section for SATB soloists with continuo accompaniment, ending in the relative major to introduce verse 3 ('Declare his honour') as a short aria for a bass soloist. Handel's aria, in E minor for an alto soloist, sets verses 2 and 3 in a rather cleverly designed structure. The modulation to the relative major key is marked by an orchestral ritornello as if the aria is to have a regular binary scheme, but the following section with the second clause of verse 2 goes decisively to the dominant minor instead of returning to the tonic; following another ritornello the soloist continues with verse 3 to complete the movement and return to the tonic key, via G major again. After the soloist's first phrase Handel seems to have abandoned the flute as an accompaniment to the voice, confining it to the ritornellos. The tone of Handel's minor-key music is perhaps a little dark for the text, but his compositional skill keeps the music alive through the interplay between vocal and instrumental parts. He did not

[45] *Divine Harmony*, 80.

[46] The autograph of Weldon's anthem (GB-Lbl Add. MS 41847, dated 9 Jan. [1708/9]) shows that he composed verse 5 but then deleted that section. Purcell, like Weldon, did not set verses 7–8.

[47] Neither Purcell nor Weldon included verse 11 in their settings.

[48] The only immediate antecedent for this combination seems to be 'O Lord, save thy people' from Croft's D major Te Deum. There is an obbligato part for oboe in 'When took'st upon Thee' from the Utrecht Te Deum, but in combination with a violin part.

[49] The use of small-note ornaments is a feature of the Chapel Royal autographs of this period: here and in the Caroline Te Deum such ornaments only occur in the first movement.

Ex. 5.2. (*a*) Handel (HWV 249a); (*b*) Purcell (Z. 44)

name the soloist for this movement, and the concentration of the tessitura around *a′* and *b′* for sustained notes in bars 14–15 and 38–9 suggests that it may have been written for Hughes rather than Elford: his planned transposition of the movement may reflect an attempt to bring the solo part into a more comfortable range for Elford.

The music of the following recitative and aria made full use of Thomas Baker's vocal prowess, and requires a two-octave range: one can only regret that Baker was so self-effacing as a singer later in life, when he apparently directed his ambitions to a clerical rather than a musical career (see App. C, 'Baker'). The recitative has a liveliness that is reminiscent of Purcell's best writing for John Gostling, especially in the picturesque plunge at 'He is more to be fear'd'. It is difficult to believe that Handel wrote this movement without some knowledge of Purcell's music for Gostling: in October 1714 Handel may have met Gostling himself, since even the more superannuated members of the Chapel Royal were obliged to appear at the Coronation and to take an oath of allegiance, unless seriously incapacitated.[50] The dancing ostinato patterns of the instrumental bass to the aria also seem to owe something to Purcell. Baker must have specialized in this type of movement, which has obvious similarities with his solo in the Caroline Te Deum.

The ensuing duet, No. 5, although it uses the traditional alto-and-bass combination of Chapel Royal voices,[51] really harks back in style and texture to Handel's Italian duets. As originally composed, it was written to a binary plan, the first half (bars 1–15) carrying the first half of verse 9, 'O worship the Lord in the beauty of holiness', and the second half (bars 17–33) continuing with the second clause, 'let the whole earth stand in awe of him'.[52] The texture of smooth, interwoven vocal parts that is characteristic of the Italian duets suits

---

[50] Gostling was about 65 years of age in 1714; he was still alive and nominally on the Chapel Royal roll, though not active in London, at the time of the next coronation in 1727.

[51] It was probably intended for Hughs and Weely, or possibly Elford and Baker.

[52] For the original instrumentation, see *HG* 36, p. 228 and *HHA* III/9, p. 68.

the 'beauty of holiness' but not the the text for the following verse: the second half of the duet as originally composed is rather sterile and Handel was right to replace it with the chorus setting, in which the 'whole earth' stands in awe to thunderous effect against held pedal notes, and the effect is enhanced because the chorus enters in the mid-point key of B flat major and gradually leads back to the G minor tonic. In the exuberance of this movement and the next Handel seems to be thoroughly enjoying himself: they provide the first hints in his English church music of one type of chorus that would eventually enliven his oratorios. The final chorus movement introduces the trumpets for the first time in the anthem and, though brief, it is the model for much of Handel's later church music: he applies to an English text the experience and techniques of his Latin church music of 1707, in particular from the first movement of the D major setting of *Laudate pueri*. There is exuberance, almost self-indulgence, in his musical reflection of the sea making a noise, with its echo effects, broken-chord figures, and pauses.

This may have been the first orchestrally accompanied anthem ever to have been performed in the Chapel Royal at St James's Palace, and indeed the first orchestrally accompanied anthem to have been heard in London since 1702. (If it was performed at the Chapel Royal on 17 October 1714, Croft's *The Lord is a sun and a shield* followed three days later at George I's coronation in Westminster Abbey.) As far as is known, neither the Thanksgiving service nor the service for the Festival of the Sons of the Clergy in the intervening years had included performances of orchestrally accompanied anthems. Modest as it is in some respects, *O sing unto the Lord* is therefore the earliest English anthem of its type in the eighteenth-century Baroque style. Handel recomposed the anthem on a broader timescale but for smaller forces during the Cannons period. The Cannons version is a much more mature, rounded, well-considered composition, yet in the process something was lost. The Chapel Royal anthem has a youthful vigour, completely in accord with the nature of its text, which is lacking in the later work. Like its companion Te Deum, it deserves renewed performance.

Autograph

Elford was named by Handel (as 'Mr Eilfort') for the alto solos in the opening and closing movements, including the revised version of 'Let the whole earth'.[53] As already noted, there is no soloist's name on the second movement, but 'Mr Baker' (spelt more correctly than on the Caroline Te Deum) is named for the central recitative, and is implied as the soloist for the following aria.

---

[53] GB-Lbl RM 20.g.6, fos. 1–11.

In common with the Caroline Te Deum, but no other items from Handel's Chapel Royal music, the autograph is unusual for the bulk of the paper gathering (8 leaves) that constitutes the majority of the score. The chorus revision to No. 5 is an insertion of two conjunct leaves (fos. 7 and 8). The autograph ends with a single leaf, with a watermark of a type that is also found in the Caroline Te Deum.

The second and third movements were deleted in ink by Handel, but perhaps not for the same reasons, and it is possible that the removal of the recitative was an accidental mistake. He wrote a transposition instruction in the second movement in German,[54] which suggests that he was working with a German copyist or one who was expert enough in the language and orthography to understand his instructions. The annotations that may have been addressed to copyists on the autographs of HWV 251a and the Utrecht music are in French: perhaps the copyist involved with HWV 249a was one of the Hanoverian court musicians who had come to England with the royal parties in September–October 1714.[55] An unidentified copyist, presumably working closely with the composer, wrote the link into the revised setting of 'Let the whole earth' in the autograph (fo. 7^r, staves 10–12); the insertion for this revision is on poorer-quality paper of a type that is unique in Handel's autographs, but which occurs frequently in those of contemporary English anthem composers.[56] He seems to have used whatever old sheets of paper came to hand when he had to do last-minute revisions. He must have kept the autograph of this anthem among the odds and ends of his sketches, for there are no early copies of this anthem: it is unlikely that it even reached Charles Jennens's relatively comprehensive collection of Handel's music.

Conditions of Performance

With the Caroline Te Deum and the anthem that probably formed its companion we reach the first works by Handel that were with certainty performed at the Chapel Royal, St James's Palace. Compared with the monumental spaciousness of St Paul's Cathedral, the Chapel Royal is small and intimate, a single hall in which the principal area was less than 25 ft. wide and about 70 ft. long, with the Royal Closet on first-floor level at the West end facing the altar.[57] Plate IV, although drawn in 1816, shows the Chapel interior substan-

---

[54] See Ch. 19 and Fig. 19.1.

[55] Two trumpeters, and possibly other musicians, came to London among the official parties: see Beattie, *The English Court*, 220, 258–9

[56] Another leaf of an isolated paper type is found Handel's single-page inserted revision for 'Let flocks and herds' in the birthday ode (see Ch. 4).

[57] The liturgical 'West end': see Ch. 18.

tially as Handel and the Hanoverian court would have known it. According to a memorandum in a notebook kept by William Loverove, the Chapel's Serjeant of the Vestry from 1752, the Chapel's Lutenist and Violist were included with the Organists and Composers as 'Instrumental performers in the Organ Loft'.[58] A further memorandum, dated 1742, suggests that the choir also sang from the organ loft,[59] but this must only have been applicable to the occasional soloist in verse anthems, because of limitations on space (see Ch. 18). As a body the choir presumably sang, in the usual facing-side arrangement, at floor level, and the protrusions from the front of the pews in Pl. IV are music desks for the choristers.

The music that Handel composed for performance in the Chapel Royal in 1714 and during the 1720s was performed in the context of somewhat enhanced regular services: the canticles and anthems would have been performed during Morning Prayer, the service that was regularly attended by the King and various other members of the royal family when in London. Accordingly we may assume that half of the full complement of Priests and Gentlemen were in waiting, with the current group of choristers. The special status of the music was given by the orchestral accompaniment and the opportunity for slightly more expansive composition, itself partly a consequence of the involvement of an orchestra. The location of the instrumentalists in the Chapel on these occasions remains uncertain (see Ch. 18). A group of string players comprising half of the King's Musicians would have been of appropriate size to accompany the Chapel Royal forces. As will be seen in Chapter 7, there are records of payments to additional players for Handel's Chapel Royal services in the 1720s. No such payments are known for 1714, but Handel's music would have required the addition of two trumpet players, one or two woodwind players, and presumably a double bass player, to the ensemble provided by the King's Musicians. Handel's transposition direction in *O sing unto the Lord* may reflect a considerable practical problem posed by the sharp pitch of the Chapel Royal organ, a matter that is considered further in Chapter 19.

---

[58] Ashbee and Harley, ii. 58.   [59] Ibid. 39.

6

Interlude, 1714–1719

Handel, the Chapel Royal, and Court Politics after 1714

THE performances of Handel's music in the Chapel Royal before King George I and his family in September and October 1714 demonstrated that the composer had been accepted by the new regime. The established position of the former Hanover Kapellmeister at the English court was confirmed: a year later, George I (in his role as Elector) even went so far as to grant some retrospective payment for his Hanoverian services.[1] Since Handel had received such signal marks of royal favour, and was still in receipt of the pension, further contributions to court music might have been expected from him: more music for Chapel Royal services, or perhaps a birthday ode. This did not happen, and the change in his situation appears to be anomalous. During Queen Anne's reign Handel, a foreigner and a representative of a court that was treated with some suspicion in London, was admitted as the favoured composer for state and court occasions. During the early years of George's reign, by contrast, his professional association with the court suffers an eclipse so complete as to suggest that his participation would have been unwelcome. He made no contribution to a Chapel Royal service for another eight years. Even in the opera house, royal favour does not seem to have advanced Handel's position. It was rumoured that the King did not intend to patronize the London opera house, but this was proved wrong within a week of the Coronation.[2] Nevertheless, Handel's operas were not given a place in the Haymarket repertory for another two months, and his re-entry into the programme was with a revival of *Rinaldo* rather than a new opera.[3] Thereafter there is no sign that he was particularly favoured in the programmes of the opera company.

---

[1] In Oct. 1715, the King ordered a payment to Handel for six months' salary for the half-year beginning Midsummer 1712: Hannover, Niedersächsiches Hauptstaatsarchiv, Hannover Des. 76 (Kammer-Rechnungen) Nr. 237, p. 393. See Burrows, 'Handel and Hanover', 40, 46.

[2] *WP*, 6–13 Nov. 1714. The King attended *Arminius* (not by Handel) at the Haymarket opera house on Tuesday, 26 Oct.; during Nov. and Dec. the Prince and Princess of Wales probably attended the opera more regularly than the King.

[3] *Rinaldo* was revived on 30 Dec. 1714; the King, with the Prince and Princess of Wales, attended the second performance on 15 Jan. 1714/15. In the absence of the autograph, it is not

Far from being an advantage, Handel's previous Hanoverian associations may have been an embarrassment during the years immediately following 1714. In London some resentment naturally grew up against the 'German' party at court, with which Handel must have been identified. This continued until the fall of Bernstorff in 1719–20,[4] though even after that 'German domination' (an assertion that the government was following policies that favoured Hanover at the expense of Britain) remained a rallying cry for opposition politics in London. The Chapel Royal, one of the repositories of traditionally English court culture, could not remain unaffected by the political climate. If the King wished to demonstrate his good faith in his new country, he did well to patronize British musicians. Although the Chapel Royal was the King's private chapel, his weekly Sunday appearances there were part of the public functions of British monarchy and were closely observed. It was politically expedient that the music for the King's devotions, like that for the court odes,[5] was once again seen to be provided by native-born English talent.

William Croft composed the orchestrally accompanied anthem *The Lord is a sun and a shield* that was performed at the King's coronation on 20 October 1714.[6] This was only to be expected, since Croft was the senior Chapel Royal Composer and Handel was not a British subject: if George I had thought of suggesting Handel's involvement, he was probably wise not to press the point. Croft's anthem, though rather more solid in style than the orchestrally accompanied anthems that had been composed around the turn of the century, nevertheless mainly remained in the harmonic and expressive world of Blow and Purcell, characterized by lyrical gravity rather than extrovert jubilation. The next state event to call for a similar musical contribution was the first Thanksgiving day of the reign. On 20 January 1714/15 the King went to St Paul's Cathedral on the day appointed for the Thanksgiving 'for bringing His Majesty to a Peaceable and Quiet Possession of the Throne, and thereby Disappointing the Designs of the Pretender and all his Adherents'. The service followed the traditions of the grand Thanksgiving services of the previous reign, with all the attendant ceremony, and the liturgy was, as usual, based on the order of Morning Prayer, followed by the Litany and Holy Communion.

---

certain when Handel composed *Amadigi*, first performed in May 1715: he may have hoped for a performance earlier in the season.

[4] See Beattie, *The English Court*, 238–9, also 258. By 1720 many of the King's Hanoverian advisers had become considerably anglicized. Hatton, *George I*, describes a change of emphasis in George's policies after 1718 from a 'Hanoverian' to a 'British' bias.

[5] Eccles composed all of the New Year and Birthday odes of the reign: there is a complete record of payments to him for the odes from New Year 1715 to Birthday 1727 in GB-Lpro LC5/156–159 and LC5/18.

[6] Copy in the hand of James Kent, GB-Lbl RM 24.g.2. Croft had also composed the organ-accompanied anthem for Queen Anne's funeral.

It was rumoured that Handel would once again be providing the music, as he had done at the previous Thanksgiving:

Extraordinary preparations are making for the Solemnity on the Thanksgiving Day; and we are inform'd that a Throne will be erected in the Choir for His Majesty, who is expected there with their Royal Highnesses the Prince and Princess of Wales. Mr. Hendel, a Native of Hannover, who set the Anthem that was sung at St. Paul's, on Account of the Peace with France, is now composing the Anthem to be set to Musick, and to be performed on the above-mentioned occasion. (*WJ*, 8 Jan. 1714/15)

If Handel did compose anything new for this Thanksgiving, no trace of it now remains: the autographs of the works described in the previous chapter name Elford as a soloist, and therefore cannot have been written as late as January 1715. Possibly some of the early amendments to the autograph of the Caroline Te Deum relate to tentative plans for this service, though Handel would probably have considered the scale of that work too small for the occasion and the venue. By 8 January arrangements for the music must have been initiated from the court, and the favoured composer was Croft: his contributions were a newly composed anthem *O give thanks unto the Lord, and call upon his name*, with solos for Hughes and Weely and accompaniment for string orchestra, and the Morning Prayer canticles Te Deum and Jubilate.[7] For the canticles Croft returned to the setting that he had originally composed for the Thanksgiving at the Chapel Royal in February 1708/9, and brought it up to date.[8]

Croft's revisions to the Te Deum and Jubilate are instructive, and fall into two categories. First, Elford's solos were adapted or rewritten to bring them within Hughes's range. The alterations reveal the differences between the voices of the two alto soloists and lend support to the suggestion that Elford might have been a 'countertenor' and Hughes an 'alto'.[9] The most extended alto solo, 'Vouchsafe, O Lord' from the Te Deum, demanded the most alteration: in two places Croft effected the necessary changes by adjusting the voice part (see Ex. 6.1), but for the last twenty bars he had to recompose the music to suit the new soloist. The second group of revisions was directed

---

[7] The canticles are those specified in the printed liturgy. The set psalms included *Rejoice in the Lord, O ye righteous*, but Croft's setting was not composed for this particular Thanksgiving: see below, App. F.

[8] GB-Lbl Add. MS 17845 is the score prepared for the 1715 Thanksgiving. James Kent was given the task of copying material from the earlier version, which was then revised by the composer. The Te Deum can be compared with the original version in GB-Lcm MS 840. The performing parts, GB-Bu Barber MS 5007a–b, were prepared in 1709 and revised in 1715. The two versions will be elucidated in my forthcoming volume of Croft's orchestrally accompanied church music for *MB*.

[9] See also Ch. 19, on the subject of the Chapel Royal altos.

towards strengthening the music with increased participation of orchestra and chorus. String parts were added to movements that had previously received only basso continuo accompaniment, and one movement was recomposed into a form that included orchestral parts.[10] In the Jubilate, 'O go your way into his gates', originally a solo for Elford (though the music is lost), was recomposed as an extended chorus movement. These alterations modified the character of the music considerably: the revised version is altogether more robust, and it is not extravagant to characterize the difference as the

Ex. 6.1. Croft, Te Deum in D major, 'Vouchsafe, O Lord' (orchestral parts omitted): (*a, c*) original 1708/9 version for Elford; (*b, d*) 1715 revisions—?for Hughes

The revisions in (*b*) and (*d*) were made by the composer in red ink in GB-Lcm MS 840.

[10] The main alterations in the Te Deum were: Nos. 2 and 3, strings added; Nos. 4 and 9, solo range altered; No. 12, new movement composed with orchestral accompaniment; No. 15, solo range altered bars 85–end, and recomposed; No. 16, end of chorus extended, from 21 bars to 38 (movement nos. from Croft, *Te Deum*, ed. Shaw).

transmutation of a 'Purcellian' work into a 'Handelian' one. Croft may have made his revisions partly to accommodate the differences between performing conditions at St James's Palace and St Paul's Cathedral,[11] but it seems equally likely that he brought the music up to date in the light of his experience of Handel's 'Utrecht' service. The new choral movement for the Jubilate in particular shows the influence of Handel's long movement for this text, in the same alla breve style.[12]

The newspaper reporting of Croft's music reflects the changed outlook that affected Handel's relationship to the Chapel Royal. Whereas all accounts of the Utrecht music had been consistently complimentary, the notice of Croft's 1714/15 music ends with a sting in the tail that was surely directed at Handel, and may have been intended as a direct riposte to the item from *The Weekly Journal* that was quoted above:

Dr Croft's Te Deum and Jubilate, were this Day perform'd at St. Paul's before the King by the Gentlemen of the Chappel Royal, and the rest of His Majesty's Musick, which, to the Honour of our Nation, are for their Aire, Contrivance, and Solemnity of the Harmony, esteemed by good Judges, the best Compositions; and the Te Deum comes up to the Performance of the famous Dr. Henry Purcell, who far exceeded all Foreigners. (*Dawks*, 20 Jan. 1714/15)[13]

For the next five years Croft had the monopoly in providing music for Court services involving instrumentally accompanied music, though the King gave few opportunities in that direction. George I did not go to St Paul's on the next Thanksgiving day[14] and this set a new precedent: no British monarch set foot inside the Cathedral for a Thanksgiving service until George III went to celebrate the recovery of his health and sanity in 1789,[15] though circumstantial evidence from the scores suggests that Handel was expecting George II to go there following the Dettingen victory in 1743 (see Ch. 14). The discontinuance of the grand combined state Thanksgiving services probably had several causes. During the quarter-century following the 1715 Thanksgiving Britain

---

[11] Although the royal service for the 1708/9 Thanksgiving took place at St James's Palace, Croft may reasonably have anticipated a service at St Paul's when he composed the music.

[12] Purcell (as also Blow and Turner) had set this verse as a chorus. However, Croft's movement (141 bars) is closer in scale to Handel's (162 bars) than to Purcell's (34 bars), and Croft also follows Handel in his excursion into 'flat' keys.

[13] See also *WP*, 15–22 Jan.: 'Dr. Crofts excellent Te Deum, equal to that of his celebrated Master Dr. Blow, that is plac'd in the Vatican for its rare merit in Letters and Notes of Gold, was sung to instrumental Musick there.'

[14] The Thanksgiving was celebrated on 7 June 1716 and the newspapers (e.g. *Dawks*, 5 May) expected the King to go to St Paul's. According to one correspondent on 4 June 'The King do[e]s not go next Thursday to the thanksgiving, and when he was asked said it was fit to give God thanks but he would not triumph over his subjects' (GB-Lbl Add. MS 47028, fo. 155ᵛ).

[15] See Burrows, *Dissertation*, ii. App. 12.

was not heavily involved in military operations that called for such events, and George I himself seems to have been temperamentally averse to grandiose public display. Another important factor in the situation may have been a dispute that seems to have arisen between the clergy of the Chapel Royal and St Paul's Cathedral about their relative status at such events: John Dolben, the Chapel Royal's Sub-Dean, recorded the Chapel's right to precedence in the Cheque Book in a manner that suggests that there had been some controversy.[16]

It would be unrealistic to view Handel's disassociation from the Chapel Royal in the period after 1715 as affecting more than the periphery of his life, and he continued in any case to receive the £200 pension which seems to have been the reward for his earlier contributions to English court music. The central part of his career in London, at the opera house, was more seriously affected by the division in social and political life that took place in 1717, and which started at court. Patronage of the opera house by the royal family and by a sufficient number of the aristocracy was essential to its continuance in London:[17] with this support the operas survived the Jacobite scares and upheavals in 1715,[18] but when this patronage became divided in the political crisis of 1717 they could not continue. The crisis was precipitated by a separation between the King and the Prince of Wales after a dispute at the christening of one of the Prince's sons in November 1717, but this was the culmination of a polarization in political life that had been developing over the previous six months, as the Prince of Wales had become the focus for opposition to his father's government.[19] Very soon the dispute escalated to the extent that the Prince and Princess of Wales (but not their children) were ejected from St James's Palace: they left on 30 November 1717, and about a month later the King issued a 'circular letter' ordering that those who attended the Prince would be forbidden the King's presence. One of the first effects was that the Prince and Princess ceased to attend the Chapel Royal, going instead to the parish church of St James's, Piccadilly. The King and Prince were thereafter not to be seen together at the opera, or anywhere else, and courtiers had to make partisan choices. One of the opera soloists, the soprano Pilotti, was under the patronage of the Princess of Wales,[20] but this would not have been an insurmountable obstacle to the continuance of the operas if the division had

---

[16] *OCB*, fo. 54ʳ; Ashbee and Harley, i. 139.

[17] See Hunter, 'Patronizing Handel'.

[18] The opera season closed at the end of July 1715; there were no performances during the rest of that calendar year, and the next season began in Feb. 1715/16. See Deutsch, *Handel*, 68.

[19] See Hatton, *George I*, 193–210.

[20] This patronage was recorded in the published word-books for Handel's operas *Rinaldo* (Nov. 1712) and *Amadigi* (May 1715): see Harris, *The Librettos*, ii. 12, 262–3.

simply been a domestic one within the royal family. The social and political divisions among the nobility and leading politicians ran much deeper. By the end of the 1716–17 season the opera company was in any case rather exhausted, artistically and financially. The doors of the King's Theatre closed after the performance of Ariosti's *Tito Manlio* on 29 June 1717, and would not reopen for the performance of Italian opera until nearly three years later.

Handel must have been placed in a difficult position by the 1717 crisis, especially if he had been welcome in a private capacity among the inner circle of the royal family during the years 1714–17. If he went abroad during the second half of 1716 this would have been diplomatically convenient,[21] since those who had attended the Prince in England during the King's absence at that time were later suspected of supporting the opposition. Handel was of the same generation as the Prince of Wales, and had probably received encouragement from the Princess, with musical consequences in the composition of keyboard music and Italian duets back in his Hanover days. The music that Handel provided for the famous royal water party on the River Thames on the night of 17–18 July 1717 seems to align him with the King: the Prince and Princess of Wales were not of the party.[22] It is the last we hear of Handel's association with the royal family until the King and the Prince were reunited in 1720. Presumably Handel found it invidious to have to choose between the two mutually exclusive courts. The King made strenuous efforts to make his own court lavishly attractive in 1718–19,[23] but Handel took no part in the festivities: Croft provided a harpsichord, and probably the music, for the King's theatrical entertainments at Hampton Court.[24]

Private Patronage:
James Brydges and the Cannons Anthems

Handel's activities following the closure of the opera house in 1717 are thinly documented, but two things can be said with certainty: that he composed music for James Brydges, Earl of Carnarvon, during 1717–18, and that he was abroad for most of 1719.[25] There is no evidence that Handel ever lived as part of Brydges's entourage, nor do we know of any financial arrangements for the

---

[21] See Ch. 7 n. 24, concerning the evidence for this visit.

[22] A previous water party in 1715 may have marked the formal resolution of Handel's relationship with the court of Hanover: see Burrows, 'Handel and Hanover', 46.

[23] Beattie, *The English Court*, 264 et seq.

[24] GB-Lpro LC5/157, p. 157.

[25] Evidence from Handel's letters and a newspaper report suggests that he left London at the end of Feb. 1718/19: see Deutsch, *Handel*, 84–8.

composer's support.[26] A letter from Brydges to John Arbuthnot dated 25 September 1717[27] reveals that Handel had composed half of the Cannons anthems at that time: the remainder, plus the Cannons Te Deum and *Acis and Galatea*, were probably composed during the following twelve months.[28] From Handel's point of view, it was a fortunate coincidence that this patronage came at the right moment in Brydges's own career. Since 1713 Brydges had concentrated on the development of his estate at Cannons, about ten miles north-west of Westminster, a project that included the building of a large mansion.[29] A long wrangle over his former period of public office as Paymaster was finally concluded when his accounts were audited in the early months of 1717,[30] after which he was free to devote more time to his own affairs. Between 1717 and 1720 he was at the height of his fortune: by the end of 1721 he had lost money in the South Sea bubble and, although the house at Cannons was maintained, his ambitions had moved on to the project of a new residence in central London.[31] Brydges seems to have been favoured by the King.[32] He had attended the Prince of Wales's water party on the Thames in June 1716,[33] but he dined with the King at Hampton Court on 22 August 1717,[34] by which time Handel was probably engaged on the composition of the Cannons anthems. He, like Handel, no doubt took the opportunity to remain out of court life as much as possible as the political climate grew more difficult.

In his letter to Arbuthnot, referred to above, Brydges invited him to 'take Cannons in on your way to London' to hear Handel's music. The chapel in Cannons house was not opened until August 1720,[35] so there can be no doubt that the anthems and canticles that Handel composed for Brydges in 1717–18 were first performed in the nearby parish church of St Lawrence. Brydges had

[26] Brydges himself was musical, and had been an early member of the Oxford Music Club when he was an undergraduate in the 1690s: see Crum, 'An Oxford Music Club'.

[27] Deutsch, *Handel*, 78.

[28] For the date of *Acis and Galatea*, see Rogers, 'Dating Acis and Galatea'. *Esther* was probably also composed for Brydges, perhaps late in 1718 or early in 1719, but no certain details are known.

[29] Baker and Baker, *The Life and Circumstances*, ch. 6.

[30] Ibid. 107. Brydges had resigned the office in 1713.

[31] US-SM MS ST 44 includes lists of the Duke's establishments at New Year 1720/1 and New Year 1721/2. The former has about 140 names, including twenty at 'The Musick Table': the latter has ninety-three names, of which three at most are musicians. It is doubtful that there was a substantial regular musical establishment at Chandos during the 1720s.

[32] Hatton, *George I*, 155.

[33] *GEP*, 2–5 June 1716.

[34] *PB*, 22–4 Aug. 1717. At this period Brydges was trying to obtain his Dukedom: see *WJSP*, 20 July 1717. He was created Duke of Chandos in April 1719.

[35] See Deutsch, *Handel*, 112.

begun his development programme at Cannons by 'modernizing' this church, which reopened with its new furnishings on Easter Sunday, 1716.[36] In its new form the church was arranged like a private chapel—in fact, just like the Chapel Royal—with west-end galleries for the Duke and his servants. Handel's anthems were almost certainly performed in the unpewed area behind the altar at the east end. The parallel between a box at the opera and the west-end gallery at St Lawrence's church is one that is still apparent to the visitor to this well-preserved church today.

The players employed at Cannons in 1718 included (though not necessarily all at the same time) three violinists, three players distributed between cello and double bass, and one each for oboe, flute, recorder and trumpet; the singers were three trebles, three tenors and two basses.[37] The constitution of Brydges's performing group may have fluctuated from month to month, or even from week to week, around a regular core of permanent players and singers.[38] Handel presumably directed the performances of his music from the organ.[39] Nicola Haym, a leading musician from the opera house who had joined Brydges's establishment towards the end of 1715, would have played the cello for Handel and may have been in charge of the other musicians; he had composed anthems for Cannons during 1716–17.[40]

Both Haym and Handel left the musical life of Cannons in 1718, and their place was eventually taken by Johann Christoph Pepusch, who was appointed Composer and Musical Director in 1719. The musical establishment had probably expanded gradually since 1716, and this trend continued for a time

---

[36] *WR*, 7 Apr. 1716: 'The same Day [Sunday 1 Apr.] the Reverend Dr. Bridges preached an excellent Sermon on the Parish Church of Edgeworth; which Church was lately beautified by the Right Honourable the Earl of Carnarvon, at his own Cost and Charges, with curious workmanship. The said Noble Peer, after Divine Service (which he attended) made a splendid Entertainment, at his Lordship's Seat at Canons-House, where were present several persons of Note.'

[37] See Beeks, 'Handel and Music for the Earl of Carnarvon', 8; unfortunately there is no comparable documentation for 1717, and calculations on instrumentation cannot be precise on account of the extent of 'double-handedness' among the players.

[38] From Handel's indications of instrumentation on the autographs, it is even possible that the Cannons anthems in 'pair IV' of Table 6.1 were performed with bassoon and double bass but no cello.

[39] The opening to Handel's autograph of HWV 251b (almost certainly his first Cannons anthem) has two figured bass parts: the use of a harpsichord may be implied (though only the organ is named), but more likely the composer was making speculative provision that was not followed through in practice.

[40] For the beginning of Haym's association with Brydges, see the letter quoted in Beeks, 'The Chandos Anthems',16; US-SM MS ST 87 records payments to him up to Michaelmas 1718. A volume of six of Haym's anthems 'for the use of Witchurch' (now GB-Lbl Add. MS 62561) has a dedication to Brydges dated 29 Sept. 1716. The autograph of his 'Antifona' *The Lord is King* (GB-Cfm MU MS 177) is headed 'Cannons 1717', and I have identified two further similar Cannons works: see Burrows, 'Some Misattributed Eighteenth-Century Anthems'.

after 1718, reaching its greatest numbers in 1720–1, after Handel had departed.[41] Among those who entered Brydges's service were several singers associated with the Chapel Royal: the 'List of His Grace the Duke of Chandos's Family at New Years Day 1720/1'[42] includes Chapel Royal Gentlemen Thomas Gethin and Thomas Bell sharing the 'Counter Tenor' place, and William Perry as one of the Basses. George Angel, employed as a double bass player for Chapel Royal services in the 1720s, appears there as the Cannons cellist. Of the two soloists (both tenors) that are identified on Handel's autographs of his Cannons works, Blackley's name appears in the surviving household accounts, but Rowe's does not: James Blackley had no known association with the Chapel Royal, but Francis Rowe subsequently became a leading Chapel Royal singer (probably as an alto) in the 1730s.[43] During the 1720s the 'Cannons concert' declined even more quickly than it had grown in 1716–21, cutbacks probably being forced on the Duke as a result of his losses on South Sea and Mississippi stock. Perry was the only Chapel Royal Gentlemen to have some connection with Cannons after 1721: he was paid in 1725 for 'his performance (in singing) at Cannons'.[44]

Handel put his previous experience of English church music to good use at Cannons. Four of the Cannons anthems are based on previous Chapel Royal works, and three others contain material derived from Chapel Royal music, in various proportions from limited motivic references to arrangements of complete movements. His procedure in adapting the Chapel Royal music was to reduce the scoring and increase the length. In place of the Chapel Royal choir and the King's Musicians he was dealing with a chamber group with one, or at most two, singers to a part and a handful of instrumentalists, again with only one or two players per part. This naturally shifted the musical balance towards the inclusion of more extended movements for solo singers, in alternation with 'chorus' movements that were ensembles for between three and five vocal parts. In *As pants the hart* and *O sing unto the Lord*, probably the first two Cannons anthems to be composed, the choruses from the Chapel Royal anthems were used as framing pillars for new structures, supporting fresh solo movements.[45] The addition of new solo movements in itself increased the length of the anthems. Most of Handel's compositions intended for

[41] See above, n. 32.

[42] US-SM MS ST 44, Part 1, p. 28.

[43] I identify Rowe, named on the Cannons Te Deum and on *Acis and Galatea*, with Chapel Royal Gentleman 65.

[44] US-SM MS ST 82, p. 185.

[45] Ensemble movements for the full forces in the Cannons anthems will be referred to as 'choruses', while recognizing that fact that in may cases there may have been only one singer to a part.

performance in the Chapel Royal are of about fifteen to twenty minutes' duration;[46] the Cannons anthems are generally about five minutes longer,[47] with the tendency for the later ones to run longer still, towards half an hour. It seems that Brydges was able to enjoy more leisurely devotions than the King.

Material from each of Handel's previous Chapel Royal compositions was pressed into service for the Cannons anthems: the Utrecht Te Deum alone escaped with but a small levy. As will be seen in Chapters 8 and 9, many of the newly composed Cannons anthems were reworked in their turn to suit later Chapel Royal conditions. Brydges's letter to Arbuthnot reveals that Handel composed the first anthems in pairs, and Table 6.1 lists these pairings in a sequence which is probably that of composition.[48] If the order is correct, then it appears that Handel began his assignment by reworking his two existing Chapel Royal anthems as the first pair. In the next two pairs, one work from each was based largely on pre-existing Chapel Royal music. After that Handel had consumed most of his earlier music, and the later Cannons anthems contain less material derived from Chapel Royal sources. Consideration will now be given to the revisions that Handel made to the Chapel Royal music in the composition of the Cannons works, following the chronology presented in Table 6.1.

As pants the hart (HWV 251b)

The mongrel text that Handel had set earlier in the decade in HWV 251a obviously held an attraction for him. It seems that the composer's certainty about the content of this anthem led him to treat it as a 'starter' when he began the composition of a new series of anthems: just as HWV 251a was probably his earliest English anthem, so HWV 251b was probably his first Cannons anthem.[49] For the Cannons version he amended details of the verbal text. In the

---

[46] The exception is the Dettingen Te Deum, which may have been composed in anticipation of a service at St Paul's Cathedral: see Ch. 14.

[47] HWV 249b is the only Cannons anthem that can be performed comfortably within twenty minutes if the timings include the opening Sinfonia movements, which are clearly connected to their anthems in the autographs. Brydges's letter to Arbuthnot includes a rather enigmatic reference to 'Overtures to be plaied before the first lesson'. To divorce the Anthems from their present overtures would present artistic problems, for example in HWV 246 where the Sinfonia ends on the dominant chord, or in HWV 250a where the first chorus entry has to pitch the note from the Sinfonia. HWV 254 (possibly the last Cannons anthem to be composed) lacks any separate Sinfonia, as also does the Cannons Te Deum.

[48] See Beeks, 'Handel and Music for the Earl of Carnarvon', 4.

[49] An indicator of this is the elaborate layout of the bassi parts in the Sinfonia, with separate staves implying two chord-playing instruments: this is not repeated later, when Handel presumably had a more accurate knowledge of the resources available.

Table 6.1. *Cannons anthems and canticles, grouped into pairs and arranged in probable order of composition*

Pair	Title	Chapel Royal
I	*As pants the hart* (HWV 251b)	★ †
	O sing unto the Lord (HWV 249b)	★
II	*My song shall be alway* (HWV 252)	★ †
	Let God arise (HWV 256a)	★ †
III	*Have mercy upon me* (HWV 248)	★ †
	O be joyful in the Lord (Jubilate) (HWV 246)	★
IV	*In the Lord put I my trust* (HWV 247)	
	I will magnify thee (HWV 250a)	†
V	*Te Deum in B flat major* (HWV 281)	★ †
	O come, let us sing unto the Lord (HWV 253)	†
VI	*O praise the Lord with one consent* (HWV 254)	
	The Lord is my light (HWV 255)	

Note: The works marked ★ include material derived from earlier Chapel Royal music; those marked † include material that was drawn upon by Handel for later Chapel Royal works. A movement from the Sinfonia of HWV 247 was also used in Handel's 1738 version of *As pants the hart* (HWV 251e).

John Arbuthnot's letter of 25 Sept. 1717 (Deutsch, *Handel*, 78) refers to the composition of three pairs of anthems. The works in the last two pairs may not have been as closely linked to each other as the earlier pairs. In pairs I–IV the anthems in each pair require the same voices; Handel wrote for alto-clef voices only in pair II.

first movement 'As paints the hart' was duly corrected to 'As pants the hart', and 'for thee, O Lord' became 'for thee, O God'; in the second movement 'When thus they say' became 'While thus they say'. These alterations bring the text closer to the forms of the sources suggested in Chapter 3 (see Table 3.2) and, were it not for some relapses in later settings, they might be taken as a sign that Handel's command of the English language had become more assured. He still retained 'In the voice of praise of thanksgiving', however, and indeed never corrected this form in his later versions of the anthem. The concluding 'Amen' did not survive the transfer from HWV 251a and never returned in the later settings.

The process of turning HWV 251a into a form suitable for Cannons involved reworking the music in a manner that would employ the orchestral instruments most effectively. In the first two chorus movements this could be done by simple rearrangement. The solo movements had to be recomposed in any case, but even they include some features that had originated in the earlier anthem; only in the final chorus did Handel depart completely from his previous setting. The music derived from the Chapel Royal anthem was transposed downwards: the implications of this are considered in Chapter 20.

The opening instrumental Sinfonia of the Cannons setting has no parallel in the anthem's Chapel Royal predecessor.[50]

For the first vocal movement, the musical source in HWV 251a had been for six voices with basso continuo accompaniment. Handel made two attempts at laying out the opening bars for the new scoring but, once the initial decisions had been made, it was a fairly straightforward matter for him to redistribute the material for three voices, violins, oboe, three instrumental bass parts, and organ. Two of the instrumental bass parts (Contra Basso and Bassoon) largely double the vocal bass line, and some of the independent material from Bass 1 in the Chapel Royal anthem is used an octave higher.[51] The amount of new material in the main body of the movement is very small. There are odd bars of additional instrumental counterpoint, some of them (such as the oboe part at bars 14–16, and Violin 2 at bars 43–4) of thematic significance; only one new passage is of any length (Violin 2, bars 18–26) and this is undistinguished except for the cunning with which its end incorporates the former tenor part in such a way as to avoid the interval of an augmented 4th that had occurred at this point in HWV 251a. There are one or two changes to details: a tempo (Adagio) is specified,[52] and the dotted rhythm of the opening bars of the main theme is amended to plain crotchets. Handel transferred his solo (verse) and tutti (chorus) indications from the Chapel Royal anthem, but it is doubtful whether the size of the Cannons establishment allowed any significant difference. The only recomposition in this movement occurred in the final bars. Up to bar 47 the Cannons version can be regarded as an arrangement of the Chapel Royal version, but the succeeding two bars were rewritten, replacing the former rhetorical pause with an echo phrase before the final choral cadence. Handel reduced the instrumental postlude from four bars to two: this is perhaps a surprising alteration in view of his tendency towards expansion rather than contraction in the Cannons anthems.

For 'Tears are my daily food' Handel discarded his previous ground-bass type movement,[53] but retained the principle of setting these words in triple time in a related minor key,[54] and both movements end with similar imperfect cadences: otherwise it is the differences rather than the similarities that are most readily apparent. The Cannons movement has a much larger timescale and

---

[50] The title 'Sonata' which appears on the autograph may have been added in the 1730s in connection with the preparation of Handel's set of Trio Sonatas, Op. 5.

[51] HWV 251b: S, bars 8–12; Violin 2, bars 16–17.

[52] HWV 251a has no tempo indication; it is probable that Handel took this movement more slowly at Cannons than at the Chapel Royal.

[53] The bass of the new movement has a resemblance to that of 'Why so full of grief?' in HWV 251a.

[54] Both settings of this movement are in the same key, A minor, but this has a different relationship to the tonal centres of the two anthems.

follows a binary plan: the second half, beginning at bar 68 after the dominant cadence, repeats the complete verbal text. The musical content seems more mature, but part of the dramatic impact was lost in the repetition. There is some compensation for this in the new interest provided by a dotted-rhythm orchestral figure, which grows from a decorative commentary (bars 35–6) into a powerful outburst reinforcing the text at bar 55. In HWV 251a Handel had riveted attention at 'Where is now thy God?' by returning to the opening bass and tonality: in the Cannons anthem this focus is achieved by the instrumental entry at bar 55. Both methods are effective, though the later one is perhaps rather less subtle. Some features of the earlier version are retained. Both settings include angular melodic shapes outlining augmented or diminished intervals. The long note on 'Tears', entering on a weak beat, is also an idea carried forward from the Chapel Royal version.

As in HWV 251a, Handel seems to have felt that the part of the text beginning 'Now when I think thereupon' demanded some novel instrumental obbligato part. In HWV 251b the novelty is the 'Harpeggio' violin solo against a background of quaver chords. The structure of the movement follows the previous setting, breaking into recitative (this time orchestrally accompanied) at 'I went with the multitude'. The addition of the word 'For' at bar 19 does something to eliminate the hiatus that was one of the previous weaknesses at this point. There are echoes of the melodic line from the earlier setting at bar 9, and the text of the recitative section also suggested the same rhythms, if not exactly the same melodic shapes, as before. Strangely enough, where Handel changes the rhythms the result is not always an improvement in the stress patterns (see Ex. 6.2).

The chorus 'In the voice of praise of thanksgiving' in HWV 251a is twenty-nine bars long. For the first twenty-five bars Handel kept to the track of the original, rearranging the material to suit the Cannons forces; as with the previous chorus, this entailed the addition of very little new material. String chords that were added at bars 22–3 give strength to a passage that was previously rather thin. There was one significant detailed amendment to the movement's subject, in the addition of semiquavers to the second phrase (see Ex. 6.3). Handel also made a minor modification to the rhythm of the bass part

Ex. 6.2. Handel, *As pants the hart*: (*a*) HWV 251a; (*b*) HWV 251b

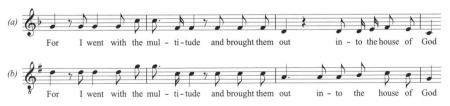

Ex. 6.3. *As pants the hart:* (*a*) HWV 251a; (*b*) HWV 251b

at bar 13, replacing a dotted rhythm with plain crotchets.[55] (He modified the rhythm in the vocal bass part, wrote crotchets in the basso continuo, but forgot to amend the bassoon part, which has the dotted-rhythm form.) From bar 26 onwards he extended and recomposed the last part of the movement, adding a new sixteen-bar passage comprising two sections. Bars 26–35 are an additional exposition, based mostly on an inverted form of the subject (5 entries),[56] but culminating in a tonic re-entry of the subject in its original presentation. In the closing section, bars 36–41, there are three inverted entries of the opening bar of the subject and three normal entries, over a dominant pedal; the cumulative effect of these entries is heightened by a stretto in bar 38, where inverted and normal entries overlap. The final bars of the movement (42–4) are an expanded version of the last two bars of the source movement in HWV 251a.

For 'Why so full of grief?' Handel rejected the movement from HWV 251a in favour of a new version, though he retained the idea of setting the text as a minor-key duet in triple time. The replacement naturally gains from the opportunities provided by the use of orchestral instruments, but some striking features of the earlier movement are lost, in particular the repetition of 'Why?' at the opening. The new movement appears to be totally original, but closer inspection reveals that Handel must have had the earlier movement in mind when he wrote it. The opening figure may have developed from a hint found in bar 9 of the earlier version, and the second important figure of the movement is also an elaboration of a parallel passage from the Chapel Royal movement; the principle of one part moving against a sustained note in the other voice also reappears (see Ex. 6.4). There are some improvements to the text: Handel now remembered, as he had not done in HWV 251a, to include the word 'so' consistently in the phrase 'Why so disquieted', and he improved things by arranging for the long note to fall on the middle syllable of

---

[55] Compare the similar alteration to the rhythm of the subject in the opening chorus of the anthem.

[56] The inverted form of the subject was not used at all in the original movement from HWV 251a.

Ex. 6.4. *As pants the hart* (HWV 251a and 251b): (*a*) opening phrase; (*b*) second figure; (*c*) continuation with pedal notes (voices only, text omitted)

'disquieted' rather than on the word 'me'.[57] In spite of differences in melodic material, Handel followed the overall musical structure from the Chapel Royal movement remarkably closely.

The last movement of HWV 251a had been the weakest part of the plan in that anthem, and its music gave very little opportunity for the addition of interesting orchestral material, so something completely new was needed. The Cannons movement provided metrical variety, avoiding two consecutive movements in triple time, and also a tonal completion for the anthem with a movement in the same key as the opening. The addition of the Sinfonia at the beginning of the Cannons version gives a stronger sense of a tonic area to the anthem as a whole, and this perhaps produced the complementary need for a clear tonic ending. The opening tenor solo in the new final movement is not a flawless example of composition, but the piece as a whole is a great improvement on its predecessor and the lead-in from solo to tutti at bar 32 is particularly well handled.

O sing unto the Lord (HWV 249b)

Only the outer framework of the previous Chapel Royal anthem (HWV 249a) was used for the Cannons anthem: Handel adapted the opening and closing choruses but the remainder was composed afresh. He also altered the selection of verses. Verse 2 of the psalm (an alto solo in HWV 249a) was omitted, and verse 3, which had not found a place in the earlier anthem, now generated a substantial chorus movement. Verse 4, previously an accompanied recitative, was recomposed as the continuation to the new chorus, in as massive a style as the conditions at Cannons would allow. Verse 6, not included in the Chapel Royal anthem, was now set as a solo movement for tenor, and the first part of verse 9 ('O worship the Lord'), was recast in a completely new duet setting; it is only with the succeeding chorus that the music returns to the track of Handel's earlier anthem.

---

[57] One rather less happy alteration to the word-setting in the autograph occurs at the cadence in bars 45–7. Handel originally set the text thus, presumably to be treated as a hemiola:

dis - quiet - ed with - in me

He then altered it to:

dis - quiet - ed with - in me

The first vocal movement was transposed from G major to F major to accommodate a treble soloist in place of the Chapel Royal alto. The voice part is therefore generally a seventh above its previous pitch, which seems rather a large transposition until it is remembered that Elford was a 'second Alto', and that the performing pitch at Cannons may have been lower than that at the Chapel Royal.[58] The structure of the Chapel Royal movement is preserved almost exactly. In the solo section an extra bar (bar 7) was added, improving the line of the soloist's second phrase. Later on, a weak spot in the earlier anthem was tightened up by the omission of a bar (bar 16 of HWV 249b replacing bars 15–16 of HWV 249a). Apart from some small details, the melodic contours of the solo are retained intact: presumably the treble soloist was competent enough to cope with music originally written by Elford. The chorus section into which the solo leads is a straightforward rearrangement of the Chapel Royal music.[59] A second violin part was added in the closing ritornello, but otherwise hardly any additional music was called for.

In the Chapel Royal version, the chorus 'Let the whole earth stand in awe of him' had originally replaced the second half of a binary movement beginning in B flat major and leading back to the tonic G minor. As it happened, it was convenient to Handel's plan to have a movement in G minor at this point in the Cannons anthem. This, of course, entailed rewriting the opening section of the Chapel Royal chorus from B flat major into G minor, so that the movement could stand by itself. The striking short phrase on which the chorus was built was amenable to presentation in successive contrasted keys, and Handel found that he could use some sections of the earlier chorus as they stood. The omission of the former closing instrumental ritornello eliminated the buffer to the next chorus and in doing so emphasized a jolt between the tonality of the two movements.[60]

The final chorus was transposed from D major to F major and recomposed considerably. Handel's treatment of tonality in the Cannons anthem is rather more stable, and accordingly rather less exciting in its interpretation of this text, than in the Chapel Royal version: more time is given for the listener to recognize the path of the modulations, and an element of surprise is thereby removed.

---

[58] See Ch. 19. Handel decided on the key of the anthem as whole before he commenced the composition: it is particularly clear in the autograph of this anthem that the Sinfonia and the first vocal movement were composed together.

[59] There are some alterations to melodic details, but only one significant change in the harmony: the sharpening of the third in the chord at bar 25, beat 3. (The bar numbers of both versions coincide at this point.)

[60] In context, the G minor–F major sequence of the Cannons anthem is more of a jolt than the G minor–D major of the Chapel Royal anthem.

Handel's rejection of the echo effects from the earlier setting also lessens the immediate impact of the chorus. Handel excised the broad final bars of the Chapel Royal movement and, in spite of the rhetorical silence four bars from the end,[61] the conclusion of the Cannons anthem is rather abrupt. Perhaps this is because Handel did not originally intend the anthem to end at the same point as the Chapel Royal setting. In the autograph of the Cannons version the chorus is followed by a tenor solo in F minor to the text of verse 13 ('For he cometh to judge the earth'), which is the last verse of the psalm.[62] This can hardly have been intended for the last movement of the anthem, but it is none too clear what Handel did intend: perhaps he planned to follow the tenor solo with a repeat of one of the earlier choruses (as Blow had done in his setting of the psalm), or with an Alleluja (as Purcell had done). He cancelled the solo movement by crossing out the first pages and reused the discarded music in another anthem.

My song shall be alway (HWV 252)

Handel may not have foreseen that he would eventually produce a setting of the Te Deum for Cannons forces, for he used up much of the musical material from the Caroline Te Deum in this anthem. The sections that presented themselves as most suitable for adaptation were the longer self-contained movements, and he rearranged three complete movements—two solos and a chorus. There is also one passing reference to music from the Utrecht Te Deum in the first vocal movement, when the entry of the lower voices under the treble solo with the words 'The heav'ns shall praise thy wondrous works' echoes a very similar phrase in the Utrecht Te Deum, 'The heavens and all the Powers therein'. The parallel between the two passages is the more striking because in both works the phrase is given two repetitions,[63] and the text complements that which is being sung by the upper voice(s).

   The aria 'God is very greatly to be fear'd' is based on music from the third movement of the Caroline Te Deum, 'When thou took'st upon thee', transposed from G minor (alto soloist) to E minor (tenor soloist). The source movement has already been described in detail in Chapter 5. For the first half of the movement (bars 1–52), Handel followed the Te Deum music quite closely, adding or subtracting the odd bar here and there and altering details of the melodic writing, but thereafter he worked with only occasional reference to his previous music. The return to the tonic key is retained, but the

----

[61] There is no authority for the pause printed over this bar in *HG* 34.

[62] GB-Lbl RM 20.d.6, fos. 41–2; *HHA* III/4, pp. 172–3.

[63] In the anthem the phrase also reappears again in the upper voices, in the course of the later working out of the chorus.

intermediate perfect cadences of the source movement are avoided, the wind-instrument obbligato is removed, and the descending dotted figure, introduced at bars 22–3 in the Te Deum, now takes on a leading role in the accompaniment for which there is no parallel in the earlier movement. Nevertheless, the lineage of the two movements is clear when taken as a whole: the binary structure and main rhythmic and melodic motifs are readily recognizable. Handel used the oboe as the obbligato instrument in place of the transverse flute from the Chapel Royal Te Deum; the Cannons movement lacks the 'staccato' direction to the string parts, as well as the tempo indication that is present in the Te Deum.

The source for the aria 'Blessed is the people' is bars 1–47 of the second movement from the Caroline Te Deum, transposed from A minor (alto soloist) to E minor (treble soloist).[64] Handel's adaptation is strikingly parallel to that in the movement just described. In both, the choral conclusion is replaced by a solo section in the tonic, and he drew heavily on the Te Deum source for the first half, but only in a general way thereafter. The revisions to the roulades and the harmonic movement in the first half (bars 1–24) result in the loss of one bar overall: thereafter, although the music is recomposed, the original harmonic plan remains. The landmarks of the instrumental ritornellos, which were prominent features in the Te Deum, are clearer still in the anthem. Handel took the opportunity to add some new obbligato accompaniments for solo oboe, probably taking advantage of the chamber-group conditions at Cannons. The alteration to the tempo (Allegro in the Te Deum, Andante in the anthem) may have been inspired by the character of the new text. Handel's alterations to the melodic writing (violins, bars 3 and 5, bass part, bar 4 and elsewhere) seem to indicate a general desire to smooth the lines out.

The closing chorus of the anthem is a revised adaptation of the closing chorus from the Caroline Te Deum (No. 6) transposed from D major to G major and with a tempo indication (Allegro) added. Not much recomposition was required. Handel added extra half-bars at bars 10 and 17 in order to expand short episodic links which lead to the re-entry of the subject. The final bars demanded slightly different treatment, but he preserved the principle of a perfect cadence followed by a plagal cadence. As in the previous movement, his revisions to the melodic writing are generally in the direction of smoothness. The octave leaps in the vocal lines of the Te Deum are replaced by melodies more conjunct, but also rather more conventional: some of the original liveliness from the Te Deum has been lost.

---

[64] As noted in Ch. 4, No. 2 of the Te Deum is really two movements in one, the first forty-seven bars forming a complete unit.

Let God arise (HWV 256a)

The first vocal movement includes two fragmentary references to music from Handel's birthday ode for Queen Anne.[65] More significant is the derivation of the opening of the anthem's last movement from the last movement of the Utrecht Te Deum. Both movements use the stepwise 'Non nobis' theme as a cantus firmus against a running bass part and as a foil against shorter choral phrases ('let me never be confounded' in the Te Deum, 'alleluja' in the anthem). Handel cleverly extracted the bass of his cantus firmus theme from material that was present in the Te Deum accompaniment (Ex. 6.5). The opening of the movement 'Praised be the Lord' bears a striking resemblance to the opening of Croft's anthem *Blessed be the Lord*,[66] composed for the Thanksgiving service in December 1705.

Have mercy upon me, O God (HWV 248)

In this anthem Handel drew on music from the Utrecht Te Deum: it is noteworthy that the Cannons arrangement of the Utrecht Jubilate is probably paired with this anthem. The first movements of the anthem have no borrowings from the Te Deum: he seems to have turned to the Utrecht music for inspiration as he progressed towards the later movements. In 'Against thee only

Ex. 6.5. (*a*) Utrecht Te Deum, No. 9; (*b*) *Let God arise* (HWV 256a), No. 8

---

[65] At bars 26–7 (compare ode No. 2, bars 78–9) and at bars 107–19 (compare the final bars of ode No. 8).

[66] Scandrett, 'The Anthems of William Croft', Anthem 64.

have I sinned' the instrumental introduction is arranged from 'Vouchsafe, O Lord' in the Utrecht Te Deum with only minor modifications; the timing of the vocal entry was improved by bringing it in a bar earlier, before the final cadence of the introduction. Although the structure of the rest of the movement generally follows that of the Utrecht movement,[67] this resemblance is a red herring. From bar 5 Handel rearranged the discarded movement from the end of HWV 249b, cunningly working string motifs derived from the Utrecht introduction into the solo, wind obbligato, and instrumental bass parts from the anthem movement.

The first part of 'Thou shalt make me hear of joy and gladness' is a straightforward transcription of 'Thou art the King of glory' from the Utrecht Te Deum, in the same key but with note values halved. The source had five voice parts, but the texture of the imitative sections involved only three genuinely independent parts, so it lost nothing at all in transcription. The transferred music is followed by another, apparently original, imitative section beginning at bar 16. and there is a short reprise of material from both sections in the closing part of the movement (bars 43–55). In 'Make me a clean heart, O God' Handel extended the opening section of 'When Thou took'st upon Thee' from the Utrecht Te Deum; the scoring of the original (oboe obbligato, unison violins, solo voice, basso continuo) exactly suited the Cannons anthem without rearrangement. Allowing for adaptations to fit the new words, the addition of some dotted rhythms,[68] and some minor alterations to the solo line, the music of the first fourteen bars is a literal transcription, transposed from D minor (alto soloist) to C minor (treble soloist). The original music was the first part of a binary structure in the Te Deum, ending in the relative major and introducing a succession of chorus movements; for the anthem Handel composed a new second half to complete the movement. There is an interesting coincidence between the bass part of the first two bars of this movement and the bass of the first two bars of the opening sinfonia to the anthem.

O be joyful in the Lord (HWV 246)

If the chronology of the Cannons anthems suggested at the beginning of this chapter is correct, it seems that Handel moved from restructuring earlier Chapel Royal anthems to recomposing previous Chapel Royal music to new

---

[67] e.g. in the modulation to the dominant and its relative major in bars 13–16: compare Te Deum, bars 17–19. The second halves of both movements also have chromatic descending figures in the bass.

[68] The new notation at bar 12 may suggest retrospectively that the semiquaver figure had been performed with dotted rhythms throughout in the Te Deum.

texts. The present anthem reverses the trend, for it is a transcription of the
Utrecht Jubilate with no changes at all in musical content until the final bars of
the last movement. Reasons can be adduced for the preservation of this
particular work intact. Psalm 100 has only four verses, so reselection or
expansion of the text on the lines of HWV 249b was impracticable; if it
was performed at St Lawrence's Church during a service of Morning Prayer
that included the Jubilate as a canticle, then this would have required the
preservation of the psalm's integrity. (The retention of the Gloria from the
Utrecht setting may indicate that this was indeed intended to be performed as a
canticle, rather than as an anthem, in Morning Prayer.) The scoring of the
choruses needed rearrangement, but the solo movements from the Utrecht
Jubilate could easily be adapted to the reduced forces. Handel may have been
pressed for time, but even if this was the case the thoroughness with which he
reproduced the original music in its new arrangement suggests that he was
musically satisfied with the Utrecht setting.[69]

His single revision to musical content may conveniently be considered first.
He shortened the final phrases of the last movement; half a bar of redundant
material was removed from bar 77, and the final 'Amen' was shortened by
three bars. A less grandiose ending was probably appropriate to the performing
conditions at St Lawrence's Church, yet in practice the amendments make
only a tiny difference to the overall effect: the rhetorical silent bars remain,
though notated slightly differently.[70] The recomposition of the Amen replaced
the overworked descending phrases of the original with something more
varied and shapely, mixing ascending and descending forms.[71]

Some general principles can be identified behind Handel's rescoring. In
movements 2, 3, 7, and 8 the oboe took over trumpet parts from the Utrecht
Jubilate, a particularly important function in the transference of the first
movement from the original setting, which had featured a duet for trumpet
and alto voice; this adaptation was accomplished with complete success.[72]
There is no transposition: Handel chose to keep the music in the 'trumpet'

[69] It has already been noted in Ch. 4 that the Utrecht Jubilate seems to be in a rather later style
than its companion Te Deum. If he was indeed satisfied with the Utrecht Jubilate, this could
explain why Handel did not compose a new setting of the canticle to accompany the A major or
Dettingen Te Deums, but there is no evidence for his revival of the Jubilate at the later periods.

[70] The six-beat silence of the Utrecht version is restored, in principle, by Handel's pause over
the four-beat rest in the Cannons anthem. The change in notation seems to have been motivated
by a desire to move the following choral entry back onto the first beat of the bar.

[71] Handel seems to have had a recurring uneasiness about the way that he ended movements.
As may be seen from the previous descriptions, he recomposed the closing bars of nearly every
chorus movement which he transferred from previous Chapel Royal works into HWV 251b and
249b.

[72] This use of the oboe for trumpet parts may have been repeated by Handel for his revival of
the Caroline Te Deum in the 1720s. See Ch. 7 and Ch. 19.

key of D major for the Cannons version. The musical establishment at Cannons did not generally have the alto-clef voices for which much of the solo work in the Utrecht version had been composed,[73] and Handel found various ways of dealing with their music: either he adapted the alto lines to bring them within the range of a solo tenor, or he used a treble soloist and rewrote sections that had included low notes.

Both movements of the Sinfonia are based on thematic material from Handel's earlier Te Deum settings.[74] The Adagio takes the introduction to the Caroline Te Deum as its starting point, with note values halved and a new continuation when the original music runs out after three and a half bars. The Allegro is worked up from the introduction to the first chorus of the Utrecht Te Deum: bars 5–16 of the Te Deum are the basis for the first eleven bars of the Sinfonia movement, after which Handel had once again to compose a suitable continuation. He did this so skilfully that the final product is one of his most closely argued instrumental movements. In 'O be joyful in the Lord' he gave the former alto solo to his tenor, with consequent alterations to the melodic lines; comparison of the chorus entry at bar 32 with that in the Utrecht Jubilate supports the probability that the tenor soloist at Cannons was also the only tenor singer in concerted passages. The reduction in the number of voice parts entailed reallocating some of the vocal music to the oboe in bars 36–7, where the part slips from its 'trumpet' role in order to fill out the texture. The autograph reveals that Handel thought of keeping his original soprano entry at bar 41, but then decided to leave this little point of imitation to the orchestra.

For 'Serve the Lord with gladness', Handel's original chorus might almost have been written with foreknowledge of transcription for Cannons.[75] Although there are five vocal parts in the Utrecht version, they rarely include more than three simultaneous essential contrapuntal lines. In the Cannons anthem, only two independent entries of the subject that were formerly in vocal parts needed to be transferred into the orchestra, at bar 42 (Violin 1) and bar 50 (Violin 2).[76] The oboe doubles the cantus firmus theme from bar 12

[73] The only works written with alto-clef vocal parts were the second pair of anthems in Table 6.1. Differences in pitch standards need to be taken into account when observing the differences between 'altos' and 'tenors' at different locations: see Ch. 19.

[74] The Sinfonia was published separately by Arnold, but Handel's autograph is headed 'Ψ [Psalm] 100', which conclusively links the instrumental movements with the anthem. The Allegro movement should end with an imperfect cadence: the alternative tonic ending was probably added later by Handel for the Trio Sonata Op. 5 No. 2.

[75] Compare also the similar situation with 'Thou shalt make me hear' in HWV 248.

[76] The second of these was in any case originally an incomplete statement of the subject. The density of the bass parts at bars 42–4 perhaps suggests that Handel had a little difficulty with the rearrangement here: the texture is not, however, as curious as that printed in HG 34, p. 11, which omits the important tenor part in bars 43–7.

onwards, providing support that had not been necessary with the larger forces at St Paul's Cathedral. The role of the viola part in the original movement was so limited in the Utrecht Jubilate that its omission is hardly noticed.[77] Only in one place (bar 19) does the reduction in the number of string parts make a noticeable difference to the contrapuntal texture: at this point Handel could have introduced the missing line into one of the violin parts, but apparently chose not to do so. In 'Be ye sure that the Lord he is God' the instrumental parts inherited from the Utrecht music were exactly what was needed for Cannons, and only the former solo alto part presented something of a problem: Handel gave this to a treble, keeping the c′ at bar 14 but otherwise rewriting the line when it went into the lower register.

'O go your way into his gates' demanded more rearrangement than the previous chorus movement, because most of the original vocal writing was in four real parts, and the alternation of instrumental and vocal expositions at the beginning of the movement limited the opportunities for transferring parts between the forces. In general, Handel gave the former chorus alto part to the treble and transferred the former treble part to the oboe. By judicious re-arrangement all of the main entries and parts, both vocal and instrumental, are covered, even in the stretto passage following bar 109. In two brief passages interesting contrapuntal strands were lost in the pressure of the arrangement, both of them from the original alto part. Handel clarified the chording and word underlay at bars 89–92 in a way that reveals his intentions about the Utrecht original, which is otherwise ambiguous. 'For the Lord is gracious' required little rearrangement. The soloists in the movement from the Utrecht Jubilate had included Chapel Royal altos: Elford and Hughes as the 'second' and 'first' altos, respectively. The obvious solution for Cannons was to give the former part to a tenor and the latter to a treble: the tenor part worked with hardly any alteration, and the treble needed only occasional upward transpos-ition to avoid the note d′. The solo bass part needed no adaptation. Handel made some limited rearrangement of the upper instrumental parts, in the course of which he removed a set of consecutives in bars 27–8.

'Glory be to the Father' necessarily underwent a change of character when it was scaled down to Cannons proportions. The effect of the choral entries in the original was primarily one of massiveness, with widely spaced voices in eight parts topped by descant-type trumpet parts. Handel made no attempt to reproduce the spacing of the chords in the Cannons version, and he did not even preserve the integrity of the top notes of the chords: yet his arrangement

---

[77] The same is true of the preceding movement as well.

is the soundest and most musical imaginable for the forces at his disposal. The voices are concentrated into close triads and chords to gain the maximum concerted effect: there could be no clearer demonstration of Handel's awareness of the needs dictated by different acoustic conditions. The instrumental introduction to the movement originally included an essential viola part: the oboe was pressed into service in the Chandos version, taking over the second violin part while the second violin acquired the previous viola line.

As in 'Serve the Lord with gladness', a little ingenuity enabled Handel to persuade us that the original five-part chorus with full orchestral accompaniment for 'As it was in the beginning' was really (once again) a three-part chorus. He succeeded in putting all of the entries of the main subject into the voices except one—that at bar 39, where an alto lead had to be transferred to the Violin 1/Oboe parts. His reduction of five parts to three in the passage from bar 63 onwards is particularly successful. In the earlier part of the movement he dealt with the problem of transcribing two treble parts by giving the first part to the oboe: since most of the important thematic work was in Soprano 2 this does no harm, and the quaver counter-melodies proved effective in their various new instrumental and vocal combinations. It is difficult to know whether the doubling of the treble lead by the oboe in bars 10–15 was a deliberate choice or an accident of transcription from the former first treble part.

Cannons Te Deum in B flat major (HWV 281)

Of Handel's two previous settings of the Te Deum, the Caroline version was closer in scale to the requirements of Cannons than the more monumental Utrecht setting. As already noted, most of the music from the Caroline Te Deum had already been used up in HWV 252, so perhaps it is not surprising that the debt to previous works in the Cannons Te Deum is to be found in isolated passages rather than in complete movements.

In 'All the earth doth worship thee', after some new and apparently original chorus work Handel was able to call on music from the Caroline Te Deum for the passage from bar 41, beginning 'To thee all angels cry aloud'. The solo part, transposed for tenor, was transferred intact up to bar 48, and the ensuing chorus entry is also based on Caroline material, though its continuation (bar 57 et seq.) is new. The following solo (bar 77) was developed from the parallel passage in the Caroline Te Deum, but at considerably greater length. It is interesting that Handel for the first time followed Purcell's model by repeating 'continually do cry' between the choral outbursts of 'Holy'. The idea of repeating 'Heaven and earth are full' (bars 108–11) may owe something to the Utrecht Te Deum.

The general scheme for 'The glorious company of the Apostles' (triple time with oboe obbligato, and a change to slow quadruple metre at 'The Father of an infinite Majesty') may have been derived from the Utrecht setting, but it is only in the closing stages of the movement that music from the earlier work is used. The vocal parts in bars 101–7 are based on bars 100–6 of the movement in the Utrecht Te Deum to the same text. In 'Thou art the King of Glory/When thou tookest upon thee', similarities with the previous settings are only fragmentary. The rhythm of the opening subject is somewhat reminiscent of the parallel passage in the Utrecht setting, and the succeeding movement is in triple time, as in the Caroline Te Deum, but there the similarity ends: the Cannons version is rather more bland in character and does not attempt to run a large number of verses of the text into a single movement.

The two short movements 'When thou hadst overcome/Thou didst open the Kingdom of Heaven' are expansions of the musical material to the same texts in the Utrecht Te Deum, from which the contrast between unaccompanied soloists and full chorus is retained.[78] In the Utrecht setting 'When thou hadst overcome', in A minor, had followed directly from a movement in F major, adding a sudden contrast of key to those of texture and accompaniment. The preceding movement in the Cannons Te Deum also ends in F major, but this time Handel smoothed over the join by beginning the new movement in D minor, adding an extra phrase to the Utrecht material to effect the subsequent transition from D minor to A minor. Both settings conclude in the same way, on the dominant of A minor. In the ensuing Allegro, 'Thou didst open the Kingdom of Heaven', Handel slotted in an extra twelve bars after the second bar of the Utrecht material. He also took the opportunity to add some semiquaver figuration to the string accompaniment: the new busy-ness disguises the fact that the vocal rhythms of the Allegro are based on the same dactylic pattern as the preceding Adagio.

In 'Thou sittest at the right hand of God' the similarity of the quaver passages first heard in bars 9 and 17–19 to those found in the solo bass part of the second movement of the Caroline Te Deum, bars 57–62, is sufficiently strong to suggest that Handel associated it with the setting of the word 'glory'. From

---

[78] In the Utrecht Te Deum the passage is marked 'Sol'. In the Cannons Te Deum Handel named two tenor soloists (Mr Blacley/Mr Row): this is the only place in the autograph where such names occur. On the autographs of the Cannons anthems Handel only named a singer on HWV 253, which is 'paired' with the Te Deum. Evidently he was in the unusual position of having a number of tenors available at this time, which necessitated the identification of soloists.

the chorus entry at bar 11 onwards, much of the music of 'We believe that thou shalt come' is recomposed from the Utrecht Te Deum,[79] transposed from G minor to E minor, but the settings of the following verses ('Day by day', 'And we worship') are new movements. Neither of Handel's previous settings had rendered these sections of the text in triple time. There are, however, two small similarities with the Utrecht version: the opening figure (trumpet and voice) for 'Day by day', and the treatment of 'And we worship thy name' as an imitative chorus.

It has already been noted that in the Cannons anthem *Have mercy upon me* (HWV 248) Handel reworked music from the instrumental introduction to 'Vouchsafe, O Lord' in the Utrecht Te Deum, but based the subsequent movement on a rejected aria from another Cannons anthem (HWV 249b). A complementary situation obtains with the setting of 'Vouchsafe, O Lord' here: Handel rethought the opening prelude, but returned in a general way to the main body of the movement from the Utrecht Te Deum when he came to the same text in the Cannons version. In the instrumental introduction the string motifs from the Utrecht music are retained, but their significance is substantially reduced.[80] The flowing quaver bass part, the interrupted cadences, and the descending quaver melody in bar 3 are all new features with no ancestry in the comparable movements from the Utrecht Te Deum and HWV 248. Ex. 6.6 illustrates how Handel recomposed the music of the ensuing movement, taking the first couple of phrases as an example: both versions follow the same general harmonic framework—modulation to the relative major, return to the tonic, interrupted cadence, perfect cadence—but the landmarks are spaced rather differently within the same seven-bar span, and the Cannons version shows a greater sense of harmonic and melodic direction. In overall structure the movement follows the same tripartite plan as before: verse 26 of the Te Deum ends on the relative major of the dominant key; verse 27 moves to the dominant minor; verse 28 returns to the tonic and introduces the chorus voices. However, Handel's treatment of the music is far superior in the Cannons version, and it is perhaps significant that he found more to rewrite in the solo section than in the choral part of the movement.

[79] The preceding bars have some similarities with the Utrecht setting, in the use of the wind instrument obbligato and a comparable metrical treatment of the text, but there are no real 'borrowings'. The opening theme is a development of material previously used in the opening bars of 'Have mercy upon me' in HWV 248.

[80] The complete ritornello in the Utrecht setting is built from these answering figures. In the Cannons Te Deum they appear only in the first two bars, and their character is changed by a new rhythmic disposition and by the different direction of the bass part, now falling instead of rising as previously.

Ex. 6.6. (*a*) Utrecht Te Deum, No. 8; (*b*) Cannons Te Deum, No. 12 (transposed)

7

The King's Return; Handel's Re-establishment at the Chapel Royal

Developments at Court

THE waves of political, social, and domestic pressures at the British court that had swept Handel away from the Chapel Royal after 1714 brought him back again in the 1720s. Much can only be surmised about the forces involved, but the route of Handel's return to the occasional life of the Chapel can be established in relation to the wider background of contemporary court history and musical activity in London.

The reconciliation between the King and the Prince of Wales which took place at court on St Georges's Day 1720 was a rather stage-managed affair, the front-of-house gloss to the backstage drama that had already been played out by Whig politicians.[1] Nevertheless, it brought to an end an uncomfortable chapter in the life of the court. The Prince of Wales was given his guardsmen back, the Wales's were once again acceptable visitors (though not residents) at St James's Palace, and the King no longer refused to see those who also patronized the Prince's court. A gradual movement towards reconciliation had taken place during 1719–20. The formation of the Royal Academy of Music, which drew its Directors from a wide political spectrum,[2] is as symptomatic of the trend towards the reunification of the aristocracy's cultural life as the closure of the opera house in 1717 had been symptomatic of its disintegration. It seems that the Directors of the Royal Academy had a desire to see Handel, as well as the opera company, established in London on a permanent, secure, and well-financed basis.[3] His chances of success were obviously much greater if he had a united source of patronage behind him.[4]

---

[1] See Plumb, *Sir Robert Walpole*, i. 282–92; Hatton, *George I*, 213–16, 245–6.

[2] See Hatton, ibid. 266. For the early history of the Academy, see Dean and Knapp, *Handel's Operas*, ch. 16.

[3] See Deutsch, *Handel*, 89–91.

[4] Handel himself described the foundation of the Academy as something on which all his fortunes depended: see the letter of 20 Feb.1718/19, Deutsch, *Handel*, 84–5.

The timing of the reconciliation in the royal family had a direct effect on Handel's music. He composed the opera *Radamisto* in preparation for the Academy's first season, and Handel himself was regarded as an important factor in the company's potential for success. Yet the Academy opened not with his specially composed opera, but with Giovanni Porta's *Numitore*. The calendar of events thereafter was as follows:

2 April:	first Royal Academy of Music performance, of *Numitore*. Repeat performances on 5, 9, 19, 23 April.[5]
23 April:	the Prince of Wales goes to St James's Palace, and is formally reconciled to the King, meeting in the King's Closet.
24 April (Sunday):	the King and the Prince of Wales attend a Chapel Royal service together for the first time since 1717. At the meeting of the court following the service, Walpole and Townshend are received by the King and accepted into the government.
27 April:	the King and the Prince of Wales go to the first performance of *Radamisto*, whose published word-book contains a dedicatory preface to the King over Handel's name.[6]
1 May:	the King and the Prince of Wales go to the Chapel Royal.
8 May:	the King, Prince, and Princess of Wales go to the Chapel Royal.
11 May:	the King, Prince, and Princess of Wales attend *Radamisto*.
15 May:	the King, Prince, and Princess of Wales go to the Chapel Royal, where an anthem by Clayton is performed.
22 May:	the King, Prince, and Princess of Wales go to the Chapel Royal.
28 May:	the King's Birthday: the King, Prince, and Princess of Wales attend the Drawing Room at court and hear the ode composed by Eccles, with soloists including Francis Hughes and Bernard Gates.
	The King, Prince, and Princess of Wales attend Chapel Royal together each Sunday until the King leaves for Hanover on 14 June. The King and the Prince of Wales also attend performances by French comedians at the Opera House, but not on the same nights. The Princess of Wales and Princess Anne attend *Radamisto* together on 26 May.

It is obvious that the opera calendar was engineered so that *Radamisto* would be the first performance that the King and the Prince attended together after their reconciliation.[7] The sequence of opera productions must have been decided before the beginning of April. The performance on 27 April was the first Academy opera to which the newspapers paid any particular attention: the

---

[5] I have not been able to find any evidence that either the King or the Prince of Wales attended any of these performances. On the printed word-book for *Numitore* Porta is described as 'Virtuoso de S.E. il Signor Duca de Wharton'. Wharton was probably a supporter of the Prince of Wales: see *PB*, 31 Mar.–2 Apr. 1720.

[6] See Deutsch, *Handel*, 103–4, and Harris, *The Librettos*, iii. 5–7.

[7] The postponement of the first performance (see Deutsch, *Handel*, 103), if it occurred, may have been made to suit the Royal family. In view of the correct date on the libretto, however, it seems more likely that the original announcement printed an erroneous date.

coverage is understandable, since it was an occasion of considerable social and political consequence, but it is rather more surprising that the opening of the Academy itself had not been reported as a significant event.[8] Handel must have had good contacts at court who gave him advance information of the reconciliation, which took some politicians by surprise. He had an obvious professional interest, and probably also a personal one, in the affairs of the royal family. The division of 1717 had driven him away from the warring factions at court: the performances of *Radamisto* provided a celebration of the Hanoverian armistice, and it was the only London opera to bear a dedication from the composer. Nevertheless, Handel's return closer to the affairs of the court did not extend immediately to the Chapel Royal; as will be seen, other composers received more favour in the immediately succeeding period. The only special music in the Chapel Royal that is reported during the period following the reconciliation is an anthem by Thomas Clayton, a former court violinist and an insubstantial composer, who had no obvious previous connections with the Chapel. It is uncertain whether Clayton's anthem, or the 'other Musick' that was performed at the same service, involved orchestral accompaniment.[9]

As noted in Chapter 5, Handel received formal patronage from the court, apart from the indirect assistance that he received through the encouragement of the Royal Academy,[10] through the continuance of the annual pension of £200 originally granted by Queen Anne, which was paid to him until his death.[11] No specific duties seem to have been attached to the pension and, if George I had hardly received anything for his money during 1717–20, at least Handel had the good sense to keep out of the court intrigues. Paradoxically William Croft, who had actively supported the musical life of the King's court during the difficult period, received less royal favour after 1720. The possibility that Handel kept up some contact with the royal family at this time by teaching the King's grandchildren needs to be considered. When the Prince of Wales was ejected from St James's in December 1717 his three daughters were retained at the Palace,[12] as a lever by which the King could continue to exert a disciplining influence on his son. A separate establishment for these Princesses was set up by the King, with the Dowager Duchess of Portland as

---

[8] Deutsch, *Handel*, 104–5.

[9] See below, App. F, Service 9.

[10] The King contributed £1,000 per year to the Academy. The financial terms of Handel's association with the Academy are uncertain, but at the foundation it was agreed that he should be 'Master of the Orchestra with a Sallary': see Deutsch, *Handel*, 97.

[11] See Ch. 4 n. 4 and Hunter, 'Royal Patronage'. Such pensions were normally granted 'during pleasure', which usually meant for life, unless the pensioner was involved in political opposition to the court or emigrated.

[12] Anne, Amelia, and Caroline, born in 1709, 1711, and 1713 respectively: see App. D. Prince Frederick (born 1707) remained at Hanover in 1714. The children born to the Prince and

Governess.[13] Inevitably this forcible separation of children from their parents soon became a party issue between the rival supporters of the King and the Prince.[14] In view of this, it hardly seems credible that Handel would have allowed himself to be drawn into a compromising position by accepting a post as Music Master to the Princesses. It is not possible to be completely definite on the matter, since the payments to the Princesses' establishment were made in lump sums to the Governess and therefore do not normally appear in detail in the official Treasury papers,[15] but it is unlikely that Handel was employed in this capacity before 1720. The Princesses' household was listed at its official opening on the King's birthday in May 1719:[16] the appointments include a Dancing Master, a Drawing Master, and a Writing Master, but no Music Master, nor is Handel mentioned by name. The first newspaper reference to Handel holding the position of Music Master to the Princesses comes from August 1724, when Handel took the two eldest Princesses to hear him perform on the organ at St Paul's,[17] and there is a documentary reference to the Princesses' lessons with Handel in June 1723.[18] A picture of the Princesses' apartments that may include a representation of Handel playing the harpsichord shows a scene from the 1720s.[19] There is no doubt that Handel was being paid an annual salary of £200 (in addition to, and separate from, his regular pensions) as Music Master to the Princesses by the end of the reign,[20] and it seems most probable that he took up this role in 1722–3, about the time of the Chapel Royal appointment which is shortly to be described.

Princess of Wales in London after 1717 (William, Mary, and Louisa) lived with their parents at Leicester House.

[13] Princess Anne fulfilled the formal role of hostess for the King's 'Drawing Rooms' after the departure of her mother.

[14] The Princess of Wales was permitted occasional access to her daughters, but this was not granted to her husband, or not taken up by him, for a long time, possibly as long as eighteen months: see Boyer, *The Political State*, xvii. 511, and Hatton, *George I*, 208. The Prince of Wales's family remained divided even after the 1720 reconciliation, and this may have caused some rancour which lasted even after George I's death. There is some doubt as to whether the Countess of Portland was given the expected pension when her services as governess were no longer required in 1727: *WEP*, 26–8 Sept. 1727 expected the Countess to receive a pension, but most London newspapers carried emphatic denials at the end of October that she was to be given one.

[15] GB-Lpro T52/30 et seq.: quarterly payments, usually of £5,000, to Joseph Eyles for the Princesses' establishment under the Countess of Portland.

[16] See *SJEP*, 26–8 May 1719 and Boyer, *The Political State*, xvii. 511–12. Both Handel and the King were out of the country at the time: the ages of the Princesses were 9, 7, and 5.

[17] See Deutsch, *Handel*, 173.

[18] See King, 'On Princess Anne's Lessons with Handel'.

[19] Reproduced in Schazmann, *The Bentincks*. It is not at all certain that the musician at the keyboard is Handel, nor is it easy to establish the ages of the children on the picture.

[20] GB-Lpro T1/260(10), referred to indirectly in Deutsch, *Handel*, 213. The unique survival of this itemized list of the Princesses' establishment can be attributed to the fact that it was a

Special Court Services in the Reign
of King George I

To explain the background to Handel's return to the life of the Chapel, it is necessary to pick up again the story of the occasional services that provided opportunities for the performance of special music. The old style of state Thanksgiving services was discontinued after January 1715, and in any case there were relatively few official Thanksgiving Days to celebrate during the reigns of the first two Georges.[21] Other occasions, however, prompted the introduction of instrumentally accompanied anthems and canticle settings into Chapel Royal services. The most important recurring court occasions of this type were those following the King's return from abroad. There was a precedent in the services of Thanksgiving for the King's 'Safe return to his People' from the 1690s, referred to in Chapter 2, but there was also a fundamental difference. At the earlier period William III was usually returning from the year's military campaign as titular head of the British forces, and the Thanksgiving for his return was usually coupled with sentiments of thanksgiving for the successes (such as they might be made out) of the year and the preservation of the King's person from the dangers of war. George I's visits to Hanover were of a different order: he went there to sustain his role as Prince-Elector and to renew his association with the social activities of the Hanover court. The attention that the King had necessarily to give to his German responsibilities did not enhance his political popularity in London. He also used the visits to advance his diplomatic plans in areas of European foreign policy: these might be variously interpreted as forwarding Hanoverian or British interests, though George I's view was naturally moulded by his pre-1714 experience.[22]

retrospective statement for payment of arrears up to the end of the Countess of Portland's period of management. The Princesses were given a new establishment in the reign of George II: the lists of their household were printed in Chamberlayne's *Magnae Britanniae Notitia*, 29th (1728) edn. and subsequent edns., and the lists include 'Musick Master Mr. George Frederic Handel £200'. See also the reference dated 19 Mar. 1729 (from GB-Lpro T52/37) in King, 'On Princess Anne's Patronage'. No lists of the Princesses' household were published during George I's reign.

[21] Following that on 7 June 1716 (see App. F), there was only one further Thanksgiving day in George I's reign (25 Apr.1723, for preservation from a 'dreadful Plague': no special music reported). Between the accession of George II in 1727 and 1757 two occasions received single Thanksgiving prayers: 17 July 1743 (Dettingen victory) and 4 May 1746 (victory over the rebels in Scotland). There were two full Thanksgiving liturgies during this period: 9 Oct. 1746 (suppression of the rebellion) and 25 Apr. 1749 (Peace of Aix-la-Chapelle). For full details, see Burrows, *Dissertation*, ii. app. 12.

[22] George was deeply committed to his own foreign policy ambitions: see Hatton, *George I*. Contacts with family relations from the Prussian court during the Hanover visits had both personal and diplomatic significance. In the next reign the diplomatic aspect was somewhat

Nevertheless, at least one of the British Secretaries of State usually accompanied him to Hanover, and his need to maintain active contact with his Electorate was recognized with the repeal of the Act forbidding the monarch to leave the country without the consent of Parliament. Although the safe return of the king was an important public matter,[23] it did not merit commemoration with a Thanksgiving Day, and liturgies were not issued as they had been for William III. Nevertheless, there was normally considerable activity at St James's Palace in the days after the king's arrival, including a well-attended gathering at the first court Drawing Room and at the dinner on the Sunday after his return. (The King was described as 'dining in public', which presumably meant that he was available to those who had access to the court, rather than dining in the seclusion of his own apartments.) It is therefore not surprising that the morning services at the Chapel Royal on these Sundays, which preceded the dinner, received some form of celebratory enhancement.

The documentary evidence for all of the special services during George I's reign involving the Chapel Royal is summarized in Appendix F, including what is known about the music performed at these services. Services 1–5 have been considered in Chapters 5 and 6. The combined silence of the official records and the newspapers after the King's first return from Hanover (Service 6, 20 January 1716/17) is strong circumstantial evidence that no special music was performed, and none can be identified from musical sources. It is possible that Handel himself went abroad while the King was in Hanover, though this is not supported by any evidence from the newspapers, or from the surviving official records of the British and Hanoverian courts.[24] He may have travelled in one or both directions with the court party, but none of his music is known to have been performed in Hanover during the King's visit.[25] It seems much

reduced, except in the matter of negotiating royal marriages, but George II took part in a military campaign during his 1743 visit: see Ch. 14.

[23] Apart from the fact that the King's presence promoted stability in the face of possible Jacobite plots, the return of the monarch also had important constitutional significance, in that power was immediately returned from the Guardian of the Realm and the Commissioners who had acted on the King's behalf during his absence.

[24] Handel's name does not appear at all in the records of the King's journeys. Such evidence as there is (admittedly thin) for Handel's 1716 visit is summarized in Schoelcher, *The Life of Handel*, 44–5: the two sources (Coxe, *Anecdotes* and Mattheson, *Grundlage*) may both be unreliable. The best evidence for Handel's visit seems to lie in his withdrawal of his South Sea dividend (see Deutsch, *Handel*, 71), which might imply a forthcoming excursion; it is perhaps significant that Mainwaring, *Memoirs* makes no mention of Handel leaving the country until 1719.

[25] I have searched the Hanover archives in vain for any reference to Handel during the King's visit. The only identifiable major theatrical performance was of Destouches's comedy *Le Médisant*: see Wallbrecht, *Das Theater*, 225. Wallbrecht's section dealing with Handel (176–7) goes no further than 1714, and I interpret her silence as confirmation that there are no references to Handel in the Hanoverian theatrical papers after 1712.

more likely that, if he indeed travelled abroad, Handel used the opportunity to visit old haunts in Halle or Hamburg rather than to stay with the King in Hanover. There is nothing to suggest that he wrote any music to celebrate the King's return to London in January 1717, nor that anyone at court thought that a musical celebration was specially called for: although the court was well attended on the day after the King's return, there was no special commemoration.

The situation was different when the King returned from his next visit, in November 1719. The rivalry between the King's court and that of the Prince of Wales was still of considerable importance at that time, and there was therefore a special incentive for the King's court to make itself as attractive and influential as possible. If anyone had thought of asking Handel for music to celebrate the King's return, the composer was not there to be asked, since he was in Europe gathering singers for the Royal Academy and he did not return to London until after the King.[26] It is not surprising to find that Croft provided the music for the relevant Chapel Royal service: Croft was the Chapel Royal Composer with the appropriate experience—indeed, he had already composed a repertory of suitable music—and he had faithfully fulfilled the musical demands of the King's court since the ejection of the Prince of Wales.[27] The service on 15 November 1719 set important precedents. It established the practice of celebrating the King's return with concerted music in the Chapel Royal, and it set the scale of the vocal and orchestral forces for future performances: in so doing it also established the practice of employing additional performers. In all subsequent performances of the same type the Chapel Royal singers and the King's Musicians were supplemented with a few additional players who received payments that are recorded in the Warrant Books of the Lord Chamberlain's department.

A year later Croft again provided similar music for the Chapel Royal service on the first Sunday following the King's return from Hanover.[28] In the meantime, some of his orchestrally accompanied music had also been included in the Chapel Royal service attended by the King on New Year's Day 1720: there appears to have been no precedent for special music at the New Year

[26] The exact date of Handel's return is unknown, but it is doubtful that he was back in London by the end of 1719. The main purpose of his visit had been to secure singers for the new opera company, and the Royal Academy did not order him back to England until their meeting on 27 Nov., nearly a fortnight after the King's return.

[27] See Ch. 6. The second Chapel Royal Composer of the period, John Weldon, seems to have left the musical duties for all the major events to Croft.

[28] See the reports of the service on 13 Nov. 1720, reproduced in App. G. *WJSP*, 12 Nov., reported that there had been an unsuccessful attempt to assassinate the King while he was in Germany, and this probably explains the reference in *WEP*, 10–12 Nov., to 'Deliverance from his Enemies'.

service, nor did it recur in subsequent years.[29] After that, however, Croft falls
away from such events at the Chapel as suddenly and as certainly as Handel had
done in 1715, and with as little evidence to explain it. Croft was certainly not
inactive in the following years: he was busy preparing the scores of his Oxford
Doctoral odes and of *Musica Sacra*, an anthology of his anthems, for publication,[30] and he appears to have continued his routine work in the Chapel. His
verse anthem *Blessed are all they that fear the Lord* was performed in January 1725
at the first Chapel Royal service that the Princess of Wales attended after the
birth of Princess Louisa;[31] later in the same year his orchestrally accompanied
anthem *Rejoice in the Lord, O ye righteous* and his Te Deum were performed in
Westminster Abbey at the first installation service for the revived Order of the
Bath.[32] His last known composition, the anthem *Give the King thy judgements*,
was composed a month before his death in August 1727 and may have been
intended for the forthcoming coronation.[33] If so, it may be significant that it is
a normal verse anthem without orchestral accompaniment, as if Croft expected
that someone else would be called upon to write the large-scale music that
had been his responsibility in 1714. Within the Chapel Royal itself, however, Croft's orchestrally accompanied church music was not heard again
after 1720.[34]

There is no direct evidence to explain Croft's loss of initiative, but we can
trace some of the events that worked against him. Most likely there was a
combination of circumstances, involving Croft's withdrawal and some competition among the musicians who saw an opportunity for their own advancement. The reconciliation between the King and the Prince of Wales reopened
the normal opportunities for patronage, making it possible once again for a
musician to put himself forward to the court without necessarily becoming

[29] The King usually attended the Chapel Royal service of Morning Prayer on New Year's
Day.

[30] An advertisement in *PB*, 5–8 Mar. 1720, indicates that engraving of the music was already
in progress by then, though *Musica Sacra* (eventually in two volumes) was not published until
1724–6. See Johnstone, 'Music and Drama', 207.

[31] *PB*, 12–14 Jan. 1725. This anthem, possibly in a slightly different version, had also been
performed at a similar service in 1721 after the birth of Prince William: see *A Collection of
Anthems*, 1724, and Burrows, 'Sir John Dolben', 150–1.

[32] *EP*, 15–17 June 1725, and *SJEP*, 17–19 June. The King was out of the country at the time,
but the Prince of Wales was present. Croft was also Organist at Westminster Abbey.

[33] Though not necessarily so: the new King and Queen attended their first Chapel Royal
service at St James's on 25 June, and Croft's anthem may have been intended as a topical offering
for a subsequent Sunday morning service. This does not affect the substance of the argument:
Croft may have felt the need to produce special Chapel Royal anthems as the result of
discovering the Coronation music was being taken away from him.

[34] It is possible that the delay in the publication of Croft's scores (see n. 30) was in some way
connected with his loss of leadership in the Chapel, or with a personal problem that limited his
activity in both areas.

involved in intrigues and the attendant dangers of offending influential parties. In 1713 Handel had brought himself to the notice of the court and wider London society with the Utrecht canticles: in 1721 it appears that Maurice Greene set out to promote himself in the same way, probably with the assistance of some aristocratic patrons who had influence at court. The King did not go to Germany in 1721, so there was no special service on his return, but somehow Greene managed to arrange for the inclusion his music in a Chapel Royal service that the King attended during the summer.[35] Greene had been Organist of St Paul's Cathedral since 1718, and he regularly composed and directed performances of orchestrally accompanied anthems and canticles at the Cathedral for the annual service of the Festival of the Sons of the Clergy.[36] The 1721 Chapel Royal service brought his music before the King, and Greene no doubt had his sights on an eventual court appointment.[37] From the payments to additional performers it is apparent that the scale of Greene's performance followed the patterns established in the two previous services celebrating the King's return from Hanover. It is not known which music of Greene's was performed: he may have repeated or adapted some of his earlier pieces from the Sons of the Clergy Festivals. (The same soloists would have been involved in performances at the Chapel Royal and at St Paul's.) As far as the evidence of the Public Records goes, Greene himself did not receive any immediate reward. He came into his own at the Chapel after Croft's death in 1727, when he succeeded him as Organist and Composer, and the 1721 service probably gave him the necessary introduction at court.

The newspapers are tantalizingly silent about the music that was performed in October 1722 on the occasion of the next special Chapel Royal service. As far as we know, Greene was not involved, and Croft did not resume his old position. This was almost certainly due to reintroduction of Handel's music in the Chapel. The evidence for this lies in a warrant for Handel's appointment as 'Composer of Musick for His Majesty's Chappel Royal' (see Fig. 7.1).[38] The warrant is dated 25 February 1722/3, a couple of days after Handel's thirty-eighth birthday and thirteen days after a warrant for payments to extra performers for the Chapel Royal service in October 1722. This appointment must

[35] The sermon at this service was preached by John Hoadly. The Hoadly family were supporters of Greene, and John Hoadly junior (nephew of the 1721 preacher) was later the author of libretti for Greene: see *NG II*, Greene. It was rather unusual for the court to be at St James's in July; the summer move to Kensington was made surprisingly late in 1721, on 2 Aug.

[36] From 1719 to 1730 Greene's music shared the honours only with Purcell's famous D major canticles: here again, Croft was the loser.

[37] This matter is considered further in Ch. 10. By 1736 Greene had acquired all the major court appointments available to a musician.

[38] The copy of warrant (GB-Lpro LC3/63, p. 282) was first discovered by the present writer in 1975.

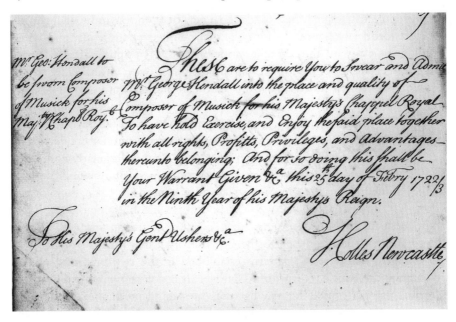

Fig. 7.1. Copy of the warrant for Handel's appointment as 'Composer of Musick for his Majesty's Chappel Royal', 25 February 1722/3. Public Record Office, LC3/63, p. 282

surely have followed Handel's re-entry into the life of the Chapel, and the 1722 service is the only relevant occasion of the period to which he can have contributed. Subsequent events provide retrospective confirmation of his status in the musical life of the Chapel: during the remainder of George I's reign, Handel's music was performed at each of the Chapel Royal services celebrating the King's return from Hanover.[39] The appointment may have come at about the same time that Handel was appointed Music Master to the Royal Princesses, and also at a period when he may have considered that his future in London was more secure: in the opera company he was making a better showing than the other house composers, Bononcini and Ariosti,[40] and in the summer of 1723 he moved into the house in Brook Street that was to be his home for the rest of his life.

[39] There is ample documentary evidence for this in 1723/4: see App. I. In 1725/6 Handel is not named, but the presence of 'Christopher' Smith's name as one of the additional performers is sufficient to establish that Handel's music was involved. During the period 1720–60 Smith's name appears in the documentation of the Lord Chamberlain's Department only in connection with Handel performances.

[40] Dean and Knapp, *Handel's Operas*, 314, 318.

Handel's Chapel Royal Appointment

No mention of Handel's appointment is found in the Chapel Royal Cheque Books. His place was an addition to the regular strength, which already included two incumbent Composers, and the instructions on the warrant make it clear that it was a 'court', rather than 'Chapel' appointment. Chapel Royal appointees were sworn in by the Sub-Dean, who periodically forwarded certificates of appointment to the Lord Chamberlain for inclusion in the general departmental records.[41] The instruction for Handel's admission was issued to the Gentlemen Ushers, who dealt with admission to the 'Servants of the King above Stairs', such as the King's Chaplains, Chemists, and Tailors. Nor does Handel's name appear in the usual accounting system through the Lord Chamberlain's department relating to the Chapel Royal. There are no salary payments to Handel as Composer for the Chapel in the Public Records, but a sudden leap in Handel's annual pension from £200 to £400 is a disguised payment for this office. (The original £200 was, of course, the pension granted by Queen Anne.) Handel's £400 pension began from 25 March 1723, when a new list was established.[42] There had apparently been a plan in 1714, during the last months of Queen Anne's reign, to appoint Thomas Tudway as a third Composer for the Chapel Royal establishment.[43] An uncompleted draft warrant for this survives,[44] whose wording suggests that the intended appointment of a third Composer was regarded as innovative: Tudway was to 'continue during our pleasure, any Article or Clause in the Book of Establishm[en]t of our Chappels to the contrary thereof notwithstanding'. Tudway was never appointed and, as with Handel, the post may have been intended as honorific rather than functional, but there was a significant difference: the warrant showed that Tudway was to receive the regular salary of a Chapel Royal Composer at £73 per year.

---

[41] Copies of these certificates are therefore found in the Admissions Books, GB-Lpro LC3/63–65. Under exceptional circumstances the admissions were made by the Dean, or an approved deputy to the Sub-Dean. For the procedure, see Ashbee and Harley, ii. 50.

[42] GB-Lpro T52/32, p. 364 et seq.: 'An Establishment of certain Annual Pensions and Bountys, which Our Pleasure is shall commence from the 25th Day of March 1723 and be paid and accounted payable Quarterly during our Pleasure, and apon the Death of any of the Persons receiving the same or other determination of our Pleasure therein', and on p. 368: 'George Frederick Handel [£]400 – –'.

[43] In 1702 Tudway had petitioned unsuccessfully for an appointment as third Organist for the Chapel Royal (Ashbee, *Records*, viii. 300). According to Hawkins (*A General History*, ii. 795), Tudway 'obtained permission to style himself composer and organist extraordinary to Queen Anne.'

[44] GB-Lbl Add. MS 70267, folder misc. 46.

The unusual nature of Handel's appointment explains the apparently anomalous entries in the tables of court office-holders published in John Chamberlayne's *Magna Britanniae Notitia* that have puzzled some of his biographers.[45] It is not surprising that Chamberlayne did not catch up with Handel's appointment in time for the 1723 (26th) edition. It was also omitted in the next edition, dated 1726,[46] but in the 28th edition (1727) a single-line entry 'Composer of Musick for the Chapel Royal Mr. George Handel' appears on p. 29, not with the Chapel Royal lists, but in the section devoted to Above Stairs Servants, immediately after the list of the King's Musicians and in company with the Instrument Keeper (William Norton), Instrument Maker (Walsh), Organ Maker (Shrider), and Tuner of the Organs (Croft).[47] Because Handel was rewarded through a pension, his Chapel Royal appointment was effectively lost from the routine Treasury/Audit system of court accounts, as his name did not appear in the regular itemized lists of payments to the King's Servants. Administratively speaking, if a Composer for the Chapel Royal was not paid as such, he did not exist. This explains the confusion in subsequent editions of Chamberlayne's work. Having included the entry for Handel as Composer in the 1727 list, Chamberlayne lost the scent, presumably because he based his published work on lists supplied from the court:[48] the next two editions (1728 and 1729) have blank entries for the Chapel Royal Composer in the parallel place. The appearance of Greene's name from the 31st (1735) edition onwards seems to have been a rationalization from the information in the Chapel Royal list: in 1727 he had been appointed as one of the Composers in the regular way. Later court records reveal that Handel continued to be paid his £400 pension for the rest of his life; there is no evidence that Greene ever received an additional payment of the same sort outside the normal run of Chapel Royal salaries.

One reason for the irregular manner of Handel's appointment may have been the provision in the Act of Settlement of 1701, to which George I owed his title to the British throne, that 'no person born out of the kingdoms of

---

[45] The state of knowledge prior to my investigations of the Public Records is summarized in William C. Smith, *Concerning Handel*, 52–3; the most thoroughgoing previous work on Chamberlayne's lists had been Chrysander, 'Der Bestand'. Smith's knowledge of the Treasury documents was largely based on the printed Calendars of Treasury documents, ed. William A. Shaw. Handel's £400 pension continues to appear regularly in the lists from George II's reign: see Hunter, 'Royal Patronage'.

[46] Chamberlayne's lists were often out of date, but the Chapel Royal list in this edition was more current than most.

[47] The lists obviously represent the period in the early part of 1727, before Croft's death.

[48] Chamberlayne's source, directly or indirectly, may have been GB-Lpro LC3/7. The entry on fo. 21ʳ for Handel as Composer of Musick for the Chappel Royal, accompanied by the warrant date, in this list of court appointees is particularly interesting because it directly couples the appointment with the payment of £200 under the 'Treasury' column.

England, Scotland or Ireland, or the dominions thereunto belonging (although he be naturalised or made a denizen, except such as be born of English parents) shall…enjoy any office or place of trust, either civil or military.'[49] It is doubtful that this was applied strictly in some areas—the King's Musicians, for example, included a number of people with foreign names—but the appointment of Handel to a regular (and prominent) salaried court post might have attracted unwelcome political attention in view of sensitivities over undue Hanover influence. In any case, there was no question of Handel performing the same sort of duties as the two established Chapel Royal Composers, taking his turn on the rota in the Chapel for the daily services.[50] The Chapel was one of the most 'English' parts of the court establishment and Handel, who was not at that stage even a member of the Church of England, would probably not have been acceptable to the Dean and Sub-Dean even if the legal obstacles had been overcome. The Chapel Royal service on 7 October 1722 was the first occasion with orchestrally accompanied music since the appointment of Edmund Gibson as Dean of the Chapel. Whether or not Gibson approved of such musical activity, the process of Handel's appointment was probably intended from the first to avoid any interference from the Chapel's clerical authorities.[51]

Since the warrant resulted not in a conventional salaried position, in either the Chapel Royal or the Above Stairs servants of the court, but in remuneration through a pension, it is not surprising that it did not generate the subsequent documentation that was normal for members of staff in the Lord Chamberlain's department. In that respect, the warrant was not executed in the normal manner, but the procedures were sidestepped rather than abandoned. Handel may well have been sworn in and admitted to the 'place and quality' of the post, taking the Oath of Allegiance, in order to give him the title of 'Composer of Music for the Chapel Royal'. The title would have had resonances for both the composer and the Hanoverian family with that of 'Kapellmeister', which at many German courts generally implied a wider range of responsibility for court music-making than that relating only to the private chapel: indeed, it had been Handel's title at Hanover.[52] Probably both Handel

[49] E. Neville Williams, *The Eighteenth-Century Constitution*, 59. This clause was originally intended to prevent William III from filling court places with Dutchmen.

[50] There had been three Chapel Royal Organists at the time of Charles II's coronation in 1661 (*OCB*, fo. 44ʳ; Ashbee and Harley, i. 120), so there would have been a precedent for a third appointment within the normal establishment, if this had been envisaged.

[51] From the wording of the warrant, the same may also have been true of Tudway's intended appointment. I take a different view of Handel's Chapel Royal appointment from that given in Hunter, 'Royal Patronage'.

[52] If the appointment was intended to give Handel a broader remit for the court's music, his sphere of action would have been limited by the traditional rights and duties of the Master of the

and members of the royal family wanted to ensure that he had a title that implied comparable status in London, and would be understood as such on continental Europe.[53] In that case the title itself would have been regarded as significant, and the procedure that was adopted was a way of securing the desired result through the administrative system of a court that did not have any precedent in this area. In practice, the appointment carried relatively light and occasional duties, though these were associated with high-profile events and sometimes required substantial musical compositions. Most importantly, the appointment gave both the composer and the royal family the grounds for Handel's future participation in special services involving the court.

There were currents in the musical and political life of London society that may have prompted and supported Handel's appointment at this time. One of the most significant events of the preceding year had been the funeral of the Duke of Marlborough. The Duke died in June 1722, and his funeral took place in Westminster Abbey on 9 August, with a pomp and magnificence that certainly made it the most memorable church service of the year for the London musicians.[54] Handel was not asked to compose the music. The newspapers heralded the event thus:

The Dean of Westminster has appointed Dr. Croft's to compose an Anthem on that Occasion: the Deans and Prebends are to walk in their Copes as upon a Coronation, and Dr. Croft's in his mantle; and we hear the Choirs of St. James's and St. Paul's are likewise to attend. (*EP*, 26–8 July 1722)

In the event the most important music for the funeral was composed by Bononcini: his anthem, *When Saul was king*, was performed in King Henry VII's Chapel at the Abbey by a large force of instrumentalists and singers, the latter led by Weely, Freeman, Gates, Laye, and Baker from the Chapel Royal, and Charles King from St Paul's.[55] Croft's Burial Service was also performed.[56] The rehearsals and the service received a great deal of attention in the press,

Music in relation to court odes. One area that is unclear is the extent to which he may have contributed music for court balls.

[53] See the references to Handel as 'Capellmeister' in German sources from Scheibe and Dreyhaupt, in Deutsch, *Handel*, 470, 768.

[54] The event, which was on the scale of a state funeral, cost the Duchess more than £5,000: see Hibbert, *The Marlboroughs*, 318.

[55] The Chapel Royal soloists, named in *DP*, 8 Aug. 1722 and elsewhere, were all also members of the Westminster Abbey choir. Reports on the size of the orchestra vary between '38 Pieces of Musick' (*SJEP*, 7–9 Aug.) and '46 Violins, 13 Bass Viols and other Musical Instruments' (*PM*, 7–9 Aug.), but leave no doubt that a sizeable force was employed. Bononcini was paid £100 for composing the anthem.

[56] The first part was performed during the opening procession, possibly by the Westminster Abbey choir alone (see Boyer, *The Political State*, xxiv. 150–1). Croft published the Burial Service in *Musica Sacra*, i (1724), but this may have been a revision of music originally composed for the funerals of Prince George (1708: see Ch. 2, p. 41) or Queen Anne (1714).

and indeed the funeral was a major public event.[57] The Prince and Princess of Wales, with their three eldest daughters, watched the funeral procession from houses in Pall Mall, but the King did not turn out, nor was any public mourning ordered in honour of the national hero.[58] The Duchess of Marlborough's consistent support for Bononcini, which culminated in the commission for the anthem, was part of a wider web of political and social intrigue,[59] so perhaps the King had a motive for rewarding his own favoured composer to counterbalance her patronage of Bononcini.

On 24 August, just over a fortnight after the Duke of Marlborough's funeral, Francis Atterbury, the Dean of Westminster who had been in charge of the arrangements for the Duke's funeral, was committed to the Tower of London on a charge of high treason. This event marked the mid-point in the exposure of a Jacobite plot in which Atterbury was certainly involved.[60] For political reasons Robert Walpole magnified the seriousness of the Jacobite threat, but it was true enough that in 1722 the Hanoverian court faced its most serious challenge since the 1715 rebellion, and Walpole's fears found many echoes in Parliament and at court. The first public references to the plot had been made at the beginning of May,[61] and early rumours of its seriousness were sufficient to force George I to cancel his intended visit to Hanover.[62] He went to Kensington for the summer instead, leaving St James's Palace on 1 June.[63] When the court returned on 5 October Atterbury had not yet been brought to trial, but the immediate danger was clearly over. It was appropriate to the mood of the moment that the King's safe return to St James's should be celebrated with a service in the Chapel Royal comparable to those that normally followed his return from Hanover. Handel's contribution therefore

[57] Nearly every London newspaper published between 26 July and 11 Aug. included some reference to the music, and many printed the text of Bononcini's anthem.

[58] The King and the Prince of Wales were officially represented in the funeral procession by the presence of their coaches, but it may have been against court protocol for them to be present at the funeral in person. Hatton (*George I*, 122) considered that there was no personal animosity between the King and the Duke.

[59] See Lindgren, 'The Three Great Noises'. Although the Marlborough family were Whigs, there was also a substantial Whig lobby that distrusted their influence.

[60] See Fritz, *The English Ministers*, chs. 7 and 8. The charge of treason against Atterbury could not be sustained, and his eventual sentence of deportation was made on the strength of the rather unsatisfactory Bill of Pains and Penalties. Evidence now available shows that Walpole's instinct that Atterbury was a dangerous man was correct: he had been an important agent for Jacobite plans since at least 1716 (ibid. 18–19).

[61] Walpole's investigations were in full swing by then: he had stepped up the pressure after the death of the Earl of Sunderland on 19 Apr.

[62] Fritz, *The English Ministers*, 83. *WEP*, 10–12 May: 'We hear, the King has laid aside his Intention of going to Hanover this Summer': it had previously been expected that the King would leave London soon after the celebrations for his birthday on 28 May.

[63] *PM*, 31 May–2 June.

came at a time when the King was most likely to favour his supporters and allies: no doubt some of the new names on the 1723 pension list were being rewarded for their part in pursuing the Jacobite plot. Handel's petition for naturalization four years later said that he 'hath constantly professed the Protestant Religion, and hath given Testimony of his Loyalty and Fidelity to His Majesty and the good of this Kingdom'. He was demonstrating these allegiances at the Chapel Royal service in October 1722. It is possible that the political intensity at this time worked against Croft while it flowed in Handel's favour, for Croft may have been regarded as too close an associate of Atterbury's, through his connections at Westminster Abbey and, more specifically, through the patronage that he had received from Sir John Dolben, the former Sub-Dean of the Chapel Royal and an undoubted friend of Atterbury's. That Croft was in some difficulties around 1721–2 is indicated by the delay to the publications of his music;[64] in terms of the most important Chapel Royal events, he may have been outmanoeuvred momentarily by Greene in 1721, but the longer-term effect was to provide an opening for Handel.

Such were the terms of the Act of Settlement, quoted above, that Handel's successful petition for naturalization in February 1727 made no difference to his status with regard to office-holding, and it is doubtful that his decision to pursue naturalization was stimulated by the desire to advance his position within the Chapel establishment: this matter will be considered further in Chapter 10.

Handel's Chapel Royal Music from the Second Period

The music composed by Handel for Chapel Royal services of the 1720s can be readily identified. A consistent group of soloists is named by Handel on the autographs, and the orchestral accompaniments have a characteristic scoring for strings (including violas) with solo woodwind players.[65] The repertory is as follows:

I will magnify thee (HWV 250b)
    singers named: Hughes, Gethin, Weely
    orchestra: oboe, strings

As pants the hart (HWV 251c)
    singers named: Hughes, Bell, Gethin, Weely, Baker, Edwards
    orchestra: oboe, strings (including double bass)

---

[64] See n. 30.
[65] All of the works also include organ continuo.

Let God arise (HWV 256b)
 singers named: Hughes, Weely
 orchestra: oboe, bassoon, strings (including double bass)

A Major Te Deum (HWV 282)
 singers named: Hughes, Bell, Gethin, Weely, Gates
 orchestra: flute, oboe, bassoon, strings

To this list must also be added:

Caroline Te Deum (HWV 280): revival of the earlier work with a new substitute movement
'Vouchsafe, O Lord': see Chapter 5.
 singer named: Hughes
 orchestra: Flute, strings

As pants the hart (HWV 251d)
 singers named: Hughes, Bell, Weely, Gates
 accompanied by basso continuo (organ and violoncello named on the autograph)

Hughes, the principal soloist for all of these works, ceased to be active soon
after 1730, and Gethin emigrated in 1732. Bell was not associated with the
Chapel until 1719/20.[66] Handel ceased to provide music routinely for Chapel
Royal services celebrating the King's return after the accession of George II in
1727,[67] so the complete group of works can be attributed with confidence to
the years 1720–7. The autographs are not dated, and there is no direct evidence
that would establish the chronological distribution of this music over the three
Chapel Royal services in 1722, 1724, 1726 (services 12–14 of App. F) for which
Handel provided the music. Nor do the texts of the anthems provide any
assistance in this matter: none is particularly more suitable for the service in a
specific year, though the moods of the psalm texts may have had topical
resonances. Rubrics in the Prayer Book specified a daily sequence for the
recitation of all of the Psalms each month, but there are no convincing matches
between the anthem texts and the dates of particular services.[68] This is not
surprising: the moment of the King's return to London was unpredictable, and
in any case Handel's music would have been performed in Morning Prayer at
the places where the Prayer Book liturgy provided for the canticles and an
anthem, rather than where the Psalms were designated.

There is nevertheless a limited amount of evidence, from the musical
sources and from the documentary information that is summarized in App.
F, that enables a conjectural reconstruction of the sequence of Handel's pieces

---

[66] See App. C for biographical details of all the soloists named.
[67] See below, App. H. I have found no references to any other special Chapel Royal services
before 1733 for which Handel might have provided music.
[68] The same is true of the Cannons anthems. This situation is in marked contrast to the
identification of J. S. Bach's church cantatas with specific Sundays in the Lutheran calendar.

from this period. (The documentary records of payments from the Lord
Chamberlain's Department are transcribed in App. I.) The autographs of the
A major Te Deum and *Let God arise* (HWV 256b) have identical paper and
handwriting characteristics, so they were presumably composed together for
performance at the same service. The instrumentation of the Te Deum and
HWV 256b includes a bassoon part with a substantial solo role; the payments
for extra performers in 1722 do not include a bassoon player, and therefore
these pieces cannot have been performed in that year. In 1724 Handel was paid
for 'the Anthem' and the newspaper reports, though ambiguous, seem to
suggest that the anthem was new but the Te Deum setting was not necessarily
original; the 1724 payment was presumably for music-copying, comparable to
the one made in 1726 to Smith for 'the Te Deum'. The payment in 1726 was
about twice the size of the previous one. The obvious inference is that in 1726
both the Te Deum and the anthem were new, and therefore needed to have
performing parts copied: in 1724 the anthem was new, but the Te Deum may
have been a revival, using pre-existing parts. This leads to the conclusion that
the A Major Te Deum and HWV 256b were probably performed in 1726. It
may be noted in passing that the 1724 service was the first one of its type for
which copying charges were recorded: presumably Croft in 1719 and 1720,
Greene in 1721, and Handel in 1722 had had to pay their own copying costs.

   The payments for additional performers reveal that Handel employed a
slightly different orchestra from that used by Croft and Greene in previous
years. In particular there was a move away from using the trumpets. Handel's
Caroline Te Deum, which has trumpet parts, was revived at one (or possibly
two) of these services (see Ch. 5), and this would have been perfectly feasible if
the music for solo trumpet was reallocated to the oboe.[69] The absence of
payments to flautists in the official records is not necessarily significant: the
flute parts in the Caroline Te Deum and the A Major Te Deum could have
been played by Kytch or by a 'double-handed' string player. The paper
characteristics of the autographs do not provide conclusive evidence on the
distribution of the music between 1722 and 1724.[70] There are some grounds
for suggesting that HWV 251c was composed first, for 1722,[71] in which case
HWV 250b followed in 1724. The Caroline Te Deum could have been
revived in 1722 or 1724, or both.

---

   [69] As noted in Ch. 6, Handel successfully dealt with the trumpet solos of the Utrecht Jubilate
by giving them to oboe when he reduced the scoring for Cannons. The same procedure could
have been used in the Caroline Te Deum, which has no independent woodwind parts in the
'trumpet' movements.

   [70] For full details, see Burrows, *Dissertation*, i. 265–6, and Burrows and Ronish, *Catalogue*.

   [71] It is, for example, the only work from the period with a separate opening sinfonia, a feature
that may be a legacy from the Cannons version.

Putting all of this together, the following tentative scheme for the three services results:

7–10–1722:   *As pants the hart* (HWV 251c), ?and Caroline Te Deum
5–1–1723/4:   *I will magnify thee* (HWV 250b), ?and Caroline Te Deum
16–1–1725/6:   A Major Te Deum, and *Let God arise* (HWV 256b)

It will be seen that my suggested programme for 1724 does not include any works with independent bassoon parts, although a bassoon player was paid for the service in that year. The bassoon presumably just strengthened the continuo line in 1724,[72] but Handel was stimulated to provide something more imaginative on the next occasion. An outstanding player may have been involved in 1726, for the role of the bassoon in the A Major Te Deum and *Let God arise* is substantial. Handel's predilection for two double basses in all three performances (as against the single bass employed by his predecessors) is noteworthy.

If the suggested chronology is correct, there emerges the remarkable possibility that Handel began each major group of his English church music so far examined with a version of *As pants the hart*: HWV 251a was his first Chapel Royal work from the early period (*c*.1712), HWV 251b his first Cannons anthem (*c*.1717), and HWV 251c his first orchestrally accompanied Chapel Royal anthem from the second period (*c*.1722).[73] HWV 251a may have been the English work that first brought him to the attention of the court, and initiated his association with the Chapel Royal singers; HWV 251c may have been the work that ultimately led to his Chapel Royal title and the doubling of his pension. The case for suggesting that HWV 251c was the first in Handel's series of orchestral anthems from the 1720s is strengthened by its relationship to the one non-orchestral anthem of the period, HWV 251d. These two anthems are the subject of the next chapter, and the remaining music is considered in Chapter 9, in the order suggested above. For each of the occasions on which Handel's music was performed in the Chapel Royal, the same conditions of performance can be assumed as in the previous decade (see Ch. 5), the only important difference being that we have slightly better information about the orchestra as a result of the records of payments for additional players.

When composing this music Handel picked up the trail that he had started with the Caroline Te Deum and *O sing unto the Lord* in 1714: settings of anthems and canticles specifically designed for performance in the Chapel

[72] The bassoon would have played from a part like many of those in the 'Aylesford' sets, extracted by the copyist from the general orchestral bass part.
[73] Compare the compositional procedure in Handel's use of borrowings and 'generating themes' suggested in Abraham, *Handel*, 262–74.

Royal by the Chapel's singers and an instrumental group founded on the King's Musicians. However, his musical materials were to a large extent derived from the intervening anthems and canticles that he had composed for Cannons, which he refashioned to make new pieces suitable for the circumstances of the Chapel. For that reason, the format for the descriptions for the works in Chapters 8 and 9 will treat the movements individually. As far as we can tell, allowing for the imperfect documentation of the music by Clayton and Greene that was performed in 1720–1, Handel was not significantly influenced by the various orchestrally accompanied anthems and canticles that had been performed there between 1716 and 1721. He did not reset the texts from any of Croft's three orchestrally accompanied anthems from that period, nor was he influenced creatively by their music, in which Croft had developed his own style. *Rejoice in the Lord, O ye righteous* has a broader harmonic style than Croft's previous anthems, for which a general influence from Handel's music may have been responsible, but there is no evidence of traffic in the opposite direction.

8

New Versions of As pants the hart

THIS chapter is concerned with the versions of *As pants the hart* that Handel composed during the 1720s. It will refer also to his other settings of the anthem, because the topic relates both to the chronology of the various versions and to the processes of composition in which Handel utilized or rejected material from his preceding settings of the text. The versions will be identified by letters deriving from the suffixes to the HWV numbers in the thematic catalogue.[1] These differ from the letters designated by Friedrich Chrysander for 'Anthem 6' in the Händelgesellschaft edition, to which reference has often been made in previous literature on the subject.

A = HWV 251a (early verse anthem = *HG* Anthem 6C)
B = HWV 251b (Cannons anthem = *HG* Anthem 6A)
C = HWV 251c (anthem with orchestra = *HG* Anthem 6B)
D = HWV 251d (later verse anthem = *HG* Anthem 6D)

Handel produced a further version based on a revision of HWV 251c: the history of this version had not been established when the HWV catalogue was prepared, but the music was subsequently published in the Hallische Händel-Ausgabe volume of Chapel Royal anthems with the designation HWV 251e, and it will be referred to as version E.[2] Versions A and B have been considered in Chapters 3 and 6 respectively; this chapter will be mainly concerned with versions C and D, but also with E because the musical sources for that version are entangled with those for C. In order to trace the course of Handel's treatment of the anthem text in the 1720s, it is necessary first to establish the order in which he composed versions C and D.

---

[1] *HHB*, ii. 692–9.
[2] *HHA* III/9, ed. Gerald Hendrie (Kassel, 1993); the versions HWV 251c and 251e were first distinguished in my edition of *As pants the hart* for *NHE* (1988).

Anthems HWV 251d and HWV 251c: Order of Composition, and Function

In an important article on Handel's versions of *As pants the hart*, published in 1931,[3] Paul Mies described the two versions of *As pants the hart* without orchestral accompaniment as sketches, and saw the relationship of the versions thus: $A \rightarrow D {\overset{B}{\underset{C}{<}}}$. Neither of these assumptions is correct. Versions A and D are complete works of the verse anthem type, certainly not 'unready and unfinished'.[4] Nor can D have been written before B: the presence of Bell's name on the autograph of D gives the *terminus ante quem* as 1720, about three years after the Cannons version. Schoelcher had previously interpreted the chronology of the four versions more accurately from the evidence of the singers' names: he guessed that D was written in 1721 and C in 1727, though giving no reason for these dates.[5] The chronological sequence of versions A, B, and C is not in any doubt, but the position of D in the sequence demands attention. Two alternative positions are possible. Either D was composed in the period 1720–2, before C, or it was composed later, between 1722 and *c.*1730. The motives for the composition of D must also be considered. If Handel had intended it as a contribution to the routine repertory for the daily services of the Chapel Royal, then it might have been composed at any time during the 1720s.

Reference must be made at this point to some strange titles that were added to manuscript copies of version A in the 1770s,[6] which obviously reflected a belief on someone's part that Handel had recomposed or rearranged one of the orchestral versions of *As pants the hart* as a verse anthem, by command of King George II, for the Chapel Royal. Since the existence of D was apparently unknown after Handel's death, it was then a reasonable assumption that the available copies of A embodied just this arrangement. Leaving aside the reference to George II, which may have been a mistake, musicians in the 1760s could point to one piece of evidence in support of the hypothesis that Handel had provided the Chapel Royal with a 'repertory' version of the anthem. The 1724 edition of the printed word-book of texts of anthems 'as the same are

---

[3] Mies, 'Das Anthem'.

[4] 'C und D erwiesen sich sofort als unfertig und unvollendet' (ibid. 2).

[5] GB-Ckc Mn 17.18 (transcription/translation of Schoelcher's catalogue), p. 466 et seq.

[6] US-NBu M2038. H14A5, vol. ix, p. 99; GB-Ob MS Mus.d.57, p. 149. The heading on the latter was probably derived from the former, which originated in the collection of Sir Watkins Williams Wynn: see Burrows, *Dissertation*, i. 95–6.

now performed in his Majesty's Chapels Royal' included, as the last of the verse anthems in the main section, the text of *As pants the hart* 'By Mr. GEORGE FREDERICK HANDELL, Composer to his Majesty' (see Fig. 8.1).[7] This was reprinted in the two following editions of the word-book, in 1736 and 1749.[8] Handel's versions of the anthem all followed basically the same literary text, but there are some minor variations. As will be seen from Table 8.1, the word-book version is marginally closer to D and C.

It is very unlikely that any of Handel's versions of *As pants the hart* were accepted into the Chapel Royal's day-to-day repertory. The anthem is not to be found in the surviving Chapel part-books from the 1720s, and there is circumstantial evidence that the Chapel did not retain copies of the music.[9] An innovation in the 1749 word-book was the inclusion of marginal entries specifying the solo voices used in each verse anthem. Handel's text is the only one in the collection with no such entry: it seems that the compiler looked in vain for the music to which the text was supposed to refer. The next edition of the word-book appeared in 1769. By then William Boyce had adapted the Cannons version of Handel's anthem as a verse anthem for the Chapel.[10] Boyce's arrangement, which probably dates from the 1760s,[11] may have been made at the request of King George III: the need for this arrangement is in itself a clear demonstration that A and D were unknown at the time.

If version D was not composed for the day-to-day Chapel Royal repertory, it must have been intended for some special occasion. Since all of the relevant 'occasions' in the early 1720s for which there is documentary evidence have been accounted for (see App. F), a more fruitful line of enquiry lies in examining more closely the relationship between D and C. These two versions have several movements with music in common, and a close examination of Handel's amendments to details of composition in the autographs reveals the

---

[7] *A Collection of Anthems* (1724), 81. I have been unable to find any newspaper advertisements to supply the exact date of publication, but there is no reason to doubt the accuracy of the year on the title page.

[8] *A Collection of Anthems* (1736), 102; *A Collection of Anthems* (1749), 71.

[9] It would perhaps have been rather uncharacteristic of Handel to allow his music into the part-books, where it would be out of his own control. His music for the orchestrally accompanied pieces did not reach the part-books, and the performing material remained with J. C. Smith: see Burrows and Dunhill, *Music and Theatre*, 199.

[10] Boyce shortened the solos and ritornellos, transposed the music to D minor, and composed his own arioso/recitative setting of 'Now when I think thereupon'. See Beeks, 'William Boyce's Adaptations', 48–51.

[11] Text printed in *A Collection of Anthems* (1769), 91: 'Composed for Voices with Instruments, but adapted to voices only by Dr Boyce'. The music occurs in Thomas Barrow's hand in the set of Chapel Royal part-books based on Organ Book GB-Lbl RM 27.d.8, probably from the mid-1760s. The confused headings to manuscript copies of HWV 251a, already referred to, may partly be explained by the existence of Boyce's version.

priority of D. At bar 17 of the first chorus, 'As pants the hart', Handel copied the Alto 1 part from A into D, but then changed his mind and cancelled the entry with a bar's rest.[12] This arrangement was carried forward without further alteration into C. At bars 37–8 of the next chorus, 'In the voice of praise',

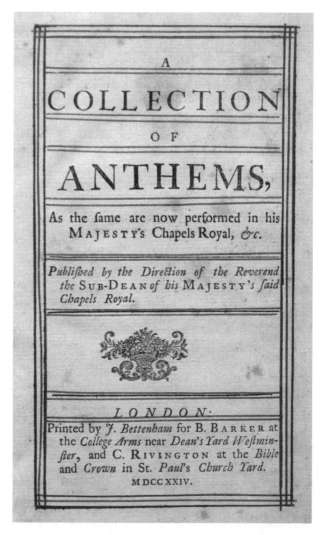

Fig. 8.1. Title page from *A Collection of Anthems* (1724), and the page with the text of Handel's anthem. Her Majesty's Chapel Royal

[12] The original Alto 1 entry doubled the Alto 2 part, coming in halfway through the phrase; Handel's alteration produced a much more satisfactory result, using Alto 1 to strengthen the Soprano entry at bar 18.

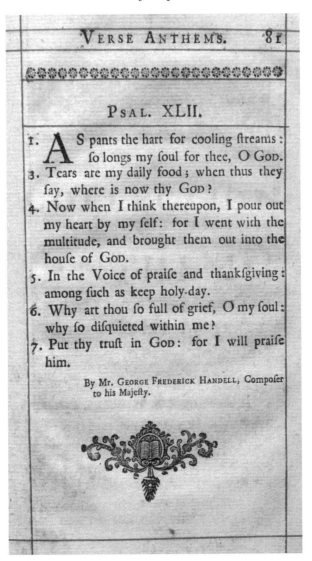

Fig. 8.1. *Cont'd*

Handel originally copied into D the chorus bass part from the parallel passage of B (Ex. 8.1(*a–b*)).[13] He recomposed this into a simpler form (Ex. 8.1(*c*); see Fig. 8.2) and the revised form was carried forward 'clean' into C.

The verse anthem HWV 251d must therefore have been composed between 1720 and 1722, the date speculatively ascribed to HWV 251c. Although D is a

---

[13] As noted in Ch. 6, there is no parallel passage in version A.

Table 8.1. *Variants in the texts of Handel's versions of* As pants the Hart

---

As paints[a] the hart for cooling streams, so longs my soul for Thee, O Lord.[b]
  [a] B, C, 1724: 'pants'; D: 'paints' altered (mostly) to 'pants'
  [b] B, D, C, 1724: 'God'

Tears are my daily food, when[c] thus they say: where is now thy God?
  [c] B: 'while'

In the voice of praise of[d] thanksgiving, among such as keep holy day
  [d] 1724: 'and'

Why so full[e] of grief, O my soul?
  [e] 1724: Why art thou so full

Put thy trust in God, for I will praise him. Amen.[f]
  [f] B, D, C, 1724: no 'Amen'

Other inconsistencies in Handel's spelling ('daly' for 'daily', 'powr' for 'poor', etc.) have been ignored. The texts are quoted from Version A (HWV 251a): variants are recorded from Versions B, D, C, and *A Collection of Anthems* (1724).

Ex. 8.1. *As pants the hart*, No. 3: (*a*) HWV 251b original; (*b*) as copied into HWV 251d; (*c*) revised form in HWV 251d

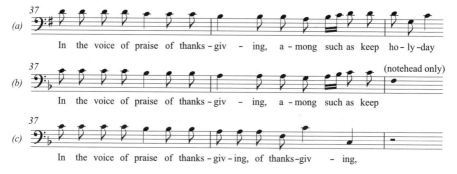

finished composition, Handel seems to have revised it into the orchestrally accompanied version almost immediately. The absence of secondary copies of D and the absence of any relevant documentary references may suggest that it remained unperformed: the most likely hypothesis is that Handel composed it for the Chapel Royal service of 7 October 1722 and then discovered (or was informed) that the employment of the King's Musicians was in order, following the precedent set by Greene's music in July 1721, and so he recomposed the anthem in a grander form. The literary text of D, or possibly C, was circulated by some means to those responsible for the 1724 anthem word-book.[14]

---

[14] It may be doubted whether the Chapel Royal regularly performed all of the verse anthems whose texts appear in the word-books; some of the longer occasional anthems seem to have

Fig. 8.2. A page from Handel's autograph of *As pants the hart* (verse anthem, HWV 251d), showing his alteration to bars 38–9 of 'In the voice of praise'. British Library, RM 20.g.10, fo. 31ᵛ

If HWV 251d was never performed, it is not surprising that it did not reach the Chapel Royal part-books: hence there was nothing to discover when the compilers of the 1749 word-book searched for the music that tallied with their text.

Whatever the precise dates for the genesis of the two versions, the clarification of HWV 251d's place in the sequence enables us to explain one apparent anomaly in the autographs: Handel's confusion over Bell's voice. Handel originally thought that Bell was an alto and wrote accordingly in version D, perhaps before actually hearing him sing. By the time he composed C he knew better: he lowered the tessitura of Bell's part in the new version of the first chorus and wrote for him as a tenor in the later movements.[15]

The Verse Anthem, HWV 251d

When Handel composed HWV 251d he had versions A and B available to him, and he drew on both. It is hardly surprising that the chorus movements

been included on account of their commemorative associations. The inclusion of Handel's text in the word-book may have been in the nature of an advertisement of the Chapel's association with the composer.

[15] Bell was employed at Cannons in 1720–1, where he appears on the list as a 'Countertenor': see Beeks, 'Handel and Music for the Earl of Carnarvon', 17.

were reworked from A, which had been composed for Chapel Royal forces including some of the same singers, rather than B, which had been written for Cannons. Certain difficulties attended the use of any material from the Cannons anthem: transposition was necessary, orchestral parts had to be revised or eliminated, vocal parts had to be adapted to different voices, and from a three-part ensemble to a larger one. In terms of the overall design, the most interesting revision for version D lies in the transposition of the last movement. When Handel composed A, his first setting of the anthem, he was apparently not concerned about overall tonal orientation: he began in D minor and ended in B flat major. In HWV 251d he followed the general design of A up to the central chorus, 'In the voice of praise', but in the last two movements he seems to have felt the need for a tonic-related ending, and this change of outlook explains the transposition of the last movement down a semitone. Table 8.2 gives the key schemes for all of Handel's versions of the anthem.

The other aspects of the composition have to be considered movement by movement. Handel's successive settings of *As pants the hart* present a fascinating case study in his adaptation of the music to varying performance conditions, and in his compositional choices concerning the reuse, adaptation, or rejection of music from previous versions of the anthem.

No. 1: As pants the hart

Handel took this movement over from version A with very little alteration. Bell was given Elford's former music virtually unchanged, save for an exchange of parts with Hughes at bars 28–31. Some details of the voice-leading were tidied up, and Handel was a little more careful about specifying the word underlay

Table 8.2. *Key schemes of all versions of HWV 251*

	A	[B]*	D	C	E
Sinfonia	—	d	—	d	d
As pants the hart	d	d	d	d	d
Tears are my daily food	a	g	a	a	a
Now, when I think thereupon	a–e	d–a	C	C	d–F
For I went with the multitude	C	F–C	C	C	d
In the voice of praise	F	F	F	F	F
Why so full of grief?	g	a	d	d	d
Put thy trust in God	B♭	d	A	d	d
Alleluja	—	—	—	—	d

*Keys for all movements from HWV 251b are shown a tone lower to facilitate comparison.

than he had been in A.[16] There were some minor improvements to the
continuo bass line and there are many more continuo figurings than in A,
some of them derived from B and one manifestly in conflict with the harmony
above.[17] It is interesting that Handel intended the movement to be taken faster
than in the Cannons version: A tempo Ordinario in D as against Adagio in B.
The only substantial change to the musical content of the movement was in the
final bars. Handel took over the idea of repeating 'for Thee' at bars 47–8 from B,
but incorporated it within material that was based on A. Departing from his two
previous settings, he decided to dispense with a final ritornello at the end of the
chorus: reference will be made to this again in connection with version C.

No. 2: *Tears are my daily food*

In this movement Handel reworked ideas that he had developed in version B.[18]
Comparison of the two movements is facilitated by the fact that both are in the
same key (A minor), though their relation to the overall tonic key is different,
owing to the transposition of the framing movements. The balance of the
movement was altered: Handel compressed the first half from fifty-four bars to
nine, while keeping the second half comparable to its previous length. The first
vocal phrases have the same rhythmic ideas as version B, except that Handel
eschewed the use of dotted rhythms until 'Where is now thy God?'. The chorus
entry at bar 17 is so effective an arrangement of the previous orchestral material
that it is tempting to believe that Handel had already thought of it in choral
terms when he wrote B. The dramatic differentiation of roles between soloist
and chorus appears only in this version of the anthem: it works well but Handel
did not repeat it in version C. As in all of Handel's versions of the anthem, this
movement ends on the dominant of A minor: the relationship to the key of the
subsequent movement is slightly more distant than in the previous settings.

No. 2a: *Now, when I think thereupon*

This, a straightforward recitative for bass voice, is the simplest and most
compressed setting of the text encountered so far. There are a few rhythmic

---

[16] Handel's verbal cues in HWV 251a are rather rudimentary, but generally his intentions are
clear; they were not followed in the version in *HG* 36, which was based on secondary MSS.
Most of the uncertainties from HWV 251a can be cleared up by reference to HWV 251d, but
Handel did make some deliberate changes in the word-setting as well: he improved bars 23–4 of
the Soprano part, for example, by changing the word underlay.

[17] Bar 39, beat 1. There is nothing in the previous settings to explain Handel's '9' here, except
possibly a 4–3 suspension which he removed in this version. The '6' at bar 23, beat 2, in *HG* 36 is
a misreading of Handel's '3'.

[18] The opening is also related to the third movement of the Recorder Sonata HWV 365,
composed later.

echoes of the previous settings, and a reminiscence of version A in the treatment of the continuo bass part at bar 8.

No. 3: In the voice of praise of thanksgiving

For the first twenty-five bars Handel took over the chorus as it stood in version A, except that he modified bar 3 of the subject at each appearance with the addition of the semiquavers from version B (see above, Ex. 6.3), and revised the inner parts in bars 19–25. He wanted to replace the short four-bar ending from A with the extended coda, with its inverted entries of the subject and long dominant pedal, that he had worked out in B. From bar 26 to the end he transcribed and adapted the three voices of the Cannons 'chorus' into a four-voice version: the small amount of additional material needed to supply the extra voice part owes little, if anything, to the orchestral parts from B. The musical substance was unchanged, but some of the part-writing was tidied up in the course of transcription. In bars 33–4 Handel simplified the bass part, rather surprisingly removing the semiquavers from the subject in bar 34.

No. 4: Why so full of grief, O my soul?

This movement is a straightforward rearrangement of the setting from version B, transposed from B minor to D minor and amended here and there. Bars 6–65 are basically a transcription from B bars 18–79, losing a couple of bars (B bars 27 and 58) and gaining another (D bar 51); bars 31–3 of B were recomposed and reduced by a bar to form bars 18–19 of D. The basso continuo part was improved and the rhythm of the motif for 'Why so disquieted?' consistently simplified.[19] The ritornellos were drastically shortened, but elsewhere in the movement the Chapel Royal cellist took over the role previously taken by violin and oboe in the Cannons version. With three melodic strands to play with (two voices and cello), Handel found it convenient to redistribute some of the material between them.[20] Alterations in the autograph of D bars 59–62 reveal that Handel was working out the redistribution as he went along; interchange between vocal and instrumental parts was fairly easy because the obbligato parts in B had, in any case, been based on melodic figures from the vocal parts. It is interesting to observe that, for the first time, Handel's cadences at the words 'within me' treat the last syllable as a weak one (see Ex. 8.2).

---

[19] There is one exception to the general pattern, in the obbligato cello part at bars 25–6 (compare A, bars 39–40): in this case D is more decorated than A.

[20] e.g. D Alto 1 bars 60–4 is based on B Oboe bars 74–8.

Ex. 8.2. No. 4: (*a*) HWV 251d; (*b*) HWV 251a; (*c*) HWV 251b

No. 5: *Put thy trust in God*

No. 5 was transposed from version A with no significant differences in the main body of the movement (bars 1–42), though there were some trivial alterations to the word underlay and the bass line. The consecutive unisons between tenor and bass at bars 20–1 do not seem to have troubled Handel when he made the transposition, for he did not change them. He wrote the chorus in four parts throughout, ignoring the pretence at a fifth part from the opening bars of version A. For the final bars he discarded the 'Amen' from A in favour of a short Adagio conclusion rather similar to the end of the movement in version B. The tempo indication at the opening (Allegro ma non troppo) is new. Handel added tempo directions with great care throughout: it is one of the signs that the anthem, whether performed or not, was a finished composition.

Autograph

Singers are named as follows:[21]

No. 1:   Mr Hughs (Alto 1); Mr Bell (Alto 2); Mr Whely (Bass 1); Mr Gates (Bass 2)

No. 2:   Mr Hughs (Alto)

No. 2a: Mr Whely (Bass)

No. 4:   Mr Hughs (Alto 1); Mr Bell (Alto 2)

In No. 1 Handel altered 'paints' to 'pants' at most occurrences of the word: a sign that he was working directly from the autograph of version A. In No. 4 he

[21] GB-Lbl RM 20.g.10, fos. 23–36.

named the obbligato instrument as 'Violoncello' on fo. 32ᵛ, at bar 13 where the part becomes independent of the continuo, and he wrote 'Organo' against the treble-clef part in the closing bars. The continuo instruments are not named in any other movement.

There are no early copies of the anthem and it was not printed until Chrysander's edition in 1872.

Conditions of Performance

Although it is likely that this version of the anthem was superseded by version C before it came to performance, it remains possible that it was sung at a routine Chapel Royal service at some time in the 1720s. If so, it would have been performed by the Children and the Gentlemen currently in waiting. The organ may have been played by Handel, or more likely by the current Chapel Royal Organist, and the cello part was presumably composed for the Chapel's Violist Francisco Goodsens. By then, 'Violist' probably designated the office rather than the specific instrument that was in use. There is no sign from the autograph of any role for the Chapel's Lutenist.

The Orchestrally Accompanied Anthem HWV 251c

When Handel composed this setting he had experience from three previous versions behind him: A, B, and D. Version D, his most recent setting, had been composed for the Chapel Royal, so it is not surprising that he drew mainly on this version when he composed HWV 251c. Version A was not directly used at all: Handel probably regarded it as having been superseded by D. The Cannons version, B, provided material for the solo movements, the opening Sinfonia, and the final chorus. It is remarkable that he drew so little on B, his only previous version with orchestral accompaniment, for the concerted movements: he seems to have thought it more efficient to add orchestral parts to the four-part and six-part choruses that he had worked out in D than to rearrange the Cannons version for larger forces.

In order to examine HWV 251c as composed for the Chapel Royal *c.*1722, it is necessary to disentangle the work's textual history. Handel revised the anthem for use as the first item in his benefit performance *An Oratorio* on 28 March 1738 at the King's Theatre, Haymarket, and for that occasion he had to turn a relatively small-scale anthem into a work appropriate to his oratorio forces and to the expectations of the theatre audience, which he did by adding extra movements and composing a new setting of 'Now, when I think thereupon'. The alterations will be described in a later section of this chapter. His autograph

of HWV 251c contains various cues and amendments that date from 1738, but
the two versions of *As pants the hart* can be distinguished on the basis of evidence
from a manuscript copy (now GB-Lbl Add. MS 31557) that was taken from the
autograph before the anthem was revised, and evidence from the printed word-
book for Handel's 1738 performance.[22] The manuscript score, which is described in more detail below, is the only secondary copy of Handel's Chapel
Royal music to have an amendment that is probably in the composer's hand, and
it may have originated as the score prepared for the anthem's first performance
*c.*1722. If so, its existence strengthens the hypothesis that HWV 251c was
Handel's first orchestrally accompanied Chapel Royal anthem of the 1720s
series: after the first occasion he probably discovered that he did not really
need a separate performing score. Whether or not this manuscript served a
practical function, it dates from the same period as the composer's autograph of
the anthem: Smith's handwriting is in the style he cultivated in the 1720s,[23] and
the paper characteristics of the copy are similar to those of the autograph. This
source is therefore of the highest value as evidence for establishing the 1722 text,
free from the additions that Handel made in 1738.

In view of the importance of this manuscript, some mention must be made
of its title page. The score is bound with a copy of HWV 251b in the hand of
J. C. Smith junior, and the calligraphic title page to the complete volume reads
'Two Anthem's / Composed for his Grace the / Duke of Shandous by / G. F.
Handel Esquire / London 1719'. This title is not in the hand of either of the
Smiths and may have been added during the second half of the eighteenth
century. The possibility that the writer of the title page had some information
which has not otherwise come down to us, and that version C was Handel's
second attempt at a setting for Cannons, can be dismissed for two reasons: the
paper characteristics of the anthem's autograph point to the 1720s rather than
to the Cannons period, and the singers named on the autograph of HWV 251c
include Hughes, Baker, Edwards, and Whely—Chapel Royal Gentlemen
who, as far as is known, never performed at Cannons.[24] Whoever wrote the
title page must have made a misguided guess about the anthem on the strength
of its fortuitous coupling with HWV 251b, which is a genuine Cannons work.

As we would expect, the groups of solo singers named on the autographs of
HWV 251c and HWV 251d are very similar. The most arresting difference is
the absence of Bernard Gates's name from version C. Presumably he was
indisposed, unavailable, or out of waiting when the anthem was performed.

---

[22] See Burrows, 'Handel's 1738 *Oratorio*'.

[23] In particular, this is true of the style of his semiquavers. This feature has already been noted in
Ch. 5 (p. 128), in connection with Smith's insertion in the autograph of the Caroline Te Deum.

[24] Since D (which includes Bell's name among the soloists) preceded C, C cannot have been
composed before 1720.

The solo part in the first chorus formerly given to him in version D was reallocated to Baker, who also gained a new solo in the last movement. In version C Handel named the leading voices for the chorus 'In the voice of praise': the basses included Edwards as well as Whely and Baker. I have suggested above that Handel discovered while writing version D that Bell did not have as high a voice as he had expected. In version C the solo part for Alto 2 in the first chorus was retained by Bell from version D with some adaptation, but in No. 4 he is named as leader of the chorus tenors, and his solo part in the duet 'Why so full of grief' is written in the tenor clef.[25] Gethin is named as the tenor soloist in the first chorus, but Handel omitted to give him any solo music.

Each setting of the anthem was produced under different circumstances. In version C Handel seems to have been aiming for simplicity and directness when he adapted earlier music. The orchestral accompaniment provides an additional dimension compared to versions A and D, but the scoring is tidier and more practical than in version B. If version C has a fault, it lies in the lack of tonal variety towards the end, where two D minor movements follow in succession.

No. 1: Sinfonia

The single-movement introduction is derived from the first movement of the Sinfonia to version B, transposed down a tone.[26] Although Handel shortened the music, the three-part structure of the original was preserved. The first section was left largely intact, the second section shortened by eight bars, cutting the former bars 33–40,[27] and the final section recomposed: bars 33–9 are derived from the former bars 41–7, but the remainder of the movement thereafter is only loosely based on the preceding version. Apart from a descending scale at bar 46, which reappears in Violin 1 and Oboe at bar 49, hardly any of the thematic material of this third section is new, but it is worked in a tighter, less repetitive, manner than in version B. Handel gave the Sinfonia a broad tonic ending, closing it off as an independent movement rather than ending on the dominant, which would still have been possible since the following vocal movement is in D minor.

---

[25] Handel did, in fact, lay out his stave in the alto clef at the beginning of the duet, but changed it to the tenor clef before proceeding with the composition.

[26] The movement is untitled in the autograph, but Smith labelled it 'Sinfonia' in Add. MS 31557.

[27] The section from bars 33 to 40 is crossed out in pencil in the autograph of HWV 251b. Although this is the same cut as that made for HWV 251c, I think it more likely that Handel marked it when he prepared the movement for the publication of the Trio Sonata Op. 5 No. 3, *c.*1739.

Ex. 8.3. Sinfonia: (*a*) HWV 251b (violin); (*b*) HWV 251c (oboe)

The instrumental resources for the Chapel were slightly larger than those at Cannons, but the differences between versions B and C tend towards simplification rather than elaboration of the texture. In the outer sections the oboe doubles the violins much more in the Chapel Royal version, and in bars 12–16 Handel removed an independent oboe counterpoint altogether. This alteration can hardly have been prompted by a deficiency in the player, since Jean Christian Kytch (who was paid as one of the additional performers) was probably London's best oboist.[28] The middle section demonstrates how well Handel understood his instruments: the violin solo from B, with its leaps and string crossings, was transformed into an idiomatic oboe solo (Ex. 8. 3).

It is difficult to read Handel's mind on one point of performance practice. The trills in the violin parts in bars 2, 4, and 6, which are clear enough in the autograph of version B, were not transferred to version C. This might have been carelessness on Handel's part, but it might also have been deliberate: conditions in the Chapel perhaps dictated a plainer style.[29] When Handel used the music of the Sinfonia again for the Anthem on the Peace in 1749, he headed the movement 'Larghetto e staccato', the staccato part of the direction possibly warning against the addition of trills. The Larghetto on the autograph of HWV 251c itself is in the hand of Smith.

No. 2: As pants the hart

Handel worked this movement from version D, transcribing the basso continuo and the vocal parts with minor revisions. When he added the orchestral accompaniment he did so without reference to his previous version of the movement in B: the orchestral lines of the two versions are not merely independent of each other, but they fulfil different functions. In both, the first 'orchestral' entry is the oboe at bar 11: for the Cannons version it provides an additional part, while in the Chapel Royal anthem its role is to strengthen

---

[28] The oboe player for the Cannons anthem was probably Biancardi: Kytch seems to have joined the Cannons establishment in 1719. See Beeks, 'Handel and Music for the Earl of Carnarvon', 17.

[29] Another reason might have been a desire to increase the dynamic contrast of the echo effects: trills tend to increase the volume of the *piano* bars.

the vocal treble line. The first entry of the upper strings in the Cannons version (bar 16) promised to be the start of a separate orchestral exposition: in the Chapel Royal version the orchestra is withheld at this point, entering later to heighten the tutti at the climax of the chorus entries. The sequence in C is therefore 'solos–chorus–orchestra added', instead of 'chorus–orchestra–chorus-and-orchestra' as in B. The doublings of the voice parts and the contrapuntal additions are rethought from first principles throughout the movement. In one place (bars 42–3) Handel even simplified the texture by removing one of the entries of the counter-melody which had appeared in all of the previous versions.

As might be expected, the main alterations to the voice parts in the autograph occur where Handel decided to improve on, or experiment with, his source from version D. The first real amendments come in bar 22, where he tackled the previously unsatisfactory layout of the Soprano and Alto parts.[30] His better information about the range of Bell's voice prompted him to rearrange the central solo entries from bar 28: Bell was given the former first bass part (at the same pitch), with consequent rearrangement to the succeeding entries. The opportunity was also taken to redistribute the treble solo in this passage, perhaps confirming a current weakness in the treble voices which is suggested by his use of the oboe to strengthen their line.

A remarkable by-product of Handel's reliance on version D as the copy-text for this movement can be seen in the final bars. Versions A and B concluded with an instrumental epilogue after the final choral cadence, but in version D Handel had decided against this. In version C he faithfully copied the ending from D and scored it up as it stood, finishing at bar 52. This ending was subsequently subjected to three revisions:

1. Handel added a new five-bar orchestral epilogue, using the empty staves on the verso of the autograph of the completed movement.[31]
2. The epilogue was crossed out in pencil, and the original short ending was restored. It is not possible to tell who made the deletion, but the word 'Fine', added in ink next to the short ending, is in Smith's hand.
3. Handel restored the epilogue, writing 'Stat' in pencil at the top of the page and crossing out Smith's 'Fine'.

---

[30] At bars 21–2 D had taken over the upper parts from version A, including a technically unsatisfactory unison doubling of Soprano and Alto 2, the former ending a phrase and the latter in mid-phrase.

[31] The epilogue occupies exactly the one (verso) side of the paper. It was not unusual for Handel to leave a blank side at the end of anthem movements that he finished on a recto: there are several instances in the autographs of the Cannons anthems. There was good reason, in any case, for him to treat movements 2 and 3 as physically separate units: he changed copy texts from D to B between them.

Since the orchestral epilogue appears in Add. MS 31557, we may assume that it was added in 1722 and that it should be an integral part of the text of the Chapel Royal version of the anthem. The clef forms for this epilogue in the autograph are sufficiently different from those in the main body of the movement to suggest that Handel made the revision after he had proceeded with, or even completed, the rest of the anthem. The conclusion of this movement presented him with a continual difficulty: in his successive versions he kept changing his mind between a forceful tutti ending and a ritornello buffer to diffuse the tension before the next movement. The diminuendo epilogue in version C, carefully marked 'pian/piu pian/pianiss' by Handel, repeats a technique from the end of No. 1 of the Utrecht Te Deum. The second and third revisions probably both date from 1738: Handel apparently decided to cut back the end of the movement but then changed his mind.

The tempo direction Largo at the start of the movement in the autograph is in Smith's hand; the source movement from version D was marked 'A tempo ordinario' by Handel.

No. 3: Tears are my daily food

This movement was adapted, with some compression and a certain amount of recomposition, from the parallel movement in version B. Handel did not even have to transpose the movement: A minor is conveniently related to D minor (the framing key of version C) as well as to E minor (the key of version B). He was actually returning to the key scheme of his previous Chapel Royal versions here, all of which followed the D minor chorus with a solo movement in A minor. The replacement of a treble soloist with an alto entailed some reworking of the voice part. Table 8.3 shows how the compression of length was effected whilst still preserving the structure, and indeed the notes, of the original.

There are a couple of interesting points of detail. The Chapel Royal version consistently lacks some trills that are present in the orchestral parts of the Cannons version (C bars 9–15; compare B bars 18–26), perhaps reflecting a difference in performance practice, as in the opening Sinfonia. The movement, in common with all of Handel's earlier settings, ends with an imperfect cadence in A minor. In version B the rhythmic disposition of the last three bars had followed a hemiola pattern: Handel did not repeat this, but adopted instead the rhythm from version D. This is one of the few places in the movement where the direct influence of D can be felt.[32]

---

[32] Another place might be bars 48–9, which are mainly derived from B bars 75–6, with material exchanged between oboe and solo voice: the b in the vocal part at bar 48, however, seems to come from D bar 28.

Table 8.3. *HWV 251c: derivation of 'Tears are my daily food' from HWV 251b*

Bar nos.	Section	Commentary
1–18	Opening ritornello	Ritornello from B shortened by 10 bars near the beginning (C bar 6 = B bar 16). This alters the proportions of the binary design: the first section (modulating to the relative major) is foreshortened, while the second section remains the same.
18–32	Vocal section 1	Derived from B bars 28–35 (bars 22–4 of C recomposed), and 48–54 (bars 28–31 of C recomposed); C follows the same key scheme as B.
32–41	Vocal section 2	Derived from B bars 55–63 (bars 38–41 of C recomposed); the same key scheme as B.
42–54	Vocal section 1A	Orchestral ritornello from B (bars 63–8) omitted. Section newly composed, but following the same tonal scheme as B: the comparable passage in D follows a different plan. C bars 50–4 are equivalent to B bars 77–80.
54–66	Vocal section 2A	Based on B bars 81–95, shortened by the omission of B bars 87 and 89.

The tempo direction in the autograph (Larghetto) is in Smith's hand: the parallel movement in version D carries the indication in Handel's hand, but that from the movement in version B is Un poco adagio.

No. 4: Now, when I think thereupon

This is based on the recitative from version D, with orchestral accompaniment added. The final bars are broadened a little, improving the effectiveness of the imitations between voice and accompaniment, and also rendering the cadence less perfunctory.

No. 5: In the voice of praise of thanksgiving

This movement is based on the version that Handel had worked out in version D. As had been the case with No. 2, he must have copied out the vocal parts first and then added the orchestral parts, because once again the orchestral material is independent of that found in version B. Furthermore, there are the same types of differences as before: the doubling of voice parts follows different principles, and independent orchestral additions to the texture (such as the viola part in bars 13–15) are completely different from those of version B. Handel's arrangement in C is simpler than in B: in general he doubled the voices at the unison or the octave with the string parts that represent the same register, and strengthened the Violin 1/Soprano part with the oboe wherever convenient.

Up to bar 23 Handel followed the track of version D precisely. He seems to have had doubts about the exposition on the inverted form of the subject which began at bar 26 of D, so he removed this, approaching the dominant pedal more directly. Consequently, there is no separate exposition of the inverted subject in version C, but the inverted form contributes to a fine cumulative climax over the dominant pedal-point. The shortening of this section was effected by composing a new bar (bar 26) to replace bars 26–34 of D, and in order to make the link smoothly Handel had to recompose the preceding bars 23–5. He tried to make sense of the tenor entry from version B bar 25 before abandoning it for something simpler: the descending scale excised in the process from B bar 24 reappeared in the bass at the new bar 26. Once back on course, Handel returned to his source from version D for the closing bars of the movement: C bars 27–36 are copied and orchestrated from D bars 35–44.[33]

In the autograph, 'Allegro' in Smith's hand at the beginning of the movement has been crossed out in pencil: there is no tempo indication at all in Add. MS 31557. The movement was probably designated Allegro in 1738 before Handel composed a new setting of No. 4, and it is an appropriate tempo for No. 5 when it follows the original 1722 recitative. The Allegro marking was probably deleted in 1738 when the new version of No. 4 provided a different context.

No. 6: *Why so full of grief, O my soul?*

This is the only movement of the anthem for which Handel used two sources simultaneously. He drew mainly on version B for the instrumental parts, and mainly on version D for the vocal parts. On the entry of the voices at bar 18 his principal source crossed over from B to D, but one source was always subject to possible modification from the other: at bar 69, for example, the main source is D bar 56, but the bass part owes something to B bar 70. Nevertheless the influence of D grows noticeably stronger as the movement proceeds, though with two significant departures: at bar 27 Handel restored a bar from B that he had cut in D, and bars 73–7 had a mixed derivation from D (bars 60, 61, 63) and B (bars 74, 76–8). In bars 55–67 he followed the revised text that he had worked out in D, and the closing ritornello was orchestrated from D's organ postlude (bars 80–5), with a couple of extra bars added.

It is not difficult to guess the reasons for the general dominance of D as the main source. Version D, unlike B, had the movement in the key that Handel wanted, and it embodied some of his previous decisions about textual revisions. Furthermore, D had been composed for the same Chapel Royal singers

---

[33] This had been derived, in turn, from B, but Handel was clearly using D, and not B, as his source here.

Ex. 8.4. No. 6: (*a*) HWV 251d and HWV 251c; (*b*) HWV 251d; (*c*) HWV 251c

as C. Such revisions as Handel made to the vocal parts between versions D and C are nearly all directed towards the same end, the lowering of the tessitura of Bell's part. Passages including top *a'* and *b'* are removed, producing a radical change in the shape of the opening entries: see Ex. 8.4. At bar 54 a high *b'* was transferred from the voice into the oboe part; at bars 73–5 Handel resorted to downwards octave transposition. The top notes in bars 84–7 were avoided by inverting the two voice parts. The obbligato oboe and violin parts in version C are indebted to their ancestors in version B, but most of the rhythms are presented in simpler forms in the Chapel Royal version, ♩ ♫♩|♩ ♩ becoming ♩ ♩♩|♩ ♩ : there is just one exception to this, at bar 70, where Handel did exactly the reverse.

Handel wrote 'Larghetto' at the start of the movement but changed languages at bar 87, where he wrote 'slow' rather than 'adagio'.[34] There is no 'slow' or 'adagio' at the parallel places in the versions previous to C (i.e. A, B, and D). The rhetorical treatment of the text at the end of the movement can be traced back to A, Handel's first setting. His addition of a rudimentary bass part to the instrumental echoes in bars 79, 81, and 83 in Add. MS 31557 hardly seems to improve the overall musical effect. It is conceivable that he was playing for safety here: perhaps some hazard of performance conditions in the Chapel Royal separated the obbligato instruments and they needed the continuo to keep them together.[35]

[34] Handel's 'slow' in the autograph of C seems to have been part of the original 1722 text: it was copied by Smith into Add. MS 31557.

[35] These additional basso continuo notes were not copied into the autograph, so they do not appear in any of the secondary MS copies which were derived (at various removes) from it.

No. 7: *Put thy trust in God*

Handel used the Cannons setting of this text as the basis for the final movement
of the anthem. His judgement was sound. The original Chapel Royal settings
from versions A and D were unpromising material for adaptation with orchestral accompaniment, while the music from version B provided a lively but
dignified conclusion, reflecting the confidence of its text in solid, if rather
four-square, vein, and with orchestral accompaniment as an essential element
to the musical content. It introduced variety since it did not repeat the triple-
time metre of the previous movement, though at the same time it introduced
the problem of overbalancing the key scheme tonally: the choice was between
two successive movements in the same metre or two successive movements in
the same key. The tempo indication Andante is Handel's: there is no marking
for the chorus in version B.

His treatment of the opening section of the movement provides an insight
into the differences between the Cannons and Chapel Royal establishments.
The Cannons version begins with a florid, almost concerto-like, tenor solo of
thirty bars over an independent continuo bass part. In the Chapel Royal this
sort of music was the perquisite of the alto soloists. Handel could have arranged
the music for alto: the opening phrase, transposed down from E minor to D
minor, would have been too low for alto as it stood, but it might then have
survived octave transposition. Instead, Handel gave it to a bass soloist, treating
the opening phrase as the bass line of the harmony, and the result is clearly
reminiscent of the opening to 'In the voice of praise of thanksgiving'. The
music follows the Cannons version for the first eleven bars, with a little
strengthening of the orchestral parts, but then Handel elided the subsequent
florid section by writing a short five-bar cadential link to terminate the solo.
This link includes a reference, possibly accidental, to the discarded triple-time
setting of the movement (Ex. 8.5). Handel retained from the Cannons version

Ex. 8.5. No. 7: (*a*) HWV 251c; (*b*) HWV 251a

the idea of overlapping the chorus entry with the end of the solo, so that the multitude bursts in to support the affirmations of the soloist. Thematic material from the Cannons violin part supplied some of the music for the additional voice part that was required by the Chapel Royal chorus. In revising the choral section of the movement Handel excised one statement of the theme from version B completely, losing thirteen bars in the process, and tightened up one of the other entries. As a finale, the movement was strengthened by the compression of the music from its source in version B: the Chapel Royal version is direct and to the point. The new Adagio termination to the movement is similar to that at the end of version B, though the values of notes and rests are augmented.

As in the previous choruses, the orchestral parts are sufficiently different in layout and texture to indicate that Handel thought out the scoring afresh, rather than copying his working from version B. Sometimes the orchestral texture is more transparent (e. g. at bars 19–20; compare B bars 33–4); at other times it is more dense (bars 22–4; compare B bars 38–40). Even the violin figuration in the decorative link bars (28, 30) is differently constructed from the parallel passages in version B. Throughout the anthem, in fact, there are examples which show that Handel rethought the arrangement from first principles in preference to the easier alternative of copying down pre-composed orchestral parts and then providing additional instrumental lines to match.

Autograph

The additions relating to Handel's 1738 version are described later in this chapter. As already noted, Smith added tempo indications to certain movements of the autograph, GB-Lbl RM 20.g.1: on the evidence of Add. MS 31557 (see below) most of them date from 1722 rather than 1738. In 1722 the Sinfonia (fos. 1–3) may have been composed last and added to the autograph after the completion of the rest of the anthem; Handel headed the Sinfonia 'Ψ [Psalm] 42', but otherwise there is no title.

Handel wrote in the following singers' names, all relating to the Chapel Royal version from the 1720s:

> No. 2: Mr. Hughs (Alto 1); Mr Bell (Alto 2); [Mr] Getting (Tenor); Mr Whely (Bass 1); Mr Baker (Bass 2)
>
> No. 3: [Mr] Hughs (Alto)
>
> No. 4A: Mr. Whely (Bass)
>
> No. 5: Mr. Hughs and ContrAltos (Alto); Mr Bell and Tenors (Tenor); Mr. Whely ['Baker Basses' crossed out] (Bass 1); Mr. Baker Edwards Basses (Bass 2)

No. 6: Mr. Hughs (Alto); Mr. Bell (Tenor)
No. 7: [Mr] Hughs (Alto); [Mr] Bell (Tenor); Mr Baker (Bass 1)

There are two instrumental bass lines in the Sinfonia and the chorus movements. These staves are labelled 'Violoncello / Organo et [Contra]Basso' in the
Sinfonia, but for the opposite combination in No. 2: 'ContraBasso / Organo et
Violoncello'. The use of tenor clefs on the lower staves suggests that the second
combination was also intended in Nos. 5 and 7, where the labelling of the parts
is not specific. There is no mention of a bassoon anywhere in the autograph:
no bassoon player was paid in 1722.

Possible Conducting Score of HWV 251c

GB-Lbl Add. MS 31557, written on paper of identical type to that of Handel's
autograph of the anthem, was copied by J. C. Smith senior, and has one passage
on fo. 25 (additional continuo notes for No. 6, bars 79–83) that is probably
(though not certainly) in Handel's hand. Handel probably also added 'Largo' at
the start of No. 2 (fo. 6^r). The other markings attributed to Handel by later
pencil annotations in the score were in fact written by Smith. The manuscript
also has a number of nineteenth-century annotations, most (possibly all) of
them written by Rophino Lacy. Smith included throughout the names of the
solo singers from the autograph,[36] as part of his original copy.

This score establishes unambiguously the original 1720s version of the
anthem, before Handel's 1738 revisions. It has the following features, apparently as originally copied by Smith:

No. 1 Heading 'Sinfonia', not in the autograph; 'Larghetto', as also added
by Smith to the autograph. The crotchets in bar 1 et seq. have
staccato dashes, but no trills are shown for bar 2 et seq. (Compare
the parallel movement from the Anthem on the Peace: see Ch. 14.)

No. 2 'Largo', probably in Handel's hand, also added by Smith to the
autograph. There are no *piano* and *forte* indications at bars 48–9:
these may have been added to the autograph in 1738.

No. 3 'Larghetto', as also added by Smith in the autograph. 'Solo' and
'Tutti' indications are given for the opening instrumental parts, but
do not appear in the autograph. Smith copied Handel's spelling of
'daly' for 'daily'.

No. 4 Heading 'Accomp', as in the autograph. The word 'pour' from the
autograph was miscopied as 'Powr'.

---

[36] The inclusion of soloists' names was a feature of performing scores: Smith did not add
them to the manuscript scores copied for private collections.

No. 5 No tempo indication; those in the autograph were probably added in 1738. 'Praise *of* thanksgiving' copied from the autograph throughout.

No. 6 'Larghetto', as given by Handel in the autograph; also 'slow' later in the movement. The Violin part is labelled 'Violin solo': the autograph has just 'V', without indication of a solo instrument.

No. 7 'Andante', as given by Handel in the autograph.

Smith copied the labels to the staves exactly as in the autograph, and consequently this copy provides no assistance to the interpretation of the scoring for the pairs of unlabelled instrumental bass parts in Nos. 5 and 7.

Handel's 1738 Version of the Anthem, HWV 251e

The opera season of 1737–8 was an unusual one in Handel's London career. At the end of the 1736–7 season the opera company at the King's Theatre, Haymarket (usually referred to as the Opera of the Nobility) faced a difficult future, its financial problems compounded by the loss of two of its star singers, the castrati Farinelli and Senesino, over the previous two seasons, and by the ruinous competition for the London audience between two opera companies. By then Handel had performed three seasons at Covent Garden theatre that had been artistically successful but had probably involved accumulating financial losses; furthermore, the end of his 1736–7 season had been interrupted by health problems, a 'paraletick disorder' for which he sought a health cure at Aix-la-Chapelle. Upon his return to London the managers of the company at the King's Theatre asked him to compose two operas for the following seasons and he accepted this commission rather than pursuing another rival opera season of his own. He was reputedly offered £1,000 for providing the operas,[37] and it is likely that the terms also included the right to a benefit performance towards the end of the season. His operas *Faramondo* and *Serse* were performed in the 1737–8 season at the King's Theatre, though it is uncertain how much practical involvement he had in the productions, and the cast of solo singers was built on that surviving from the previous seasons of the Opera of the Nobility.

For his benefit night on 28 March 1738, however, there is no doubt that Handel himself arranged and directed the miscellaneous concert of his music that was given under the simple title *An Oratorio*.[38] According to contemporary reports, the King's Theatre was crowded, with additional seats for the audience on the stage, and Handel gained a vast sum, variously estimated between £800

[37] See Burrows and Dunhill, *Music and Theatre*, 31 (letter of 1 June 1737).
[38] See Burrows, 'Handel's 1738 *Oratorio*'.

and £1,500. For the performance he had the musical resources of the opera company, comprising Italian solo singers (including the castrato Caffarelli) and the orchestra; in addition he employed some English singers including William Hayes, the Professor of Music from Oxford, to strengthen the chorus movements. The programme opened with Handel's revised version of *As pants the hart*, based on the Chapel Royal version HWV 251c, composed about sixteen years previously. The autograph of HWV 251c carries various revisions by Handel relating to this performance, but he did not add the names of the solo singers for the occasion. While it is possible that the solo movements of the anthem were sung by the Italian singers from the opera company, it seems more likely that Handel used his English singers, perhaps even some from the current Chapel Royal.[39] The orchestral accompaniment to the anthem in the theatre would have been richer than in the Chapel Royal, employing about twenty-five string players and at least two oboes and two bassoons; the principal keyboard continuo role may have been played on the harpsichord rather than the organ. The scale of the performance was larger, but so was the venue, and the occasion required a longer piece than at a Chapel Royal service: the King's Theatre audience was different in size, variety of experience, and expectations. Handel's method for matching the music to the occasion was to increase the amount of concerted music in the anthem.

The word-book for the benefit performance gives the text of the anthem and helps to define the musical content of the 1738 version (HWV 251e).[40] A final 'Alleluja' was added, and this must be the D minor movement that is found in several secondary sources of the anthem, though not in the composer's autograph score. There is no doubt that this movement was added in 1738 and was not part of the original Chapel Royal anthem: it had originally been composed in 1733 as the final movement to Part I of *Athalia*.[41] A section of the basso continuo part copied by J. C. Smith for the 1738 *Oratorio* fortunately survives today.[42] This was apparently used by Handel, probably for the performance itself, in conjunction with the anthem's autograph: a pencil line down the score halfway through bar 40 of 'Put thy trust in God' in the autograph (fo. 24ʳ) provides continuity to the continuo part, which

[39] The 'singer from Windsor' mentioned in a letter of 14 Mar. 1738 (Burrows and Dunhill, *Music and Theatre*, 43) may have been Prince Gregory, who joined the Chapel Royal in 1740.

[40] See Burrows, 'Handel's 1738 *Oratorio*', and the music edns. referred to at n. 2.

[41] Autograph GB-Lbl RM 20.h.1, fos. 26–8. The movement was obviously part of the original composition score of *Athalia*: Dean (*Handel's Dramatic Oratorios*, 254, 643) states that the 'Alleluja' was composed for the anthem and reused in *Athalia*, but this goes against the evidence of the sources.

[42] GB-Cfm MU MS 265, pp. 53–5, 61; the part was presumably with the collection of Handel's autographs that was acquired by Viscount Fitzwilliam in 1799. The musical origin of the continuo part was first identified in Dean, *Handel's Dramatic Oratorios*, 261.

commences with a new linking passage in score but then goes over to a
continuo bass line only as soon as the Alleluja is established.

Two further amendments which are now found in the anthem's autograph
must have originated with the revisions for the 1738 performance. The final
bars of the Sinfonia from HWV 251c were recast to give a close on the
dominant instead of the tonic, leading into an additional second movement
taken from the Sinfonia to one of the Cannons anthems, HWV 247 (see Ex.
8.6); the more substantial two-movement Sinfonia was appropriate for the
beginning of Handel's theatre performance. 'Now, when I think thereupon' in
the Chapel Royal anthem had been an eleven-bar accompanied recitative in C
major for bass voice and strings (HWV 251c, No. 4). Handel reset this in D
minor, dividing the verse into two sections. The first clause remained an
accompanied recitative with bass soloist (6 bars), but it now led into a movement for unison chorus tenors and basses with orchestral accompaniment (30
bars). This strengthened the choral element in the anthem, providing a striking
new concerted movement which also joined well with the following chorus
movement. Handel crossed out his original recitative setting in pencil, and
wrote 'mutato'; his autograph of the new setting (GB-Lbl Add. MS 30308, fos.
27–8) was written on paper of a different format from the main autograph, so
Smith copied the movement on paper of the appropriate dimensions and his
copy was inserted (RM 20.g.1, fos. 12–13). Some other alterations, of less
significance, may also have been made in 1738, though they are difficult to date
with certainty. These involve additional or amended speed indications, and a
revision to the closing ritornello of the first chorus; most of them have already
been noted in connection with the description of HWV 251c.

Ex. **8.6.** Sinfonia: (*a*) original ending (HWV 251c); (*b*) 1738 revision (HWV 251e)

The addition of the second movement to the Sinfonia hardly needs explanation: it brought the instrumental introduction into the two-movement form
that was the normal minimum for overtures to Handel's theatre works.
Although he could have composed a new movement instead, he chose a
particularly good movement from the Cannons repertory which, as far as we
know, he had never previously performed to the London theatre public,
though John Walsh had printed it about four years before in the fifth concerto
from the set that he published as Handel's Op. 3.[43] Walsh's publication, which
was probably assembled without the composer's involvement, gave the movement in an orchestral guise arranged from the Cannons chamber texture, with
Oboe 2 doubling Oboe 1 and the original bass line largely doubled by violas an
octave higher. Handel's cue for the insertion of the movement into the anthem
consists of only two bars (violin parts), but it is likely that the orchestration of
the movement was arranged somewhat on the lines given in Walsh's edition.
Handel's cue does, however, include a tempo marking (Allegro) which is not
found on the Cannons anthem original, and the title 'Fuga'.

The other revisions to the anthem served to increase the choral contribution. The new setting of 'For I went with the multitude' is remarkable because
it is based on the Lutheran chorale melody for 'Christ lag in Todesbanden',
slightly adapted, and labelled by Handel 'Bassi e Tenori Canto fermo'.[44] The
use of the men's choral voices in this way was a novelty in Handel's English
church music, though he had written a brief solo phrase for the basses in 'Day
by day we magnify thee' in the Caroline Te Deum, and had effectively used
the men's voices against solo altos for 'the Heavn's and all the Powers therein'
in the Utrecht Te Deum. In addition to making rhythmic alterations to
accommodate the English text, Handel adapted the chorale melody by cutting
(at bar 30 of the anthem movement) from the fourth note of the fourth phrase
to the final cadential phrase.[45] He seems to have taken a new interest in
German chorales at this period, perhaps on account of some contact that he
made during his convalescent trip to the Continent: the influence is also
apparent in his *The ways of Zion do mourn*, his anthem for the funeral of
Queen Caroline, composed a few months before the revision to this anthem,
and it will be referred to again in Chapter 13. Perhaps Handel's continental

[43] The authority for the musical texts published in Walsh's Op. 3 is variable; Op. 3 No. 5,
which includes several Cannons-derived movements, has an independent early source (as a
'Sonata') in a manuscript from the Malmesbury Collection.

[44] The use of the chorale melody in this movement was first identified in Schering, 'Händel
und der protestantische Choral', 29–31. See also Roberts, 'German Chorales', 98.

[45] Handel did not include the repeat of the first two phrases, which was necessary in the
original to accommodate the German text. It is possible nevertheless that this movement was
based on a borrowed German source, perhaps a chorale setting for organ.

experience restored his contact not only with the chorale but with the genre of the chorale prelude, for his figural accompaniments in the orchestral parts of the anthem movement resemble one style of treatment in organ chorales. This seems to be the first example of a movement in which Handel combined the simple statement of a vocal cantus firmus with independent instrumental counterpoint: the result is engaging, and sufficiently interesting for us to regret that the two statements of the short text did not provide opportunity for a longer treatment. The second of the chorale-derived musical phrases produced a gravitation towards a central perfect cadence in the tonic, so the second statement of the text has the effect of a varied repeat of the first.

The revision of 'Now when I think thereupon' probably took place at the last moment, for the word-book for *An Oratorio* heads the movement simply 'Recit. Accomp.'. Given that Handel wanted to increase the choral element in the anthem, the logic of introducing the full tenors and basses at the first mention of the multitude is defensible, though his original scheme in the anthem perhaps brought out more clearly the fact that the psalmist was referring to his *memory* of going with the multitude. The music of the preceding brief accompagnato recitative was newly composed: the vocal line owes virtually nothing to the previous settings, and it is the only version to set 'I pour out my heart by myself' as a rising phrase. The melodic contour may have been partly influenced by the need to provide a good lead into the ensuing chorus. Handel's tempo direction Largo for the accompagnato bars suggests that his resetting of the text 'For I went with the multitude' as an Andante movement required a broader pace for the preceding recitative section. On the autograph no bass soloist is named for the opening accompagnato. On the succeeding Andante Handel labelled the uppermost orchestral line 'VI e HI e 2', reflecting the resources available from the opera house orchestra, and in contrast to the single oboe for the original Chapel Royal version of the anthem. There is no double bar at the end of the autograph, which continues after a single bar-line with a cue for the beginning of the following chorus: the layout of this ending clearly implies that 'In the voice of praise' should start without a hiatus, picking up the same beat as the previous Andante section. This provides an explanation for the deletion of the Allegro tempo indication on No. 5 in the autograph, referred to on p. 205. The alteration makes musical sense: the original accompanied recitative (4A) seems to demand the reaction of a faster chorus, but the second setting (4B) can continue satisfactorily under its own weight, flowing into No. 5 with gathering momentum as the upper voices enter, without the need for a change of speed.

The concluding 'Alleluja' chorus, joined seamlessly onto the previous ending of the anthem with a rebarring from 2/4 to common time, is also a fine movement. The chorus was composed in the original score of *Athalia*, which was performed at Oxford in 1733; it is uncertain whether Handel had included it in his London performances of the oratorio at Covent Garden in 1735.[46] Superficially, like the additional movement to the Sinfonia, we might attribute his use of this chorus in the anthem to the coincidence that it was a ready-made movement in D minor, the tonic key of the anthem. However, there is a remarkable similarity in style and character through all of the new D minor contributions—the Sinfonia, the chorale movement, and the final chorus—and we might wonder whether Handel recognized a 'D minor style': serious and contrapuntal, yet in its way quite tuneful. Consciously or unconsciously, he may have gone even further and seen the opportunities that the 'Alleluia' chorus provided for unifying motivic cross-references within the anthem. The rhythm of the chorus's counter-subject echoes the figural accompaniment to the new 'chorale prelude' movement, and indeed relates also to 'So longs my soul, O Lord' in the opening chorus: when it comes in the relative major key at bar 64 it even echoes 'In the voice of praise and thanksgiving' (see Ex. 8.7).

Ex. 8.7. HWV 251e: (*a*) No. 7; (*b*) No. 4b; (*c*) No. 2; (*d*) No. 7; (*e*) No. 5

[46] See Burrows, 'Handel's 1735 (London) Version of *Athalia*', esp. 209.

A quarter of a century separates Handel's final version of this anthem from his first verse anthem setting. His various successive versions seem to reflect the composer's fascination with the musical possibilities in a text that he had first encountered during his early years in London, and his choice of *As pants the hart* as the opening item in his benefit performance indicates the value that he placed on the piece. The anthem would have been virtually unknown to the theatre audience in 1738 in any version, and it largely remained so in London, though a form of HWV 251c with organ accompaniment (and transposed to C minor) had entered the choirbooks of Durham Cathedral by the middle of the century.[47] Oxford musicians seem to have performed a version with orchestral accompaniment, possibly as early as the 1740s: a fragment of their score and performing materials for HWV 251c survives, with amendments showing that they had access to the 1738 revisions.[48] An organ-accompanied version of the anthem that was copied by John Mathews into the choirbooks for Christ Church Cathedral, Dublin, in the last decades of the eighteenth century incorporates considerable ornamentation in the music for the soloists, but the source of this ornamentation is uncertain and it cannot at present be taken as representing Chapel Royal practice from Handel's lifetime.

[47] See Crosby, *A Catalogue*, 163.
[48] See Burrows, 'Sources for Oxford Handel Performances', 180–1.

9

Other Chapel Royal Music from the Second Period, 1722–1726

Revival of the 'Caroline' Te Deum

THE evidence for a revival of the Caroline Te Deum in the 1720s has already been presented in Chapter 5. It remains only to note some features of its performance at this time and to examine the musical construction of the new setting of 'Vouchsafe, O Lord'.

The artistic weight of the work now fell heavily onto the alto soloist Francis Hughes, who must have performed all of the music originally composed for Elford in addition to his own previous music; the new movement was also composed for him. Gates took over the bass solo in No. 2, originally composed for Baker. No singer is named against the solo tenor part at the opening of No. 1, but the alto/tenor/bass line-up was probably Hughes/Gethin/Weely. Kytch was paid for playing the oboe: in the absence of trumpets, he would have played the Trumpet 1 part on the oboe in Nos. 1, 4, and 6, and may also have doubled Violin 1 in No. 2. As noted in Chapter 5, the autograph shows a series of alterations by Handel in Nos. 3 and 4 changing the obbligato parts from flute to oboe and back again. Kytch may have played these on the oboe in the 1720s but, in view of the difficulties suggested by Handel's annotation to the movement of HWV 249a which also involves the flute, the oboe alternative more likely dates from 1714, and the restoration of the flute from the 1720s.

No. 5b: Vouchsafe, O Lord

The immediate ancestor of this movement is Handel's setting of the same text from the Cannons Te Deum, which was in itself indebted to the parallel movement from the Utrecht Te Deum (see Ch. 6). Unlike those two versions, the new movement is a continuous solo aria. In the Utrecht and Cannons settings the solo music (verses 26–7 of the canticle) took up about two-thirds of the movement, ending in the dominant key and introducing a chorus entry (for verse 28) which returned the music to the tonic. In this setting the proportions of the movement are about the same, though verse 28 receives slightly shorter measure, but there is no chorus entry and the dominant cadence is avoided. Indeed, Handel avoids strong cadences throughout the movement: there are clear harmonic cadences in the relative major (bar 14) and the subdominant (bar 22), but the melodic line and the musical impetus is carried over them in both cases.

The movement is in the same key (B minor) as that in the Utrecht setting: it suited the range of the alto soloist and provided a contrast to the overall D major tonic of the Te Deum. The recomposition of music from the Cannons setting (which had been for a tenor soloist, in G minor) followed a pattern already observed with some of the Cannons anthem revisions in Chapter 6: Handel based the first part of the movement on his previous working, with some tightening up, but recomposed the second part afresh from bar 18 onwards. The opening ritornello employs motifs that are found in both the Utrecht and Cannons settings of this movement; the bass part is closer to the Utrecht version. The three-strand scoring (strings with flute/voice/bass) was inspired by the Cannons version, though in this case Handel seems to have regarded the flute as contributing to a synthetic tone colour with the strings, rather than as a solo instrument. Most of the independent flute notes are merely conveniences of scoring to avoid lower notes that were only available to the violins, though the contrast of registers is put to good effect momentarily in bars 4–5.

I will magnify thee, O God my King (HWV 250b)

Handel's procedure in this anthem is in marked contrast to the one that he had adopted for *As pants the hart*. Whereas the outline of the latter remained constant throughout the various revisions and the integrity of its literary text was maintained, *I will magnify thee* was completely reconstructed, retaining only the outer framework of the Cannons anthem (HWV 250a). This is a pattern similar to that found in the relationship between the Chapel Royal version of *O sing unto the Lord* and the Cannons anthem HWV 249b, as described in Chapter 6. The void between the movements derived from HWV 250a was not filled with original material, but with rearranged or recomposed movements selected from other anthems: Handel drew on three other Cannons anthems to provide four movements and ended up with settings of verses from three different psalms (see Table 9.1). He was perhaps influenced by the fact that one of these anthems, *O come, let us sing unto the Lord* (HWV 253), had the same key centre as the Cannons version of *I will magnify thee*. The text of HWV 253 comprised verses selected from a number of different psalms,[1] but the

---

[1] Psalms 95, 96, 97, 99, and 103. By contrast, the Cannons original of *I will magnify thee* (HWV 250a) was based entirely on Psalm 145, with the exception of the aria 'Happy are the people' from

Table 9.1. I will magnify thee, O God my King (*HWV 250b*): *Derivation of movements from previous anthems*

Anthem movement	Text	Key	Source	Key of source
1. I will magnify thee	Ps. 145, v. 1	A major	HWV 250a, No. 1	A major
2. O worship the Lord	Ps. 96, v. 9	A major	HWV 249b, No. 5	B♭ major
3. Glory and worship[a]	Ps. 96, v. 6	D major	HWV 253, No. 4	D major
4. Tell it out	Ps. 96, v. 10	A major	HWV 253, No. 5	A major
5. Righteousness and equity	Ps. 89, v. 15	F♯ minor	HWV 252, No. 6	D major
6. My mouth shall speak	Ps. 145, v. 21	A major	HWV 250a, No. 8	A major

[a] Handel had also previously set this text, to different music, in anthem HWV 249a (No. 4, Bass solo in G major).

verses of the movements that Handel extracted for use in *I will magnify thee* came from Psalm 96, and in their new context they were reunited with another verse from the same psalm in a musical setting derived from yet another Cannons anthem. This reunion may have been fortuitous, though it points up the similarity between the tone of Psalm 96 and that of Psalm 145 which provided the outer movements of this anthem.

There is certainly nothing haphazard about the artistic construction of the anthem as a whole. The key scheme, although rather heavily loaded towards the tonic, is sufficiently varied, and contrasts of speed and metre are satisfyingly balanced. The first four movements of the anthem form a good musical sequence: the end of each movement sets up the beginning of the next. The musical material from which each of the six movements was derived is of first-rate quality: we might almost suspect that Handel was putting together his own favourite movements. The choice must surely have been his own, for it is not likely that the Sub-Dean of the Chapel accidentally supplied Handel with a text that happened to be made up entirely of passages from the psalms that the composer had set before. Nevertheless, the construction of texts from diverse scriptural verses was not unfamiliar to the official clerical mind: as noted in Chapter 2, the passages to be used in place of the *Venite* in the Thanksgiving Services are testimony to the literary ingenuity of highly placed ecclesiastics, and some of the anthems composed for these services also have texts selected from several psalms.[2]

Psalm 144, a movement that may not, in any case, have been part of Handel's original plan for the anthem: see Beeks, 'Handel's Chandos Anthems: More "Extra" Movements'.

[2] For example, Weldon's *O give thanks unto the Lord* and Croft's *Sing unto the Lord* (texts printed in *Divine Harmony*, 59 and 69); see also Ruth Smith, *Handel's Oratorios*, ch. 3. The selection of verses for anthems from two or more psalms had a longer history from the previous century: see John Morehen, 'The English Anthem Text', 66.

Regardless of musical considerations, the text as constructed in this anthem has a shape and coherence that could hardly have been bettered by one of the librettists for Handel's London oratorios. The ideas in the text form an arch pattern:

Nos. 1 and 2:   Call to praise (No. 1) and worship (No. 2)
No. 3:   Four attributes of the Almighty, in pairs (glory and worship/power and honour)
No. 4:   The faithful are enjoined to tell the heathen about the power of the Almighty
No. 5:   Four attributes of the Almighty, in pairs (righteousness and equity/mercy and truth)
No. 6:   Praise and thanksgiving, expressed, as in No. 1, in the first person

Movement 4, the central climax, is surrounded symmetrically by Nos. 3 and 5, and by Nos. 1–2 and 6. Within the general intention of a laudatory text, the emphasis is subtly varied from movement to movement.

Handel's music is ideally matched to the structure. The opening solo movement with its first-person text leads into a duet for the invitation to 'worship the Lord in the beauty of holiness'; the process of expansion in vocal resources continues in No. 3, with its scoring for seven vocal parts, but this is less powerful in effect than No. 4, where the chorus voices come together in a concentrated manner to assert that 'the Lord is King', and that 'he made the world so fast it cannot be moved'. The divine attributes of justice and mercy demand the quieter, more serious, treatment that Handel provides in No. 4; in the last movement the chorus voices respond to the soloists' 'Let all flesh give thanks' with cries of 'Amen'. The transferred music, particularly Nos. 3 and 4, is at least as effective in its new context as it had been in the original Cannons anthems.

Handel's composition of the new sequence of movements from material supplied by previous anthems gives us an insight both into the nature of his genius and into the quality of his literary discrimination. The anthem is one of the best in the canon of his Anglican church music,[3] and the only questionable aspect of its musical design is the long delay before the first entry of the chorus. If Handel used HWV 250a as his starting point, he may have made a deliberate decision to move away from the 'chorus' setting of the first movement as in the Cannons anthem, in favour of a solo aria that was suggested by the first-person voice in the text for the first verse. Although Francis Hughes did not receive the same level of public commendation that was devoted to the memory of Elford's voice and manner of delivery,[4] the music that Handel wrote for him

---

[3] There is a striking parallel with the wedding anthems composed by Handel a decade later: *This is the day*, greatly indebted to music from *Athalia*, is at least as successful as the more 'original' *Sing unto God*. See Chs. 12–13.

[4] For example, in the Preface to Croft's *Musica Sacra*, which was published around the time that Handel composed HWV 250b.

indicates a similarly effective singer, particularly strong in the type of sustained lyrical phrases with which the Chapel Royal version of *I will magnify thee* opens. The phrase lengths and the vocal range are more modest than those characteristic of the music for contemporary opera singers, but Handel, working within the expressive manner of the English anthem, treated Hughes as a serious vocal performer. The Chapel's particular strength throughout the first half of the eighteenth century was in the alto and bass voices, and HWV 250b is typical of its period in that it relied to a large extent on the musical and expressive talents of Hughes and the bass-baritone Samuel Weely. The years 1722–6 might, indeed, be fairly described as the 'Hughes and Weely' period of Handel's Chapel Royal music, and their professional relationship with the composer must have provided a creative stimulus comparable to that exerted by the opera singers on his contemporary theatre work.

Every movement of the anthem was subjected to a different type of revision in the process of adaptation. The techniques used include rearrangement to suit different forces, the simple reduction of lengthy movements by cutting, detailed recomposition and improvement of individual passages, and the composition of completely new movements from thematic material supplied by earlier versions. The anthem thus clearly demonstrates one of the anomalies of Handel's compositional processes: the amount of work involved was surely greater than that which would have resulted from beginning the composition again.

No. 1: *I will magnify thee*

In the Cannons version of the anthem Handel had set the text as an ensemble movement for soprano, tenor, and bass voices, beginning with a musical subject derived from the opening of his Latin psalm *Dixit Dominus*, which conveyed an atmosphere of rejoicing but was perhaps rather brash for this particular text; it was succeeded by a more cantabile theme for 'and I will praise Thy name'. This material could have been worked up as a chorus movement, but as already noted Handel instead composed a solo movement for alto, reflecting the first-person voice of the text, using thematic ideas derived from the opening movement of the Sinfonia to the Cannons anthem. It is possible that he began the Chapel Royal anthem by recomposing music from the Sinfonia as an introductory orchestral movement, and that it was only when he began work on this that the idea of adapting the music for the first verse struck him,[5] but there is no trace of such an introduction in the autograph of the anthem as we have it, which has a stave for Hughes from

[5] Comparison can be made with the Anthem on the Peace in 1749, where Handel discarded his original idea for the first movement, 'How beautiful are the feet', but used this material for the third movement instead. See Ch. 14.

the start of the first movement. Handel's previous Chapel Royal works, with the single exception of HWV 251c, do not have independent orchestral introductions, while his Cannons anthems, with the single exception of HWV 254, always include them.

The opening and closing bars of the Cannons Sinfonia movement, with a little revision, generated the ten-bar instrumental introduction for the Chapel Royal anthem. The first theme (Ex. 9.1), built over an ostinato bass, is never given to the voice (it is hardly a very characteristic vocal melody in any case), but it functions in the manner of a ritornello from a concerto movement,[6] confirming the tonic at bar 12½ after the soloist's first phrase and reappearing to mark the movement's central cadence in the dominant at bar 23½. The ostinato extends and develops to carry the construction of the whole movement: the first entry of the soloist is accompanied by a two-bar version of the bass (Ex. 9.2), and two other, more fragmentary, themes from the Cannons Sinfonia are put to good use in the voice part (Ex. 9.3). All of the music of the main part of the movement grows from these three ideas, newly developed. The binary structure allows three statements of the text, and it is instructive to compare Handel's treatment of the opening words at the repetitions. He does not repeat the broad opening melody from Ex. 9.2 at the later entries. Instead, the central entry in the dominant compresses the rhythm of the opening but preserves the shape of the consequent phrase; the third entry, occurring when the music is poised ambiguously between the dominant key and a return to the tonic, tightens up the second phrase as well and introduces a sense of urgency in the overlapping orchestral answer (Ex. 9.4). The movement develops greater activity at each repetition: the more leisurely ritornello theme, Ex. 9.1, is crowded out as the musical sinews tighten. A certain degree of relaxation is provided by the coda from bar 43 onwards, which develops a semiquaver motif derived from bar 26 in the string parts. The coda modulates once again to end in the dominant, preparing the way for the next movement. The idea for this may have come from the Sinfonia in HWV 250a, which also ended in the dominant, but even so the sureness of pacing is remarkable: no composer of the Classical period used this tonal procedure with a finer sense of preparation. The second movement follows without an intrusive ritornello.

No. 2: O worship the Lord in the beauty of holiness

The originating movement from the Cannons anthem *O sing unto the Lord* was subjected to transposition, rearrangement, a limited amount of detailed

---

[6] It is an elaboration of a melodic/harmonic formula which occurs in Corelli's music at the opening of the Trio Sonatas Op. 4 No. 3 and Op. 3 No. 2; the latter may also have been in Handel's mind as a source for the last movement of the Utrecht Te Deum.

Ex. 9.1. *I will magnify thee* (HWV 250b), No. 1

Ex. 9.2. *I will magnify thee* (HWV 250b), No. 1

Ex. 9.3. *I will magnify thee* (HWV 250b), No. 1

Ex. 9.4. *I will magnify thee* (HWV 250b), No. 1

recomposition, and some cutting. Transposition was necessary to suit the tonality of the new anthem, but downwards transposition by a semitone was not sufficient in itself to turn a treble/tenor duet into an alto/bass one.[7] Handel overcame this problem ingeniously by exchanging the parts: the former tenor part became the new alto part, and the former treble part was transposed down a ninth for bass voice. Fortunately Handel's original counterpoint in the vocal parts was invertible, and the bass voice after transposition still remained safely above the independent instrumental bass. By rearranging the parts in this way he was able to introduce some variety at the beginning: the bass provides a contrast which enhances the effect of the subsequent re-entry of the alto. Most of the compositional revisions are minor improvements, but two substantial cuts (bars 23–37 and 65–81 from HWV 249b) are significant, since they were not merely aimed at shortening the movement but follow a definite plan in removing redundant matter. The tied-note figure for the word 'holiness', first heard in bars 6–7, had been rather overplayed in the previous setting, and Handel's cuts fall mainly on passages devoted to it, including the lengthy coda (bars 65–81), which was rather out of proportion with the rest of the Cannons movement and was redundant harmonically because the main business had finished with the perfect cadence at bars 64–5. Handel's judgement in removing this coda was surely correct.

No. 3: *Glory and worship are before him*

The Cannons anthem *O come, let us sing unto the Lord* from which this movement was adapted was one of the later ones, employing a four-part chorus. For the Chapel Royal Handel expanded the layout to a seven-voice arrangement, using solo alto, tenor, and bass voices (Hughes, Gethin, and Weely) in conjunction with 'Ripieno' chorus voices (see Fig. 9.1). He did not divide the treble part, which was presumably sung by all of the boys even though it has some florid passages. It is unlikely that the ripieno singers numbered more than two or three to a part, and the soloists' music is not particularly independent or demanding, with the exception of the odd bar or two of Hughes's part. Handel's object in this movement was to gain a richer texture, using the seven parts to fill out the chordal outbursts on 'Glory, worship, power' and to provide various combinations of solo and ripieno voices. In some passages the soloists act as strengtheners to the next highest voice. If the choir sat divided in the facing choir stalls, Handel's scoring might have been intended to ensure that some strands of the music were sung from both sides; in bars 25–6, for example, this might explain the coupling of Solo

[7] If Chapel Royal pitch was a semitone (or more) above 'Cannons' pitch, the real difference in sounding pitch would have been substantial. See Ch. 19.

Fig. 9.1. The opening of the movement 'Glory and worship are before him', from Handel's autograph of the anthem *I will magnify thee*, HWV 250b. British Library, RM 20.g.8, fo. 13ᵛ

Bass/Ripieno Tenor, and Solo Tenor/Ripieno Alto. The overall aim of the arrangement is clear enough: Handel was seeking the richest effect from his Chapel Royal resources: sonority rather than volume.

The rearrangement from four vocal parts to seven and the addition of a viola part to the orchestral texture were straightforward tasks, but Handel also made some significant revisions to musical content. He added a two-bar instrumental introduction, from aesthetic choice rather than technical necessity: the key sequence from the preceding movement in the Chapel Royal version is more closely related than in the Cannons anthem, and the singers needed no special help to focus the pitch of the first notes. The addition of the introductory bars gives weight to the first chorus entry: it also makes the canon between bass and treble parts in the first two bars a little more explicit. Within the body of the movement Handel made a four-bar cut (bars 28–32½ from the Cannons version) which removed the emphasis on the dominant key at that point, accelerating the return to the tonic and the opening thematic material.

At bars 24–5 Handel added half a bar at the approach to the cadence, making this rather broader and incidentally improving the verbal stress at the same time (see Ex. 9.5). He similarly recomposed the final choral cadence of the movement (bars 39–42, comparable to bars 40–4 of the Cannons movement), expanding the approach, adding a momentary touch of the subdominant key, and improving the vocal lines. Throughout the movement he also took some care to improve the shape of the instrumental bass part, in particular replacing repeated-note figures of Ex. 9.5(*a*) with something a little more varied.[8] The final instrumental ritornello is shorter than its predecessor, providing a tighter link to the next movement, which begins (like its parent movement in the Cannons anthem) without an instrumental introduction. Handel obviously regarded movements 3 and 4 as a coordinate pair, comparable to a keyboard prelude and fugue, and transferred them from HWV 253 as a unit.

No. 4: Tell it out among the heathen

Handel's setting of this text is particularly striking: the rhythms and melodic shapes of the opening theme provide a lively and appropriately forceful treatment of the words in the best Purcellian manner.[9] It may be that Handel was deliberately imitating Purcellian models here, though it is doubtful that he regarded the rhythm of bar 4 as an archaism characteristic only of English church music, since he uses this triple-time pattern in his oratorio-type works.[10] He began the movement with his principal soloists and there is a

---

[8] Handel also eschewed the dactylic rhythm from the first vocal movement of the Cannons anthem, derived from *Dixit Dominus*.

[9] This was noted by Basil Lam in Abraham, *Handel*, 171, in the context of a description of the original movement from HWV 253: unfortunately the quotation of the theme there (as Ex. 52) contains an error in the word underlay at bar 4 which removes one of its most Purcellian features.

[10] In 'Bacchus' blessings are a treasure' from *Alexander's Feast* Handel may have intended this rhythmic device to represent a state of inebriation.

Ex. 9.5. *O come let us sing unto the Lord* (HWV 253): (*a*) No. 4; (*b*) *I will magnify thee* (250b), No. 3 (upper orchestral parts omitted from both examples)

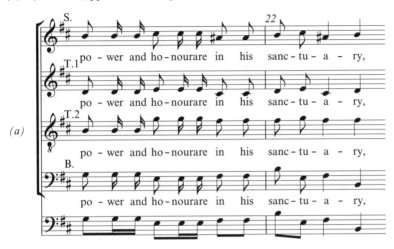

fine cumulative build-up, solo voice → orchestra → duet → chorus. The
sequence was derived in outline from the original in HWV 253,[11] but the
Cannons movement had one major defect: it was too long, even given the
more leisurely circumstances at Cannons, and its 150 bars of continuous four-
part choral writing hold diminishing interest for the listener. This is a pity,
because the material of the movement's second section, 'and that he made the
world so fast', is excellent, and its subsequent combination with the opening
subject is effective. For the Chapel Royal Handel reduced the first section by
41 bars,[12] but curtailed the remainder less dramatically: either he became less
conscientious about arranging the cuts as he went along or, more likely, he
found that the second half could not be reduced without serious musical losses.
The movement as a whole is greatly improved by the two-bar cut in the
opening theme after bar 15, which eliminates a rather flabby melodic continuation. An even more compressed form of the theme appears among Handel's
fragmentary sketches, but this was written long after the Chapel Royal anthem
and therefore has no direct relevance to the composition of the anthem
movement.[13] The three versions of the theme are given in Ex. 9.6. The
movement's second theme also received an interesting alteration. Since composing the Cannons anthem Handel seems to have discovered that 'can't' was
not good form,[14] and amended the subjects beginning at bar 72 to accommodate 'it *cannot* be moved'. As in the previous movement he recomposed
important cadences, at bars 34–5 and at the end. The first revision introduced
a hemiola harmonic rhythm into the orchestral parts against a regular triple-
time entry in the voices; at the end the hemiola implications from the Cannons
version were removed, the declamation was improved, and the passage as a
whole was made more direct in expression. From bar 138 onwards the close of
the movement was subjected to more radical revision.[15] The single extended
climax over the dominant pedal in bars 141–55 is a great improvement on the
previous double-take in the Cannons anthem, and the strength of the final
assertion left no room for the orchestral postlude from the Cannons original,
which was omitted in the Chapel Royal version.

[11] The duet section was achieved by omitting the entries of the third and fourth voices from
bars 42–3 of the Cannons version.

[12] Bar 55 in HWV 250b is equivalent to bar 96 in the movement from HWV 253.

[13] GB-Lbl RM 20.g.14, f. 51, commencing stave 3: see Burrows, 'Handel's Teaching
Exercises', 111, 115–21. This version of the theme cannot have been intended for the words
of the anthem, since it omits the cadence theme carrying the words 'that the Lord is King'.

[14] Compare the replacement of 'flee' with 'fly' in the first movement of HWV 256b, noted
later in this chapter.

[15] Bar 137 is equivalent to bar 185 in HWV 253.

Ex. 9.6. *I will magnify thee*: (*a*) HWV 253 (Cannons); (*b*) HWV 250b; (*c*) sketch, GB-Lbl RM 20.g.14

All three were written by Handel in A major.
Original clefs: *(a)* Tenor *(b)* Bass *(c)* Two-stave systems, Soprano and Bass.

No. 5: Righteousness and equity

This movement owes only two features to the setting of the same text in the Cannons anthem *My song shall be alway of the loving-kindness of the Lord*: the shape of the opening four bars of the theme, and the rhythm for the phrase 'shall go before thy face' which appears at bar 25. The two movements serve different roles in their respective anthems: the Cannons movement is a D major chorus falling between two minor-key arias, whereas the Chapel Royal movement is a minor-key aria between two assertive concerted movements in major keys. Even within the predominantly cheerful text of *I will magnify thee* some contrast was needed, and this aria makes a good foil to the surrounding movements. The text, with its emphasis on the judicial attributes of the Almighty, has an emotional ambiguity which renders it suitable for more serious treatment: God's justice and mercy are fit subjects for celebration, but the prospect of judgement also carries the darker possibilities of rejection.

There is an obvious parallel between the emotional function of this movement within the anthem and that of the verse beginning 'We believe that thou shalt come to be our judge' in the Te Deum settings: both introduce serious matters without unduly interrupting the general rejoicing.

Handel develops the initial melodic ideas using techniques similar to those employed in the first movement of the anthem. The music unfolds within a binary structure, with instrumental ritornellos based on the opening theme acting as concerto-style landmarks. The strings answer the voice in close imitation at bars 10–13 and 47–50, but elsewhere the aria has a simple trio texture for oboe, voice, and basso continuo. It is remarkable that this was not one of the movements that Handel quarried for his Op. 5 Trio Sonatas, for it could have been rearranged relatively easily and effectively into that medium. The basic thematic material derives from a subsidiary idea in the aria 'Amor, nel mio penar' from his opera *Flavio*, composed in May 1723,[16] whose main theme the composer also used a couple of years later for a new movement in the A Major Te Deum, described later in this chapter.

No. 6: *My mouth shall speak the praise of the Lord*

This movement received the least revision. Handel took the final movement of the Cannons anthem, slowed down the speed from Allegro to Andante, made some rhythmical alterations to the subject[17] and some improvements to the shape of the bass part, but otherwise he simply adapted the music to the new forces. One bar was removed, but this was a stenographic rather than an aesthetic alteration: a bar's rest before the concluding 'Amen' was replaced by a pause over the rest at the end of the previous bar. The tenor solos from the Cannons anthem provided material for the Chapel Royal alto and bass soloists in the first half of the movement, the former oboe part supplying the music for the second vocal soloist in bars 10–12. The addition of an extra chorus part and an extra orchestral part in the tutti sections presented Handel with few difficulties. It is interesting that, as in No. 3, Weely's part in chorus sections of the movement commutes between the chorus bass and tenor parts.

Autograph

Handel wrote in the following singers' names into the autograph (GB-Lbl RM 20.g.8):

---

[16] *Flavio, Re de' Longobardi*, HHA II/13, p. 137 (bar 45 et seq.).

[17] These alterations may be more apparent than real. Dotted-rhythm groups in the oboe part were replaced by plain quaver groups at bar 2 beat 1, bar 4 beat 1, and bar 6 beat 3; however, they remain as dotted groups when the soloists repeat the theme. The autograph of this movement is lost, but the earliest MS copies leave no doubt that Handel's notation was inconsistent here.

No. 1:   Mr. Hughs (Alto)
No. 2:   Mr. Hughs (Alto); Mr. Whely (Bass)
No. 3:   Mr. Hughs (Alto); [Mr] Getting (Tenor); [Mr] Whely (Bass); the other parts for A,
            T, B are designated 'Ripieno' (see Fig. 9.1)
No. 4:   Mr H[ughs] (Alto); Mr W[hely] (Bass); the other parts for S, A, T, B are designated
            'Rip:'

The autograph includes the following pencil emendations in Handel's hand, dating from 1744, when movements from the anthem were adapted for use in his oratorio *Belshazzar* (see Ch. 11, pp. 302–3).

No. 1:   Cut indicated with 'NB' from bar 46 to the end of the movement, where he wrote
            out a new ending on the spare staves on fo.10^v, linking this with a cue to the last
            movement of the anthem, 'Vide infra my mouth shall'.
No. 4:   Direction at the top of fo. 18^v: 'ex g. un tono piu basso'. There is a cue for the
            adaptation of the opening alto solo to the soprano clef for 'Franc[esina] solo'; the
            voice entries at bars 35 and 38 are marked 'Contr' and 'Ten' respectively, and at 50–1
            the chorus bass part is cued in an octave higher. From bar 61 beat 2 to bar 63 the
            chorus bass part has pencilled note heads a seventh higher: Handel was presumably
            thinking of the music in G major at this point, which was the key for its use in
            Belshazzar.

The autograph is now incomplete, lacking the pages with the music from no. 4 bar 69 onwards: it seems likely that the second part went astray when the anthem was used in the preparation of the conducting score of *Belshazzar*. Later, probably towards the end of the 1750s, J. C. Smith the younger made up the deficiency by copying the remainder of the anthem: his manuscript was probably bound (or secured) with the section in the composer's autograph, but is now separated as GB-Lbl RM 18.b.7. Some early manuscript copies of the anthem were made before the second part of the autograph was lost, and two copies are particularly valuable because the scribes included the singers' names from the original, and probably even followed the layout of the pages from the autograph.[18] From these copies the following inferences can be made about the lost section of the autograph:

No. 5   Tempo: Larghetto. Singer named: Mr. Hughs (Alto). Oboe and Violin 1 shared the
            same stave up to bar 32; thereafter the staves were rearranged with Oboe on stave 1
            and both violin parts on stave 2 until bar 52, when the original arrangement was
            restored. The movement ended with the cue 'Chorus My Mouth Shall Speak the
            Praise of the Lord'.
No. 6:   Tempo: Andante. Singers named: Mr. Hughs (Alto); Mr. Whely (Bass); chorus parts
            labelled 'Rip[ieno]'. At the end: 'Fine' three times, after Violin 2, Solo Bass and
            Chorus Bass staves.

---

[18] GB-Mp MS 130 Hd4 v. 47(3), and US-Cu MS 437.

In the surviving section of the autograph two substantial passages were revised during composition and deleted by Handel before the orchestral parts were fully scored: they occur in No. 1 (2 bars, long melisma on 'ever', after bar 40) and No. 4 (3 bars, including an entry of the main subject in the tenor part, after bar 63). The first movement occupies a complete bifolium (fos. 7–10) and ends with the apparently redundant cue 'O Worship the Lord a 2'. As noted above, there is evidence from secondary copies that a similar redundant cue occurred in the autograph between Nos. 5 and 6. Their existence suggests that Handel began the composition of the anthem by adapting the outer movements from HWV 250a and then composed and inserted the inner movements.

Te Deum in A Major (HWV 282)

For some movements of this setting Handel drew upon the Cannons Te Deum, but his reworking of that music along with new material changed the balance of the work as a whole, and the most closely comparable setting is the Caroline version, his previous 'short' Chapel Royal Te Deum. Both works are characterized by compression and economy in their paragraphing of the text: some sections that were emphasized or dwelt upon in the longer Utrecht and Cannons versions are passed over quickly here, and the brisk transitions from one section to the next provide moments of dramatic contrast which are absent from the more spacious versions. The compact settings depend for their artistic success upon the balanced placing of short sections, arranging pieces of the mosaic to form a coherent picture: by contrast, in the Cannons Te Deum many clauses of the text receive the luxurious treatment of individually developed movements. Paradoxically, the latter procedure tends towards a more fragmented overall effect: there are several places in the Cannons setting where the listener has to wait rather too long for a half-verse to play itself out. In the A major Te Deum, on the other hand, there are sequences of sections in which there is only just enough time to digest one event before the next is presented. This also has the effect of throwing into greater prominence the two substantial arias for Francis Hughes, which become more extended contemplative episodes within the overall scheme of the Te Deum: in terms of external features these arias, featuring the obbligato woodwind players as well as Hughes, are the most characteristic elements in this Chapel Royal setting. If the scoring of the A major Te Deum lacks the glamour that the trumpets contributed to the Caroline setting, the imagination with which Handel employs the chamber-music potential of his vocal and instrumental forces is ample compensation.

It will be seen from Table 9.2 that the paragraph structure of the A major Te Deum closely follows that of the Caroline setting (compare Table 5.1), with

Table 9.2. *Te Deum in A major, HWV 282*

Verse		No.	Key	T/s	Voices[a]	Orch.[b]
1–2.	We praise thee	1	A	¢	sAatBbb	full
3.	To thee all angels	2	b, f♯		T, chorus	full[c]
4.	To thee Cherubim	3	f♯		A	str.
5–6.	Holy, holy		b, f♯		chorus	full
7.	The glorious company	4	b	¾	B, chorus	full
8.	The goodly fellowship		D		T, chorus	
9.	The noble army		f♯		A, chorus	
10.	The holy Church		f♯, b		A, chorus	
11–13.	The Father		B, F♯	¢	chorus	
14–15.	Thou art the King	5	D	¢	chorus	full
16–18.	When thou tookest	6	D	¾	A	full[d]
19–20.	We believe	7	e	¢	B, A	full[c]
	(help Thy servants)				chorus	full
21.	Make them to be numbered		G		B	str.
22–3.	O Lord, save		e		chorus	full
24–5.	Day by day	8	C	¢	chorus	full
26–8.	Vouchsafe, O Lord	9	a	¾	A	full[c]
29.	O Lord, in thee	10	A	¢	chorus	full

[a] chorus = sAatBBb. No distinction is made for this, except where A and B have solo music within chorus movements.

[b] full = ob. or fl., bn. and str.; 4-part strings throughout.

[c] obbligato parts for ob., bn.

[d] obbligato parts for fl., bn.

only one significant change: in Caroline Te Deum verses 7–23 are treated as two sections, breaking at verses 15/16, while the A major Te Deum has a three-section arrangement, dividing at verses 13/14 and 18/19. Seven paragraphs result: verses 1–6; 7–13; 14–18; 19–23; 24–5; 26–8; 29. The third and sixth paragraphs receive more extended treatment than in the Caroline Te Deum, as the two aria movements. There is one other respect in which this Te Deum is individual and remarkable. Handel's previous settings of the text had included excursions to relative minor keys for verse 3, 'To thee all Angels cry aloud'. He makes a similar move here, but this time it introduces a substantial structure around B minor and F sharp minor that transcends changes of tempo and metre (and even decisively final-sounding cadences), running all the way to verses

11–13. More remarkably still, it culminates in a remarkable conclusion in B major and F sharp major, the most colourfully distant relationships to the tonic in any of his Te Deum settings. Unlike any of the others, the emotional climax of this version is 'The Father of an infinite Majesty; Thine honourable, true and only Son; Also the Holy Ghost the Comforter'.

No. 1: *We praise thee, O God*

This is arranged from the first movement of the Cannons Te Deum. Handel's alteration to the tempo, Non troppo allegro in place of Andante, presumably indicates that a slightly slower interpretation was appropriate for the Chapel Royal. The springing dotted rhythms immediately convey both the exaltation of the text and the scale of the work: their effect would have been lost in a larger building such as St Paul's Cathedral. The previous version was composed for the fullest complement of vocal forces in the Cannons establishment, with parts for treble, three tenors, and bass. Handel adapted this to give seven vocal parts for the Chapel Royal,[19] with short solos for Hughes and Weely derived from the former Cannons parts for Oboe and Tenor 2. For the first sixteen bars his alterations to the movement, apart from transposition, were matters of layout and detail. The most interesting revision occurs in bar 13, where the string parts are brought in half a bar earlier in order to provide interest to a slack part of the bar. The remainder of the movement, covering the second clause of the first verse and all of the second verse, is dispatched in a mere seven bars of new, basically homophonic, music, with the orchestral dotted-rhythm theme providing a unifying link in bars 17–18. The strong dispatch of verse 2 in the final four bars provides the transition to the minor-key area, and the movement ends on the dominant of B minor. This is the same key, and the same cadence, as the Utrecht setting at this point in the text, but as already noted the long-term consequences are very different. The immediate transition is smoother, since the opening of the following movement picks up the dominant chord.

No. 2: *To thee all angels cry aloud*

In general character this movement is indebted to the Utrecht Te Deum, where the same text is set in the same key and with the same type of jagged

---

[19] This did not entail seven 'real' contrapuntal parts: the layout was useful mainly for distinguishing the solo alto and bass parts from the chorus lines. Although Gates was given a separate stave, his part differs from the chorus bass part (Bass 3) only in small details. In bars 10–13 the principal soloists, Hughes and Weely, operate in tandem; nevertheless, Handel did not apparently think of them as a 'concertino' group. Compare the layout of this movement with HWV 250b No. 3.

accompaniment.[20] The treatment of the text is also similar, with the chorus answering the soloist at 'The Heav'ns and all the Powers therein', though this time there are only two statements instead of three. In other respects this is a completely new movement. The leading solo melodies are independent of the Utrecht version,[21] the accompaniment is differently handled, and the harmonic progressions are more forceful. The opening string figuration recedes into an accompaniment to a duet for oboe and bassoon: this in turn gives place to the entry of the tenor soloist, and finally the chorus completes the ensemble. By contrast the Utrecht setting, with its 'till-ready' string accompaniment that never grows into anything more significant, is underdeveloped. Within a mere sixteen bars Handel here created a fully rounded movement in a more mature style.

No. 3: To thee Cherubim and Seraphim

The verbal text completes that from the previous movement, and this is faithfully reflected in the music, which completes the binary structure left in mid-air at the end of No. 2 by returning the tonality towards B minor. Pianissimo staccato quavers replace the broken rhythms of the previous movement as the principal accompaniment figuration. As in all of Handel's previous settings, verses 5–6 of the text receive straightforward homophonic choral treatment after the threefold repetition of 'Holy': there is one momentary resemblance to the parallel movement of the Cannons Te Deum, in the rhythm of the solo part at bar 5.

No. 4: The glorious company of the Apostles

The first section of the movement is similar in character to its predecessors in the Utrecht and Cannons settings: the words are set in triple time, in the minor mode, and with a running quaver accompaniment. The general scheme and some of the melodic formulae can be traced back to the Cannons version, as also the choral responses on 'praise thee', but the alternations with the soloists are more direct and to the point.[22] As to the Grave at 'The Father of an infinite Majesty', the Utrecht and Cannons settings have a similar change of speed and

[20] This type of accompaniment is usually associated with rather anguished texts, as for example in the choruses 'Doleful tidings' from *Deborah*, 'The people shall hear' from *Israel in Egypt*, and 'How dark, O Lord' from *Jephtha*. Perhaps a question still remains as to the sense in which Handel interpreted the word 'cry' in this verse of the Te Deum.

[21] The opening phrase of the solo part is related to the bass aria 'Mein Vater' from Handel's *Brockes Passion* (HWV 48), HHA I/7, p. 26.

[22] The plan of giving each clause (Apostles/Prophets/Martyrs) to a different soloist goes back much further, to Purcell's setting, but the addition of the chorus on 'praise Thee' seems to have been an original idea of Handel's in the Cannons and A major settings.

metre at this point, and the declamation in the A Major Te Deum is closer in rhythm to the former than to the latter, but the throbbing quaver accompaniment, anticipating that in 'O Lord, save thy people', is a new feature. The details of recomposition are, however, subsidiary to the novel overall effect of this passage in context, which floats off into airy regions to conclude on F sharp major: a sublime moment, created with the simplest chordal word-setting and modest performing resources. The words 'the Holy Ghost, the Comforter' conclude the first section of the Te Deum text, the hymn to the Trinity, so this is a logical place for a pause, before moving on to the second, Christ-centred, section. Even so, the effect of the climax here is startling, in relation to all the comparable previous English settings.

No. 5: *Thou art the King of Glory, O Christ*

The unprepared shift of the key centre to D major and the change in tempo brings matters back to earth rather abruptly. The music is taken from the Cannons Te Deum, where it had been worked into an extended imitative movement of more than seventy bars. Handel now gives a précis of it in nine bars, and at the opening he does not even allow a full statement of the theme from the Cannons version: the subject is presented in tandem with a loose countersubject derived from the subject's third bar, and the working-out closes with a perfect cadence after only four bars. The same material is adapted to lead immediately into the beginning of the second clause, 'Thou art the everlasting Son', and the parts quickly combine into groups, gravitating towards the choral homophony that is Handel's favourite time-saving device in the shorter Te Deum settings. In contrast to the end of the comparable movement from the Cannons Te Deum, the section ends with an imperfect cadence that sets up the transition to the next movement. It is arguable that in this section Handel's drive towards compression went a step too far, and rather cruelly dispersed the vision from the preceding Grave. However, its rather breathless urgency makes a good foil for the more leisurely aria that follows.

No. 6: *When thou tookest upon thee*

After a succession of short movements for solo and chorus, No. 6 is the first aria-type movement in the Te Deum, and the first one for which extended comparison with a previous setting can be made. The principal theme of the movement comes from the Cannons Te Deum, and Handel followed the key structure from the parent movement: central excursions to the dominant, relative minor, and sub-dominant keys lead to a return to the tonic at bar 61 (comparable to bar 57 in the Cannons movement). Beyond this, the music is entirely new. The introduction of the obbligato woodwind duo (flute and bassoon) led Handel to rethink the presentation of answering phrases in terms of three blocks of sound (woodwind/strings/voice).

Recomposition, rather than adaptation, was in any case rather forced upon Handel. In about the same number of bars as in the comparable Cannons movement, he encompasses three times as much of the text: in this respect the movement is almost as compact as No. 3 of the Caroline Te Deum. There are three distinct topics in the text, and Handel starts again with new melodic formulae for each verse, while at the same time preserving the overall musical unity of the aria. By running verses 16–18 together he sacrificed the opportunity for contrast at 'When Thou hadst overcome the sharpness of death / Thou didst open the kingdom of Heaven' which had provided striking moments in both the Utrecht and the Cannons settings. Instead the aria succeeds by purely musical means: the intrinsic interest of the melodic material and its development. The new ideas in this setting begin with the answering theme for 'Thou didst not abhor', based on a falling fourth and imitated by the woodwind (bars 22–30). The climbing phrase for the second verse, 'When thou hadst overcome', is derived from the parallel passage in the previous version of the aria, though to different words (see Ex. 9.7).[23] The third verse, 'Thou sittest at the right hand of God', introduces new music, enlivened by imitation between vocal and woodwind soloists. Handel did not accompany the return to the tonic at bar 61 with a reprise of the opening melodic material, as had happened in the Cannons version, and this faithfully reflects the difference between the two movements: the Cannons music carried a repeat of the opening text, but the new setting has moved on to a different verse of the Te Deum by the time the return to the tonic is reached.

Handel restored the tempo to that which he had originally designated for the comparable movement in the Cannons Te Deum, where he altered Andante to Larghetto.

Ex. 9.7. (*a*) Cannons Te Deum, No. 5; (*b*) Te Deum in A major, No. 5

---

[23] It was also, in the first place, a logical extension of the movement's opening theme.

No. 7: We believe that thou shalt come

This is a composite movement of three short sections.[24] The material of the
first two, both of which begin with soloists and culminate in chorus entries, is
derived quite closely from Handel's setting of the same texts in the Cannons Te
Deum. Such were the accidents of the key schemes in the two works that he
was even able to reuse music in the same key. The instrumental introduction
contains a technical tour de force. The Cannons version had begun with an
oboe cantilena anticipating the melody of the vocal parts, accompanied by
simple string chords. Handel introduced into this pre-composed material an
obbligato part for the bassoon soloist in the Chapel Royal version, which
imitates figures from the oboe part and immediately becomes a natural part
of the musical fabric (Ex. 9.8). The ensuing verse is adapted from the Cannons
version with minor amendments to the layout, but the second verse, 'Make
them to be numbered', received more extensive revision. In the solo section
only the background of a moving-quaver instrumental bass and the key of G
major is retained: the florid solo for the bass singer is new, replacing a duet for
two tenors in the Cannons Te Deum. In the choral continuation Handel
shifted material from his earlier version around a little, giving a more emphatic
declamation reinforced by slightly simpler harmonic progressions.[25] A remarkably sturdy product emerges as a result of some fairly simple musical carpentry:
half a bar added at bar 25, half a bar subtracted at bar 27, and bar 29 recomposed
to replace two former bars.

The most striking change to the second section lies in the simple omission of
the Cannons version's closing three-bar ritornello, so that the prayer 'Govern
them and lift them up for ever' now gives way to spontaneous rejoicing, with
an abrupt change of speed and key: only the treble e″ is a link between the two
sections. Once again, Handel produces a superbly effective progression-by-
reaction, a technique that he had successfully employed in previous Chapel
Royal works, including the Caroline Te Deum and HWV 250b.

No. 8: Day by day we magnify thee

Though the rhythm of 'Day by day' owes something to the Utrecht setting,
the material is new and so is its treatment. Handel sustains the musical interest
by alternating the chordal figure for 'Day by day' with a scalic cantus firmus

---

[24] Chrysander, following some secondary copies, made the movement appear more fragmented than Handel intended in *HG* 37 by inserting a double bar after bar 17: there is a page
turn in the autograph at this point, but Handel did not insert even a single barline.

[25] The simplification included the removal of a diminished seventh chord at bar 25 of the
Cannons Te Deum.

Ex. 9.8. Te Deum in A major, No. 4

theme,[26] heard successively in soprano, bass, and tenor chorus parts, and the last entry is accompanied by choral figures derived from the orchestral accompaniment. The scoring of the last bars is of some interest: cellos and bassoon double the tenor cantus firmus in the middle of the texture, leaving bass voices, double basses, and organ with the harmonic bass.[27]

[26] Once again, a variation on the 'Non nobis' type of cantus firmus, which was obviously a favourite of Handel's, since he also used it in the last movement of the Utrecht Te Deum (see Ch. 4) and the last movement of the anthem HWV 256b, the companion anthem to the A major Te Deum.

[27] In *HG* 37 Chrysander included most of Handel's bassoon cues but missed the last one: 'NB les Bassons colla Parte et Violoncelli' next to the tenor part at bar 56.

No. 9: *Vouchsafe, O Lord*

This movement owes nothing to Handel's previous settings of the text, but the opening thematic material comes from the aria 'Amor, nel mio penar' from Handel's opera *Flavio*, composed and performed in 1723. That movement was written for the castrato Senesino, as his final aria in the opera, so in this case there is a rare example of some comparability between the music that Handel wrote for his operatic and Chapel Royal soloists. The held notes in the opening phrases seem to require the same expressive and technical treatment as examples previously noted in Handel's music for Elford, in the same register (see pp. 66 and 94). The opera aria, in the key of B flat minor, has an obbligato part for oboe, which may have been played by Kytch (in notated A minor) on the sharp-pitch instrument that had probably been specially made or adapted for the Chapel Royal: see Chapter 19. Beyond the opening theme, the structures of the two movements are not very similar: more significantly, the livelier activity added by the bassoon part and by the introduction of a new rhythmic figure (first heard on the oboe at bar 6) gives a subtly different mood to the anthem movement. The style of the movement seems to be largely instrumental in conception, though the alto solo is lyrical in the serious vein which characterized all settings of this text from Purcell's famous original onwards. Handel's bassoonist must have been no mean executant: the instrument's complete range of more than two octaves is exploited to the full, with scarcely a pause for breath.

No. 10: *O Lord, in thee have I trusted*

This chorus is based on new music, worked in Handel's favourite theme-combination manner, on principles well tried in the previous settings. The bold opening followed by the shorter-note continuation 'let me never be confounded' is a pattern familiar from the Utrecht and Caroline settings, and indeed the quaver figure for 'let me never be confounded' is very close to that from the Caroline Te Deum.[28] The melodic contours of the opening emphasize 'Thee' as the climax more strongly than in Handel's previous settings. The minim-rhythm theme and the quaver-rhythm answer are soon combined with a running semiquaver passage which is first heard in the orchestra but is cunningly used as chorus material in the lead up to a grand reprise of the opening at bar 20. The movement, short though it is, is a fitting conclusion to a work that may be regarded as Handel's masterpiece in 'brevis' settings of this canticle: the faithful are sent on their way in confident and jubilant mood.

---

[28] The form found in the A Major Te Deum derives from Kuhnau, *Frische Clavier Früchte*, Sonata Sesta, third movement, bars 34–5.

Throughout the work he successfully compressed musical content without stemming the flow, and created big effects with small resources: this Te Deum exhibits nearly every facet of Handel's English church music, but on a miniature scale.

Autograph

The pages of the Te Deum (GB-Lbl RM 20.g.4, fos. 1–20) and *Let God arise* (HWV 256b) have stave-rulings of a type which is not found elsewhere in Handel's autographs. The autograph of the Te Deum lacks the second movement, and this presents something of a puzzle. It seems that for some reason Handel wrote the movement on a separate sheet, which was not part of the original gatherings. His cue 'To the [*sic*] all Angels from the other score' is written at the end of No. 1 on fo. 3^r, and fo. 3^v continues with No. 3: the cue is not crammed onto the page, nor does it seem to have been added as an afterthought. The appearance of the autograph at this point does not support the possibility that he simply forgot to set the words of No. 2 and had to make it good afterwards; neither does the musical construction of this section, since Nos. 2 and 3 clearly belong together. The reference to 'the other score' only compounds the mystery. The possibility cannot be completely ruled out that some Te Deum setting composed by Handel in the 1720s, from which the composer salvaged No. 2, has been lost. Such a work might, for example, have been composed for the Chapel Royal service on 5 January 1723/4: see the proposed chronological scheme at the end of Chapter 7. Whatever the nature of the 'other score', it was lost by the 1740s.[29] The text of No. 2 can, however, be confidently established from manuscript copies.

The following singers were named by Handel:

No. 1:	Mr Hughs (Alto 1); Mr Wheely (Bass 1); Mr Gates (Bass 2)
No. 3:	Mr Hughs (Alto)
No. 4:	[Mr] H[ughs] (Alto 1); Mr Getting (Tenor, at bar 12); [Mr] W[hely] (Bass 1); [Mr] G[ates] (Bass 2)
No. 5:	Mr Hughs (Alto)
No. 6:	Mr Hughs (Alto); Mr Getting (Tenor); Mr Whely (Bass 1); Mr Gates (Bass 2); Canto part at bar 41 marked 'all'
No. 7:	Mr Hughs (Alto)

Early copies of the anthem indicate that the following names also appeared at the start of the lost autograph of No. 2: Mr Hughs (Alto), Mr Getting (Solo Tenor).

---

[29] The copyist of the 'Aylesford' score (GB-Mp MS 130 Hd4 v.325) copied Handel's cue and left a page of empty staves for No. 2, but apparently could not trace the music.

It is remarkable that, although his part is named throughout, Gates was given virtually no solo work. The solo parts in No. 4 were subjected to some rearrangement by Handel during the course of composition. The bass solo at bar 5 was begun on Gates's stave and then transferred to Weely's; the alto solo at bar 18 was originally given to 'Mr Bell' (who is otherwise not named on the autograph) on Alto 2, and then transferred to Hughes on Alto 1. One possible inference is that Handel discovered or remembered during the composition of the movement that Bell was not 'in waiting' for the month of the performance.

There are a few uncertainties as to Handel's intentions on some practical details. In Nos. 5 and 7 he wrote the music for Violin 2 and Viola on the same stave but did not show the viola part consistently throughout. Although the bassoon obbligato part in Nos. 2, 5, and 7 is obviously for a soloist, and only one bassoonist is accounted for in the payments to performers, Handel's cues in No. 6 (bars 53 and 55) mention 'Bassons'. In the alto part at bars 25–6 of No.7 he wrote two alternative versions of the melodic line.[30] The upper line appears to have been written slightly later than the lower, and this is what we would expect, knowing that Hughes was a 'high' alto: Handel probably realized that the low cadential ending did not suit his singer very well and supplied the higher version as a more practical alternative. Only the lower version appears in secondary manuscript copies.

Let God arise (HWV 256b)

This is the shortest of Handel's Chapel Royal works from the second period: it comprises only four movements and takes less than a quarter of an hour in performance. Compressed though the A major setting of the Te Deum is, Handel may have felt that his music was still on the long side for the intended Chapel Royal service, and so he deliberately provided a short companion anthem. If the suggested chronology of his Chapel Royal music is correct, this would have been the last of his anthems for George I, and perhaps some allowance has to be made for the advancing age of the King,[31] or even for the possibility that Handel composed the music so close to the King's return from Hanover that he took account of the effects of a particularly bad North Sea crossing on the King's stamina.

Handel used only the framework of the opening and closing choruses from the related Cannons anthem *Let God arise* (HWV 256a), placing two newly

---

[30] *HG* 37 reproduces them exactly as in the autograph.
[31] The king perhaps remained standing during the performance of the anthem at Chapel Royal services: see the reference to George II in Ch. 19 (p. 509).

composed solo movements between them. The psalm text was rather more warlike than those of the previous anthems in the series, and this might reflect a time of instability in Britain's foreign affairs: there was growing tension during the period following the Treaty of Vienna (April 1725), with occasional scares throughout 1726–7 that a war with Spain might be imminent.[32] However, it is more likely that in his composition of this anthem Handel was more influenced by the pre-existing Cannons anthem than by the diplomatic climate. There is, in fact, little reason to see any specific contemporary messages behind any of the Chapel Royal anthems from the 1720s. They and the canticles were composed for inclusion in services of Morning Prayer on Sunday mornings at the Chapel Royal that were distinguished from the normal routine only because they marked the King's return to St James's Palace: the key factor was the enhancement of the music that was provided by the orchestral accompaniment. It was all to the good when, as in Psalm 68, the text provided stimulating images for musical setting. The pre-existence of his Cannons setting of *Let God arise* must have been a major factor when Handel planned the anthem: his choice may also have been influenced by the fact that HWV 256a had been one of the Cannons anthems that included a specified (though admittedly not very independent) bassoon part in the scoring.

Although the Chapel Royal version of *Let God arise* is 8–10 minutes shorter than the Cannons anthem, Handel lost surprisingly little from the text. 'Let the righteous be glad' (verse 3 of the psalm, an aria for a treble soloist in the Cannons anthem, and not included in HWV 256b) largely repeated sentiments that are present in other movements. Handel's new short duet version of 'O sing unto God' is an improvement on the Cannons setting, which had been a rather overextended movement. The Cannons anthem incorporated a verse from Psalm 36 with some lively imagery referring to the crossing of the Red Sea; the loss of this is perhaps regrettable, but it was in the nature of a parallel commentary and its omission left no hole in the coherence of the anthem text.

No. 1: *Let God arise*

This movement, derived from the first 'chorus' of the Cannons anthem, falls into two sections: a common-time opening (Allegro ma non troppo in the Cannons version, but no tempo indicated for HWV 256b), followed by a faster triple-time section (Allegro in both versions) for the second half of the verse, 'let them also that hate him fly before him'. The Cannons material itself is excellent, the defiant chordal statements of the opening section leading to the unrighteous being thrown down with fine rhetorical effect on 'be scatter'd', and then put to flight and confusion with the descending-scale figures and

---

[32] See Hatton, *George I*, 277–8.

Ex. 9.9. *Let God arise:* (*a*) HWV 256a, No. 2; HWV 256b, No. 1

cross-rhythms of the triple-time continuation. Handel rearranged the second, triple-time, section for the Chapel Royal forces without substantial change in content, combining the quaver figures between different voice parts to give added strength and rendering the hemiola rhythms in staccato minims rather than crotchets and rests (see Ex. 9.9). He replaced 'flee before Him' (as found in the Prayer Book, and the Cannons anthem) with 'fly before Him' throughout: perhaps someone had pointed out to him the possible confusion between 'flee' and 'flea'.

The first part of the movement received more substantial revision. The original introduction served well enough in place of a separate sinfonia, with a little strengthening of the bass part and the removal of a redundant bar in the echo passage immediately preceding the chorus entry. Handel recognized that the semiquaver tremolando representing 'scattered', although an excellent idea in itself and effective in the orchestral parts, had been rather overdone in the Cannons anthem, and he shortened the choral section of the movement to remove this excess.[33] All of his amendments were effective in tightening up the drive of the movement. Some of the most striking ideas, derived immediately from the Cannons anthem, originated from Handel's earlier compositions. The scattering of the enemies at bars 22–3 uses material from the Birthday Ode for Queen Anne (No. 2, bars 78–9)[34] and from the Latin Psalm *Dixit Dominus* ('implebit ruinas', No. 7, bars 56–61).[35] The Latin borrowing is particularly interesting, since the second part of the anthem movement ('Let them also that hate him') is also musically similar to the following movement in *Dixit Dominus* ('Conquasabit', bars 62 et seq.). The instrumental ritornello at the end of the movement seems to have been inspired by the final bars of No. 8 of the Birthday Ode.[36]

---

[33] Handel cut bar 15 from HWV 256a; bars 21 and 32 replaced bars 22–6 and 37–9 from HWV 256a, respectively. One of these revisions removed a homophonic passage in which the text had received rather dubious syllabic treatment, bars 25–6 of the Cannons anthem.

[34] *HHA* I/6, pp. 13–14.

[35] *HG* 38, p. 100: movement numbering from *Dixit Dominus*, ed. Watkins Shaw (*NHE*).

[36] *HHA* I/6, p. 59.

No. 2: *Like as the smoke*

From the Cannons setting of the same words two relatively insignificant features were preserved: the semiquaver runs associated with the word 'drive' and the cadence figures for 'so shalt thou drive them away'.[37] Otherwise all, both thematically and structurally, is new. Handel changed the metre for the Chapel Royal anthem from the triple time of the Cannons setting, probably in order to introduce some variety following the triple-time section at the end of No. 1. This alteration tipped the balance in the opposite direction: HWV 256b is dominated by quadruple and duple metres, but there is enough variety in speed and mood to compensate for this.

The Cannons setting of 'Like as the smoke' in HWV 256a is a continuous minor-key aria (for tenor) in binary form, with the relative major as the mid-point key centre and a swift return to the tonic at the start of the second half of the text, 'like as wax melteth at the fire'. For the Chapel Royal version Handel took the idea a stage further and produced a novel double movement. The first half ('Like as the smoke') is given to the bass soloist in F major, and the second half ('like as wax') to the alto soloist in D minor: in terms of length, both halves are substantial enough to have been free-standing anthem movements. Pulse, metre, and principal thematic material remain constant throughout, but the movement ends in a different key from that in which it started. The effect, with the change of voice and key halfway, is very striking, comparable to a set of variations in which the composer decided halfway through to devote the rest of the piece to developing the possibilities of the theme in the relative minor mode. Both halves of the movement are complete in themselves: the bass's section is a full binary aria, but the alto's continuation is looser in structure and rather more discursive. The key scheme of the alto section includes a piece of musical irony: the first modulation is to F major, and Handel introduces the ritornello theme momentarily in bars 65–8, as if a permanent return to F major was to be expected and the movement is, after all, to be in conventional binary form. Instead, the music then sets off towards G minor and A minor before returning to D minor at the close.

The bass solo is rather more operatic in style than most in Handel's church music. Although it is not a conventional 'rage' aria, the driving away of the enemies is vividly depicted, using the full range of Weely's voice to good effect (Ex. 9.10). The alto's half of the movement, more constricted in vocal range, presents the vision of the ungodly perishing at the presence of God in music which is less aggressive, more sinuous, but no less serious in tone. The alto never sings the semiquaver figuration associated with the bass's 'drive them

---

[37] Handel's distribution of the instrumentation on the bass line also follows that of the Cannons anthem: bn. & vc./org. & d.b.

Ex. 9.10. *Let God arise* (HWV 256b), No. 2

(a)

Like as the smoke,   like as the smoke,   as the smoke van-ish-eth

(b)

so shalt thou drive them a - way,_____   so shalt thou drive them a -way.

away', but this figuration is continually present in the orchestral background and generates some tension under the sustained voice part at bars 60–2. Handel's scoring, carefully specified, seems to be deliberately bottom-heavy at this point, with a full complement of cello(s), double basses, and bassoon(s) playing the semiquaver roulades, and it is marvellously effective in performance.

No. 3: O sing unto God

This short movement is by way of a relaxation: beatific contemplation as a contrast to the prophetic threats of the previous movement. The two soloists from that movement join together in a duet, but they do not dominate the music: instead, they are part of a richer texture, interwoven with the orchestral parts. The movement opens with a duet for oboe and bassoon, anticipating the vocal duet: thereafter, over a primitive harmonic bass the voices, violins,[38] and oboe develop and extend the opening melody, with occasional assistance from the solo bassoon. The structure is binary, but the interest of the movement lies in its sonorities rather than its construction. The theme and its characteristic figuration became firmly embedded in Handel's imagination, for he reused the idea twice in works composed over the following quarter-century, in the opera *Arminio* and in his unperformed score for *Alceste*, the music for the latter surfacing publicly in *The Choice of Hercules*.[39] In none of these movements was the verbal text similar in content to that of the anthem. Musical ideas relating to melody, harmony, and texture in the anthem movement are

---

[38] Handel omitted any reference to violas, even in the final ritornello, and so provided a trap for the unwary: No. 3 was one of the movements inserted into Cannons anthem HWV 256a in the Aylesford part-books (US-Cu Ms 437) and in Arnold's published edition. Although it appears to be a plausible Cannons piece, the movement's typical Chapel Royal alto/bass vocal combination and its indifferent contribution to the key scheme of the Cannons anthem immediately arouses suspicion.

[39] Duet 'Il fuggir, cara mia vita' (*Arminio*); aria 'Ye fleeting Shades (*Alceste*); and aria 'Lead, Goddess' (*The Choice of Hercules*).

traceable to 'Be ye sure that the Lord' from the Utrecht Jubilate: that relationship extends to the duet idea, both vocal and instrumental, to the rhythmic bass, and even to the key of A minor, but the melodic treatment underwent a remarkable metamorphosis. An anticipation of the Chapel Royal anthem can be heard in the outline of the orchestral bass part in the Utrecht movement, but it is hardly noticeable on paper: this is an opposite case from many of Handel's 'borrowings', where visual similarities in the scores are often not matched by the aural experience.[40]

No. 4: Blessed be God

This movement was adapted from the final movement of the Cannons anthem. It is a chorus which sets a 'Non nobis' type of scalic cantus firmus[41] against a flowing bass and a number of lively 'Hallelujah' figures: as noted in Chapter 6, the opening material had itself been reworked from the last movement of the Utrecht Te Deum. The spacious Chapel Royal arrangement with six vocal lines (as against four in the Cannons anthem) allowed Handel some opportunity for filling in holes in the harmony,[42] but in general he preferred to dispose the voice parts with linear rather than harmonic objects in view. He combined the vocal parts in order to bring important strands of the texture to the foreground: in turn, Bass 1 helps out the Tenors, Alto 1 helps the Trebles, and the Tenors strengthen Alto 2.[43]

Handel altered the notation of the music in the course of the transfer, doubling the note values. The Cannons anthem movement is barred in 𝐜 (4/4) and the Chapel Royal movement in ¢ (2/2), one bar of the Cannons movement becoming two bars in the later version. There seems to be no obvious motive for the change, though it may have been intended to clarify the tempo of the music. In the Cannons anthem Handel had at first written 'Allegro', but then changed this to 'Andante': perhaps he thought that, if he gave the music an alla breve appearance, the musicians would know from experience how it should be treated. In the Chapel Royal anthem he did not add any tempo indication as such.

Two substantial cuts were made when Handel adapted the Cannons movement,[44] and these reveal what he was prepared to sacrifice to the cause of

[40] As e.g. in the apparent similarity of the openings to *Nisi Dominus* and *Zadok the priest*.

[41] See n. 26 above, and also Ex. 6.5.

[42] In the course of doing so, Handel introduced a set of consecutive fifths between the viola and bass parts over the barline of 21–2, but these are not audible in the general busyness.

[43] Handel did not label the parts at the start of the movement, but presumably the arrangement followed that of the first movement, with Alto 1 and Bass 1 staves intended for Hughes and Weely, respectively.

[44] Bars 16½–20 and 40–4 from HWV 256a; HWV 256b bars 37–8 were also compressed from bars 24–5 of the Cannons anthem.

strengthening the movement as a whole. The first cut, after bar 31 of the Chapel Royal version, attenuates the cantus firmus in the Bass part to its first three steps only. Although this looks rather unsatisfactory on paper, it usefully breaks up the theme just when its development is in danger of becoming predictable. The scale pattern is carried up harmonically into the Tenor part in bar 32, and the complete passage now serves to introduce the dominant entry in the Bass at bar 33. With the second cut Handel removed a passage that had included some contrapuntal interest: bars 36–41 of the Cannons anthem had presented the cantus firmus theme in stretto canon between the upper two voice parts, the only appearance of this device in the movement. It is curious that he did not wish to preserve this piece of ingenuity, though it is characteristic of the difference between the music he wrote for the two establishments that he should go for the simpler effect in the Chapel Royal version. In the final bars of the movement he broadened the ending by proportionately doubling the note values from HWV 256a.

Autograph

As already noted, the stave-rulings are of a type identical to those found in the A Major Te Deum.[45] The paper gatherings are numbered in ink, possibly by Handel, and indicate that fo. 33, which has the end of the duet movement on one side and blank staves on the other, is a separate sheet. The most likely explanation of this odd page is that, as in HWV 250b, Handel worked out the first and last movements from the parent Cannons anthem and then filled in the new inner movements: it so happened that these movements occupied an untidy number of sheets.

Assuming that Handel continued to write the last movement with much the same spacing as before, two leaves have been lost from the end of the autograph, but the missing bars can be restored with confidence from an early manuscript copy which accurately reproduces many features from the autograph.[46] It seems probable, from the evidence of this copy, that Handel did not add either of his characteristic terminal annotations, 'Fine' or 'S.D.G.', at the end of the movement. Perhaps the anthem was composed before the accompanying A major Te Deum, which does have 'S.D.G.' at the end.

The following singers were named by Handel:

No. 1:   Mr. Hughs (Alto 1); Mr. Wheely (Bass 1)
No. 2:   Mr. Wheely (Bass); Mr. Hughs (Alto at bar 50)
No. 3:   Mr. Hughs (Alto); Mr. Wheely (Bass)

[45] The anthem autograph, GB-Lbl RM 20.g.4, fos. 21–37, is now bound with that for the Te Deum.
[46] GB-Mp MS 130 Hd4, v. 47(2).

In No. 1 the staves for Alto 2 and Bass 2 are labelled 'Chorus'; there are no names at the start of No. 4, but the layout of the staves is identical to that in No. 1.

Throughout the work Handel took some care over the instrumentation of the bass line, using separate staves to clarify his intentions. In No. 1 one stave is given to bassoon and cello, leaving a separate (unlabelled) Basso Continuo part that was presumably for organ and double bass. The same arrangement is continued in No. 2, specific references being made to double basses next to the continuo stave. In both movements Handel referred to a violoncello in the singular, obviously intending that a soloist would play with the bassoon. If there were any ripieno cello players they presumably followed the continuo line:[47] there are no references to them, however, and it is possible that Handel's orchestra for this anthem included one cello and two double basses.[48] One obvious inference from his layout of the score is that the basso continuo group might have consisted of double bass and organ rather than cello and organ.[49] In No. 2 bar 42, at the bass soloist's final cadence and the place where a cadenza would have occurred in an operatic aria, Handel treated the instrumental bass line in exactly the same manner as for the theatre, silencing the solo cello/bassoon part and leaving the accompaniment to the basso continuo stave. In Nos. 3 and 4 the bassoon has a separate stave in the score, so the cello and double bass parts were presumably to be derived from the continuo line.

Probably through accidents of transmission, copies of the anthem are found in some early manuscript collections of Handel's church music that do not include its companion Te Deum and, more remarkably still, it was the Chapel Royal version that found its way into the first published collections of the 'Chandos Anthems' from 1784 onwards, in place of the Cannons anthem with the same title.[50]

The repertory of anthems and canticle settings that has been described in Chapters 5, 8, and 9 represents Handel's most characteristic 'Chapel Royal music'. It was composed for the enhancement of the regular services of Morning Prayer in the Chapel, and designed to make the most of the resources of the Chapel's voices, in collaboration with a related group of string players

[47] Two movements of the anthem were included in the Aylesford part-books for HWV 256a (US-Cu MS 437), but unfortunately the copyist arranged the parts mainly to suit his own convenience, and they provide no further enlightenment as to Handel's own treatment of the bass line.

[48] Compare also the single cello clearly specified at the beginning of Handel's Anthem on the Peace: see Ch. 14. See also Ch. 17, 'Stringed Instruments for the Bass Line and the Continuo' (pp. 474–9).

[49] In Germany the use of violone (probably at 8′ pitch) with the organ was one conventional combination for the accompaniment of sacred music.

[50] See Burrows, *Dissertation*, i. 390–1.

from the King's Musicians. The pieces could probably just be accommodated within the acceptable time limit of the routine Sunday morning services in the Chapel, the timetable for which was governed by the Royal procession into the Closet at the beginning and the 'public' dinner afterwards. The scale of the music was ideally matched to the performing forces available, and to the size of the venue. It was only with his last contributions to the Chapel Royal in 1749 that Handel returned to music of similar proportions and character. In the intervening twenty-three years a number of events involving the Chapel Royal required more grandiloquent music, and these took place in circumstances very different from those of the Chapel's regular services.

10

The New Reign and the 1727 Coronation

1727—Changes at Court and in the Chapel Royal

THE death of the King on his way to Hanover on 11 June 1727 generated some routine administrative activity for the Chapel Royal. The Gentlemen, in common with other employees of the court, had to be sworn into their places afresh and special arrangements were made for aged absentees, such as John Gostling, who could not come up to London for the purpose.[1] The establishment was tidied up: no fewer than five Children were discharged from the Chapel during June 1727.[2] The new King had, as Prince of Wales, attended the Chapel Royal regularly since 1720, so there was no break in the continuity of the services. The singers from the Chapel gained additional public attention, and those that were also members of the Abbey choir received additional financial rewards, as a result of their participation in the coronation service,[3] but unusual circumstances denied them the benefits accruing from a royal funeral: George I was buried in Germany.

The life of the Chapel was probably more directly affected by another death only two months after the King's, that of William Croft. There is a hint that he had not been in good health for some time, in a dedicatory epistle to Croft that accompanied the publication of the sermon by Thomas Bisse from the Three Choirs' meeting in September 1726: 'I will add my request to you, not to continue too hard a student; that so the present age may long enjoy you in person, as posterity will in your works.'[4] Nevertheless, Croft seems to have

---

[1] *OCB*, fo. 55ᵛ; Ashbee and Harley, i. 142.

[2] See App. B, B49–B53. Accounts were probably made up to the nominal date of 30 June, the end of the quarter-year in which George I's death occurred, so that arrears of pay could be calculated. The voices of the discharged choristers had probably changed earlier, so they could not have performed as trebles at the coronation.

[3] *WA2* records that the income from letting viewing places for the coronation in the 'Windows in the Vaulting', in which the members of the Abbey choir had a share, was £380.14.0, nearly double that from the previous coronation.

[4] Bisse, *Musick the Delight of the Sons of Men*, Dedication p. [2].

been active up to a short time before his death. His last anthem, *Give the King thy judgements*, was completed on 13 July.[5] On 22 July he received an advance of 6 guineas from his salary as organist of Westminster Abbey,[6] presumably to support a trip to Bath for the recovery of his health, but he died there on 14 August. In addition to his status as the Chapel's foremost native-born composer, he had been at the centre of the institutional framework, holding the offices of Composer, Organist and Master of the Children at the Chapel Royal, as well as the post of Organist at Westminster Abbey. Maurice Greene was Croft's obvious successor, but it is doubtful that Greene could have taken on all of Croft's former offices in the Chapel unless he first gave up his post at St Paul's Cathedral; in particular, it would have been difficult for him to have fulfilled the post of Master of the Children and combined this with his duties at St Paul's. When Greene was recommended as Croft's successor as Organist of the Chapel Royal, Edmund Gibson as Dean predictably made 'some difficulty about Mr. Greene's having another Post'.[7] In the event, the Chapel Royal offices were divided: on 4 September Greene was appointed Organist and Composer of the Chapel Royal, retaining his post at St Paul's, and Bernard Gates became Master of the Children.[8] Gates had already been appointed to Croft's former court office as Tuner of the Organs on 21 August.[9] Later in September John Robinson, a former Child of the Chapel Royal, succeeded to Croft's place as Organist at Westminster Abbey.

The distribution and timing of these appointments is of some importance. For the first time in the eighteenth century the leading musician at the centre of the life of the Chapel did not combine all three principal offices. The appointment of Gates as Master of the Children was to have momentous consequences for the development of Handel's oratorios, and the fact that he had control of this part of the Chapel's life also opened up the possibility of friction in the future between himself and Greene. The date of the Chapel Royal appointments does not suggest an undue or deliberate delay: a fortnight was quite a short period for the normal administrative process to operate, especially in view of the fact that many of the people who would have taken an interest in this matter had the preparations for the coronation on their minds at the same time.

---

[5] Dated autograph, GB-Lbl Add. MS 17861: see Ch. 7 n. 33.
[6] *WA1*, entry dated 22 July 1727.
[7] GB-Lpro SP 36/3(2), fos. 3–4.
[8] *NCB*, 31; Ashbee and Harley, i. 220–1.
[9] GB-Lpro LC3/64, p. 80, where the post has the antiquated form 'Tuner of the Regalls, Organs, Virginalls and Flutes'.

Handel's Naturalization

Handel's decision to adopt British nationality in February 1727, just before his forty-second birthday,[10] has already been referred to in Chapter 7. The timing of his naturalization is intriguing. The signing of the Naturalisation Bill to which his name had been added was one of George I's last public acts, and the naturalization may have made Handel's status a little more secure in London during the following years. The continuance of his pensions under George II was not endangered following George I's death, but an 'English' Handel was in a better position to face his critics as the situation in the opera house became more contentious. It is not likely that he foresaw the imminence of the King's death, and the synchronization of events in 1727 seems to have been fortuitous: when George I signed the Naturalisation Bill on 20 February 1726/7 he appeared to be in good health, and his death on the way to Hanover four months later took everyone by surprise.[11]

If Handel's naturalization was not motivated by uncertainties about his future at court under a new king, then other reasons must be considered. The possibility that he was trying to make some political point in taking British nationality, to ingratiate himself with the London opera patrons and to diminish his 'German' image, also seems unlikely as the primary motivation. His naturalization took place with as little publicity as his Chapel Royal appointment had attracted four years before: there is no mention of it at all in the newspapers,[12] who would surely have registered some comment if it had been regarded as a matter of prime public concern. Handel did not reduce any of his former German connections, nor was such a self-denying stance required in the following reign: George II was as regular a visitor to Hanover as his father had been. It has been suggested that Handel's naturalization was motivated by a desire to succeed Croft at the Chapel Royal:[13] if Croft was showing signs of ill-health in the autumn of 1726, then Handel, while he could not have foreseen the imminence of the King's death, might have predicted Croft's. As a reason for Handel's naturalization, however, this also will not stand scrutiny. He never participated in the day-to-day life of the Chapel and probably never had any

---

[10] For the official records relating to Handel's naturalization, see Deutsch, *Handel*, 202–5, and Simon, *Handel*, 284–5.

[11] Plumb, *The First Four Georges*, 66–7; Hatton, *George I*, 280–1.

[12] The most detailed reports in the newspapers for 18–21 Feb. (and the weekly papers dated 25 Feb.) state only that the King gave his assent to 'two Private Bills'.

[13] This suggestion was proposed and elaborated in Fiske, *English Theatre Music*, 174–5; at that time, however, the warrant for Handel's appointment as Composer had not been discovered, and the details of his pension were unclear.

desire to do so. He participated by providing the Chapel with music for special occasions, but was not attracted to a full-time career in church music: he had rejected that path when he left Halle, and there is no sign that he ever went back on his decision. The financial rewards to be gained from the regular Chapel Royal posts were not so significant that it was in Handel's interest to pursue them. In connection with his appointment as Composer for the Chapel Royal in 1723 he had received an additional pension of £200 per year in return for very light duties; an Organist or Composer in the normal establishment of the Chapel received less than half of that amount and had to be in attendance week by week for half of the year.[14] If he accumulated two of Croft's posts Handel could perhaps have added nearly another £200 to his income, but the additional labour involved was out of proportion to the benefits. It is rather unlikely that Handel would have been able to take over more than one of Croft's offices, since he already held one substantial pension to reward him as Composer, and was probably not a suitable candidate for Master of the Children,[15] so the additional salary as Organist would only have been in the order of £73, an amount of only moderate significance compared with his other income. Regular duties at the Chapel Royal would not have fitted in with his theatre-based career, and Handel, accustomed to being his own master, would have been the first to realize this: the prospect of having to manage Bishop Gibson in addition to the opera singers was not one to be seriously contemplated.

The remaining explanation for Handel's decision to take British nationality is much more prosaic. However uncertain the future of the Royal Academy of Music appeared to be in 1727, Handel had decided to settle in London permanently and it was logical to back this up by pursuing the appropriate legal status. There may have been some pressing personal motive in the background, such as the need to hold money or property under particular conditions.[16] There was indeed political and social benefit to be gained at court by adopting British nationality, even though this does not seem to have been Handel's primary consideration. As already noted in Chapter 7, the legal status acquired by naturalization still did not in itself qualify him to hold public office under the crown.

---

[14] The employment of a more or less permanent deputy might have been possible, though this would have involved a reduction in the income from the post, and the practice might have been less acceptable in the Chapel Royal than in London's parochial appointments.

[15] Although it is unlikely that all of the choristers lived in the Master's house, a settled married life seems to have been a tacitly understood qualification for the post.

[16] The last-minute addition of Handel's name to another petition might suggest that he took the decision quite suddenly. The terms of his occupancy of the house in Brook Street were not affected, since he rented the property.

The timing of Handel's naturalization probably had one immediate musical consequence, because it enabled him to contribute to the coronation service for King George II and Queen Caroline in October 1727. In spite of his pension relating to the Chapel Royal appointment, this privilege might well have been denied to him, or become the subject of political controversy, if he had not taken up naturalization: otherwise, as in 1714, the responsibility (and the opportunity) would have gone to one of the regular Composers for the Chapel. The coronation proved to be a landmark in Handel's association with the Chapel, but also in his wider relationship with British society. It was a well-attended event of major social significance, and his Coronation Anthems repeated the success of his Utrecht music fourteen years previously by providing the listeners with a memorable musical experience. The Chapel Royal was naturally at the centre of events for the coronation service,[17] but the Chapel singers formed the core of a much larger body of performers. Thirty-four years later the coronation was still remembered as 'the first Grand Musical Performance'[18] and in 1727 Handel apparently put together the best of London's available vocal resources, probably including some from the theatres, on a scale that was new and was applied to novel musical effect. The experience moulded Handel's outlook when he produced English oratorios in the theatre five years later, the first performances of which were promoted on the recollection of the coronation music.

The Coronation Service and the Anthems

Although the coronation service followed liturgical patterns that had been long established by historical precedent and practice,[19] circumstances had introduced considerable variation into the coronations preceding 1727. That of James II and Mary of Modena in 1685 had been the most recent coronation of a king and queen consort, but had deviated from normal practice by omitting the Holy Communion component; in 1689 the Communion service was restored, but William III and Mary II were invested as joint monarchs, an unusual proceeding that required the hurried manufacture of a second coronation chair and a second set of regalia. In some respects Anne's coronation returned to a more regular pattern, but little attention was paid to George of Denmark as the consort. Following the Act of Union in 1707, George I's coronation was the first one of a monarch of Great Britain, and also the first

---

[17] All of the soloists named on Handel's autographs of the Coronation Anthems were Chapel Royal Gentlemen.

[18] William Boyce's description in 1761: see below.

[19] See Legg, *English Coronation Records*.

one for the Hanoverian line, but there was no Queen consort: George's marriage to Sophia Dorothea had been dissolved in 1694, and if he had subsequently taken Melusine von der Schulenburg as his morganatic wife, this relationship was not recognized in Britain.

The coronation was one of the most sumptuous court occasions in every reign, and possibly the only one that regularly demanded the attendance of the full complement of the court's servants, including the Royal Musicians and the Chapel Royal. Furthermore, the coronation of 1727 saw a return to royal display on a scale that had probably not been seen since 1685. In the words of Lord Hervey, 'the Coronation was performed with all the pomp and magnificence that could be contrived; the present King differing so much from the last, that all the pageantry and splendour, badges and trappings of royalty, were as pleasing to the son as they were irksome to the father. The dress of the Queen on this occasion was as fine as the accumulated riches of the City and suburbs could make it.'[20] The traditional site for coronations was Westminster Abbey, and the service involved the Abbey staff, including the choir: at the beginning of the ceremony the royal procession was received at the West door of the Abbey by the Dean and Prebendaries with the Abbey choir, who then sang an anthem while they led the procession to the nave. In the detailed and sumptuously illustrated commemorative volume for the 1685 coronation by Francis Sandford, Lancaster Herald of Arms,[21] the individual singers from the choirs of the Chapel Royal and Westminster Abbey are named, and the illustrations show the choirs ending up in separate galleries, with yet another gallery for the principal band of instrumentalists. Whether or not this arrangement was followed exactly in 1727, the musical resources for the event included the combined choirs, supplemented by as many appropriate extra musicians as could be found. The overlap in membership between the choirs in any case implied the employment of a substantial number of deputies: in 1727 only one adult member of the Westminster Abbey choir did not also have a Chapel Royal place.

The liturgy for the 1727 coronation was prepared by William Wake, the Archbishop of Canterbury, in consultation with the Privy Council. Wake made a draft based on the coronation services in 1702 and 1714, adding in the Queen's coronation from the 1685 service; he brought this to the Privy Council on 5 September, and a final form was approved on 20 September, with the direction that 'his Grace do take care that One Hundred Copies be forthwith printed, fifty of which are to be delivered for the use of the Lords of His Majesty's most honourable Privy Council and the other Fifty, for the

[20] Sedgwick, *Some Materials*, 66.
[21] Sandford, *The History of the Coronation*.

Service of those who are to officiate at the Abbey'.²² At the same meeting the date of the coronation was moved to 11 October, a week later than originally planned, because of a tidal forecast for the River Thames that might have affected Westminster Hall, where the banquet was held following the service. Greene had been appointed to his Chapel Royal posts the day before the earlier Privy Council meeting in September.

The first mention of the music for the coronation in the London newspapers already named Handel as the composer:

London. Sept. 14 Circular letters are sent by the Lord Great Chamberlain to all Peers and Peeresses to provide themselves with suitable Habits and Equipages to attend the Coronation, and the famous Mr Handel is appointed to compose the Antheim [*sic*], which is to be sung at that Grand Ceremony. (*PM*, 12–14 Sept. 1727)²³

Two later authorities, both of them anecdotal in nature, provide some clues to the background. In the margin of his copy of John Mainwaring's biography of Handel, King George III added an annotation referring to

that wretched little crooked illnatured insignificant Writer Player and Musician the late Dr. Green Organist and Composer to King George II. who forbad his composing the Anthems at his Coronation Oct 22d. [*sic*] 1727. And ordered that G. F. Hendel should not only have that great honour but except the 1st. choose his own words. He had but four Weeks for doing this wonderful work.²⁴

We may indeed take it as probable that George III's grandfather had specifically requested Handel to compose the new music for the service and, while making due allowance for the tendentious tone of the annotation, it nevertheless seems remarkable that Maurice Greene, the Chapel Royal's new Composer, and described by the Bishop of Salisbury in his letter of recommendation as 'the greatest Musical Genius We have',²⁵ was apparently given no creative role in the service.

Secondly, Charles Burney related the following story about the 1727 coronation nearly sixty years later:

At the coronation of his late majesty, George the Second, in 1727 HANDEL had the words sent to him, by the bishops, for the anthems; at which he murmured, and took offence, as he thought it implied his ignorance of the Holy Scriptures: 'I have read my Bible very well, and shall chuse for myself'.²⁶

---

²² See Burrows, 'Handel and the 1727 Coronation', 469–70.

²³ Handel is similarly named in other newspapers for 16 Sept.

²⁴ William C. Smith, 'George III', 790, where the annotation is illustrated; the original volume was destroyed in the Second World War. '1st' probably refers to *Zadok the priest*. King George III was not born until 1738; it is unlikely that the 'great man' in Mainwaring, *Memoirs*, 83–4 that prompted the annotations was originally a reference to Greene.

²⁵ GB-Lpro SP 36/3(2).

²⁶ Burney, *An Account*, Sketch, 34.

This may have had a basis in fact, for Handel had probably begun, and even possibly completed, the composition of one or two of the anthems before the official order of service was circulated following its final approval on 20 September: prior to that date, he would in any case have been pacing his activity in expectation that the coronation would take place on 4 October. There are differences between the anthem texts specified by Wake and those set by Handel, and the composer may have designed some of the anthems for slightly different places in the liturgy. He seems to have used Sandford's account of the 1685 coronation, probably in a contemporary edition,[27] as the source for the anthem texts when he began composition, since he followed Sandford's texts of *Let thy hand be strengthened* and *Zadok the priest* exactly, except for the addition of 'Amen' to the first and 'Allelujah, Amen' to the second. These are the first two anthems of the coronation service proper (discounting the processional introit) in the 1685 liturgy as printed by Sandford, and we can assume that they were also the first two to be composed by Handel. The remaining two anthems follow neither Sandford's texts nor Wake's, and it seems plausible that Handel went his own way when he found that the printed order of service was not going to conform to what would be performed even in the first two anthems: perhaps from then on he referred directly to the Bible and to the Prayer Book, as well as to any accessible texts from previous coronation liturgies.

The autographs are undated, but the composition of the Coronation Anthems must have been completed by the end of September. There were at least two rehearsals at Westminster Abbey, on 6 and 9 October. The newspaper reports of them echo the laudatory remarks on the Utrecht music in 1713 and comment, probably with only approximate accuracy, on the novelty of such a large group of performers:

Mr. Hendle has composed the Musick for the Abbey at the Coronation, and the Italian Voices, with above a Hundred of the best Musicians will perform; and the Whole is allowed by those Judges in Musick who have already heard it, to exceed any Thing heretofore of the same Kind: It will be rehearsed this Week, but the Time will be kept private, lest the Crowd of People should be an Obstruction to the Performers. (*PPP*, 4 Oct. 1727)[28]

Yesterday was the Rehearsal of the Musick which is to be performed at the Coronation, notwithstanding all possible care was taken to keep it private, the Crowd was exceeding great, the Composition and Performance was universally Admired. (*FP*, 5–7 Oct.)

---

[27] *A Complete Account of the Ceremonies.* The text of *Let thy hand be strengthened* is from Psalm 89; that of *Zadok the Priest* from 1 Kings: 1.

[28] Deutsch, *Handel*, 214; the report implies a previous rehearsal.

Yesterday there was a Rehearsal of the Musick that is to be perform'd at their Majesties Coronation in Westminster Abbey, where was present the greatest Concourse of People that has been known. (*RWJ*, 7 Oct.)[29]

The Musick composed for the Coronation by Mr. Hendel is to be performed by Italian Voices and above 100 of the best Musicians; the Rehearsal was this Week and is allowed to [be] the best performance of that kind that ever was. (*CJ*, 7 Oct.)[30]

Last Friday, also Yesterday in Westminster Abby there was a Rehearsal of the Musick compos'd by Hendel against the Coronation by a great Number of the best Voices, accompanied by divers sorts of Instruments of Musick, Violins, Bass Viols, Trumpets, Hautboys, Kettle Drums, Organ, &c. and the Performance in the Opinion of good Judges was extraordinary fine, and exceeding every Thing before of the like kind. (*EP*, 7–10 Oct.)

October 7. Yesterday there was a Rehearsal of the Coronation Anthem in Westminster-Abbey, set to Musick by the famous Mr. Handell: There being 40 Voices, and about 160 Violins, Trumpets, Hautboys, Kettle-Drums and Bass's proportionable; besides an Organ, which was erected behind the Altar: and both the Musick and the Performers, were the Admiration of all the Audience. (*NorG*, 14 Oct.)[31]

If any initial attempt had been made to exclude interested listeners from the rehearsal, it clearly failed. As with the Utrecht music in 1713, at these rehearsals Handel magnified his fame with a wider London public through his English church music: his success was confirmed at the coronation itself on 11 October before a royal, noble, and captive audience, even if the performances of the anthems may have had some momentary imperfections.

The Coronation Service and Handel's Music

The order of service and the texts of the anthems for the Coronation of King Charles I in 1625 had been entered into the Old Cheque Book,[32] but the Clerks of the Cheque saw no reason to repeat this practice for the next hundred years. In 1727 Jonathan Smith copied 'The Order of Performing the Several Anthems at the Coronation of their Majesties King George the second & Queen Carolina' into the New Cheque Book (see Fig. 10.1).[33] He may have had two reasons for doing so, whether on his own initiative or at the prompting of the Dean or Sub-Dean. First, there seems to have

---

[29] Deutsch, *Handel*, 214.

[30] This and the following reference were first noted by H. Diack Johnstone in *MT* 118 (1977), 725.

[31] Deutsch, *Handel*, 215.

[32] *OCB*, fos. 71ᵛ–72ʳ; Ashbee and Harley, i. 155–8.

[33] *NCB*, 103–6; Ashbee and Harley, i. 281–4.

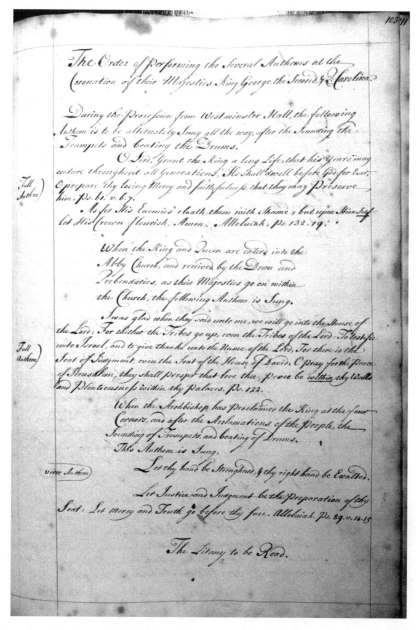

Fig. 10.1. The first two pages from 'The Order of Performing the Several Anthems' at the Coronation of King George II and Queen Caroline, 11 October 1727. New Cheque Book, pp. 103–4. Her Majesty's Chapel Royal

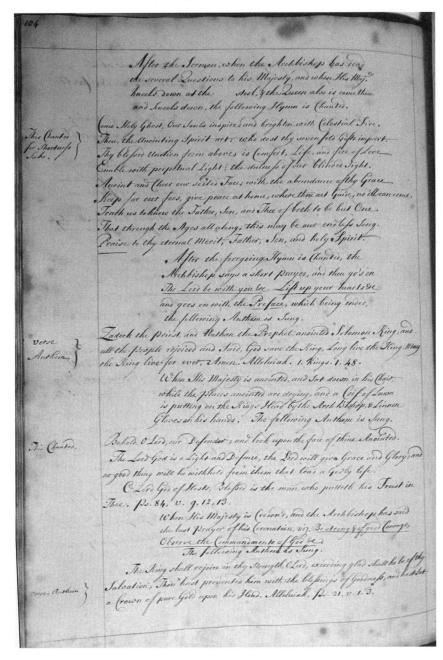

104

After the Sermon, when the Archbishop has read
the several Questions to his Majesty, and when His Maj.ty
kneels down at the   stool, & the Queen also is come there
and kneels down, the following Hymn is Chanted.

This Chanted
for Shortness
Sake.

Come Holy Ghost, Our Souls inspire, and brighten with Celestial Fire.
Thou, the Anointing Spirit art, who dost thy sevenfold Gifts impart.
Thy blessed Unction from above, is Comfort, Life, and fire of Love
Enable with perpetual Light; the dulness of our blinded Sight.
Anoint and Cheer our soiled Face, with the abundance of thy Grace
Keep far our foes, give peace at home, where thou art Guide, no ill can come.
Teach us to know the Father, Son, and Thee of both to be but One.
That through the Ages all along, this may be our endless Song.
Praise to thy eternal Merit, Father, Son, and holy Spirit.

         After the foregoing Hymn is Chanted, the
         Archbishop says a short prayer, and then go's on
         The Lord be with you &c Lift up your hearts &c
         and goes on with the Preface, which being ended,
         the following Anthem is Sung.

verse
Anthem

Zadock the priest, and Nathan the Prophet anointed Solomon King, and
all the people rejoiced and said, God save the King, Long live the King, May
the King live for ever. Amen. Alleluiah. 1. Kings. 1. 48.

         When His Majesty is anointed, and Set down in his Chair,
         while the places anointed are drying, and a Coif of Lawn
         is putting on the Kings Head by the Arch Bishop, & Linnen
         Gloves on his hands, The following Anthem is Sung.

This Chanted.

Behold, O Lord, our Defender, and look upon the face of thine Anointed.
The Lord God is a Light and Defence, the Lord will give Grace and Glory, and
no good thing will he withhold from them that lead a Godly life.
O Lord God of Hosts, Blessed is the man, who putteth his Trust in
Thee. Ps. 84. v. 9, 12, 13.

         When His Majesty is Crown'd, and the Archbishop has said
         the last prayer of his Coronation, viz. Be strong & of good Courage,
         Observe the Commandments of God &c
         The following Anthem is Sung

verse Anthem

The King shall rejoice in thy Strength, O Lord, exceeding glad shall he be of thy
Salvation; Thou hast prevented him with the blessings of Goodness, and hast Set
a Crown of pure Gold upon his Head. Alleluiah. Ps. 21. v. 1. 3.

Fig. 10.1. *Cont'd*

been a deliberate attempt to make the New Cheque Book a systematic and comprehensive record of affairs concerning the Chapel, particularly in areas that were matters of custom or which set a precedent; the coronation of 1727 was the first since the commencement of the New Cheque Book. Secondly, there may have been good reason for recording what actually happened at the 1727 coronation in view of the fact that, as we know, the printed order of service was inaccurate as to the texts of the anthems. Most likely the Cheque Book entry was a copy of another document that had recorded the final decisions about the musical content of the service, during the last stages of the preparations for the coronation: this would explain the formulation 'The Litany to be read', and also the inclusion of *I was glad*, which was probably not performed. The Cheque Book record has a number of scribal errors, but the texts of Handel's anthems are given correctly enough and the overall description seems to be authoritative, as we would expect it to be.

That description, however, differs in various ways from the printed liturgy for the Coronation,[34] not least in the placing of the anthems in the service. Another important source of evidence that also needs to be taken into account is a copy of this printed order of service with manuscript annotations that were added by William Wake himself.[35] Table 10.1 reproduces the essential information from the printed order of service (quoting also Wake's comments), and from the New Cheque Book. Wake's annotations were probably made in two stages. He seems to have made corrections before the service, recording his decision to have the Litany read instead of sung, and juggling with the anthems so that *Let thy hand be strengthened* (already composed by Handel, but not included in Wake's scheme) was inserted with as little disturbance to his overall plan as possible. The remaining comments were written either during the service or very soon after:[36] these give a vivid impression of the problems to which musical performances at big state occasions were vulnerable, but they also demand some explanation.

The first comment, on *I was glad*, reflects a situation in which there were two complicating factors, one of them probably of Handel's making. As already noted, it was the duty and privilege of the Westminster Abbey clergy and choir, as the representatives of the host church, to meet the royal party on arrival. Such was the pluralism among the choirs that only one Lay Clerk from Westminster

---

[34] *The Form and Order of the Service.*

[35] GB-Llp Cod. Misc. 1079B, signed 'WCant[uar]' and inscribed 'with notes of W[ha]t was done or omitted at that Coronation'; Wake's comments were first referred to by Winton Dean in the sleeve notes to a recording of the Coronation Anthems, Argo ZRG 5359 (1963).

[36] In his biographical entry on Handel in *NG* (1980, viii. 92) Winton Dean suggested that Wake might have written the annotations at a rehearsal; this seems unlikely, and Wake's diaries do not suggest that he ever attended musical rehearsals.

Table 10.1. *Documentary evidence for the music at the 1727 coronation*

Published Order of service	New Cheque Book	
Procession	O Lord, Grant the King a long Life [text as set by William Child]	Full Anthem
The Entrance into the Church Anthem I. I was glad *This was omitted and no Anthem at all Sung: in the Coronation of K[ing] G[eorge] 2. by the Negligence of the Choir of Westm[inste]r*	I was glad	Full Anthem
The Recognition Anthem II. The King shall rejoice *The Anthems in Confusion: All irregular in the Music (Coron G 2)*	Let thy hand be strenghned [*sic*]	Verse Anthem
The Litanie The Choir singing the Responses to the Organ *To shorten the Service let this be Read: so it was G 2*	The Litany to be read	
The Anointing Anthem III. Come Holy Ghost *This Hymn by mistake of the Music not sung; but the next Anthem instead of it*	Come Holy Ghost	This Chanted for shortness sake
Anthem IV. Zadok the Priest	Zadok the Priest	Verse Anthem
Anthem V. Behold, O God our defender	Behold, O Lord, our defender	This Chanted
The putting on of the Crown Anthem VI. Praise the Lord, O Jerusalem	The King shall rejoice	Verse Anthem
The Benediction, and Te Deum Anthem VII. We praise thee, O God [*'Anthem VII' deleted*]	Te Deum of Gibbons's was Sung	
The Inthronisation *Anthem VII. Let thy hand be strengthened*		
During the Homage Anthem VIII. The Lord is a Sun and a Shield	God spake sometimes in visions	This Chanted
The Queen's Coronation Anthem IX. My heart is enditing	My heart is inditing	Verse Anthem
The Communion The Organ plays, and the Choir singeth: Anthem X. Let my prayer come up into thy presence The Choir sings. Therefore with Angels The Choir sings. Glory be to God on high	During ye Offertory the Organ plays, till the Alms are done Collecting Sanctus &c. sung in Musick The Gloria in Excellis [*sic*], sung in Musick	

Italic indicates comments or amendments by William Wake in GB-Llp Cod. Misc. 1079b.

(Francis Rowe) was not also currently in the ranks of the Chapel Royal. In the procession the pluralists almost certainly walked with the Chapel Royal and arranged deputies, who may or may not have been competent singers, to take their places in the Westminster Abbey section.[37] Under normal circumstances this would still not have presented an insuperable problem: some arrangement could have been made for the processions, as in previous coronations, so that the Abbey choir could sing their anthem and then join the main body of musicians for the rest of the service. In 1727, however, the galleries for the musical performers seem to have been larger than for previous coronations and possibly rather differently arranged. (See below, 'Conditions of Performance'.) Given conditions of crowded galleries and bad communications, the arrangement was less flexible than previously, and it would not have been surprising if the singers made for their stations in the main body of the Abbey at the earliest opportunity, rather than delaying to perform their anthem.

Wake's second comment brings home the extent of the communication problems in the Abbey. At that point in the service some musicians (following the printed order) may have begun *The King shall rejoice* while others commenced *Let thy hand be strengthened*, which would explain Wake's comments about 'confusion' and 'irregularity'. Such an accident is not as unlikely as it might seem today, when large-scale musical events have the benefit of modern communication systems. The musicians were probably distributed in two or three widely spaced galleries, and some of them might have had access to the printed liturgy, which appeared to be authoritative. The performers, reading from part-books, could have proceeded for quite a long time before one party or the other gave way: the opening movements of both anthems are in the same metre and are similar in tempo. Apart from his insertion of the text for *Let thy hand be strengthened* (which may have been made before the service), Wake's manuscript comments thin out as the service proceeds, no doubt because he was fully occupied with his own duties, but we may tentatively conclude that any subsequent mishaps in the musical performances were not sufficiently memorable to prompt him to further annotations. Whatever 'confusion' had overtaken Handel's first anthem, matters were presumably sorted out by the time it came to perform *Zadok the priest*, and indeed before the first movement of *The King shall rejoice* had run its course.

The order of the anthems as given in the Cheque Book makes better sense, both in terms of the practical demands on the musicians the service and in relation to the earlier liturgical tradition, than that in Wake's version. *Let thy hand be strengthened* was associated with the Recognition in the 1685 service: in

---

[37] Contemporary descriptions of the procession, probably based on the ceremonial from previous coronations, listed the musicians in the following order: Children of Westminster Abbey, Children of the Chapel Royal, Choir of Westminster, Gentlemen of the Chapel Royal.

1727, as in 1685, it followed 'the sounding of the Trumpets and the beating of the drums', and Handel's setting is the only one of his four Coronation Anthems that does not include these instruments, whose players may have been temporarily separated from the main body of musicians in order to perform their fanfares.[38] The positions of *Zadok the priest* and *My heart is inditing* in the service are not in any doubt: they are appropriate only to the Anointing and the Queen's Coronation respectively.

Handel's scoring for the anthems was innovative in its inclusion of parts for three trumpets and timpani, and in a thoroughly modern orchestral use of oboes and bassoons. Croft's anthem for the 1714 coronation had followed the combination of two trumpets and strings that had been established by Purcell's 1694 Te Deum and Jubilate. Handel's music seems to have been the first to include timpani in the anthems for a British coronation,[39] and indeed the first to incorporate them into the score of an anthem for an English service: timpani do not appear in Maurice Greene's anthems and canticle settings until the 1730s.[40] In Handel's own music, the closest precedent for the instrumentation was the inclusion of four trumpets and timpani in two movements from his first London opera *Rinaldo*.[41] The step upwards to the inclusion of timpani as well as trumpets in the orchestral accompaniment to choral movements was a significant one that would be followed up by Handel in some of his subsequent Chapel Royal music and in his English oratorios, though usually in combination with two rather than three trumpet parts. In the Coronation Anthems Handel's use of trumpets and drums with a full choir and orchestra increased both the majesty and the jubilation of the music: while it was probably not possible for the combined sound of the trumpets and drums to shake off their military associations, Handel to a large extent diverted their use into an independent orchestral resource that contributed colour, variety, and a sense of completion to the ensemble.

Let thy hand be strengthened

As already noted, this is more lightly scored than the other Coronation Anthems, for five-part chorus (SAATB) accompanied by strings and oboes. As in many of Handel's Chapel Royal chorus movements, the two alto parts in the anthem separate and merge in a fluid manner, as the texture variously requires harmonic richness or contrapuntal strength. The form of the anthem resembles

[38] The illustrations in Sandford, *The History of the Coronation*, show the Trumpeters in position on the screen at the West end of the Choir area.

[39] Trumpets and drums had, of course, regularly contributed fanfares to the Coronation service, and to the subsequent ceremony of the 'King's Champion' in Westminster Hall.

[40] See Ch. 17 n. 92.

[41] A march and the subsequent aria 'Or la tromba', *HHA* II/4.1, 176–83.

that of the three-movement Italian sinfonia, with two lively movements in quadruple time framing a triple-time slow movement: the same plan is also found (for example) in Croft's organ-accompanied full anthem *God is gone up with a merry noise*. The use of a semi-chorus of soloists at the first vocal leads also resembles Italian concerto grosso practice, in which movements begin with the concertino group of performers for the initial entries, with the ripieno players joining in once the music has become established. The outer movements of the anthem begin as if they are to be built on imitative treatment of their opening themes, and indeed the last movement's subject resembles that of Handel's keyboard fugue HWV 606,[42] but contrapuntal gestures soon give place to varied chordal homophony. Intricate contrapuntal textures were incompatible with the strong, straightforward effects that Handel sought in these anthems, and he never leaves more than two melodic strands in the foreground simultaneously. However, the entries of the main subjects in both movements are cleverly prepared, and the listener is therefore occasionally deceived into thinking that serious fugal business is going on, only to find the music dissolve back suddenly into continuo-homophony. The first movement is cast in a binary structure, with substantial independent orchestral participation; the last movement is more continuous, with only momentary modulations away from the tonic. The use of pedal points is an interesting feature of both movements. The D pedal in the first movement comes at the top of the binary arch and eventually effects the return to the tonic key, while the pedal in the last movement fulfils the usual function of dominant preparation for the final cadence.

The limited employment of imitation and the use of pedal points are also features of the central Larghetto, although in that movement their musical significance is secondary to the strong harmonic rhythm and sighing melodic figures. The text's references to 'justice and judgment' gave Handel an opportunity for a reflective contrast in this movement: six years later he found the music exactly appropriate for the text 'Despair all around them shall swiftly confound them' in *Deborah*. It is just possible that Handel knew Blow's 1685 setting of *Let thy hand be strengthened*,[43] which is a modest affair in one movement, but the central section for 'Let justice and judgment' has some affinities in melody, mode, and rhythm with Handel's setting of the same words.

Zadok the priest

This, Handel's shortest and best-known anthem, is also in many ways his most original. Like the preceding anthem, it is in three movements, but there the

---

[42] Probably composed during the Cannons period: the music was also arranged in an orchestral form in the Concerto Grosso published by John Walsh as Handel's Op. 3 No. 3, *c.*1734.
[43] *MB* 7 (Lewis and Shaw, *Blow* I), 46–7. The text is from Psalm 45.

resemblance ends. Where *Let thy hand be strengthened* is made up of three separate, contrasted movements, *Zadok the priest* is a continuous anthem in three sections: the movements are cumulative, each one leading on to something grander. The choral writing in Purcell's 1685 coronation anthem *My heart is inditing* is in eight parts, and that of the first movement of *Zadok the priest* is in seven parts, yet the effect is utterly different. Purcell's part-writing is richly intricate, as if it were a greatly expanded form of chamber music: Handel's music is concentrated and monumental, displaying the dynamic mass of his forces. In spite of the elaborate orchestral preparation, Handel's seven-part choral entry is not an end in itself: the composer knew well enough that the multiplication of parts produced richness rather than volume,[44] and as the excitement mounts in the following movements the number of parts is reduced. Although the Chapel Royal forces were supplemented by additional singers for the coronation, the balance and distribution of the voices follows the layout that we would expect for the Chapel Royal choir, with division of the strong alto and bass sections, but not of the tenors.

Zadok the priest is Handel's apotheosis of the grand choral and orchestral sound, and it fulfils the specification that the composer himself is reputed to have given for success with the 'English taste'—'something striking, which has its effect directly on the eardrums'.[45] Even today, when this anthem has become part of our regular musical experience, the effect of the first chorus entry as the climax to the orchestral prelude remains spectacular: at the first performance it must have been overwhelming. Introductions based on broken-chord figuration are found in Handel's earlier church music, both English and Italian,[46] but here Handel set a completely new scale of application. The opening twenty-two bars have the effect of a stage-curtain rising, very slowly: the tonic cadence is delayed cleverly with a false alarm at bar 16, when the chord movement appears to be returning in the direction of D major but switches suddenly to B minor. Handel made full use of the opportunities provided by a large string section (with violins divided into three parts) and an abundance of woodwind. When the chorus does finally enter, the chord is capped not by the trebles but by the trumpet: perhaps Handel did not feel that a treble entry on top *a′* was safe.

The second movement is built from cadence figures around which the string parts dance with French-style dotted rhythms: the crescendo effect is propelled

[44] The spacing and balance of the choral sonority were Handel's prime consideration, rather than the maintenance of seven independent contrapuntal parts, hence his apparent indifference to the consecutives between Alto 1 and Bass 1 at the opening entry.

[45] See Howard, *Gluck*, 17.

[46] For example, in the openings to *Nisi Dominus* and to 'Sing praises unto the Lord' from the Cannons anthem *The Lord is my light*.

towards the final cadence, and thus on to the next movement: in retrospect, even the delayed entry of the trumpets and drums at the beginning of the movement is part of an overall plan to make 'God save the King' the musical target. The hammer strokes of the last movement have forerunners (though on a more modest scale) in Handel's previous church music, for example in the outburst on 'Holy' in the Te Deum settings. Both the chordal blocks in bars 5–7 of the last movement and the combination of running semiquavers with staccato chords that follow have a more specific ancestry in his English and Italian works:[47] the unaccompanied unison passage at bar 4 seems to have been a new effect as an answering phrase, though Handel had begun movements with a strong unison theme in his earlier music, as for example 'O Lord, in thee have I trusted' from the Caroline Te Deum. He was careful not to overuse the unison passage, however: it comes only twice, and to complement the chordal affirmations of 'God save the King' at the most concentrated points in the anthem. Handel's setting has little relationship to Henry Lawes's rather primitive, though modestly effective, chordal setting of the text from the coronation of Charles II,[48] and it is doubtful that Handel would have had access to Lawes's music. A setting of a longer version of the text was performed at the 1702 coronation,[49] but the composer for this is not known and no music survives.

The King shall rejoice in thy strength, O Lord

This anthem is the most formal in tone of the four, and the least varied in effect, though the scheme of movements is well planned. The four main movements (all designated Allegro) follow a logical key sequence (D major–A major–B minor–D major). The outer two are in quadruple time, the inner pair in triple: the first two are mainly homophonic, while imitative and contrapuntal writing play a larger part in the last two. The most striking moment is provided by the insertion of a short passage of simple but powerful choral homophony between the triple-time movements. This was surely Handel's idea, a dramatic musical interjection that interpolates a phrase from verse 5 of Psalm 21 ('Glory and worship hast thou laid upon him') between verses 1 and 3. Four of the seven bars of this movement are taken up with musical image-painting that is familiar from the Utrecht Jubilate: a halo of string semiquavers around the word 'glory'. Elsewhere, however, the anthem seems in places to get by through technique rather than imagination.

---

[47] See e.g. 'Let me never be confounded' in the Caroline Te Deum, and the passage quoted at Ex. 1.4.

[48] The opening is quoted in le Huray, *Music and the Reformation*, 345.

[49] Planché, *Regal Records*, 122; GB-Lbl Add. MS 6336, fo. 19ᵛ.

The first movement has the festive spirit of the more heavily scored movements of the *Water Music*, and its main interest lies in the orchestral material: a good interplay between the treble and bass lines, and a concertato-type use of trumpets and oboes who receive solo 'breaks' in the opening and closing ritornellos. The dotted rhythms of the second movement resemble those in the middle movement of *Zadok the priest*, and indeed there is a similar dance-like spirit, though of a less exultant, more refined, nature. There is a teasing question of rhythmic interpretation in this movement: the sudden appearance of triplets at bar 14 suggests that the opening dotted rhythm may be a false notation, though the situation is complicated by the even duplets at bars 21–2, which are probably to be taken literally. The movement has some well-written smooth counterpoint, based on rising and falling entries of a new subject that first appears at bar 31, against which the dance rhythm continues in the background.

The second triple-time movement, 'Thou hast prevented him', includes some of the most carefully worked imitative writing in the Coronation Anthems. Although complex imitative activity was not really suitable either to the occasion or to the forces, Handel worked effectively with a long, flowing subject, which is tuneful enough to establish itself firmly with the listener, and is accordingly easy to follow through later entries. As might be expected, this does not develop beyond the initial exposition (five entries). A chordal passage for the words 'and hast set a crown of pure gold upon his head', melodically almost monotonic, acts as a foil to the previous counterpoint: the most interesting part of the movement lies in the ensuing alternating contrast between the gentle imitative material and the more forceful chordal passages. In the final 'Alleluia' movement a short theme is worked in imitation and in contrast to other more homophonic material, in a manner very similar to the final chorus of *Let thy hand be strengthened*. This time, however, trumpets and drums add an extra dimension to the contrasts available. The movement is framed by a fully scored ritornello which appears first at bar 8, at the final (bass) entry of the opening exposition, and is repeated exactly at the end, immediately before the final cadential chords.

A similar text had previously been set to music by William Turner on two occasions, once accompanied by an orchestra of trumpets and strings for the St Cecilia's Day celebrations in 1697, and once as a full anthem without orchestra for Queen Anne's coronation in 1702.[50] Neither of these has serious points of comparison with Handel's setting. Turner himself would have been among the Chapel Royal singers in 1727.

---

[50] Copies in Tudway's collection, GB-Lbl Harl. MSS 7339, 7341.

My heart is inditing of a good matter

Purcell's impressive anthem *My heart is inditing* for the 1685 coronation has already been mentioned. The settings by Purcell and Handel display fundamental differences in style and approach,[51] and there is nothing to suggest that Handel was musically influenced by Purcell's setting. Although the anthems have the same title and set the same biblical verses for opening and closing movements,[52] the structures for the middle movements are entirely different: Purcell set verses 10, 15, 16, 11, and 17 from Psalm 45 and a verse from Psalm 147, while Handel created two movements from Psalm 45 verse 10, supplemented with a phrase from verse 12. He thus dealt with a much shorter text, and made more of the individual movements. Even though this was the anthem associated with the Queen's coronation, he seems to have been principally concerned with making a good finale; certain parts of the text called for a gentle response, and received appropriate treatment, but the outer movements have a dignified exuberance. It may be anachronistic to look for 'gendered' aspects in this anthem, beyond those inherent in the choice of text, but it is hardly less jubilant and extrovert than the others, and this perhaps reflects the lively influence that Caroline had in court life, and indeed in consequent political activity: by all accounts, she was not a recessive consort.

For the first movement Handel returned to a structure that had been well tried and proved in his earliest Chapel Royal music: a two-part scheme beginning with a long solo section, at the end of which the chorus enters as the music returns to the tonic key.[53] The opening thematic material is gentle and suave, almost a minuet in spirit.[54] Single soloists would have been ineffective in the Abbey: Handel paired his voices Alto/Bass and Treble/Tenor and put two of the leading Chapel Royal Gentlemen on each of the alto and bass parts. No names are given for the second set of entries: Handel wrote 'Solo' against the tenor part, but 'all' for the trebles—an interesting reflection on the balance of voices, and on the comparative anonymity of Chapel Royal tenors. The graceful dialogue of the soloists is transmuted into something more muscular at the tutti entry, though based on the same thematic material.

The second movement, 'Kings' daughters were among thy honourable women', is one of the best individual movements in the Coronation Anthems. From the same musical stable as the opening movement of *I will magnify thee*,

---

[51] Even by the time of the Te Deum and Jubilate in 1694, Purcell was experimenting with a different musical style for orchestrally accompanied church music than in his 1685 anthem.

[52] Psalm 45: 1; Isaiah 49: 23; Purcell adds a final 'Alleluja' movement.

[53] See e.g. 'Vouchsafe, O Lord', from the Utrecht Te Deum, and other movements from the Caroline Te Deum and the Birthday Ode for Queen Anne.

[54] It was developed from a theme by Telemann: see Roberts, 'Handel's Borrowings from Telemann', 153.

it develops by melodic extension over a walking quaver bass. Through this movement and the succeeding one there is a cumulative build-up of voices,[55] even though these movements function as the relatively relaxed centre to the anthem. In 'Upon thy right hand' contrast is obtained from substantial ritorn-ellos for the strings alone without oboes,[56] which eventually enter to double the voices. (Handel may have intended a similar scoring for the central movement of *Let thy hand be strengthened*, though his omission of labels to the orchestral staves leaves his intentions uncertain there.) There is a slightly unusual key jolt between the E major conclusion of 'Upon thy right hand' and the succeeding D major movement, ameliorated by the spacing of the first orchestral chord in 'Kings shall be thy nursing fathers'. The autograph of the anthem is continuous here, so there is no sign that Handel planned an intermediate movement in another key. As already noted, the text that Purcell set in 1685 (and was printed by Sandford) had several more verses from Psalm 45 at this point; some of the text that Handel did not set in *My heart is inditing* would be used, just as appropriately, in one of his royal wedding anthems a few years later (see Ch. 12). The last movement, which displays its vigour from the beginning, keeps the trumpets and drums in reserve for nearly two thirds of the movement: the combined effect of a return to the tonic and the entry of these instruments at bar 53 gives a fine climax to this anthem, and indeed to the complete cycle of the four coronation anthems. At the opening of the movement Handel wrote 'Allegro' next to the running violin parts, but 'Allegro e staccato', apparently with deliberate distinction, next to the crotchets in the bass.[57]

Although there are few points of comparison between Handel's and Pur-cell's anthems for *My heart is inditing*, there is a fascinating resemblance between Handel's theme for 'Kings shall be thy nursing fathers' (first heard in full in the bass voice) and Purcell's second setting of these words in 'Praise the Lord, O Jerusalem', his anthem for the joint crowning of William and Mary in 1689:[58] see Ex. 10.1. The similarity is not very prominent in performance, largely because of the diversion provided by Handel's independent orchestral writing. The appearance of triple-time dotted rhythms in the accompaniments to 'with joy and gladness' in Purcell's *My heart is inditing*[59] and 'the King shall have pleasure in thy beauty' in Handel's anthem seems to be a coincidence.

---

[55] 'Upon thy right hand' was apparently sung by soloists up to bar 42.

[56] This is the first occurrence of the scoring in the Coronation Anthems, though the voices were also accompanied by strings alone for the opening entries of 'Thou hast prevented him' in *The King shall rejoice*.

[57] Compare the similar distinction between the flute obbligato and the string accompaniment in No. 3 of the Caroline Te Deum.

[58] PS 17, pp. 150–2. In Purcell's *My heart is inditing* this verse had been followed by the final 'Alleluja' movement, but in the 1689 anthem it came near the beginning.

[59] PS 17, p. 89.

Ex. 10.1. (*a*) Handel, *My heart is inditing*, No. 4; (*b*) Purcell, *Praise the Lord, O Jerusalem*
(Z. 46)

Conditions of Performance

Like St Paul's Cathedral, Westminster Abbey is a large and resonant building,
though the sound is rather clearer because the Abbey does not have the
acoustic complications that are caused at St Paul's by the dome and by the
more rounded ceiling profile: instead, the sound spreads into the lofty spaces of
the Gothic vaulting. While the Thanksgiving services at St Paul's were conducted in the Choir area at the East end, the scene of activity for coronation
services at Westminster Abbey was the central crossing, giving a wider distribution of sound through the building. Sandford's book describing the 1685
coronation includes some large and detailed engravings representing the service, and these show the musicians dispersed in several locations: the Chapel
Royal in a gallery with a specially built organ on the south side of the crossing,
the Royal Musicians in a facing gallery on the north side, the Westminster
Abbey choir in another gallery to the north-west of the crossing, and the
trumpets and drums in the gallery at the west entrance to the Choir area.[60]
Unfortunately there are no similarly authoritative images of the succeeding
coronations, though it is certain that all coronation services required rearrangement of the furnishings within the Abbey and the building of large temporary
constructions.

The best evidence about the arrangements for the 1727 coronation emerges
incidentally from a memorandum that William Boyce wrote at the time of the
next coronation, in 1761:

Dr. Boyce most humbly begs leave to represent to his Grace The Lord Chamberlain,
That the upper-part of the A[l]tar at Westminster Abbey, as it now stands, will be in

---

[60] See also the section on Westminster Abbey in Ch. 19, concerning the arrangement of the
galleries.

the middle of the Gallery appointed for the Music, which renders it impossible for the Musicians to join in the Performance as they ought to do, and will intirely spoil the Composition.

The first Grand Musical performance in the Abbey, was at the Coronation of King George the Second, and the late Mr. Handel, who composed the Music, often lamented his not having that part of the Altar taken away, as He, and all the Musicians concerned, experienced the bad effect it had by that obstruction.

The D[ean] has been informed by Workmen in that branch of business, that it may be taken down & re-placed, at a small expence, & without damage to the Work.[61]

Probably the principal galleries were built on the north and south sides at the East end of the crossing in 1727, as in 1685, but it is noteworthy that one of the newspaper reports mentions that an organ was built 'behind the altar', suggesting the possibility of an additional gallery at the eastern end, and in a position comparable to the East-end galleries that were constructed for the weddings in the Chapels Royal during the 1730s. A special organ that would have matched the pitch standards of the orchestral instruments was provided by Christopher Shrider for the coronation. Although the trumpets and drums may have played fanfares from the gallery at the East end of the Choir (and elsewhere), the relevant players would have joined the main body of performers for Handel's anthems.

As already noted, the incorporation of the timpani as well as trumpets into the Coronation Anthems was an innovation. While it is possible that improvised timpani parts may have been added to Handel's English church music prior to 1727, it seems more likely that the Purcellian combination of trumpets and strings without drums represented both the preferred scoring and the most practical one. The already modest space for performers in the Chapel Royal itself would not have encouraged the inclusion of the drums, and even at St Paul's Cathedral the space in the organ gallery was probably better used for the accommodation of other additional performers: Trevitt's picture shows no timpani at the 1706 Thanksgiving (see above, Fig. 4.3), and the stairwells to the gallery restricted the background space in which drums could have been located. For the Coronation Anthems, notwithstanding the remarkably large total body of performers, it is likely that only three trumpeters and one timpanist were involved, although it is just possible that (as later with the *Fireworks Music*, though for open-air performance) two or three players doubled each part. There are no special payments to the trumpeters and timpanist, who were presumably on duty as servants of the royal household.[62]

[61] GB-Lpro LC2/32. For correspondence between Boyce and the Archbishop of Canterbury over the music for the 1761 coronation, see Knight, 'Resources for Musicologists', 4–6.

[62] *LJ*, 7 Oct., reported that 'The Kettle-Drums and Trumpets of the four Troops of Life-Guards' were to be 'employed in the Procession, in the Abbey, and Westminster Hall'.

There is no possibility that the parts could have been played, equally divided, by the complete court establishment of trumpeters and drummers, since Handel's music for Trumpet 1 and 2 calls for specialized playing skills that were only cultivated by a few players. It may be significant that he labelled the third part for 'Trumpet 3' rather than 'Principale',[63] and the balance of the parts would in any case have been undermined if a group of fanfare trumpeters had been diverted to the Trumpet 3 part.

The sheer number of performers was an aspect of Handel's music that seems to have caught the attention of the press in 1727, and presumably also the listeners at the service and the rehearsals. Documents from the Lord Chamberlain's Department record payments for additional players (see App. I), though unfortunately (as with all such warrants from the period) the accompanying bills that would have listed the names of the players do not survive. Bernard Gates was paid 42 guineas for additional singers and J. C. Smith senior was paid for fifty-seven 'supernumary' instrumentalists at three guineas each: if the extra singers were paid at the same rate, there would have been fourteen of them. The additions would bring the adult voices to about forty in number, but the total for instrumentalists (adding the supernumeraries to the King's Musicians and to trumpet and drum players from the court establishment) still falls short of the 160 mentioned, perhaps with more enthusiasm than accuracy, by one newspaper report. The only hint about orchestral numbers from Handel's autographs is his specification next to the Bassi stave of *The King shall rejoice*: 'Organ et 12 Viol[oncelli]'.[64] Liveries for the coronation were provided for the Master of the Musick and thirty-three musicians, though only the twenty-four members of the King's Musicians were entitled to Coronation medals: the Chapel Royal also nominally brought their players of the lute and bass viol, though the musicians concerned doubled with court offices among the trumpeters and string-players. Maurice Greene and John Weldon, the Chapel Royal Organists, were presumably present and must have contributed at least to the performances of the other musical items in the service apart from Handel's anthems. Whatever the precise number of players, it seems that the orchestra substantially outnumbered the singers, and the supplementation with additional performers exceeds anything recorded in the court documents for any coronation since the restoration of the monarchy in 1660.

The regular body of singers from the choirs of the Chapel Royal and Westminster Abbey was insufficient for Handel's musical designs. Doubtless the unfortunate timing of Croft's illness and death had caused a lapse in the training (and probably also the recruitment) of the Chapel Royal Children, but

---

[63] Compare Handel's designation 'Principale' for the Dettingen music: see Ch. 14.
[64] GB-Lbl RM 20.h.5, fo. 18ʳ.

with experienced musicians on hand such as Bernard Gates and John Church (Master of the Choristers at Westminster Abbey) the effects should have been short-lived. Nevertheless, as already noted, five of the ten Chapel Royal boys had gone from the choir in June, and only one adult member of the Westminster Abbey choir was not also a member of the Chapel Royal. The adult membership of the choir at George II's accession was listed in the New Cheque Book: see Fig. 10.2. On the first page of the autograph of *The King shall rejoice* Handel labelled the vocal parts as follows:[65] C[anto—i.e. Treble] 12 /H[ughes] et 6 (Alto 1) /Freem[an] et 6 (Alto 2) / Church et 6 (tenor) / Wheely et 6 (Bass 1) /Gates et 6 (Bass 2). He repeated the same specification just before the chorus entry: see Fig. 10.3. The numbers are obviously rounded figures, with a section leader and six supporters for each part, and represent approximately what might have been expected from a full muster of the combined Chapel Royal and Abbey choirs, including deputies for all of the simultaneously held places. As already noted, with the addition of fourteen extra singers this would have brought the vocal strength up to a little over forty adult voices. Most likely the occasion drew in all of the competent musicians that could be found from London's church singers, including any otherwise unaccounted-for men from the St Paul's choir, and any singers who were currently serving as deputies while awaiting the availability of a full place in one of the main establishments. If the St Paul's choristers were also involved, it is possible that they included William Boyce himself, though at the age of 17 his voice may already have broken. Some independent singers may also have been available from St George's, Windsor.[66] No doubt, if the hunt was on for London's most capable singers, this extended to some who had primarily followed careers in the theatre: perhaps Richard Leveridge was among the supernumeraries. The mention of 'Italian voices' in one newspaper report is intriguing: if correct, it suggests the incorporation of voices from the opera company. (Players from the opera orchestra would certainly have been included.) The opera season began at the King's Theatre on 30 September, so the singers would have been in London at the time of the rehearsals for the coronation music. Perhaps the castrati Senesino and Baldi sang with the altos, Boschi and Palmerini with the basses: it seems rather less likely that the voices of Faustina and Cuzzoni were mixed with the trebles. One factor

---

[65] GB-RM 20.h.5, fo. 18[r]. F. G. Edwards, 'Handel's Coronation Anthems', 154, suggested that these labels might have been added by Handel in connection with a subsequent concert performance, but this is very unlikely. The second and third annotations may have been altered initially by Handel from 'H. et 4' and 'Freem et 4'.

[66] Fellowes, *Memoirs*, 115, stated that the Minor Canons, Lay Clerks, and Choristers of St George's Chapel, Windsor 'have a traditional claim to be included in the special choir to sing at the coronation': I have found no evidence for this from the 18th c., though many individuals sang by virtue of their dual posts, and Windsor was a source for additional competent performers.

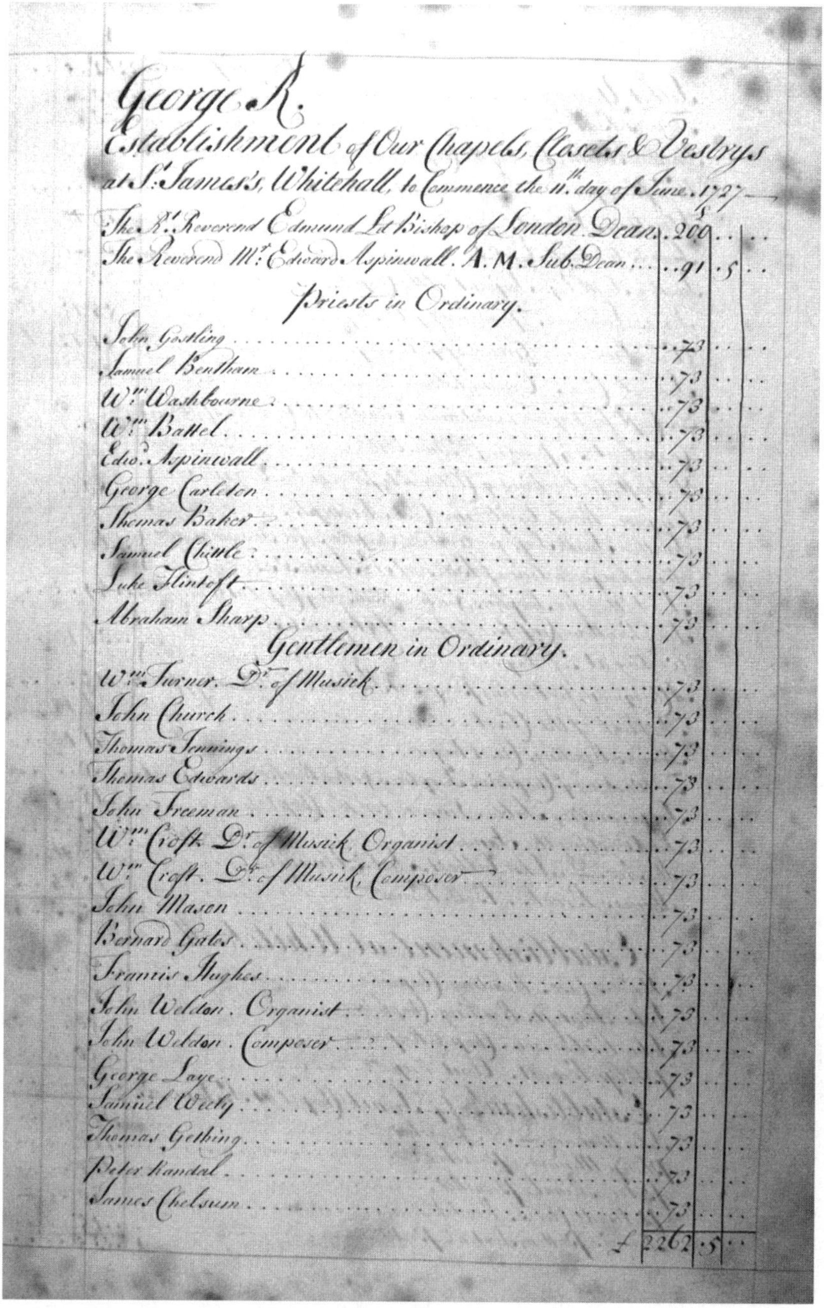

George R.

Establishment of Our Chapels, Closets & Vestrys at St. James's, Whitehall, to Commence the 11th. day of June. 1727

	£	s
The Rt. Reverend Edmund Ld Bishop of London Dean	200	..
The Reverend Mr. Edward Aspinwall. A. M. Sub Dean	91	5
Priests in Ordinary.		
John Gostling	73	..
Samuel Bentham	73	..
Wm. Washbourne	73	..
Wm. Battel	73	..
Edw. Aspinwall	73	..
George Carleton	73	..
Thomas Baker	73	..
Samuel Chittle	73	..
Luke Flintoft	73	..
Abraham Sharp	73	..
Gentlemen in Ordinary.		
Wm. Turner. Dr. of Musick	73	..
John Church	73	..
Thomas Jennings	73	..
Thomas Edwards	73	..
John Freeman	73	..
Wm. Croft Dr. of Musick Organist	73	..
Wm. Croft. Dr. of Musick Composer	73	..
John Mason	73	..
Bernard Gates	73	..
Francis Hughes	73	..
John Weldon. Organist	73	..
John Weldon. Composer	73	..
George Laye	73	..
Samuel Weely	73	..
Thomas Gething	73	..
Peter Randal	73	..
James Chelsum	73	..
£	2262	5

Fig. 10.2. List of the Chapel Royal establishment at the accession of King George II, 11 June 1727. New Cheque Book, pp. 15–16. Her Majesty's Chapel Royal

	£		
Brought forward	2262	5	
Talbot Young	73		
Thomas Bell	73		
Jonathan Smith, Clerk of the Cheque	73		
Wm Perry	73		
John Shore, Lutenist	41	10	
Francis Goodsens, Violist	40		
Jonathan Smith Esqr Serjeant of the Chapel	73		
Thomas Langhorne, Yeoman of ye Vestry	54	15	
Wm Duncum, Groom of ye Vestry	51	12	6
Samuel Clay, Organ-Blower	20		
Dr Croft, for keeping, maintaining & teaching 10 Children of the } Chapel, at 24 pounds p.^r Ann. Each	240		
Dr Croft, for teaching ye Children to play on the Organ, and } Compose, Read, Write and Cast Accompts	80		
Jonathan Smith Esqr for Washing Surplices, for Strewings, and } all necessary's, in lieu of Bills at St James's	60		
To Ditto, for Surplices, & in lieu of Bills for ye Chapel at Whitehall	49	2	
Saml Bentham, Confessor, for himself & to provide Surplices and } Washing at 2.^s p.^r Day	36	10	
A Clergyman, for Reading Prayers at St James, in ye Absence of ye Court	15		
The Clerk of the Closet	6	18	
Thomas Reading, Closet Keeper	41	10	
For Washing ye Chaplain's Surplices, & other Necessary's for ye Closet	50		
For providing Table Linnen for the Chaplains	18	5	
For Washing the Same	13		
The Revd Dr John Gilbert, Sub-Almoner	97	11	8
Thomas Brooks, Bell-Ringer	15	4	2
£	3485	3	4

Establishment at Whitehall.

Thomas Case, Reading Chaplain	80		
Luke Flintoft, Reading Chaplain	80		
John Richardson, Chapel-Keeper	50		
Philip Bennet, Closet-Keeper	50		

Establishm.^t of y.^e French Chapel at St James's.

	260		
John Menard, L.L. Preacher	160		
Philip Menard, Preacher	160		
Peter Rival, Preacher	160		
Peter de Cloris, Reader	40		
Francis Dalton, Sexton & Porter	15		
£	575		

Fig. 10.2. *Cont'd*

Fig. 10.3. The chorus entry in the Coronation Anthem *The King shall rejoice*, HWV 260. At the left margin Handel indicated the Gentleman who were chorus leaders for each part. The alternative text on the lowest stave relates to the use of the movement for *Deborah* in 1733. British Library, RM 20.h.5, fo. 19ᵛ

that should be borne in mind is that, beyond the 'big four' choirs from London and Windsor, the pool of music-reading professional singers of sufficient vocal accomplishment available in London was probably quite small, and certainly smaller than that for the instrumentalists: this was not the era of the efficient amateur singer, nor perhaps would non-professionals have been acceptable at this period for a major public performance. The coronation music may well have involved every professional orchestral player and every professional singer then in London.

Although the Chapel Royal singers had an important status at the coronation because they were the court's establishment of professional singers, their musical prominence must have been rather diluted in the larger group. Nevertheless, it is significant that, in the annotation already quoted, Handel named only singers from the Chapel Royal as the section leaders. Chapel Gentlemen are also named, in pairs, for the opening vocal entries in the first movement of *Let thy hand be strengthened*, and the first and third movements of *My heart is inditing*. What is not known is whether, when he first drafted the anthems, Handel intended some movements to begin with a semi-chorus of a handful of leading voices, or whether this was an expedient that proved necessary on account of the dispersal of the performers, in order to secure good ensemble at the first entries, the remaining voices entering once tempo and style were well established. The musical character of the Coronation Anthems was not, however, conducive to the use of solo voices, which would have sounded thin in their surroundings, architectural and musical. Rather, the character of the anthems depended on an effective use of weighty choral sound and voluminous orchestral accompaniment: the Coronation Anthems were grand music for a grand occasion and a grand building.

Autographs

The autographs of the anthems[67] were written on independent paper gatherings, and no particular significance can be attached to the order in which they are now bound, especially since anthems or sections of them were temporarily separated in the 1730s for use in the preparation of performing material for oratorio performances. The following annotations by Handel relate to these subsequent uses:

Let thy hand be strengthened
Alternative texts written in ink for the first two movements, beginning 'Let thy deeds be glorious' and 'Despair all around them' respectively, for use in *Deborah* (1733), along with the 'Alleluja' movement.

---

[67] GB-Lbl RM 20.h.5.

Zadok the priest
Alternative text written in pencil for the first movement, beginning 'Blessed are all they'; this text was also added by J. C. Smith senior in ink. Further relevant pencil amendments by Handel are the deletion of the second movement, accompanied by 'out', and 'stat' for the last movement; also 'End of ye 2d part' in ink on the empty-stave verso to the last page of music. All of these relate to *Esther*, 1732.

The King shall rejoice
Alternative text written in ink for the first movement, beginning 'the great King of Kings' (see Fig. 10.3), and 'NB Littera A' in ink above the start of 'Thou has prevented him'; both for *Deborah*, 1733.

The first page of *Let thy hand be strengthened* seems to have been lost at an early stage, and the present music for the first twenty-five bars is a make-up copy provided by J. C. Smith the younger in the 1750s: the loss of the page may suggest that this anthem was for some time at the top of the autographs. Smith junior also filled in the music in a section of the last movement of *The King shall rejoice* (bars 59–65) which Handel had originally left empty with a cue for the repetition of a passage from earlier in the movement. These completions may have been in some way associated with Smith's similar make-up copy for the lost section of the autograph of the Chapel Royal anthem *I will magnify thee* (see Ch. 9).

Handel's specifications for performers at the beginning of *The King shall rejoice*, naming Chapel Royal Gentlemen, have already been quoted.[68] In addition, he wrote the following singers' names on the autographs:

Let thy hand be strengthened
No. 1 bar 26, Bass 'Wh[eely] et Bell', followed by 'Tutti Bassi' at bar 28. No similar indication appears next to the tenor entry at bar 26; the previous alto entries at bar 25, which might also have been annotated, would have been on the leaf that has been lost.

The King shall rejoice
At bar 54 of the final 'Alleluja' movement, an annotation to the Bass 1 part probably reads 'Whe[l]y'.

My heart is inditing
No. 1, bar 22, Bass, 'Mr Whely/Mr Bell'; bar 24, Alto, 'Mr Hughs/Mr Lee'. There are no comparable annotations at bars 45 and 47, though Handel wrote 'all' before the treble stave preceding bar 45. At the beginning of

---

[68] Handel repeated them at the beginning of 'Glory and worship' later in the same anthem (fo. 26ʳ).

the movement he wrote a number of indications for soloists, probably 'H[ughes] et L[aye]' (Alto 1), 'F[reeman]' (Alto 2) and 'Church' (Tenor), but he then replaced them with part-names, largely obliterating the original markings. In No. 3 bar 34, Bass, 'Mr W[heely] & B[ell]', but there are no comparable annotations to upper voices.

Handel's skeleton first draft for the opening to the final movement of *The King shall rejoice* survives in the autograph because he reused the pages.[69]

Most of the early manuscript copies of the Coronation Anthems seem to be derived from a source, possibly the original conducting score, that has not survived. They preserve an important, and probably authentic, revision: the insertion of an extra word in a passage from *The King shall rejoice*, turning 'Glory and worship' into 'Glory and great worship' by splitting the original crotchet for 'and' into two quavers. There is no sign of this amendment in the autograph. An early chorus part for HWV 261 is noted on p. 293.

Handel and the Chapel Royal during the Reign of King George II

The changes at the Chapel Royal during August and September 1727 affected Handel, though not immediately. The pattern of events that followed George I's accession in 1714 was repeated almost exactly after his son's accession in 1727. In September–October 1714 Handel's music had been performed before the King in the Chapel Royal, but for the following six years it was Croft who provided the music for special court services: in October 1727 Handel's music was performed at the coronation, but during the succeeding six years it was Maurice Greene who provided the Chapel Royal music for special occasions.

Between 1722 and 1726 Handel's main duty as Composer had been to provide music for the Chapel Royal services following the King's return to London from Hanover. Following his accession, King George II did not visit his Electorate until 1729. When he came back to London in September of that year the court remained for a time at its summer residence at Kensington, returning to St James's at the end of October. On 2 November, the first Sunday after the court's return, 'the new Anthem, composed by Mr Green, was sung before their Majesties in the Royal Chappel at St. James's'.[70] Greene

---

[69] Fos. 30, 35: see Burrows and Ronish, *Catalogue*, 213.

[70] *DJ*, 3 Nov. 1729. The King had returned to St James's on 29 Oct., the day before his birthday, on which the regular court ode (composed by Eccles) was performed: in this reign the court normally returned in time for the birthday. Greene's anthem was rehearsed in the Chapel Royal on 23 Oct. and 1 Nov. (*LJ*, 25 Oct.; *DJ*, 31 Oct.).

provided the music for similar services celebrating the King's return from Hanover regularly thereafter, with the single exception of 1743, the year of the King's participation in the battle of Dettingen (see Ch. 14). Neither Handel's nominal Chapel Royal appointment nor his naturalization maintained him in the musical niche that he had carved for himself at the end of the previous reign: either he withdrew from this activity, or Greene edged him out. As was the case in 1715, however, there is insufficient evidence from which to judge whether the pressures that dissociated Handel from the Chapel in 1729 were primarily political, musical, institutional, or personal. In other respects his relationship with King George II, in so far as it affected his personal career, seems to have been much the same as it had been with George I: if anything, he came to receive more support from the royal family, through the influence of Princess Anne and possibly also Queen Caroline. We do not know how the various sensitivities over status, recognition, and creative opportunity were resolved between Handel and Greene in the course of 1727–9, though the outcome in November 1729 is clear enough. There were no changes in the personnel responsible for the running of the Chapel during that time: Edmund Gibson was the Dean and Edward Aspinwall the Sub-Dean throughout. Gibson's translation from the see of Lincoln to London in April 1723, soon after Handel had secured his Chapel Royal pension, may possibly have increased his opportunities for involvement, or interference.

Nevertheless, something must be said about Handel's relationship with Greene, because of its possible relevance to the nature of his association with the Chapel during the period after 1727.[71] Both Burney and Hawkins, writing half a century after the event, explicitly state that, following an initial period during which Greene stood in admiration of Handel, there was some personal animosity between the two composers.[72] Their testimony may be regarded with caution in the absence of supporting contemporary evidence, but it need not be dismissed, even if some anecdotes were garbled or misapplied in their narratives. The principal professional interests of Handel and Greene lay in different areas of London's musical life, but both were directly involved (though in different ways) with the Chapel Royal, so it is appropriate to chart their paths in relation to the Chapel. For reasons already stated in this chapter, it is unlikely that Greene's appointments as Composer and Organist to the Chapel Royal provoked Handel's jealousy: it seems improbable that Handel wanted those offices in the regular establishment, and there seems to have been no cause for serious animosity between the two during the 1720s,

---

[71] See H. Diack Johnstone, 'Handel and his Bellows-Blower', which gives references to the early documentation.

[72] Hawkins, *A General History*, ii. 879, 884; Burney, *A General History*, ii. 489.

although Greene did receive two niggling setbacks that might have fuelled later mistrust. The Chapel Royal service for which Greene provided the music in 1721 yielded him only limited benefits: his music was well received at the time, but in the long term Croft's withdrawal presented the opportunity to Handel for the rest of the reign. In 1727 Greene, newly appointed as Composer to the Chapel, received no recognition at the coronation: the fact that his appointment was made only a month before the coronation is hardly relevant, for nothing is known of Handel's music for the coronation until a fortnight after Greene's appointment. Perhaps, as George III's partisan commentary suggests,[73] Greene's claim to contribute to the coronation was rebuffed by the King himself. This would hardly have been an encouraging start to Greene's Chapel Royal career, and would have strengthened his resolve to establish himself thereafter. He had many influential supporters, including the Hoadly family of ecclesiastical grandees, Henry Godolphin the Dean of St Paul's Cathedral, and the Duke of Newcastle, who had been Lord Chamberlain between 1717 and 1724. His sister-in-law was married to George Carleton, a priest who served in all three of the London choirs and who became Sub-Dean of the Chapel Royal in 1732. Perhaps the influence of Greene's supporters was fully stretched in 1727 in obtaining for him the Chapel Royal posts of Organist and Composer, and they were reluctant to press further for his involvement in the coronation.

By 1729 Greene had reversed the previous uncertainty in his position through the performance of his music at the Chapel Royal service following the King's return from Hanover, a task that had formerly been Handel's perquisite. Handel may have been offended by this, but not necessarily: in the autumn of 1729 his energies were probably fully absorbed in sorting out the future of Italian opera in London, forming his own company in collaboration with John Jacob Heidegger following the collapse of the Royal Academy.[74] Provided his Chapel Royal pension continued, Handel was probably content for Greene to undertake the music for the King's return, though this in itself might have added to Greene's eventual sense of grievance: Handel was well rewarded for a Chapel Royal sinecure while he did the routine work for a considerably smaller salary.

To make sense of the relationship between Handel and Greene it may be more relevant to consider the general division of London's musical life in the

---

[73] See n. 24 above.

[74] The singers that Handel had engaged for the new season began to arrive in London at the end of Sept. (*CJ*, 20 Sept. 1729). Presumably some of Oct. was spent in rehearsals; a concert was given before the royal family at Kensington by Handel and some of the opera company on 10 Oct. (Deutsch, *Handel*, 245). By the time the King heard Greene's new anthem on 2 Nov., Handel was probably at work on the composition of *Lotario*.

1730s. Once again, there is a parallel with events from the previous reign. In 1717 the rift between the King and the Prince of Wales shut the opera house: in the 1730s a similar hostility between the generations of the royal family encouraged the development of two rival opera companies.[75] The polarization in the opera world had been preceded by a division among the musicians associated with the London choirs. Matters came to a head at the Academy of Vocal Musick in a controversy over the authorship of Antonio Lotti's madrigal 'In una siepe ombrosa'.[76] By supporting Bononcini here, Greene may have aligned himself with Handel's operatic rivals,[77] though this in itself would hardly have provoked a reaction from Handel, since Greene was not a force to be reckoned with in the operatic world. The serious problem in personal relationships in the early 1730s may well have been not between Handel and Greene, but between Greene and Bernard Gates,[78] which would have caused a double division: it ranged the Chapel Royal Composer against the Master of the Children, and it generated a conflict of loyalties between the Gentlemen whose partial allegiance was to St Paul's (where Greene was Organist) and those associated with Westminster Abbey (where Gates was a leading member of the choir). Greene withdrew the support of himself and the St Paul's choristers (and possibly some of the St Paul's choirmen) from the Academy, which reformed as the Academy of Ancient Music in May 1731.[79] It is unlikely that Handel himself was involved in any of this, since he was not a member of the Academy, but singers from the Chapel Royal, St Paul's, and Westminster Abbey had been deeply involved in its original foundation,[80] just as musicians

[75] See Burrows, 'Handel and the London Opera Companies'.

[76] See Hawkins, *A General History*, ii. 862, 884, and Lindgren, 'The Three Great Noises'. Hawkins's date (p. 884) of 1728 for the first performance of the madrigal is dubious, and his version of the Academy's origins (Hawkins, *An Account*; also *A General History*, ii. 805) certainly seems to be wrong: on the evidence of GB-Lbl Add. MS 11732 the first meeting of the Academy of Vocal Music was in 1725/6 and the original membership, which did not include Needler, was based on the three London choirs.

[77] I interpret Hawkins's references to the Handel–Greene–Bononcini triangle (Hawkins, *A General History*, ii. 879, 884) in terms of the period around 1731 rather than the 1720s.

[78] Lowell Lindgren ('The Three Great Noises', 567–9) and I arrived at a similar conclusion independently, though the suggestion that the actions of Greene and Gates have to be seen in the context of the domestic politics of the London choirmen is my own.

[79] Hawkins, *A General History*, ii. 884. It is apparent from GB-Lbl Add. MS 11732 that the first meeting of the Academy of Ancient Music took place in May 1731. The emphasis on 'Ancient' music was intended to prevent further controversies about contemporary music, but the word-books for the Academy's later performances show that this self-imposed restriction did not last long. If Hawkins is to be believed, the restriction did not achieve its object in any case, since Gates and the Chapel Royal Children left in 1734 (*A General History*, ii. 885).

[80] It is uncertain whether John Church, a key singer from the Chapel Royal and Westminster Abbey, was ever a member; the Academy, perhaps on account of the situation of its performing venue, had a slight bias towards St Paul's Cathedral rather than the Abbey among its dual-membership singers.

from the Chapel Royal and St Paul's had been involved in the earlier Cecilian Society, as described in Chapter 2. Divisions in the Academy precipitated or reflected divisions among the London choir-men themselves

Such evidence as there is suggests that Gates used two weapons in an attempt to embarrass or outdo Greene: his own Chapel Royal position and Handel's music. On 14 January 1730/1, at a crucial stage in the Lotti madrigal controversy and before Greene's departure from the Academy, Gates was responsible for a performance at the Academy that included the disputed madrigal (attributed to Lotti in the newspaper advertisements) and Handel's Utrecht canticles.[81] The canticles were also introduced a month later into the programme of the service for the Festival of the Sons of the Clergy, which took place in Greene's territory at St Paul's Cathedral. The Festival services had previously been one of the main platforms for Greene's church music,[82] but he could hardly have objected to the inclusion of Handel's music without seeming petty. This was, as far as is known, the first year in which Handel's music had featured at the annual Sons of the Clergy service. The musical programme for the service was presumably drawn up by the Stewards in some sort of consultation with the performers:[83] we may suspect the hand of Gates behind the inclusion of Handel's music, but it is doubtful that the composer himself was involved, beyond perhaps lending Gates performing materials for the concert at the Academy.[84] (He also presumably lent Greene the same materials for the Sons of the Clergy service.) A year later Gates promoted Handel's music again through private performances of *Esther* by the Chapel Royal Children, which turned out to have a significant role in the history of Handel's English oratorios and will be considered further in Chapter 11.

Gates's actions need not, in themselves, have resulted in alienation between the two composers: at this stage Greene may have had cause for irritation with

[81] It is significant that the Academy programme appeared in the 'news' section of contemporary newspapers, and not as a concert advertisement. I discovered the programme in *LEP*, 14–16 Jan. 1730/1 (see Burrows, 'Thomas Gethin', 1006); Lindgren ('The Three Great Noises', 567) quotes a similar report from *DJ*, 16 Jan.

[82] Orchestrally accompanied anthems and canticles by Greene, many specially composed for the occasions, had featured at the services since 1719; for details, see Burrows, *Dissertation*, ii. app. 4.

[83] The only Steward in the 1730/1 list who is known to have had musical interests was Humphrey Wyrley [Birch], who joined the Academy of Vocal Music on 19 Dec. 1726. He seems to have been an enthusiast for English church music, and in particular Croft's: see Hawkins, *A General History*, ii. 796. The Academy performance was probably engineered as a final rehearsal for the Sons of the Clergy service, in addition to being one stage in the diplomatic battle against Greene: compare the similar performance/rehearsal in 1733/4 recorded in the Earl of Egmont's diary (Deutsch, *Handel*, 358).

[84] The performance at the Sons of the Clergy Festival service may have prompted the publication of the score of the Utrecht canticles soon afterwards: see William C. Smith, *Handel*, 157.

Handel but his main problem may have been with Gates. However, the situation was changed radically in 1733–4 by the circumstances surrounding the provision of music for the wedding of Princess Anne, George II's eldest daughter, which will be described in Chapter 12. Any suppressed resentment from his treatment over the 1727 coronation would probably have exacerbated his feelings in 1733. It seems plausible that Greene and Handel lived in a state of distant mistrust after the contretemps over the wedding: there are even hints that Greene made a point of defending the artistic programme of the Middlesex opera company in the 1740s, which Handel viewed with rather amused disdain.[85] If Greene's self-esteem received a blow in 1733, he had some compensation two years later when he gained the post of Master of the King's Musick on the death of John Eccles,[86] thereby accumulating all of the major court appointments that were available to a musician simultaneously. This gave him a new outlet for his talents through the composition and performance of the odes for the court festivals celebrating the New Year and the King's birthday. It is not known whether Handel would have had an interest in the post of Master, which was worth another £200 per year: in 1735 this may have seemed rather attractive to him, since competition between the opera companies was threatening the financial base of his theatre productions. In the Chapel Royal a new pattern emerged from 1734 onwards: Handel composed the music for services closely concerning the royal family and the bigger national celebrations, while Greene continued to be responsible for the services that followed the King's return from Hanover (see App. H).

It is notable that Handel and Greene seem to have avoided composing anthem texts that had been set by the other composer. Both set verses from Psalm 145 (*I will magnify thee*) as orchestrally accompanied anthems, but the duplication must have been accidental: Greene's anthem was composed for the Sons of the Clergy in 1719, when he is hardly likely to have known the recent Cannons anthem that provided the framework for Handel's subsequent Chapel Royal setting in 1723–4. In principle, the recurring demand for new settings of the Te Deum involved a repertory in which comparisons could be made,[87] but several factors prevented this from becoming a live issue: as the repertory increased, the composition of music on the Purcell/Croft model but adapted to newer harmonic styles became almost a matter of routine, while Purcell's 1694 settings and Handel's Utrecht music retained their hold in continued

[85] See Burrows and Dunhill, *Music and Theatre*, 129 (Greene); Deutsch, *Handel*, 532 (Handel).
[86] Greene's first court ode was for the King's birthday at the end of Oct. 1735: it was followed only three days later by Greene's music in the Chapel Royal marking the King's return.
[87] There are fewer new settings of the Jubilate Deo, the principal accompanying canticle for Morning Prayer: either older settings were repeated or the Jubilate was sung in settings without orchestral accompaniment.

performance. When Handel next composed a new version of the Te Deum in 1743, his determination to produce a memorable and original treatment of the text led him to an extension of the style from his Coronation Anthems, to produce the loudest and grandest version so far. Coincidentally, some of the major landmarks in Handel's Chapel Royal career occur at ten-year intervals: the Utrecht music in 1713, the pensionable appointment in 1723, the wedding anthem in 1733, and the Dettingen music in 1743.

11

The Chapel Royal and Handel's Oratorios

PASSING mention was made in the previous chapter of the performances of Handel's *Esther* initiated by Bernard Gates in 1732, which led Handel towards the introduction of English works into his Italian opera seasons, and ultimately to the creation of the genre of English theatre oratorio that formed the basis of his later career.[1] In 1785 Charles Burney related the history of these performances in two separate sections of his book recording the Handel Commemoration of the previous year. First, in the course of the biographical essay 'Sketch of the Life of Handel':

Esther, composed for the Duke of Chandos, in 1720, was the first Oratorio which HANDEL set to music. And eleven years after its performance at Cannons, a copy of the score having been obtained, it was represented, in action, by the Children of his Majesty's Chapel, at the house of Mr. Bernard Gates, master of the boys, in James-street, Westminster, on Wednesday, February 23, 1731. The Chorus, consisting of performers from the Chapel-Royal and Westminster-Abbey, was placed after the manner of the ancients, between the stage and orchestra; and the instrumental parts were chiefly performed by Gentlemen who were members of the Philharmonic Society. After this, it was performed by the same singers at the Crown and Anchor, which is said to have first suggested to HANDEL the idea of bringing the Oratorios on the stage.[2]

This is supplemented in Burney's commentary to the Fifth Performance of the Commemoration, with the introductory explanation that 'the following information has been obtained from Dr. Randall, the musical professor at Cambridge, and Mr. Barrow, who were among the original performers, when it was dramatically represented':

On the first performance of ESTHER, in action, at the house of Mr. Bernard Gates, Master of the Children of the Chapel-Royal, in 1731, the parts were cast in the following manner:

---

[1] See Dean, *Handel's Dramatic Oratorios*, 203–7.
[2] Burney, *An Account*, Sketch, 22–3.

Esther - -	by Mr. John (now Dr.) Randal.
Assuerus, and first Israelite	- James Butler.
Haman - -	- John Moore.
Mordecai, and Israelite Boy	- John Brown.
Priest of the Israelites -	- John Beard.
Harbonah - - -	- Price Clevely.
Persian Officer, and 2d Israelite	James Allen.
Israelites	Samuel (late Dr.) Howard.
and } - -	Mr. Thomas Barrow.
Officers	Robert Denham.

Soon after this, it was twice performed by the same children, at the Crown and Anchor, by the desire of William Huggins, esq. a member of that Society, and translator of Ariosto, published 1757, who furnished the dresses. Mr. HANDEL himself was present at one of these representations, and having mentioned it to the Princess Royal, his illustrious scholar, her Royal Highness was pleased to express a desire to see it exhibited in action at the Opera-house in the Hay-market, by the same young performers; but Dr. Gibson, then bishop of London, would not grant permission for its being represented on that stage, even with books in the children's hands. Mr. HANDEL, however, the next year, had it performed at that theatre, with additions to the Drama, by Humphreys; but in *still life*: that is, without action, in the same manner as Oratorios have been since constantly performed.[3]

The introductory pages to an eighteenth-century manuscript score of *Esther* repeat much of Burney's information, including the cast list,[4] but also give further details about the dates of the performances, concluding as follows:

The instrumental parts ... were performed by Members of the Philharmonic Society, consisting only of Gentlemen; at the Crown and Anchor Tavern, in the Strand –

on Wednesday 23 February 1731 }
& Wednesday ... 1 March 1731 }   for the Philharmonic Society
& on Friday ... 3 March 1731.   for the Academy.

On the strength of this, it has been assumed in modern times that Burney was incorrect in placing the first performance at Gates's house, except that there might have been a previous rehearsal there.[5] Since Burney was in touch with two of the original performers, it seems strange that he should have been so definite about the location if it was incorrect, and indeed he repeated the statement about the venue in his history of music, published four years later.[6]

---

[3] Ibid. Fifth Performance, 100–1. See also Perceval's diary, Deutsch, *Handel*, 286.

[4] The MS is now in the Gerald Coke Handel Collection (*HHA* I/8, source M): the introductory pages appear to have been written by the same (unidentified) scribe as the music.

[5] Dean, *Handel's Dramatic Oratorios*, 204.

[6] Burney, *A General History*, ii. 775. In 1770 John Hawkins had referred to the Chapel Royal performances of *Esther* (*An Account*, 6–7), implying that even the first performances were under

The writer of the manuscript may have known less than it appears about the first performance, though the descriptions there convey useful information about the dates and sponsorship of the second and third performances, which would certainly have taken place at the Crown and Anchor tavern. Gates's house in James Street, Westminster, had a room that was large enough to accommodate musical performances on quite a substantial scale,[7] as is revealed by a report in November 1730: 'On Thursday last the Coronation Musick (compos'd by Mr. Handel) was perform'd at Mr. Gates's, Master of the Children of the Chapel Royal, where were present the Right Hon. the Marquess of Blandford, and several other Persons of Distinction' (*LEP*, 26–8 Nov. 1730). The house was also the venue for at least one of the final rehearsals, possibly semi-public, of Handel's anthem for the Prince of Wales's wedding in 1736, and again for a similar event in 1740 (see Ch. 13). A performance of *Esther* there by a modest-sized group of singers and players is therefore not implausible. Whether that performance would have been fully staged is rendered rather uncertain by an ambiguity in Burney's description, which might imply that Huggins provided the costumes for the subsequent performances at the Crown and Anchor.[8]

A principal, though unacknowledged, source of information about the performance, for both Burney and the annotator of the music manuscript, was a word-book for *Esther*, which according to its title page gave the text of the oratorio as 'Perform'd by the Children of His MAJESTY'S Chapel, on *Wednesday, Feb. 23. 1731*' and was 'Printed in the Year M.DCC.XXXII'.[9] The title page of this word-book is the source for 1720 as the year (almost certainly erroneous) for the composition of the original version of *Esther* for James Brydges. The Old Style year date for the Chapel Royal performance was incorrectly interpreted by Burney, which is curious in view of his communications with former members of the cast. The word-book also provided the cast list of the Chapel Royal boys, and the text below the cast list, which was obviously the source for later descriptions, reads as follows:

the auspices of the Academy, but he may have given unsupported credit to the Academy because he was at that time trying to save its future; he probably had no better evidence than Burney.

  [7] The house was on the south side of James Street, and survived into the early years of the 20th c. as 30 Buckingham Gate. Rate books for the parish of St Margaret's, Westminster (Absey), record Gates's occupation of the house from 1729 until his retirement from London in 1757, after which it passed to his successor as Master, James Nares. It is not known whether any of the Chapel Royal Children also lived in the house. A report of a concert in Gates's house in July 1728 (*LEP*, 29 June–2 July 1728) may indicate the earliest known date for his occupation, or it may refer to a previous residence.

  [8] William Huggins was probably the son of John Huggins, Warden of the Fleet Prison, who had been involved in a court case concerning the death of Edward Arne, one of the prisoners, and was finally acquitted of the murder charge in Nov. 1730.

  [9] *Esther: an Oratorio; or, Sacred Drama*; facs. in *HHA* I/8, pp. xxv–xxviii.

Mr. BERNARD GATES, *Master of the Children of the* Chapel-Royal, *together with a Number of Voices from the Choirs of St.* James's, *and* Westminster, *join'd in the* Chorus's, *after the Manner of the Ancients, being placed between the* Stage *and the* Orchestra; *and the Instrumental Parts (two or three particular Instruments, necessary on this Occasion, excepted) were performed by the Members of the* Philharmonick Society, *consisting only of* Gentlemen.

This is clearly a description of an event that had already happened, and the word-book must therefore have been published afterwards, perhaps printed very quickly in time for the subsequent performances at the Crown and Anchor.[10] No venue for the Chapel Royal performance is named, either in the description or on the title page, though the latter is specific about the date of the performance. The absence of any reference to a venue is rather frustrating, and the possibility that the performance took place at Gates's house must remain open. 23 February 1732 was Handel's 47th birthday, and he may have been an honoured guest at the performance. It was also Ash Wednesday, when the Chapel Royal would have had regular duties:this was one of the days in the year on which the Dean (that is, Edmund Gibson) preached at the Chapel, and there would also have been the usual service of Evening Prayer. The timing of the *Esther* performance would therefore have been regulated by the Children's other duties.

All of the singers named in the cast list were identifiable Children of the Chapel Royal except John Brown,[11] and were discharged from the Chapel between 12 June 1733 (Howard) and 12 June 1737 (Denham) (see App. B, p. 575). Gates's early years as Master of the Children had obviously brought him a talented group of youngsters, and *Esther* represented an ambitious project under his training, since the boys formed the complete cast of principals, for both male and female roles. The printed word-book shows that Chapel Royal production gave the Cannons form of *Esther* without compromises in musical content, though the original six scenes were arranged into a three-act structure, with three scenes in each act. If the manuscript score with the introductory pages referring to the 1732 performances represents the version of the oratorio that was performed then, the orchestral introduction to *Zadok the priest* was inserted before the final chorus.[12] Presumably the tenor roles were sung an octave higher, and perhaps more substantial adaptation was made so that John Moore could play the role of Haman, composed for a bass voice. Although the Chapel may occasionally have retained some talented boys for a brief period after their voices had broken, that seems unlikely to have been a

[10] In print style it does not resemble the surviving word-books for the Academy of Ancient Music.

[11] He was possibly a younger brother of Henry Brown (App. B, B54); his dismissal may have been accidentally omitted from the records, or he may have died while still a chorister.

[12] See the description of Source M in *HHA* I/8.

factor here, since the earliest departure did not occur until more than a year after the *Esther* performances. Historically, the Chapel Royal choristers had been actors in theatrical performances, and had indeed had their own theatre at Blackfriars in Shakespeare's time, but this activity had ceased by 1626.[13] Gates's production of *Esther* a century later relates only indirectly to this past, however, since it was an all-sung piece performed in circumstances that were not open to the general public. Performances at the Crown and Anchor tavern took place in the context of the private clubs of London 'gentlemen' connoisseurs: most likely the audiences included lady guests as well as members. Not only were the leads taken by Chapel Royal choristers, but men from the Chapel Royal and Westminster Abbey choirs provided the tenor and bass voices for the chorus movements. It was not accidental that the description in the word-book did not mention St Paul's Cathedral singers, since Greene had withdrawn from the Academy the previous May: the *Esther* performances may, indeed, have marked a new level in the ongoing competition between Gates and Greene.

By 1732 Handel had been intermittently involved with the Chapel Royal's music for twenty years. His association with Gates went back at least to 1712–13, when he had named him as a soloist for his first setting of *As pants the hart* and the Utrecht Jubilate, as well as giving him a solo aria in the Birthday Ode for Queen Anne. His attendance at one of the 1732 performances of *Esther* would therefore not have been surprising. Neither is his subsequent reported conversation with Princess Anne implausible, since she would have had a double interest in the matter: she was Handel's student and supporter, and the performances involved musicians closely involved with the court. Court protocol would presumably not have permitted her to attend one of the Academy's meetings in a Fleet Street tavern, hence her request for a public performance at the opera house. No doubt Handel gave a suitably polite answer, but he must have realized that it was impracticable to transfer Gates's production to the theatre, since it would have been lost in the larger spaces of the stage at the King's Theatre. Although the choristers probably included two or three boys with strong voices, the cast as a whole would have been inadequate for the theatre, especially when accompanied by the opera orchestra. Handel subsequently used treble soloists in his oratorio performances at the London theatres, but these would have been the best singers at the peak of their voices: it was not to be expected that every chorister would be an effective soloist in a large theatre with radically different acoustic conditions from those in which he normally performed.

[13] See Baldwin, *The Chapel Royal*, ch. 5.

The *Esther* performances of February–March 1732 created sufficient interest for Handel to try the experiment of presenting the oratorio in the opera house. He adapted and expanded the Cannons score for his current Italian opera company, producing a version of comparable length to his operas,[14] which he performed at the end of his current opera season, in May 1732, at the King's Theatre. Princess Anne therefore had the opportunity to hear performances of *Esther*, though not in Gates's Chapel Royal production, within a couple of months.[15] The version at the opera house was given in English throughout, though a contemporary pamphlet commented that '*Senesino* and *Bertolli* made rare work with the *English* Tongue you would have sworn it had been *Welch*; I would have wish'd it *Italian*, that they might have sang with more ease to themselves, since, but for the Name of *English* it might as well have been *Hebrew*'.[16] Nevertheless Handel's theatre performances of *Esther* seem to have been a success with the London audience and ran for six performances. These fell after Easter; the previous performances, including Gates's, had taken place during the Lenten period that was later to be Handel's regular oratorio season.

The pamphlet from which quotation has just been made also described the arrangements for the theatre performances as follows:

I saw indeed the finest Assembly of People I ever beheld in my life, but, to my great Surprize, found this Sacred *Drama* a mere Consort, no Scenary, Dress or Action, so necessary to a *Drama*; but H[andel] was plac'd in a Pulpit, I suppose they call that (their Oratory) [and] by him sate *Senesino*, *Strada*, *Bertolli*, and *Turner Robinson*, in their own Habits; before him stood sundry sweet Singers of this our *Israel*.[17]

The 'sundry sweet Singers' were presumably the chorus voices, and perhaps the soloists for the subsidiary roles. This description needs to be read in conjunction with a statement in the newspaper advertisements for the performances: 'N.B. There will be no Action on the Stage, but the House will be fitted up in a decent Manner, for the Audience. The Musick to be disposed after the Manner of the Coronation Service.'[18] 'Musick' here refers to the performers, and perhaps the implication is that there were galleries for the

[14] Handel's introduction of English theatre works has also been seen as a reply to the productions by the Arne family in 1732 at the Little Theatre, Haymarket, which included *Acis and Galatea*. However, Handel performed *Esther* before he gave *Acis and Galatea* himself, while the Arnes' repertory did not include *Esther*.

[15] Burney's statement that this took place the next year was based on his misinterpretation of the old-style year on the word-book. The first theatre performance of *Esther*, on 2 May 1732, was attended by Princess Anne, along with the King, the Queen, the Prince of Wales, and Princess Amelia.

[16] *See and Seem Blind*, 16. A soprano chorus part for *My heart is inditing* with phonetic English text (US-NYp JOD 72–75) originated from these *Esther* performances: see Burrows, 'Handel's 1738 Oratorio', 22–4.

[17] Ibid. 15.   [18] *DJ*, 19 Apr. 1732; Deutsch, *Handel*, 289.

orchestra and chorus singers on either side of the central 'pulpit'.[19] As described in Chapter 10, Handel incorporated a shortened version of *Zadok the priest* into his 1732 score of *Esther* at the end of Act II, and the complete Coronation Anthem *My heart is inditing*, with its original text, into the body of Act I; his new setting of the chorus 'The Lord our enemy has slain' at the end of Act III was also scored in full 'Coronation Anthem' style, including three trumpets and timpani. He would have needed a number of chorus singers in addition to the soloists in order to do justice to the performance in a manner comparable to the Coronation.

Such chorus singers at the *Esther* performances would have been a distinctive innovation in Handel's London theatre career, and the question arises as to whether any of them came from the Chapel Royal, if Burney's report of Bishop Gibson's ban is correct. Burney's account implies that Gibson's original objection was to the choristers' participation in a proposed staged and costumed production at the opera house: it sounds as if someone had returned to Gibson with the suggestion (also rejected) that a compromise with theatrical impersonation might be made by the children holding their music throughout. Furthermore, Handel's decision to perform the oratorio 'in still life' suggests that it was still hoped to involve the choristers in some way: otherwise, a staged or semi-staged production with the opera soloists would have been a possible option. Probably Gibson, as Dean of the Chapel, was able to exert a greater degree of control over the choristers, who were directly educated and maintained under the Master of the Children, than he could over the adult members of the Chapel Royal. Nevertheless he may have had the power to discourage the participation of the Gentlemen in theatrical performances, as the parallel authorities at the Dublin cathedrals did when it came to Handel's concert performances in that city a decade later.[20] The administrative records of the Chapel Royal suggest that Gibson's principal concern as Dean was to ensure that the Gentlemen performed their duties in the Chapel adequately. In all probability some Gentlemen took part in the *Esther* performances at the King's Theatre, and the choristers may also have done so. We may assume that Gates himself would have been supportive, even though his charges did not repeat their solo roles.

Gibson's intervention may have occurred under an exceptional set of circumstances. Day-to-day administration of the Chapel was normally exercised by the Sub-Dean, who in February 1732 was Edward Aspinwall.

[19] There are no contemporary pictures of Handel's theatre oratorio performances; pictures of performances from the period around 1800 show an arrangement of galleries whose relevance to Handel's practice is uncertain: see Burrows, 'Handel's Oratorio Performances'.
[20] See Barra Boydell, *Music at Christ Church*, 112–13, and Deutsch, *Handel*, 536–7.

Aspinwall signed no entries in the Chapel's Cheque Books between 1 December 1731[21] and his death in August 1732, so it is possible that he was incapacitated in February 1732 and that therefore the Dean was more directly involved in the running of the Chapel than usual. Gibson had been Dean since 1721, and Handel would surely have had to deal with him at some point during the 1720s in connection with his music for the Chapel Royal. There is no direct evidence of personal animosity between the two men, though Gibson may have harboured a long-term resentment that Handel's appointment as Composer for the Chapel Royal had been made in a manner that put him beyond the Dean's control. Winton Dean has interpreted Gibson's ban on stage performances by the Chapel Children as the product of a generally obstructive temperament, reinforced in this context by a puritanical opposition to public entertainments, and influenced by his campaign against the masquerades that took place at the opera house.[22] This may well have been an important motivating factor, but it was probably not the principal one, which more likely originated from Gibson's view of his role as Dean of the Chapel, against the background of his general opposition to anything that he regarded as secular interference in the affairs of the church.[23]

In spite of the circumstance that the Deanship of the Chapel Royal was only one of Gibson's offices, he had a concern for efficient administration and was willing to spend time in order to ensure that the Chapel ran as he wished; in this, he seems to have differed from most of his immediate predecessors.[24] It was Gibson who turned the Chapel Royal cheque book into the 'old' Cheque Book: when he became Dean he probably took one look at the existing volume, with its antiquated arrangement and disorganized entries, and decided immediately that a fresh start was needed. The New Cheque Book was made up to begin from the day of his appointment, and he seems to have decided that the day-to-day operation of the Chapel needed reform, for he prepared an elaborate set of rules that defined precisely the duties of the members of the Chapel, described standards to be observed in behaviour at services, and set up a system of enforcement; this reached a definitive form in 1728.[25] The rules did

---

[21] *NCB*, p. 32; Ashbee and Harley, i. 222.

[22] Dean, *Handel's Dramatic Oratorios*, 205–6. Dean's view was challenged by Arthur Jacobs: see the extended correspondence in *MT* during 1969–70.

[23] Lord Hervey, who seems to have taken a particular dislike to Gibson, described him as having 'so haughty, so insolent and so sour a disposition' (Sedgwick, *Some Materials*, 544), but his descriptions leave no doubt about Gibson's attitude to church appointments (ibid. 400, 404).

[24] Sykes, *Gibson*, provides ample supporting evidence of Gibson's characteristic concern for efficient administration.

[25] Original draft, signed by Gibson, GB-Llp Fulham Papers 124; copies of the final text in *NCB*, pp. 8–13 (Ashbee and Harley, i. 202–7) and Windsor, Royal Archives RA 36. See also Ch. 16.

not make any direct reference to musical activities outside the Chapel, except in relation to those Gentlemen who held simultaneous posts in the other London choirs. Chapel Royal singers regularly took part in the court odes for the New Year and the King's birthday, and there are occasional newspaper reports of their participation as soloists in London concerts; several of them were involved with the Academy of Vocal Music from 1726 onwards,[26] and probably also with other similar societies in London that gave regular, though private, performances. Gibson was apparently not concerned about any of this, provided that the services in the Chapel were properly maintained with due attendance. Having established tidy and efficient procedures to make sure that the staff of the Chapel performed their duties as he wished, he would naturally resist anything which threatened to upset the system,[27] and would have particularly discouraged any move that appeared to involve Chapel Royal personnel in activities that would render them unreliable for their day-to-day work: it was difficult enough to maintain good order when so many Gentlemen also served in the other London choirs. We can imagine the questions that ran through his mind when he heard of the proposal to put *Esther* onto the public stage. Would the Children's attendance at Chapel suffer? Was Mr Handel proposing a series of performances? Was Mr Gates going to abuse his Chapel Royal office by creating a theatrical agency? Perhaps Gibson saw the future more clearly than most of his contemporaries.

There is no definite evidence for the participation of singers from the Chapel Royal in the performances of *Esther* at the King's Theatre in 1732, or indeed any evidence about the number and affiliations of Handel's chorus singers in the early years of his theatre oratorios. Taking a broader view of Handel's oratorio performances between 1732 and his final season in 1759, the evidence is sporadic but a number of aspects are worthy of consideration, regarding the singers both as a group and as individuals. The only detailed information about his performers comes from the surviving account lists for *Messiah* performances at the Foundling Hospital chapel during the composer's last years: the original accounts, or copies of them, survive for 1754 and 1758, and also for the performance in 1759 that took place soon after the composer's death.[28] The 1754 list has the following entries for singers:

---

[26] Seven of the thirteen members at the foundation of the Academy in January 1725/6 (as recorded in GB-Lbl Add. MS 11732) currently held places at the Chapel Royal.

[27] If there was bad feeling between Greene and Gates, this would also have produced an unstable situation in the Chapel. Aspinwall's successor as Sub-Dean, George Carleton, was related to Greene by marriage and may have exerted some pressure on Gibson.

[28] See Burrows, 'Handel and the Foundling Hospital', 283–4.

[name]	[£. s. d.]
Beard	[—]
Frasi	6. 6. –
Galli	4. 14. 6
Passerini	4. 14. 6
Wass	1. 11. 6
Boys	3. 3. –
Baildon	10. 6
Barrow	10. 6
Cheriton	10. 6
Ladd	10. 6
Baildon Junr	10. 6
Vandernon	10. 6
Champness	10. 6
Courtney	10. 6
Wilder	10. 6
Dupeé	10. 6
Walz	10. 6
Cox	10. 6
Legg	10. 6[29]

The first five names were the soloists; they included John Beard, who had been a Child of the Chapel (and had taken the role of Priest of the Israelites in Gates's 1732 production of *Esther*), and Robert Wass, who was a current Gentleman of the Chapel. The 'Boys' would have been four in number, since a later account indicates payments of 15s. 9d. (three-quarters of a guinea) for each;[30] the minutes of the Foundling Hospital regularly record thanks to Gates (and then to William Boyce from 1752 onwards) for the participation of the trebles, so these must have come from the Chapel Royal.[31] It is curious that Gates himself was not named among the singers: perhaps he was already reducing his own performing activity by 1754.[32]

Of the thirteen chorus singers in the list, five (Baildon, Barrow, Cheriton, Ladd, and Vandernan) were currently Chapel Royal Gentlemen; of the others, Cox joined the Chapel in 1755, 'Dupeé' was probably Dupuis (Child until 1751, Organist and Composer from 1779), and Champness, a former Child of

[29] Deutsch, *Handel*, 751, and facs. in Burrows, 'Handel's Oratorio Performances', 272; the fourth name was incorrectly written on the original as 'Passesini'.
[30] 1758 account, Deutsch, *Handel*, 801. The rather awkward sum may have included the cost of a coach for transport to the performance.
[31] See Burrows, 'Handel and the Foundling Hospital', 273.
[32] He was nevertheless named as a singer for the court odes at New Year 1754 and 1756.

the Chapel, joined as a Gentleman later in life (1789) after a career in the theatre.[33] Gustavus Waltz, probably the only chorus singer not of British birth, was a theatre singer who had sung as a soloist in operas and oratorios for Handel in former years. Legg was subsequently a Vicar Choral at Westminster Abbey: Courtney and Wilder were probably theatre singers. Enough is known of the group as a whole, however, to indicate that the pool of potential chorus singers for Handel's oratorios in London relied to a considerable extent on current Chapel Royal Gentlemen and other singers who had some association with the Chapel. It is unlikely that the availability of the Gentlemen was greatly affected by their 'months of waiting', since most also served alternately at Westminster Abbey or St Paul's Cathedral and thus lived permanently in London. There was probably never any question of Handel employing the complete Chapel Royal choir for his chorus: rather, the Chapel provided one of the main sources for competent professional singers in London. The Gentlemen he employed were presumably good music readers as well as competent vocalists: this was an important consideration in view of the intense repertory, and probably limited rehearsal time, of the oratorio seasons. The Foundling Hospital list of chorus men seems to be arranged by voices: as far as can be determined, Baildon, Barrow, and Cheriton were altos, Ladd, Baildon junior, and Vandernan tenors, and the remainder basses. This implies a bass-heavy vocal balance, perhaps compensated by the strength of the soloists in the upper voices. In spite of the uniformity of payments to the chorus singers, the section leaders may have been those who were named first, in which case the altos and tenors were led by Chapel Royal men.

Two issues arise from this list: did the chorus for the Foundling Hospital performances differ radically from the chorus that sang for Handel in the theatre in the same year, and what documentary evidence is there that might indicate the participation of the Chapel Royal singers in earlier seasons? While the first question cannot be answered with complete certainty, there is one aspect of the 1754 list which suggests that it may also be relevant to Handel's theatre performances. None of the Chapel Royal Gentlemen named on the list are Priests, and this is what we would expect for a group that sang in the theatre as well. Leaving aside Gibson's personal scruples, it would have been regarded as improper for men in holy orders to perform in the public theatres. George Harris, a clergyman who had no personal reservations about attending oratorios and plays at the London theatres, nevertheless reflected the nature of ecclesiastical constraints when he commented sardonically on the first performance of *Messiah* in the Foundling Hospital Chapel that 'two or three of the

---

[33] There is some ambiguity over the names, but the most likely identifications for Baildon (sr.) and Champness in App. B are Gentleman 82 and B83/W15.

bishops were there; so that I hope, in a little while, the hearing of oratorios will be held as orthodox'.[34] Curiously, there seems to have been no inhibition on the Priests of the Chapel performing as soloists in the court odes. With due caution, the 1754 list may taken as a guide to the type of chorus singers, and their numbers, that Handel may have employed for the theatre oratorios, at least in some seasons.

Unfortunately, specific information on Handel's chorus singers in previous seasons is so thin and so sporadic that it is impossible to draw firm conclusions. If Handel did manage to include some Chapel Royal singers, men or boys, in his 1732 *Esther* performances, then no doubt he called upon them again in 1733, when the score of his new oratorio *Deborah* also drew on music from Coronation Anthems and required an appropriate number of performers; similarly, his ambitious programme of oratorios at Covent Garden theatre in 1735 implies the participation of chorus singers, though the opera scores from the season indicate that he also employed a number of additional non-Chapel singers as a regular part of his resources at that time.[35] Concerning his benefit night at the King's Theatre in March 1738, a correspondent referred to Handel's employment of extra singers, but those named were William Hayes from Oxford and a 'singer from Windsor', rather than Chapel Royal Gentlemen.[36] The grand choruses in *Saul* and the double choruses in *Israel in Egypt* imply the employment of a substantial number of chorus singers for Handel's 1739 season at the King's Theatre; for his subsequent seasons at Lincoln's Inn Fields there are very few clues about the chorus singers. His programme swung rather capriciously between operas and oratorios in the years between 1732 and 1741, according to the opportunities of the moment, and it seems unlikely that he was able to establish any regular arrangement for the employment of chorus singers. From 1743 onwards, however, his London performances settled into a regular rhythm of Lenten 'oratorio seasons', and fairly early on in the series there is one valuable clue: in June 1744 J. C. Smith senior apologized in a letter to James Harris that he could not lend him some of Handel's performing parts for oratorio performances in Salisbury because 'as he is to have the choir and boy's, he would give them their parts in time to be perfect in every one of them'.[37] The implication of this is also, however, that Handel may not have employed these singers in the previous season, and indeed Smith had apologized to Harris in October 1743 that he could not supply any duplicate vocal

---

[34] Burrows and Dunhill, *Music and Theatre*, 270.

[35] On the autograph of *Alcina* (GB-Lbl RM 20.a.4) Handel named the following singers in addition to the soloists on the final coro: 'Howard, Corf, Tomson [tenors], Leveridge, Stoppelar [basses]'; he also wrote 'Negri etc' for the alto stave.

[36] Burrows and Dunhill, *Music and Theatre*, 43.

[37] Ibid. 194. Handel's next oratorio season began unusually early, in Nov. 1744.

parts (probably for *Messiah*) because 'Mr Handel had but one done per Parte'.[38] In connection with Handel's performance of *Deborah* at the King's Theatre on 3 November 1744 the Earl of Shaftesbury reported that 'wee had al the boys from the chapell, and abundance of other voices to fill up',[39] and when Handel outlined the performers that he hoped to have for the season that began that night he included 'Mr Gates with his Boyes's and several of the best Chorus Singers from the Choirs'.[40] It was perhaps in the second half of the 1740s, at Covent Garden, that Handel's chorus regularly took on the sort of composition that we find in the 1754 Foundling Hospital account, although there can be no certainty on the matter on the basis of the sparse documentation that we have. What does seem certain, however, is that the Chapel Royal singers, men and boys, were a significant resource when Handel needed a substantial chorus. The timing of the rehearsals and performances must have enabled the singers also to fulfil their regular duties for Evening Prayer at the Chapel Royal, Westminster Abbey, or St Paul's Cathedral on the same days; it is unlikely that all of the men could have employed deputies, every time. We must assume, also, that in the long run Gibson either acquiesced in the boys' participation or was powerless to prevent it.

Robert Wass was the only Chapel Royal Gentleman to be a principal soloist for Handel's oratorio performances while holding his Chapel post. The 1754 list shows that, although Wass was no doubt musically competent, he did not command as high a fee as the other soloists.[41] He had become Handel's regular bass soloist for the oratorios after the death of Henry Reinhold in 1751: by the time of the 1758 Foundling Hospital list he had been superseded as the principal by Samuel Champness (also paid £1.11.6), but was nevertheless listed with the soloists and paid £1.1.0. Two other Chapel Royal men (Baildon and Barrow) were also paid £1.1.0 for the 1758 performance, perhaps as section leaders since the other chorus singers still received 10s. 6d.[42] A year later Wass's name moved down the list to the chorus voices, while still retaining the payment differential, joining Baildon and Barrow.[43] Two further Gentlemen, Hugh Cox and Francis Rowe, performed secondary solo roles in Handel's oratorios, Rowe perhaps only for his Oxford performances in 1733.[44] Handel's

[38] Burrows and Dunhill, *Music and Theatre*, 171. Handel's annotations on the autograph of *Samson* relating to the 1743 performances include one reference to 'Boys' (GB-Lbl RM 20.f.6, fo. 139ʳ) but no mention of other chorus singers.
[39] Ibid. 204
[40] Letter to Charles Jennens, 9 June 1744; Deutsch, *Handel*, 591.
[41] Beard regularly donated his services for the Foundling Hospital performances.
[42] Deutsch, *Handel*, 801.
[43] Ibid. 825.
[44] Some of the biographical material in Dean, *Handel's Dramatic Oratorios*, 654–60 is incorrect. I identify Cox with App. B B80 and Gentleman 85. Wass is unlikely to have sung in the 1737

teams of soloists from time to time included boy trebles, identified by the composer on his autographs and performing scores simply as 'the Boy' in each case. In view of the good evidence for a working relationship between Handel and Gates, it is tempting to suppose that the boys always came from the Chapel Royal, but this was not always the case: Handel's best-documented treble soloist, William Savage, came from St Paul's Cathedral. Perhaps Handel had a better relationship with Charles King, the Master of the Choristers at St Paul's in the 1730s, than he had with Greene. Following King's death in 1748, Savage himself succeeded him, and the soloists for the Foundling Hospital *Messiah* performance in 1757 included 'Mr Savage's celebrated Boy'.[45] It seems likely, however, that Handel's other treble soloists came from the Chapel Royal, and it may be significant that the solo treble from St Paul's in 1757 coincided with the time of Gates's retirement.

Of the Children from the Chapel who did not proceed to a place of Gentleman, by far the most significant was John Beard. He was discharged as a chorister at the end of October 1734 and went straight from the Chapel into Handel's opera company at Covent Garden, appearing on stage as a (tenor) soloist in *Il pastor fido* on 9 November. He remained Handel's leading tenor as the composer's career moved from opera to oratorio, eventually performing more new oratorio roles for him than any other singer. Although he does not feature much in the story of Handel's relationship with the Chapel Royal after 1734, he maintained contact with the Chapel musicians through his regular employment as a soloist in the court odes.[46] Another Chapel Royal boy of Beard's generation, Samuel Howard, was among the chorus singers employed by Handel at Covent Garden in 1735.[47]

Some generalizations can be made concerning the Chapel Royal music that Handel incorporated into his oratorios. As already noted, for his theatre oratorios in 1732 and 1733 he turned first to the Coronation Anthems. All four of them were used, in full or in part, in the course of *Esther* and *Deborah*:[48] the Old Testament stories gave plenty of opportunity for working in the

---

Funeral Anthem. Dean's entry for Abbot (p. 651), who was a Priest of the Chapel, must unfortunately be removed from the canon: see Ch. 12.

[45] See Watkins Shaw, *A Textual and Historical Companion*, 64. By 1757 the performances advertised under Handel's name were in practice organized by the Smiths, and Gates was no longer in charge of the Chapel boys: see Burrows, 'Handel and the Foundling Hospital', 273.

[46] The soloists for the court odes came from the Chapel Royal, with the addition of Beard from New Year 1736 and Savage from Birthday 1744.

[47] See n. 37 above.

[48] *Athalia*, composed a short time after *Deborah*, does not include any music from the Coronation Anthems. Since he planned also to perform both *Esther* and *Deborah* in Oxford, Handel probably felt that he had already consumed all the available music from the anthems in these oratorios.

anthems as the Jews celebrated various triumphs.[49] They were retained when
the oratorios were revived in later years,[50] and *Zadok the priest* also found a
place in the *Occasional Oratorio*, composed when the uncertainties of the
outcome of the '45 Jacobite rebellion prompted the patriotic inclusion of
'God save the King'. In general, solo movements from the Chapel Royal
works were not used in the oratorios, probably because their music was too
closely linked to the particular styles of the Chapel's alto and bass soloists. The
only work associated with the Chapel singers from which Handel drew
substantially for solo music in his earliest theatre oratorios was the secular
court ode *Eternal source of light divine*, composed in 1713.[51]

In two subsequent oratorios Handel used music from the Chapel Royal
anthems that he had composed before 1727. As described in Chapter 8, the
orchestrally accompanied Chapel Royal version of *As pants the hart* was presented in a revised form to open his benefit-night *Oratorio* in March 1738 (see
Ch. 8). Part One of this performance concluded with a chorus 'Blessed be
God. Allelujah', which was almost certainly the last movement of *Let God arise*,
HWV 256b.[52] More substantial was Handel's use of *I will magnify thee* (HWV
250b) at the conclusion of *Belshazzar*, composed in the autumn of 1744. In a
letter to the librettist Charles Jennens on 2 October 1744, Handel mentioned
that Jennens had suggested the inclusion of 'anthems' at the end of Part III, as
the Persians and Israelites join together in praise of the Almighty after the
defeat of the Babylonians.[53] The letter implies that Jennens had suggested the
incorporation of at least one complete anthem and that Handel was disturbed
by the effect of this in what was already a long oratorio, but the text that he
quotes in the letter reveals that he was thinking in terms of using three
movements from the Cannons anthem *I will magnify thee* (HWV 250a) to

[49] Movements from a later Chapel Royal work, the Dettingen Anthem, served a similar
function in *Joseph* (1743) and in the 1756 revival of *Athalia*.

[50] Music from all four Coronation Anthems was also included in Handel's *Oratorio* in March
1738.

[51] See Dean, *Handel's Dramatic Oratorios*, 207, 642. It is interesting that solo movements from
Cannons anthems were drawn upon, but not those from Chapel Royal anthems.

[52] The text as printed in the 1738 word-book, which is the only evidence for that part of the
performance, leaves it open as to whether the music performed was the last movement of HWV
256a or HWV 256b. Two pieces of circumstantial evidence point to the latter, however: the
scoring of HWV 256b was more appropriate to Handel's forces in the *Oratorio*, and the key of
A major makes a more logical sequence after the previous item in the programme, the aria
'Bianco giglio' in D major.

[53] Deutsch, *Handel*, 595–6; see also Dean, *Handel's Dramatic Oratorios*, 434. Handel's use of
'anthems' in the plural presumably means that, at that stage, he was thinking of 'Tell it out
among the Heathen' in its Cannons anthem context as part of HWV 253 rather than HWV
250b. He may, however, have been using 'anthems' in a generic sense to mean anthem-style
chorus movements.

'conclude well the Oratorio'.[54] In the event he used music from the Chapel Royal anthem instead, which had three advantages: the Chapel Royal version was shorter, the music had been improved in the course of revision from the Cannons version, and it suited his oratorio performing forces better. The composer's emendations to the autograph of the anthem for use in *Belshazzar* have been described in Chapter 9. The chorus 'Tell it out among the heathen' was transposed to G major, the opening solo being given to the soprano Francesina. A newly composed recitative followed this chorus in the oratorio, and then Handel put together the first and last movements of the anthem, retaining their texts, as a single-movement finale: the sections from the anthem were Andante movements with 'walking' quaver basses, so the join was seamless. The opening music of this final movement, originally composed for Hughes, was given to Miss Robinson in the character of Cyrus, and Weely's former contribution to the continuation 'My mouth shall speak the praise of the Lord' was converted into a soprano part for Francesina: Hughes's music in that section was originally allocated to Mrs Cibber for *Belshazzar*, but was given to Miss Robinson in a last-minute alteration.[55] Both movements from HWV 250b were subjected to further cuts and revisions after they had been copied into the conducting score.[56] Handel's selection of music from the Chapel Royal anthem for use in the oratorio was both effective and practical, but twelve years later J. C. Smith senior showed less common sense, or perhaps greater ignorance of what was available, when he introduced 'My mouth shall speak the praise of the Lord' into a revival of *Athalia*.[57] He began by copying the opening from the Cannons anthem, but then realized that that version, with its three-part chorus and lack of orchestral viola parts, would require considerable alteration as soon as the chorus and orchestra entered, so he welded the chorus section from the Chapel Royal anthem onto the solo opening from the Cannons version.

   Through the incorporation of substantial sections or complete movements into the oratorios, the Chapel Royal music that Handel had composed for particular occasions came into a wider and more durable use. Before returning

[54] The text quoted by Handel in the letter includes 'The Lord preserveth', one of the movements from HWV 250a that was not used in HWV 250b.

[55] The preceding recitative was for the character Cyrus, and Handel's plan as he composed the oratorio was clearly that the recitative should introduce the final anthem, Mrs Robinson (in the character of Cyrus) singing both the recitative and the ensuing solo at the beginning of 'I will magnify thee'. A last-minute illness in the cast forced Handel to redistribute the roles and Cyrus was given to a bass, but it is probable that Mrs Robinson kept 'I will magnify thee'.

[56] See Clausen, *Händels Direktionspartituren*, 121–3.

[57] Ibid. 119. Although Handel was nominally responsible for the oratorio performances in his last years, the artistic decisions were probably mainly taken by J. C. Smith junior, and various errors of judgement like the one described here seem to confirm this.

to take up the story of his compositions for the Chapel Royal in the 1730s, it is convenient at this point to note the earliest occasions on which his Chapel Royal pieces were taken up by other people for performance, since the first substantial examples come from the 1730s. One possible performance by Handel himself must be mentioned first. During his visit to Oxford in 1733, his music was performed in services at St Mary's Church on Sunday 8 July. The reports of the event are rather sketchy: the most detailed account says that a Te Deum and an orchestrally accompanied anthem were performed in the morning, a Jubilate and another anthem in the afternoon.[58] It is probable, though not certain, that the Utrecht settings of the canticles were performed; the anthems were not specified. Some performing parts for the Cannons version of *I will magnify Thee*, associated with Oxford musicians from the 1730s, have an amendment substituting the first movement from the Chapel Royal anthem:[59] these may be connected in some way with the 1733 event, perhaps deriving as secondary copies from part-books that were used then. One first-hand report on 'the Act at St Maries and the Theatre' said that Handel 'conducted the whole',[60] and one advance newspaper report suggested that the church music was part of his planned programme.[61] Otherwise there is no explicit evidence that Handel directed the church performances, though the reported participation of three of his oratorio soloists (Powell, Waltz, and Rowe) is suggestive.[62] There are no annotations on surviving musical sources that might relate to a performance by Handel at this time, and it is possible that the music for the services was the responsibility of Richard Goodson, the Professor of Music.

With regard to performances of Handel's Chapel Royal music by others, it is convenient to separate the Utrecht Te Deum and Jubilate from the rest. As noted in Chapter 4, this music became popular for special services in provincial churches and cathedrals, the earliest recorded example occurring at Bristol on St Cecilia's Day in 1727. After its inclusion in the service for the Festival of the Sons of the Clergy at St Paul's Cathedral in 1731 the Utrecht music became

[58] *The Oxford Act*, 33–4. Of the various sources quoted in Deutsch, *Handel*, 326–9, the fullest report is from the *London Magazine* (p. 329).

[59] In GB-Ob MS Mus.Sch.c.104, and GB-Occ MSS 70, 81, 73, 1141. One part is labelled 'Verse Mr Powell', and the oboe part is transposed to G major.

[60] Letter from William Warren to Thomas Brett; see Johnstone, 'Handel at Oxford', 252. Warren does not seem to have been very interested in music, and was giving a very general description.

[61] *DA*, 20 June 1733.

[62] There is some circumstantial evidence from the financial records of the Vice-Chancellor of Oxford University that the University Organist was not responsible for these performances: see Burrows, 'Sources for Oxford Handel Performances', 178 n. 9. There is no record of a payment to Handel in these accounts. It is unlikely that he had any involvement in a performance of his church music while he was at Dublin in 1741–2: see Burrows, 'Handel's Dublin Performances', 53–4.

well established in the musical programme for that annual event. (The performance in 1735 stimulated an enthusiastic poem from Aaron Hill.)[63] Walsh's publication of the score soon followed; thereafter the Utrecht canticles were easily accessible, and became part of the regular repertory for performances at Dublin (from 1735),[64] Salisbury (from 1740),[65] and the Three Choirs Festival (probably from the 1730s).[66] The Utrecht Te Deum maintained its place even after the appearance of Handel's equally popular Dettingen setting. The Coronation Anthems were also readily available following the publication of Walsh's score in the early 1740s, and they were taken up even earlier. The performance at Gates's house in 1730 has already been mentioned; early performances of all four anthems were advertised in the programmes for public concerts in London on 28 March 1735, 4 March, and 16 April 1736, and two of them were performed at William Savage's benefit concert at the Castle Tavern in London in May 1737.[67] *Zadok the priest* was performed at Windsor Town-Hall in concerts for the Benefit Fund for the choir of St George's Chapel in August 1737, and in the same year 'God save the King' from that anthem was performed at the opening and the close of the summer season at Vauxhall Gardens.[68] It seems probable that most of the many subsequent references to Handel's 'Coronation Anthem' in reports and advertisements for concerts and services are to *Zadok the priest* or to this chorus, which seems to have developed an independent life for performances.

The rest of Handel's Chapel Royal repertory composed before 1730 remained less accessible, and performances seem to have been rare. Although it had been stimulated by the conditions specific to the Chapel's performers, the music would have been ideally suited in style and scale to the resources that were available for many cathedral-style provincial performances. The recurring vagueness of advertisements that refer to 'two anthems' or 'two new anthems' by Handel renders it impossible to estimate the number of early performances of the Chapel Royal repertory. *O sing unto the Lord* was performed at Hickford's Room in April 1740,[69] and an anthem with the same title was performed at Salisbury in October 1754, along with *I will magnify thee*,[70] but probably the Cannons versions of the anthems were given on both

---

[63] Deutsch, *Handel*, 306–7. See also p. 285 above for the 1731 Academy performance.

[64] See Brian Boydell, *A Dublin Musical Calendar*, 60 (8 Apr. 1736).

[65] *RMARC* 8 (1970), 24.

[66] The programmes from the 1730s are poorly documented. See the summary in Young, 'The First Hundred Years', 11–13, and Watkins Shaw, *The Three Choirs Festival*, 8–9.

[67] The first three were advertised in *DA*, 4 Mar. 1735, 2 Mar. and 16 Apr. 1736; for Savage's concert, see Deutsch, *Handel*, 432.

[68] *DA*, 12 Aug., 30 Apr., and 23 Aug. 1737.

[69] Deutsch, *Handel*, 497–8.

[70] *RMARC* 5 (1965), 54.

occasions. The performances for which the identity of the Chapel Royal works is beyond question are few indeed:

Dublin, Mercer's Hospital Benefit, and Philharmonic Society
The repertory of the Mercer's Hospital charity performances before 1750 can be established from the earliest layers of the surviving part-books now in the library at Trinity College, Dublin: in addition to the Utrecht service and two Coronation Anthems, these parts include the Chapel Royal version of *I will magnify thee* (HWV 250b), transposed to G major. The first benefit performance was at a service on 8 April 1735, at which the Utrecht canticles and two of Handel's Coronation Anthems were given.[71] The Dublin Philharmonic Society's word-book dated 1741 includes the texts of HWV 250b and HWV 256b, as well as the Coronation Anthems.[72]

London, Sons of the Clergy Festival Services[73]
1731/2 One 'anthem for his late Majesty', possibly repeated in the next two years.
1734/5 Te Deum in A major ('Te Deum in Airy')

Oxford Musical Society
Surviving musical sources, including performing parts, deriving from Oxford musicians in the 1730s and 1740s indicate performances of the Chapel Royal version of *As pants the hart* (HWV 251c) with the amendments from the 1738 *Oratorio* (HWV 251e) and, as already noted, a movement from the Chapel Royal version of *I will magnify thee*.[74]

London, The Academy of Ancient Music
A text for a Te Deum setting by Handel is printed in the programmes of the Academy's concerts on 28 February 1751 and 29 April 1756:[75] the arrangement of the verses is that for the A major Te Deum.

Some early manuscript copies of the Chapel Royal music may have been associated with other, undocumented, performances: for example, John Alcock's scores of the Caroline and A major Te Deums, the surviving part-books for the A major Te Deum and HWV 250b now in the Guildhall Library, London, or some of the early scores that couple the A major Te Deum with HWV 256b.[76]

---

[71] See Brian Boydell, *A Dublin Musical Calendar*, 60–1.
[72] For the word-book see Dean, *Handel's Dramatic Oratorios*, 186–7. It may have been published in two separate sections, and the 1741 date on the title page may apply only to the first section, in which all of the Chapel Royal works are represented.
[73] See Burrows, *Dissertation*, ii. App. 4.
[74] See Burrows, 'Sources for Oxford Handel Performances' and n. 62 above.
[75] GB-LEc R 780.73 Ac12.
[76] See Burrows, *Dissertation*, i. 364–6, 369–70, 387–8.

One other performance claims special attention. In 1729 a mutual Fund was established for the Chapel Royal, the Gentlemen's subscriptions being invested in South Sea stock in order to provide an income for their widows or legatees.[77] The moving force behind the scheme was John Church, who acted as secretary-treasurer for the Fund in the early years;[78] most of the Gentlemen, including the Priests, participated. In order to accumulate some capital the Chapel mounted a series of three mid-day concerts at the Banquet-

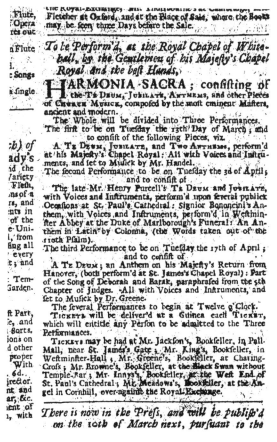

Fig. 11.1. Advertisement for the performances at the Banqueting House Chapel, Whitehall, in support of the Chapel Royal Fund, *The Daily Journal*, 28 February 1732/3. British Library

[77] GB-Cfm MU MS 1011, 'The Chapel Subscription Book for a perpetual Fund', commenced at Lady Day (25 Mar.) 1729.

[78] *WA1* shows that Church was also the accountant for the choir income at Westminster Abbey.

ing House Chapel, Whitehall, in March and April 1733 under the title
Harmonia Sacra: see Fig. 11.1.[79] The first programme, on 13 March, was
devoted to music by Handel, comprising 'a Te Deum, Jubilate and Two
Anthems, perform'd at his Majesty's Chapel Royal: all with Voices and Instruments, and set to Musick by Mr. Handel'. The two anthems were presumably
taken from the repertory that had been composed for the Chapel during the
period 1722–6. The Jubilate must have been the Utrecht setting, but this could
have been coupled with any one of Handel's three Chapel Royal settings of the
Te Deum—Utrecht, the Caroline, or A major: the last two would probably
have been better suited to the forces available. The performances were perhaps
conducted by Greene; Handel presumably cooperated by lending the necessary performing material, and may have attended at least the concert of his own
music.

   All three concerts were accompanied by orchestra, and the programmes
included music directly associated with the Chapel Royal. The second performance of the series included Purcell's D major Te Deum and Jubilate, and
Bononcini's Funeral Anthem for the Duke of Marlborough; the third performance was devoted to music by Greene—a Te Deum, an anthem, and *The
Song of Deborah and Barak*. The venture as a whole was extremely successful and
produced £130 profit for the Fund. It was the only time that the Chapel Royal
choir gave concert performances of their music in the eighteenth century, and
the only occasion on which a wider London audience could have heard
Handel's Chapel Royal music performed in a public concert by some of the
singers for whom it had been composed. It might also have been the last
occasion on which Hughes and Weely sang solo parts together in Handel's
music.

---

[79] Initial notice in *DPB*, 22 Feb. 1732/3; also *DJ*, 24 Feb. After the first performance this
footnote was added to subsequent advertisements: 'NB The Performances of Church Musick at
Whitehall are for augmenting a Fund for the Widows, &c. of the Gentlemen of the Chappel Royal,
who die in his Majesty's Service.' No information on the performances is to be found in Deutsch,
Handel, but a laudatory verse inspired by the Handel concert is reprinted on pp. 339–40.

12

Princess Anne's Wedding Anthem, 1733–1734

Princess Anne's Wedding

THE Hanoverian family was part of a large dynastic structure, characterized by much intermarriage and an instinctive concern to preserve and increase power, influence, and territory through marriage. There were no royal marriages during George I's reign: the King's two children were already married by 1714 and his grandchildren were too young to be of marriageable age. Nevertheless, dynastic plans for the future would have been second nature to George I, and involved both political and personal considerations. His main ploy against his son during the period of estrangement had been to take over the three eldest granddaughters with a possessiveness that was politically driven but which also seems to have involved a certain amount of personal affection, and it is hardly surprising that he also began negotiations in the 1720s for the future marriages of his grandchildren. His plan was for a double marriage involving his Prussian grandchildren: Frederick, the eldest son of the future King George II, was to marry Friedrich Wilhelm of Prussia's eldest daughter, and one of George II's daughters (preferably Anne, the eldest) was to marry Friedrich Wilhelm's eldest son. This was one of the pieces of business that George I had hoped to finalize on the visit to Hanover in 1727.[1] The thought that Princess Anne might have become the wife of the future King Frederick the Great of Prussia is an intriguing one, but this dream was never realized. Shifts in political allegiances intervened, and George II as King dropped the double marriage plan. The vacuum that was left behind was not absolute, for George I had also made other forward matrimonial plans for his grandchildren: in particular, the young Prince of Orange-Nassau (son of King William III's nephew) had in 1721 been offered one of the granddaughters as a marriage partner when he came of age. This was a generous political gesture at the time on the part of George I, who took a long-term view and hoped that the influence of the British relationship would increase Prince Willem's chances of eventually

---

[1] See Hatton, *George I*, 271–2, 280–1.

being elected Stadholder.[2] Speculation about a marriage between Willem and Princess Anne reached the London newspapers within a couple of months of George II's coronation.[3]

Prince Willem came of age in 1732, by which time the Prussian project had been abandoned and he was the main candidate for Princess Anne's hand. He had inherited the rather frail physical constitution of the Orange family, and was a safe, useful, Protestant match rather than a prepossessing suitor. Nevertheless, the wedding of the King's eldest daughter was a prospect that aroused expectations of a special event in London, and Willem himself, whether on account of his own personality or on account of what he represented, proved popular with the public during his time in England. Princess Anne holds a special place in the story of Handel's relationship with the court. She is the member of the royal family for whom there is the best authoritative contemporary documentary evidence that she was an active partisan supporter on Handel's behalf: Lord Hervey's memoirs describe her personal advocacy.[4] Handel had been active as Anne's music teacher since 1723:[5] a later anecdote reported that she was the only pupil whom he enjoyed coaching.[6] Such was her own interest in music that, on the day that her prospective husband arrived in London, she was still 'in her own apartment at her harpsichord with some of the Opera people'.[7]

It has already been seen that church services for state and royal occasions (including the Utrecht Thanksgiving, the 1727 coronation, and the Chapel Royal services marking the King's return to London) were prone to postponements and delays: the timing of both public and private events involving the royal family was often rather capricious on account of various political, diplomatic, and personal factors. Royal proclamations and announcements concerning the dates and arrangements for celebrations were often held back until the last possible moment, delayed until all negotiations had been completed; the negotiations themselves often involved cross-channel communication, requiring journeys by ambassadors and messengers as well as by the persons directly concerned. Even after an announcement had been made, circumstances could modify the intended dates and arrangements. It is prob-

---

[2] See Hatton, *George I*, 267–8; Willem eventually became Stadholder in 1747. I have retained the Dutch form of his name to distinguish him from Prince William, Duke of Cumberland, George II's younger son, and from the various other members of the House of Orange who were relevant to British history.

[3] *WEP*, 28–30 Nov. 1727, and *LEP*, 16–18 Jan. 1727/8: Willem is referred to as the Prince of Nassau-Friesland.

[4] See Sedgwick, *Some Materials*, 273–4, 371.

[5] See Ch. 7 nn. 17 and 18. By 1739 other people are named as Music Masters for the remaining royal children (in Lpro LC5/21), though Handel continued to receive the pension.

[6] Jacob Wilhelm Lustig in 1771: see Deutsch, *Handel*, 360.

[7] Sedgwick, *Some Materials*, 231.

able that much of the rumour and gossip reported in the newspapers (often under the formula 'we hear that . . .') was derived from informal messages that were circulated at the twice-weekly royal 'Drawing Room' gatherings. Those involved with providing the music for royal occasions no doubt had to pay attention to such rumours, but the situation was often one of uncertainty up to the time of the official announcement and intense activity thereafter, since there might be barely enough time for proper preparation. On some occasions music was composed and rehearsed, but the event for which it was intended was delayed: it was even possible that the event, or the performance of the music, might be abandoned, as happened from time to time with the court odes.[8] Under these conditions the musicians most closely involved must have had mixed feelings when the announcement of a postponement was made. The circumstances leading up to the wedding of Princess Anne in March 1734 combined nearly all of the hazards that made for uncertainty. The timing of the Prince of Orange's arrival in England was unpredictable; the announcement of the wedding was delayed, so that both the date and the venue were the subject of successive rumours; eventually a celebration on an ambitious scale and involving considerable building work was planned, but time for its preparation was on the short side; then at the last moment an unforeseen illness changed the course of events completely.

The original double marriage plan with the Prussian relatives was finally abandoned in May 1730:[9] on 8 May 1733 the King announced to Parliament that 'a Contract of Marriage was far advanc'd' between Anne and Willem.[10] Soon afterwards the Prince was elected one of the Knights of the Garter and a party was sent over to Holland to invest him, though at that time negotiations were still in progress concerning details of the marriage contract and the arrangements for the wedding itself. The latter was apparently intended to take place as soon as was feasible, initial rumours indicating that the Prince would come to England early in July.[11] This proved too optimistic, because the contractual arrangements were complex and Dutch political business kept Willem in Holland for longer than anticipated.[12] His departure for London

[8] As e.g. with the New Year odes in 1738, 1744, and 1749, which were not performed, though Greene nevertheless received the regular payments of £25 for music-copying, additional players, and the hire of a rehearsal room, recorded in GB-Lpro LC5/20, 22, and 23.

[9] *BJ*, 23 May 1730; Boyer, *The Political State*, pp. xxxix, 626. There had apparently been one final and short-lived attempt to resuscitate the Prussian match: see *SJEP* and *LEP*, 4–7 Apr. 1730.

[10] *DA*, 9 May 1733.

[11] Ibid.; there was also a rumour (in *DA*, 6 June) that the Princess would be appointed Governor of the Electorate of Hanover, and that she and Willem would reside in Hanover after their marriage.

[12] *US*, 29 Sept. 1733. Negotiations for the marriage were also used as convenient opportunities for diplomatic activity on matters of foreign policy: see Sedgwick, *Some Materials*, 230.

was successively expected in mid-August, early September, and then mid-October.[13] At the beginning of October the King was away from St James's, having been in residence at Hampton Court Palace since July,[14] and the preparation of apartments for the Prince at Hampton Court indicated that he was expected to join the King there in the first instance.[15] The reports in the newspapers at that stage expected that the wedding ceremony itself would take place at Hampton Court.[16] The month of October included a number of royal anniversaries, and the wedding was variously expected to take place on the 11th (the 1727 Coronation anniversary), the 22nd (Princess Anne's birthday), or the 30th (the King's birthday).[17] All of these dates came and went, and still Willem had not arrived.

In the meantime several important developments had taken place: the Bishop of London established his right to perform the wedding ceremony, in his capacity as Dean of the Chapel Royal, and the ratified marriage contract was signed at Hampton Court on 18 October.[18] The King returned to St James's Palace on 27 October, and the following announcement was made concerning his birthday the following Tuesday:

His Grace the Lord Chamberlain has notify'd to the Lords and Ladies of the Court, &c. that as it is uncertain whether the Prince of Orange will come over in Time to celebrate his Nuptials with the Princess Royal on the King's Birth-Day, as was intended; his Majesty is so good as to dispense with the Appearance of new Cloaths on his Birth-Day, and to defer them to their Highnesses Wedding-Day, in order to celebrate the same with the greater Splendour. (*LEP*, 23–5 Oct.)

Nevertheless there was the usual meeting of the court on 30 October at which the birthday ode was performed; for the rehearsal of Eccles's music the previous day the solo vocalists were named as Gates, Rowe, and two Chapel Royal boys.[19]

Following the court's return to St James's Palace, accommodation was prepared for the Prince of Orange at Somerset House.[20] By then a new

[13] *DA*, 28 June, 30 Aug., 15 Sept.

[14] The principal summer residence for the Hanoverians was usually Kensington Palace, but at this period the royal family engaged in frequent hunting parties, for which Hampton Court was a convenient base.

[15] *LJ*, 1 Sept.

[16] *US*, 1 Sept.

[17] *WEP*, 8–11 Sept.; *BBEP*, 4 Oct.; *WEP*, 4–6 Oct.

[18] *LEP*, 13–16 Oct.; *DC*, 22 Oct.

[19] Some reports suggested that the court for the birthday would be deferred, but *DJ*, 31 Oct., confirms that the ode was performed; however, the usual ball in the evening did not take place and the King went to the opera instead. Advance notices of the rehearsal of the ode (e.g. *DP*, 24 Oct.) include Hughes among the soloists, but his name is omitted from the reports after the event (*DC* and *DJ*, 30 Oct.).

[20] *GEP*, 20–3 Oct.

Pl. I. Robert Trevitt, 'A Prospect of the Cathedral Church of St. Paul, on the General Thanksgiving the 31st of Decem.' 1706', with figures drawn and engraved by Louis Du Guernier. Detail from the engraving, showing the west end of the Choir, including the organ and gallery

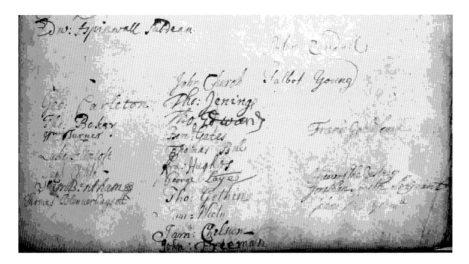

Pl. II. Signatures of Chapel Royal Gentlemen who attended the Vestry meeting of the Chapel on 23 April 1720. Handel named ten of these as leading singers on his autographs of Chapel Royal music

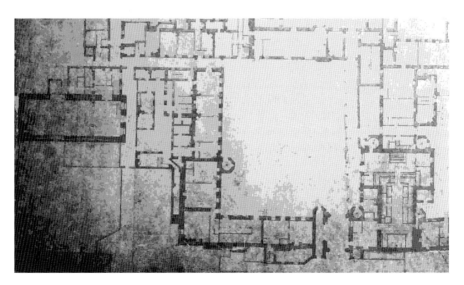

Pl. III. Survey of St James's Palace (ground floor) in 1729 by Henry Flitcroft. Detail showing the two principal Chapels: the Queen's Chapel is at the left, the Chapel Royal is at the bottom right, next to the gateway facing St James's Street

Pl. IV. Sketch of the Chapel Royal, St James's Palace, by Robert Bremnell Schnebellie, 10 February 1816, the basis for the engraving of the Chapel interior that was published in Robert Wilkinson's *Londina Illustrata* (1819)

Pl. V. The wedding of Anne, Princess Royal, and the Prince of Orange in the French Chapel, St James's Palace, 14 March 1733/4. Engraved by J. Rigaud from drawings by William Kent. The engraving has a caption in Latin with a dedication by Kent to King George II

venue for the wedding had been established, and the papers quickly reported the lavish preparations that were to be made. Two items from the London newspapers on consecutive days illustrate the instability of the information that came from the court in mid-October. On 16 October *The Daily Courant* sounded authoritative: ' No Day us yet fix'd for solemnising the Nuptials between the Prince of Orange and the Princess Royal; but certain it is, that the same will be performed at Hampton-Court, before the Royal Family returns to St. James's.' However, the next day *The Daily Post* had more up-to-date news: 'The Marriage of the Prince of Orange with the Princess Royal will now be in the Royal Chapel at St. James's.' Better and more substantial information followed a few days later:

The Nuptials between his Royal Highness the Prince of Orange and the Princess Royal will be celebrated in a grand and magnificent Manner at the French Chapel adjoyning to the Royal Palace at St James's; great Preparations being making for the same. Yesterday the Workmen took down all the Pews and the Pulpit of the said Chapel, in order to make Seats for the Reception of the several Nobility that will be present at the Solemnity. (*DP*, 20 Oct. 1733)

Newspapers over the next few days described in detail the arrangements for refurnishing, draping, and lighting the Chapel for the wedding. (The lighting was particularly important, since the wedding would take place in the evening.) It was calculated that the Chapel's capacity when refurnished would be 500 people,[21] and a procession gallery was built between St James's Palace and the Chapel to accommodate the rest of the guests who were entitled to attend the event. The newspapers devoted much attention to the construction of this gallery, and to the arrangements for the procession, as for example:

The Day is not yet fixt for the Marriage of the Princess Royal with the Prince of Orange, but it has been agreed on, that the Procession to the French Chapel (where the Ceremony is to be perform'd) shall be made from his Majesty's Privy Chamber in St. James's House round the Garden, and so to the Door of the said Chapel, thro' a Scaffolding cover'd over, which is to contain about 2000 Persons, for the Admittance of whom Tickets will be deliver'd by his Grace the Lord Chamberlain. The Procession is to begin at Six in the Evening exactly, and to be made by the Light of Flambeaux. (*LEP*, 20–3 Oct.)

The constructions inside the Chapel included additional side galleries, and special galleries for the musicians at the East End: the descriptions of the interior arrangements of the Chapel tally with what is seen in Plate V. On the day of their return to St James Palace, the King and the Queen 'went to view the necessary preparations that were making at the French Chapel'.[22]

---

[21] *DA*, 31 Oct.   [22] *DC*, 29 Oct.

It is obvious that lavish provision was made for this wedding, more so than for the succeeding royal wedding ceremonies of 1736 and 1740, and the scale of the operation may have grown as a result of the investigation of relevant precedents.[23] The previous wedding of a king's eldest daughter had been that of Mary, daughter of King Charles I and the first to bear the title of Princess Royal, as long ago as 1641. Little is known about the arrangements or the music for that occasion, but it may have been conducted without elaborate ceremony: the bride was only 10 years old, and the King's political circumstances were difficult at the time.[24] More relevant and accessible as a precedent was the wedding of King James I's eldest daughter in February 1612/13, the ceremonial for which was entered in the Old Cheque Book of the Chapel Royal.[25] The same arrangements were not followed exactly in 1733, but the 1613 wedding gave licence for considerable extravagance. As one newspaper noted in 1733, James I had spent more than £85,000 on the wedding, and had 'demanded Aid-Money of his Subjects, according to the antient Custom when the Kings marryed their eldest Daughters', raising £20,500 thereby;[26] the Cheque Book noted that the Banqueting House had been built specially for the wedding feast that followed the Chapel ceremony. In 1613 the throne arrangements in the Chapel (a different building from that prepared in 1733) were not the same as for the later wedding, but on both occasions the chapels were decorated with 'rich hangings'. The grander processions for Princess Anne's wedding, involving considerable participation of trumpets and drums, may have reflected George II's tastes, or may have been influenced by Hanoverian practice.

The first mention of music for the wedding preceded the notice of the new venue by one day:

A fine Anthem is compos'd by Dr. Green on Account of the Nuptials between his Highness the Prince of Orange and the Princess Royal, which will be performed at the Chapel Royal at St. James's, by Mr. Gates, Mr. Hughs, Mr. Rowe, the Children belonging to the Chapel, and the Gentlemen belonging to his Majesty's Band of Musick. (*DP*, 19 Oct.)

Similar reports in newspapers of the following week named a different combination of soloists:

---

[23] The College of Arms was asked to 'send the Records in what Manner the Marriages of the Princesses of England were performed when contracted to Foreign Princes' (*DC*, 7 Sept.), and later the records of the House of Lords were consulted (*DJ*, 3 Nov.).

[24] The bridegroom was Prince William II of Orange, grandfather of the bridegroom at the 1734 wedding. King William III was the son of the 1641 marriage.

[25] *OCB*, fo. 77; Ashbee and Harley, i. 172–5. The bride on this occasion was subsequently grandmother to King George I, and thus the link to the Hanoverian succession.

[26] *LEP*, 13–15 Nov. 1733.

The Marriage of the Princess Royal with the Prince of Orange is to be conducted in the most splendid and magnificent Manner imaginable; their Majesties having given Orders that no Costs should be spared to make it as grand as may be. The Ceremony is to be performed not in the Chappel Royal, but in that elegant one built by Inigo Jones, to which there will be a grand Entrance made from the Garden. The Chappel is to be hung with Velvet and Tapestry, and will be splendidly illuminated and richly ornamented. There will be performed a very fine Anthem suitable to the Occasion, composed by Dr. Green for Voices and Instruments; the Verses are to be performed by the Reverend Mr Abbot, Mr Hughes and Mr Chelsam; the other Vocal Parts by the rest of the Gentlemen of his Majesty's Chappel Royal. (*DPB*, 25 Oct.)

The reconstruction of the Chapel interior included special provision for the royal listeners as well as the performers: 'The Area before the Altar is to be rais'd some Steps, and a sort of a Throne made thereon for their Highnesses [i.e. the bride and bridegroom] to repose themselves whilst the Musick is playing'.[27] A couple of newspaper reports said that a Te Deum would also be performed, but this was almost certainly a mistake.[28] A rehearsal of Greene's anthem was planned to take place in the 'Royal Chappel at Whitehall' (i.e. the Banqueting House Chapel) on Saturday 27 October.[29]

Hardly had the announcement of this rehearsal appeared, however, before Handel had replaced Greene as the favoured composer: 'The Musick to be perform'd in the Royal Chapel at the Solemnity of the Princess Royal's Marriage, is now composing by Mr. Handel.'[30] Probably as a consequence of incompetence in the production of the newspapers through the delivery of bad copy, rather than with any deliberate intention of irony, this news item continued: 'The Words of the Anthem are as follows. *The* NUPTIAL AN-THEM, *by Dr.* GREENE', followed by the text of Greene's anthem, beginning 'Blessed are all they that fear the Lord'.[31] Perhaps the text of the anthem had been given to Greene by the Dean or Sub-Dean of the Chapel and it was expected that Handel would set the same words.

Greene's displacement over the music for the wedding, potentially more humiliating than that for the Coronation since his music had already been composed and publicly announced, must have seriously worsened the personal relationship between himself and Handel. As in the 1720s, the forces that substituted Handel's music for Greene's are hidden from us. The request for

[27] *GEP*, 23–5 Oct.

[28] *SJEP*, 25–7 Oct., and *DA*, 27 Oct.

[29] *DPB*, 27 Oct. The Banqueting House may have been out of commission, during a period of renovation (see *DA*, 28 June 1733).

[30] *SJEP*, Oct. 27–30; also *LEP*, 27–30 Oct., *PLP*, 31 Oct. and *LJ*, 3 Nov., but this item did not appear in the daily papers. *LEP* and *LJ* omitted 'all' in the first verse.

[31] The text does not conform precisely to that found in the musical sources for Greene's anthem, but is recognizably related.

Handel to compose the music probably came from the Princess herself, or possibly from the King or the Queen; since the wedding was a matter of Hanoverian family interest as well as a British royal occasion, Greene's supporters may have been unable to defend his position, even though his anthem had already been composed.[32] For Greene this meant that the edge of influence that he had won in 1729, with the music for the King's return from Hanover, was now lost again. Even though he was paid for his unperformed anthem (see App. I), he must have felt some grievance against Handel. It is not recorded whether Greene played the organ at the wedding, though this should surely have been part of his official duties.

On 3 November *The Universal Spectator, and Weekly Journal* printed 'The Words of the Anthem to be sung at the Prince of Orange's Marriage with the Princess Royal. Set to Musick by Mr. Handel.' This gave the text of movements 5, 6 (without the middle section), and 8 from the anthem *This is the day that the Lord has made* (HWV 262) as we now know it, but also inserted the words for an extra movement 'Instead of thy Fathers, thou shalt have Children', which it is unlikely that Handel ever composed.[33] The arrangement of the page conjunctions in the conducting score of Handel's anthem is such that it is improbable that he began the composition with No. 5, or that he put the last movements together first. Perhaps the verse referred to in the newspaper was included in the original scheme for the text, but was replaced by the words of the present No. 7 before Handel composed the music;[34] the version given in the newspaper may even reflect a suggested addition or variant to the text that had already been composed by Greene. It is noticeable that Handel avoided most of Greene's text, setting only versions of the verse beginning 'The King's daughter is all glorious within' (as a solo, not a chorus) and the last verse. The full text of Handel's wedding anthem in the form known to us (with the minor variation of 'ariseth' for 'arises') was printed in newspapers for the following week, in some of them with the preamble: 'Yesterday [Monday 5 November] the Musick Compos'd by Mr. Handell, to be perform'd at the Nuptials of the Princess Royal with the Prince of Orange, was perform'd before the Royal Family, at St. James's.'[35] This must have been a rehearsal, probably in the Chapel Royal, and we can therefore be sure that the anthem was composed in late October/early November 1733. The various anthem texts from the newspapers are given in Table 12.1.

---

[32] The wedding seems to have been regarded as a 'private' rather than 'state' occasion.

[33] The unset verse had been included in Purcell's *My heart is inditing*, but Handel avoided it when selecting the text for his own Coronation Anthem, perhaps because he thought it indelicate to make reference to Queen Caroline's future fecundity.

[34] Handel also set another text for the B section of No. 6.

[35] *DA*, 6 Nov.; *WEP* and *SJEP*, 3–6 Nov.

Table 12.1. *Texts of the wedding anthems by Greene and Handel, as printed in London newspapers*

The NUPTIAL ANTHEM, *by Dr.* GREENE

2 *Voc.*	Blessed are all they that fear the Lord, and walk in his ways.	[Ps. 128, v. 1]
Cho.	The king's daughter is all glorious within, her clothing is of wrought Gold.	[Ps. 45, v. 14]
2 *Voc.*	Upon her right hand did stand the queen in a vesture of gold.	[v. 10]
Cho.	The king's daughter &c.	
Solo,	The virgins that be her fellows, shall bear her company, and shall be brought unto Thee. Full of grace thy lips: for God hath blessed thee for ever.	[v. 15, v. 3]
Cho	Prosper thou with thine honour.	[v. 5, not Prayer Book]
Solo,	Hearken, O daughter, and incline thine ear: forget thine own people, and thy father's house. Instead of thy father's, thou shalt have children, whom princes may'st make.	[v. 11, v. 17]
Cho.	I will remember thy name from one generation to another; therefore shall the people give thanks unto thee, world without end. Amen.	[v. 18]

(*SJEP*, 27–30 Oct. 1733)

The Words of the Anthem to be sung at the Prince of Orange's Marriage
with the Princess Royal. Set to Musick by Mr. Handel.

Ecclesiasticus 26. *Ver.* 16 As the Sun when it ariseth in the High Heaven, so is the Beauty of a good Wife.

Proverbs 31. *Ver.* 28. Her Children arise up, and call her Blessed; her Husband also, and he praiseth her.

Psalm 45. *Ver.* 17. Instead of thy Fathers thou shalt have Children, who thou mayest make Princes in all Lands.

Hallelujah, &c.

(*US*, 3 Nov. 1733)

Several additions having been made to the Nuptial Anthem, the Words are now as follow.

This is the Day which the Lord has made, we will rejoice and be glad in it.
The King's Daughter is all glorious within, her Clothing is of wrought Gold.
She shall be brought unto the King in Raiment of Needle-work, the Virgins her Companions shall be brought unto thee.
With Gladness and Rejoycing shall they be brought.
Blessed is the Man that has a virtuous Wife, for the Number of his Days shall be double.
A good Wife is a good Portion, which shall be given in the Portion of them that fear the Lord.
Strength and Honour are her Clothing, and she shall rejoice in time to come.
She opens her Mouth with Wisdom, and in her Tongue is the Law of Kindness.
As the Sun when it ariseth in the high Heaven, so is the Beauty of a good Wife.
Her Children arise up and call her blessed; her Husband also, and he praiseth her.
Many Daughters have done virtuously, but thou excellest them all.
We will remember thy Name from one Generation to another, therefore shall the people give Praise unto thee, World without end. Amen.
Hallelujah. Amen.

(*WEP*, 3–6 Nov. 1733)

The Prince of Orange finally arrived in London two days after the rehearsal of Handel's anthem. The newspapers carried speculations on the date for the wedding, Thursday 15 November being thought likely, but the official decision, when it came, was for the following Monday, 19 November.[36] There is no report of another rehearsal, but probably one took place at some time during the previous week. However, on Sunday 18 November the Prince of Orange was taken ill and the ceremony had to be deferred.[37] Various rumours appeared in the papers—that the wedding was only to be delayed for a short time, with 2 December as a possible alternative date, and that it would be performed privately—but doctors attending the Prince advised that the wedding would have to be delayed for some considerable time to ensure his recovery. The French Chapel was boarded up, some of the decorations were taken down and put into storage, and a minimum of alteration was made to the external procession gallery to allow free access to the area for the normal course of business.[38] The Prince moved to Kensington on 11 December. It was rumoured that the wedding would take place soon after New Year's Day, that the Prince's doctors had advised that 'the Inconveniences that may attend his Highness by a Publick marriage, the Fatigue of the Ceremony, &c' would produce 'too great a hum of Spirits for his Constitution to bear', that the procession gallery would be dismantled, and that the marriage would be performed 'as private as possible' in the French Chapel; however, the King and Queen announced at their levée on 19 December that the marriage 'would be Solemnized as in the manner first intended'.[39] Early in 1734 the Prince paid an extended visit to Bath, and 1 March (the Queen's birthday) or the previous evening were rumoured as a likely dates for the wedding on his return,[40] but no action followed, partly because the Queen was incapacitated for a time with gout. The Prince made a leisurely return from Bath, taking in Oxford on the way, where he received the honorary degree of Doctor of Laws; he was back in London on 2 March. Workmen restored and extended the galleries in and around the French Chapel, and on Thursday 7 March the Lord Chamberlain was able to announce that the wedding would take place on the 14th 'between the hours of Four and Ten in the Evening'.[41] A subsequent announcement said that the procession would form up at 6 o'clock.[42] There are no reports of another rehearsal of Handel's anthem, though presumably at least one took

[36] *DPB*, 9 and 10 Nov.
[37] *DA*, 12 Nov.
[38] This was not done until Jan 1733/4: see *DPB*, 8 Jan.
[39] *LEP* and *GEP*, 15–18 and 18–20 Dec., 1733.
[40] *DPB*, 30 Nov. 1733, 2 Feb. 1733/4. Other predicted dates were 4 Mar. (*DC*, 26 Feb.) and 12 Mar. (*DC*, 7 Mar.).
[41] *SJEP*, 7–9 Mar. 1733/4.
[42] *DA*, 14 Mar.

place: as a newsworthy event this was probably crowded out by reports of the wedding itself, and by reports of Handel's topical serenata for the wedding season, *Parnasso in Festa*, the first performance of which was attended by the royal family and the Prince of Orange at the King's Theatre the evening before.[43]

Apart from a last-minute delay caused by the enthusiasm of the London crowd to see the Prince, which resulted in his journey from Somerset House to St James's taking an hour and a half in place of the expected half an hour, the wedding passed off as planned on 14 March. The marriage service itself took place about 10 o'clock at night, followed by supper at midnight and a ball. Newspaper reports of the service were rather disappointing in their coverage of the music, since even the more informative ones only mentioned the organ music at the beginning of the service as the main procession arrived, and the fact that Handel's anthem was performed at the end:[44]

The Lord Bishop of London, Dean of the Chapel, and the Lord Bishop of Winchester, Clerk of the Closet, stood before the Communion Table with Prayer-Books in their Hands; and after the Organ had play'd some time, his Highness the Prince of Orange led the Princess Royal to the Rails of the Altar, and kneel'd down, and then the Lord Bishop of London perform'd the Service; after which the Bride and Bridegroom arose and retir'd to their Places, whilst a fine Anthem, compos'd by Mr Handell, was perform'd by a great Number of Voices and Instruments. (*LEP*, 14–16 Mar. 1734)

If this coverage seems rather mean, there is some compensation from the engraving of the scene in the Chapel (Pl. V), which shows the musicians in place.

Later in 1734 John Walsh published a set of orchestral concertos as Handel's 'Opera Terza'.[45] The earliest print of the title page included the following note: 'N.B. Several of the Concertos were perform'd on the Marriage of the Prince of Orange with the Princess Royal of Great Britain in the Royal Chappel of St. James's.' This rubric was soon removed in subsequent printings, presumably either because it was factually wrong or because it had ceased to be topical. The edition had almost certainly been prepared without any involvement from the composer, and the concertos concerned were derived from his earlier music. There is no mention of the performance of concertos in the

[43] *WEP* 12–14 Mar.; *DA*, 11, 14 Mar.

[44] Many newspaper reports do not name Handel, deriving their descriptions from *LG*, 12–16 Mar.: 'the married Couple rose and retired to their Stools on the Haut-pas, where they remained while the Anthem was sung'. The processions involved fifes, drums, and trumpets, which apparently did not enter the Chapel itself. See also the descriptions in Sheppard, *Memorials*, ii. 68–71, 363–7.

[45] The earliest known advertisements date from Dec. 1734: see William C. Smith, *Handel*, 218.

reports of the wedding, though the assembled musicians may have played some before the wedding procession arrived at the Chapel, or during the dinner.

As with the 1727 coronation, the gathering of the rich and the powerful who attended the wedding in 1734 provided a significant audience for Handel's music. The performance of his anthem was apparently the only time during the service when the bride and groom sat on the specially provided seats: the implication is that everyone's full attention was given to the music. This wedding was an event on a much larger scale than others that followed, and the service was much grander than those in the Chapel Royal for which Handel had previously provided music. The anthem itself was much longer than those that he had composed for the Chapel Royal services of the 1720s, and its scoring was more comparable to the Coronation Anthems. Greene must have felt considerably aggrieved about the treatment that he and his music received, but the delay in the wedding doubled Handel's opportunities for extending his reputation, since his anthem was heard both in November 1733 and March 1734.

This is the day which the Lord has made (HWV 262)

With this anthem the texts set by Handel in his English church music enter a new phase. The outer framework of the anthem is conventional enough: after the initial call to rejoicing from Psalm 118, the words of the remainder of the first movement and of 'We will remember thy name' (No. 7) are taken from Psalm 45, the 'Queen's psalm', already drawn upon in the settings of *My heart is inditing* by Purcell and Handel.[46] But within this framework the inner movements venture into the Wisdom literature, taking their texts from the books of Ecclesiasticus and Proverbs. Someone, possibly Handel himself but more probably a clerical adviser, did the work well in selecting appropriate texts: the author may have been the same as that for the text of the 1737 Funeral Anthem, which similarly drew on the Wisdom literature.[47] As noted above, Handel may have received the text in two instalments, but the Wisdom component was there from the start. As far as I have been able to discover, no previous anthem by a composer associated with the Chapel Royal between 1660 and 1733 had drawn on either Ecclesiasticus or Proverbs for its text.

Some attempt may have been made in 1733 to investigate the texts of the anthems that had been performed at previous royal weddings. As already

---

[46] Greene's anthem was also based on verses from Psalm 45, after the initial verse from Psalm 128.

[47] The anthem texts preceded Cruden's *A Complete Concordance* (which also covered the Apocrypha), published in June 1737 and dedicated to Queen Caroline.

noted, the most recent comparable weddings had been in 1612/13 and 1641. It is unlikely that anyone in 1733 knew what music was performed in 1641, any more than we do today, nor was there much to be found about the music performed at the weddings of the daughters of the Duke of York in 1677 and 1683. The more accessible information about the 1612/13 wedding in the Old Cheque Book referred to the singing of four anthems, of which only two are identified, one by title ('The Psalme, Blessed art thou that fearest God'—i.e. Psalm 128, in the metrical version by Sternhold and Hopkins) and one by composer ('Doctor Bull') without reference to a text.[48] Whoever was responsible for the text of Handel's anthem must have started again from first principles in selecting and assembling words appropriate to the occasion.

Handel did not start from first principles in composing the music, most of which was lifted from the oratorio *Athalia*, composed earlier in 1733 and performed by him at Oxford, but not yet heard in London. His theatre serenata *Parnasso in Festa* for the wedding season in 1734 (and thus composed after the anthem) was similarly indebted to the same source, and even used four of the same movements as the anthem:[49] this degree of overlap is extraordinary. Handel gave Princess Anne every opportunity to hear the best of his recent music before she left London to live in the Netherlands: she would be gone before Handel could perform *Athalia* in London, and she may have specifically asked to hear some of its music, as she had also reputedly done with *Esther* the previous year.[50] The skill with which the music was selected from the oratorio score and arranged to make up the anthem provides the surest evidence that, if Handel did not select the texts himself, his adviser worked very closely with him, choosing texts that could use the available music, and providing a scheme that accommodated both solo and chorus movements. Most of the movements were transferred from *Athalia* without key transposition and the selection resulted in an acceptable key scheme, even though the individual movements were culled from different places in the oratorio. The musical source explains the unique feature of this anthem in Handel's Chapel Royal canon, the inclusion of two full da capo arias. However, we need not attribute the pasticcio-style construction simply to haste on Handel's part: he was here experimenting with an oratorio-type anthem, just as in the Funeral Anthem three years later he experimented with an extended fully choral anthem. In any case English oratorio itself was still an experimental medium for him in the

[48] *OCB*, fo. 77ᵛ; Ashbee and Harley, i. 174–5. The setting of Psalm 128 was probably that by the Andrew Blackhall, as in MB 15 (*Music of Scotland*, ed. Elliott), 120–3.

[49] See Burrows, 'Handel's 1735 (London) Version of *Athalia*', 194.

[50] In addition, the report of Handel 'waiting on their Majesties with his New Opera of *Ariodante*' (Deutsch, *Handel*, 372) may relate to a private preview of arias from that opera at Kensington in October 1734, when Anne was in England.

1730s. The Chapel Royal singers and the Coronation Anthems had played a significant part in the experiment: this is, in short, just the period when some interchange between oratorio and anthem might have been expected.

It is necessary to outline the unusual source situation for *This is the day* before considering the musical content further. There is no surviving holograph of the complete anthem, nor did one ever exist except for the Andante allegro section of 'We will remember thy name', the autograph of which is now lost. At most, Handel may have provided a rudimentary continuity sketch, directing the copyist to the movements that were to be taken from *Athalia*, and their order.[51] The only primary source for the anthem is the conducting score that was prepared by J. C. Smith senior to Handel's directions.[52] Smith must have been given precise instructions: for the movements derived from *Athalia* he laid out the score and copied the orchestral parts, leaving Handel to fill in the vocal parts and any other new material which was required (see Fig. 12.1). Handel marked up the conducting score of *Athalia* at various places in connection with the preparation of the anthem,[53] a circumstance that has led to some misunderstandings concerning the history of the oratorio: the situation is further confused by the fact that the *Athalia* conducting score also contains markings relating to further the use of some of the music by Handel for his 1738 *Oratorio*.[54] Table 12.2 shows the sources of the anthem movements, the relevant cues written by Handel in the autograph and in the conducting score of *Athalia*, and his written contribution to the conducting score of the anthem.

The first movement of the anthem originally opened Part II of *Athalia*. For the anthem Handel applied the ternary structure of the movement (chorus–alto solo–chorus) to excellent purpose, moving from the general ('This is the day'—chorus) to the particular ('The King's daughter'—solo), and then returning to the chorus for 'With gladness shall they be brought', 'they' being the psalmist's 'virgin companions' of the bride. The alto solo suited the Chapel Royal's traditional strength in solo voices: in Handel's previous performances of *Athalia* this music, for the character Joad, had been sung by Walter Powell, a leading alto from the Oxford college choirs. No change was needed to the melodic lines except those necessary to accommodate the rhythms of the new words and, remarkably, Handel did not specify which of the Chapel Royal altos was to take the solo in the anthem: it may eventually

---

[51] A similar set of instructions may also have been written in 1749 for the Foundling Hospital Anthem. See also the directions relating to the construction of a score for the opera *Poro*, GB-Cfm MU MS 258, pp. 89–91.

[52] D-Hs M C/266.

[53] D-Hs M C/264. There are no markings on this score, or on the autograph of *Athalia*, relating to the adaptations for *Parnasso in Festa*.

[54] See Burrows, 'Handel's 1738 *Oratorio*', 21.

Fig. 12.1. A page from Handel's performing score of the anthem *This is the day*, HWV 262, for the wedding of Princess Anne and the Prince of Orange. Handel added the vocal part and text to the score prepared by Smith. Staats- und Universitätsbibliothek, Hamburg, M C/266, fo. 16ᵛ

Table 12.2. This is the day: *sources of movements, and material relating to the anthem*

Anthem movement	Source	Amendments by Handel in *Athalia* sources	Elements written by Handel in anthem conducting score
1 This is the day	*Athalia*, 'The mighty Pow'r'	GB-Lbl RM 20.h.1: cues in ink for text, bars 68–108 (solo) and 110–132 (chorus)	Vocal parts (notes and words) bars 31–45, 128–34, 137–44
2 Blessed is the man	*Athalia*, 'Gentle airs, melodious strains'	D-Hs M C/264: cues in pencil 'Ex G' and (for voice) 'In Bass for Abbot'	Vocal part (notes and words)
3 A good wife is a good portion	*Athalia*, 'Through the Land'	—	Vocal part (notes and words)
4 Strength and honour	*Athalia*, 'My vengeance awakes me'	GB-Lbl RM 20.h.1: 'Bird' in pencil, but possibly added after 1734	Vocal part (notes and words)
5 As the sun when it arises	(original)	—	Vocal and orchestral notes
6 Her children arise up	*Athalia*, 'Ah, canst thou but prove me'	—	Vocal part (notes and words)
7 We will remember Thy name, bars 1–6	*Nisi Dominus*, 'Gloria Patri' bars 1–8. (Double SATB chorus, Orchestra I and II)	—	Trumpet parts
bars 7–55	(?original)	—	—
8 Alleluja, Amen	Caroline Te Deum, 'O Lord, in Thee'	—	—

have been sung by Hughes, Bell, or even Laye. When Handel adapted the movement in the autumn of 1733 Hughes was undoubtedly still the Chapel's leading alto soloist, and he sang in the court ode for New Year 1734. Thereafter, however, his career is difficult to trace and he may have retired from his leading position in the course of 1734.

The rich eight-part vocal layout for the chorus in the first movement was suitably sumptuous for the wedding: although it is somewhat reminiscent of the spread in the opening movement of *Zadok the priest* and 'Glory and worship are before him' from HWV 250b, it was derived directly from the oratorio. The chorus part for Bass 1 is consistently lower in tessitura than Bass 2, and this apparent anomaly can also be traced to Handel's score of *Athalia*, where he named the singer Montagnana for Bass 1.[55] The directions for the use of both organ and cembalo on the bassi staves at the opening of the movement in the conducting score, which were reproduced in Chrysander's edition,[56] are not relevant to the anthem, still less are they evidence that both instruments were in use at the wedding, for the cues were merely copied mechanically from the *Athalia* score by Smith. However, he did omit the horns from the stave labels when he transcribed the movement from *Athalia*, where horns had doubled the trumpet parts: no horn-players are visible on the picture of the wedding, and it seems certain that horns should not be included in the wedding anthem, though Chrysander 'restored' them in his edition. Smith copied the 'Tympano' stave from *Athalia* into the anthem score, but there are no drum parts in the later movements and it seems doubtful that they were used for the anthem: again, no drums appear in the picture of the wedding. This is the only movement of the anthem for which Smith had to use the *Athalia* autograph (in conjunction with the oratorio's conducting score) as his copy-text: Handel provided enough cues to enable him to work out the vocal parts for most of the movement, but Smith handed a few tricky passages back to the composer for completion.

The music from the *Athalia* aria 'Gentle airs, melodious strains' proved very apposite for the text of the second movement, 'Blessed is the man that has a virtuous wife', which is a gentle miniature da capo movement for bass voice with cello obbligato. Originally for tenor soloist in A major in *Athalia*, this is the only movement whose key was transposed in the transference from the oratorio. Handel's cue in the *Athalia* conducting score (see Table 12.2), provides the only certain soloist's name for the anthem. Both Winton Dean and Hans Dieter Clausen have interpreted this cue in relation to Handel's

---

[55] Montagnana may not actually have sung in the oratorio at Oxford, on account of the break-up of Handel's London opera company at the end of the 1732–3 season. (Handel completed *Athalia* on 7 June, just before the night of the last opera performance.)

[56] *HG* 36, p. 27.

planned revival of *Athalia* in 1743,[57] but, quite apart from the fact that it links with the key of the movement in the anthem, the circumstance that Abbot was one of the Priests of the Chapel makes it very unlikely that he would have been allowed to sing in the theatre. With some regret, therefore, Abbot must be deleted from Winton Dean's list of Handel's oratorio singers.[58] Handel needed to alter the melodic line very little to accommodate the new words: the only really significant alteration is in bar 16, where the anthem text called for something rather simpler than the original musical illustration of 'sweetly soothe her as you flow'. As in the first movement, Chrysander's edition preserved a feature of the *Athalia* scoring that Smith had been careful to omit from the anthem's conducting score, where there is no mention of 'Contra-basso, Cembalo ed Archliuto' on the continuo part.[59] There is no evidence for the participation of harpsichord or archlute in the wedding anthem. Although brief, the movement is written out in the traditional da capo format in the conducting score: it is probable that the Adagio direction at bar 10 should refer to the second time only (i.e. bar 22).

In 'A good wife is a good portion' the text of the anthem is again similar in spirit to that of the source movement. The *Athalia* aria is a full da capo movement of generous proportions: Handel kept only the first section, which still left him with a substantial movement of 129 bars. In context, the succession of the solo arias in the anthem creates gradually increasing interest, as each one proves slightly more weighty than its predecessor. This movement, originally for soprano, was sung by a Chapel Royal treble in the wedding anthem, which no doubt partly accounts for its shorter span. Handel's recasting of sections of the vocal line will be considered further in Chapter 19, as providing valuable evidence for the music that he thought technically appropriate for a Chapel boy. Sometimes the line is only marginally altered, avoiding top notes and providing more direct rhythmic phrasing,[60] but in other places he recomposed the vocal part over the given bass (see below, Ex. 19.1) The instrumental obbligato parts are an important feature of the movement: in *Athalia* they were specified for 'Flauto ou Travers.', but in the anthem Smith (presumably at Handel's instruction) came down on the side of transverse flutes rather than recorders. Certain phrases combining pedal notes with these obbligato parts (e.g. bars 36–9) anticipate the third movement of the Anthem on the Peace (see Ch. 14); at other times (e.g. bar 109) the triplet figures look backwards to the Sinfonia to the Cannons anthem 'In the Lord put I my trust'.

---

[57] Dean, *Handel's Dramatic Oratorios*, 261; Clausen, *Händels Direktionspartituren*, 119.

[58] Dean, *Handel's Dramatic Oratorios*, 651.

[59] HG 36, p. 54; D-Hs M C/266, fo. 16ᵛ.

[60] Handel also avoided the note *a″*, to the detriment of the melodic line, in the chorus treble part at No. 1 bar 60.

'Strength and honour are her clothing' is the most surprising transfer from *Athalia* in terms of its text, since the original aria expressed a determination to seek revenge and the new topic concerns the virtues (strength, honour, wisdom) of the king's daughter. The transference was helped by the major-key mode of the aria, which perhaps originally conveyed the energy of Athalia rather than her specific desire for vengeance. Yet the conversion worked well in the details as well as in mood, demonstrating (as also do many similar transfers in works by J. S. Bach) the interchangeability, within limits, of many musical symbols. Thus the string figures in the opening section of the anthem movement serve to illustrate strength and rejoicing rather than vengeance, and the arpeggio leaps in the voice part represent exultation rather than the dismissal of compassion. This movement is in the same key as 'Rejoice greatly' in *Messiah*, and there are also other similarities: many of the same musical figures are used to the same purpose, and even the contrast in the middle section is similar. Both in scoring and in general character this is the most operatic-style movement in the whole of Handel's church music.

Some aspects of the history of this movement are rather uncertain. It was originally composed in *Athalia* for the soprano voice, and was sung by Mrs Wright in the title role at Oxford in July 1733. The next stage was its transference to the anthem in the autumn of that year. In the score of the anthem Smith copied out the orchestral parts as they stood in *Athalia* and Handel adapted the vocal part to the new words, but for tenor: this works well enough, though the solo part at times becomes rather entangled with the basso continuo. Nevertheless Handel must have been more or less satisfied with the arrangement, since the aria was also sung in other contexts (to its *Athalia* words) by a tenor on subsequent occasions. In the anthem the solo part may have been sung by John Beard, but the evidence for this is complex and equivocal: see below, under 'Conditions of Performance'. The aria was certainly copied from the conducting score (rather than the autograph) of *Athalia* when Smith prepared the anthem movement. 'Organ soft, tasto solo' appears next to the bass line in the autograph but not in the conducting score of *Athalia*, and it was not included in the anthem score: in any case this direction reflected oratorio performance practice rather than that relevant to the anthem. The direction for the oboe (or oboes) to double the voice part is derived from *Athalia*, where it had Handel's authority but was more appropriate with the original soprano voice than in the anthem where it doubles the tenor at the octave. One implication of the shadowing of the voice part by the oboe may be that the soloist was not expected to ornament the da capo repeat until the final couple of bars, where the doubling ceases.

There was a need for some musical contrast after this movement, and the key sequence of the arias required a buffer between movements 4 and 6, which were brought forward to the anthem in their original keys from *Athalia* (B flat major and A minor). Handel's accompanied recitative 'As the sun when it arises' is straightforward, with passing illustration of 'in the high heaven' and a slightly ungainly ending as the secondary accent in the final bar falls on the word 'a'. Movements 4–6 form the climax of the anthem, and the main function of No. 5 is to introduce No. 6, which has no opening ritornello. The recitative and aria may have been sung by Abbot, Gates, or even Weely. For the recitative Smith laid out the clefs for the stave systems in the conducting score and wrote in the text: Handel filled in the notes for all of the parts, vocal and orchestral. For good practical reasons, it was normal for the organ to play the bass line tasto solo in accompanied recitatives that had sustained string chords, as here, but Handel figured the bass line in the penultimate bar: this may perhaps have been in order to remind himself of the harmony for the upper parts, if he wrote the vocal line and instrumental bass first.

In 'Her children arise up' the change of subject in the text from *Athalia* is only slightly less remarkable than in No. 4: in the oratorio aria Abner declares his loyalty, if the rightful heir to the Israelite kingdom should be discovered, while the anthem movement is another in praise of the king's daughter. Although the music has not the bluster of a traditional 'rage' aria, the accompaniment is perhaps rather bellicose for the anthem text: the transfer of association in the movement's motivic material (semiquaver figuration and unisoni passages) to the expression of jubilation is less successful than the conversion in the previous aria. Perhaps the minor key has something to answer for in this: Handel's choice of this particular music from *Athalia* may have been motivated by a desire to introduce the contrast of a more serious mood, through the minor key and the strong, pithy theme (which provided for the right number of syllables). It seems unlikely that, by 1733, Handel would have misconstrued the meaning of 'arise up', and still less likely that he intended deliberate reference in this aria to the currently deteriorating state of relations between the King and the Prince of Wales. The forceful melodic lines and elaborate ornamentation in bars 40–3 might have given away the theatrical origin of this movement even if the original had been lost: the difference is a matter of degree, however, for similar passage-work can be found in Handel's earlier Chapel Royal music, such as the Caroline Te Deum and *O sing unto the Lord* (HWV 249a). The full use of the wide range of an octave and a half for the bass voice was also a common feature in Handel's music for the theatre and the Chapel. He set the biblical text as it stood, including the rather awkward phrase 'he praiseth her', which Chrysander altered to 'he praises her' in his edition.[61]

[61] *HG* 36, pp. 66–7.

The chorus movements in this anthem serve as the opening and closing framework: this is the only Chapel Royal anthem apart from *O sing unto the Lord* (HWV 249a) to have no central chorus. The choral movements at the end of the anthem provide a balance to the very substantial opening movement. 'We will remember thy name' is introduced by a short passage of choral homophony that also brings the music back towards the anthem's trumpet-orientated tonic key of D major. Possibly the most surprising aspect of the anthem as a whole is that Handel took even this six-bar Grave section from a previous composition, as if he was determined not to write anything afresh. The music derives from the opening of the double-chorus 'Gloria Patri' from the Latin psalm *Nisi Dominus*, composed by Handel in Rome and dated 13 July 1707: see Ex. 12.1. He amended the music and entered the English text on his autograph of the movement from *Nisi Dominus*. The autograph was destroyed in a fire in 1860, but the following description had been given in a sale catalogue two years previously: 'Handel appears to have contemplated a setting of this composition to English words, having on the first page inserted under the Latin text, "Wee will remember thy name" with a repetition of the music adapted to English syllables.'[62] In fact the changes that were made when this music was transferred to the wedding anthem went beyond the simple alteration of rhythms to accommodate the English text: the harmony was altered in bar 2 and suspensions were removed in bars 3 and 6. (Smith absent-mindedly copied the superseded basso continuo figures from *Nisi Dominus* into the conducting score of the wedding anthem, nevertheless.) This must have involved more labour than the composition of a new six-bar passage. Handel added new trumpet parts, but the adaptation of the double-choir/double-orchestra scoring from the 'Gloria Patri' may have been done by Smith, and perhaps not too successfully: there is a curious doubling of Alto 2 and Tenor 1.[63]

In the subsequent Andante allegro movement the initial chorus entry repeats the text from the Grave introduction.[64] It becomes apparent as the movement progresses, however, that this text was not complete, but only the opening phrase of a more extended verse. The movement develops in Handel's best choral manner, with homophonic and polyphonic elements alternating. The cantus firmus subject which begins with the new second clause of the text at bar 16 is worked against some lively contrapuntal tags, to the dominant key and then back towards the tonic: a majesterial reprise of the opening at bars 39–40

---

[62] Puttick and Simpson, *Catalogue*, Lot 187. The sale included the 'Granville' collection of manuscript scores of Handel's works, but the catalogue title stated that the 'Gloria Patri' was 'from another collection'.

[63] See the commentary in Handel, *This is the day*, ed. Burrows.

[64] The Grave forms an introduction to the Andante allegro and it seems best to regard them as a single musical unit, though they are numbered as separate movements in *HHB*.

Ex. 12.1. (*a*) *Nisi Dominus*, No. 6; (*b*) *This is the day*, No. 7

Coro II, A., bar 2: early sources show the first note an octave lower.

Figures are reproduced from Handel's conducting score of the anthem

leads to the whole process beginning again, this time with the contrapuntal elements in stretto from the start (bar 48 onwards) and with an excursion to the subdominant key. Throughout the movement the orchestral parts alternatively provide an independent commentary to the voice parts and recede into the background as required. The Andante allegro is the only newly composed movement for the anthem (apart from the accompanied recitative No. 5), though the autograph is lost and thus there is no evidence to confirm the date of its origination. The music has some resemblances to other works by Handel. The chorus 'The clouded scene begins to clear' from *Athalia* has a similar opening, but in the minor key: rather closer, and in the major mode, is the opening music of the orchestral Sonata with obbligato organ from Handel's early oratorio *Il trionfo del Tempo*.[65]

For a short rousing final movement, suitable for maintaining the impetus set up by 'We will remember thy name', Handel returned to the closing movement of the Caroline Te Deum, composed twenty years before. Its success in the new context is remarkable: Handel must have felt pleased that his old music had worn so well. Even the join to the preceding movement was smooth: 'We will remember Thy name' ends on a dominant chord, and 'Alleluja, amen' begins with a unison theme that starts on the dominant note. As noted in Chapter 5, it is possible that the oboe cues on the autograph of the Caroline Te Deum were added when it was used as a copying source for the wedding anthem. There are no marks on that autograph, or any other surviving copy of the Te Deum, that can be interpreted as sketches for the rearrangement of the notes to fit the words for the wedding anthem: either Handel drafted the word-setting on a source which is now lost, or he left the job to Smith. The former seems rather more likely, since Smith's copy in the anthem's conducting score is fluent and does not suggest that he was working things out as he went along. The arrangement is not at all indebted to the adaptation of the music to a rather similar text at the end of the Cannons anthem *My song shall be alway* (HWV 257). It is interesting that the octave-leap figures of the original Te Deum setting were removed from the vocal parts but retained in the orchestra for the wedding anthem. The alterations to the music are purely rhythmic: there are no cuts or revisions to musical substance.

Conditions of Performance

The 'French Chapel' at St James's was slightly larger than the principal Chapel Royal, but still a relatively intimate venue (see Ch. 19). The building received only very light usage from the 1690s onwards and it was easy to put out of commission for a time in 1733–4 so that major additional furnishing and

[65] *HG* 24, p. 33.

decorations could be installed for the wedding. The congregation of the French Chapel Royal, which had use of the building in the 1730s, was presumably not large and could be accommodated elsewhere for as long as necessary. As already noted, the preparations for the wedding involved the construction of extra temporary galleries, both outside and inside the Chapel. The French Chapel already had an extensive first-floor west-end gallery, covering about one third of the floor area below, and additional galleries were built on the north and south sides, probably at the same height, to accommodate more wedding guests. At the east end a musicians' gallery, or rather a series of galleries at different levels, was built, rising from the level at the top of the existing screen behind the altar to the uppermost window.

The scene at the wedding was recorded by William Kent in astounding detail which was reproduced, as far as the chisel would allow, in Rigaud's etching (see Pl. V).[66] It shows that the main decoration of the Chapel consisted of drapes and carpets, which would have deadened most of the building's normal reverberation. It also shows the additional side galleries built for the occasion and, most importantly of all, the musicians' galleries at the East end above the altar: see Fig. 12.2. The altar screen and the walls adjoining are draped, obscuring the carving and panelling: nevertheless, the distance from the screen to the window and door openings on the North and South walls appears to be the same in Pl. V as in Flitcroft's plan of 1729 (see Pl. III) and indeed also the same as it is today, so there is no reason to suppose that the screen was moved for the wedding.

Assuming that the screen remained in its original position, the arrangement of the galleries for the musicians appears, at first sight, highly improbable. The main gallery is about 8′ deep,[67] which does not seem to allow space either for the number of performers shown on the picture or for staircase access to the higher levels. The upper galleries for the musicians must have been specially constructed, and the ease with which the French Chapel could be released from regular services gave the Surveyor of the Works freedom to adapt the building considerably. From the engraving it appears that the windows at the east end were removed completely, so the musicians' galleries were probably built up with access from the rear. Because of the thickness of the walls the window openings themselves would have added about 5′ to the depth of the

---

[66] *DA*, 14 Nov. 1733, said that Hogarth would be at the wedding to 'take a view' and 'oblige the Publick with a fine Print': it seems that Kent displaced Hogarth, as Handel displaced Greene. Kent had been responsible for designing the furnishings and decorations in the Chapel for the wedding: payment to him for this is recorded in LGB-pro AO1 413/168.

[67] The gallery is 8′ deep at its outer extremities and about 4′ deep in the centre. It appears from the engraving that the first level of the musicians' galleries was built up by running a platform across the shallower central section, above the area of the communion table.

main galleries, and this would have enabled sufficient performers to have a place within the Chapel, though hardly in comfortable circumstances. They are obviously packed closely together, and their vertical distribution, with the topmost group about 20′ above the main gallery and about 30′ above ground level, must have posed considerable communication problems.

The importance of Kent's picture hardly needs further emphasis. It is the only known overall view of the performers for one of Handel's own performances.[68] In spite of the small size of the human figures on the engraving, most of the musical activity is identifiable. A key to the performers shown on the picture is given in Table 12.3. More musicians, about fifteen at the most, are hidden from sight by the chandelier, and this would bring the total performing force to about seventy-five. Some twenty-five of these were additional performers (see below), and this leaves fifty regular court musicians to be accounted for. Perhaps for this particular wedding a full turnout of the Gentlemen and King's Musicians was the order of the day:[69] this would have provided about thirty performers (Priests, Gentlemen, Violinist, Lutenist) from the Chapel Royal in addition to the Children, and about twenty string-players. As far as can be seen from the picture, the additional singers did not include any sopranos. The absence of timpani from the picture is noteworthy: the drums might have been hidden by the chandelier, but it is more likely that they were not included in the orchestra.[70]

The records in the Lord Chamberlain's papers, transcribed in Appendix I, provide only limited assistance for interpreting the performing group shown in the picture. Assuming that music-copying accounted for about £25 of the amount that Smith was paid, the remainder would represent about twenty-five additional performers.[71] This, as we would expect, indicates a larger performing group than for the Chapel Royal services of the 1720s, but smaller than that for the 1727 coronation. Presumably the 'extraordinary performers' included both vocalists and instrumentalists, so on this occasion Smith seems to have been responsible for arranging (or at least accounting for) both. Bernard Gates, who had been responsible for the additional singers at the Coronation, was paid instead for supervising the arrangements for the provision of the organ, the first recorded commission-type payment to a 'Tuner of the Organs' (i.e. the former office of 'Tuner of the Regals') during the eighteenth century. This

---

[68] Vanderbank's picture of an operatic scene in the 1720s (Deutsch, *Handel*, Pl. 9) shows only the singers. It is doubtful that the picture reproduced in Ceci, 'Handel and Walpole', 18–19, relates to any performance under the composer.

[69] This may not have been the case for the subsequent royal weddings in 1736 and 1740.

[70] See Ch. 17 concerning the chronology of Handel's use of timpani.

[71] The sums paid per performer varied on different occasions: the usual rate for balls at court was £25 for ten extra performers, but the rate was 3 gns. per musician at the 1727 coronation.

Fig. 12.2. Musicians' galleries at the wedding of Princess Anne and the Prince of Orange, 15 March 1733/4. Detail from Plate V

is also the only occasion in the period 1700–60 when an organ for a royal chapel or for a royal occasion was not provided by Bernard Smith or Christopher Shrider. The employment of Knoppel may have been motivated by the desire to place the work with a Dutchman as a compliment to the Prince of Orange.

Table 12.3. *Key to Kent's picture of the musicians' galleries at the royal wedding in 1734*

Upper Gallery
7
inc. 1 ?fl., 1 vn./va., 1 boy

Side Gallery
?5

? organ

?2

? organ

Side Gallery
?5
inc. 1 vc.

Second Gallery
?5
inc. 2 vn./va., 1 singer

6
inc. 1 vn./va., 2 obs..

5
inc. 2 ?tpts.

Main Gallery
4
inc. 1 boy

7
inc. 1 fl., 3 vn./va., 1 singer, 2 boys

6
3 singers, 3 boys

Side Gallery
?5
inc. 1 vc.

8
2 d.b., 1 keybd.
2 vn./va.
3 singers

Total number of visible performers: 66
Identifiable performers: 2 fl., 2 obs., 2 tpts., 9 vns./vas., 2 vc., 2 d.b., 1 keyboard (?organ); 8 singers, 7 boys

Unfortunately the surviving performing parts for William Boyce's anthem for the wedding of King George III on 8 September 1761 do not provide useful assistance for retrospective interpretation of the pictorial and documentary evidence from 1734. Coincidentally, the surviving part-books for that anthem are adequate for about seventy performers, but the set must be seriously depleted,[72] and the payments for the 1761 wedding suggest that about three times as many additional performers were hired compared with 1734.[73] Furthermore, the 1761 wedding took place in the Chapel Royal and not in the French Chapel.

The performing score of Handel's wedding anthem is the only original complete musical source for his Chapel Royal music, apart from the autograph of the Utrecht Te Deum, on which the composer did not name the intended solo singers: this is particularly surprising in view of the fact that the anthem (unlike the Te Deum) included a number of substantial and self-standing aria movements. The newspaper reports are uncharacteristically silent about the names of the soloists: perhaps the exclusive nature of the guest list for the Chapel at the wedding restricted their sources of information. The only soloist who can be named with certainty is Abbot for the second movement, thanks to Handel's transposition cue on the *Athalia* conducting score. That leaves an alto soloist unaccounted for in No. 1, a treble in No. 3, a tenor in No. 4, and a bass in Nos. 5 and 6. Abbot may possibly also have sung the last two, though Handel seems more often to have spread the solo music around the leading singers in each voice, except during the period of dominance by Hughes and Weely in the 1720s.

The most intriguing aspect with regard to the soloists concerns the music that might have been sung by John Beard. The anthem was composed in the autumn of 1733 and performed in March 1734; Beard was officially discharged from the Chapel, following the changing of his voice, on 29 October 1734. He should therefore still have been a treble at the time of the wedding. However, he could have been retained for a time after his voice had changed on account of his general usefulness to the choir; he may, for example, have deputized for an indisposed or senior Gentleman. It is even possible that Beard stayed on at the Chapel Royal hoping for a vacancy in one of the Gentlemen's places, but found himself unpopular with Greene at this time, at first because he was one of Gates's students and subsequently because he had taken part in Handel's

---

[72] GB-Ob MS Mus.Sch.c.117a–c. The surviving parts tally with the list (possibly made at the time of the sale of Boyce's music in 1778) on the organ part MS Mus.Sch.c.117; there are twelve parts for violins but only four for trebles.

[73] GB-Lpro LC5/168, p. 246.

wedding anthem.[74] Less than a fortnight after his dismissal from the Chapel, Beard appeared on stage at Covent Garden in the tenor role of Silvio in Handel's opera *Il pastor fido*, and this might suggest that his voice had been a settled tenor for some time. In the autograph score of the opera *Ariodante*, begun in August 1734 and completed on 24 October, Handel wrote the music for the role of Lurcanio in the soprano clef for Acts I and II (which he completed on 9 September), but went over to the tenor clef in Act III;[75] when the opera came to production in January 1735, Beard played Lurcanio. Perhaps Beard's voice changed while Handel was composing the score, though it is more likely that Handel composed the first two acts in the expectation of a different singer, since Gibson would not have countenanced the appearance of one of the Children in a public opera performance.[76] Another curious piece of evidence is a letter dated 21 November 1734 describing the new young singer at Covent Garden as 'A Scholar of Mr. Gates, Beard (who left the Chappel at Easter)' in direct contradiction to the institutional records,[77] but perhaps reflecting some knowledge that his voice had changed earlier in the year.

At the beginning the movement 'My vengeance awakes me' in the conducting score of *Athalia* Beard's name is written in pencil three times: Handel apparently wrote 'Bird' and then 'Beard' over the top,[78] and the third entry, 'Beard', is in the hand of J. C. Smith.[79] The aria was originally part of Athalia's role and so the solo part was written in the soprano clef, but as already noted Smith wrote tenor clefs for the vocal stave when he laid out 'Strength and honour are her clothing' in the conducting score of the anthem for Handel. The music of the aria was given to a tenor for the first time in the anthem, but for the London performances of *Athalia* in 1735 it may have been transferred (with its original oratorio text) to the role of Mathan, which was sung by Beard.[80] In the same season the aria was also almost certainly sung by Beard in

[74] Beard did, however, sing regularly in the court odes from New Year 1736, which was only the second composed by Greene after succeeding as Master of the King's Music.

[75] GB-Lbl RM 20.a.7; see Burrows and Ronish, *Catalogue*, 17–18.

[76] The date of Beard's dismissal from the Chapel nevertheless suggests that his voice changed at this time.

[77] Deutsch, *Handel*, 375; Beard may also have been the 'extreme fine English Voice' referred to in the newspaper quotation on p. 374.

[78] The spelling 'Bird' suggests an early annotation: both forms are found in Handel's autograph of *Alexander's Feast* (Jan. 1736), where he corrected 'Bird' to 'Beard' on GB-Lbl RM 20.d.4, fo. 67.

[79] D-Hs M C/264, fo. 78ʳ.

[80] See Burrows, 'Handel's 1735 (London) Version of *Athalia*', 201, correcting Dean, *Handel's Dramatic Oratorios*, 260–1. This also explains the presence of Beard's name on 'Gentle airs' in the *Athalia* conducting score.

Deborah.[81] The aria was used again by Handel (to the *Athalia* text) for his *Oratorio* of March 1738, and Beard would have sung it in Handel's revival of *Athalia* in 1756. Handel also planned a performance in 1743, for which Beard would probably also have been a soloist if it had come to fruition. It seems probable from the style of the handwriting that Smith's entry for Beard's name in the *Athalia* conducting score dates from 1756 (though the word-book for that year still attributes the aria to Athalia, not Mathan),[82] so Handel's entries could have been made for oratorio performances in 1735, 1738, or 1743, as plausibly as in 1733 in connection with the preparation of the wedding anthem score. The evidence is therefore inconclusive and it may be best to consider Beard as a possible treble soloist for 'A good wife is a good portion', in spite of his subsequent association with the music of the tenor aria. It is, of course, possible that his voice changed between the time the anthem was composed in autumn 1733 and its eventual performance the following spring.

We might perhaps expect that the cello obbligato in No. 2 was intended for, and performed by, the Chapel Royal's Violist Francisco Goodsens. The style of the cello part is, however, very similar to that of the obbligato to the aria 'Softly sweet, in Lydian measures' in *Alexander's Feast* (1736) which was written for Andrea Caporale, and there is little evidence that Goodsens undertook anything beyond straightforward continuo work. Perhaps Caporale had been one of the additional instrumentalists that Handel took with him to Oxford, where *Athalia* was performed, and he played again for the wedding.

Conducting Score

The important features of this manuscript, which is partly in Handel's autograph, have already been described. As with the autograph of the Chapel Royal anthem HWV 251d, it eluded the attention of those responsible for providing scores of Handel's music for eighteenth-century collectors: no manuscript copies are known, and the music was not published until Chrysander's edition of 1872.[83] However, a copy was presumably available in Dublin within a decade of the anthem's composition, since the text of the anthem was included in the Philharmonic Society's word-book dated 1741, referred to in Chapter 11. Movements from the anthem, presumably copied from this score, may have contributed to the royal wedding anthem of 1740, which is described in Chapter 13.

---

[81] Pencil cue in Handel's hand: 'Ex Athalia Mr Bird/My vengeance awakes me' in the conducting score of *Deborah* (D-Hs M C/258, fo. 85ᵛ).

[82] Athalia's name was at some stage deleted in pencil on the aria in the conducting score.

[83] Included in *HG* 36.

13

Anthems for Other Royal Family Occasions: Two Weddings and a Funeral

The Wedding of the Prince of Wales, 1736

FREDERICK, Prince of Wales, had been born and brought up at Hanover, where he remained as the family's representative when his parents came to London in 1714. Following his father's accession to the British throne in 1727 it was inevitable that he too would move to London, but the King showed no impatience for his company: he eventually arrived at St James's Palace early in December 1728, never to return to Hanover again. He was 21 years old and had been separated from his immediate family since the age of 7: indeed, this was his first opportunity to meet his younger brother and two of his sisters, who had been born in London. Since he was the heir to the throne, the arrangement of a marriage for him was of political importance, and the need for it was brought to attention by the Prince's liaisons during his early years in London with Lady Diana Spencer, the granddaughter of the Duchess of Marlborough, and with Anne Vane, a mistress by whom he had at least one child. The situation was complicated by the recurring antipathy between the generations of the royal family, but also by two other factors: George II was reluctant to grant the greater political and financial independence that might follow from his son's marriage, and there was the practical problem of finding a suitable consort among Europe's Protestant ruling families. According to Lord Hervey, Princess Anne's marriage (which had brought her a settlement of £80,000 a year) had been a cause of jealousy in her brother, whose supporters had encouraged him to 'think it very hard that the first establishment provided by Parliament for one of the royal progeny should be for any but the heir-apparent to the Crown'.[1] As noted in the previous chapter, shifts in Europe's political alliances had by 1730 destroyed George I's plan for Frederick's marriage to Wilhelmina of Prussia. During his visit to Hanover in 1735 George II seems to have taken the matter in hand, and settled upon a suitable partner in

---

[1] Sedgwick, *Some Materials*, 196.

Augusta, the younger daughter of Frederick II, Duke of Saxe-Gotha.[2] The couple were married at the Chapel Royal, St James's Palace, on 27 April 1736: Frederick was 29 years old, his bride 16.

In November 1735 the newspapers had expected that the wedding would take place the following March,[3] but early in the new year they reported a delay and anticipated that 'the Nuptials are to be celebrated in the Month of May'.[4] The King announced the 'intended marriage' at a Council meeting on 5 February, and the Prince gave his formal approval to the proposal.[5] In mid-March the Earl of Delawar was dispatched to Gotha to stand proxy for the Prince at the espousal and to bring the Princess to London:[6] as usual, the negotiations relating to the marriage contract took some time, and the ratification from London was not returned until 6 April.[7] The previous month a rather curious announcement had appeared in one newspaper:

The Marriage of his Royal Highness the Prince of Wales to the Princess of Saxe-Gotha, will certainly be solemniz'd at St. Paul's, the beginning of May; and the Procession from St. James's will be with the utmost State and Magnificence. The rich Cloathing and Equipages that are preparing on this Occasion will exceed all that ever came before. (*LEP*, 13–16 Mar. 1736)

It would have been unprecedented for a royal wedding to take place at any other venue than one of the Royal Chapels. Perhaps the rumour reflected an attempt by some of Frederick's political supporters to promote a scheme that would trump the extravagance of Anne's wedding; if so, it is hardly surprising that it found no favour with the King. A fortnight later the same newspaper reported that on 31 March 'the Surveyors of his Majesty's Works measur'd and survey'd the Chapel Royal at St. James's, in order to prepare and make the same more commodious' for the wedding, and they returned a couple of weeks later, presumably with more specific plans for refurnishing the interior:

Yesterday some of the Surveyors belonging to his Majesty's Board of Works, took a Survey of the Royal Chapel at St James's, in order to get the same in Readiness against the Marriage of his Royal Highness the Prince of Wales; and the same will be set about immediately after Easter Sunday. (*DJ*, 15 Apr.)

On 17 April the bride-to-be set out from Gotha and travelled through Germany to Holland; on 24 April she left Helvoetsluys for a North Sea crossing in which 'it blew a very hard Gale, and her Highness was extremely

---

[2] Rumours that an espousal had already taken place at Hanover were, however, denied: see *DA*, 25 Oct. 1735.

[3] *SJEP*, 15–18 Nov. 1735.

[4] *LDP*, 5, 16 Jan. 1735/6; *DG*, 5 Jan., however, still predicted the wedding to take place on 1 Mar., the Queen's birthday.

[5] *DA*, 5, 6 Feb. 1735/6.   [6] *DA*, 12 Apr. 1736.   [7] *DG*, 12 Apr.

Sea-Sick'.[8] She landed at Greenwich about 1 p.m. the next day, which was Easter Sunday. The Prince of Wales visited her that afternoon, and he returned again the next day (26 April), when the couple dined together and took a river trip on the Prince's barge 'attended by two other Barges full of Persons of quality, and preceded by a third with a fine Concert of Musick'.[9] Next morning the King's coaches went to Greenwich to collect Augusta: she left about noon, arrived at Lambeth at 1.15, and was met by the King's barge which carried her to Whitehall; from there she was carried in 'his Majesty's own Chair' to St James's Palace, arriving just after 2 o'clock.[10] She was presented to the Royal Family, dined with the Duke of Cumberland and the Royal Princesses, and retired before 7 o'clock to be dressed for her wedding. The procession formed up at 8.30 and the marriage service, conducted by Bishop Gibson, began about half an hour later.

The wedding preparations involved a last-minute rush. Not only did the bride have just two days between her arrival in Britain and the ceremony,[11] but the reconstruction of the Chapel Royal interior had to be accomplished during the same time: 'As soon as Divine Service [probably Morning Prayer followed by Holy Communion] was over in the Chapel on Easter Sunday, about 40 Men were set at Work to get the Chapel in Readiness against the Marriage, which is to be Solemnised To-morrow Evening.'[12] The initial labour force proved to be insufficient, and had to be increased the next day: 'The Workmen were Yesterday augmented to above 100, in order to prepare the Royal Chapel for the Marriage; and made such Haste, that by Night the King's and Queen's Thrones were finished, and the Canopy for the Prince; and this Morning at Eight o'Clock the Velvet Hangings are to be placed, and the Chapel is to be ready by Six in the Evening.'[13]

According to Lord Hervey, the process was hurried by the King's desire to see his new mistress in Hanover: 'The King, being very impatient to return to Hanover to the arms of Madame Walmoden, declared to his Queen and his Ministers, that if matters could not be so managed as to bring the Princess of Saxe-Gotha into England before the expiration of the month of April the marriage should either be put off till the winter or solemnised without him.'[14]

---

[8] *DA*, 26 Apr.

[9] Boyer, *The Political State*, li. 444; on 26 Apr. the Prince was accompanied by the Duke of Cumberland and Princess Amelia.

[10] *DA*, 29 Apr.

[11] The intended timetable may have been even more severe, that the Princess would be married on the same day that she landed (*DA*, 9 Apr.).

[12] *DJ*, 16 Apr.

[13] *DJ*, 27 Apr., with 'popare' for 'prepare'.

[14] Sedgwick, *Some Materials*, 549. According to *DG*, 22 Apr., the object of the King's journey to Hanover was 'to confer with German princes' over a European peace settlement.

There may also have been a desire at court to see that no accident delayed the wedding in the same way as that of the Princess Royal two years previously. The timing of Augusta's arrival in Britain on Easter Sunday at least gave her an additional day to recover from the sea crossing, while the Chapel was being prepared against the clock. One rehearsal of the anthem, probably convened at short notice, was reported:

Yesterday there was a Practice of a fine Anthem compos'd by Mr. Handel, to be perform'd at the Nuptials of the Prince of Wales, at Mr. Gates's, Master of the Boys belonging to the Chapel Royal, St. James's: The Vocal Parts were perform'd by Mess. Row, Gates, Lee, Abbot, Beard, the Gentlemen of the Chapel, and the Boys. The Instrumental parts by twenty of his Majesty's band of Musick, and the same Number of Performers from Mr. Handel's Opera. (*DA*, 27 Apr.)

On that day it would probably have been impossible to rehearse in the Chapel itself, on account of the construction work that was being undertaken by the 'workmen', and the second most convenient rehearsal venue, the Banqueting House Chapel, was probably similarly unavailable because of renovation work to the ceiling.[15] The description of the size of the performing forces for the rehearsal confirms that Gates's house must have had a room of substantial size.

Concerning the wedding itself, Hervey commented that it was 'performed in much the same manner as that of the Princess Royal had been, only there was no gallery built. Consequently there could be no procession in form, and they were married in that Chapel to which the King constantly goes on a Sunday.'[16] 'Gallery' here refers to the special procession gallery between St James's Palace and the French Chapel that had been built for the previous wedding in 1734. Inside the Chapel Royal itself a special east-end gallery was constructed in 1736 to accommodate the musicians, but the reports make no mention of side-galleries and it seems probable that the guest list was more modest than in 1734.[17] The Prince's wedding was apparently provided for decently, but not on the lavish scale of that for his elder sister: as noted in Chapter 12, there may have been precedents, derived ultimately from feudal practice, for more extravagant celebrations on the marriage of the King's eldest daughter. Given the history of personal difficulties between the generations of the Hanoverian family, it is not likely that George II would have been troubled

[15] See Colvin, *The History of the King's Works*, v. 301. In Apr. 1736 the service for the Royal Maundy, which usually took place at Whitehall, was held in Duke Street Chapel (*DJ*, 23 Apr.); the progress in the renovation at Whitehall was viewed by the Queen and Princess Caroline in August (*DA*, 27 Aug.).

[16] Sedgwick, *Some Materials*, 552.

[17] 'Necessaries for the Chapel against the Prince of Wales's wedding' in GB-Lpro LC2/29 gives a description of the furnishings and decoration. It includes 'To cover with new Crimson Baze the Musick Gallerys', but nothing about other galleries.

by the more modest arrangements for his son's wedding. Nevertheless, the wedding was another important social event: Hervey commented that 'the whole Court, and almost indeed the whole town, resorted to St James's in their wedding-clothes to see her [the Princess's] arrival',[18] but only a limited number of these people could have been in the Chapel for the ceremony.[19] One of them was Katherine Knatchbull, who reported that 'it was a noble sight & the young princess is a fine young lady'.[20]

Unfortunately, the journalists' reports of the wedding service are devoted mainly to the processions, and their references to the music are as meagre as in 1734. While the processions entered the Chapel, 'During all this Time the Organ play'd, but as soon as the Persons were thus seated the Organ ceased, and Divine Service began'; then, 'When the Dean had finished the Divine Service, the married Pair rose and retired back to their Stools upon the Hautpas; where they remained while an Anthem composed by Mr. Handel was sung by his Majesty's Band of Musick, which was placed in a Gallery over the Communion Table.'[21] The words of the anthem, accompanied by biblical references for the verses, were published in the newspapers: the text matches that set by Handel, except that in No. 3 the phrase 'upon the walls of thine house' is omitted.[22] The Earl of Egmont's diary provides the only documentary description of the performance: 'Over the altar was placed the organ, and a gallery made for the musicians. An anthem composed by Hendel for the occasion was wretchedly sung by Abbot, Gates, Lee, Bird and a boy.'[23]

For the period of the wedding, as in 1734, Handel composed a topical piece for his current theatre programme, this time the opera *Atalanta*. He completed the autograph on 22 April; the score had occupied him for most of the month.[24] The preparation of the opera's performances involved considerable activity, since he had to secure some good Italian singers at short notice and the production itself required construction work at Covent Garden theatre that sounds almost as ambitious as that in the Chapel Royal: 'We hear that Mr. Handel has comps'd a new Opera, on the Occasion of his Royal Highness's Marriage to the Prince[ss] of Saxe-Gotha, and as the Wedding was solemnized sooner than expected, great Numbers of Artificers, as Carpenters, Painters, Engineers, &c. are employed to forward the same in order to bring it on the Stage with the

---

[18] Sedgwick, *Some Materials*, 549.

[19] *LDP*, 9 Apr., estimated that 'only 100 of the Nobility and Quality' would attend the wedding, and *DG*, 24 Apr., reported a rumour that 'none would be admitted except Peers, Peeresses and Privy Counsellors'.

[20] Letter of 8 May 1736, Burrows and Dunhill, *Music and Theatre*, 16.

[21] *DJ*, 28 Apr.

[22] *LDP*, 30 Apr.; no composer was named for the anthem.

[23] Diary, 27 Apr.; Deutsch, *Handel*, 405; the wedding 'ended about nine'.

[24] GB-Lbl RM 20.a.9. Handel did not date the beginning, but he finished Act I on 9 Apr.

utmost Expedition, and that several Voices being sent for from Italy, for that Purpose, are lately arrived.'[25] In fact, some of Handel's singers arrived in London on Easter Sunday, the same day as the Princess,[26] but *Atalanta* did not come onto the stage at Covent Garden until 12 May. Although it is possible that he might have written the wedding anthem first, it seems more likely that Handel worked on it concurrently with the composition of the opera score. In a letter of 22 April (the day on which Handel dated the completion of *Alatanta*), the Earl of Shaftesbury described how he was experiencing a delay in the delivery of some music that he had ordered from Handel's copyists, because they were fully occupied: 'We are not to hope for the musick I bespoke till the latter end of next month; for the Nuptial Anthem, & a new opera Handel has just finished & some other things, have employ'd Smiths people sufficiently, not to do any-thing else at this time.'[27] From this, it seems unlikely that Handel put the anthem together in the couple of days following his completion of *Atalanta*.[28]

The inclusion of his anthem at the wedding must have been a consequence of favour from the King and Queen, and in fulfilment of his 'Chapel Royal' pension, rather than a response to any encouragement from the Prince of Wales himself. For the theatre seasons of 1734–5 and 1735–6 Frederick had not supported Handel's performances at Covent Garden, but had maintained his subscription to the rival Opera of the Nobility at the King's Theatre.[29] Hervey related that their support for different opera companies was one source of contention between Frederick and Princess Anne in the period around her marriage,[30] and the residue of this situation may have continued for a while after Anne had left London.[31] In the weeks following their wedding, the Prince and Princess of Wales attended performances of Porpora's *La festa d'Imeneo* at the King's Theatre, but stayed away from *Atalanta* at Covent Garden, on the first night of which Frederick 'order'd a play at Drury Lane, which carry'd away most of the Company, though the rest of the Royal Family were at Covent Garden.[32] In such circumstances the Prince would hardly have taken an initiative to invite Handel to compose the anthem for his wedding, though he may have been unable to prevent its inclusion.

---

[25] *LDP*, 29 Apr.   [26] *DA*, 26 Apr.   [27] Burrows and Dunhill, *Music and Theatre*, 15.
[28] The earliest references to Handel's anthem in the newspapers were in *DA*, 27 Apr. and *LEP*, 24–7 Apr.
[29] Carole Taylor, 'Handel and Frederick', 91.
[30] Sedgwick, *Some Materials*, 273–4.
[31] See King, 'On Princess Anne's Patronage'; also id., 'Anne of Hanover' 171.
[32] Taylor, 'Italian Opera-going', 229; hence the absence of the Prince's name in the report on the royal family's attendance at *Atalanta*, Deutsch, *Handel*, 407–8. In spite of the statement in *DA*, 9 Apr. that Handel had engaged the Italian singers 'to perform eight Operas, for the Entertainment of her Royal Highness the future Princess of Wales', the Prince and Princess are not reported as attending any of his performances.

Sing unto God, ye kingdoms of the earth (HWV 263)

In this anthem Handel repeated the same pattern from *This is the day*. General texts of jubilation from the Psalms (in this case, Psalms 68 and 106) frame texts that have more specific relevance to a marriage, the first five verses from the 'family' Psalm 128. Only verses 3–4 of the Psalm (set as the third movement of the anthem) refer specifically to wife and family, the verses either side providing transitions to the more general theme of rejoicing. The texts of neither of Handel's wedding anthems give any prominence to the husband. *This is the day* is almost entirely devoted to the wife, and her husband only features on account of his good fortune in having a 'virtuous wife'; in *Sing unto God* the husband is perhaps implied in 'Blessed is the man that feareth the Lord', but if so he is presumably blessed with a wife and family as a result of his faith and trust in the Lord God of Israel.

Handel also repeated the musical structure from *This is the day*, with choruses for the outer movements, a succession of separate arias (one with cello obbligato) to follow the opening chorus, and a brief accompanied recitative towards the end. The proportion of known borrowed or transferred music is smaller than in *This is the day*: the chorus 'Blessed is the man' was adapted from a movement in a German passion setting by C. H. Graun, and the final movement was derived from Handel's *Parnasso in Festa*, lifted complete but with a recomposed vocal line for the soloist. Although the text sequence is at least as good as in the previous wedding anthem, the key scheme is effective enough (D major, A major, A minor, F major, linking recitative, D major) and the newly composed material includes some good music, yet the anthem as a whole hangs together rather less well than its predecessor, whose musical agenda seems to have been influenced mainly by the desire to reuse as much music as possible from *Athalia*. The problems come mainly towards the end of *Sing unto God*. 'Blessed is the man' has the character of a medial chorus, marking the furthest distance from the anthem's tonic, and the succeeding recitative seems rather perfunctory as a means of achieving the trajectory back to the final chorus and tonic key; the final chorus itself can be made effective by determined performers, but constitutes one of Handel's few practical miscalculations in the transference of his musical movements between one work and another. The scoring of the anthem is identical to that for *This is the day*, except that there is no movement involving flutes. It also shares a similar anomaly concerning the participation of the timpani, which (in the received version of the musical text) have a part only in the first movement.

The first movement itself, like that in the previous wedding anthem, alternates the chorus with an alto soloist, but in a different structure. In *This is the day* the chorus had contributed the opening and closing sections of a three-part scheme to which the alto solo provided the middle section: in *Sing unto God* Handel adopted a binary plan, using the chorus music as ritornello material successively in the tonic, dominant, and tonic keys, between which the passages for the alto soloist provide intermediate episodes. The choral sections, which are much shorter than in the previous anthem, once again have fully scored accompaniment for trumpets, oboes, and strings (with bassoons, and organ continuo), while the solo sections return to the Purcellian texture of a continuo-accompanied duet for alto voice and solo trumpet. The prelude for strings and oboes outlines the melodic material that will be taken up in a varied form by the voices: a rising-third opening followed by a falling phrase with a characteristic semiquaver-rhythm component, presented initially as a sequential passage. The soloist's music beginning at bar 20 recalls a phrase in 'Day by day we magnify thee' from the Caroline Te Deum, and indeed the alternation of the solo and chorus material is also very similar, even down to the outline of the choral rhythms, though the wedding anthem movement is more substantial. The second solo is a little prolix but leads back into the chorus in splendid fashion, and in the continuation Handel works in the orchestra's sequential passage from the opening as an accompaniment to the chorus. Chrysander's edition is misleading in showing the opening alto leads of the movement for the soloist: the first two phrases should be for full chorus, with the soloist's music beginning at the end of bar 16.

About a year after the wedding Handel reused the movement with an Italian text to open his Italian oratorio *Il trionfo del Tempo e della Verità*, an expanded version of the oratorio *Il trionfo del Tempo e del Disinganno* that he had composed in Rome thirty years previously. The first performance of the oratorio was at Covent Garden on 23 March 1737. The alto solos in the movement, originally composed for performance by one of the Chapel Royal altos, were adapted only to the extent of accommodating the Italian text, without altering the range of the part. The words of the chorus in the oratorio, beginning 'Solo a goder', were for the supporters of Piacere (Pleasure), but the solo music in this movement would not have been sung by the soloist for the role of Piacere, Gioacchino Conti, who was a castrato with a soprano-range voice: the solo may perhaps have been taken by another alto-range singer from Handel's current opera company, perhaps Maria Negri. When the score was rearranged twenty years later into an English oratorio, *The Triumph of Time and Truth*, the allegiance of the text was changed, to 'Time is supreme'.[33]

---

[33] The text for the English oratorio was by Thomas Morell. The chorus is printed in *HG* 20, pp. 8–14, but the Italian-text version was not included in the movements from the 1737 oratorio that were published in *HG* 24.

The treble aria 'Blessed are all they that fear the Lord' is accompanied by unison violins and bassi, a regular scoring from Handel's operas (and oratorios) that he had also used in 'Strength and honour', accompanying a tenor voice, in the previous wedding anthem; this time the voice is not doubled by oboe, which would perhaps have masked the solo treble. It is a flowing, unhurried movement in binary form, the central dominant-key ritornello beginning at exactly the halfway point. Melodic motifs from the first movement reappear here, whether by accident or by subconscious connection on the composer's part: the rising third at the beginning and the tied rhythmic figure at bar 30. The opening rising third is particularly interesting because it shows how Handel varied the music that gave him the idea for the movement, an aria in the same key from C. H. Graun's 'Brunswick Passion' *Kommt her und schaut:*[34] see Ex. 13.1. The opening, and the related violin figure at bars 7–8, are the only specific elements from Graun's music that Handel used in his own composition.

In 1737 he included the anthem aria in *Il trionfo del Tempo e della Verità*, close to (but not immediately following) the opening chorus. Unlike the chorus, however, the aria was recomposed rather than simply retexted. The music from the anthem movement became the basis of an A section for a full dal segno aria for Piacere, and the words assumed a different mood: the beatific message from the anthem became a warning that gloom and despair need to be chased from the heart before they multiply ('Fosco genio'). (This message was retained in the subsequent English version, with a text beginning 'Pensive sorrow'.)[35] The change of emphasis probably accounts for the alteration of the tempo from Larghetto in the anthem to Andante in the oratorio. The recomposition of the music, although it preserved the main melodic material and the binary structure, was so thorough-going that it required a new autograph; Handel retained some passages but rewrote others, developing parts of the melodic line differently, and in the process adding or shortening, by the odd bar and by more substantial sections. The music came out at nearly the same length overall (46 bars in the anthem movement and 47 bars in the A section of the oratorio aria), but the central ritornello shifted further on (to bar 28), because he added a couple of bars at the vocal entry, introduced a new figure (bars 15–18), and reworked the approach to the dominant in a more leisurely manner (bars 20–7, comparable to bars 20–2 of the anthem), compensating by shortening the return to the final cadence. Comparison of the second part of the music is particularly revealing with regard to the difference in Handel's

---

[34] See Roberts, *Handel Sources*, v, p. xiv and music pp. 58–62; Handel copied bars 1–7 of the ritornello in his transcript of extracts from the Passion, GB-Cfm MU MS 251, p. 25.

[35] For the English version, see *HG* 20, pp. 18–21; the Italian version was not included in *HG* 24.

Ex. 13.1. (*a*) Graun, Brunswick Passion, 'Ihr Jünger Jesu lernt die Tücke'; (*b*) Handel, *Sing unto God*, No. 2

This shows the ritornello omitting va, as copied by Handel in GB-Cfm MU MS 251, p. 25. His alternative variants are shown in small-size notes.

writing for a young treble and for an experienced theatre soprano. In the anthem the tied-note figure at bar 30 commences a build-up with longer phrases towards a tonic cadence at bar 36, but the singer is then given shorter 'recovery phrases' before the approach to the final cadence at bar 40. In the oratorio movement Handel shortens the process, going more directly to the final cadence with a climax that refers to the opening rising melody, and in a register that demands adult breath support: the highest note of the movement (*a''*) is reserved for the final vocal phrase in both cases, but approached in entirely different ways.

As in *This is the day*, Handel seems to have felt that the anthem needed a minor-key movement to provide variety, and a more serious (though not pessimistic) mood is supplied by 'Thy wife shall be as the fruitful vine'. The opening cello theme sets a lyrical framework, introducing variety by the triple-time metre as well as by the minor mode. The movement is in binary form: at the mid-point in the dominant minor key the violins make a rather unexpected entry to accompany the second verse of the text ('Thy children like the olive branches'), playing a figure which is derived from bar 11 in the cello solo but is never heard from the voice. In the midst of the second half the music returns to the tonic, and to the original text, with a variant of the opening theme, and this runs into a repeat of the second verse incorporating the violins. In the first half there are well-managed excursions to C major and G major. Overall the movement is pleasingly constructed, but it needs careful management in performance to maintain lyrical continuity, particularly in the transitions between the sections.

For the chorus 'Lo, thus shall the man be blessed' Handel returned to Graun's 'Brunswick Passion', from which he lifted the first chorus ('Lasset uns aufsehen': see Ex. 13.2 for the opening) completely and with very little alteration apart from that required by the English text.[36] He scored the movement up with written-out orchestral parts—Graun's original had vocal parts and basso continuo, with the direction 'Gli Stromenti colle Voci'[37]—but even here he added little of his own. Yet the movement works surprisingly well: something must have connected for Handel between Graun's theme and the syllabic possibilities of the English text. There is also a strong family resemblance between this movement and 'In the voice of praise' from *As pants the hart* (used in all versions of Handel's anthem), even down to the key. Graun's composition probably dates from the 1720s:[38] the rather short-winded theme and close-worked style of counterpoint represent a style that Handel was beginning to leave behind in 1736, but nevertheless he thought enough of the chorus to incorporate it into his Italian oratorio the next year, as 'Pria che sii converta in polve' to conclude Part II, whence it later reappeared in the English version of the oratorio as 'Ere to dust is chang'd that beauty'.[39] Handel's indebtedness to Graun in this movement was discovered by William Crotch in 1822, and was the subject of an interesting article by Ebenezer Prout in 1894.[40]

The function of the accompanied recitative 'Blessed be the Lord God of Israel' is to provide a transition back to D major for the final movement. As already noted, the last movement was the anthem's principal self-borrowing,

---

[36] Roberts, *Handel Sources*, v, p. xiii and music pp. 2–6.
[37] Ibid., music p. 2.
[38] Ibid., p. x.
[39] *HG* 20, pp. 128–33; Italian version not included in *HG* 24.
[40] Prout, 'Graun's *Passion Oratorio*'.

Ex. 13.2. (*a*) Graun, Brunswick Passion, No. 2; (*b*) Handel, *Sing unto God*, No. 4

taken from the closing movement of *Parnasso in Festa*, Handel's theatre serenata originally composed for the period of the previous Royal wedding in 1734: in the serenata Apollo leads the chorus in acclaiming the marriage of Peleus and

Thetis.[41] This is one of the least successful musical transfers in Handel's Chapel Royal music. The movement itself is jolly enough, and the cries of 'Giove il vuole' from the chorus were easily converted into 'alleluia, amen', but it outstays its welcome in the context of the anthem, and Apollo's music, written for the castrato Carestini, did not transfer comfortably for a tenor. At the first entries of the soloist Handel began a radical attempt to recast the music, but from bar 20 (equivalent to bar 18 in the *Parnasso* movement) he made only the minimum alterations necessary to accommodate the change of voice. Mostly the music came out an octave lower: the adjustment to the higher octave in one of the passages that did receive attention (bars 34–8) sits awkwardly for a tenor. Carestini had a particular style as a singer, and the music for his strongest register did not adapt well for the lower voice: the version in Handel's anthem is hard work for the tenor soloist, without much benefit in terms of musical effect. The solo part also has a few uncomfortable near misses in consecutive octaves with the basso continuo, for example at bars 16 and 46: contrary to his received image, Handel was usually careful about these things, and it is difficult to resist the impression that he had lost interest in the anthem, or ran out of time for its preparation, in the last movement.

Conditions of Performance

This is the only item of Handel's music for the Chapel Royal that was composed for an occasion on which special physical arrangements were made for performers in the regular Chapel Royal at St James's Palace. The newspaper reports reveal that the work of the carpenters included the construction of a gallery for the musicians at the east end of the Chapel at first-floor level:

A Gallery is built over the Communion-Table for the Musick, who are to perform a fine Anthem, compos'd by Mr. Handel. (*LEP*, 24–7 Apr.)

The Organ is to be taken down, and a Gallery to be erected at the North Window for the Musick. (*DG*, 24 Apr.)

The reference to the 'North Window' is ambiguous, owing to the north–south orientation of the Chapel, but the scheme for the construction is clear: as at the French Chapel in 1734, a gallery was built across the area above the communion table, presumably at the same height as the organ gallery, which was taken into the available performing space through the removal of the regular instrument. Also as in 1734, the arrangements probably involved the removal of the Chapel's windows in order to provide access and additional

---

[41] *HG* 54, pp. 125–36.

depth. If the choir normally sang the services from floor-level choir stalls, on this occasion they were dispatched to the gallery, to make room for more guests in the body of the Chapel. It might just have been possible to build a two-level gallery in the window space, but height was much more restricted than in the French Chapel and, apart from the limitations imposed by the short time available for refurnishing, there would have been reluctance to interfere in any way with the sixteenth-century ceiling which is the decorative glory of the Chapel Royal. Shrider was paid to take down the Chapel's regular organ and to build a new one in the specially constructed gallery. This was probably done to release performing space in the organ chamber, since the organ for the wedding was probably much smaller, but also to provide an instrument that matched orchestral pitch: this may have been the first service in the Chapel during the eighteenth century to involve a large enough orchestra to make the problem of pitch difference serious. It seems unrealistic that Shrider completed the dismantling of the Chapel organ and the building of a new one in the gallery within forty-eight hours: perhaps the framework for the musicians' gallery had already been constructed off-site by Easter Sunday and Shrider had a suitable chamber organ in storage. The payment to Gates, as the officer responsible for the organs, for 'his attendance at several Rehearsals of Musick' (see App. I) may have covered expenses for the rehearsal at his house as well as his formal duty relating to the work in the Chapel Royal: it seems unlikely, given the short preparation period, that Shrider would have wasted time setting up an organ in one location for the rehearsals, only to have to dismantle the instrument, move it, and reassemble it again in the Chapel gallery.

The payment to Smith for the wedding relates to music-copying and the cost of additional performers. It is the only such payment in connection with the wedding, and so (as in 1734) it presumably covered both vocal and instrumental performers: the former would have included Beard and the latter would have included oboe and bassoon players. The sum paid to Smith was smaller than the comparable one for the 1734 wedding and, if calculated on the same basis, would suggest about fifteen to twenty additional performers. The difference between the two weddings may reflect both a different policy in court spending and the practical limitations imposed by the size of the gallery. A total of about forty to fifty performers seems to be a realistic estimate. The report of the rehearsal mentioned an orchestra of forty, though obviously describing the participants in round numbers, and it is very likely that the players were more numerous than the singers. Egmont's reference to 'Abbot, Gates, Lee, Bird and a boy' presumably described the principal singers, who were probably placed at the front of the gallery: if his identifications were correct, Laye sang the alto solos in the first movement, the boy sang the second movement, either Abbot or Gates (probably the former) sang the third, leaving

Beard with the accompanied recitative and the solos in the last movement. The treble soloist may have been one of the Children who were discharged the following February: James Allen, Thomas Barrow, or James Butler. The principal singers would have been supported by the other Children and Gentlemen of the Chapel, or at least such of the latter as were currently in waiting, and perhaps a few additional voices.

As with *This is the day*, the first movement has a part for timpani but the drums are not employed thereafter, even though trumpets are included in the last movement. Perhaps the timpanist improvised a part in the last movement, perhaps the arrangement was designed to enable him to slip away during the later movements of the anthem because he was on duty in a procession from the Chapel at the end of the wedding. It seems just as likely, however, that the inclusion of the drums seemed a good idea when Handel began the composition of the anthem, but proved impractical once the limitations of the gallery space became known. If timpani were used in the anthem, it may have been the first occasion on which they were included in any music at the Chapel Royal: see Chapter 17. The textual history of the anthem's first movement is a little uncertain because the composer's autograph does not survive, though on the evidence of early manuscript copies the timpani part was integral to the anthem and was not a subsequent addition for the oratorio. None of the copyists in early manuscripts of the anthem sought to remedy the anomaly by providing a drum part for the last movement.

Musical Sources

Of Handel's autograph material for the anthem, which would probably have covered all of the movements apart from the last one and the preceding recitative, only a fragment survives, for the chorus 'Lo, thus shall the man be blessed' beginning at bar 14.[42] It is rather ironic that it should have been this music, since it is a lightly adapted transcription from the Graun source. The only authoritative early manuscript of the anthem is a score in the hand of S4, one of the scribes from the 'Smith circle', which is written on paper that dates it to 1736–7.[43] The copyist added 'Mr Beard' against the solo part of the last movement but there are no other soloists' names. This manuscript is unlikely to have been Handel's conducting score for the anthem, in which we would have expected to find his amendments to the solo part in the last movement, and probably also the music of the accompanied recitative in his hand. The score has a cue for bassoons to double the bass voices in 'Lo, thus shall the man

[42] GB-Cfm MU MS 251, pp. 51–4; for Handel's transcript of Graun's movement, see pp. 21–3 of the same MS.

[43] GB-Ob MS Tenbury 618.

be blessed', probably conveying a feature from the lost section of the auto-graph. The anthem was published in Samuel Arnold's collected edition of Handel's works in 1795,[44] but in an inflated form, preceded by an overture derived from Handel's opera *Il pastor fido*, incorporating a couple of extraneous movements (one arranged from an aria from Handel's opera *Rodelinda*), and with the addition of horn parts to the scoring. Arnold's version seems to have no authenticity, and it possibly relates to a performance at the wedding of Prince George (subsequently King George IV) at the Chapel Royal in April 1795: he married a cousin, and so both bride and groom were grandchildren of the royal marriage from 1736.

Handel's Royal Wedding Anthem of 1740

Although it takes events out of chronological sequence, it is convenient at this point to deal with Handel's one further contribution to a British royal wed-ding. At the time that Princess Anne's wedding was in prospect during the autumn of 1733, there were also rumours of marriage plans for her sisters: newspapers related the possibilities of matches between Princess Amelia and the Duke of Holstein-Gottorp, and between Princess Caroline and Frederick, heir to the Landgrave of Hesse-Cassel.[45] The latter was related both to the King of Sweden and to the Prince of Orange. Rumours resurfaced again in October 1735, when the Prince of Wales's wedding was being arranged, that the Landgrave of Hesse-Cassel (i.e. Frederick's father) would be coming to London the following February to negotiate a marriage contract between his son and one of the younger royal princesses.[46] At that stage there were four unmarried daughters of George II: Amelia and Caroline of the elder group (now possibly moving out of the most eligible age bracket for marriage), and Mary and Louisa from those children born after their parents' removal to London in 1714.[47] Eventually an arrangement was agreed for the marriage of Princess Mary and Frederick of Hesse-Cassel; negotiations may have been delayed following the death of the Queen in 1737, and in any case Mary was probably then regarded as being too young for immediate marriage. The match was concluded in 1740, when Mary was 17; the King sent messages to

---

[44] *Anthem. For the Wedding of Frederick Prince of Wales, and the Princess of Saxa-Gotha. Composed in the Year 1736, by G. F. Handel.* Nos. 153–4 of Arnold's edition: see William C. Smith, *Handel*, 155.

[45] *DA*, 27 Sept. and 24 Oct. 1733.

[46] *DPB*, 30 Oct. 1735.

[47] For a survey of the matrimonial history of George II's daughters, see Baker-Smith, 'The Daughters of George II'. See also Appendix D.

the Houses of Parliament on 6 March 'to acquaint them with the intended Marriage' and the newspapers' information was that it was 'to be consummated in May next'.[48] For once, the prediction about the date held good, though the occasion was very different from the royal weddings of 1734 and 1736. According to Lord Hervey,

the King long ago determined that Prince Frederick should not come over to marry his daughter, because he would not be at the expense of it; and now he was as peremptory in saying his daughter should be married before she went [abroad], because it was below his dignity to send his daughter to a man who, when she came to him, had it in his power to call her his wife or not.[49]

The principal ceremony took place in Kassel on 28 June 1740, Modern Style, but it was preceded by one of espousal at the Chapel Royal on 8 May. Like the previous weddings, this took place in the evening: there was a court Drawing Room at 6 p.m., the procession to the Chapel formed up at 8 p.m., and the ceremony was over about 9.15. At the beginning of the service the Duke of Newcastle, Principal Secretary of State, read the Latin document of Procuration, to which assent was given, and then the Duke of Cumberland, acting as proxy for the bridegroom (who was not present), exchanged vows with Princess Mary in an adapted version of the form of the marriage service in the Book of Common Prayer and placed a ring on her finger. The Archbishop of Canterbury read a Latin speech and gave an English prayer of Benediction, after which the reports of the service merely state that 'an Anthem was sung',[50] and seventy-two witnesses present, most of them noblemen, signed the 'Instrument' confirming that the ceremony had taken place. This was clearly not an event on the same scale as the previous Royal weddings. The ceremony was conducted by the Archbishop of Canterbury rather than the Bishop of London, as Dean of the Chapel,[51] but the Chapel Royal and the King's Musicians were in attendance and the event justified the performance of an orchestrally accompanied anthem. It appears that Handel's contribution was a pasticcio of movements from his previous anthems for the weddings of 1734 and 1736.

---

[48] *DA*, 7 Mar. 1740, where the prospective bridegroom is wrongly identified as Prince William.

[49] Sedgwick, *Some Materials*, 931. Hervey's note of the Council meeting on 9 May 1740 (ibid. 929–32) describes the constitutional and dynastic problems relating to the wedding arrangements. *LG*, 6–10 May, described the London event as 'The Ceremony of the Espousals, or Contract of Marriage'.

[50] *LG*, 6–10 May, repeated in subsequent newspaper reports.

[51] Hervey records the dispute between the Archbishop and the Bishop over which of them should officiate, concluding 'The Bishop of London was absent [from the ceremony]': Sedgwick, *Some Materials*, 930, 932.

For information about the content of Handel's anthem we are entirely reliant on a text that was printed in the newspapers, introduced in *The Daily Gazetteer* for 8 May as 'the Wedding Anthem for the Princess Mary, as composed and set to Musick by Mr Handell' (see Fig. 13.1). This text is reproduced in Table 13.1, which indicates the source of the movements from the previous wedding anthems. No musical source survives for an anthem in this form, nor are there any markings on musical sources for the contributory movements that relate to their reuse in 1740. However, the scheme works well enough as both a literary and a musical sequence, apart from a key jolt between movements 2 and 3, so perhaps the pre-existing movements were simply laid together without any alteration to musical content. The framework is that of the 1736 wedding anthem, with three movements from the 1734 anthem replacing the bass aria 'Thy wife shall be as the fruitful vine': perhaps it was noticed that the relevant 'thy' would not be present in 1740 to be told of his felicity. The unoriginality of the anthem's music was apparently no secret to those who had an interest in the matter, such as Thomas Harris, who wrote to his brother on 10 May: 'There was nothing

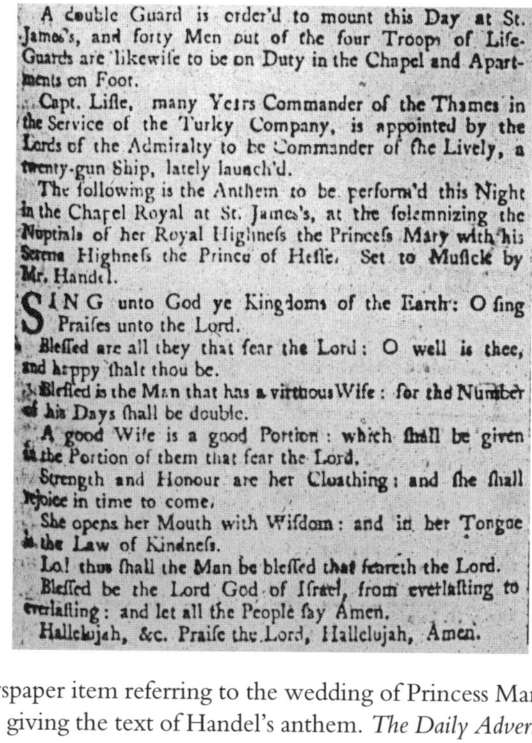

A double Guard is order'd to mount this Day at St. James's, and forty Men out of the four Troops of Life-Guards are likewise to be on Duty in the Chapel and Apartments on Foot.

Capt. Lifle, many Years Commander of the Thames in the Service of the Turky Company, is appointed by the Lords of the Admiralty to be Commander of the Lively, a twenty-gun Ship, lately launch'd.

The following is the Anthem to be perform'd this Night in the Chapel Royal at St. James's, at the solemnizing the Nuptials of her Royal Highnefs the Princefs Mary with his Serene Highnefs the Prince of Heſſe. Set to Muſick by Mr. Handel.

SING unto God ye Kingdoms of the Earth: O ſing Praiſes unto the Lord.

Bleſſed are all they that fear the Lord: O well is thee, and happy fhalt thou be.

Bleſſed is the Man that has a virtuous Wife: for the Number of his Days fhall be double.

A good Wife is a good Portion: which fhall be given to the Portion of them that fear the Lord.

Strength and Honour are her Cloathing: and fhe fhall rejoice in time to come.

She opens her Mouth with Wiſdom: and in her Tongue is the Law of Kindnefs.

Lo! thus fhall the Man be bleſſed that feareth the Lord.

Bleſſed be the Lord God of Iſrael, from everlaſting to everlaſting: and let all the People fay Amen.

Hallelujah, &c. Praiſe the Lord, Hallelujah, Amen.

Fig. 13.1. Newspaper item referring to the wedding of Princess Mary and the Prince of Hesse-Cassel, giving the text of Handel's anthem. *The Daily Advertiser*, 8 May 1740. British Library

Table 13.1. *The 1740 Wedding Anthem*

Text[a]	Music	Key	Voice[b]
Sing unto God ye Kingdoms of the Earth: O sing Praises unto the Lord.	1736	D Major	Ch, A
Blessed are all they that fear the Lord: O well is thee, and happy shalt thou be.	1736	A Major	S
Blessed is the Man that has a virtuous Wife: for the Number of his Days shall be double.	1734	G Major	B
A good Wife is a good Portion: which shall be given in the Portion of them that fear the Lord.	1734	D Minor	S
Strength and Honour are her Cloathing: and she shall rejoice in time to come.	1734	Bb major	T
She opens her Mouth with Wisdom: and in her Tongue is the Law of Kindness.		[continuation of aria]	
Lo! thus shall the Man be blessed that feareth the Lord.	1736	F major	
Blessed be the Lord God of Israel, from everlasting to everlasting: and let all the People say Amen.	1736	D major	T, Ch[c]
Hallelujah, &c. Praise [ye] the Lord, Hallelujah, Amen.		[continuation of movement]	

[a] As given in *DA*, 8 May 1740, introduced by: 'The following is the Anthem to be perform'd this Night in the Chapel Royal at St James's, at the solemnizing the Nuptials of her Royal Highness the Princess Mary with his Serene Highness the Prince of Hesse. Set to Musick by Mr. Handel.' The version of the text printed in *DG*, 8 May, was identical in content but divided verses 1, 2, 4, and 8, producing 13 verses.

[b] 'Ch' indicates a chorus movement.

[c] Accompanied recitative for tenor, leading into chorus with tenor solos.

new in the anthem which was performed at Princess Mary's wedding, being partly that made for the Prince of Orange, partly for the Prince of Wale's.'[52] It was perhaps by accident rather than by design that the assembly process ended up with a more extensive anthem than that for the Prince of Wales's wedding.

The performance of the anthem received the usual minimal coverage in the newspapers. The *Daily Gazetteer* followed up the publication of the anthem text quoted above with the following report the next day, 9 May: 'The Anthem mentioned in our last was perform'd, the Vocal Parts by the Gentlemen belonging to his Majesty's Chapel Royal, and the Instrumental Parts by his Majesty's band of Musick etc.' The 'etc' is accounted for by a payment to Smith 'for Extraordinary performers of Music, and for Writing the Anthem' (see App. I): the sum involved was slightly more than that for the 1736 wedding, possibly representing one more performer at a rate of 3 gns. plus office fees. If Smith charged the usual rate for providing the music he probably

[52] Burrows and Dunhill, *Music and Theatre*, 97; Thomas Harris had visited Handel the previous day.

did rather well, since the performing material could have been adapted from that used for the anthems at the previous weddings. There was a report of one rehearsal:

Yesterday, at Mr. Gates's, was a Practice of a fine new Anthem compos'd by Mr. Handel, for her Royal Highness the Princess Mary's Marriage; the Vocal Parts by Mess. Abbot, Chelsum, Beard, Church of Dublin, Gates, Lloyd, and the Boys of the Chapel Royal; the Instrumental by his Majesty's Band of Musicians, and several additional Hands from the Operas, &c. (*DA*, 6 May 1740)

'Church of Dublin' was John Church, a cathedral singer from Dublin, and subsequently one of the soloists for Handel's performances of *Messiah* in that city in 1742. He was probably related to John Church, a senior member of the choirs of the Chapel Royal and Westminster Abbey who died in January 1740/1. John of Dublin may have been in London to visit his namesake, and also to pursue the prospects of a London appointment for himself: in 1741 he took up a place as Vicar Choral at Christ Church, Dublin, instead.[53] In the 1740 wedding anthem Abbot and Beard presumably repeated their solo roles in 'Blessed is the man' and 'Blessed be the Lord God of Israel / And let all the people say amen' respectively. Beard probably also sang 'Strength and honour', though another Chapel Royal tenor (such as James Chelsum) may have done so if he had also sung the movement in 1734. Edward Lloyd may have sung the alto solos in the first movement: a Priest of the Chapel, he had been a soloist in the court odes since New Year 1735.[54] The letter of Thomas Harris quoted above continues with 'I hear that Beard is gone off together with his lady, who I believe had contracted debts before her marriage': the wedding anthem may have been Beard's last appearance before he left London, where he did not perform during the season of 1740–1. The solo chorister may just possibly have been William Randall, who was named as a soloist for the birthday ode in November 1742;[55] it is also possible that the two treble arias were taken by different boys.

According to the newspapers, orders were given to the Board of Works at the beginning of April 'for fitting up the Chapel Royal at St. James's, in the same manner it was at his Royal Highness the Prince of Wales's Wedding', and on 29 April, when the wedding was only just over a week away, orders were again given for preparing the Chapel.[56] In contrast to the 1736 wedding, there

---

[53] He had previously held a half place at St Patrick's Cathedral: see Brian Boydell, *A Dublin Musical Calendar*, 274.

[54] Lloyd's vocal range is uncertain: his name appears on a tenor part in GB-Lcm MS 224 (Greene, Te Deum).

[55] *DA*, 1 Nov. 1742.

[56] *DA*, 3 Apr., 29 Apr. 1740.

was on this occasion plenty of time for refurnishing the interior, since the ceremony took place according to the predicted timetable, and there was a period of more than a month following Easter Sunday for the preparations. However, it seems doubtful that the gallery over the altar was constructed again in 1740: this time, the newspapers have no reports of activity by workmen in the Chapel, and there was no payment to Shrider for taking down the organ and supplying a replacement. We can only guess how any problems of pitch difference would have been resolved.

The anthem came at an interesting time in Handel's career. On 23 April he had, at Lincoln's Inn Fields theatre, completed his first season of all-English works, which had included the first performances of the *Song for St Cecilia's Day* and *L'Allegro, il Penseroso ed il Moderato*. Two days before the end of the season his Concerti Grossi Op. 6 had appeared, 'Publish'd for the Author': the subscribers included Princess Mary, the Princess of Orange, Princesses Amelia, Caroline, and Louisa, and the Duke of Cumberland (but not the Prince of Wales). Soon after the wedding both Handel and the King left London for visits to the Continent—in the King's case, very soon afterwards, on 14 May. Princess Mary did not depart until 6 June.

There were no more royal weddings in London during the lifetime of either Handel or George II. Princesses Amelia and Caroline remained unmarried (Caroline died before Handel, in 1757), as did the Duke of Cumberland. Princess Louisa married Frederick, son of the King of Denmark, at Christiansborg in December 1743, but there was no court ceremony in London because the betrothal by proxy was conducted in Hanover. Louisa died in 1751, just after her 27th birthday. By 1740 the Princess of Wales had given birth to three of her eventual nine children: the first of those to be married would be her eldest son in 1761, about a year after his accession as King George III.

The Funeral of Queen Caroline, 1737

Queen Caroline was not as actively involved with music-making as her eldest daughter, but she was nevertheless an important supporter of Handel's music. While political and domestic motives may have played a part in this support, for example in the conspicuous attendance of the King and Queen at Handel's 1734–5 opera season which the Prince of Wales boycotted, it seems likely that she also had a liking for the composer and his music, originating from his period of activity at the court of Hanover in 1710–11.[57] Her death in 1737 was caused by complications arising from a long-term gynaecological problem that

---

[57] See Burrows, 'Handel and Hanover', 39, 54.

had probably undermined her health for some years, but her end was relatively sudden and unexpected. At the beginning of 1737, indeed, there was more concern over the condition of the King than the Queen. On his return journey from Hanover he experienced unusually dangerous conditions for the North Sea crossing, which gave the Queen (who was, as usual, Regent during the King's absence) a considerable period of anxiety: at one stage there was a possibility that the King's boat had been destroyed at sea. Furthermore, once the King returned he was unwell for a time because a chill that he had caught during his journey turned into a fever. The year was marked by growing tension between the Prince of Wales and his parents, which came to a head following the Prince's decision on 31 July to move his wife back from Hampton Court to St James's when she went into labour with their first child. This was done without consulting or informing the King, and a dispute ensued which led to a complete breakdown in the relationship between the King and the Prince, culminating in the ejection of the Prince and Princess from St James's Palace, in the same manner that his parents had been forced to leave by George I in 1717. There was a difference in the situation, however, because Frederick had by the mid-1730s had attracted a range of supporters, and as a result the dissension within the royal family took on a more serious political dimension, at a time when there were also various incidents of civil disorder. By the end of 1736 the King and the Queen had already experienced personal unpopularity of a type that had not previously been significant for the Hanoverians, while the Prince's popularity was rising: the fractured atmosphere was reflected in satirical literature, including theatrical productions which eventually prompted the Licensing Act of June 1737.[58]

The situation was stressful for Queen Caroline, but there was no sign in the early autumn of 1737 that her health was endangered, or that her normal activities were impaired. On 29 October the King and Queen attended a performance of the pasticcio *Arsace* on the first night of the opera season at the King's Theatre, having just returned from Hampton Court in order to be at St James's Palace as usual for the King's birthday. The birthday itself (30 October) fell on a Sunday, so the usual court celebrations, including the performance of Greene's birthday ode, took place the next day. At St James's Caroline was occupied with establishing a new library, and it was while she was giving directions to the workmen in the library on 9 November that she was taken ill. Within a couple of days it became apparent that her condition was critical and she was no longer seen in public: after eleven days of patiently borne suffering she died on 20 November. The tragi-comical scenes of her last

---

[58] See Liesenfeld, *The Licensing Act of 1737*, esp. pp. 64–70, concerning the unpopularity of the King and the Queen at this time.

conversations with George II and her children are recorded in one of the most vivid and moving sections of Lord Hervey's memoirs.[59]

For Handel also, 1737 was a year of health problems, though the consequences for him were not in the end so grievous. Towards the end of April, while still in the midst of a very busy opera season at Covent Garden, he was afflicted, apparently without warning, with a 'rheumatick palsie' which paralysed his right arm.[60] He managed to complete the opera season with the assistance of J. C. Smith junior (who played the harpsichord and probably acted as musical director): the last performance was on 25 June. John Mainwaring, the composer's first biographer, recorded that as a result of Handel's illness 'his senses were disordered at intervals', but he survived various medical treatments including the 'vapour-baths' at Aix-la-Chapelle in September–October, and made a prodigiously successful recovery.[61] He probably returned to London at the end of October, about the time of the King's birthday, to a very unusual situation in relation to the forthcoming performances of Italian opera. At the close of the 1736–7 season the Opera of the Nobility had faced a crisis which led to the end of that institution in its previous form: the financial problems of the company had become severe and its star singer—the castrato Farinelli—left London, never to return. The company was re-formed, probably under the executive control of directors from the Nobility Opera, including the Earl of Delawar. Handel was offered, and accepted, the opportunity to compose two operas for them on commission, instead of running his own season at Covent Garden: the deal was apparently done before he left London for Aix-la-Chapelle.[62] He made a start on the composition of the first of the operas, *Faramondo*, on 15 November.

By then the gravity of the Queen's condition was public knowledge: the newspapers reported the 'utmost Consternation' and a 'perfect State of Despondency' at court, and also the hurried return to London of Robert Walpole after his wife's funeral in Norfolk.[63] Nevertheless Handel pressed on with his work as usual, completing the draft of Act I of *Faramondo* on 28 November and Act II on 4 December. Then he laid the score aside in order to compose the Funeral Anthem. His annotation at the completion of Act II of *Faramondo* is unusually explicit in recording the exact moment as 10 p.m. on Sunday evening:[64] perhaps he broke his normal working routine by continuing until

[59] Sedgwick, *Some Materials*, 889–914.

[60] Burrows and Dunhill, *Music and Theatre*, 26.

[61] Mainwaring, *Memoirs*, 121–3, and Landgraf, 'Aachen und Burtscheid'.

[62] See Burrows and Dunhill, *Music and Theatre*, 31; also Burrows, 'Handel and the London Opera Companies', 160–2, and Ch. 8, p. 210.

[63] *SJ*, 21 Nov., report headed 'London, Nov. 15.'; *DA*, 15 Nov.

[64] GB-Lbl RM 20.a.13, fo. 60ᵛ.

late Sunday evening, bringing the act to a conclusion in order to clear the way for the other, previously unscheduled, task. The autograph of the anthem is not dated at the beginning, but Handel completed it on 12 December; most likely, he had begun on 5 December. In a footnote to his history of music, written nearly forty years later, John Hawkins related his timetable for the anthem as follows: 'It was on a Wednesday that he received orders from the King to compose it, the words having been previously selected for the purpose and approved. On the Saturday se'ennight after[wards] it was rehearsed in the morning, and on the evening of the same day it was performed at the solemnity in the chapel of King Henry VII.'[65] Hawkins does not indicate the source of his information, and his timetable cannot be quite correct, though the general picture of the concentrated period of composition is true enough. If indeed Handel received a specific command on a Wednesday to compose the anthem under the terms stated, this could have been on 30 November: a week later he would already have been engaged on the composition of the anthem, and must have received the text. In view of his association with the royal family and the Chapel Royal, Handel no doubt anticipated that he would be called upon, if special music was to be performed at the funeral. The most remarkable aspect of the situation is perhaps that he appears to have left the composition of the anthem so late, instead of breaking off work on *Faramondo* sooner: the Queen had been dead three weeks before he began on the Funeral Anthem, and it was completed only a week before the funeral itself.

The extended period of nearly a month between the Queen's death and burial, which gave Handel time to continue work on the opera as well as composing the anthem, is attributable to the extensive building works that were required at Westminster Abbey. Because of the relative suddenness of her decline and death, no advance planning seems to have been in place for the ceremonial of the Queen's funeral or the disposal of her remains. The preceding monarchs who had died in Britain (Mary II, William III, Anne) were buried in King Henry VII's Chapel at Westminster Abbey, and this would be the site for Queen Caroline's burial, as also eventually for her husband and some of her children.[66] Space in King Henry VII's Chapel was limited, so large galleries were built in the procession area of the Abbey itself in order to accommodate people who had a right to attend the funeral service,[67] but these (as with the galleries in the Royal Chapels for the weddings) were temporary wooden structures. More serious and extensive was the major structural masonry work that was undertaken on the vault in King Henry

---

[65] Hawkins, *A General History*, ii. 913.
[66] Prince George William, her son who had died in infancy, was already buried there.
[67] See the description in *GEP*, 10–13 Dec.

VII's Chapel, and the preparation of a large outer coffin of marble that would eventually receive the coffins of both the Queen and the King.[68] (The new arrangements for the vault affected most of the area under the floor of the Chapel, and its completion effectively closed off the history of royal burials: George II and Caroline were the last monarchs to be buried at Westminster.) There was an initial delay because of a dispute between the Board of Works and the Abbey over their relative responsibilities,[69] but this was quickly resolved and the progress of the work was reported regularly in the newspapers. As usual with royal events, the date for the funeral was the subject of successive rumours, though in this case the situation was made more difficult because of the unpredictable timetable for the completion of the vault. An early estimate was that it would not be ready until after Christmas; concerning the Queen's funeral, it was expected that the 'Manner of her Interment will be like that of Queen Mary, King William's Queen'.[70] On 30 November the speculation was that 'her late Majesty's Funeral will be on Tuesday the 20th of December, in a private Manner'.[71] In the event Caroline received a 'private' funeral, instead of a state funeral as had been accorded to Mary II in 1695, but this did not involve a dramatic reduction in the ceremonial or the lavishness of the provision.[72] On 1 December it was rumoured that the Queen would be interred on 23 December 'between the hours of one and three in the Morning',[73] but soon afterwards a definite date was set for 17 December, and orders for the funeral procession were issued on Wednesday 7 December.[74] The details of the funeral ceremony were probably agreed the same day, including provision for the anthem at the end of the service.

The first public reference to the anthem followed soon afterwards, on 10 December: 'The Anthem to be sung in Westminster-Abbey, at her Majesty's Funeral, it's reckon'd will take up near an Hour in performing. The Musick, which is said to be exceedingly grand and solemn, is compos'd by Mr. Handell, and the Words by Dr. Green.'[75] By that date the composition of the music had not been completed, though perhaps an estimate of the duration of the anthem

---

[68] The Queen's coffin had a removable side panel that was withdrawn when her husband was buried next to her.

[69] *OW*, 1 Dec., repeating an item from an unidentified newspaper for 26 Nov.

[70] *DA*, 23, 22 Nov.

[71] *DA*, 30 Nov.

[72] On the nature of 'private' royal funerals, see Fritz, 'From "Public" to "Private" '. *DG*, 2 Dec., printed the ceremonial from Queen Anne's 'private' funeral, having given that from Queen Mary's state funeral the previous week. *LEP*, 20–2 Dec. reported that 50,000 yards of bays and black cloth had been provided for the mourning in 1737.

[73] *SJEP*, 29 Nov.–1 Dec.

[74] *GEP, LEP*, 3–6 Dec.; *SJEP*, 6–8 Dec.

[75] *LEP*, 8–10 Dec.

could have been made from the text. The inclusion of the anthem in the scheme for the service entailed further special construction, as reported on 12 December: 'They are putting up a Gallery in King Henry the Seventh's Chapel, where an Organ is to be built by Mr Schrider, his Majesty's Organ-Builder, as fast as possible, for the Performance of a solemn Anthem the Night her Majesty is interr'd.'[76] Another report gives the location of the gallery: 'They are erecting a Scaffold at the West-End to hold an Organ, and the Gentlemen of the Choir who are to perform the Anthem.'[77] It seems probable that the organ and the gallery were not sufficiently ready to be used for a rehearsal until shortly before the day of the funeral. Meanwhile, opportunities were taken to hold public rehearsals in a number of more comfortable and convenient venues.

The first rehearsal, on Wednesday 14 December, was reported in the newspapers the next day, preceded by the text of the anthem: 'The above Anthem was yesterday Morning rehears'd at the French Chapel adjoining to St. James's Palace; there were about 140 Performers; it took up just 50 minutes in the Rehearsal, and the Music was extremely grand and solemn; his Majesty and some of the Royal Family were *incognito* in the Closet at the said Chapel to hear it.'[78] The rehearsal was also mentioned in a letter of 16 December from Princess Amelia to Princess Anne in the Netherlands: 'We had Handel's Anthem last Wednesday in the French Chapel, that the King might hear it in Carolin's Bedchamber, and it's the finest cruel touching thing that ever was heard.'[79] Smith's team must have worked intensively to provide the performing materials within forty-eight hours of Handel completing the composition. The principal public rehearsal followed on Friday in the Banqueting House Chapel, and was reported next day: 'the fine Anthem, set to Musick by Mr Handell...was rehearsed yesterday twice at the Chapel at Whitehall to a crowded Audience.'[80] As with the performance of Handel's music for the Chapel Royal Fund in the same building in 1733, the rehearsal prompted a commemoration in verse, this time a two-stanza poem by John Lockman beginning 'Struck with the Beauties form'd by magic Dyes', the 'Magic Dyes' referring to Rubens's painted ceiling at the Banqueting House Chapel.[81] There may also have been some last-minute rehearsal in the organ gallery of the Chapel at the Abbey on the Saturday itself.

[76] *DA*, 12 Dec.
[77] *LEP*, 10–13 Dec. The wording of the report suggests that it may not have been possible to begin construction of the gallery until some of the work on the vault had been completed, perhaps because the flooring had been removed.
[78] *LEP*, 13–15 Dec.
[79] Quoted in Richard G. King, 'Handel's Travels', 384.
[80] *WEP*, 15–17 Dec.; *LEP*, 10–13 Dec., had predicted a rehearsal 'in the Choir of Westminster Abbey' on 15 Dec., but there is no subsequent report that this took place.
[81] *OW*, 4 Jan. 1738, *WM*, 6 Jan.; Deutsch, *Handel*, 448.

Meanwhile other arrangements for the funeral had proceeded. The Queen's body was moved from St James's Palace to the Prince's Chamber next to the House of Lords, and the additional furnishings in King Henry VII's Chapel included a large chandelier with 200 wax candles and a canopy throne for Princess Amelia as the chief mourner. (Neither the King nor the other immediate members of the family were to be present at the funeral.) In an echo of the arrangements from the recent weddings, the seat was provided 'for the comfort of the Princess during the Funeral Solemnity and the Anthem'.[82] Around the period of the funeral, ''Tis computed, that the Servants to the Board of Works and the Gentlemen of the Choir of the Abbey, receiv'd between 5 and 600 £, in shewing King Henry the VII's Chapel and the new Vault.'[83]

It had been variously expected that the funeral would begin at 10 p.m. or at midnight on Saturday 17 December,[84] and there may have been a deliberate attempt to conceal the real plans from the wider London public. Eventually, 'The Funeral of her late Majesty was performed between the hours of Six and Nine last Saturday Night. . . . The Funeral being much earlier than expected, the Concourse of People was not so great as was thought, and we do not hear of any Mischief that happened.'[85] Nevertheless, the quantity of people attending the funeral must have been considerable. The participants in the procession would have crammed King Henry VII's Chapel, and there were many onlookers in the Abbey: tickets for seats in the galleries in the Choir, which had a good view of the procession as it passed down the Abbey to the Chapel, changed hands at a guinea each for the first three rows and half a guinea each for the remainder.[86]

The procession for the funeral began at 6 p.m. and, like the coronation procession, it was met at the North Door by the Dean and Prebendaries of the Abbey, 'with the Masters, Scholars and the Choir belonging to the same, and the Choir of the Chapel Royal, attending there in their proper Habits, with Wax Tapers in their Hands'; they joined the procession and 'the Moment the Royal Corpse entered the Church, they began to sing the Anthem in the Burial-Service [probably Croft's setting of the Burial Sentences], which lasted till the whole Procession passed thro' the North and South Isles of the Church, to King Henry the Seventh's Chapel'. In the Chapel, the Dean of Westminster read 'that Part of the Burial-Office [from the Book of Common Prayer], appointed to be read at the Grave: Which being finished, and the Royal Body interred, Garter King at Arms proclaimed Her late Majesty's titles. Then followed another Anthem composed on Purpose for this Solemn

---

[82] *DA*, 16 Dec.
[83] *RWJ*, 24 Dec.
[84] *GEP*, 10–13 Dec.; *WEP*, 15–17 Dec.
[85] *WEP*, 17–20 Dec.
[86] *AOWJ*, 17 Dec.

Occasion.'[87] After the performance of Handel's anthem the procession left the Chapel 'the nearest way' to the North Door of the Abbey, and so presumably not returning through the Choir. As at the 1727 coronation, there may have been some imperfections in the musical arrangements (though this time not affecting Handel's music) resulting from bad communications: George Carleton, Sub-Dean of the Chapel Royal and Chanter of Westminster Abbey, recorded the events in King Henry VII's Chapel as follows:

> Being come there, it was order'd that Both the Psalms in the Burial-Service should be sung to the Organ: which (by some Accident) was omitted. The Hymns in the Burial-Office were sung in the Organ Loft. The Organist of West[minste]r perform'd in the Church of West[minste]r and the Organist of the King's Chapel in H[enry] the 7ths Chapel. After the Anthem (compos'd for voices and instruments) was perform'd, the Stiles being pronounced by the King at Arms, the whole Ceremony ended.[88]

Newspaper reports of the service and the rehearsals comment on the length of Handel's anthem and the number of performers. The length of the anthem is also noted in letters written the next day by two men who were named as taking part in the procession, and would therefore have been in the Chapel, the Duke of Chandos:

> The Solemnity of the Queen's Funeral was very decent, and performed in more order than any thing I have seen of the like kind. . . . It began about a quarter before 7, & was over a little after ten; the Anthem took up three quarter of an hour of the time, of which the composition was exceeding fine, and adapted very properly to the melancholly occasion of it; but I can't say so much of the performance.

and the Bishop of Chichester:

> The funeral service was performed by the Bishop of Rochester as Dean of Westminster. After the service there was a long anthem, the words by the Sub-dean, the music set by Mr. Handel, and is reckoned to be as good a piece as he ever made: it was above fifty minutes in singing.[89]

One newspaper reported that 'the fine Anthem of Mr Handel's was perform'd about nine', which would have been about right.[90]

A handsomely printed folio-size sheet with the text of the anthem, headed simply 'THE ANTHEM.' and saying '*Compos'd by Mr.* HANDEL' below the text (see Fig. 13.2),[91] seems to have been issued officially for the funeral; this is

---

[87] *LG*, 20–4 Dec., repeated in other newspapers and *GM*, vii (Dec. 1737), 765–6. For further details of the procession and ceremonial, see Landgraf, 'Die Begräbniszeremonie für Queen Caroline'.

[88] *WA2*, pp. 39–40.

[89] Letters of the Duke of Chandos and Francis Hare, 18 Dec. 1737; Deutsch, *Handel*, 443.

[90] *DA*, 19 Dec., the source for the newspaper extract for 22 Dec., Deutsch, *Handel*, 444.

[91] Copy at GB-Lwa Muniments 6269.

THE

ANTHEM.

LAM. I. ver.4. **T**HE ways of *Zion* do mourn, and she is in bitter-
ver. 11. nefs; All her people figh, and hang down their
II. ver. 10. heads to the ground.

1 SAM. i. 19. How are the Mighty fall'n ! She that was Great among
LAM. i. 1. the nations, and Princefs of the provinces !

JOB xxix. 14 She put on righteoufnefs, and it cloathed her : Her judgment was a robe and a diadem.

ver. 11. When the ear heard her, then it bleffed her ; and when
the eye faw her, it gave witnefs to her.

ver. 12. She deliver'd the poor that cried, the fatherlefs, and him
that had none to help him.

ECCLUS. Kindnefs, meeknefs, and comfort were in her tongue.
xxxvi. ver. 23.

PHILIP. iv. 8. If there was any virtue, and if there was any praife ; fhe
thought on thofe things.

PSAL. cxii. 6. The Righteous fhall be had in everlafting remembrance ;
DAN. xii. 3. and the Wife fhall fhine as the brightnefs of the firmament.

ECCLUS. xliv. Their bodies are buried in peace, but their name liveth
ver. 14. evermore.

ver. 15. The people will tell of their wifdom, and the congregation will fhew forth their praife.

WISD. v. 15. Their reward alfo is with the LORD, and the care of them
is with the MOST HIGH.

ver. 16. They fhall receive a glorious kingdom, and a beautiful
crown from the LORD's hand.

PSAL. ciii. 17. The merciful goodnefs of the LORD endureth for ever
on them that fear him, and his righteoufnefs on chil-
drens children.

Compos'd by Mr. HANDEL.

Fig. 13.2. The text of Handel's anthem for the funeral of Queen Caroline, 1737.
1500 copies of the sheet were printed. Westminster Abbey Muniments 6929

probably the item referred to in the Chapel Royal Cheque Book, 'Fifteen hundred Papers of the Anthem for the Funeral were printed'.[92] Another, rather smaller, sheet also seems to have been in circulation, less accurate in the text and the biblical references for the verses, and not naming the composer;[93] yet more versions of the text with different inaccuracies were printed in the newspapers for 13–15 December.[94] After the funeral some newspapers gave the text again, with the introduction, 'There having been some Mistakes made in the Publick Papers in Printing the Anthem performed at Her MAJESTY's Funeral; it may not be improper to publish a Correct Copy of the Words chose on so Solemn an occasion',[95] but in fact the former mistakes had only been in details (of words and biblical references) and the substance of the anthem text had been presented. The tone of the comment suggests that the compiler of the text had made a complaint to one or more of the newspapers.

Very soon after the funeral, and perhaps even interleaved with the preceding rehearsals of the anthem, Handel picked up his work on *Faramondo*, which still required the composition of Act III. This he completed on 24 December, exactly a week after the funeral service. Following normal London practice upon the death of a monarch, the theatres had been closed, since 20 November. They reopened on 2 January and *Faramondo* was performed the next day, the first available opera night in the calendar. Of the first performance one newspaper reported that 'It being the first Time of Mr. Handel's Appearance this Season, he was honour'd with extraordinary and repeated Signs of Approbation'.[96] The newspapers also noted a rehearsal of the opera on 28 December.[97] Perhaps it was coincidental that a 'Genealogy of the late Illustrious and most Excellent Queen Caroline', published in one of the newspapers on 10 December 1737, had begun with 'PHARAMOND, Duke of the East Franks, AD 404'.[98]

The Ways of Zion do mourn (HWV 264)

The anthem text, probably the work of George Carleton, Sub-Dean of the Chapel Royal,[99] was assembled from disparate scriptural verses and part-verses.

---

[92] *NCB*, p. 155; Ashbee and Harley, i. 317.
[93] *The Anthem, To be Sung at Her Majesty's Funeral* (no composer named): copy in GB-Lbl C.145.a.25, bound with a commemorative poem on the Queen's death.
[94] *GEP*, *LEP*, *SJEP*, and *WEP*, 13–15 Dec.; also *AOWJ*, *CJ*, and *RWJ*, 17 Dec.
[95] *SJEP*, 17–20 Dec., repeated in *Common Sense*, 24 Dec.
[96] *LDP*, 4 Jan.   [97] *WEP*, 27–9 Dec.   [98] *RWJ*, 10 Dec. 1737.
[99] From Hare's letter (see p. 366) it is usually attributed to Edward Willes, Sub-Dean of Westminster, but see p. 379. The attribution to 'Dr Green' (see p. 363) cannot at present be explained; Carleton was related by marriage to Maurice Greene.

This procedure was to be found in the texts of previous English anthems, and in the introductory verses for the special Fast and Thanksgiving liturgies, but in those the integrity of the original verses had usually been preserved. Here the scriptural material contributed to a new mosaic, without any apparent restraint in reshaping the stones to make them fit.[100] In the verses from the Book of Job, the original author's 'I' and 'me' were replaced with 'she' and 'her'; the 'she' of the opening chorus, in its original context from the Book of Lamentations, referred to the city of Jerusalem; 'How are the mighty fallen' comes from David's lament over Saul and Jonathan; 'If there was any virtue' was adapted from an exhortation given to the early Christians by the writer of Philippians. The verses do not repeat any from the funeral sentences in the Burial Service which were sung during the procession, and there are no obvious English precedents for the anthem text as a whole, though 'How are the mighty fallen' and 'She that was great among the nations and princess of the provinces' were used in Bononcini's funeral anthem for the Duke of Marlborough in 1722,[101] in which the latter text retained its original context of the 'solitary city'. The eclectic selection of the source texts is remarkable: this may have been the first English anthem for which an author made full use of Cruden's concordance to the English Bible.[102] The Psalm texts follow the forms from the Book of Common Prayer, but the rest of the verses were directly adapted from the Authorized Version of the Bible and the Apocrypha: apart from obviously intentional amendments, the only significant change is 'their name liveth evermore' rather than 'their name liveth for evermore'. If we accept the legitimacy of the procedure for creating the anthem text, which formed an afterpiece to the liturgy of the Burial Service itself, then the carpentry and reapplication of the texts is effective. Verses from Samuel and Lamentations joined up well for 'How are the mighty fall'n' / 'She that was great', and verses from a Psalm and the Book of Daniel similarly for 'The Righteous shall be had in everlasting remembrance'/'and the wise shall shine': in the latter the sequence continued particularly happily with verses from Ecclesiasticus and Wisdom, 'Their reward' even preserving the original subject (the Righteous) of the verse from Wisdom.

There is no evidence for any influence from Handel over the selection of the text of the anthem: most likely Handel set the text in the form it was sent to

---

[100] See Ruth Smith, *Handel's Oratorios*, 103–7, which gives a detailed table of the anthem text and the biblical source texts: Smith describes this as 'the greatest collage anthem of Handel's time'.

[101] Bononcini, *When Saul was King*, nos. 2 and 3.

[102] *DA*, 22 Nov., noted the publication of Cruden, *A Complete Concordance*, 'which he had the Honour to present to their Majesties a few Days before the Queen's Illness, the Book being dedicated to her Majesty'.

him, though perhaps introducing the subsequent repetitions of 'How are the mighty fall'n' on his own initiative.[103] He treated the text as a continuous sequence and, particularly in the first half, did not follow the grouping of the scriptural sources for his musical movements. The three verses from Job 29 'She put on righteousness/When the ear heard her/She delivered the poor' are divided, the first serving to conclude the opening block of movements, the second forming a separate movement, and the last beginning a new movement that also takes in verses from Ecclesiasticus and Philippians. It is possible that Handel had originally been given the verses in biblical order ('When the ear/ She delivered/She put on righteousness'), and that the composer made the rearrangement: the verses would have made sense in either order, but 'She delivered the poor' did not fit Handel's musical scheme, as it developed, for the first position.

The musical challenge that Handel set himself was to produce a totally choral setting, with an orchestral accompaniment for strings and oboes (and organ continuo) throughout, in extended movements, serious in tone, yet with sufficient variety to sustain interest.[104] Inevitably the music would be mainly in minor keys, though the text provided opportunity for a substantial major-key area in the section beginning (in Handel's scheme) 'When the ear heard her'. The words implied a moderate, or slower, pace for most of the movements, and Handel extended the challenge by choosing to set all but two movements in quadruple time. The triple metre provides some welcome relief in the second half of the anthem, and indeed 'The righteous shall be had in everlasting remembrance', the first triple-time movement, is also the most energetic in the anthem. In the tonal scheme he also seems to have deliberately chosen a restrained, even severe, pattern. The tonic key of G minor pervades the first quarter of the anthem rather obstinately, and he hauls the music back to that key in the subsequent repetitions of 'How are the mighty fallen', finally to introduce the pivotal movement 'The righteous shall be had in everlasting remembrance'. Thereafter there is an obvious relationship between the key centres of 'Their bodies are buried in peace' (F major) and 'The people will tell of their wisdom (D minor), but the sequence of the final movements (D minor, A minor, G minor) shows no Classical-style logic in the path back to the tonic: rather, it seems that Handel may have seen these movements as having individual and contrasted key characters.

---

[103] The phrase is not repeated in the printed text of the anthem, but this may have been following a literary convention in which such repetitions would not have been included: the same applied to the anthem's adapted text in the printed word-book for *Israel in Egypt*.

[104] In this I make the assumption that, if he had so wished, he could have employed more varied resources, for example by including flutes or by writing some movements for soloists.

A remarkable feature of the Funeral Anthem is Handel's prominent use of musical phrases derived from Lutheran chorales. The opening theme of 'The ways of Zion do mourn' derives from a chorale melody which is associated in the works of J. S. Bach with the text 'Herr Jesu Christ, du höchstes Gut', though it was used for other texts as well in Handel's time, including one beginning 'Herr Jesu Christ, ich weiss gar wohl dass ich einmal muss sterben', the recollection of which could have provided the link to the composer's use of the melody in the anthem.[105] The same theme also formed the basis of the fugue for 'And the congregation shall shew forth their praise' later in the anthem. Another chorale melody, associated with the text 'Du Friedefürst, Herr Jesu Christ', is explicitly used (though without the initial note) for the text beginning 'Kindness, meekness and comfort were in her tongue' in 'She deliver'd the poor that cried', and less explicitly it also generated the theme at the start of that movement. (The same melodic shape is also found at 'Thou art the King of Glory, O Christ' in the Cannons Te Deum, subsequently reworked in the Chapel Royal A major Te Deum.)[106] The fugue for 'And the congregation shall shew forth their praise' may have originated from a keyboard piece based on the chorale, and that for 'She put on righteousness' derives from a keyboard fugue by J. P. Krieger.[107] It has been suggested that when composing the anthem Handel went back to an old notebook of pieces that he had copied when studying under Zachow in Halle forty years previously;[108] given the short timescale of the composition, some reliance on musical borrowings is not at all unlikely, and much of the source material may plausibly have come from German composers. As suggested in Chapter 8, it is also possible that Handel renewed some contact with German music during the Continental visit in 1737 that was necessitated by his health cure at Aix-la-Chapelle. Perhaps he discovered or collected a chorale book and some keyboard pieces then: he would certainly have had time on his hands for looking at pieces of music during the period of his treatment. The two strands of possible influence may have complemented each other; what is certain is that, creatively speaking, chorale melodies and keyboard pieces (some of them based on chorales) in the styles of German composers from his youth became matters of both use and interest to him in the winter and spring of 1737–8. Also of possible relevance is *Psalmodia Germanica*, a book of chorales collected by John Christian Jacobi, the Keeper of the Lutheran Chapel Royal at St James's Palace, which was published in London in the 1720s with English texts.[109]

---

[105] Roberts, 'German Chorales', 78.   [106] Ibid. 91–3.
[107] Ibid. 89; Krieger, *Gesammelte Werke*, 192 (fugue from Toccata in A minor).
[108] Roberts, 'German Chorales', 94–5.
[109] Ibid. 83–4. The music was presented as melodies and figured basses. The texts were in English, but the titles were given in German; the chorales include a large number of those that

What is less certain is that there was any connection between Handel's use of 'German' musical sources and the commemoration of a British Queen who had originated from Germany. It seems most likely that he, as ever, used his borrowing sources primarily because they suited the mood of the music and his own compositional purposes. Most remarkable of all, perhaps, is his use of music from the motet *Ecce quomodo moritur justus* by the Slovenian composer Jacobus Gallus (or Handl; 1550–91) for 'But their name liveth evermore', where the chord on the flat seventh of the scale provides a startling and rather antique musical gesture. Another striking momentary harmonic gesture is the sudden subdominant lurch at one of the repetitions of 'She thought on those things'.[110] The harmonic tensions in the chordal passages for 'How are the mighty fall'n' that introduce 'She deliver'd the poor that cried' and 'The righteous shall be had in everlasting remembrance', on the other hand, seem more naturally part of the musical rhetoric for their type of material, whose ancestry can be traced back to 'Juravit Dominus' in Handel's *Dixit Dominus* and 'Quis sicut Dominus' in his D major setting of *Laudate pueri Dominum*.

The introductory Sinfonia to the anthem, almost certainly composed last, sets the tone with a serious yet lyrical miniature movement, ideal for concentrating and settling the listeners' thoughts after the interment. In its elegiac tone it bears obvious comparison with 'Nimrod' from Elgar's *Enigma Variations*, though the latter acquired its solemn associations after the event since Nimrod himself was very much alive at the time of Elgar's composition. All string parts have a wavy-line ornament over the held note in bars 1–2 which was clearly intended for expressive effect, though the interpretation of the sign here is uncertain. Following the initial four-bar phrase there is a succession of brisk sequential modulations that hint at the musical gestures that are to come later, particularly in the extension of the first phrase from the tonic G minor to B flat major, subsequently confirmed by a full cadence in the major key at bar 9. The opening also sets forth a balance of falling and rising phrases that is to be a feature of the anthem: it is perhaps not too fanciful to see a deliberate (though perhaps unconscious) representation of sighing and 'hang down their heads' on one hand, and the hope of renewed life beyond the immediate circumstances (or at least memorialized reputation) on the other. At some stage Handel cut four bars of the music near the end of the movement, perhaps because he felt that they gave too much weight to the downwards melodic trajectory.

are now familiar from the works of J. S. Bach. The 2nd edn. (1732) represented ninety-three German texts and had fifty-eight chorales. The chorales as given would not have been used in the Lutheran Chapel Royal, which in any case had no musical staff and no musical instrument. See Burrows, 'German Chorales and English Hymns'.

[110] Bars 105–9, *HG* 11, p. 41; *HHA* III/12, p. 44.

The first choral movement sees Handel at his best. The simple chordal opening may have had a direct influence on the similar passage that opens Mozart's *Requiem*. The first violins outline the chorale melody, and then strings are joined by oboes for a sighing figure which introduces the chorus voices. At the end of the first statement of the chorale-derived melody the orchestra prefigures the two short themes that the voices will take up for 'and she is in bitterness' and 'all her people sigh': the material of each of the three elements is developed separately, moving towards the key of C minor, in which the shorter themes are then worked against the chorale melody.[111] In a leisurely and expansive way the music returns to the tonic key of G minor, and there is a grand final statement of the chorale phrase (in canon between alto and bass voices) over a tonic pedal, leading to a concentrated chordal peroration with rhetorical pauses between the sighs. The opening 'movement' turns out to be the first of three sections forming a lengthy paragraph that sustains the tonic key of G minor: it is arguable that the three sections in fact together constitute one movement, since Handel indicates no new tempo for 'How are the mighty fall'n' and 'She puts on righteousness'. Certainly he intended this as one interconnected musical sequence: the first two sections end with dominant pedals.

At the end of the first section the voices, gathered together, descend into gloom as they 'hang their heads to the ground': the reaction in 'How are the mighty fall'n' comes as a protest as much as a lamentation. This text must have needed careful treatment, if the minds of the original listeners were not to be diverted towards a more worldly interpretation relating to Caroline's constant political support for Robert Walpole: Handel almost invites the listener to confront such a possibility by choosing to emphasize these words in his setting.[112] The fallen city from the Book of Lamentations perhaps bore some comparison with the passing of Queen Caroline, as a general parallel could be made in relating present desolation to the recollection of past glories. Handel builds the section around threefold statements of the motto phrase, successively in G minor, F minor, and C minor, followed by a single statement in B flat major before returning to the closing repetitions in the tonic. The intermediate sections are notable for the contrast between the orchestra's descending chromatic phrases and the generally ascending lines for the choir's 'She that was great'. While the conclusion to the first section had included rhetorical cries of 'sigh', this time the word is 'how': it is not impossible that Handel had a slight

---

[111] Roberts, 'German Chorales, 90–1, suggests that the movement might have been based on an earlier German piece, possibly by Alberti, with a single counter-subject to the chorale phrase which provided Handel with his shorter themes.

[112] Compare the very similar situation with his setting of 'Bless the true church and save the King' in *Athalia*, first performed in Oxford where there was some sympathy for Jacobitism.

recollection of 'Howl, howl O ye fir trees' in Bononcini's funeral anthem for the Duke of Marlborough. After the intensity of this section the relative formality of the closing fugue for 'She put on righteousness' comes as a necessary emotional release. As in the first movement, the varied character of the musical material must have been agreeable to Handel, particularly in the cumulative effect introduced by a new figure at bar 8 and the dactylic-rhythm counter-subject at bar 14: the latter provides the lead for a free stretto over a dominant pedal beginning at bar 41 which winds up the opening three-section block in fine style. In the fugue there is the first hint in the anthem of Handel's characteristic way of playing off the rhythms and inflections of the music against the words: for 'a robe and a diadem' this works well enough, but sometimes 'it clothed her' does not sit so easily. The issue arises more prominently later in the anthem, with Handel's treatment of 'It gave witness of her' and 'If there was any virtue'. It seems too simplistic to dismiss these passages as reflecting an imperfect command of the English language on the part of the composer: rather, it shows his preference for striking and strong syllabic treatments, many of which seem deliberately to avoid a bland 'sing-song' option and to present instead a particular, sometimes unconventional, way of reading the text.[113]

'When the ear heard her' begins a major-key block of movements with a more relaxed Andante character. The first of these is straightforward in expression and form: the duet texture for the voices immediately introduces a cooler expressive mode, which is sustained when the four parts come together. Following this movement and the next Handel hauls the music back to the minor key with strong homophonic interjections of 'How are the mighty fall'n', though not using the same rhythms as in the first movement. The verbal logic of repeating 'She that was great among the nations, and princess of the provinces' to introduce 'She delivered the poor that cried' is clear enough, and it was presumably Handel's idea: in practice the transition from the dominant chord of G minor to a movement in B flat major is quite colourful, since we expect the music to revert again to the tonic. Sharp dotted rhythms from 'How are the mighty fall'n' reappear in a different context for 'The fatherless and him that hath none to help him'. The interweaving of the movement's opening material with the chorale-derived melody is effectively managed, and Burney was enthusiastic about the effect at the entry of the unharmonized chorale theme at the 1784 Handel Commemoration:

The trebles singing alone, and only accompanied in unison by treble instruments, at the words—'*kindness, meekness, and comfort were in her tongue*' had an admirable effect, in

---

[113] Burney noted another example, of elision rather than accentuation, in Handel's setting of the word 'deliver'd': Burney, *An Account*, First Performance, 34 n. (a).

point of contract, with the full harmony of this charming Chorus. . . . The beauties of this strain are of every age and country; no change of fashion can efface them, or prevent their being felt by persons of sensibility.[114]

The chorus takes up new treatments of 'Kindness, meekness and comfort were in her tongue' at bars 62 and 89, on both occasions bringing the music briefly back to G minor from the surrounding F major, the conventional mid-movement dominant key. The varied musical materials are integrated with fine rhetorical effect as the movement proceeds; as Burney put it, the movement 'contains all the requisites of Good Music, in plain counterpoint: as good harmony, melody, rhythm, accent, and expression.'[115] When the movement ends, 'How are the mighty fall'n' once again drags the music back to G minor, but this time the tonal invitation is taken up and a movement in G minor follows, 'The righteous shall be had in everlasting remembrance'. It might perhaps have seemed rather dangerous to the scheme of the anthem as a whole to revert back to the tonic and the minor mode so clearly at this point, given the long dose of G minor in the opening sections, but the change of metre to triple time and the generally energetic character of the string writing introduce a new element. It is with this movement, in fact, that the anthem begins a transition in mood: regret and mourning are succeeded by celebration of the completion of a virtuous and model life. As in 'When the ear heard her', the first half of the movement uses the voice parts in various duet combinations, and then all four parts are brought together, returning to the tonic key.

With the following double sequence of 'Their bodies are buried in peace / But their name liveth evermore' Handel produced the same type of alternation as the more famous group beginning 'Since by man came death / By man came also the resurrection of the dead' in *Messiah*, composed nearly four years later. In both cases minor-key passages with restrainedly intense harmony for un-accompanied chorus give place to more optimistic major-key music in the second clause of the text. Here the passages concerned are more extended, and in some aspects more colourful: at the second sequence Handel moves straight from F major to D flat major for 'Their bodies are buried in peace' before proceeding to F minor, and in the major-key sections the cross-rhythms (partly derived from, and presumably suggested by, the Gallus/Handl source) provide a dance-like element. Handel designated the contrasted sections 'piano' and 'forte' but, unlike the *Messiah* parallel, did not indicate any change of speed from the initial 'Grave': it seems unlikely that he was careless in this matter three times over. This sequence of movements subsequently became the best-known part of the Funeral Anthem in Britain because it was extracted as a

[114] Ibid. 34.   [115] Ibid.

separate piece for liturgical use:[116] in context, it clearly functions as the transitional stage in the subject and mood of the anthem. Although the subsequent movements are in minor keys, the cloud of mourning has lifted: 'How are the mighty fall'n' does not recur again. A comparable, but very brief, chordal passage introduces 'The people will tell of their wisdom', but it does not have the harmonic tension of the earlier interjections, and it gives place to the anthem's second smoothly moving fugal movement. As already noted, the subject of this fugue relates closely to the melody of the chorale line that was used in the first choral movement, and it shows a variety of continuations after the initial five-note figure: the more chromatic form first heard in the soprano part is a particularly striking variant. As usual, Handel draws the threads together with broad chordal passages at the conclusion.

In 'They shall receive a glorious kingdom' Handel returns to the duet-type texture for the voices, in various combinations and eventually building up to the full four parts. The opening theme itself is not treated in imitation by the voices, and the various entries suggest a fecundity of invention in different thematic ideas that are subsequently worked together, though the tenor entry at bar 24 is derived from bar 4 of the opening ritornello and the alto's phrase for 'and a beautiful crown' beginning at bar 28 can be seen as a variant on the shape of the original alto theme at bars 17–19. The orchestral bass line cunningly provides harmonic direction and security without committing to a clear cadence until bars 41–2, overlapping with the entry of the bass voice. Perhaps surprisingly, this also marks a point of arrival at the key of D minor, the tonic of the previous movement: as in the anthem's opening movements, it seems as if Handel is deliberately keeping his tonal framework under tight rein in this anthem, in spite of incidental patches of colourful chromatic harmony. The movement returns to the tonic key with the bass-voice entry at bar 60 and various rather attractive excursions ensue, including a descent through the four voices in turn between bars 79 and 87, just before all the parts are brought together. Both in its tonal organization, which is quite free-ranging in some places, and in its melodic diversity this is an interesting and well-composed movement, easily underrated because of its less than prominent position in the anthem. The final movement takes consolation that 'The merciful goodness of the Lord endureth for ever' in simply-expressed phrases, mainly for full choir over a raft of repeated-quaver accompaniment. The opening ritornello provides a final essay in the balance of rising and falling melodic lines, the phrases also becoming progressively longer. A new phrase at bar 28 (returning to the epigrammatic style of bar 1) is echoed between voices and orchestra and provides the stimulus for the anthem's closing ritornello. Although firmly

---

[116] It was included in Davies and Ley, *The Church Anthem Book*.

based in G minor, the movement's brief excursions to B flat major and F major come as memorable moments of relief. Nevertheless, in the end the anthem comes to rest with the open G strings of the orchestra, the violins' lowest note: the passion is spent, but dignity remains.

Handel must have regarded the Funeral Anthem highly, for he made unusually strenuous efforts to secure its further circulation. The opportunities for the reuse of a sequence of choral movements, all serious in tone, were obviously limited. For his benefit night at the King's Theatre in March 1738 he apparently hoped to include the anthem in the programme, but according to the Earl of Shaftesbury the King would not 'suffer the Funeral Anthem to be performed'.[117] It seems most likely that the Italian text which Handel added in pencil to the autograph of the anthem related to this plan, since the singers from the opera company were to take part in his benefit performance. In September 1738 he planned to use most of the anthem in Part III of *Saul* as the Elegy on the death of Saul and Jonathan, though in the end he developed a sequence of new movements for the purpose, in collaboration with Charles Jennens the librettist.[118] The idea had presumably been prompted by the fact that the anthem text included one verse from the biblical elegy. Finally, and probably again in collaboration with Jennens, the complete anthem was used a few weeks later, with only slight changes to verbs and pronouns, to become Part I of a new oratorio, *Israel in Egypt*, where it functioned as 'The Lamentation of the Israelites for the Death of Joseph'. The anthem was balanced in Part III of the oratorio by another extended choral anthem-like sequence, 'The Song of Moses' celebrating the liberation of the Israelites at the Red Sea; Part II comprised the narrative of the plagues and the escape of the Israelites, again primarily related through choral movements. The resulting work was apparently none too popular with the audiences at the King's Theatre because it had gave too little prominence to the solo singers, but it seems to have found favour with a group of connoisseurs, who publicly requested a further performance of the oratorio.[119] The concept of a fully choral anthem with orchestral accompaniment was ambitious in itself: by extending the idea to a complete oratorio Handel seems to have run too far ahead of his theatre audience. It is perhaps surprising that an anthem designed for a solemn royal funeral should have been considered at all for the theatre, but the genre of English oratorio that Handel developed was still at a stage where experiment was possible. The 1739 season during which *Israel in Egypt* was first performed

[117] Letter to James Harris, 14 Mar. 1738; Burrows and Dunhill, *Music and Theatre*, 43.

[118] Handel wrote cues for the use of movements from the anthem in the autograph of *Saul*, GB-Lbl RM 20.g.3, fo. 98ᵛ. See Dean, *Handel's Dramatic Oratorios*, 309, also Hicks, 'Handel, Jennens and *Saul*', 204.

[119] See Burrows and Dunhill, *Music and Theatre*, 68–9.

was unusual because Handel briefly returned from Covent Garden to the King's Theatre: he obviously wanted to fill the space in the theatre with a grand choral sound, on as extensive a scale as possible.[120] When *Israel in Egypt* was revived in the later 1750s the anthem was replaced by a more diverse pasticcio of Handel's music for Part I, but by then artistic control of his oratorio performances had probably passed into the hands of J. C. Smith the younger. Handel had in the interim raided movements from the Funeral Anthem for the Foundling Hospital Anthem in 1749, to be described in Chapter 15.

Conditions of Performance

The newspaper report of the first rehearsal on 14 December, already quoted, referred to 140 performers, and the reports of the funeral itself similarly emphasised the size of the performing group:

After the Burial Service was over, the fine Anthem, set to Musick by Mr. Handel, was performed by upwards of 140 Hands, from the Choirs of St. James's, Westminster, St Paul's and Windsor. (*DG*, 19 Dec.)

The Vocal Parts were perform'd by the several Choirs of the Chapel Royal, Westminster-Abbey and Windsor, and the Boys of the Chapel-Royal and Westminster-Abbey; and several Musical Gentlemen of Distinction attended in Surplices, and sung in the Burial Service. There were near 80 Vocal Performers, and 100 Instrumental from his Majesty's Band and from the Opera, &c. (*DA*, 19 Dec.)

This is one of the few occasions for which all four major choirs are named,[121] though it is unlikely that the choirs of St Paul's Cathedral and Windsor participated as distinct units, since the records of their institutions have no reference to their participation: more likely, singers from these choirs covered for those Chapel Royal singers who had double places or dual memberships. As with the coronation ten years previously, Handel (or Smith on his behalf) probably sought out as many competent singers and players as could be found and, as in 1727, there is mention of performers from the opera company, though these may have been restricted to orchestral musicians. It is not clear from the wording of the second report whether the 'Gentlemen of Distinction' sang in Handel's anthem, or only in the Burial Sentences during the procession.[122]

---

[120] Remarkably, 'The Song of Moses' and the Funeral Anthem were performed by the Academy of Ancient Music on 10 May 1739, only a month after Handel's performances of *Israel in Egypt*; programme in GB-LEc R 780-73 Ac 12.

[121] They were also referred to in *WEP*, 15–17 Dec., and several other newspapers for 19 Dec.

[122] See, however, the curious note in Hawkins, *A General History* (ii. 796) concerning Humphrey Wyrley Birch: 'At the funeral of queen Caroline, for the greater conveniency of hearing it [Croft's *Burial Sevice*], he, with another lawyer, who was afterwards a judge, though

It is striking that the payments to Smith and Shrider in the Lord Chamberlain's records are comparable to those for the coronation (see App. I): Smith was actually paid more for copying the music for the funeral, and Shrider was paid more for the specially provided organ than he had received for the coronation. The payment for additional performers is rather smaller than in 1727, and was made as one payment to Smith, whereas in 1727 Gates had been responsible for the additional singers. Nevertheless the sum involved is obviously more comparable to that for the coronation than to those for the intervening royal weddings. The scoring of Handel's anthem is for oboes, bassoons, strings, and organ continuo only, accompanying a four-part choir (with some division of the Soprano part in 'She deliver'd the poor that cried'), but restraint in orchestral colour through the absence of trumpets and drums did not entail a restraint in solidity of tone. Although the newspaper reports may have been a little exaggerated as to numbers of performers, this was nevertheless the second largest force to be assembled for a church service in London during the first half of the eighteenth century. Samuel Arnold's edition of the Funeral Anthem, published *c.*1795, indicated 'Soli' for the vocal entries in 'When the ear heard her' and gave the heading 'Quartetto' for 'They shall receive a glorious kingdom', but this seems to reflect a later performing tradition and there is no hint of the use of soloists in earlier musical sources.[123] It is, of course, possible that Handel used fewer voices to establish some of the opening vocal entries in various movements, as he had done in the Coronation Anthems, but nevertheless he obviously regarded the Funeral Anthem as a fundamentally all-choral piece. The Lord Chamberlain's records also include a payment to George Carleton, the Sub-Dean of the Chapel Royal, for 'writing Anthems and for printing a Great number of the Same' for the funeral: the sum involved is less than half of that paid to Smith for his copying activity. Perhaps extra copies of the music were needed for the singers in the procession; the wording also suggests that Carleton had been responsible for organizing the printing of the single-sheet anthem text.

As with Handel's anthems for the 1727 coronation, there were no precedents for the performance of an anthem of this scale and type for a royal funeral. The surviving performing material for Boyce's anthem *The souls of the Righteous* for the funeral of King George II on 11 November 1760 may provide information that is of retrospective relevance to the performing group in

---

neither of them could sing a note, walked among the choirmen of the abbey, each clad in a surplice, with a music paper in one hand and a taper in the other.'

[123] 'When the ear heard her' may have been performed by soloists at the Handel Commemoration of 1784, though it is not possible to tell from Burney's comments in *An Account*, First performance, 33.

1737.[124] A checklist of performing parts on the organ copy suggests the following forces, assuming that the orchestral musicians apart from double basses, brass, and timpani shared two to a part:[125]

> Voices: 52 (22 trebles, 9 contratenors, 11 tenors, 10 basses)
> Strings: 54 (16/16/10/8/4)
> Wind: 8 oboes, 8 bassoons, 2 trumpets, 2 horns, plus timpani and organ

This would give a total performing strength of 138. Ninety-five additional performers were hired,[126] which, if added to a full turnout of the Chapel Royal and Royal Musicians, would give 155 in total. The difference between these two figures is not so large as to be inexplicable: a 'full' turnout of the court establishments would probably in practice have been fewer than ten Children, twenty-six Gentlemen, and twenty-four string players, and there have almost certainly been some losses from the set of parts. (The number for Contratenor is particularly suspicious.) The overall picture for the mix and balance of forces is probably quite accurate, however, and the 1760 performance probably owed something to Boyce's experience at the 1737 funeral: in 1736 he had succeeded to a post as Composer at the Chapel Royal, with responsibility also for part of the duty of an Organist.[127] There are some obvious differences between the musical contribution to the two funerals: Boyce's score includes trumpets, horns, and timpani, and the payments indicate that fewer additional performers were hired in 1737 than in 1760.

The special gallery that was constructed for the organ and the performers at the west end of King Henry VII's Chapel was presumably located over the entrance to the Chapel from the Abbey, and possibly extended a little round the side walls. It is unlikely that this allowed as much space for the performers as they had received in the galleries for the 1727 coronation in the main area of the Abbey, so conditions for them must have been very crowded. If the 1737 payment refers to about fifty extra musicians, then with a full turnout of the Court's musicians and those from Westminster Abbey, and cover by deputies for dual places, the total performing force would certainly have been more than 100. This is on the assumption that all members of the Chapel and the Musicians attended, and not merely the half-numbers that were in waiting: the complete establishments were undoubtedly required to attend for the state

---

[124] GB-Ob MS Mus.Sch.c.115b. The 1760 funeral was the first one since 1737 to include an orchestrally accompanied anthem; the funeral of the Prince of Wales in 1751 had not even involved an organist.

[125] This is supported by the presence of two performers' names on several of the performing parts, including those for bassoons.

[126] GB-Lpro LC5/168, p. 20.

[127] *OCB*, fo. 58ᵛ; Ashbee and Harley, i. 145.

funerals of monarchs, since mourning liveries were provided for the full numbers in 1714, 1727, and 1761.

Autograph

Handel's autograph of the anthem is remarkably fluent, occupying twelve regular four-leaf gatherings with very little sign of hesitation or revision, suggesting that he must have worked from the complete and final form of the text as supplied to him.[128] There are some small variants between the printed anthem text and what Handel wrote in his score, almost certainly reflecting his own choices when composing the music. He preferred 'It gave witness of her' to 'It gave witness to her', and showed some indeterminacy between 'shall' and 'will' in 'The wise shall shine' and in 'The congregation shall show forth thy praise'. (In the first he seems to have gradually settled on 'will', and in the second on 'shall'.) He subsequently made various alterations and amendments to the autograph in connection with the re-use of some of the music for the Foundling Hospital Anthem in 1749: these included the alteration of 'She deliver'd the poor that cried' to 'They deliver the poor that crieth'. There are, however, no alterations to pronouns relating to the use of the anthem as Part I of *Israel in Egypt*: these may have been made in a performing score of the anthem, or in a separate score copied for the oratorio. There is a strong probability that a performing score was also copied for the anthem (and may have been part of the work for which Smith was paid), but it cannot be identified with any of the early manuscripts of the anthem that are known at present.[129]

A number of Handel's alterations to the autograph, in ink and in pencil, do not relate to either of these later uses of the music. The most substantial amendments concern the adaptation of the complete anthem, except for the two movements 'The people will tell of their wisdom' and 'They shall receive a glorious kingdom', to an Italian text; as suggested above, Handel probably planned to include this version of the anthem in the programme of his benefit *Oratorio* in March 1738. There are also a number of other alterations that may or may not relate to the same plan, but which were certainly made during the earliest months of the autograph's existence:

1. The opening Sinfonia. Handel wrote the title to the anthem at the beginning of the chorus 'The ways of Zion do mourn':[130] the Sinfonia is a single-leaf addition, clearly separate from the main paper gatherings.

---

[128] GB-Lbl RM 20.d.9.

[129] See the sources described in the commentary to *HHA*, III/12.

[130] Handel altered his first thought for the title, but not completely: in the final form it reads 'The Anthem at the Queens Caroline's Funeral'.

2. A cut, shown in pencil, of four bars beginning at bar 11 of the Sinfonia.
3. A substantial cut, bars 34–70, in 'The ways of Zion do mourn'. This is indicated in pencil, and clearly applied to the Italian version of the movement, but the added notes in pencil at bar 33 are accompanied by the English text 'The', as well as 'Il'.
4. A pencil amendment, with both English and Italian texts, providing an alternative beginning (three bars instead of one) for the reprise of 'For their name liveth evermore'.
5. A cut of three bars, shown in pencil, in the closing ritornello of 'They shall receive a glorious kingdom'.

These alterations may relate to pre-performance revisions to the anthem, or to revisions that were made when Handel was planning to include the anthem in his benefit performance but had not yet decided to convert to an Italian text:[131] furthermore, they may not all date from the same stage, though the pencil marks look fairly consistent in style. Musically, it would be a pity to lose either the Sinfonia or the original form of the first chorus from the anthem. Early secondary manuscripts of the anthem include the Sinfonia in some form, have the longer version of the first chorus and the variant for 'For their name liveth evermore', but their evidence in relation to the form of the work as performed at the funeral in December 1737 is rather insecure since none was copied from the autograph (or a derivative source) before spring 1738.

---

[131] The Italian text, a 'singing translation', was probably not Handel's own, and he may have revised the music before receiving the text. The complete Italian-text version of the anthem is included in *HHA* III/12.

14

War and Peace: Commemorations in the 1740s

LIKE his father, King George II paid regular visits to Hanover. The principal function of these visits was to sustain direct contact with the administration of the Electorate, but they served other purposes as well. At Hanover he was well placed geographically to undertake formal and informal diplomatic contacts, on behalf of Britain as well as Hanover, with other European powers, and also to deal with family matters such as the choice of marital partners for his children; in 1736 the visit took on an additional aspect when he acquired a new mistress, the wife of the Hanoverian Baron von Walmoden.[1] When the King left London for Hanover late in April 1743, however, he was also anticipating a rare opportunity for personal participation in military activity. During the 1730s the political stability of Europe, already potentially threatened by the break-up of previous alliances, had dissolved and given way to a succession of conflicts. By the end of the decade Britain had been drawn into a war against Spain, and in 1740 the invasion of Silesia by the new King of Prussia, Frederick II, signalled a new phase of opportunistic fragmentation in European politics. The death of the Emperor Charles VI, also in 1740, triggered a series of disputes as various states found ways to avoid or repudiate their obligations under the Pragmatic Sanction to support the succession of Maria Theresa in Austria. In April 1741 the British government agreed to provide a cash subsidy to Maria Theresa, supplemented by the funding of 12,000 Danish and Hessian troops. French military action was successful against Bavaria, and for a time it would have threatened Hanover also if George had not managed to come to an agreement with Frederick of Prussia to guarantee Hanover's neutrality. Following Walpole's fall from office in 1742, Lord Carteret (the Secretary of State for the Northern Department) persuaded the King to abandon Hanover's neutrality, but this came at a price: Hanoverian troops, and a contingent of Hessians, were taken into British pay, and this led to some controversial scenes in the House of Commons. In 1742 Carteret sent

---

[1] After the death of Queen Caroline she moved to London, where she took British nationality in 1740 and was created Countess of Yarmouth.

an army of British, Hanoverian, and Hessian troops to the Low Countries in order to create a diversion on Maria Theresa's behalf against the French, but the range of effective action was limited in the absence of further support from Dutch troops. In 1743 the Dutch joined the military alliance and more serious campaigning was anticipated: specifically, some gesture to curb French dominance of Bavaria. George II was given command of this combined army, supported in various roles by his younger son, William Duke of Cumberland, and by Carteret. The King had seen significant military service once before in his life, with the Duke of Marlborough at Oudenarde in 1708; in 1743 his British principal military adviser was Marlborough's former Field-Marshal the Earl of Stair, now 70 years old. The King himself was approaching his sixtieth birthday, and the expedition seems to have represented for him the fulfilment of a personal dream for a last chance to prove himself as a soldier.[2]

On 27 June 1743 George's troops set forth from their camp at Aschaffenburg on the River Main to join the Hessians and Hanoverians encamped at Hanau, and they were shadowed by French troops on the opposite bank of the river. The French army crossed the river to occupy the village of Dettingen, and it was in front of the French position there that George led the army into action, first responding to French attack and then turning the situation round so that the French troops were forced back over the river—symbolically, to the defence of their own country. The French losses, some 4,800 men, were about double those of their opponents: they included troops who were drowned when they tried to return over the river. It was subsequently rumoured by George's detractors in London that his battle response had commenced not through any will of the King but because his horse took fright and carried him towards the enemy. In fact he seems to have behaved with considerable valour, leading the later part of the battle dismounted; the Duke of Cumberland was also reported to have made a good impression and was wounded in the leg during the action. Dettingen was neither the most militarily heroic nor the most politically critical battle in history, but George fulfilled his personal ambition by fighting and winning. It was also the only battle ever fought by the 'Pragmatic army' and it was, from Britain's point of view, a battle fought by proxy. France was officially not at war with Britain (or, indeed, with Maria Theresa) until 1744: the skirmish took place between the auxiliaries of the Emperor of Bavaria (France) and of Maria Theresa as Queen of Hungary (Britain). On the battlefield George wore Hanoverian uniform, and indeed had taken command in his capacity as Elector of Hanover. Both Hanoverian and British troops had been involved.

---

[2] For George II's personal military ambitions, see Sedgwick, *Some Materials*, 340–1; Walpole had dissuaded him from accepting the offer of a command in the Imperial army in 1735 (ibid. 467).

Nevertheless, the King of Great Britain had led the troops in a victorious continental battle, and arguably the composite army at Dettingen was not significantly different in character from the miscellaneous allied troops that Marlborough had led forty years previously. In Britain a thanksgiving prayer was issued for the 'late Glorious Victory obtained by His Majesty at Dettingen and for imploring the Divine Blessing for the Preservation of his Majesty's Sacred person, and upon the Future Progress of his Arms', which was commanded to be read in all churches after the Prayer of General Thanksgiving at Morning and Evening Prayer on Sunday 17 July. On that same day Handel began the composition of a setting of the Te Deum. The last page of the autograph of the Dettingen Te Deum (which probably carried a completion date) is lost, but we may assume that as soon as it was finished he moved on to the companion anthem *The King shall Rejoice*, which he wrote between 30 July and 3 August. His work on the Te Deum was referred to by John Christopher Smith in a letter to the Earl of Shaftesbury on 28 July:

He is now upon a new Grand Te Deum and Jubilate, to be performed at the King's return from Germany (but He keeps this a great secret and I would not speak of it to any Body but to your Lordship) and by the Paper he had from me I can guess that it must be almost finished. This I think perfectly well Judg'd to appease and oblige the Court and Town with such a grand Composition and Performance.

But how the Quality will take it that He can compose for Himself and not for them when they offered Him more than He ever had in His life, I am not a Judge.[3]

The context for the last two sentences is that Handel had apparently indicated that he would be willing to write one or two operas on commission for the current Italian opera company at the King's Theatre (for which Lord Middlesex was the principal Director), but had then declined to do so. Handel's 'composing for himself' involved not only the Dettingen Te Deum and Anthem but also two major works that he would present in an all-English oratorio-style season at Covent Garden in February and March 1744. *Semele* was drafted before the Te Deum, between 3 June and 4 July 1743; *Joseph and his Brethren* followed the composition of the anthem, Parts I and II being completed on 26 August and 12 September respectively.[4] There is no completion date for Part III of *Joseph*: the autograph ends with a cue to the final chorus from the Dettingen Anthem to conclude the oratorio.[5]

While news of the King's part in the Dettingen victory was treated with some levity by opposition politicians, George II himself was apparently well received by crowds when he passed through the City on his eventual return to

[3] Matthews, 'Unpublished Letters', 265–6; *HHB*, 364.
[4] See Hurley, '"The Summer of 1743"'.
[5] GB-Lbl Zweig MS 38: see Burrows and Ronish, *A Catalogue*, 302.

London. Nevertheless it seems that Handel made an uncharacteristic political miscalculation when he composed the Te Deum and anthem. The large orchestration (including three trumpet parts and timpani) and the expansive musical treatment for these pieces were in the style of the Coronation Anthems, and it seems almost certain that Handel expected a big combined state Thanksgiving Service, probably at St Paul's Cathedral, on the pattern of the Utrecht Thanksgiving thirty years previously.[6] Two circumstances went against this. First, since the King's role in the battle was principally as Elector of Hanover, a public celebration on a grand scale in London might have encouraged unwelcome dissention, providing an occasion for protest by opposition politicians who claimed that Britain's interests were being relegated to those of Hanover. Secondly, there was a series of delays, with the result that the performance took place several months after the battle of Dettingen, and also did not follow immediately after the King's return to London: the military victory was no longer topical, and the first Sunday service at the Chapel Royal following the King's return received no special musical enhancement. Handel might perhaps have foreseen the first problem, but not the second.

After the battle George II's duties with the army had detained him for a time before he could travel to Hanover, and once there he was in no hurry to leave for London. No doubt he was pleased to remain in Hanover, basking in his enhanced reputation, but he was also kept there by family business, the conclusion of the arrangements for the last marriage of one of his daughters. This time, as noted in Chapter 13, the wedding involved no ceremony at all in London. Princess Louisa left Britain in mid-October 1743, and on 30 October the betrothal took place in Hanover,[7] when, as with the 1740 ceremony for Princess Mary in London, her future husband was represented by proxy. Her marriage to Prince Frederick of Norway (subsequently King Frederick V of Denmark) took place at Christiansborg on 11 December. 30 October, the day of the betrothal ceremony, was also the King's birthday, which he usually celebrated at St James's Palace: the customary court celebrations in London were postponed until his return from Hanover. The first documented public rehearsal of Handel's music took place on 26 September, presumably in the expectation that the King would return soon: 'Yesterday their Royal Highnesses the Princesses were at the Chapel Royal at St. James's to hear the Rehearsal of Mr. Handel's new Anthem and Te Deum, to be perform'd on his Majesty's safe Arrival in his British Dominions.'[8] The Princesses who

---

[6] *GEP*, 2–5 July, expected at least the announcement of a General Thanksgiving.

[7] 10 Nov. Modern Style. According to *LDP*, 1 Sept., the treaty of marriage was signed at Hanover by Carteret and the Danish Ambassador on 14 Sept. (= 3 Sept. Old Style). Newspapers in July (e.g. *DA*, 19 July, also 3 Aug.) expected Princess Amelia to accompany Louisa.

[8] *DA*, 27 Sept. 1743; also advance notice in *DA*, 26 Sept.

attended would have been Amelia, Caroline, and Louisa. There was also another rehearsal in the same week, the evidence for which comes in a letter dated 4 October from John Christopher Smith to James Harris at Salisbury: 'We had last week two rehearsals of Mr Handels new anthem & Te Deum, which went off with general approbation; the musick is very grand & in a new cast, differend from his former Te Deum.'⁹ The day before that of Smith's letter, the newspapers had reported that ''Tis now said his Majesty will not be at home till the Middle of November.'¹⁰

The King finally left Hanover on 9 November and arrived back at St James's Palace on the evening of Wednesday 15 November. Further rehearsals took place, this time at the Banqueting House Chapel in Whitehall, before and after his arrival:

Yesterday [9 November] Mr. Handel's new Anthem and Te Deum, to be perform'd in the Chapel Royal at St James's as soon as his Majesty arrives, was rehears'd at Whitehall Chapel. (*DA*, 10 Nov. 1743)

Yesterday [18 November] a Te Deum and Anthem, composed by Mr Handel for his Majesty, were rehearsed before a splendid Assembly at Whitehall Chapel, and are said by the best Judges to be so truly masterly and sublime, as well as new in their kind, that they prove this great Genius not only inexhaustible, but likewise still rising to a higher Degree of Perfection. (*DA*, 19 Nov.)

The final comment was apparently intended to counter the idea that Handel's great days were over, an image no doubt fostered by the opera supporters who were offended by his non-cooperation.¹¹ The opera company had opened their season at the King's Theatre on 15 November with *Rossane*, a version of Handel's *Alessandro* (1726):¹² it may have been rumoured that he was not now capable of fulfilling a commission for a new opera, since it was known that he had had a return of his illness earlier in the year.¹³ Concerning the rehearsal on 18 November, an advance notice said that the Dettingen music would be 'rehearsed for the Second and Last Time at Whitehall Chapel on Friday next, between the hours of Ten and Eleven in the forenoon'.¹⁴ Mrs Delany attended the rehearsal 'in the morning' on 9 November and was as enthusiastic about the music as the journalist who wrote up the subsequent rehearsal: 'It is excessively fine, I was all rapture and so was your friend D[r] D[elany] as you may imagine; everybody says it is the finest of his compositions; I am not

⁹ Burrows and Dunhill, *Music and Theatre*, 167.
¹⁰ *DA*, 3 Oct.
¹¹ See also the letter of Prince Frederick of Prussia in Oct. 1737 (Deutsch, *Handel*, 441), no doubt relaying gossip from London.
¹² Handel may possibly have cooperated in this, perhaps by lending a score.
¹³ See Burrows, *Handel*, 271–2.
¹⁴ *LDP*, 17 Nov.

well enough acquainted with it to pronounce that of it, but it is heavenly.'[15] However, another person who attended the same rehearsal found the music 'vastly loud & I thought not agreable'.[16]

The expectation at the time of these rehearsals was that the music would be performed, according to established precedent, on the first Sunday after the King's return from Hanover, which would have been 20 November. However, there was a further delay, as *The Daily Advertiser* reported the next day: 'His Majesty did not see Company at St James's Yesterday as usual, because it was the Day on which the late Queen died; and the new Te Deum and Anthem, which were to have been perform'd at the Chapel Royal, were put off till next Sunday on that Account.'[17] It is possible that one further rehearsal was held as a result of the postponement, as *The London Daily Post* indicated on 23 November: 'We hear, that the Te Deum and Anthem, compos'd by Mr Handell which is to be performed before his Majesty, will be rehearsed again at Whitehall Chapel on Friday Morning next.' There was probably no pressing musical need for this rehearsal, but it would have given more people a chance to hear the music and there may have been some financial benefit to the performers, either through a charge at the rehearsal or through a larger claim on the expenses from the Lord Chamberlain.

Handel's music finally came to performance at the Chapel Royal service on the morning of Sunday 27 November: 'Yesterday [27 November] his Majesty was at the Chapel Royal at St. James's, and heard a Sermon preach'd by the Rev. Dr. Thomas; when the new Te Deum, and the following Anthem, both set to Musick by Mr. Handel, on his Majesty's safe Arrival, were perform'd before the Royal Family.'[18] This report, which appeared in several London newspapers, was accompanied by the text of the anthem *The King shall rejoice*, accurately presented. In the preceding week another postponed musical event had taken place at court, the performance of Greene's ode for the King's birthday. This was given on 22 November (coincidentally St Cecilia's Day) in the usual venue (the Great Council Chamber at St James's Palace) before the King, the Prince of Wales, the Duke of Cumberland, the Princesses (Amelia and Caroline), and 'several of the Nobility'.[19] One newspaper report of the performance of the ode is important because it indicates the leading singers from the Chapel Royal at the time: 'the Vocal Parts by Mess. Abbot, Beard, Bailey, Gates, and the Boys of the Chapel Royal; the Instrumental by his Majesty's Band of Musicians, and several extraordinary Performers'.[20] Beard

---

[15] Letter to Mrs Dewes, 10 Nov. 1743; Deutsch, *Handel*, 573.
[16] Letter of Jemima, Marchioness Grey, Bedfordshire and Luton Archives, Wrest Park (Lucas) Collection, L 30/9a.
[17] *DA*, 21 Nov.   [18] *DA*, 28 Nov.   [19] *CJ*, 26 Nov.   [20] *DA*, 23 Nov.

was never a Gentleman of the Chapel, but he was probably one of the 'extraordinary Performers' for the Dettingen music: he had, earlier in the year, created the leading role in Handel's successful performances of *Samson* at Covent Garden theatre. As usual in Handel's Chapel Royal music, the Dettingen Te Deum and Anthem feature alto and bass voices in the solo sections, and Abbot and Gates are named on the autographs for the bass music. No alto is named, though in the anthem Handel wrote 'Mr.....' against the Alto part in 'His honour is great' without filling in the name. His hesitation or uncertainty may have arisen because in 1743 the Chapel was in a transition between the generations of its principal singers. The years 1743–4 saw the deaths of many key singers for whom Handel had composed in the 1720s, most particularly Francis Hughes (died March 1744) and Samuel Weely (died 3 November 1743); the toll also included James Chelsum (died August 1743) and Thomas Bell (died May 1743), and indeed John Abbot himself in February 1744. Of the seven leading singers named on the autograph of the Coronation Anthems in 1727, only Bernard Gates and George Laye were still alive in November 1743. Although Weely was still on the Chapel's member-ship at the time of the composition and first rehearsals of the Dettingen music, he had apparently retired from prominence.[21] Formally, at least, all of the Gentlemen held their places until death, and the only customary exception from regular attendance was for the senior Gentleman, who at this time was John Mason. Abbot's obituaries do not indicate the cause of his death, but there is no reason to suppose that he was debilitated in November 1743, and he was only 38 years old. The music for solo alto was almost certainly sung by Anselm Bayly, who had been appointed a Gentleman of the Chapel Royal in January 1741 and had been a regular soloist in the court odes during 1741–3: not only was he named in the newspaper report of the 1743 birthday ode, but when in 1744 James Harris wanted to borrow Handel's performing materials of the Dettingen music for use in Salisbury, John Christopher Smith apologized that he could not provide all of the music because 'there is a principal part still wonting, which is Mr Baily's'.[22] Bayly had succeeded to the place in the Chapel that had fallen vacant by the death of John Church, and he also followed into Church's place as a Lay Vicar at Westminster Abbey. He was one of the Chapel's leading soloists during the 1740s, but he subsequently followed a clerical career, becoming Sub-Dean in 1764.

Greene had provided the special music for the Sunday services in the Chapel Royal following all of the King's previous returns from Hanover (see App. H) but, given the circumstances of 1743, there was perhaps less reason for his

---

[21] His last recorded appearance in a court ode was for the King's birthday in 1737.
[22] Letter of 30 Sept. 1744, Burrows and Dunhill, *Music and Theatre*, 199.

resentment of Handel's participation than over the royal wedding in 1733–4. In any case Greene received some recognition through the performance of the birthday ode, an event that might well have been cancelled rather than postponed, and his public status as a composer had been enhanced by the publication of his *Forty Select Anthems* in January 1743. Although Handel's Te Deum and anthem were described in the newspaper report of one of the rehearsals as being 'new in their kind', they were basically a renewed application of his style from the Coronation Anthems. This was certainly the first time that an orchestra involving three trumpet parts had been heard in the Chapel Royal; timpani had been introduced there in 1736–7.[23] The scale of Handel's music, in both resources and style, seems to have been designed for a large building such as St Paul's Cathedral or Westminster Abbey. The scoring may have been tolerable at the Chapel in Whitehall, but it would surely have been uncomfortably overpowering at St James's, even for the King whose tastes favoured 'martial music'.[24]

Dettingen Te Deum (HWV 283)

The Dettingen Te Deum is more spacious than its predecessors,[25] but it is clearly in the lineage of Handel's previous settings of the text, and in particular the Utrecht setting. The new version followed much the same pattern as his earlier settings in combining verses into paragraphs suitable for more extended musical movements (see Table 14.1), and indeed many aspects of the scheme can be traced back to Purcell's 1694 Te Deum. The movements thus created mainly begin and end in the same key, and their conclusions are marked by closing instrumental ritornellos or emphatic final cadences. The principal musical movements articulate the following structure:

    verses: 1; 2; 3; 4–6; 7–13; 14–15; 16; 17; 18; 19–23; 24–5; 26–8; 29

The first two verses receive substantial independent movements of their own (as in the Utrecht setting), but then the arrangement becomes more fluid. 'To Thee all Angels' introduces a minor-key contrast and arrives at a clear cadence on A major at bar 12, setting off thereafter in F sharp minor as if to make a binary-form movement; however, instead of completing this scheme

---

[23] See Ch. 17, esp. n. 92.

[24] See the Duke of Montagu's letter concerning the *Fireworks Music* in 1749, Deutsch, *Handel*, 661.

[25] Comparative timings from recorded performances are *c*.25 min. for the Utrecht Te Deum (Hogwood, 1980) and *c*.40 min. for the Dettingen Te Deum (Preston, 1982).

Table 14.1. *The Dettingen Te Deum*

Verse		No.	Key	T/s	Voices	Orch.[a]
1.	We praise thee	1	D	¢	ssatb, A	full
2.	All the earth	2	D	¾	A, ssatb[b]	full
3.	To Thee all angels	3	b, A	¢	stb	bn. and str.
4–6.	To Thee Cherubim	4	D	¢	ssatb	full
7.	The glorious company	5	G	¢	b, sa	str.[c]
8.	The goodly fellowship				b, at	
9.	The noble army				b, st	
10.	The holy Church		G, b		satb	
11.	The Father		b	¢	ssatb	ww. and str.
12–13.	Thine honourable	6	b, A	¢		
14–15.	Thou art the King	7	D	¢	B, ssatb	tpt, full
16.	When thou tookest	8	A	⅜	B	str.
17.	When thou hadst	9	g, d	¢	ssatb	str.[c]
	(thou didst open)	10	D	¢	ssatb	full
18.	Thou sittest	11	B♭	¾	atb[d]	obs. and str.
19.	We believe	12	B♭, g	¾	atb[d]	b.c.; tpts.
20.	We therefore pray	13	g	¢	ssatb, ss	b.c.[e], unacc.
21–3.	Make them	14	B♭, g	¢	ssatb	ww. and str.
24.	Day by day	15	D	¢	ssatb	tpt., full
25.	And we worship	16	D	3/2	ssatb	full
26.	Vouchsafe, O Lord	17	b	¢	B	str.
27.	O Lord, have mercy		e			
28.	O Lord, let thy		b			
29.	O Lord, in thee	18	D	¾	A, ssatb	full

[a] full = 3tpt., timp., 2 obs., bn., str; ww. = obs. and bn.; No. 3 has bn. parts without obs.

[b] Some sections possibly for SST, though not marked for soloists.

[c] With obs. and bn. doubling voices.

[d] Not indicated for soloists, but perhaps intended so.

[e] + obs doubling voices.

the music at bar 21 reverts rather abruptly to A major, which this time clearly functions as a dominant to reintroduce D major. The key scheme through verses 3–6 thus follows the same broad outline as in the Utrecht setting

(B minor, A major, D major: see above, Table 4.1), but while the Utrecht scheme arrives back at the D major tonic in verse 5, the Dettingen setting compresses all of the key contrast into verse 3: there are only twenty-six bars of excursion before the tonic returns again for another substantial movement. The further return to the tonic for another coupled pair of movements at 'Thou art the King of Glory' (verses 14–15) and again at 'Thou didst open the Kingdom of Heaven' (verse 17) also marks a departure from Handel's previous plans. The recurring slabs of the tonic key (verses 1–6, 14–15, 17a, 24–5 and 29—the last being the longest movement in the Te Deum by bar count) is a feature that gives the Dettingen setting a more static and ceremonial character than its predecessors. There is also an unmistakable extended fanfare on D major to represent the last judgement at 'We believe that Thou shalt come to be our judge', but in context this functions as a dominant chord in G minor, and not as a further return to the tonic key.

The interruption of the trumpet fanfare draws attention to the reference to judgement in verse 19, giving it greater emphasis than in Handel's previous settings of the Te Deum. The other characteristic feature of the Dettingen setting is the exuberantly emphatic treatment that the first six verses receive. Instead of the simple threefold statement of 'Holy', the voices hammer away at this word while '*continually* do cry' is represented to the verge of excess. Trumpets and drums play an important role in this: as in the Coronation Anthems, Handel turns these battlefield instruments into enhancements of jubilation. The first, second, and fourth movements exhibit the side of Handel's music that George Bernard Shaw admired for its 'force of assertion':[26] it is, indeed, a very different aspect of the composer from that seen in his previous, A major, setting of the Te Deum. Handel's style in the more extrovert sections of the Dettingen Te Deum, as with all such powerful rhetoric, requires the listener to share rather uncritically in the emotions of the moment. Even in the more lyrical and restrained 'To thee all Angels cry aloud' he was unusually careful to avoid any possible ambiguity by marking the voice parts 'tutti' at the opening accolade and the first entry: he wanted *all* the angels on duty. Celebration and judgement are the two topics that remain in the memory of the listener at the end of the Te Deum.

In composing his Te Deum, Handel drew on musical ideas from a Latin setting of the text by Francesco Antonio Urio, an Italian composer whose biography remains rather vague.[27] Urio's Te Deum survives in three later British manuscript copies, one of which is said to have been transcribed from

---

[26] In a 'Causerie on Handel in England' (1913); Laurence, *Shaw's Music*, iii. 639–40.

[27] See 'Urio, Francesco Antonio', *NG II*, xxvi. 156–7. In Robinson, *Handel and his Orbit*, it was suggested that the Te Deum was composed by Handel, but this is now discredited.

an Italian copy (now lost) that Handel owned.[28] The other two copies attribute composition dates of 1660 and 1682 to the Te Deum, but the style of the music suggests that both dates may be too early. Urio's Te Deum has a scoring comparable to Handel's Utrecht setting, with five-part chorus voices (SSATB) and an orchestral accompaniment for trumpets, oboes, and strings.[29] Handel must have known the work by at least 1738, since he drew on some of its music in *Saul* and *Israel in Egypt*.[30] His use of Urio's material involved relatively short thematic ideas: there are no whole-movement (or whole-section) transcriptions comparable to his use of Kerll's keyboard piece for 'Egypt was glad when they departed' in *Israel in Egypt*, or the chorus from Graun's Passion for 'Lo, thus shall the man be blessed' in the 1736 wedding anthem. In the Dettingen Te Deum he only employed Urio's ideas for parallel English texts sporadically, most prominently near the beginning of the work. At the very opening Handel preceded a Urio-derived motif with a military-style fanfare, and in the second movement Urio provided Handel with the idea for the opening ritornello (see Ex. 14.1 and Ex. 14.2),[31] but beyond some similarities in the choral textures there is little influence on the parallel movements thereafter. For 'To thee all Angels cry aloud' Handel drew on the ritornello to a later movement of Urio's, his equivalent setting of 'The glorious company of the Apostles' (see Ex. 14.3), but the ensuing vocal writing owed more to Handel's own Utrecht setting than to Urio, in its contrast between a rather angular initial phrase and a cantus-firmus-like response from the lower chorus voices for 'The Heavn's and all the Powr's therein'.

Comparison of Handel's setting with Urio's serves to illustrate a difference in approach to the text, and the extent of the Dettingen Te Deum's relationship to previous English settings. In general Urio treats each verse of the Te Deum as a separate musical movement and does not combine sequences of verses into broader musical paragraphs, though in some places he runs together texts that are presented as two separate verses in the English Prayer Book version (e. g. 7–8, 11–12, 14–15, 24–5). He treats 'We believe that thou shalt

[28] GB-Lbl Add. MS 31478: the transcriber in 1781 said that it derived from an Italian copy formerly owned by Handel, and subsequently by Samuel Howard, who as a Chapel Royal chorister had sung in Gates's production of *Esther*. Handel may have acquired a copy of the Te Deum in his early years at Rome, through some connection with Cardinal Ottoboni, to whom Urio had dedicated a set of motets in 1690; however, a thirty-year delay in Handel's use of the material seems uncharacteristic.

[29] A score of the Te Deum was published in 1902 as Supp. 2 to *HG*; Chrysander's preface lists the borrowings relevant to the Dettingen Te Deum, including some that are not referred to here.

[30] See Dean, *Handel's Dramatic Oratorios*, 643, and the preface to *HG* Supp. 2.

[31] This also contributed material for 'Their land brought forth frogs' and 'The Lord is a man of war' in *Israel in Egypt*. In No. 2 Handel used the ritornello with the voice in bars 11–13, and with the chorus when the same theme returns at bar 68.

Ex. 14.1. (*a*) Handel, Dettingen Te Deum, No. 1; (*b*) Urio, Te Deum, 'Laudamus te'

come to be our Judge' as the B section of a dal segno aria beginning 'Thou sittest at the right hand of God', thus breaking up what the English settings construe as a connected sequence 'We believe that thou shalt come / We therefore pray thee, help thy servants'. Handel's paragraph movements for

Ex. 14.2. (*a*) Handel, Dettingen Te Deum, No. 2; (*b*) Urio, Te Deum, 'Te eternum Patrem'

verses 7–13, 19–23, and 26–8 are set by Urio as five, five, and three movements respectively. Perhaps most striking of all, in contrast to Handel's settings, is Urio's treatment of 'Dignare, Domine' (= 'Vouchsafe, O Lord') as a sprightly D major Spirituoso movement with trumpet obbligato, at the point where Handel (following Purcell) moves into a reflective minor-key movement, the most lyrical solo-voice interlude in the Te Deum, falling between the more

Ex. 14.3. (*a*) Handel, Dettingen Te Deum, No. 3; (*b*) Urio, Te Deum, 'Te gloriosus Apostolorum chorus'

extrovert choral movements for 'Day by day' and 'O Lord, in thee have I trusted'. Strange to the English tradition also is Urio's treatment of 'Thou art the King of Glory, O Christ' as a Siciliana-style duet accompanied by strings. Some ideas in Urio's setting may have appealed to Handel's imagination even though he chose not to set the text in that way himself: when the Cherubim and Seraphim continually cry 'Holy', Urio's angels are represented by an ethereal continuo-accompanied trio of soprano and alto voices who indulge in eighteen bars of ornamental luxury, while Handel consistently preferred simple, forceful, threefold tutti affirmation, followed in the Dettingen setting by a coda in grand style for 'Heaven and Earth are full of the Majesty of thy Glory'. He resisted the temptation of Urio's rather whimsical semiquaver babble on 'incessabili' for 'continually do cry'.

For the musical paragraph beginning 'The glorious company of the Apostles' (verses 7–13) Handel set the first three verses as a movement in G major: there seems to be a deliberate reference back to the texture of 'To thee all Angels cry aloud' as the cantus firmus-like phrase in the bass voices, always in the tonic, is answered in turn by a different duet combination the upper voices. The fourth clause of the text, 'The holy Church throughout all the world', slides seamlessly into a full choral texture and a transition away from G major to a simple Grave homophonic statement of 'The Father of an infinite Majesty' in B minor, and then a faster short imitative chorus for 'Thine honourable, true and only Son' which rounds off the paragraph off in A major, preparing for the return to the tonic in the next movement, 'Thou art the King of Glory'. The latter is in two parts, a complete bass aria for Bernard Gates with trumpet obbligato, followed by a chorus to the same text: Gates's opening phrase forms the bass line for the parallel phrase of the chorus, and his theme for the repetition of the initial words at bar 13 generates a short imitative section in the chorus (bars 49 onwards).[32]

In the verse 'When thou tookest upon thee' Handel departed most clearly from the plan that he had followed in the Utrecht setting, preferring to treat this as an extended aria, as he had done in his Caroline, Cannons, and A major settings.[33] Like the earlier aria versions this is in triple time: the conjunct phrases also display a similar musical approach, though the shapes of the melodic lines differ. The movement was designated by Handel for the bass soloist John Abbot, and its more lyrical lines perhaps reflect a contrast between this singer's style and that of Gates. It has a leisurely, well-developed structure in which the soloist's statements of the text move successively between orchestral ritornellos in E major, F sharp minor, and the tonic A major. A chorus movement follows that uses one of Handel's well-tried schemes: a minor-key Grave homophonic introduction ('When thou hadst overcome') leading to a major-key Allegro that begins as if it is to be imitative, but quickly develops in other ways ('Thou didst open the Kingdom of Heaven'). As already

---

[32] The figure in bar 4 may possibly have been an echo from the ritornello of Urio's 'Te gloriosus Apostolorum' (*HG* Supp. 2, 43).

[33] The opening vocal phrase appears on John Beard's monument at Hampton Church, even though Beard would not have sung this movement.

noted, this returns the key to the tonic D major and, although chromatically coloured, the introductory Grave is clearly in D minor. Nevertheless the opening chord is G minor, a hint of the flat-side excursion to come.

The extensive three-voice movement for 'Thou sittest at the right hand of God' marks a departure from Handel's previous schemes, in which this verse had been part of longer 'paragraph' movements; it also sees the Te Deum's first decisive move away from the tonic-key area. The style of the movement is comparable to Urio's setting of the same text; furthermore, the violin parts in bars 7–9 and the combination of voices and basso in bars 19–20 reflect a more specific, if momentary, stimulus from Urio. Handel did not designate the movement for soloists, and it seems most likely that, as with the duet-texture movements in the Funeral Anthem, this was performed chorally. At 'We believe that thou shalt come' Handel slips from B flat major into G minor, and abandons extended musical movements: the thoughts of judgement leave no leisure here for contemplation, either by soloists or chorus. In a sequence of short sections, and with very little repetition of the text, Handel moves effectively through the successive petitions, presented in the full texture of collective utterance but echoed by unaccompanied soprano voices at 'We therefore pray thee', presumably representing the prayer being carried up to heaven. Only with the rising phrase for 'And lift them up for ever' is the basic homophonic texture broken. In spite of the transitional brevity of the individual sections, and the apparent interruption of the last trumpet(s), the sequence is firmly framed in the key of G minor.

With the chorus 'Day by day' Handel returns to thematic material that is rather uncomfortably similar to that from 'Thou art the King of Glory', not only in the opening rising arpeggios (an almost inevitable consequence of the leading thematic role played by the trumpet) but also in the rhythm for 'We magnify thee' (bar 10). This section, however, serves as an introduction to its pendant chorus 'And we worship thy Name' in a different style and metre. The latter was wondrously developed by Handel from Urio's 'Per singulos dies' (= 'Day by day'), building the imitative phrases into a cumulative movement that is finally crowned by the entry of trumpets and drums, and concludes with a grand coda in Handel's sublimest manner. Between this and the Te Deum's extended final movement comes 'Vouchsafe, O Lord', a minor-key aria for Abbot which provides a lyrical interlude that seems rather brief in context. As far as the technical capacities of natural trumpets allowed, the final movement is also somewhat lyrical, though in the grand manner: the fanfares of war that opened the Te Deum do not dominate its conclusion. This is Handel's only setting of 'O Lord, in thee have I trusted' in triple metre. The recapitulation from bar 94 onwards builds to a conclusion that is confident and triumphal, but not triumphalist.

Most modern listeners will recognize the cross-reference to 'The trumpet shall sound' in *Messiah* in the trumpet fanfare that follows 'We believe that thou shalt come to be our judge'. The oratorio had received its first London performances, somewhat controversially, earlier in 1743. There are also other echoes that suggest that *Messiah* was on Handel's mind when he composed the Te Deum: 'Glory to God' in the first chorus entries of 'To thee Cherubim'[34] and in the echo triads (e.g. bars 27–8) of the first movement, also 'And the glory of the Lord' in the Te Deum's final movement (e.g. bars 76–8). Bars 5–6 of 'Day by day we magnify thee' may also recall a memory of 'The trumpet shall sound', though they are in a passage that is derived from Urio's 'Dignare Domine'.[35] In more general aspects, the Te Deum relates closely to Handel's earlier Chapel Royal music in its use of a solo alto voice as a contrast within chorus movements, in the first movement (bar 36 onwards) and the opening sections of 'All the earth doth worship thee' and 'O Lord, in thee have I trusted'. Though not so indicated, Handel may also have intended an alto soloist in the duet passages with trumpet at bars 20–6 of 'Day by day'. Within the English traditions of orchestrally accompanied church music, the combination of alto voice with trumpet was a regular one, and this makes the use of the bass voice with trumpet in 'Thou art the King of glory' more remarkable: perhaps Handel was not confident at this time that the Chapel had a worthy heir to Elford and Hughes, and perhaps also he was recollecting 'The trumpet shall sound' in *Messiah*. As in the Funeral Anthem, there are a couple of places where Handel's English word-setting is idiosyncratic. His treatment of 'the Holy Ghost, the comforter' conforms to what we would expect until a variation in the very last bar; similarly, in 'Day by day' there is one apparently anomalous stress pattern for 'without end' in Soprano 1 part at bar 49. As far as is known, Handel never contemplated matching the Te Deum with a new setting of the Jubilate (as implied in Smith's letter to Shaftesbury, quoted above), and there are no signs that he revived the Utrecht Jubilate to accompany the Te Deum in 1743—or indeed for any of the other Chapel Royal services from 1722 onwards at which his music was performed. The combined duration of the Dettingen Te Deum and Anthem probably stretched the regular Sunday morning timetable for the court to its limit in November 1743, and this would have discouraged the inclusion of an extended setting of the Jubilate at the Chapel Royal service.

From 1744 the Dettingen setting largely displaced Handel's Utrecht Te Deum at the annual festival service for the Sons of the Clergy at St Paul's Cathedral. Elsewhere, and particularly for those provincial festivals that could

[34] This follows a ritornello indebted to the parallel movement in Urio's Te Deum.
[35] *HG* Supp. 2, 136.

run to orchestrally accompanied church music, it would be an oversimplification to say that the Dettingen Te Deum simply displaced the Utrecht setting: rather, the new version joined the established settings by Purcell and Handel as an additional alternative. In order to distinguish Handel's two best-known settings, the Dettingen Te Deum continued to be referred to as his 'new' Te Deum in advertisements and newspaper reports long after it had ceased to be so. Walsh had published a score of the Utrecht canticles in the 1730s, but that for the Dettingen Te Deum did not follow until the 1760s, after Handel's death,[36] and this must have limited the music's accessibility. In 1744 Greene borrowed Handel's own performing materials for the Te Deum in order to perform it at the Sons of the Clergy, and James Harris made a similar arrangement for the Salisbury Festival later in the year. The relevant section of Smith's letter to Harris on this subject, partly quoted above, is as follows:

> I... should have answerd you sooner, if it had not been for Dr Green, whom Mr Handel lend the score and parts of the new Te Deum for the performance at St. Pauls, for the Sons of the Clergy. Ever since I could not have them again compleatly, though I sent so often, and there is a principal part still wonting, which is Mr Baily's, which you'll be pleased to have done out of the score (which my Lord Shaftesbury had of me) and have the other singers parts look'd over that there is nothing wonting.[37]

The Earl of Shaftesbury, possessing his own manuscript score, would have been one of the few people with easy access to this music for the next decade.[38] The Academy of Ancient Music included the Te Deum in their concerts on 24 April 1746 and 1 March 1759, on the latter occasion with the Dettingen Anthem.[39] By the time of the Handel Commemoration in 1784, however, Burney regarded the Dettingen Te Deum as a repertory work: 'This splendid production has been so frequently performed at Saint Paul's and elsewhere, that nothing could be added to its celebrity by my feeble praise.'[40] Something was certainly added to Handel's score for the Commemoration, however: 'as it was composed for a military triumph, the fourteen trumpets, two pair of common kettle-drums, two pair of double drums from the Tower, and a pair of double-base drums, were introduced with great propriety; indeed, these last drums, except the destruction, had all the effect of the most powerful artillery'.[41]

Since Anselm Bayly was almost certainly the alto soloist in the first performance of the Dettingen music, and in the performance at the Sons of the

---

[36] See William C. Smith, *Handel*, 155.
[37] Letter of 30 Sept. 1744, Burrows and Dunhill, *Music and Theatre*, 199.
[38] The Earl of Shaftesbury's copy is now in the Gerald Coke Handel Collection.
[39] Programmes in GB-LEc R 780.73 Ac 12.
[40] Burney, *An Account*, First Performance, 28.
[41] Ibid. 28–9.

Clergy Festival in April 1744, some enlightenment concerning the Te Deum might be expected from his *Practical Treatise on Singing and Playing*, although published more than twenty-five years later. Unfortunately this gives no hint of the circumstances or the effect of the first performances, and the reader would not guess from the text that Bayly had been involved. In his critical comments Bayly treats the Dettingen Te Deum along with the famous Purcell and Utrecht settings, and a simpler organ-accompanied setting by Henry Aldrich. He is far from complimentary about the first movement of the Dettingen Te Deum, in which

the musick is too complex and noisy, one voice and instrument pursuing another as fast as they can, crying out with quick notes 'O God, O God' just as if each were pricking on the other behind with a needle, and in a tedious division, first down hill then climbing up the same way back; 'till at length arrived at the top again, with much ado and out of breath, all bawl out again, 'Thee O God' on the same spot, from which the countertenor began the race; surely he might have varied his ground.[42]

In 'All the earth doth worship thee' Bayly finds the Dettingen version preferable to the fugue in the Utrecht setting, saying with approval that 'this verse opens simply with a solo, and ends in unison, grand and solemn'.[43] Other aspects of the setting also meet with his approbation: ' "To Thee all angels", taken by the boys in verse, and "the heavens with all the powers therein" by the whole choir in unison makes a fine contrast.'[44] As to 'Let me never be confounded', 'The air should not be, as it often is, in the extreme too grave, or too triumphant, but modest and pleasing even to exceed, if it be possible to exceed, that of *Handel* in his last *Te Deum*.'[45] Burney also thought that Handel had made a good conclusion:

The symphony of this Chorus, which is chiefly constructed on a *ground-base*, beginning by two trumpets, that are afterwards joined by the other instruments, is stately and interesting, though in the measure of a common minuet. The long solo part, after the symphony, for a contralto voice, with soft and sparing accompaniments, renders the sudden burst of all the voices and instruments the more striking. And the latter part, in fugue, with an alternate use of the ground-base, seems to wind up this magnificent production by

'Untwisting all the chains that tie
The hidden soul of harmony.'[46]

---

[42] Bayly, *A Practical Treatise*, 82–3; punctuation modernized in all quoted extracts.
[43] Ibid. 84.
[44] Ibid. 84.
[45] Ibid. 86.
[46] Burney, *An Account*, First Performance, 30–1. The quotation is from Milton, *L'Allegro* (line 143).

Dettingen Anthem (*The King shall rejoice*), HWV 265

This anthem shares a title with one of Handel's Coronation Anthems because both commence with musical settings of the first verse from Psalm 21. Both anthems are indeed built on verses from that Psalm (the Coronation Anthem exclusively so), but they are independent compositions as regards both text and music. The Coronation Anthem divides verse 1 into two movements, and then inserts a phrase from verse 5 before continuing with a movement for verse 3, and concluding with an 'Alleluia' chorus; there are variants from the Prayer Book forms of some verses (in tenses, and the substitution of 'hath' for 'shalt'), accounted for by the influence of texts that had been set as anthems in previous English coronations.[47] The Dettingen Anthem treats Psalm 21: 1 as one movement, and then proceeds to three movements that set verses 5, 6, and 7 from the psalm in turn, before concluding with a 'Hallelujah' movement that also incorporates verse 5 from Psalm 20. Thus although the two anthems end with a 'Hallelujah' chorus,[48] and have some words from Psalm 21 in common, the overall schemes are different. The most distinctive aspect of the text in the Dettingen Anthem is the inclusion of verses 6–7, which emphasize the position of an anointed King as an agent of the Almighty: he achieves strength and honour because he 'putteth his trust in the Lord'. While this implies a rather simplistic interpretation of the military and political fortunes of national leaders, it also sets human achievement, even that of a king at the head of a victorious army, in a perspective of wider responsibility. Given the limitation imposed by the convention of using scriptural verses for an anthem, the selection could have been more embarrassingly bellicose. In Psalm 21: 6 the Prayer Book version has 'Thou shalt give him everlasting felicity, and make him glad with the joy of Thy countenance', and this is what appeared in the text of the anthem as it was printed in the newspapers; Handel's setting omits 'and', though his musical theme for the phrase could have accommodated the word. It is perhaps curious that the text of this anthem, which is relatively brief and straightforward, was considered sufficiently interesting or significant for publication.[49]

---

[47] At least as far back as Charles I's coronation in 1625: see *OCB*, fo. 72[r]; Ashbee and Harley, i. 157.

[48] Handel consistently wrote 'Hallelujah' in the Dettingen Anthem, 'Alleluja' in the Coronation Anthem.

[49] The first of Handel's Chapel Royal anthem texts to see such publication was *This is the day* (1733), though the texts of the court odes (by the Poet Laureate) were routinely printed. Handel may have chosen the anthem text himself, but more likely it was suggested to him, perhaps in a longer version than he actually set. The libretto of *Joseph*, into which the anthem's last movement was incorporated, was by James Miller, but the anthem was composed first and Miller was presumably not responsible for its text.

As with Handel's other pairings of a Te Deum and an anthem for the Chapel Royal, the Dettingen Anthem is more straightforward in design than its companion canticle because the psalm verses provided an easier structure for independent movements. Compared with Handel's Chapel Royal anthems from the 1720s for the King's return, this one naturally displays the features that we would expect of his more expansive musical style in the 1740s; it is also rather better balanced in overall design than the wedding anthems from the 1730s. The common-time outer movements, in his best 'Coronation Anthem' style, are the only ones to use trumpets and drums; the second and fourth movements are contrasted by the use of triple-time metres and by extended sections for soloists that introduce music which is subsequently taken up by the chorus; the central movement is an alla breve contrapuntal chorus. In the second, third, and fifth movements Handel drew on ideas from a set of *Sonates sans basses* by Georg Philipp Telemann for two flutes, violins, or recorders, which had been published on the continent in 1727; Walsh also published an edition in London, but not until 1746.[50] As with the Urio Te Deum, Handel used his source only for some basic ideas and motifs; in this case, the potential that he saw in these modest chamber pieces, as material suitable for chorus and orchestra, is remarkable. More direct and substantial was the indebtedness of the choral section of the fourth movement to the chorus 'Bless the glad earth' in the score of *Semele*, composed just over a month previously, which had itself incorporated an idea from the Telemann sonatas.[51]

The anthem opens with a fanfare-like figure quite distinct from that which began the Te Deum: in other circumstances the version in bars 1–2 might have formed the basis for a ground-bass movement. As already noted, Handel took the whole of the psalm verse as the basis for the movement, and its second clause ('Exceeding glad shall he be of thy salvation') generated a contrasted musical subject that could be treated contrapuntally and extended. The movement has a simple binary structure, but the return to the initial choral theme at bars 38–40 is rather subtle: the opening of the original version of the theme is in the violin and oboe parts and not (as might be expected) in the bass voices, and although the original D major chord returns, it is in the context of a passage that is A major.[52] In the second movement ('His honour is great') the opening duet for alto and bass soloists presents the theme in B minor,[53] but at bar 42 the

[50] See Roberts, 'Handel's Borrowings from Telemann', 149, 164, the latter also listing a borrowing in the Te Deum. Walsh's edition numbered the sonatas in a different order.

[51] See Hurley, '"The Summer of 1743"'.

[52] In bars 39–42 Handel avoids the note G, whose inflection would have clarified the key: he sketched, but did not complete, a longer passage at this point that was more clearly in D major.

[53] The vocal parts begin with the interval of a falling third, though the orchestral parts had prepared the melody with a rising third.

Ex. 14.4. Dettingen Anthem, No. 2

alto moves it colourfully to D major: a new theme for the second clause, 'Glory and great worship hast Thou laid upon him' introduces quaver movement into the voices against an angular violin line that traverses two and a half octaves to end up below them (see Ex. 14.4). The duet section ends in F sharp minor, which soon adjusts itself to become the dominant of B minor and leads into the chorus, where the main theme is first introduced by the sopranos, but the D major statement at bar 90 is, as before, led by the alto part. The chorus voices do not take up the soloists' material for the second clause: instead they have strong chordal statements accompanied by violin semiquavers derived from the movement's opening ritornello. A second statement of the main theme, beginning in D major at bar 118, leads back to the tonic of B minor.

The chorus 'Thou shalt give him everlasting felicity' begins with a shortened version of Telemann's theme, and proceeds to a second exposition for 'Make them glad with the joy of Thy countenance', based on Telemann's counter-theme (see Ex. 14.5). The two themes are then presented together (at bar 48) and worked at some length, culminating in a final brief combined-theme exposition beginning at bar 88. The successive expositions all begin in the tonic, but the movement passes smoothly around the related keys, and this is one of Handel's most successful contrapuntal movements of its type. Although there is a clear and definite final cadence in D major, the beginning of the next movement (in G major), 'And why? Because the King putteth his trust in the

Lord' makes both a verbal and musical continuation. After the initial 'And why?' from the chorus, the alto soloist replies with a short aria that moves to the dominant, the closing echo ritornello leading into the chorus entry and a return to the tonic. The chorus music is directly derived, with revisions, from

Ex. 14.5. (*a*) and (*b*) Handel, Dettingen Anthem, No. 3 (orchestral doublings omitted); (*c*) Telemann, *Sonates sans basse* VI/2 (III/2 in Walsh edn.)

Cont'd

Ex. 14.5. *Cont'd*

the *Semele* chorus movement. At first sight the music of the alto solo bears little thematic relationship to the chorus: the soloist's opening music is constructed in rising phrases, while the opening melody of the chorus has a falling contour. There is, however, some similarity between the opening chorus music and the alto's phrases for 'and in the mercy' at bars 15–19, while the alto's sequential and cadential phrases in bars 27–39 relate to the music near the end of the chorus (bars 71–81). The closing orchestral ritornello was added for the anthem and did not feature in the *Semele* chorus movement. The flowing quavers of 'He shall not miscarry' in the chorus section of the movement are reminiscent of the soloists' phrases for 'Glory and great worship' in the second movement: this may be a coincidence, or Handel may have been aware of the musical echo.

The last movement is a rumbustious piece, and the opening promises a contrapuntal working of the two contrasted subjects: however, while the livelier phrase for 'We will rejoice in thy salvation' does indeed set off some lively chatter, the angular 'Hallelujah' subject is all the more effective for being sparingly used as a foil: there are only four statements of this subject in the movement, one in each vocal part. The contrapuntal material in any case dissolves quite quickly into assertive choral homophony for the words 'And triumph in the Name of the Lord our God', in a style resembling the description of the destruction of the Egyptians at the Red Sea in *Israel in Egypt*.

Conditions of Performance

'Christian' (i.e. John Christopher) Smith was paid £25. 4s. 5d. for copying the music of the Te Deum and Anthem, and £91. 4s. 6d. for additional performers (see App. I). This does not suggest the employment of performers on the scale of the 1727 coronation or the 1737 funeral, but nevertheless the figures imply slightly greater numbers than for the wedding anthems in 1736 and 1740, and more comparable to those for the 1734 wedding. The total sums paid for copying and performers were: £118. 8s. 11d. (1734), £86. 2s. 6d. (1736), £96. 15s. 10d. (1740), and £116. 8s. 11d. (1743). As already noted, there are no records of payments for the construction of additional galleries in the Chapel Royal in 1743, or reports of such work being undertaken, so somehow the musicians and instruments (possibly including timpani) must have been squeezed into the available spaces in the Chapel: the occasion must have been more crowded, as well as noisier, than any previous service in the Chapel. Allowance in the calculations must be made for the fact that, if Smith was paid by the page for music-copying, the Dettingen music was more extensive than the wedding anthems: it is also possible that the payments to additional musicians were higher pro rata on account of the number of rehearsals.

Nevertheless, the 1734 wedding seems to have been the closest comparable event in terms of numbers of singers and players, and there were certainly many more performers for this celebration of 'His Majesty's safe arrival from beyond the Sea' than for the similar occasions in which Handel had been involved during the 1720s. As already noted, on the Dettingen music Handel named Gates and Abbott for the solo music for bass voice, and the identity of Anselm Bayly as the alto soloist is established from a letter written by John Christopher Smith.

Autographs (Te Deum and Anthem)

For the Dettingen music Handel returned to the large-format paper that he had used for the Coronation Anthems, though not for the intervening wedding and funeral anthems.[54] In both the Te Deum and the Anthem Handel labelled the third trumpet part 'Principal', instead of 'Trumpet 3' as in the Coronation Anthems: the practical implications of this, if any, are uncertain. The SSATB chorus scoring that was in the lineage of Purcell's (and Urio's) settings of the Te Deum survived throughout the Dettingen Te Deum and into the first movement of the anthem, but thereafter Handel combined the 'Canto' (soprano) lines into one part. As already noted, in 'To thee all angels cry aloud' he was careful to designate the parts for tutti (rather than solo) voices, which makes it perhaps the more surprising that he did not mark up 'Thou sittest at the right hand of God' or 'We believe that thou shalt come'. At the beginning of 'All the earth doth worship thee' he wrote 'Solo' (without a singer's name) at the first alto lead, and again at bar 32, but there are no such markings on the following leads for soprano and tenor voices, which may have been sung chorally. As also noted, there is no solo indication at bars 20–6 of 'Day by day we magnify thee', though context and style here suggest the possibility of a solo voice. At 'The Father of an infinite Majesty' (fo. 15ᵛ) he laid out staves for trumpets and drums, though he did not need them until well into 'Thou are the King of Glory' two folios later: perhaps he had wondered about bringing these instruments in earlier. The last page of the Te Deum autograph (which probably carried a completion date) seems to have been lost during the eighteenth century: Smith junior copied a replacement, probably *c*.1760, just as he did for the lost first leaf of *Let thy hand be strengthened* (see Ch. 10). The autographs of the Te Deum and the Anthem were the first of Handel's music for the Chapel Royal to carry dates of composition: as already noted, he began the Te Deum on 17 July 1743, began the anthem on 30 July, and completed it on

---

[54] GB-Lbl RM 20.h.6 (Dettingen Te Deum); Lbl Add. MS 30308 (Dettingen Anthem).

3 August. His date annotations, as usual on his musical autographs from this period, were written in German.

The autographs of both works suggest that the composition ran fairly smoothly, since they comprise mainly regular paper gatherings.[55] Visually, however, there is a considerable contrast, for the autograph of the Te Deum has very few corrections except to minor details, while that for the anthem shows considerable structural revisions to several movements, clearly under-taken during compositional drafting since many deleted passages were left in a skeletal form without completion of the parts for all voices and instruments. There is only one such major alteration in the main run of the Te Deum autograph, in 'When thou tookest upon Thee', where Handel slightly delayed the arrival at a cadence in F sharp minor (eventually, bar 73). A couple of other alterations required inserted folios. In one case he extended 'Make them to be numbered with thy saints' slightly, replacing his original scalic figure for 'and lift them up for ever' with the more characterful one in rising thirds.[56] The other inserted leaf carries 'Vouchsafe, O Lord':[57] either he omitted to set this in the first instance, or his single-page version replaces an earlier setting. (The latter seems less likely, since the following paper gatherings are undisturbed.) Interestingly, corrections to the word-setting in this movement suggest that Handel may have been considering a longer treatment of the text, but then decided to incorporate all three verses in one short movement.[58]

The revisions to the Dettingen Anthem began in the opening ritornello, where he cut a substantial (fully scored) passage that had included an excursion to the dominant key. Later in the movement (beginning at bar 41 in the final version of the movement) he removed a lightly drafted eleven-bar passage that, for the only time in the movement, would have used the opening fanfare figure as the basis for the vocal parts; he also cut a brief fanfare-based ritornello at the end of the movement. In the second movement he shortened the semiquaver passage in the opening ritornello and excised two substantial passages, of ten and nineteen bars, that extended the repetitions of 'Glory, worship, honour' (with semiquaver string accompaniment): it is possible that, in addition to deciding that this extension was out of place, Handel recognized that he had done something rather too similar nearly twenty years before, in 'Glory and worship are before him' from the Chapel Royal anthem *I will magnify thee* (HWV 250b). The last movement of the anthem is virtually

---

[55] The pattern of the paper gatherings is clear, but Handel added apparently anomalous folio numbers: see Burrows and Ronish, *A Catalogue*, 288.

[56] GB-Lbl RM 20.h.6, fo. 25.

[57] Ibid., fo. 30.

[58] Handel originally set bars 11–16 to 'O Lord, have mercy upon us', and then amended the music to accommodate the additional verse.

revision-free, and many of the alterations to the preceding movement are related to the recomposition and adaptation of the *Semele* chorus,[59] though a more structural choice in the fourth movement was the deletion of a thirty-five-bar solo section for Abbot, that had originally complemented the alto solo, following bar 42. The most fascinating revisions, however, are in the chorus 'Thou shalt give him everlasting felicity', in which Handel shifted around the musical building-blocks (including tonal centres) within the movement, as well as simply making extensions or excisions. It seems likely that he began by trying out the two-subject exposition[60] before he composed the beginning of the movement (as it became in the final version), which he started on the vacant previous folio. According to Handel's dates, he completed the anthem in five days, a rate of one movement per day: the autograph shows that a lot of serious and constructive compositional thought went into the job, and that he was not content with an easy path.

The Peace of Aix-la-Chapelle

The victory at Dettingen marked a glorious end to George II's personal military career, but it was also the beginning of Britain's involvement in the next round of European continental warfare, exacerbated and complicated by the necessity to secure Britain itself against Jacobite activity that came close to at least the appearance of success in challenging the Hanoverian succession. European alliances at this time were both complex and unstable, and inter-connections between various political interests in Britain and Europe made for a particularly dangerous situation: the security of both Britain and Hanover was at stake in various phases of the conflict, and it suited France's continental interests to encourage domestic mayhem in Britain that would draw off the country's resources. The events of 1745–6 brought the facts of war close to home for most Britons: the Jacobite army reached as far south as the Midlands, and fears for security led to a longer-term anxiety about invasion that spread a blight of constant military presence across the southernmost (France-facing) counties of England from the 1750s until at least the end of the Napoleonic wars. The political, dynastic, and territorial issues involved in the continental war were so intricate that probably no long-lasting solution was possible, but there were times when the smouldering fires of conflict flared up into actual warfare, and other times when relatively honourable compromises looked more attractive than the continuance of destructive campaigning. In the later

---

[59] See Hurley, '"The Summer of 1743"'.
[60] Now GB-Lbl Add. MS 30308, fo. 9^r.

1740s shifting political interests and war-weariness encouraged a move towards a negotiated pause in the competitive aggression. It is not surprising that Londoners, in particular, were more ready than usual to celebrate the relief that was represented by the Peace of Aix-la-Chapelle.

International negotiations for the Peace were necessarily protracted: many interests were involved, and specific proposals had to be ratified separately by national governments. A draft form of the 'definitive treaty' was prepared by mid-October 1748, at which time the King was in Hanover. Already on 31 October *The General Advertiser* began to refer to the firework display that was expected for the Peace celebrations in London, and on 2 November it made a couple of other predictions:

> We hear that Thursday Se'ennight is appointed for the Proclaiming of the Peace, in case his Majesty is not detained abroad by Contrary Winds; and
> We likewise hear that his Majesty has been pleased to signify his Intention of going to St. Paul's on Thanksgiving Day, which will be afterwards appointed.

By mid-November work had started in Green Park on the preparations for the firework display, which involved the erection of a wooden building from which the fireworks were to be played off, and stands for the spectators,[61] but the Peace negotiations were not completed by the end of the year. Early in January 1748/9 a description of the building for the forthcoming fireworks included: 'There are handsome Steps, which go up to a grand Area before the Middle Arch, where a Band of a Hundred Musicians are to play before the Fireworks begin, the Musick for which is to be compos'd by Mr. Handel.'[62] Probably Handel anticipated that suitable music would also be needed from him for the service that would be attended by the King on the Thanksgiving Day, as well as for the Royal Fireworks, but his experience with the Dettingen music would have led him to be cautious over the venue for the service, and his recollection of the negotiations for the Peace of Utrecht would have reminded him that such agreements were not completed quickly. *The Daily Advertiser* on 18 November 1748 expected that 'that the publick Thanksgiving for the Peace will be on the 10th of January next, when his Majesty will repair to St. Paul's with the usual Ceremonies; and that the Fireworks that have been so long preparing, will be play'd off the same Evening in the Green-Park'. The suggested date was too optimistic, and the eventual Peace celebrations were not concentrated into one day.

---

[61] *DA*, 5 Nov. reported the marking-out of the ground for the building and the stands; *GA*, 8 Nov. reported the commencement of work on the fireworks building, and (11 Nov.) the clearing of the ground.

[62] *GA*, 3 Jan. 1748/9.

The King returned to England late on 22 November, arriving back at St James's Palace at 2 a.m. the next morning. In the following fortnight it was Greene's music that was heard at court: a Te Deum and an anthem 'vocally and instrumentally perform'd' at the Chapel Royal on 27 November, the first Sunday after the King's return, and then a performance of the delayed ode for the King's birthday on 2 December. The soloists for the ode included Anselm Bayly and two singers who had become Gentlemen of the Chapel in 1744: Benjamin Mence (alto) and Robert Wass (bass).[63] A new generation of singers was now established at the Chapel, and other changes had taken place as well: Edmund Gibson died in September 1748 and Thomas Sherlock, his successor as Bishop of London, was sworn in as Dean of the Chapel Royal on 20 December. The British proclamation of the Peace, dated 1 February 1748/9, was publicly read in London the next day, and by that time Handel was no doubt preparing for his forthcoming oratorio season at Covent Garden theatre, which opened on 10 February. Information and speculation about the forthcoming Peace celebrations continued to flow from the newspapers:

We are now credibly informed that Thursday the 6th of April is fix'd for the Thanksgiving on account of the Peace: when his Majesty will go to St. Paul's with the usual State.

And that the Fireworks in the Green Park will be play'd off the Day following. (*GA*, 1 Mar. 1749)

We are informed that his Majesty will not come to St. Paul's on Thanksgiving Day, as has been so confidently asserted. (*GA*, 4 Mar.)

Rumour gave place to more solid information when a proclamation was issued on 16 March naming 25 April as the day for the Public Thanksgiving on which the service would take place;[64] the printed liturgy for the occasion (see Fig. 14.1), comprising Morning Prayer and the Communion Service, was advertised for sale as early as 29 March.[65]

According to one newspaper Handel received a formal request for music for the Thanksgiving soon after the proclamation: 'We hear that last Monday [20 March] Mr. Handell received Orders to compose a new Anthem, which is to be perform'd before his Majesty at the Chapel Royal the Day of the Thanksgiving for the Peace.'[66] There is no documentary record of the order in the Lord Chamberlain's papers,[67] but the report seems plausible both as to

---

[63] *GA*, 1 Dec.: the complete list of named singers was Bayly, Wass, Mence, Savage, and Beard.

[64] The proclamation was printed in *LG*, 14–18 Mar.

[65] *DA* and *GA*, 29 Mar.

[66] *WEP*, 21–3 Mar.

[67] Few such orders are recorded in the Warrant Books: a rare exception is the command in Apr. 1746 to the Bishop of London (as Dean) for a 'New Anthem to be composed & performed

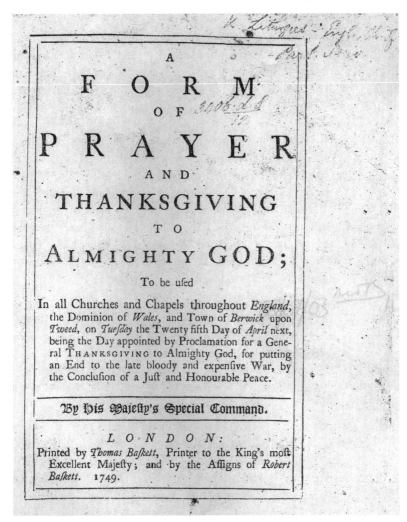

Fig. 14.1. Title page from the official order of service for the Thanksgiving for the Peace of Aix-la-Chapelle, 1749. British Library

content and timing. Handel completed his oratorio season with a performance of *Messiah* at Covent Garden on 23 March, and this gave him about a month in which to prepare and rehearse the music for both the Royal Fireworks and the Thanksgiving Day. Throughout the various stages of rumour, it seems to have been assumed that the Fireworks would not be held on the Thanksgiving Day

at the Chapel Royal . . . on Sunday next . . . upon the Account of His Royal Highness the Duke of Cumberland's good Success against the Rebels in Scotland' (GB-Lpro LC5/161, p. 220).

itself, and indeed this turned out to be the case. The timetable for the Fireworks and the preceding musical rehearsals underwent some changes, and in the end Handel must have interleaved the final preparations for the two events. According to newspaper reports there was a preliminary rehearsal for the *Fireworks Music* (presumably with principal performers only) at Handel's house in Brook Street on Monday 17 April,[68] and the famous full public rehearsal took place at Vauxhall Gardens on 21 April. Only one rehearsal for the Chapel Royal service was reported, for the following day: 'We hear that this Day [22 April] there will be a Practice of a new Anthem and Te Deum in St. James's Chapel, which is to be perform'd on the Thanksgiving Day before his Majesty and the Royal Family.'[69] On the Thanksgiving Day the following Tuesday, the Estates and the City attended church services at their separate venues, as they had done for Thanksgivings since 1715: the King went to the Chapel Royal, the House of Lords to Westminster Abbey, the House of Commons to St. Margaret's Church, Westminster, and the Mayor and Corporation of London to St Paul's Cathedral.[70] The Chapel Royal service was reported as follows:

> Tuesday being the Day appointed by Royal Proclamation, for a General Thanksgiving on Account of the late Peace, his Majesty and the Royal Family went to the Chapel Royal, where a new Te Deum and Anthem, the Musick whereof was composed by Mr. Handel, was performed, and also heard a Sermon preached by the Rev. Mr. Denne, one of his Chaplains, and Archdeacon of Rochester, from the 29th. Psalm, and the 10th Verse. (*WEP*, 25–7 Apr.)

Another newspaper report, which did not mention Handel's music, named the members of the Royal Family attending the service as the King, the Prince and Princess of Wales, Princess Amelia, and the Duke of Cumberland.[71] The Royal Fireworks took place in Green Park two days later: the fireworks themselves were preceded by an extended military review in the afternoon, and it seems to have been then that Handel's music was performed, rather than during the firework display itself.

The references to Handel's 'new Te Deum and Anthem' for the Thanksgiving service were no doubt made in good faith and followed a conventional formula that was probably encouraged by the musicians themselves: the

---

[68] *PLP*, 17–19 Apr.; *DA*, 18 Apr. The reports said that the 'Band consists of upwards of a Hundred...Instruments', but this was not necessarily a description of those attending on 17 Apr.

[69] *DA*, 22 Apr.

[70] Canaletto's magnificent picture of a colourful procession leaving from the west door of Westminster Abbey in 1749 relates to an installation service for the Knights of the Bath in June and not to the Thanksgiving.

[71] *DA*, 26 Apr.

payments for music-copying would have been made on the basis that the music was 'new'. In fact, neither the Te Deum nor the anthem for the occasion was strictly 'new', though they departed from this description in different ways: for the Te Deum Handel revived the Caroline setting in the form that he had given it at the Chapel Royal during the 1720s, and for the anthem he constructed a work from music that he had previously written, though in this case some new composition was also involved.

Revival of the Caroline Te Deum

The evidence for a revival of the Caroline Te Deum in 1749 is provided by one set of singers' names on the autograph, given here in Handel's spellings:[72]

We praise Thee, O God	Mr Bayly★, Mr Menz (altos), Mr Wase (bass)
To Thee all angels	Mr Menz★
To Thee Cherubim	Mr Bayly★
When Thou tookest	Menz
And we worship Thy name	Mr Menz★
Vouchsafe, O Lord	Mr Bayly

Handel made further subsequent alterations to these names. On 'When Thou tookest upon Thee' he deleted 'Menz' and wrote 'Mr Baily'; the entries marked ★ were deleted and in each case replaced by 'Mr Leigh'. These reallocations may refer to a further performance of the Te Deum, actual or planned, after April 1749 (see Ch. 15), or to last-minute changes that were made before the Thanksgiving service. If the latter, perhaps George Laye (who was senior in the Chapel to Bayly and Mence) was found to be serving a period of waiting in late April, and a solo part was carved out for him from the music previously assigned to Bayly and Mence.[73] Laye's name (as 'Lee') name appears among the chorus leaders on Handel's autograph of the Coronation Anthems, but he does not seem to have been very active or prominent as a soloist after 1730: although he probably served his duty regularly at the Chapel Royal, his principal centre of activity was at St George's Chapel, Windsor.

Other annotations on the autograph of the Te Deum, in pencil and not written by Handel, also relate to a performance in 1749 or later. Above the beginning of the movement 'When Thou tookest upon Thee' is written

---

[72] See above, Table 5.2, for the names on the autograph from which this list is extracted.

[73] The alterations may also possibly reflect a plan, though not recorded comprehensively next to every passage for solo alto, to give Laye the music previously allocated to both Bayly and Mence.

'Teede and Richter', the names of two well-documented woodwind-instrument players who presumably needed to be supplied with the music for the obbligato part. Handel's original designation 'Traversiere' for this part has been deleted in pencil and replaced by 'Hautb', probably by Handel, but the latter was then subsequently deleted in ink. Among Handel's performances of the Te Deum in 1714, the 1720s, and 1749 this part was taken at various times by flute or oboe, but the names of the performers do not help to identify the instrument that was used in 1749: Teede and Richter, like many contemporary players, were probably double-handed on flute or oboe. Their names appear again above the obbligato line in the aria version of 'Vouchsafe, O Lord', where the 'Trav' indication has not been amended. (For this movement, a copy of the aria written by J. C. Smith was inserted into the autograph, and it was on this that Handel wrote 'Mr Bayly', so there is no doubt that this aria was the setting of the text that was performed in 1749.) The evidence that the obbligato parts were at some stage doubled by two players is interesting with respect to performance practice: it is clear on the manuscript that the names are in fact coupled and were not added at different times. While the payments for the Chapel Royal services in the 1720s, including at least one occasion on which the Caroline Te Deum must have been performed, consistently indicate a single player for oboe (possibly doubling flute), Handel expected two upper woodwind players to be available in April 1749, since the Anthem on the Peace has obbligato music for flute and oboe, playing together but not doubling the same music. In the absence of the 'annext list' for the payments that would have given the names of the additional players, we cannot be sure that Teede and Richter played in 1749, but it seems very likely. Below the orchestral bass part in 'Vouchsafe, O Lord' another pencil annotation (not in Handel's hand, and probably no earlier than 1749) reads 'Bass part for Deidrich and Gillier', also referring to identifiable musicians: Christian Dietrich was a double bass player and the cellist Peter Gillier was the Chapel Royal's Violist, having held that office since 1742.

There is no evidence from the autograph, or from any secondary manuscript copy, that the Te Deum was changed in any matter of musical substance in 1749: indeed, the manner in which the soloists' names were added indicates that the work was repeated in the form that Handel found it—that is, the 1714 score, amended by the aria version of 'Vouchsafe, O Lord' that he had substituted for the original accompanied recitative in the 1720s (see Ch. 9). It is remarkable, and a tribute to the musical quality of the original, that Handel could repeat the music thus thirty-five years after its composition, without any sense of incongruity. The Caroline Te Deum clearly fulfilled the specification, in terms of scoring and performance duration, that was needed for the Chapel Royal service in 1749. Although he was probably very busy in April of that year with preparations for the performances at the Chapel Royal and the Royal Fireworks, Handel could have replaced all or part of the work with new composition. Perhaps he decided, on reflection, that he could not do better for a compact setting of the English Te Deum text with accompaniment for trumpets and strings, and designed for Chapel Royal singers.

The Anthem on the Peace
(*How beautiful are the feet*), HWV 266

Handel's anthem does not survive in one integral score, but can be reconstructed with some confidence from a number of different sources. About a month after the 1749 Thanksgiving service, he gave his first performance at the Foundling Hospital Chapel, a concert on 27 May in which the first part, as described in the newspaper announcement, comprised performances of '*The Music for the Late* Royal Fireworks *and the* Anthem *on the* Peace'.[74] The printed word-book for the concert gives the text of 'The ANTHEM composed on the Occasion of the PEACE' in the following form:[75]

VERSE DUET.
How beautiful are the feet of them that bring good Tidings of Peace!
that say unto Sion, thy God reigneth!
CHORUS.
Break forth into Joy, Thy God reigneth.
CHORUS.
Glory and Worship are before Him, Power and Honour are in his Sanctuary.
VERSE and CHORUS.
The Lord hath given Strength unto his People:
The Lord hath given his People the Blessing of Peace.
Full CHORUS.
Blessing and Glory, Power and Honour be unto God for ever and ever. Amen.

This represents four musical movements, in which the opening Verse Duet and the following Chorus run together as one movement. The texts of the first and third movements have obvious relevance to the Peace celebrations, while the other two have a more generalized theme of praise and thanksgiving; together they provided the opportunity for two successive two-movement sequences. The individual verses were taken from disparate places in the Bible, and for three of the four movements they relate directly to texts that Handel had set previously. For the music of all four movements he drew in various ways on his previous compositions. The eclectic assemblage of texts resembles

---

[74] *GA*, 19 Apr.   [75] *A Performance of Musick*, [5]–6.

the sequences of verses from equally diverse scriptural sources that appeared in the section of the printed Thanksgiving liturgies for Morning Prayer headed 'Instead of the *Venite*, this hymn shall be used' (see Ch. 2). The verse beginning 'The Lord shall give strength unto his people' that Handel set (in a slightly altered form) for the anthem was included in this section of the 1749 Thanksgiving liturgy,[76] and it was also the text (Psalm 29: 10) that Dr Denne took for his sermon at the Chapel Royal service.

The words and the music of 'How beautiful are the feet' are familiar from *Messiah*, but the relationships between the movements in the anthem and the oratorio are not simple, regarding both the text and the music. In the Authorized Version of the Bible there are two very similar texts:

How beautiful upon the mountains are the feet of him that bringeth good tidings, that publisheth peace; that bringeth good tidings of good, that publisheth salvation; that saith unto Zion, Thy God reigneth! Break forth into joy, sing together, ye waste places of Jerusalem. (Isaiah 52: 7, 9)

And how shall they preach, except they be sent? as it is written, How beautiful are the feet of them that preach the gospel of peace, and bring glad tidings of good things! (Romans 10: 15)

It is obvious from the context that the author of the Epistle to the Romans was making reference to the Isaiah text: the apparent misquotation may have been accidental or deliberate. In the libretto of *Messiah* Charles Jennens used the Romans text (with some adaptation), followed by a version of words from verse 18 ('Their sound is gone out into all lands'), and in his original autograph of the oratorio Handel set these verses as a full dal segno soprano aria, with 'Their sound is gone out' as the middle section.[77] However, in Dublin before the first performance of *Messiah* he recomposed the movement as a sequence for alto duet and chorus, using the Isaiah text and bringing in the chorus at 'Break forth into joy'.[78] This version, but with soprano and contralto soloists in place of the two altos, was included in the first London performances of *Messiah* in March 1743, and it may have been one of the causes of Jennens's dissatisfaction with the work at that time; Handel, probably rather hurriedly, tacked on a short aria setting of 'Their sound is gone out'.[79] At the next revival of *Messiah* in 1745 he reverted completely to the Romans text, using the opening section of his original soprano aria and composing a new chorus

---

[76] *A Form of Prayer and Thanksgiving to Almighty God; To be used . . . on Tuesday the Twenty Fifth Day of April next* (see Fig. 14.1), 5.
[77] GB-Lbl RM 20.f.2, fos. 89ᵛ–90ᵛ; see *HHA* I/17, 170–2.
[78] *HHA* I/17, 159–69.
[79] Ibid. 170. For the history of these movements in *Messiah*, see Watkins Shaw, *A Textual and Historical Companion*, 112–14; Burrows, 'Handel's Performances of *Messiah*', 327–8; and id., 'The Autographs and Early Copies', 214–15.

setting of 'Their sound is gone out'. From that moment he seems to have abandoned the 'Isaiah' duet-and-chorus version in his performances of *Messiah*.

In March 1749 Handel revived *Messiah* for a single performance at the end of his Covent Garden oratorio season: this was only his sixth performance of the oratorio in London. No doubt the *Messiah* music was still on his mind when he came to compose the Anthem on the Peace soon afterwards: perhaps he had turned over his autograph of the Isaiah setting when he was preparing the *Messiah* performance. There are autographs of two versions for the first movement of the anthem, both on the Isaiah text;[80] in the 1950s their association with the anthem was still unrecognized and they were assumed to have been composed for alternative use in *Messiah*.[81] One version is a triple-time movement in D major for treble soloist and chorus (see Ex. 14.6).[82] Handel recomposed the music from a movement for soprano and chorus that he had written early in 1746 for 'Be wise at length, ye kings averse' in the *Occasional Oratorio*, which had itself been based on thematic material from an aria movement in a serenata by Alessandro Stradella.[83] In the anthem movement, at the entry of the chorus with a new fanfare-like figure for 'Break forth into joy', he brought in the trumpets and drums, with an effect similar to that in the first movement of the Coronation Anthem *My heart is inditing*; eventually the theme and text from the solo return, to be treated in imitation by the chorus (as in the earlier oratorio movement).

Handel did not quite complete this version. Following one of his usual methods when drafting a choral movement, in the second section he began by writing out the chorus parts and then went back to fill in the orchestral accompaniment: most unusually, he abandoned this filling-up process about fifteen bars from the end—literally within sight of the end, on the last page of his manuscript. The text of his movement was a mixture from Isaiah and Romans: 'How beautiful are the feet of them that bringeth good tidings of peace, that say unto Sion, thy God reigneth; break forth into joy'. In the merger the syntax had gone awry, coupling 'them' with 'bringeth': Handel seems to have been quite comfortable with this usage, for he repeated it when

[80] They were reproduced in facsimile in Chrysander, *Das Autograph*, 285–309, along with the duet-and-chorus setting for *Messiah* (310–20). The remaining autograph material for the Anthem on the Peace was not included.

[81] Herbage, 'The Oratorios', 99, following the implications of the inclusion of the movements in Chrysander's *Messiah* facsimile; Larsen, *Handel's 'Messiah'*, 230–2, distinguished the movements as 'Chapel Royal versions' but did not connect them with a context in the Peace Anthem.

[82] GB-Lbl RM 20.g.6, fos. 34–9. This movement is HWV 267.

[83] Stradella's serenata, *Qual prodigio è ch'io miri?*, was published as *HG* Supp. 3, where the relevant movement begins on p. 28.

Ex. 14.6. Handel, Anthem on the Peace (first version, HWV 267)

setting a text in the Foundling Hospital Anthem about a month later, 'Blessed are they that considereth the poor and needy'.

For the other version of the movement Handel returned to the D minor setting for alto duet and chorus that he had composed in 1742 for *Messiah*, and used that as the basis for a new composition.[84] Although it is just possible that he composed this version first, and then tried the triple-time setting, the alternative sequence of events seems more likely: that he wrote the D major setting first, but abandoned it at the last moment and pursued the *Messiah*-related idea. Perhaps he had initially deliberately avoided going over the *Messiah* ground again for setting the text, but subsequently decided that this material provided a good solution after all: in the other version, notwithstanding the appropriateness of the major key for the mood of the text, the music derived from the *Occasional Oratorio* did not really fit the words very well. What is certain is that the *Messiah*-related setting became the one that finally formed the first movement of the Anthem on the Peace: not only is it a fully completed movement, but its autograph runs directly into music for the second movement, while the incomplete D major version is followed by empty manuscript pages. Probably, in addition to reconsidering his original decision to avoid the *Messiah* music, Handel also saw opportunities relating to the broader musical strategy for the anthem. Effective as the entry of the trumpets and drums had been at 'Break forth into joy' in the D major version, a better scheme still would be to delay these instruments until the second movement, producing a larger structure with cumulative effect: How beautiful are the feet (soloists) → Break forth into joy (chorus) → Glory and worship are before him (with trumpets and drums). Furthermore, the *Occasional Oratorio* music could be used for the text of the third movement of the anthem. The *Messiah* duet proved to be a very appropriate basis for the first movement, since it had originally been composed for two male altos from the Dublin cathedral choirs:[85] the music was a ready-made resource, in terms of musical style and register, for Bayly and Mence at the Chapel Royal. (Greene had also composed a duet movement for them in his 1747/8 New Year ode.) As far as Handel's future performances of *Messiah* itself were concerned, the duet-and-chorus setting was now obsolete. In melodic outline the theme of the duet version was similar to that of the aria setting of 'How beautiful are the feet' which was now his regular version for the oratorio, but in fact the two movements were clearly distinguished by metre as well as text: the compound-time setting of the aria implied a different style of performance and a different tempo from the triple-time duet.

[84] GB-Lbl RM 20.g.6, fos. 25^r–31^r.
[85] Ward and Lamb: see Burrows, 'Handel's Performances of *Messiah*', 327. It is possible, however, that one or both of these singers had been replaced by Sigra Avolio or/and Mrs Cibber for this movement before the first performance.

Having decided to revert, after all, to using the *Messiah* duet as the basis for a new movement, Handel brought considerable ingenuity and care to the task. The Dublin *Messiah* duet had opened with a short ritornello for strings introducing the theme: for the Peace Anthem he used the opening of the introductory Sinfonia from his Chapel Royal version of *As pants the hart* from the 1720s (HWV 251c) to begin the movement. As a Larghetto movement in D minor and in 3/4 time, this fitted the tempo, key, and metre for the duet, but Handel also saw the possibility of coupling the music from the two sources more closely. He must have copied and adapted the opening of the anthem directly from his autograph of *As pants the hart*:[86] although the scoring of the orchestral staves is slightly different, he reproduced the same bar layout on the opening pages. He followed his Sinfonia source as far as the dominant modulation and then, returning to the tonic, introduced the 'How beautiful' theme as a duet for flute and oboe:[87] again this marks a more interesting approach than in his earlier *Messiah* setting, or in his first attempt at setting the text for the anthem. The duet music, for 'Mr Bayly solo' and 'Mr Menz solo', extended the *Messiah* material by half a dozen bars, and set the opening text in a more strongly syllabic manner.[88] The words from the other draft of the anthem were carried forward intact, with their defective syntax: the *Messiah* movement had followed Isaiah more closely with 'How beautiful are the feet of him that bringeth'. For the chorus section of the movement Handel began by following the track of the *Messiah* movement, but then (from bar 94) worked a thematic idea from the *As pants the hart* Sinfonia into the orchestral accompaniment: he even managed to fit this material together when, as in the *Messiah* movement, the chorus reintroduces the music of the duet: see Ex. 14.7.

Instead of the perfect cadence that concluded the *Messiah* movement, the chorus ends on the dominant of D minor, to introduce the next movement, 'Glory and worship are before him', in D major. The latter was transferred, complete and with its original text, from the anthem *I will magnify thee* (HWV 250b) that Handel had composed for the Chapel Royal in the 1720s (see Ch. 9), but enhanced with new additional parts for trumpets and drums (see Fig. 14.2).[89] Just as the first movement showed remarkable cunning in integrating music from the *Messiah* movement with material from the Sinfonia to *As pants the hart*, so the addition of the trumpets and drums to the second movement involved some creative ingenuity: it is a comparable case to

---

[86] GB-Lbl RM 20.g.1.

[87] Solo instruments are implied, but not actually specified; it is unlikely that the additional players for the Chapel Royal service in 1749 included more than two for flute/oboe.

[88] See the music example in Larsen, *Handel's 'Messiah'*, 232.

[89] The additional parts for trumpets and drums (GB-Lbl RM 20.g.6, fos. 31^v–32^r) begin on the verso of the last page of the duet-and-chorus movement.

Ex. 14.7. Anthem on the Peace (No. 1)

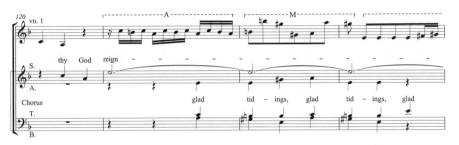

A = *As pants the hart* (HWV251c); M = *Messiah*

Handel's addition of the obbligato bassoon part to the pre-existing introduction to 'We believe that thou shalt come' in the A major Te Deum, described in Chapter 9. In the movement from HWV 250b the vocal parts were for alto, tenor, and bass soloists with ripieno four-part choir, arranged in such a way that the soloists were concertists within the overall texture, so the addition of the trumpets and drums enhanced a texture that was already quite elaborate, as well as adding formal weight. The opening of the movement is particularly striking. In bars 1–2 the orchestra introduces the theme in canon between the bassi and the violins; the theme is taken up by the chorus in bar 3, and then the entry of the trumpets and drums in bar 4 adds an extra gloss.[90]

For the third movement Handel used the *Occasional Oratorio* material from his abandoned draft of the first movement, returning the key to E major as in the oratorio and adding an extended opening ritornello for his flute and oboe soloists (with basso continuo accompaniment) before the entry of the treble soloist. The music generally worked well to the new text, and recomposition was needed only in a few details; curiously, at one place (bar 36) the anthem movement introduced a difficulty into the word-setting that had not been

[90] Handel had followed a similar pattern in the discarded setting of 'How beautiful are the feet', where he brought in the trumpets and drums two bars after the chorus entry.

Fig. 14.2. A page of Handel's autograph of music for his Anthem on the Peace, HWV 266, for the 1749 Thanksgiving. The trumpet and drum parts were to be added to the movement from HWV 250b shown in Fig. 9.1. British Library, RM 20.g.6, fo. 31^v

present in the oratorio version. The aria had originally been composed in the *Occasional Oratorio* for the soprano Francesina; in the anthem Handel labelled the solo part, in his usual anonymous manner, for 'the Boy'. After the solo section he composed a fourteen-bar link for the opening of the chorus music, but then the autograph ceases.[91] The continuation of the music is, however, to

---

[91] The autograph material for the movement is GB-Lbl RM 20.g.6, fos. 32–3.

be found in scores relating to the later use of the chorus as a separate movement in revivals of *Israel in Egypt* under Smith junior in the 1760s;[92] Handel also wrote some fragmentary verbal cues into the autograph of the *Occasional Oratorio* that relate to the preparation of the anthem.[93]

There are no complete primary or secondary sources for the last movement, but it seems certain that Handel used the music from *Messiah* to a similar (but independent) text: the section 'Blessing and honour, glory and pow'r' from 'Worthy is the Lamb'.[94] On the conducting score of *Messiah* he wrote in the adaptation for the anthem text on the first phrases of the music, and at the end of the movement he wrote a cue (as a vocal bass line) to show an alternative final cadence: this showed how the anthem was to end, incorporating the 'Amen' from the final bars of the last movement of *Messiah*.[95] Thus the Anthem on the Peace, Handel's last composition for the Chapel Royal, ended with a simple 'Amen', as his first Chapel Royal anthem (HWV 251a) had done more than thirty-five years previously. The 'Blessing and honour' section in the autograph of *Messiah* has pencil marks indicating a fourteen-bar cut in the middle of the movement, but it is unlikely that these relate to the anthem: the cut would have shortened the movement too much for its context in the anthem, and it seems that the conducting score rather than the autograph of *Messiah* was primarily used for the preparation of the anthem.[96] The transition from third movement's key of E major to the D major of the final movement is smoother than at the parallel place in *My heart is inditing*, because 'Blessing and glory' begins with a unison entry on the note A, the dominant of D major.

In spite of the attention that Handel paid to the recomposition of the first movement and the solo section of the third movement, it might be thought that the Peace Anthem as a whole was rather opportunistically cobbled together. He probably had to work quickly to produce the anthem, but the overall musical scheme is both effective and coherent: he judged well the picture that could be made from the various elements. The fact the movements draw in various ways upon his pre-existing music suggests that Handel influenced the selection of the text for the anthem, knowing in advance both the music that he wanted to use and (after a false start on the first movement) the

---

[92] The chorus had been included in the new form of Part I for the performances of *Israel in Egypt* at Covent Garden in 1756–8, but no musical source survives from this: the extant scores relate to performances from 1765 onwards. See Handel, *The Anthem on the Peace*, ed. Burrows, p. vi, and the commentary to *Israel in Egypt*, HHA I/14.2.

[93] GB-Lbl RM 20.f.3, fos. 45–8.

[94] The anthem text is from Revelation 7: 12, the *Messiah* text from Revelation 5: 13.

[95] GB-Ob MS Tenbury 347, fos. 125ᵛ–126ʳ, 132ʳ.

[96] There is, however, a linking 'NB' cue for the final 'Amen' of the anthem in the autograph of *Messiah*, GB-Lbl RM 20.f.2, fo. 132ᵛ.

distribution of this music within the overall scheme of the anthem. If the Peace Anthem, in combination with the Caroline Te Deum, created a kind of retrospective exhibition of Handel's music in 1749, it also formed a worthy conclusion to his creative association with the music of the Chapel Royal. As already noted, Handel repeated the anthem, probably with the same perform-ers, at his concert in the Foundling Hospital Chapel on 27 May 1749, about a month after the Chapel Royal service; thereafter it was not heard until a performance that I directed in December 1973. The reconstruction of the anthem was my first Handelian project, and I have had no regrets about its value in the performances that I have attended and conducted.[97]

Conditions of Performance

In spite of the monster-sized orchestra that was assembled for the Fireworks Music in the same week, it is unlikely that the 1749 Thanksgiving Service involved an exceptionally large group of musicians, or even as many perform-ers as the Dettingen music had done in 1743. J. C. Smith was paid £58. 1s. 0d. for providing the music and for the hire of additional performers (see App. I): this is less than half of the amount that he had received in 1743, and indeed considerably less than any of the comparable payments relating to Handel's other Chapel Royal performances during George II's reign. The music was similar in scale to that composed by Handel for Chapel Royal services during the reign of George I: the Caroline Te Deum itself was music that had been composed and performed at the earlier period, though a slightly larger number of players and singers may have been involved for its performance in 1749. The Te Deum included trumpet parts, but the work had probably been performed by Handel at least once during the 1720s in a reduced scoring, with an oboe taking the Trumpet I part: in view of the inclusion of trumpet parts in the Anthem on the Peace, there is no doubt that the original instrumentation was restored in 1749, and perhaps a timpani part was added for which we have no notational record. The players of the trumpet and drum parts may have performed as part of their duties as members of establishments in the Royal household, but the necessary players for double bass, flute, oboe, and bassoon must have been among the 'extraordinary performers' that were hired for the service, and it is likely that there were a few additional singers as well, probably including John Beard. On his autograph of the first movement of the Peace Anthem, Handel specified 'Violoncello' and 'Contra Basso', but plural 'Bas-sons'. The basic complement of Chapel Royal Gentlemen and Musicians in Ordinary who were currently in waiting, plus the Chapel Royal choristers, were supplemented by perhaps about a dozen extra players and singers in all.

---

[97] See Burrows, 'Handel's Peace Anthem'.

No special gallery or organ was provided in the Chapel for the occasion. Over the years, Smith may have been able to establish a more favourable remuneration for his provision of the music.

On his autographs Handel identified Bayly, Mence, and Wass as the principal soloists from the Gentlemen for the Chapel Royal performance in 1749. In the anthem he wrote for Mence in the alto clef, but he also named him for the tenor part in the short ATB ensemble at the beginning of the Caroline Te Deum; perhaps Mence also took the 'concertino' Tenor line in 'Glory and worship are before him' in the anthem. As for 'the Boy', the senior Chapel Royal boys in 1749 included Neal Abington, from a trumpet-playing family and later to make a career for himself in London as a trumpeter and singer, and Thomas Dupuis, who would eventually succeed Boyce as Organist of the Chapel Royal. One of the most attractive features of the Anthem on the Peace is that it encompasses both musical grandeur and more intimate chamber-style elements: the alto duet and the treble solo are complemented by passages in trio-sonata style featuring flute and oboe, and the vocal layout of the transferred movement 'Glory and worship are before him' implies performing circumstances in which, notwithstanding the addition of the trumpets, all of the singers made significant contributions to the texture.

Sources

The relevant annotations for the 1749 performance on the autograph of the Caroline Te Deum, and the new autograph material relating to the Anthem on the Peace,[98] have already been described. A conducting score of the anthem was certainly prepared: presumably Smith was given the autograph component and was directed to the various cues in the scores of the *Occasional Oratorio* and *Messiah* in order to make up the rest. A score of the anthem was described in a letter to Samuel Arnold from Henry Harington,[99] who wrote from Bath on 21 June 1796 to inform Arnold of some unknown pieces that might have been of interest to him in relation to his collected edition of Handel's works:

The knowledge you have so honourably obtained, and so worthily employed, in publishing the Works of Handel, may induce you to excuse my troubling you with a trifling circumstance relating to him. On looking over the musical papers of the late Mr Smith [i.e. J. C. Smith junior] who died here, and was the friend and assistant of Handel until his Death; I found a MSS in his own hand signed G. F. Hendel July 13 1707 at Rome.

---

[98] GB-Lbl RM 20.g.4, fos. 1–20 (Te Deum); RM 20.g.6, fos. 25–39 (anthem)
[99] In a volume of miscellaneous autograph letters, formerly owned by William Hawes, GB-Lg MS 10189/1.

Harington proceeds to describe the autograph of the 'Gloria Patri' from Handel's *Nisi Dominus*, and then continues:

I also found a chorus [to] the words 'Glory and Worship are before him[,] Power and Honour are in his Sanctuary'. It is in D♯3d con Tromb et Tympan. Another in A♯3 'The Lord hath given his people strength'. These are corrected in his owns [*sic*] hand both words and music. Whether designed for parts of the Messiah, as in the same Book is 'Break forth into joy', I know not, or whether introduced in some other work you can best inform us. I observe <u>Mence</u> Bailey Waltz and a Boy were the singers.

This must surely have been the conducting score of the anthem, presumably in some form of binding since Harington refers to 'a Book', though the letter describes the movements individually. Wass's name (misconstrued as 'Waltz') was probably added to the 'concertino' bass part in 'Glory and Worship are before him'. The description of Handel's alterations to the score is intriguing: perhaps, following the same pattern as in the conducting score of *This is the day*, Handel wrote in the new texts and adapted the music for the choral parts in 'The Lord hath given strength' and 'Blessing and Glory', and copied in his trumpet and drum parts for the second movement. Unfortunately the score was almost certainly destroyed, along with the autograph of the 'Gloria Patri' from *Dixit Dominus*, in the fire at a Bristol bookseller's shop in 1860, and no further copy is known.

15

Epilogue

THE Thanksgiving Service for the Peace of Aix-la-Chapelle in April 1749 was the last occasion for which Handel composed music specifically for the musicians of the Chapel Royal. His concert in the chapel of the Foundling Hospital a month later included a repeat performance of the Anthem on the Peace, in which Bayly and Mence almost certainly repeated their solo roles in the anthem: although the Foundling Hospital Chapel was not yet consecrated, it seems likely that the nature of both the building and the charitable occasion would have removed the inhibitions that normally prevented Priests from the Chapel Royal from performing at public venues such as the theatres. (The previous death of Bishop Gibson may also have helped.) Other singers from the Chapel Royal would also have taken part in the anthem, and contributed chorus voices for the rest of the programme, which comprised (as Part II) extracts from Handel's oratorio *Solomon* and (as Part III) 'The ANTHEM composed on this Occasion'. The latter, the 'Foundling Hospital Anthem' *Blessed are they that considereth the poor and needy*, HWV 268, was Handel's last English anthem.

In the Foundling Hospital Anthem, as in the Anthem on the Peace, Handel created an effective new work on the foundation of music that was transferred, adapted, or recomposed from his previous compositions. The anthem went through two distinct versions, one for chorus and orchestra throughout, and one incorporating movements for soloists—an opening aria for tenor, an aria version of 'O God, who from the suckling's mouth' composed for the alto castrato Guadagni, and a duet 'The people will tell of their wisdom' for boy trebles.[1] The arias were resettings of texts that had already been present in the first version, but the duet introduced a new verse. The word-book for the 1749 performance presents the text of the all-chorus version: it includes movement headings such as 'Verse and Chorus', but these refer to 'verse' passages that involved less than the full complement of four vocal parts, rather than movements or sections for soloists.[2] The characteristics of the manuscript paper on

---

[1] See Burrows, 'Handel and the Foundling Hospital', 275–8.
[2] There is an anomaly in the 'Verse and Chorus' heading to 'Comfort them, O Lord', which was probably a printer's error.

which Handel wrote the autographs of the solo movements, and the related insertions in the conducting score of the anthem, suggest that his revision of the anthem dates from about 1751, probably when the official opening of the Chapel was in the offing,[3] and comparison of the autograph of Guadagni's aria with the musically-related movement 'Happy Iphis' in *Jephtha* (composed in June or July 1751) suggests that the anthem movement was written second, though probably not much later in view of Handel's encroaching blindness.

Taking the all-chorus version of the Foundling Hospital Anthem as the work that was composed and performed in 1749, the origins of the various movements can be identified as follows:

1. Blessed are they that considereth the poor	Adapted and extended from 'How are the mighty fall'n' in the 1737 Funeral Anthem, HWV 264 (*NHE* No. 5, *HHA* No. 6), bars 8–14.
2. They deliver the poor that cry	'She deliver'd the poor that cried', Funeral Anthem (*NHE* No. 6, *HHA*, No. 7), bars 1–40, with alterations to the words, shown by Handel in his autograph of the Funeral Anthem.
O God, who from the suckling's mouth	New continuation of chorus; music derived from an organ chorale prelude on 'Aus tiefer Not lasst uns zu Gott' by F. W. Zachow.[4]
3. The charitable shall be had in everlasting remembrance	'The righteous shall be had in everlasting remembrance', Funeral Anthem, complete movement (*NHE* No. 8, *HHA* No. 9) with alterations to the words. (Handel's adaptation of the music in the first part of the movement for solo voices relates to his later revised version of the Foundling Hospital Anthem.)
4. Comfort them, O Lord	New composition, drawing on music from a Mass by Antonio Lotti.[5]
Keep them alive	'Virtue shall never long be oppress'd', a discarded chorus from the oratorio *Susanna* (composed 1748), adapted to the new text by Handel.
5. Hallelujah	Transferred without alteration from *Messiah* (sixth London performance, March 1749).

---

[3] See Burrows, 'Handel and the Foundling Hospital', 273–5. It is possible that the revisions were made for an intended performance at the funeral of Thomas Coram, which took place at the Foundling Hospital Chapel on 3 Apr. 1751. This conflicts with the suggested chronology in relation to the *Jephtha* aria, and is unlikely for other reasons: there was a very short time between Coram's death and the funeral, the only music that was performed on that occasion was 'a solemn Service composed by Dr. Boyce' (*DA*, 4 Apr.), and Handel's non-involvement may have been on account of the current state of his health. He presumably composed the revised aria before Guadagni left London towards the end of 1751 to perform in Dublin.

[4] Roberts, 'German Chorales', 88.

[5] See Roberts, *Handel Sources*, v, p. xv and music fos. 58^r–63^v.

The first three movements therefore derived substantially from the Funeral Anthem: indeed, it is not unreasonable to suppose that this anthem provided the initial musical stimulant to the composition of the Foundling Hospital Anthem,[6] and also the model for a work that was entirely for chorus and orchestra, though diversified by sections with different combinations of the voice parts. The texts of the second and third movements were directly adapted from those in the Funeral Anthem: worthy as the sentiments are, the substitution of the Charitable in 'The Righteous shall be had in everlasting remembrance' was possibly near the limits of acceptable adaptation for a scriptural text.

Although 1749 saw the end of Handel's Chapel Royal music, it did not also mean the end of his association with the Chapel Royal singers. As outlined in Chapter 11, Children and Gentlemen from the Chapel Royal continued to be an important component of the chorus singers for his oratorio performances at Covent Garden theatre, as they probably had done since the 1730s. On the death of Henry Reinhold in 1751 Robert Wass from the Chapel Royal became Handel's principal bass soloist for a few years, before ceding to Samuel Champness and taking up a place in the chorus. Many of the treble soloists probably still came from the Chapel, and John Beard's continuing career as Handel's principal tenor soloist for the oratorios displayed a long-term product of Chapel Royal training. Beard had been one of the early generation of Gates-trained choristers, and Champness represented a later generation; Samuel Arnold may have been one of the last choristers that Gates initiated into the Chapel.[7] Gates himself, a crucial figure in the development of Handel's career and a long-standing soloist in his Chapel Royal works even from Handel's first years in London, retired from participation at the Chapel in the later 1750s, when he became the senior Gentleman and took up the privilege of non-attendance without losing his two places.[8] As a performer he is last named, apparently as a chorus singer, in reports of rehearsals for the New Year odes for 1754 and 1756.[9] He resigned his places as Master of the Children at the Chapel Royal and Master of the Choristers at Westminster Abbey in 1757, but he had probably been reducing his activity during the previous years: as noted in

---

[6] The connection between the two works may possibly explain a newspaper reference to Handel 'composing a Funeral Anthem for himself' in Apr. 1753, when a performance of the (revised) Foundling Hospital Anthem was in preparation for the opening of the Chapel: see Burrows, 'Handel and the Foundling Hospital', 275.

[7] Arnold was not discharged as a chorister until Aug. 1758, but he had been a soloist in the New Year ode in 1757, just before Gates's formal retirement as Master. A connection is suggested by the fact that Arnold featured in Gates's will: see Highfill, *A Biographical Dictionary*, vi. 120.

[8] Gates retired to North Aston, Oxon.

[9] *SJ*, 7 Jan. 1754; *Jackson's Oxford Journal*, 3 Jan. 1756.

Chapter 11, Boyce rather than Gates received the thanks of the Foundling Hospital for supplying the trebles for Handel's *Messiah* performances.[10] In preparation for the official opening of the Foundling Hospital Chapel, the committee of the Hospital approached Handel, Boyce, and J. C. Smith junior at various times during 1750–2 regarding the music:[11] presumably Boyce and Smith directed the performances of the Te Deum, Jubilate, and anthem by Handel when this service eventually took place on 16 April 1753, probably with the composer in attendance. On that occasion it is most likely that the Foundling Hospital Anthem (in its second version) and *Zadok the priest* were performed, and the notices also mention a Te Deum and Jubilate by Handel, so possibly the Caroline Te Deum and the Utrecht Jubilate were also given.[12] The Foundling Hospital Anthem was performed again in a memorial concert for Handel at the Chapel in 1759, shortly after the composer's death. During the 1760s Boyce made a new verse anthem arrangement of Handel's *As pants the hart* for the Chapel Royal, and arranged movements from his oratorios for use as anthems there.[13]

Handel's Chapel Royal music forms an important strand in his creative achievement as a composer, and his interaction with leading members of the Chapel influenced aspects of his career both in his church music and in his theatre music. His association with the Chapel was also an important element in his relationship to the English Court, affected by developments within the royal family and by wider political influences. At times, particularly in connection with the Utrecht canticles and the Coronation Anthems, the performance of his music had a political aspect and can to some extent be regarded as fulfilling a political role. Handel probably expected that the Dettingen music would have a similar function, though in the end the relatively private circumstances of its performance may not have had much wider public effect: nevertheless, this music was the subject of public rehearsals and it provided Handel with some degree of cover or defence against the supporters of the 'Middlesex' opera company who considered that he was being disloyal to his responsibilities to London's musical life.

Purcell and Handel have been by far the greatest composers to be associated with the music of the Chapel Royal during the last four centuries. Although Purcell was, institutionally speaking, more of an 'insider' to the Chapel, both composers brought a breadth of vision and a strength of style to their English church music which marks them out from their contemporaries. Both com-

---

[10] See Burrows, 'Handel and the Foundling Hospital', 273–4, also 276 n. 32. However, it was James Nares, not Boyce, who succeeded Gates as Master of the Children.

[11] Ibid. 271–4.

[12] Ibid. 274.

[13] See Beeks, 'William Boyce's Adaptations'; also Ch. 8, p. 189.

posers had powerful musical personalities: in Handel's case an additional important factor was that he also brought diverse experience to the composition of his English church music, from church music in Germany and Italy, and from his work in the theatre. When the Chapel Royal gave three concerts in 1733 in support of their Fund, the programmes—of music by Purcell, Handel, and Greene—accidentally also commemorated one of the greatest periods in terms of music that was specially composed for, or associated with, the Chapel's musicians and their style.

If Handel's music provided one of the high points in the musical history of the Chapel Royal, it is also the case that the composer was able to take advantage of one of the best periods in the Chapel's musical life. The strength of the Chapel at this time is attributable to several factors, including a good creative legacy from the later seventeenth century, the institutional reconstruction of the choir during Queen Anne's reign, and the quality of the Chapel's leading singers. Although they did not attract the same sort of public attention as the opera stars, nevertheless Elford, Hughes, Weely, Bayly, Mence, Wass, and their like were respected musicians, newsworthy beyond the fact that they held some of the most lucrative posts that non-theatrical performers could aspire to in London. The musical strength of the Chapel as a performing group was clearly in these leading singers (including the best of the boys): the other singers, of whom we hear little musically, presumably did their regular duty (in person or by deputy) and provided choral support. In spite of the employment of additional performers for the grander occasions with which Handel was involved, nevertheless it was the Chapel's resources that provided nearly all of the key singers for the church music on special occasions, and also for the performance of the court odes for the New Year and the monarch's birthday. The participation of the Chapel Royal singers in the court odes is well documented even before the death of John Eccles in 1735: his successors as Master of the King's Musick (Greene and Boyce) held offices simultaneously as Composer and Organist for the Chapel Royal. In its successive Composers, Organists, and Masters of the Children, the Chapel Royal had a chain of talented musicians who sustained the practical routines of the services and provided a continuous background of professional competence.

During the century following Handel's death the musical status of the Chapel Royal gradually lost lustre. It remained a secure source for professional employment, though incomes from the places dropped in real terms and institutional numbers were gradually reduced in a series of reforms to the court establishment. However, the Chapel ceased to attract public attention from those whose interests were not primarily centred on church music. To some extent this trend is even attributable to Handel and Gates, who had jointly brought the 'solemnity of church music' into the London theatres—and eventually to other venues—through Handel's theatre oratorios. The colour and energy which had vitalized the Chapel's activities therefore passed elsewhere. In 1792 the Chapel Royal musicians discovered that concerts had been held in aid of their Fund in 1733, though they found that 'no other Particulars are handed down'. A subcommittee consisting of Dupuis, Arnold, and Richard Guise was set up to consider whether a new series of concerts should be promoted in aid of the Fund. No doubt the recollection of the Handel Festivals at Westminster Abbey was fresh in their minds, and the healthy income that these had raised for the Society of Musicians. Arnold presented the subcommittee's report on 27 December 1792, and it makes gloomy reading: 'Musick being more generally diffused & better understood than formerly, it is imagined that (notwithstanding the Excellence of many Gentlemen of the Chapel) a Performance would have no Attraction without the Assistance of some Female Performers, which could not be suffered in the White Hall Chapel.'[14] At the Handel Commemoration of 1784 half a dozen sopranos had been smuggled in among the trebles, but the 'female performers' had principally been the soprano soloists: during the thirty years following Handel's death, the London audience had come to expect the participation of singers such as the Linleys, Gertrude Mara, or Sarah Harrop. The gentlemanly off-stage deportment of David Garrick, and indeed of John Beard himself in his later role as manager of Covent Garden theatre, had to some extent broken down the polarization in public perception between the lasciviousness of the stage and the virtuous culture of church music. By the 1790s verse anthems and full anthems, still the regular fare of the Chapel's daily services, had retreated in public perception to the corners of 'ancient music': the Concerts of Antient Music mixed performances from 'Female Performers' with motet-style works. The orchestrally accompanied repertory of church music with which Handel had been associated ceased to be a regular component of the Chapel's routine life, but nevertheless found a continuing place in the church services for charitable institutions such as the Sons of the Clergy, and for provincial musical festivals, which were themselves often related to local charities and relied on local cathedral musicians as performers.

It is difficult to imagine Arnold's report being presented in the age of Richard Elford and Bernard Gates. The Chapel Royal in the period between 1710 and 1750 constituted a lively, dynamic, musical, and artistic entity at the centre of London life, working at times in close collaboration with the Royal Musicians. Although extra performers were added for special events, the Chapel's singers nevertheless retained the leading musical roles. The Chapel and its music commanded the attention of the media and it was at the centre of

---

[14] Chapel Royal Fund Minute Book, p. 53.

court affairs in London, at a time when these affairs were often controversial and the objects of public attention. If the Chapel was fortunate in its association with a composer of Handel's stature, Handel was also fortunate in the cohesive artistic tradition that the Chapel offered as a musical stimulant. The fruits of the collaboration between the two are in the music that has been described in the preceding chapters.

PART II

Institutions, Resources, and Venues

16

The London Choirs

The Chapel Royal

THE Chapel Royal, the Royal Musicians, and the Royal Trumpeters were all within the Department of State administered by the Lord Chamberlain.[1] The Master of the Musick and the Musicians in Ordinary were among the 'Servants above Stairs' under the direct control of the Chamberlain, but the Chapel Royal was a separate sub-department of the Chamber and had a greater measure of independence: the management of the Chapel was the responsibility of the Dean, though (as the Cheque Books show) the Sub-Dean in practice acted for him in most matters of routine administration. There was no parallel Cheque Book for the Royal Musicians: matters such as suspensions and dismissals, which for the Chapel Royal were dealt with internally and recorded in the Cheque Books, are in the case of the Musicians recorded in the general run of government papers for the Lord Chamberlain's Department. The Musicians, like most Above-Stairs servants, were sworn into their places by the Gentlemen Ushers: Chapel Royal admissions were dealt with by the Sub-Dean, who administered the oath of allegiance and submitted a certificate to the Lord Chamberlain.[2] (As noted in Ch. 7, Handel's appointment as Composer exceptionally followed the first route, rather than the second.) The tenure of Chapel Royal posts appears to have been almost completely free of political interference during the period 1700–50, the only suspicious exception being the departure of the Dean and Sub-Dean under unrecorded circumstances in March 1717/18.[3] Chapel Royal Gentlemen could normally expect to retain their places as long as they lived. Working continuously together, the members of the Chapel formed a distinct community: there was a tendency for court service to become a family business and, although this was less prevalent

---

[1] Concerning the musical establishments of the court, see also Daub, 'Music at the Court of George II'.

[2] The Sub-Dean periodically communicated the admissions for which he had been responsible to the Lord Chamberlain's Department: the Cheque Book entries are repeated in the Appointments Books, GB-Lpro LC3/63–65.

[3] See Burrows, 'Sir John Dolben', 66. Political dismissals from the Chapel had always been rare: in the period 1660–1700 there were two, Blase White in 1675 (*OCB*, fo. 49ʳ; Ashbee and Harley, i. 132), and Bishop Compton ten years later.

in the Chapel Royal than among the Musicians and the Trumpeters, a certain amount of intermarriage and father–son continuity can be traced.[4] There was no residential accommodation at St James's Palace for the Gentlemen, though several singers who had dual membership had lodgings in the Little Cloister at Westminster Abbey by virtue of their places in the Abbey choir, and others lived at houses in Westminster that may have been regular residences for members of the choir.[5] For many of the Gentlemen, their daily performing schedules were probably supported by strong personal and marital relationships. In 1740 William Turner and his wife died within a few days of each other at their house in Duke Street, Westminster:[6] Turner was 80 years old and had been one of Purcell's contemporaries at the Chapel. The frequent deaths of children of the Gentlemen that are recorded in the registers of Westminster Abbey and St George's Chapel, Windsor, are constant reminders of the high level of infant mortality in the eighteenth century, which must have had a disturbing effect: the day-to-day background to the lives of these Gentlemen must have been very different from that of the unmarried men such as Abbot, Hughes, and Weely. No doubt the choirs included a number of men with male orientation, but this does not seem to have affected their professional activity.

The nature of the Chapel Royal changed little from reign to reign, largely on account of the overwhelming influence of precedent on the regulation of court affairs, and the durable structure for the establishment had been settled in the years following the Restoration. There were some variations—most seriously a trimming of the numbers in the 1690s and an expansion again during the following decade—but the basic membership pattern remained the same. The court's records, and publications based on them, did not always catch up immediately with changes in the Chapel such as the succession on the death of one of the Gentlemen, but on the whole the compilers of these records were on safe ground in assuming that the numbers and composition of the Chapel would continue from year to year.

One particularly compendious semi-official publication was Chamberlayne's *Magnae Britanniae Notitia*,[7] which regularly included the following description of the Chapel Royal in a chapter entitled 'Of Particular Government: and first, of the Ecclesiastical . . . Government of the King's Household':

[4] Examples of intermarried Chapel Royal families included Braddock–Blow, Clarke–Greene–Carleton and Weldon–Baildon–Champness. The list of the Children includes at least five sets of brothers, but fewer sons of the Gentlemen. There is only one example of a Gentleman being succeeded in the Chapel by his son: Thomas Baker (45) one of Handel's soloists, and his son Thomas Baker (77).

[5] The Sub-Dean of the Chapel apparently had official lodgings in Whitehall, which Dolben took up in May 1713 following Battell's death: see GB-Lpro LC5/155, p. 215.

[6] They had previously lived in Dartmouth St, Westminster (*PB*, 12–14 Sept. 1723).

[7] Published up to 1707 under the title *Angliae Notitia*.

For the Ecclesiastical Government of the King's Court, there is first a *Dean* of the *Chapel-Royal*, who is usually some Grave, Learned Prelate, chosen by the King, and who, as *Dean*, acknowledgeth no Superior but the King; for as the King's Palace is exempt from all inferior *Temporal* Jurisdiction, so is his Chapel from all *Spiritual:* It is call'd *Capella Dominica*, the *Domain Chapel*; is not within the Jurisdiction or Diocese of any Bishop, but as a Regal Peculiar, exempt and reserved to the Visitation and immediate Government of the King, who is Supreme Ordinary, as it were, over all *England*.

By the *Dean* are chosen all other Officers of the Chapel, namely a *Sub-Dean*, or *Precentor Capellæ*; thirty-two Gentlemen of the Chapel, whereof twelve are Priests, and one of them is Confessor to the King's Household, whose Office is to read Prayers every Morning to the Family, to visit the Sick, to examine and prepare Communicants, to inform such as desire Advice in any Case of Conscience, or Point of Religion, &c.

The other twenty Gentlemen, commonly call'd *Clerks of the Chapel*, are with the aforesaid Priests, to perform in the Chapel the Office of Divine Service, in Praying, Singing, &c. One of these being well skill'd in Musick, is chosen Master of the Children, whereof there are twelve in Ordinary, to instruct them in the Rules and Art of Musick for the Service of the Chapel. Three other of the said Clerks are chosen to be Organists.

There are moreover four Officers, a *Sergeant*, two *Yeomen*, and a *Groom* of the Chapel.

In the King's Chapel, thrice every Day Prayers are read, and God's Service and Worship perform'd with great Decency, Order and Devotion, and should be a Pattern to all other churches and Chapels of *England*.[8]

This version, taken from the 25th edition (1718; pp. 95–6), was a partially revised text of the description that had run through the previous two reigns.[9] By 1718 there were no longer three organists and the number of Gentlemen was out of date; there is no mention of the office of Composer, even though the Composers' names appear in the lists of Chapel Royal personnel later in the same volume. However, one significant amendment had been made to the description. The last sentence of the third paragraph had read thus up to the 22nd edition (1708, p. 123): 'Three other of the said Clerks are chosen to be Organists, to whom are joyned upon Sundays, Collar-Days and other Holy-Days, a Consort of the King's Musick, to make the Chapel Musick more full and compleat.' This was shortened in the 23rd edition (1719, p. 105), in belated recognition that regular instrumental participation in the Chapel had

[8] A description of offices not directly related to the musical part of the establishment follows—Almoners, Chaplains, and the Clerk of the Closet.

[9] I have traced back this text as far as the 18th (1694) edn., but its outline originated much earlier. The first paragraph remained intact throughout the edns. published in Queen Anne's reign, without even the substitution of 'Queen' for 'King'.

become a thing of the past, and there was no mention of the use of instruments on Thanksgiving days.

Although *Magnae Britanniae Notitia* was a commercial publication, there is no doubt that it was also regarded as a semi-official one: the volumes bear dedications to the monarch, and King George I (or his advisers) thought highly enough of its contents to order copies for the use of his closest servants, as a reference book on British affairs during their first years in England.[10] Chamberlayne's lists of the officers and servants of the court are very detailed and must have been based on official sources to which the publishers were given access, but these lists, like the descriptive texts, seem to have been subjected to varying degrees of revision.[11] By drawing on information from the institutional records of the London choirs, interpreted in the light of more refined biographical information on individual singers, it is possible to subject Chamberlayne's lists to critical examination: source dates can be given to the lists, and occasions when they were compiled from old copy can be identified. Not all of the lists within the same section were revised at the same time. The 26th edition (1723) had a correct record of the membership of the Chapel Royal as it stood on 1 June of that year, at a period when Handel was closely associated with the Chapel. On the other hand, the boys' list in the 36th edition (1743—the year of the Dettingen Te Deum and Anthem) must be dismissed immediately as extremely out of date. This was a reprint of the list found originally in the 32nd edition (1736, giving the names of the choristers as they stood in mid-1735): it is obvious that in 1743 the Gentlemen's list was brought up to date but that for the Children was not.

Gentlemen

The Chapel Royal establishment included twenty-six Gentlemen in Ordinary, of whom ten were Priests. This number is consistent from 1715 until 1760. Many of the entries in the Old Cheque Book do not distinguish between the Priests and the rest of the Gentlemen, but the Priests can be identified in various lists of the Chapel's membership[12] and from the payments of Travelling Charges in those years when the Priests alone accompanied the monarch.[13]

---

[10] Beattie, *The English Court*, 259.

[11] They were the main source material for Chrysander, 'Der Bestand', which was the first published attempt to put together systematic information about Handel's Chapel Royal singers. Chrysander observed that many of Chamberlayne's lists did not square with the information that was available to him from Rimbault, *The Old Cheque-Book*. The lists relevant to music from the editions up to 1710 are reproduced in Ashbee, *Records*, v.

[12] For example *OCB*, fo. 54[v] (1689); GB-Lpro LC5/153, p. 238 (1702); *NCB*, pp. 15–16 (1727).

[13] The Travelling Charges are described in detail below, under 'Conditions of Service'.

Though they gained a little extra in Travelling Charges, the Priests received the same basic remuneration as the rest of the Gentlemen (£73 per annum). From the time of Anselm Bayly's appointment in March 1743/4 the move from Gentleman to Priest seems to have been regarded as promotion, involving the resignation of the Gentleman's place and subsequent readmission.[14] Movements from Gentleman to Priest undoubtedly took place before that date,[15] but apparently without such formalities. Since the Priests had to take their turns at reading weekday prayers, it was probably convenient to have some additional men in orders among the ranks of the Gentlemen, whose duties could be transferred when a Priest's place fell vacant, or when a Priest was unable to fulfil his duty. The distinction between Priest and layman was apparently irrelevant with regard to musical function: the active musicians included Priests as well as laymen, though some Priests are not known to have been performers. Bayly's 'promotion' in 1743/4 did not prevent him from keeping his position as the Chapel's leading alto singer of his generation, and he continued to perform as a soloist in the court odes. There was nevertheless a cultural distinction between the Priests and the laymen that may sometimes have been divisive: the names of the Priests are found in the registers of the Universities of Oxford and Cambridge.

It is only for the first decade of the century that there is any doubt about the number of Gentlemen in post, because the Chapel began the century at less than full strength. Twelve Priests and seventeen other Gentlemen were listed at the 1685 Coronation,[16] but vacancies that occurred were not filled under James II, so that by 1689 the numbers were down to eight Priests and twelve laymen.[17] By the time of Queen Anne's coronation in 1702 the establishment was somewhat restored, to ten Priests and thirteen laymen.[18] The number of the latter seems to have remained at thirteen or fourteen in the early part of Anne's reign, but during her later years the Cheque Book was not kept very efficiently, a circumstance that affects the interpretation of several admissions

[14] *OCB*, fo. 59ᵛ; Ashbee and Harley, i. 149.

[15] The appointment of Carleton and Baker in 1713/14 was as supernumerary Gentlemen 'until a Priest's place becomes vacant' (Ashbee, *Records*, v.103). Samuel Chittle, admitted as a Gentleman in 1715, must have succeeded to a Priest's place on the death of James Hart in 1718, releasing a Gentleman's place for James Chelsum, though this process is not apparent from the Cheque Book entry (*OCB*, fo. 13ᵛ; Ashbee and Harley, i. 51).

[16] *OCB*, fo. 52ʳ; Ashbee and Harley, i. 135–6. The names of nineteen Gentlemen appear in this list, but one of them had been suspended and another held an extraordinary (i.e. non-established) place.

[17] *OCB*, fo. 54ᵛ; Ashbee and Harley, i. 140. In 1685 Blagrave is listed separately as Clerk of the Cheque, but also held a place as Gentleman, as Braddock did in 1689.

[18] The list in GB-Lpro LC5/153 does not include two Gentlemen (William Spalden and John Weldon) who had been sworn into Extraordinary Places in 1701.

dated 8 August 1715.[19] The 'four additional Gentlemen' named there bring the total back to twenty-six, but the recovery in numbers had been made some years before. The Travelling Charges for 1709 include in the lists four Gentlemen (Laye, William Battell, Aspinwall, and Weely) whose admissions had not yet received notice in the Cheque Book, though their appointments (and some others that do not appear in the Cheque Book) are recorded in other court documents from the period 1706–14.[20] The 1715 Cheque Book entry, dated about a year after George I's accession, was an *ex post facto* administrative measure which gave the Chapel's formal approval to the expansion of the establishment and protection to the tenure of those who had been appointed in the meantime.[21] By the time Handel arrived in London in 1710, the full complement of twenty-six Gentlemen had already been restored.

The records of new admissions after 1710 appear to be tidier than in previous years because some initiation and promotion procedures had been abandoned. The succession through Gospeller and Epistler to Gentleman seems to have ceased by the end of William III's reign,[22] and the practice of appointing Gentlemen to Extraordinary or Supernumerary Places, presumably with the prospect of a full place when a vacancy occurred,[23] seems to have been discontinued after Queen Anne's death, or at least not recorded thereafter in the Cheque Book.[24] In later years the practice of employing deputies may have removed the need for a probationary period. As far as can be determined, a place in the Chapel Royal was not a saleable article in the first half of the eighteenth century: there is no evidence that reversions of places were purchased (by singers or non-singers), as happened with many other offices within the government's patronage, though no doubt influential persons helped their

[19] *OCB*, fo. 13[r]; Ashbee and Harley, i. 50–1.
[20] See Ashbee, *Records*, v. 99–103. These include some 'supernumerary' places which were nevertheless designated for the full salary.
[21] This is confirmed by a Treasury Minute dated 19 July 1715: 'Upon reading a letter from the Bishop of London concerning the Establishment for the Chapel, My Lords direct a letter to be written to the Bishop that they have no objection to the Establishments being made with the allowances settled by the late Queen.' The Bishop was instructed to prepare lists of the establishment 'according to what they were at the late Queen's demise': see William A. Shaw, *Calendar 1669–1718*, xxix. 281, 643–4. The swearing-in of the new Chapel establishment on the basis of these lists seems to have taken place on 8 Aug. 1715 (GB-Lpro LC3/63, pp. 158–66), which probably explains the arrangement of the Cheque Book entries under that date (see n. 46, below).
[22] Alford, Manuscript Register, p. 41a (Ashbee and Harley, ii. 292) gives the financial arrangements of the system as it operated in 1685. Promotion was from Gospeller (£45.12.6 per annum) to Epistler (£50) and thence to Gentleman (£73). The last Epistlers and Gospellers were admitted on 2 Mar. 1699/1700 (*OCB*, fo. 11[r]; Ashbee and Harley, i. 45).
[23] See *OCB*, fo. 46[r], para. 14; Ashbee and Harley, i. 125.
[24] The last appointment of a Gentleman Extraordinary recorded in the Cheque Book was that of William Spalden on 13 Oct. 1701: *OCB*, fo. 11[r]; Ashbee and Harley, i. 46.

own candidates where possible.[25] During Gibson's term of office as Dean, the entries in the Cheque Book indicate that the Chapel was maintained first and foremost as a competent professional body, musical and ecclesiastical, from which inefficient members could face fines or dismissal.

The Gentlemen, Priests and laymen alike, received an annual salary of £73, a sum fixed in 1685 on the basis of a daily payment of 4 shillings per day throughout the year.[26] Salary payments were made quarterly, and they figure from time to time in the lists of unpaid government debts, indicating that the Gentlemen's income suffered the hazard of occasional delays.[27] The founding of the Chapel Fund in 1729 may reflect some financial insecurity at that period,[28] but it was primarily motivated by a long-standing need to provide support for the less fortunate members of their community and their dependents. Royal Funerals and Coronations brought the Gentlemen occasional perquisites, but they received only one regular privilege from the Exchequer: an annual payment of £20 in lieu of deer for their annual Feast. Two representatives of the Chapel acted as Stewards for the Feast, which apparently was not limited to the Gentlemen. In 1711, for example, the Stewards were Goodsens the Chapel's Violist and Shrider the court Organ-maker,[29] the latter not even a member of the regular Chapel establishment. There is not much information about the Feast during the period under review,[30] and it is possible that in some years the members of the Chapel shared out the money rather than having the Feast.

Children of the Chapel

The official numerical strength of the Children of the Chapel was ten. As with the Gentlemen, the number of boys had been reduced at the end of the

[25] A curious incident, though not affecting a place for a musician, occurred in 1730 when the Sub-Dean apparently tried to put forward one of his 'Domesticks' for the vacancy as Groom of the Chapel, but Richard Norton, 'Porter to the Bishop of London [i.e. the Dean]' was appointed instead (*DPB*, 13 June 1730; *WEP* 2–4 July).

[26] Alford, Manuscript Register, p. 41a; Ashbee and Harley, ii. 292.

[27] Many of the lists of debts in the Treasury papers have simple explanations, such as the delay in the final payment from a reign because the monarch died in mid-quarter; there is little evidence of accumulated delays to the routine salaries between 1700 and 1760. In GB-Lpro T1/168(15) there is a claim on behalf of the Chapel Royal for no less than twenty-seven years' payment 'for attendance on the great annual festivities' between 1684 and 1711; this was not related to the routine salaries, and the Chapel's claim may not have been allowed.

[28] For the Fund, see below and Ch. 10.

[29] Named in GB-Lpro AO/319.

[30] The Feast does not figure in the Cheque Books, and references from the newspapers, such as the following, are rare: 'On Tuesday the great feast was held at the Swan Tavern over against Somerset House in the Strand, of all the Clergymen, Choristers and Musicians belonging to the King's Chappell, his Majesty presented them with a couple of Bucks; and there was performed instrumental and vocal Musick' (*WJSP*, 7 Sept. 1717).

seventeenth century, probably in James II's reign: unlike the Gentlemen, they never recovered their former numbers. There were twelve Children in 1684, and twelve at the 1685 Coronation,[31] but from 1690 to 1760 the Master of the Children consistently received annual payments for liveries for ten boys. Chamberlayne's lists reveal that there were occasional gaps in the ranks: even the prestige of the Chapel could not guarantee a continuous supply of young musical talent. The boys received free clothing, board, lodging, and education. Some of them may have lived in the house of the Master of the Children which, in Bernard Gates's time, was in James Street, Westminster.[32] The Master received £240 per year (£24 for each boy) for boarding expenses, and an allowance of £80 for teaching the Children to 'Compose, play on the Organ and Harpsichord, read, write and cast accompts'.[33] On leaving the choir, each Child was quite handsomely rewarded. There are two sets of warrants for payments to departing choristers, one to the Treasury for the 'Customary Allowance' of £20 and one to the Royal Wardrobe for a set of clothes.[34] A receipt book for these leaving presents, signed by the boys, reveals that by 1750 some of them received a money payment of about £10 instead of the clothes.[35] The administrative records in connection with the payments to departing Children have survived virtually intact at the Public Record Office, and they demonstrate the proliferation of paperwork which was generated by even the simplest procedure: there are Original Warrants (LC5/126–131), copies of them in the appropriate Copybooks (LC5/18–24, 152–159, 167), and then another set of records among the Treasury Papers dealing with the receipt of the warrants and their processing by the Treasury. Sometimes the process of payment was completed quickly, but sometimes there was considerable delay.[36]

The list of Children and their leaving dates given in Appendix B is derived from these records: it also includes the boys' ages on departure, as far as these can be ascertained. The warrants for the 'customary payments' begin:

[31] Ashbee, *Records*, i. 212; Sandford, *The History of the Coronation*, 69.

[32] On Gates's retirement as Master, the house was occupied by his successor, James Nares. It was not, however, previously occupied by Croft, who in 1720 lived in Charles Street.

[33] The £80 allowance is first mentioned in the Cheque Book entries for Aug. 1715 (see n. 46 below) and may have been a recent innovation. It is listed in the Establishment Charges at George I's accession (GB-Lpro LS 13/44), and appears in the 1716 edition of Chamberlayne's *Magnae Britanniae Notitia*, but not in earlier editions.

[34] The 'allowance of clothes' described on the warrants consisted of '1 suit of plain cloth, 1 hat and band, 2 holland shirts, 2 cravats, 2 pairs of cuffs, 2 handkerchiefs, 2 pairs of stockings, 2 pairs of shoes and 2 pairs of gloves'.

[35] GB-Lpro LC5/91.

[36] Samuel Arnold's leaving warrant is dated 11 Sept. 1758 and Treasury approval for payment was given sixteen days later (GB-Lpro T56/19). Roger Gethin, by contrast, had to wait from 8 July 1721 until 21 Oct. 1721 for Treasury approval (T56/18).

'Whereas the Sub-dean of his Majesty's Chapel, in the absence of the Dean, has certified that [name]'s voice has changed, who was one of the Children of the Chapel', but the ages of the boys, particularly from the first decade of the century, suggest that some were retained after their voices had broken,[37] presumably because they were useful as singers in the lower parts, as organists, or even as composers.[38] Several of the Children returned to the choir as Gentlemen. The information on the boys that is provided by the leaving dates can be supplemented from the lists in Chamberlayne's *Magnae Britanniae Notitia*, which show the composition of the choir at identifiable periods. Usually ten Children are named in these lists, but there are some exceptions. Only eight names appear in the 23rd and 27th editions, with spacer lines to indicate the two unfilled places, and it can be inferred from this that the ranks of the boys were depleted in 1710 and 1726. Even when there was a full complement of ten trebles, some of them would have been new to the choir and of limited musical value.

The boys' origins were diverse. Some were probably relatives of people with court connections: Joseph Centlivre may have been related to a Master Cook and John Duncombe to the Groom of the Vestry of the Chapel.[39] Neal Abington went on to become one of the leading Royal Trumpeters in the next generation, which is no surprise since he came from a family of Royal Trumpeters; John Mason and Edmund Woodeson were sons of Gentlemen of the Chapel. Many other Children had no known previous connection with the Chapel or the court; the Gethin brothers, for example, were the sons of the Parish Clerk of Bridewell Chapel.[40] A certain amount of talent-spotting and auditioning must have taken place. Some boys were transferred from other choirs to serve their last and, presumably, most useful years before their voices broke: John Mason came thus from Windsor and James Kent from Winchester. Making due allowance for some superannuation among the Children, the successive treble soloists named 'the Boy' in Handel's autographs can sometimes be tentatively identified from the more senior choristers in the list at the time.

[37] This is true even if allowance is made for a later maturation of the boys' voices in the 18th c.: their voices seem usually to have broken at 16–17. The ages that accompany the list of the Children in App. B are based on sources of varying accuracy and certainty. The leaving date for Samuel Howard (B62) suggests that the year of birth given in modern biographies (1710) is too early.

[38] This certainly happened at Windsor, where the reasons for the retention of John Goldwin and William Lamb (around 1680) are well documented.

[39] The Purcell family also had strong connections with court service. One branch of the family probably had representatives among the servants of George II, both as Prince of Wales and as King, and Henry Purcell's own grandson was a Child of the Chapel Royal in the 1730s (B73).

[40] See Burrows, 'Thomas Gethin'.

Organists, Composers, and Master of the Children

The regular Chapel Royal establishment included two Organists and two Composers, each post carrying a salary of £73, identical to that for the Gentlemen. Except for the period 1736–58, both Organists also held the Composers' places.[41] The office of Composer was a relatively new one, first created for Blow in 1699/1700.[42] The second Composer does not appear in the Cheque Book until the formal entries dated 8 August 1715, but it is obvious from the Travelling Charges and Chamberlayne's lists that Weldon was appointed to this post much earlier, probably from the time of Blow's death in 1708.[43] As described in Chapter 7, Handel's own appointment as Composer was unusual, and an addition to the normal two places.

Croft, who was married but did not have any children of his own, combined the office of Master of the Children with those of Composer and Organist, as Blow had done before him. On Croft's death in 1727 Greene succeeded him as Composer and Organist, but the Mastership of the Children passed into the hands of Bernard Gates. The Mastership was reunited with the other offices in 1757 when Gates resigned in favour of James Nares, who had previously taken over Greene's posts as Composer and Organist.[44] It was probably an assumed requirement of the post that the Master of the Children would be a married man, and that he would fulfil a role of guardianship over the Children, providing a family ambience. In 1726 Croft was involved in apprehending a visitor to the Chapel who was attempting to molest one of the boys.[45]

Other Instrumentalists

The general Cheque Book entry dated 8 August 1715, already referred to, also records the addition of the places of Violist and Lutenist to the Chapel establishment, but again this legitimized existing appointments.[46] John Shore

---

[41] Even then, the duties of Composer and Organist were sometimes shared: see *OCB*, fo. 58ʳ; Ashbee and Harley, i. 145.

[42] According to Hawkins, *A General History*, ii. 740, the office of Composer was suggested by John Tillotson, Dean of St Paul's, in the early 1690s with the intention that Blow and Purcell, in alternate months of waiting, should produce a new anthem for the first Sunday of each month. By the time the idea was implemented, Purcell was dead.

[43] Other documents reveal that Croft had a full place as second Composer from Jan. 1707/8, following the death of Clarke, and that Weldon succeeded as the other Composer on Blow's death later in the year: see Ashbee, *Records*, v. 100–1.

[44] Some of Gates's work as Master seems to have been performed by William Boyce from 1752: see Ch. 15. Gates became the senior Gentleman on the death of John Mason in July 1752 and may have claimed the privilege of absence thereafter, but not continuously; he attended a Chapel Royal Chapter Meeting in 1756 (*NCB*, p. 116; Ashbee and Harley, i. 293).

[45] *FP*, 10–13 Dec. 1726.

[46] *OCB*, fo. 13ʳ; Ashbee and Harley, i. 51.

appears in the lists of Travelling Charges from 1705 as Lutenist,[47] and Francisco Goodsens from 1712 as Violist, and their appointments are recorded in the papers of the Lord Steward's Department. Shore, who 'hath for some time duely performed upon the Lute in Our Royall Chappels at St. James's and Windsor without any Consideration for the same' was appointed from 1 April 1706; Goodsens, who 'hath in consert with the Organ performed upon the Base Violin in Our Royall Chappells to Our satisfaction', commenced on 1 October 1711.[48] Shore is probably one of the two lutenists depicted in the picture of the December 1706 Thanksgiving Service (see above, Fig. 4.3). The surviving sets of Chapel Royal part-books from the first half of the eighteenth century include books for the Violist and Lutenist, the music in both consisting of continuo basses, with figurings in the Lute books.[49] The Lutenist and Violist had to be present in the Chapel 'on all Sundays; & at other times, when any of the Royal Family shall be present'.[50] Both offices were maintained throughout the period up to 1760; the name of Goodsens's successor as Violist, John Gillier, appears on Handel's autograph of the Caroline Te Deum, presumably in connection with the performance in 1749. By 1767 the Violist was considered dispensable, and on Gillier's death the emoluments of the office were annexed to the Master of the Children.

Both Shore and Goodsens doubled their Chapel Royal posts with places in the Royal Musicians. Goodsens was appointed to the Queen's Musicians on 19 October 1711,[51] in the same month as his Chapel Royal appointment. The nature of the instrument that the Violist regularly used in the Chapel cannot be determined with certainty, but the cello was probably the standard instrument by 1750: see Chapter 17. Before then, the Violist may have had a number of alternative instruments available; most likely he played the cello in orchestrally accompanied music, but may have continued for some time to use a bass viol sometimes with the organ in verse anthems and full anthems.

John Shore had been listed among the Musicians in Ordinary since 1695 (with a full place since 1697), and also as one of the Musicians to Princess Anne in 1699,[52] an association that probably put him in a good position for a suitable

[47] His name also appears in the list for the Establishment of Riding Charges in 1705 (GB-Lpro LC3/53, p. 24).

[48] Ashbee, *Records*, v. 99, 102.

[49] The sets of part-books, now arranged in chronological series as GB-Lbl RM 27.a to RM 27.h, cover a wide period of copying, from the 17th to the 19th cc. See Laurie, 'The Chapel Royal Part-Books'.

[50] *NCB*, p. 8; Ashbee and Harley, i. 202; also Chamberlayne, *Magnae Britanniae Notitia*, 32nd edn. (1736), in the Chapel Royal list.

[51] GB-Lpro LC5/155, p. 122. He also appears, as 'Mr Francisco', in the list of the opera house orchestra in Dec. 1707 (LC5/154, p. 288).

[52] Ashbee, *Records*, ii. 55, 59, 65.

reward when the Princess became Queen. He was, moreover, well known as a member of one of the great trumpet-playing families. From 1688 to 1697 he had been one of the Trumpeters in Ordinary; he succeeded his brother as Serjeant Trumpeter in February 1707/8, holding this office in plurality with his places as Musician and Lutenist.[53] In processions on great occasions his place as Serjeant Trumpeter took precedence over his other offices, but it is significant that the Serjeant carried a mace rather than a trumpet in the Coronation processions: it is doubtful that Shore actually played the trumpet after 1697, though he carried out the ceremonial and managerial functions of his office. He was obviously a versatile professional court musician. As one of the Musicians in Ordinary he presumably played a bowed string instrument, and may have contributed in that role to the special Chapel Royal services after 1719 which involved the Royal Musicians.

That Shore played the lute in the Chapel, joining the organ in the accompaniment of verse anthems, is certain: in addition to the statement at the time of his appointment, the evidence of the Chapel Royal lute books (which run on into George II's reign), and the picture of the 1706 Thanksgiving, he is also celebrated in a poem, probably written *c.*1710 by Richard Roach. As well as referring to Shore's Chapel Royal activities, this poem reflects the reputation that he commanded as an artist and an inventor: he is also credited with the invention of the tuning fork:

> To Mr. Serjeant Shore, *on his New-Invented Lute*
>
> What mean you, Sir T'Augment our *Joys* or *Fears?*
> Already we've submitted Hearts & *Ears;*
> Charm'd ev'n to *Statues* by your *Magic* Airs.
> And we suspect, if *beyond* This you Play,
> Airs strain'd too high may waft our *Souls* away.
> Yet what Complaint? Since by Your *Hand* who *Dies*
> From *Heavn* on *Earth's* Translated to ye *Skies.*
>   The *Lute* transcending in *Harmonious* Arts,
> Before the *Queen of Instruments,* & *Hearts.*
> But thus Improv'd, its *Rivals* turn'd to *Mutes,*
> Yours is *Queen Regent,* both of *Hearts,* & *Lutes.*
> Form'd in your *Head,* & manag'd by your *Hand,*
> For Sweet *Constraint,* & *Sovereign* Command.
>   Yet more Exalted is your Great *Design;*
> As Nature Perfected becomes *Divine:*
>   Your Lute is form'd & strung
>   For *Anthems* yet *Unsung,*

---

[53] Ashbee, *Records,* ii. 19, 93; GB-Lpro LC5/154, p. 316. He had also been appointed Musical Instrument Maker in 1687/8, but surrendered this place to John Walsh senior in 1692 (Ashbee, *Records,* ii. 17, 46).

And *Consecrated* in the Royal *Shrine*.
　For This in Service of the *King of Kings*,
Your *Little*⁺ *Angel* spreads his Golden Wings;
With *Life* Inspir'd: And while *You Play, He Sings*.
　So may *Davidic Strains* again *Return*;
And Hearts *Attun'd* in *Sacred* Ardors burn;
As with the *Royal Quire* Your Strings combine,
Vibrant in ★*Golden* Wire, & *Silver* Twine:
And *Courtiers*, now *Devote*, be lull'd to *Rapts Divine*.

⁺Carv'd on the Arm [?] of his Lute, & Gilded
★. . . . . being [?] all of Gold which express . . . . ⁵⁴

Shore's ingenuity and artistry created a place for him in the Chapel Royal establishment, but the musical opportunities provided by the presence of the Lutenist were only taken up seriously during the first decade of the century. Blow's anthems for the 1704 and 1706 Thanksgivings include obbligato lute parts that Shore must have played before his official appointment,⁵⁵ but there are few comparable solos in the later repertory.

Other Members of the Chapel Establishment

The remaining staff of the Chapel Royal consisted of a Serjeant of the Vestry, a Groom, a Yeoman, an Organ-Blower, and a Bell-Ringer.⁵⁶ Of these, only the Organ-Blower took any part in the performance of the anthems. The Serjeant of the Vestry was the most important of the servants and in 1720 Jonathan Smith, the current holder of that office, managed to raise its status further by taking on the additional post of Clerk of the Cheque. The Clerk's principal duties involved keeping a register of the Gentlemen, so that appropriate deductions could be made for non-attendance when the salaries were calculated, and maintaining the Cheque Book. He received a fee for recording the admission of the Gentlemen to their places, and qualified for the privilege of special Travelling Charges after December 1712, following a successful petition by Daniel Williams.⁵⁷ Williams, like his predecessors since 1688 as Clerk of the

---

⁵⁴ GB-Ob MS Rawl. D 832, fo. 182. Layout reproduced from the original; the bottom margin of the page is damaged, rendering part of the last line illegible.

⁵⁵ The anthems are *Awake, awake, utter a song* and *Blessed is the man that hath not walked* (D minor setting). Blow's anthem *Let the righteous be glad*, which appears in the autograph fair copy (GB-Cfm MU MS 240) with the first of these, also includes a lute part.

⁵⁶ The first three, and sometimes all five, were referred to collectively as the Officers of the Vestry.

⁵⁷ GB-Lpro LC3/53, p. 78. Thereafter, Williams (who was not a Priest) was paid Travelling Charges even in the years when the monarch was accompanied by the Priests only. He seems to have been specially favoured by Queen Anne, receiving 70 oz. of gilt plate on the christening of his child in 1706 (LC/154, p. 166).

Cheque, was also one of the Gentlemen of the Chapel, and on his death in 1720 it was expected that Thomas Edwards would succeed him as Clerk,[58] but Smith was appointed instead. Smith is included in the supplementary list in Appendix B on the grounds that he took over an office from one of the Gentlemen, though he is not known to have been a singer. He was paid Travelling Charges both as Serjeant of the Vestry and as Clerk of the Cheque: in the former role he always received two days' extra payment, presumably because he travelled in advance of the royal party during removes in order to prepare the Chapel, and returned after the rest of the Gentlemen.[59]

John Bowack's name appears from time to time in the lists of the Chapel, mainly in the Travelling Charges. Unlike Williams, he did not succeed in advancing his status: his petition that he had 'for many years taught the Children of the Chapel Royal writing and accounts under the direction of Dr. Croft in London, also at Windsor and Hampton Court', and that he had in the past received suitable travelling allowances which he wished to be continued, was rejected by the Treasury on 28 March 1718.[60] He was not paid for 1716 or 1717 but, in spite of the Treasury minute, his name reappears for the last time in 1718. The same man had been responsible for supplying the Chapel with 'Anthem Books', presumably copies of *Divine Harmony*, in 1714/15.[61]

The Sub-Dean

After 1732 the Sub-Dean was usually promoted from within the ranks of the Priests.[62] Sub-Deans who had previously been Gentlemen or Priests are automatically listed in Appendix B, and Sub-Deans from the earlier period are also included in the Gentlemen's list. The 'promoted' Sub-Deans included Anselm Bayly, who had formerly been one of Handel's alto soloists. Whether any of the Sub-Deans, while holding office, took any active part in the musical life of the Chapel (except, perhaps, in the singing of responses) may be doubted, though Battell and Dolben are known to have been interested in church music and Carleton seems to have been a singer.[63] No musical activity

---

[58] *PB*, 31 Mar.–2 Apr. 1720.

[59] William Lovegrove, Jonathan Smith's successor in 1752 as Serjeant of the Vestry and Clerk of the Cheque, had an uneasy relationship with his Sub-Dean, which is recorded in Lovegrove, Manuscript (transcribed in Ashbee and Harley, ii).

[60] GB-Lpro T1/123(40). The rejection of Bowack's petition may be connected in some way with the additional payment of £80 to the Master of the Children, from the same period (see above, n. 33).

[61] GB-Lpro LC5/156, p. 106.

[62] There was one exception: Fifield Allen, Sub-Dean 1751–64.

[63] Battell's interest in church music was outlined in Ch. 2; for Dolben, see Burrows, 'Sir John Dolben'. Carleton's name appears on a Decani Tenor part for Weldon's D major service (c.1715–17), GB-Lcm MS 2043. In 1713 the office of Sub-Dean was described as requiring 'that the Person have good judgment in Musick' (GB-LBI Add. MS 72496, fo. 56).

of this type is associated with the successive Deans. The collections of anthem words that were published in 1712, 1724, 1736, and 1749 state on their title pages that they were issued under the direction, or with the approbation, of the Sub-Dean of the Chapels Royal. A longer time interval following the 1749 publication may be an indication that Fifield Allen was not as interested in music as his predecessors, or that the Chapel repertory had become rather stultified in the last years of George II's reign; the next issue was in 1769, by which time Bayly was Sub-Dean.

Conditions of Service

Information on the size and composition of the Chapel establishment must be supplemented by an investigation of conditions of service: that is, how the establishment worked in practice. The Children seem to have attended all the year round, except for the 'Play Weeks' that all of the choir enjoyed,[64] and those summer seasons when they were not required to attend the monarch. Similar continuous attendance can hardly have been possible for the Gentlemen. The theoretical conditions of service were quite clear. For the routine daily services half of the Gentlemen attended on a month-on, month-off rotation, but all members of the Chapel 'as well out of there [*sic*] appointed month as in it' were expected to attend on 'Sundaies, holidaies and sermon daies',[65] and forfeited a double 'checke' or fine if they failed to appear. By 1742–3, when the first list giving 'months of waiting' appears in a Cheque Book (see Fig. 16.1),[66] there is no hint of the requirement for all of the Gentlemen to appear on Sundays, and there is no reason to believe that they did so. From 1730 some Gentlemen (the best musicians) were appointed to double places, clearly indicating that the monthly rotation plan was the standard arrangement for all services: no singer could have appeared as two persons every Sunday. The first double appointment was of Francis Hughes in 1730, and a marginal note in the New Cheque Book makes the motive explicit:

NB This is the first instance of one Gentleman having two places at the same time. But this privilege was granted for his extraordinary skill in singing, & his great usefulness to the Choir in the performance of verse Anthems. He is oblig'd the whole 12 months.[67]

---

[64] The Play Weeks were those following the festivals of Christmas, Easter, and Whitsun (*OCB*, fo. 57ʳ; Ashbee and Harley, i. 144).

[65] *OCB*, fo. 42ᵛ; Ashbee and Harley, i. 118. These regulations, dating from 1637 and themselves derived from an earlier formulation (*OCB*, fo. 39ᵛ), were restated in 1663 (ibid., fo. 45ᵛ, para. 9).

[66] *NCB*, p. 130; Ashbee and Harley, i. 305. The lists of the Chapel Royal Gentlemen in Chamberlayne, *Magnae Britanniae Notitia*, 32nd edn. (1736), were arranged to show months of waiting, and this format was repeated, with varying accuracy, in some subsequent editions.

[67] *NCB*, p. 32; Ashbee and Harley, i. 221–2.

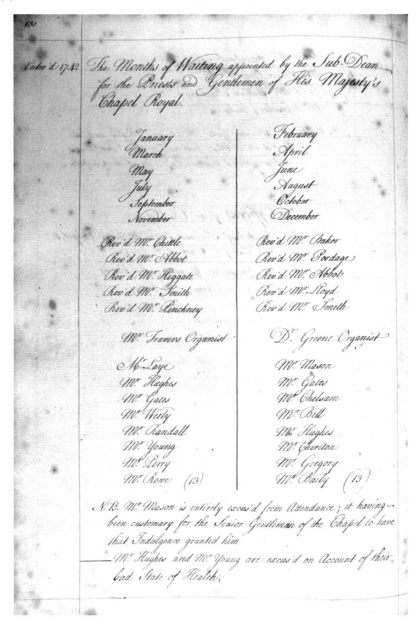

Fig. 16.1. The Months of Waiting for the Priests, Gentlemen, and Organists of the Chapel Royal in 1742. New Cheque Book, p. 130. Her Majesty's Chapel Royal

It is apparent from the lists of Travelling Charges (see below, and Table 16.1) that Hughes had already worked 'double shifts' of continuous attendance in the 1720s, as Elford had also done before him.

Further evidence that the Gentlemen were not expected to appear in full force for routine daily services comes from the *Rules for Performing due Order and Government in his Majesty's Chapel Royal* which were promulgated under Dean Gibson's direction at two Chapter meetings in July and October 1726. A fair copy of these rules appears at the front of the New Cheque Book,[68] and the original draft survives at Lambeth Palace with additions in Gibson's own hand.[69] The *Rules* reformulated the regulations found in the Old Cheque Book in the light of current practices, and dealt with a number of current abuses. The latter apparently included arriving late, leaving early, the disturbance caused by sending messages during the service because people did not know what music was to be sung, and occasions when 'one part of the Quire favouring their Voices, & another part not Joining in at all in the Choral Performance scarce any Voices have been heard in that part of the Choral Service which ought to be more Solemn and full'.

The first section of the *Rules* comprises a sub-section, *Rules for due Attendance in the Chapel*, beginning 'Every Priest Gentleman and Officer, belonging to his Majesty's Chapel shall constantly Attend Divine Service therein during their Respective Seasons of Waiting'. Gibson obviously thought that this needed further clarification, and on the draft he added the following rider, which was incorporated into the main text in the Cheque Book: 'that is to say, The Priests and Gentlemen Six Months of the Year each, according to the appointment of the Sub Dean as hath been accustomed, the Lutenist and Bass Violins on all Sundays and at other times when any of the Royal Family shall be present and the Serjeant Yeoman and Groom throughout the Year'. The implication of this is that by 1726 the attendance of the full choir on Sundays had ceased to be an established practice: if this were not so, there would have been some specific reference to such attendance in Gibson's amendment. In all probability the lapse in the requirement of full Sunday attendance had taken place before 1700, during the reduced musical activity of William III's reign.[70]

A later part of the same sub-section of Gibson's *Rules* deals with the arrangements for prolonged periods of absence on account of 'age, sickness

---

[68] *NCB*, pp. 8–13; Ashbee and Harley, i. 202–7. Another copy, probably entered in 1743, appears in Royal Archives, Windsor, RA36, pp. 14–18.

[69] GB-Llp, Fulham Papers 124.

[70] A memorandum dated 5 Apr. 1693 (*OCB*, fo. 53^v; Ashbee and Harley, i. 137) referred to Saturday rehearsals of the anthem (for the service the next day, if the King or Queen were to be present) at which the Gentlemen 'in waiting' were required to attend, from which it may be inferred that the full Chapel was not expected regularly.

or other impediment'. If the Dean granted permission for an absence, the Gentleman's place had to be supplied by another member of the Chapel (presumably one out of waiting) though difficulties could arise if the absentee was a Priest 'the most necessary parts of whose Duty he [a layman] is incapable of performing'. We have to look to a later period for further evidence concerning prolonged absences. A major overhaul of the New Cheque Book took place in 1742–3, when many new entries were added to bring it up to date, including the list of Months of Waiting referred to above.[71] A footnote to the list reveals the current situation:

N.B. Mr. Mason is entirely excus'd from Attendance; it having been customary for the Senior Gentleman of the Chapel to have that Indulgence granted him.
– Mr. Hughes and Mr. Young are excus'd on Account of their bad State of Health.
– The Revd Mr Smith (belonging to the Cathedral of Worcester) is on the Account of his Performing extraordinary Service in Singing before the Royal Family, allow'd to wait three Months only Viz. February, April and May: the other three months viz. November, December and January are supplied by a Deputy.[72]

It is easy to see how the system of waiting could break down very quickly: the absence of Hughes, with his two places, either required the employment of a continuous deputy or left the number of singers one short, and John Smith's timetable cut across the list of months of waiting for the rest of the Gentlemen. Either some members of the Chapel were deputizing for their fellows for most of the year, or the full muster of thirteen per month was not maintained, or other deputies were regularly brought in: one or more of these solutions must have been in operation from time to time, perhaps even most of the time. As already noted, the discontinuance of the probationary arrangements suggests that some singers had previous acquaintance with the Chapel as deputies.

   This annotation seems to be the earliest recorded reference to the privilege of absence for the senior Gentleman, though the description of it as a customary privilege implies, perhaps intentionally, that it was an unwritten practice of some antiquity.[73] By 1727 John Gostling, who, notwithstanding his 'great age and infirmities' was not the senior Gentleman, seems not to have been active in

---

[71] William Webster was paid in Mar. 1743 for work on the Cheque Book (GB-Lpro LC5/21, p. 395). The specific task for which he was paid was that of copying the 'Rule and Orders' (presumably *NCB*, pp. 120–1), but many other entries were made by him at the same time, most of them indicated 'Enter'd 1742'.

[72] *NCB*, pp. 130–1; Ashbee and Harley, i. 305–6 (8 words omitted).

[73] William Savage's obituary (*GM*, 1789) mentioned that he enjoyed the Senior Gentleman's privilege of absence in his last years. This may mean that Priests were excluded from the privilege: both Anselm Bayly (Sub-Dean) and Henry Evans were senior to Savage in service to the Chapel.

London for some time,[74] and the tone of the Cheque Book entry referring to him suggests that his attendance was not expected.[75] Dismissals from the Chapel were rare: in general the Gentlemen kept their places for life. Although many of them are recorded as collecting their own money for duties in the other choirs nearly up to the time of their deaths, their attendance must have been unpredictable and their musical value variable as they grew older.[76]

Some of the best evidence for the routine patterns of activity in the Chapel comes from the lists of Travelling Charges. Travelling Charges were formally established in 1703,[77] and consisted of payments to named members of the Chapel Royal for periods of attendance on the monarch at the royal palaces away from St James's. In Queen Anne's reign this usually meant Windsor, but the principle came to be extended to Hampton Court and even (from 1719) to the much closer Kensington Palace. The payments had been of an occasional nature prior to 1703, and there had always been the alternative possibility that the Chapel would be given a holiday instead: 'When wee are absent, . . . our Expresse pleasure is that our Chapell be all the yeare through kept both morning and Evening with solemn musique like a Collegiate Church, unless it be at such times in the summer or other times when we are pleased to spare it.'[78] Queen Anne's visits to Windsor with her Chapel became so regular, and so lengthy during the summer season, that it was necessary to make some extra financial provision. Payments to the Gentlemen were made on the basis of 6/- per day for the first week and 3/- per day thereafter. The lists of payments for these charges reveal three things: the names of the members of the Chapel who attended, the number of days' attendance for each member, and the scope of the Chapel's activity during each summer season.[79] No doubt some of the payments to named Gentlemen may have gone to deputies, but the lists define the attendance associated with each man's place. As already noted, the Travelling Charges are more accurate than the Cheque Book for the first decade of the century, recording the presence of singers and instrumentalists who are unknown to the Cheque Book until 1715.

[74] William Turner was the senior Gentleman 1712–40.

[75] *OCB*, fo. 55ᵛ; Ashbee and Harley, i. 142.

[76] Turner and Hughes, for example, signed for their money in the St Paul's Cathedral Rent Books up to the last year of their lives: it is almost certain that neither of them sang at the Chapel Royal in their last years, and it may be doubted whether they performed their duties at St Paul's in person. Compare this situation, however, with the description of Estwick's attendance as Minor Canon in old age, in Hawkins, *A General History*, ii. 767.

[77] GB-Lpro LC3/53, pp. 11, 24–5. The first payments were made retrospectively in 1705 (LC5/154, p. 75).

[78] Alford, Manuscript Register, p. 7a (*c*.1675); Ashbee and Harley, ii. 280. In 1687 the attendance of the full Chapel was dispensed with when James II was away from London (ibid., p. 20b; Ashbee and Harley, ii. 286).

[79] Sources for the lists of Travelling Charges are given in Burrows, *Dissertation*, ii. app. 8.

From these lists it appears that up to 1737 (the last year with a 'full' Chapel list in the Travelling Charges) even the senior Gentleman of the Chapel usually attended occasionally, and there are altogether very few absentees from the lists of names. The absentees in 1737 were accounted for by Hughes and Young, which accords with the 1743 memorandum; John Smith put in no appearance during the 1740s (with the result that there were never ten Priests in attendance), but was paid for a week's attendance in 1754 and again in 1756. The period from 1738 to 1760 was one of reduced activity, with only the Priests attending the King's summer periods of residence at Kensington Palace: it may have been during this period that a tradition of acceptable absenteeism emerged. There is very little evidence from the Travelling Charges that the Chapel's numbers were regularly depleted.

The numbers of days' attendance appearing against the Gentlemen's names in the Travelling Charges appear at first sight to be haphazard and there are wide variations within each list. This is one reason for taking the evidence of the lists at its face value, for there has obviously been no attempt to rationalize the scheme. Three typical lists, from years in which Handel had a definite association with the Chapel, are summarized in Table 16.1.[80] The lists provide confirmation that the general rule was for alternate months of waiting: even in the earliest list there were not enough 'spare' days to allow an interpretation that all of the Gentlemen were present every Sunday. In 1724 and 1737 it is possible to work out a likely roster, based on a 30/32 day division in 1724 and a 50/62 division in 1737. Secondly, the lists show that the Gentlemen with the largest number of days' attendance included the best-known musicians: Hughes, for example, was obviously an essential member of the Chapel long before he received his double place. The picture of the Chapel Royal that emerges from the lists is of a number of talented musicians at the centre of activity, surrounded by a ballast of other Gentlemen. The active members of the Chapel can be discerned from the Travelling Charges (see Table 16.2) and from the lists of attendance at Chapel's Chapter Meetings during the 1750s.[81] It was the musicians, rather than the Priests, who gave the Chapel Royal its distinctive quality, and it is no accident that newspaper reports of Chapel Royal services tend to concentrate on the names of the musical soloists. These are also the names that are mentioned in reports of the court odes.

---

[80] In 1737 Gates was paid for the full complement of days as Master of the Children, though other payments refer to him 'attending with the Children on Sundays' at Hampton Court in 1731, 1733, and 1737 (GB-Lpro LC5/18, p. 303; LC5/19, p. 162; LC5/20, p. 293).

[81] *NCB*, pp. 113–16; Ashbee and Harley, i. 290–4. The only comparable list from the earlier period is for the well-attended Vestry Meeting in Apr. 1720, *OCB*, fo. 57ʳ; Ashbee and Harley, i. 143–4. See Plate II.

Table 16.1. *Number of days' attendance recorded in Travelling Charges for members of the Chapel Royal*

	1713, Hampton Court and Windsor		1724, Windsor		1737, Hampton Court[a]	
Sub-Dean	Dolben	199	Aspinwall	51	Carleton	110
Priests	J. Hart	115	Gostling	25	Carleton	110
	Trebeck	50	Bentham	32	Baker	85
	Gostling	59	Washbourne	32	Chittle	50
	Woodeson	108	W. Battell	32	Pordage	62
	Bentham	59	Aspinwall	51	Abbot	110 (?2 places)
	Linacre	33	Carleton	32	Powell	50
	Radcliffe	159	Baker	20	Lloyd	50
	Washbourne	92	Chittle	20	Pottell	62
	W. Battell	172	Flintoft	32	Higgate	62
	Aspinwall	96	Blennerhaysett	20		
Gentlemen	Turner	62	Turner	20	Turner	62
	Damascene	74	Church	32	Church	62
	Williams	86	Jenings	20	Mason	62
	Church	83	Edwards	32	Gates	62 (?1st place)
	Jenings	138	Freeman	32	Laye	110
	Edwards	120	Mason	32	Weely	78
	Freeman	64	Gates	32	Randall	50
	Elford	172	Hughes	51	Chelsum	106
	Mason	120	Laye	20	Bell	110
	Gates	93	Weely	37	Perry	50
	Hughes	128	Gethin	20	Cheriton	99
	Laye	108	Randall	20	Gates	50 (?2nd place)
	Weely	101	Chelsum	20	Rowe	50
	Morley	145	Young	20		
	Carleton	94	Bell	32		
Master of Children	Croft	199	Croft	51	Gates	110
	Bowack	199				
	10 Children	199	10 Children	51	10 Children	110
Organists	Croft	93	Croft	32	Greene	62
	Weldon	115	Weldon	20	Travers	50
Clerk of the Cheque	Williams	199	Smith	51	Smith	110
Lutenist	Shore	199	Shore	51	Shore	110
Violist	Goodsens	178	Goodsens	51	Goodsens	110
Serjeant	Parker	199	Smith	53	Smith	112
Yeoman	Alford	199	Langhorne	51	Langhorne	110
Groom	Lenton	199	Duncombe	51	Norton	110
Organblower	Shelley	199	Clay	51	Ray	110
Bellringer	Brooks	199	Brooks	51	Martin	110

[a] In this year the Chapel was below strength numerically, hence the need for some men to attend for a larger number of days. The absence of Hughes and Young is notable. If 25 Gentlemen had been in attendance, as in 1713 and 1724, the average theoretical attendance would have been 63.6.

Cont'd

Table 16.1. *Cont'd*

	1713	1724	1737
Abstract and analysis of attendance by Priests and Gentlemen			
Total attendances	2531	716	1592
Maximum possible attendance for each Gentleman	199	51	110
Number of Gentlemen	25	25	22
Average attendance	101.2	28.6	72.3
If all Gentlemen had attended half of weekdays and all Sundays, the theoretical attendance would have been:	113.7	29	70.7
Probable rota	?	20+32 (= 52)	50+62 (= 112)

The picture of attendance at the Chapel clarified by the Travelling Charges is confused again by the Gentlemen's practice of holding other simultaneous posts which apparently conflicted with their Chapel duties. Some of the Priests even took on an impossible combination of duties within the Chapel, receiving Travelling Charges for attendance at Kensington, Hampton Court, or Windsor and also payments for preaching or reading prayers at St James's Palace during the absence of the court.[82] The leading singers combined a Chapel Royal place with at least one other in the London choirs at Westminster Abbey or St Paul's Cathedral, or in the choir at St George's Chapel, Windsor. Before 1700 various attempts had been made to end or limit this pluralism. It was expressly forbidden at a Chapel Royal Chapter Meeting in 1663[83] but with little effect, since the Treasurer's Accounts at Westminster Abbey do not reveal any resignations from the choir that would have been most affected. The reduction of numbers in the Chapel Royal after 1685, achieved by not filling vacancies as they occurred, resulted in a redistribution of salaries which was undertaken with the intention that the Chapel Royal singers would have 'no dependency upon any other Choirs but Westminster and St Paul's'.[84] However, the royal association with Windsor ensured that some Gentlemen continued to hold places there as well: members of the Chapel Royal—Woodeson, Laye, and Mason among them—are shown by the Windsor Chapter minutes to have occupied houses at Windsor in person.[85] Queen Anne, when Princess, had used the Windsor choir as a means of rewarding Elford until a Chapel Royal position became available, securing a

---

[82] Two of Handel's Chapel Royal soloists performed this double duty, though not in the years of his association with the Chapel: Baker read prayers at St James's in 1722 and Abbot in 1730–3.

[83] *OCB*, fo. 45ᵛ, para. 3; Ashbee and Harley, i. 123–4.

[84] Alford, Manuscript Register, p. 41a; Ashbee and Harley, ii. 292.

[85] GB-WRch Chapter Acts VI.B.5, pp. 71, 284: VI.B.6, p. 148.

Table 16.2. *Gentlemen of the Chapel Royal with the largest attendances recorded in Travelling Charges, 1711–1737*

1711	1712	1713	1716	1717
Gostling	Jenings	Jenings	Gostling	Hughes
Church	Edwards	Edwards	Church	Chittle
Elford	Elford	Radcliffe (C)	Radcliffe (C)	
Radcliffe (C)	Morley	Elford	Hughes	
		Mason	Morley	
		Hughes		
		W. Battell		
		Morley		

1718	1724	1728	1730	1731
Williams	Hughes	Gates	Gates	Church
Hughes	Aspinwall	Hughes	Hughes	Gates
Laye	Weely	Aspinwall	Aspinwall	Hughes
Chelsum		Weely	Bell	Aspinwall
		Young	Sharp (C)	Chittle
			Abbott	Young
				Bell
				Sharp (C)

1733	1737
Gates	Laye
Hughes	Weely
Carleton	Carleton
Chelsum	Baker
Bell	Chelsum
Abbott	Bell
	Abbott
	Cheriton

Notes:
1. Names followed by (C) are Priests who held office as Confessor to the Royal Household.
2. The Sub-Dean, Clerk of the Cheque, and Master of the Choristers normally have two entries in the lists, one of them for the maximum number of days. Their names have not been included in the lists unless the other entry, for their attendance as Gentlemen, also records a large number of days' attendance.
3. The Lutenist and Violist are always shown as having full attendance; the Organists are not. There are no entries for Composers.

place for him there with a special augmentation to the normal salary.[86] There is little sign of subsequent direct royal patronage in choir places. Windsor declined in importance as Anne's successors took less interest in that residence, but there was nevertheless a disturbance when a Chapel Royal Gentleman, Thomas Bell, was put into a place at Windsor for which he was not qualified,

[86] See App. C, Elford.

leading to a court case which seems to have resulted in his removal from a Minor Canonry into the more appropriate, though less well-rewarded, ranks of the Lay Clerks.[87] The Cheque Book reference to John Smith retaining a place at Worcester simultaneously with his Chapel Royal appointment serves as a reminder that some members of the Chapel also had interests further afield: the vast majority of the singers, however, seem to have confined their pluralism to the major choirs at London and Windsor.

Motives related to personal status and financial reward probably combined to maintain the habits of pluralism among the choirmen: a successful and secure musical career probably required such multiple membership. It will be seen from Appendix B that no person belonged simultaneously to all four choirs, and that the Gentlemen with two Chapel Royal places did not have a place at Windsor. The timing of the daily services in London was so arranged as to allow the men from the major choirs to move from one venue to another.[88] Double duty would have been easy to manage between Westminster Abbey and St James's Palace, less easy between St James's and the more distant St Paul's Cathedral, nearly two miles away. The periodic absence of the court from St James's must have necessitated the increased employment of deputies in London. While the court was in London it was obviously impossible to be at Windsor and St James's on the same day: a register of the Windsor choir survives from the period just after 1760 and confirms that the Chapel Royal men were present there in alternate months.[89]

The choirs of Westminster Abbey, St Paul's, and Windsor each had a different institutional framework; a short description of each one will indicate the demands that they made on those members of the Chapel Royal who held posts in plurality.

---

[87] See App. C, Elford, Bell.

[88] Sunday services at Westminster Abbey and St Paul's Cathedral were at 10 a.m. and 3 p.m. or 3.30 p.m., Chapel Royal services at 11 a.m. and 5 p.m. (Paterson, *Pietas Londinensis*, 220, 244, 108).

[89] GB-WRch V.B.4. The register begins from 1762, and the Clerks' attendances for the first two months were:

June	July
Vandernan(C)	Ladd (C)
Coster(C)	Denham (C)
Perry (C)	Westcote
Westcote	Rutter
Rutter	Guise
Guise	Buswell (C)
Ward	Ward

(C) indicates those Clerks who held Chapel Royal places.

Westminster Abbey

In 1700 there were four Minor Canons and twelve Lay Vicars, numbers that had an obvious convenience for a monthly system of rotation. In 1703 one of the places as Lay Vicar was converted into that of Minor Canon, and from then on there were five Minor Canons and eleven Lay Vicars. From the time of John Abbot's appointment in 1731 onwards one of the Lay Vicars was usually in orders, so that he could also perform the office of Minor Canon. One of the Minor Canons was designated Chanter, and the holder of this office would usually have been a competent musician.[90] Lay Vicars' places were sometimes shared between two men for a few years. A month-on, month-off system of attendance was in operation at the Abbey. Orders from the Dean of Westminster dated 29 November 1731 give details of the routine arrangements,[91] which can be summarized as follows:

Minor Canons:	six in all, three of whom are in waiting every month. Two of these three have to be present unless the court is out of London
Lay Vicars:	ten in all, five in waiting each month. If four are present, the fifth is excused attendance

The same orders describe arrangements that are obviously designed to facilitate the pluralists: the Chapel Royal Gentlemen could leave after the Nicene Creed at the morning service and before the Sermon in the afternoon. There is evidence from the 1730s onwards that members of the Westminster Abbey choir served a probationary period of at least one year before installation,[92] and this can be presumed to have been the practice before.

There was one Organist. This office was held successively by the Chapel Royal organists Blow and Croft, but on Croft's death in 1727 he was succeeded by John Robinson, an ex-chorister of the Chapel who never held an adult appointment there. The office of Master of the Choristers was held by one of the Lay Vicars: from 1740 to 1757 Bernard Gates was Master of the Children of the Chapel Royal and also Master of the Choristers at Westminster Abbey. Eight Westminster choristers were named in the lists for the 1685 Coronation;[93] throughout the period 1700–60 the Treasurers' Accounts

[90] The Chanters between 1700 and 1760 were Barnes, W. Battell, Carleton, Lloyd, and Bayly. All apart from Battell are named as singers on musical sources, and Battell was also probably musical: he was Sub-Dean Battell's brother and had a high attendance in the 1713 Travelling Charges (see Table 16.2).

[91] *WA2*, p. 30.

[92] Cheriton took over *WA2* in 1734 and, from his first entries, recorded dates of admission and dates of installation separately.

[93] Sandford, *The History of the Coronation*, 69.

record payments to the Master for ten Choristers, though only eight were paid for attending Queen Caroline's Funeral.[94] The annual salaries of the choir, as revealed in the Treasurers' Accounts, were as follows:

Minor Canons:	£14.8.0 (the Chanter received an additional £2, and there were additional payments to other Canons for reading prayers in King Henry VII's Chapel)
Lay Vicars:	£10.0.0
Master of the Choristers:	£10.0.0, plus £3.6.8 per boy
Organist:	£10.0.0

There were additional sources of income from the 'Tombs money' (fees for the admission of visitors to see the monuments), the letting of viewing spaces for special events, rents, and payments for performing at special services in the Abbey such as installations, weddings, and funerals.[95] There was also an income of £1 per year from St Margaret's Church, Westminster, which was divided among the choir members.

St Paul's Cathedral

At St Paul's, although institutional continuity was preserved following the destruction of the old building in the Great Fire, the choir had been virtually refounded in February 1686/7 as the new Cathedral building took shape.[96] Here the number of Priests outweighed that of the lay singers: there were twelve Minor Canons and six Vicars Choral. The Minor Canons were nevertheless part of the musical establishment: we might suspect this from the presence of the names of known musicians in their ranks,[97] and it becomes a certainty when the constitution of the Vicars Choral is considered. Of the six Vicars Choral, one was also Organist and another Almoner (a post which

---

[94] *WA1*, 'What was paid for the Funerals of Q Anne and Q Caroline', entered in 1738.

[95] *WA1* begins with Church's record of these additional incomes, 1724–40. Rents are described at various times as 'Martin's Rents', 'Rents from Duke's Head Court', and 'Rents in the Great Ambry'. A list of Martin's Rents at Michaelmas 1730 shows that Jenings and Turner occupied a property instead of receiving rent from it. The popularity of the Abbey as a burial ground for the rich and famous, and George I's revival of the Order of the Bath (the Installations for which took place at the Abbey) ensured a steady stream of additional income for the choir.

[96] For an overall survey of the building and the institutions of the Cathedral, see Keene, Burns, and Saint, *St Paul's*.

[97] These included Gostling, Barnes, Estwick, Carleton, and four of Handel's Chapel Royal soloists: Baker, Abbot, Mence, and Bayly. The practical need for joint musical participation by Vicars Choral and Minor Canons suggests that the daily services were sung from ground-floor stalls, and not from the gallery as in the Thanksgiving services.

included that of Master of the Choristers).[98] Discounting the Organist, the Vicars Choral therefore provided only five singers and the full complement can have been present only on rare occasions: in the decade 1720–30, for example, four out of the five were also members of the Westminster Abbey choir as well as the Chapel Royal, and must have served Westminster and St Paul's in alternate months. Nevertheless there appears to have been a careful spread of voice ranges among the Vicars Choral, with altos, tenors, and basses always represented.

Arrangements for a period of probation before qualifying for admission to a full place seem to have been more rigidly followed at St Paul's than elsewhere.[99] There was a complicated system of promotions among the Minor Canons, with a Sub-Dean and Senior and Junior Cardinals at the top: a new admission to the ranks of the Canons often entailed several reinstallations as others moved up the ladder. The Cathedral also had rights to considerable patronage in appointments to vicarages and rectories, the fruits of which were enjoyed by many of the Minor Canons. Accounts from the first decade of the century mention ten choristers,[100] but eight are named in 1755, in the first list of the Cathedral choir to appear in Chamberlayne's *Magnae Britanniae Notitia*.[101]

The Minor Canons were paid amounts varying between about £9 and about £20 per annum, with additional payments for Epistler, Gospeller, and Sacrist.[102] The Vicars Choral received £9.14.2¾ per annum (£2.8.6 in most quarters), with the Organist receiving in addition 2/- per year.[103] The Almoner was paid for the upkeep of the Choristers,[104] and a separate schoolmaster was also employed at £10 per year.[105] The Vicars Choral received

---

[98] An exceptional situation arose between 1708 and 1730, when Charles King appears to have been Almoner/Master of the Choristers but did not have a place as a Vicar Choral, and there was consequently slightly less of a drain on the manpower of the Vicars Choral. The income from the 5th Minor Canonry seems to have been surreptitiously diverted to King, who may have been a Nonconformist: he is shown as receiving money from this source in GB-Lsp WA 100 and WA 88, but the Canonry is shown as vacant at the Bishop's Visitation in 1724–6.

[99] One of the few examples of a lapse in the system occurred in the cases of Wass and Baildon, who joined the choir in 1743–4. On Baildon's death in 1762 the Cathedral authorities discovered that the two men had never been admitted to full places and Wass was quickly advanced, having served a probation twenty times as long as usual.

[100] GB-Lsp WA 84.

[101] 28th edn., 216.

[102] Information from GB-Lsp WA 100 (1699) and WA 88 (1717).

[103] GB-Lsp WA 100 and WA 84. According to Arnold (*Cathedral Music*, ii. 8), the Organist's salary was augmented at the time of Greene's appointment. I have found no evidence to support this, though some additional income (e.g. from rents) might not have appeared in the main accounts.

[104] In 1703 he received £47.13.04 for ten Choristers (GB-Lsp WA 84).

[105] GB-Lsp WA 88.

occasional augmentations to their salaries[106] but their main supplementary income came from rents on various properties in London and in the country, which brought in about another £16 per annum for each man.[107]

St George's Chapel, Windsor

There were seven Minor Canons[108] and eleven Lay Clerks. A register for 1762 shows that there were normally one or two Minor Canons and six or seven Lay Clerks in attendance at a time,[109] and this was probably the pattern before 1760 as well. No doubt the considerable periods of royal residence at Windsor during Queen Anne's reign, and the shorter periods during summer seasons in occasional years during later reigns, brought the Chapel to life more than at other times. There were also brief bursts of intense activity in connection with the installation ceremonies for the Order of the Garter; the Royal Musicians came from London for these, but they were probably employed at the feasts rather than the services.

The instability of some appointments at Windsor during the years 1714–20 suggests that various Chapel Royal singers experimented with appointments there, but found that their London duties were too demanding to allow them to maintain the Windsor places. The discontent among the Minor Canons over Bell's appointment in the later 1720s has already been referred to, and there may have been other occasions when some of the Windsor singers felt that places in the choir were being abused by the court in London. On the other hand some famous Chapel Royal singers, such as George Laye, were intimately associated with Windsor and were mainly resident there. In 1700 the Windsor choir had three singers in common with the London choirs: in 1760 there were eight, plus one 'Supernumerary' Gentleman. The Organists and Masters of the Choristers were independent of their London counterparts. There were eight choristers, who each received £5 on leaving the choir when their voices broke. The Minor Canons received £30 per annum, the Lay Clerks £22; the Organist's post counted as a double Lay Clerkship at £44. The Master of the Choristers received about £24, and £7.4.0 was allowed to him

---

[106] These are recorded in GB-Lsp WA 88, but no reason for the augmentations is given.

[107] Four rent books, and part of a fifth, survive; the earliest entries date from 1730. The Vicars Choral appointed one of their number annually as Pittansary to administer the rents. They collected their income from the rents quarterly, and assiduously: see above, n. 76.

[108] In the Chapter Acts the office is usually described as Petit Canon. Fellowes, *The Vicars* uses the title 'Vicar or Minor Canon', but in order to prevent any confusion between Minor Canons and Lay Clerks I have avoided 'Vicar'.

[109] GB-WRch V.B.4: see also n. 89, above.

for each of the Choristers.[110] Rights of residence at various houses at Windsor also went with adult places in the choir.

By accumulating places in the various choirs, singers were able to maintain a fairly comfortable income. We may guess that their day-to-day lives were stimulating but rather hectic, though in time some of them would have become discouraged by the grinding routine of daily services: the special events with orchestra may have provided a refreshing stimulant, and they also gave the Gentlemen and Children of the Chapel Royal access to major court occasions. The principal singers must have formed a fairly close-knit community, and for musical purposes the distinction between laymen and Priests cannot have been much in evidence among them. Annual Feasts probably helped to maintain the choirs as social institutions, at least in the first part of the eighteenth century. As already noted, the Feast tradition in the Chapel seems to have died out gradually, though the annual payment of £20 in lieu of Deer was still collected; at Westminster Abbey, the money due to the choir from St Margaret's, Westminster, was originally used for a Feast 'until Mr Baker refused to serve as Steward'.[111] As the Feasts declined, the social activity of the choirs developed in a new, thorough less festive, direction, as the members founded benefit schemes to provide for their families. The Chapel Royal Fund started in 1729,[112] at Windsor there was a 'Widows' Fund' and money was also put aside for apprenticing the children of the choir.[113] John Church's management of the accounts for additional incomes for the choir at Westminster Abbey shows an almost obsessive carefulness over accounting for the dues, and the same characteristic is apparent in the opening section of the account book for the Chapel Fund, which was also his work.[114] It is symbolic of the change of emphasis that many entries in the Fund Book are payments 'in lieu of Treat': new members of the Chapel contributed to the Fund instead of holding a party.

[110] Details of incomes from GB-WRch XII.B.4.

[111] *WA1*, entry dated 1737.

[112] The principal early sources for information on the Fund and its members are the original Account Book (GB-Cfm MS 1011), a Minute Book, and a Receipt Book (Chapel Royal, St James's Palace).

[113] GB-WRch XII.A.8.

[114] Church's industrious accounting may disguise a certain amount of manipulation in his own favour: this is implied by remarks written by Cheriton in the Chapel Fund Account Book and *WA1*, probably coloured by personal animosity.

17

Orchestral Accompaniment

Musicians in Ordinary

APART from the two verse-anthem versions of *As pants the hart* (HWV 251a and HWV 251d), all of Handel's music for the Chapel Royal has orchestral accompaniment. The core of the orchestra for his performances was provided by the Royal Musicians, whose establishment consisted of the Master of the Musick and 24 Musicians in Ordinary;[1] the full roll of twenty-four was maintained throughout the period 1700–60.[2] The contraction of musical life at court in the closing years of the seventeenth century simplifies the position with regard to instrumentalists, since the confusing additional lists of players for 'Wind Musick' and 'Private Musick' from the previous reigns are found no more;[3] from Queen Anne's reign onwards any court orchestra had to be based on the 24 Musicians. The Musicians had also been known during the reign of Charles II as the 'four and twenty violins'[4] and it can be inferred that they still comprised string-players after 1700: supplementary payments for additional players are usually for wind instrumentalists, though double bass players are also named with a regularity which indicates that the '24' did not normally include bassists. Some families had a tradition of service in the Musicians: the Eccles and Bradley families, for example, seem to have brought up their children so that they could eventually take their places in the ranks. Some of the players, including John Shore, were probably competent on both stringed and wind instruments, but it appears that their specific duties as Musicians in Ordinary were fulfilled on bowed stringed instruments.

The Master of the Musick received an annual salary of £200, with additional payments for expenses incurred in connection with music for the annual court

---

[1] This was the official title, though they were also called the Queen's Musicians or the King's Musicians, according to the reign; I have adopted 'Royal Musicians' in descriptions that cover the period 1700–60. See also Daub, 'Music at the Court', ch. 5.

[2] Only twenty-two are listed in the 1700 edition of Chamberlayne's *Angliae Notitia*, but the depletion was due to tardiness in appointments rather than a reluctance to fill vacancies.

[3] As late as 1699 a group of seven performers was described as 'musicians to princess Ann' (Ashbee, *Records*, ii. 65), but during her reign any employment of private musicians was occasional, casual, and individual.

[4] Ashbee, *Records*, i. 83.

odes celebrating the New Year and the monarch's birthday, and court balls.[5] After the death of John Eccles in January 1734/5 the office was held by Greene and Boyce successively, in plurality with Chapel Royal appointments. The Musicians in Ordinary received £40 per year,[6] with additional payments for their attendance with the Master of the Musick for special events away from London, usually in connection with the Installations for Knights of the Order of the Garter at Windsor. John Shore and Francisco Goodsens, the Chapel Royal's Lutenist and Violist, also held places in the 24 Musicians,[7] though their successors did not. It is perhaps more of a surprise to find that two of the Gentlemen of the Chapel Royal—Peter Randall and Talbot Young—also doubled with places in the Musicians.[8] These two men were supplied twice over with liveries for the 1727 Coronation, as Musicians and as members of the Chapel;[9] for such occasions they must have provided deputies in order to make up the numbers.

The interpretation of the official lists of the Musicians carries the same hazards as those encountered with the Chapel Royal lists. Resignation was more common from the Musicians than from the Chapel, probably because a number of them had families or business 'beyond sea'.[10] Even so, the majority of the players remained in office until their deaths, and the active participation of some of the more senior members is doubtful. Talbot Young was one of the Gentlemen who were excused attendance at the Chapel Royal by 1743 on account of health, so his absence from the Musicians in Ordinary during the same period can also be assumed. Musicians also absented themselves for other reasons from time to time, and the Lord Chamberlain's records contain notices of suspension from office for non-attendance at some of their court duties.[11] Perhaps communications with the Musicians, whose functions were occasional, were more difficult than with the Gentlemen of the Chapel, whose office demanded attendance at daily services. The fact that the Master of the Musick rarely had twenty-four players at his immediate command in practice seems to be reflected by the Lord Chamberlain's request to Greene in 1735 for:

[5] These payments covered the costs of music-copying, hiring a rehearsal room, and employing additional performers.

[6] According to Chamberlayne, *Magnae Britanniae Notitia*, 22nd edn. (1708), 612, they also received £16 annually for Livery. Special livery payments were also made to them, along with the other court participants, for royal funerals and coronations.

[7] Dates of appointment to the Musicians: Shore 29 Mar. 1695 ('without fee'), 28 Jan. 1696/7 (full place); Goodsens 27 Oct. 1711. See also p. 449.

[8] Dates of appointment to the Musicians: Randall 27 Aug. 1712; Young 20 Aug. 1717.

[9] GB-Lpro LC2/23, Coronation Liveries for the Chapel Royal and thirty-three Musicians.

[10] Many of the Musicians had foreign names, and 'going beyond sea' was one of the main reasons given for absence or resignation.

[11] The Master of the Musick himself was even among those suspended for non-attendance at the Court on the Princess of Wales's Birthday in 1726 (GB-Lpro LC/158, p. 224).

'an exact State of His Majesty's Band of Musick Vizt. what Instrument or Instruments each Musician plays upon, the Names of such who by old Age or other Infirmitys are unable to do their Duty, and of those that are excused, and also, an Account of the Number of different Instruments you think proper to make a Set for the Balls'.[12] A rotating system of months of waiting can be assumed for the Musicians, as for the Gentlemen of the Chapel Royal. No doubt the arrangements for this were part of an accepted routine, and the relevant records, being regarded as insignificant and ephemeral, were discarded.

The conditions regulating orchestral participation in court services can best be understood in the wider context of the association between the Musicians and the Chapel Royal during the century following the Restoration, and in conjunction with the historical framework that was presented in Chapter 2. The first precise information about the formal arrangements for the Musicians' participation in Chapel Royal services comes from the period around 1670. The '24 Violins' and the 'Chapel Musick' were specifically protected from the retrenchment of royal finances in 1668/9,[13] and in the following years fifteen members of the 'Violins' were named to serve the Chapel in rotation, five at a time; the number rose to six in 1672.[14] These Musicians were even provided with surplices, along with the Gentlemen and Children of the Chapel.[15] When string-players failed to attend for their Chapel duties they were threatened with suspension, a necessary sanction when the numbers involved were so small.[16] It can be assumed that the arrangements remained substantially the same until the extinction of anthems accompanied by strings in the Chapel after 1689.

When instrumentally accompanied canticles and anthems reappeared in the Thanksgiving Services of Queen Anne's reign, the scale of these occasions demanded a rather larger number of players, and the period coincided with the development of an orchestra for the opera house, drawing on an influx to London of some talented foreign instrumentalists. In the absence of any documentation from the Lord Chamberlain's records comparable to the instructions to the Musicians from the 1670s, we must assume that for the Thanksgiving services either the full band was expected to turn out, as happened for coronations, or that the players who were in waiting were supplemented by several,

---

[12] GB-Lpro LC5/160, p. 268, dated 24 Jan. 1734/5: an opportunity seems to have been taken to review the situation when Greene succeeded Eccles as Master.

[13] Ashbee, *Records*, i. 88.

[14] See Holman, *Four and Twenty Fiddlers*, 398. The fifteen named in 1670 were presumably an expansion on the original ten who were protected as the 'Musick of the Chapell' in 1669 (Ashbee, *Records*, i. 91).

[15] Ashbee, *Records*, viii. 220

[16] Ibid. i. 115–16.

probably many, additional instrumentalists.[17] It is probable that the normal routine for 'waiting' in London was the same as for the Chapel Royal Gentlemen, with half of the players on call at any time and each man serving for six months of the year.[18] A list of the Musicians who attended, with the Chapel Royal, for an Installation at Windsor in 1717 contains thirteen names,[19] one of whom (Goodsens) may have been acting partly in his 'Chapel' capacity: rather confusingly, later lists for attendance at Windsor indicate a nearly complete turnout, with more than twenty names.[20] The fortunate survival of sets of the original performing parts for Boyce's court odes during the period 1755–79[21] enables us to estimate the number of Musicians who participated on those occasions. The usual complement of string parts is 3/3/1/1/1, plus one additional bass part which may be for a second double bass; the rest of the orchestra comprised, in addition to the harpsichord, two oboes or flutes, one bassoon, two trumpets or horns, and drums.[22] If string-players shared two to a part, the complete orchestra would have numbered about twenty-six players. In 1758 Boyce was paid £34.10.00 for additional players in the birthday ode,[23] a figure that is known from previous payments to represent fourteen performers.[24] This leaves exactly twelve players to be made up from the King's Musicians, so it seems that the normal muster of Musicians that was available for routine court duties, whether odes or Chapel Royal services, was nominally twelve, perhaps fewer in practice.

Just as the Chapel Royal employed a group of professional singers who served several choirs, so the Musicians must have included professional string-players with interests elsewhere. Apart from the necessity of augmenting their salaries, there was scarcely enough musical employment at court to keep the Musicians busy. Many of them also played in the orchestra of the opera house,[25] and would therefore have been well known to Handel. I have only

[17] There are no records of payments for these additional performers in the 18th c. before those for the Chapel Royal service on 15 Nov. 1719.

[18] I have not found any explicit statement of the Musicians' duties, but there is circumstantial evidence for this arrangement. When they were required to attend away from St James's for an extended period, probably eight were in waiting: see GB-Lpro LC5/153, p. 418.

[19] Lpro LC5/157, p. 136.

[20] e.g. Lpro LC5/18, p. 5 (1728, 22 names), p. 207 (1730, 21 names); LC5/19, p. 148 (1733, 21 names).

[21] GB-Ob MS Mus.Sch.d.298–340. I have made allowance in my calculations for accidental depletions to some sets of parts.

[22] For the purpose of the calculation I have assumed that only two players each were accounted for by flutes/oboes and by trumpets/horns.

[23] Lpro LC5/167, p 109. This is one example from many similar ones, chosen because it is less ambiguous than some others in identifying what the payment was for.

[24] e.g. Lpro LC5/24, p. 60 (payment to Greene).

[25] Lpro LC5/154, p. 288; LC5/155, p. 3.

found one adverse comment on the multifarious nature of the instrumentalists' activities, in a newspaper report concerning the 1720 service for the Sons of the Clergy: 'some of the Musicians were taken from the Play-House, a thing which we took to be very odd, that the Sanctuary should be served by the same Men that serve the Theatre'.[26] Otherwise the issue of orchestras in church, significant in the sermons of the 1690s, seems to have been largely uncontroversial in eighteenth-century London.

Two broad levels of orchestral participation can be distinguished in Handel's Chapel Royal music: a 'small orchestra' for performances in the Chapel Royal itself, and a 'large orchestra' for big state occasions that normally took place in larger buildings. The former was built around the twelve-man string ensemble from the Musicians. On the bigger occasions the Musicians, probably in their full force of twenty-four, were supplemented by many additional instrumentalists, and the total number of players usually seems to have far exceeded the number of singers. Some works—the Utrecht canticles, the wedding anthems of the 1730s, and the Chapel Royal music from the 1740s—may have been performed by an instrumental group of intermediate size, but they can best be understood as a variation of Handel's 'large' orchestra. In the chapters of Part I, the size and constitution of the performing forces for individual occasions have been estimated under 'Conditions of Performance', and further consideration will be given to this subject in relation to venues in Chapter 18. This chapter is primarily concerned with the ways that Handel used the available instrumental resources.

Stringed Instruments—Violins and Violas

The strings, as a section, were the mainstay of Handel's orchestra, in church as in opera house. No complete movement of his orchestrally accompanied Chapel Royal music passes without their participation. In large-scale works (Utrecht and Dettingen canticles,[27] Coronation Anthems) the group of violins is sometimes divided into three parts, but he generally follows the normal division into Violin 1 and Violin 2. They are combined into a unison violin line from time to time, usually in order to give a stronger effect, as in 'Day by day' in the Caroline Te Deum, but sometimes to provide a sparser texture, as in 'They shall receive a glorious kingdom' in the Funeral Anthem. The full body of unison violins is sometimes employed to accompany solo voices, and the use

---

[26] *LJ*, 3–10 Dec. 1720. The 'Musicians' referred to were not necessarily all Royal Musicians, but the report seems to refer to instrumental rather than vocal performers.

[27] As noted in Ch. 4, the exact arrangement of the orchestral scoring in some sections of the Utrecht Te Deum is ambiguous because Handel did not label the staves, but three violin parts are strongly implied.

of a solo violin is rare:[28] Handel seems generally to have preferred the effect of a complete section of violins, marked down to the appropriate dynamic level where necessary.

D major is a favoured key for much of the Chapel Royal music, largely on account of the inclusion of trumpets in many works. The sharp-key bias also suits the stringed instruments, taking advantage of the open strings and facilitating passages of semiquaver figuration. For that reason, the opening movement of *Let God arise* (HWV 256b) in A major is both easier to play and much brighter in effect than its earlier counterpart in B flat in the Cannons version (HWV 256a). Handel's violin parts in the Chapel Royal music are practical and effective. They never go higher than one note above third position (e''')[29] and there is a natural bias towards the upper two strings in the accompaniments to chorus movements, but they make full and varied use of the violin's registers.[30] Movements that call for the 'strong snatching way of playing, to make the musick brisk and good', which Roger North saw as one of the strengths of the violin,[31] are contrasted with others in a more cantabile style. Novel effects are rare: the Funeral Anthem includes more than usual, from the wavy-line direction in the opening bars of the Sinfonia to the concluding symbolic dissolution of the music in the open G strings which are the last sound in the anthem.[32] In arias or extended sections for solo voice the violins provide ritornellos and counterpoints: in choruses they also strengthen the vocal parts, with first violins frequently doubling their chosen part (not always the Soprano) an octave higher. Passages of imitation between the violin parts perhaps suggest that some spatial separation between first and second violins may have been practised in the instrumental layout, as far as conditions in the performing areas permitted.[33]

The violas consistently remain the poor relation of Handel's string section. Although providing an essential element to the harmonic texture, they never have independent thematic material except in passages involving short imitative entries, or where they are called upon to provide a bass to the harmony in

[28] Utrecht Jubilate No. 3, and possibly HWV 251c, No. 6; in both cases solo violin is used in conjunction with solo oboe.
[29] Cannons anthem HWV 256a goes one note higher, to f'''.
[30] A particularly striking example of the immediate contrasting of different registers occurs at the beginning of the last movement of the Caroline Te Deum. See also Ex. 14.4.
[31] Wilson, *Roger North on Music*, 221.
[32] I assume here, as I believe to be the case, that the Sinfonia was intended as part of the anthem. Handel's oratorio *Theodora* ends in a similar manner to the anthem. The effects in the anthem did not included muted strings, though sordini directions are found in Handel's opera and oratorio scores.
[33] It is not possible to deduce anything further on this matter from Handel's scores alone. Passages such as HWV 256b, No. 1, bars 13–15, could have been performed with the violins arranged in opposition, in conjunction, or in no arrangement at all (as in Pl. 1 and 5).

the absence of a cello/bass part. Their most extended break of the latter kind comes at the opening of 'Glory be to the Father' in the Utrecht Jubilate, where Handel withholds the orchestral basses until the tutti chorus entry at bar 12. Some thinness of tone in the violas may be inferred from his use of them elsewhere as a quiet bass to recorders.[34] The relative underemployment of the viola section (as also in Handel's theatre music) may have had a practical advantage in releasing John Christopher Smith senior, who possibly played the viola in the Chapel Royal music,[35] to assist in the management of the performances. Handel always refers to the instrument as the viola in his scores, though the English term 'Tenor' was also in common use during the eighteenth century. In Walsh's edition of Handel's Op. 3 concerti, published in the 1730s, the viola parts carry the name 'Alto Viola' except in Op. 3 No. 1, where the part for Viola II is named 'Tenor':[36] no difference in range is associated with these names, however, and it is unlikely that two distinct genres of instruments were in use, though no doubt individual instruments differed from each other. As early as 1664/5 the Royal Musicians had been equipped with a 'Cremona tenor violin'[37] and John Walsh, as Royal Instrument Maker, supplied 'Tenor Violins' again in 1706 and 1727.[38] In the music that Handel composed in London he always wrote the viola part in the alto clef, although Croft continued to use the mezzo-soprano clef: it is found in Croft's autograph of the Te Deum of 1709, and even in the scores of the orchestrally accompanied anthems that were published in *Musica Sacra* during the 1720s.[39]

Stringed Instruments for the Bass Line and the Continuo (Cello, Double Bass, and Lute)

The Walshes also supplied the Royal Musicians from time to time with new 'Bass violins', a description that may have been either specific or generic.[40] By 1710 the cello was probably the regular bass instrument in the ensemble of the Royal Musicians, though instruments may have varied somewhat in size and

[34] For example in 'Augeletti' (*Rinaldo*), and the second setting of 'Thus long ago' (*Alexander's Feast*).

[35] This is suggested by the appearance of Christopher Smith's name as a viola player ('Tenor') in the payments for Handel's Chapel Royal music in 1724 and 1726: see App. I. Linike, another of Handel's copyists from the same period, was also a viola player.

[36] The scoring with two viola parts, and the instrumental designations, may, however, relate to the circumstances for which Op. 3 No. 1 was composed, possibly in Hanover.

[37] Ashbee, *Records*, i. 60.

[38] Lpro LC5/154, p. 227; LC5/18, p. 1.

[39] Also on Croft's autograph of the anthem *O give thanks unto the Lord, for he is gracious* (*c.*1719), now at the Brotherton Library, Leeds.

[40] Lpro LC5/154, p. 319 (1707), LC5/157, p. 165 (1718); LC5/18, p. 1(1727); LC5/19, p. 290 (1734). On Walsh's death in 1736 he was succeeded by his son, John Walsh jr.

design; in his scores, from the Utrecht Te Deum to the Anthem on the Peace, Handel refers only to that instrument ('Violoncello', 'Violoncelli', or 'Violonc:'). For the Chapel Royal performances one or more cellos were joined on the orchestral bass line by double basses, played by extra musicians hired specially. As already noted in Chapter 16, the Chapel's own Violist cannot be counted as an additional performer up to 1741, since Goodsens also held a place as Musician in Ordinary. It is doubtful that bass viols were ever mixed with cellos in any of Handel's performances of English church music.[41] Goodsens was probably 'double-handed' on viol and cello, and the only bass instrumentalist shown in Fig. 12.2 appears to be holding a cello.

With regard to the use of a bass stringed instrument in conjunction with the organ for the accompaniment of verse anthems in regular Chapel Royal services, a changeover from viol to cello may have taken place during the 1720s: the Sub-Dean was paid in 1721 and 1725 for the repair of 'the Great and small Viol used in the Chappell'[42] and in 1726/7 for the repair of 'the Double Bass and Bass Violin used in the Chapple'.[43] The earlier references to viols may, however, have been based on a standard form of words, covering up a change to the violin family that had already taken place: it is unlikely that the descriptions were used with precision in accounting systems that favoured the use of consistent forms of words. Gillier, although he still held office under the title of Violist when he succeeded to the post after Goodsens's death, was responsible for 'stringing and keeping the Violoncelloes in repair & carrying them to & from the Chapel Royal at St. James's Palace' in 1753, and in 1734/5 'Mr Francisco Goodsens Violist' had been paid for a 'Case to Violoncello' for the Chapel.[44] The regular mention of two string bass instruments for the Chapel in the 1720s is intriguing since only one Violist was employed. One possible explanation is that the ever-versatile John Shore occasionally forsook his lute in favour of a bowed string bass instrument; John Immyns, Shore's successor as Lutenist, played bowed string instruments in addition to being a self-taught lute-player,[45] and may have gained his place on the strength of being able to continue Shore's double-handedness.[46] Both Goodsens and Gillier presumably played the cello for orchestrally accompanied music in

[41] They do appear together in certain of Handel's works from the earlier Italian period, such as *La Resurrezione*.

[42] Lpro LC5/158, pp. 17, 387.

[43] Lpro LC5/159, p. 12.

[44] Lpro LC5/23, p. 388 (1753); LC5/19, p. 326 (1734/5), the earliest mention of the instrument under that name (rather than 'Bass Violin') that I have found in the Public Records.

[45] See *NG II*, Immyns.

[46] After Immyns's death in 1764 the Lutenist's place was apparently used to give an extra place for new singers until a Gentleman's place fell vacant; it is doubtful that Immyns's nominal successors (Medley and Friend) ever played the lute.

the Chapel. In the only music by Handel that seems to make specific use of the Violist, 'Why so full of grief' from the second verse-anthem setting of *As pants the Hart* (HWV 251d, *c*.1722), the composer labelled the relevant stave of the score 'Violoncello'.[47] In the previous setting (HWV 251a, *c*.1712) Goodsens may have played viol or cello: the warrant in March 1711/12 for his appointment, backdated to October 1711, said that he had 'performed upon the Base Violin' in the Chapel, but this again may be a generic description.[48]

The Lute is never specified in any of Handel's English anthem scores, and the direction for the use of the 'Archiliuto' which appears on the autograph of 'Gentle airs, melodious strains' from *Athalia* was omitted when this aria was adapted in 1734 for the wedding anthem *This is the day* (see Ch. 12). It is only in the earliest period that Handel's Chapel Royal performances may have included a lute, and it is perhaps surprising that he did not seize the opportunity to use the instrument positively if it was available. The presence of two lute-type instruments in the orchestra shown in Fig. 4.3 might perhaps suggest their inclusion in the first performance of the Utrecht Te Deum and Jubilate, even though the organ is the only chord-playing continuo instrument specified by the composer in the scores: on the other hand, Handel might have regarded the lute as both old-fashioned and musically inappropriate for those particular works. The short unlabelled melodic instrumental part in 'Now when I think thereupon' from the first version of *As pants the hart* (HWV 251a) may have been intended for lute, though Handel's treble-clef notation, mainly in a high register, is not similar to the music in the Chapel Royal part-books for Lute, or to the obbligato lute parts in the scores of anthems by John Blow. As suggested in Chapter 3, it is more likely that the organ played the melodic line in Handel's anthem and the Lutenist filled in the chords.[49]

It was Handel's normal practice to indicate changes in the weight of vocal tone by writing 'Solo', 'Soli' or 'Verse', and 'Chorus', 'Coro' or 'Tutti', next to the continuo bass line.[50] These markings were of practical service to the keyboard player, since they indicated suitable levels of volume and distinguished the textures for soloists and chorus, in which he had different roles. If the organist had only a figured bass line to play from, these labels provided a guide to the player, but English organ parts of the period (as, for example, in the organ books from the Chapel Royal part-books) were more often two-stave outlines that showed leading parts as well as the bass, and in this case

[47] GB–Lbl RM 20.g.10, fo. 32[r].

[48] Ashbee, *Records*, v. 102.

[49] See Ch. 3 (pp. 67–9), and Ch. 16, 'Other Instrumentalists'.

[50] Handel's use of 'Verse' is characteristic of his early Chapel Royal music: he normally used 'Solo' or 'Soli' thereafter. His markings are not fully comprehensive, and he tended to omit them when the musical context was obvious.

Handel's markings would also have guided the copyist: solo sections were laid out with the voice part (or parts) and the bass line, while chorus sections might show a fuller texture, with the organ doubling the principal vocal leads. The 'solo' and 'tutti' markings were also probably used as a guide for the instrumentation of the orchestral bass parts, giving indications for variations in the scoring that might be interpreted by both players and part-copyists. Orchestral ritornellos and passages marked 'Tutti' were normally played by the complete field of instruments, but the accompaniment of the 'Solo' sections probably reduced to a single cello, or sometimes one cello and one double bass, with the organ. So much must have been a matter of conventional practice that the correct interpretation of Handel's markings is only brought to attention by accident. For the revival of the Caroline Te Deum in 1749 someone had to remind the copyist that instrumental bass parts for the arias had to be provided for 'Diedrich and Gillier'.[51] (Gillier was the Chapel Royal's Violist, and Dietrich, whose name appears in the Foundling Hospital *Messiah* accounts, was a leading double bass player of the period.) Handel also used different clefs in the basso continuo part to indicate variations in the scoring: passages in the soprano or alto clefs are cues for the organ only, and those in the tenor clef are for organ and cellos (or cello, as appropriate) without double basses. He sometimes added instrumental specifications next to a change of clef, but none of these conflicts with the practice just described and some explicitly confirm it.[52]

In some movements Handel allocated separate staves in his scores to cellos and double basses, mainly where he wished to liberate the cellos from the harmonic bass: this usually leaves double basses and organ sharing the basso continuo stave. Unless it has a separate solo part, the bassoon, where employed, is also usually cued in onto one of these staves, tending to work more with the cellos than with the double basses, and usually participating in tenor-clef passages. Two places where instrumental bass staves are particularly carefully specified by Handel call for some comment. In the first movement of the Anthem on the Peace the figured continuo stave is allocated to 'Organo e Violoncello' throughout, while the second bass stave is for 'Bassons, Contrabasso'. The latter are given a typical ripieno part, playing in the opening ritornello, resting during the alto duet and then re-entering with the chorus.[53]

[51] GB-Lbl RM 20.g.4, fo. 56ᵛ.

[52] e.g in No. 4 of the Coronation Anthem *The King shall rejoice* and the last movement of the A Major Te Deum.

[53] GB-Lbl RM 20.g.6, fos. 25–31, reproduced in Chrysander, *Das Autograph*, 285–97. There are two rather surprising details in Handel's music for these bass parts. At bar 84 the d.b./bn. line enters with the chorus on beat 3, rather than beat 1; in the final bars d.b./bn. remains an octave above vc, when, on the basis of Handel's practice elsewhere, the lower octave might have been expected. In both cases it is possible that Handel confused the d.b./bn. stave with a vocal bass part.

In 'Like as the smoke vanisheth' from *Let God arise* (HWV 256b) 'Bassons
e Violoncelli' share one stave in Handel's score, except for a short passage in
bars 38–40 where the bassoon part doubles the voice and the cellos join the
harmonic bass, leaving the other stave for 'Organ' and 'Contrabassi'.[54] The
parts are notated almost throughout on separate staves, in spite of the fact that
for much of the time they play the same notes. The layout of the music seems
to indicate that the complete bass section played almost continuously throughout the aria: Handel only indicated the removal of the double basses for one
short passage in the tenor clef early in the movement, and the simplifications of
some later passages seem designed to enable the basses to keep playing through
technically difficult sections.[55] In the accompaniment to the first entries of the
voice, furthermore, Handel was careful to mark the contrabass/organ line
down to 'pp' (as against 'p' in the cello/bassoon part) rather than removing
the double basses altogether. The accompaniment of this particular movement
with its continuously rich instrumental bass line may have been unusual, but
the arrangement may alternatively suggest that the orchestral bass line elsewhere should be treated more densely than we might otherwise expect.
A similar treatment may have applied, for example, in 'Thou art the King of
Glory' from the Caroline Te Deum, and in 'Glory and worship are before him'
from *O sing unto the Lord* (HWV 249a).

It is difficult to know the relative extent to which Handel's treatment of the
orchestral bass line was influenced by the availability of players in London, and
by his own taste. Presumably he knew what forces would probably be available
when he wrote the specifications on the Peace Anthem for a bass line consisting of a single cello, a single double bass, and at least two bassoons. The
orchestra for his Foundling Hospital *Messiah* performances in the 1750s had
the same sort of balance on the bass line: three cellos, two double basses, and
four bassoons. The payments for additional players from 1722–6, on the other
hand, suggest a preference for substantial double bass tone, and indicate that
only one bassoonist was available. The performing parts for Boyce's court odes,
which commence from the same period as the surviving Foundling Hospital
accounts, include parts for two or three cellos, two double basses, and a single
bassoon, so perhaps the substantial double bass presence was a common feature
of the orchestra for court occasions. (It may also reflect a relative lack of power
in the double basses.) If one of the Chapel Royal's own instrumentalists
was a bassist, the use of three double basses against two cellos in Handel's

---

[54] As noted in Ch. 9, this division of the bass instruments follows that from the Cannons
setting of the same text, so it is probable that Handel's choice here was a general aesthetic one,
rather than something that related to the practice of the Chapel Royal.

[55] e.g. bars 38–41, 60.

performances from the period 1722–6 cannot be ruled out. In his Chapel Royal scores he frequently wrote passages including low D on the stave that includes the double basses, and bottom C in two movements,[56] without any alternative pitches, so it must be assumed that the range of these instruments went down to C.[57] He always refers to the instruments as 'Contra Bassi' (or some variant), so there seems no doubt that these sounded an octave lower than the written pitch, and that the instruments were recognizably different from the parallel families of the violone and the bass viol.

Except for the designation at the start of the Peace Anthem, Handel's markings in the Chapel Royal music seem to point towards the regular employment of more than one double bass, as revealed also by the payments for additional players in the 1720s. Indications for the number of players on the cello parts are less consistent. The first (chorus) movement of *Let God arise* (HWV 256b), for example, has 'Violoncello' in what appears to be a clear 'tutti' context,[58] while the second movement no less clearly specifies 'Violoncelli' in the accompaniment to solo voices. The 'small orchestra' Chapel Royal music may have involved quite a modest performing group, to the extent that in such works as the Caroline Te Deum a single cellist may have served both continuo and orchestral roles. The only obbligato cello solos in the Chapel Royal music occur in the wedding anthems of the 1730s and may have been played by Andrea Caporale, as one of the 'extraordinary' performers: the relevant movement in *This is the day* was directly arranged from *Athalia*.

Keyboard Instruments

The organ is regularly specified as the keyboard continuo instrument on Handel's Chapel Royal autographs.[59] Only once is any other keyboard instrument named on a primary manuscript source, a harpsichord in the first movement of *This is the day*, and this reference is itself suspect, since J. C. Smith probably copied it unthinkingly onto the score of the anthem from the

---

[56] Caroline Te Deum, 'When Thou tookest upon Thee', and HWV 256b, No. 2.

[57] C may also have been the lowest note of the Chapel Royal organ (see Ch. 18). Croft wrote down to AA for the orchestral (and continuo) bassi in the autograph of his Te Deum, but perhaps expecting that the Thanksgiving at which it would be performed would take place at St Paul's Cathedral (where the the organ range extended to FF), and perhaps at a time when the bass-line players of the Royal Musicians were not yet fully converted to C-range cellos.

[58] This may have been copied rather absent-mindedly by Handel from the parallel place in HWV 256a.

[59] All of the Chapel Royal autographs with the exception of those for the Caroline Te Deum, *O sing unto the Lord* (HWV 249a), and the Funeral Anthem include specific references to the organ. The organ is not mentioned on the surviving autograph fragment of the 1736 wedding anthem, but GB-Lpro documents show that a special organ was provided for this wedding and for the 1737 Funeral.

score of *Athalia*.[60] For the remaining Chapel Royal music the overwhelming weight of the evidence is that the organ, and only the organ, was used for the keyboard continuo. In some oratorio performances during the 1730s Handel employed two organs, and 'Organi' appears in the scores, but he apparently never expected to use two for his church music: even large-scale works such as the Coronation Anthems have consistent references to 'Organo'. A special organ was erected for the 1727 Coronation, apparently replacing the Abbey's own organ for the performances of Handel's anthems.[61] At the coronation service a Chapel Royal Organist presumably played the former and the Abbey's Organist may have played the latter, but it is doubtful whether the two were used simultaneously. Details of the organs associated with particular buildings are given in Chapter 18, but for the performances of all of Handel's Chapel Royal music between 1727 and 1737 special organs were provided; the expenses incurred are recorded in the Lord Chamberlain's papers. In 1734 and 1737 these occasional and temporary organs were required because the sites of performance (the French Chapel and King Henry VII's Chapel) did not have an instrument. On-site organs could pose practical problems, however. The Chapel Royal organ was dismantled and replaced for the wedding of the Prince of Wales in 1736, probably because it took up too much space; in any case, once a substantial orchestra was involved there would have been difficulties in matching the pitch of the regular organs to that of the orchestral instruments in every location.

With the exception of a couple of short passages in the verse-anthem settings of *As pants the hart* there are no written-out solo parts for the organ: the player fulfilled the normal continuo role, realizing the harmonies with reference to Handel's bass figurings and following the hints provided by his 'Solo' and 'Tutti' markings.[62] Continuo cues in the higher C clefs reveal that the organ was used to double leading chorus entries; the organ's role was to support the chorus in ensemble movements and to provide the chordal background for solo movements. No organ part from Handel's Chapel Royal performances survives,[63] and it is probable that, for many works, a separate keyboard part was

---

[60] The two-stave arrangement of the instrumental bass line that Smith copied reflects the typical practice for Handel's oratorio performances, where the harpsichord was the main keyboard instrument and the organ had a limited orchestral role. See also Ch. 12.

[61] This organ was subsequently presented to the Abbey by George II and replaced their previous instrument: see Ch. 18.

[62] The composer's figurings are usually rather sporadic, but an exception is the unusually comprehensive set in the first movement of HWV 251d (the second verse- anthem setting of *As pants the hart*), subsequently carried forward into HWV 251c.

[63] One 18th-c. keyboard part, GB-Lbl Add. MS 27745, claims an elaborate pedigree supposedly stretching back to Handel's time, but this cannot be supported. The organ part for the Foundling Hospital Anthem in GB-Lcm MS 2273 dates from Handel's lifetime, and may

not copied, especially if Handel directed the performances himself from the keyboard.

If separate organ parts were written out for Handel's performances, then the continuo parts from the Aylesford Collection may reflect the conventions by which a copyist prepared them. Many of the sets of part-books in this collection were written in the 1740s, close to the period of the Dettingen music, and they were copied for Charles Jennens by scribes from Handel's own circle.[64] In solo movements the copyist included the music of the voice parts as well as the bass line in the continuo part-book; in chorus movements a leading voice part was sometimes shown in addition to the basso continuo, but often the figured bass line (including the higher-clef passages just referred to) was all that was provided. Given a part of the 'Aylesford' type, an organist would have been able to rehearse with the soloists, react to any passages that went astray, and even provide some elementary assistance with the direction of the performance. The vocal solo part-books from the Aylesford sets contain, in complementary fashion, the continuo bass line under the voice part in solo movements, so that soloist and continuo player know exactly what the other should be doing. That this was normal practice is confirmed by the contemporary set of parts, dating from 1745, for a Te Deum by Maurice Greene that was almost certainly composed for the Chapel Royal.[65] No doubt these highly practical arrangements had been evolved much earlier. An early organ part for the Foundling Hospital Anthem consists principally of a two-stave reduction of the vocal parts with the basso continuo,[66] and other eighteenth-century keyboard parts follow much the same style: this may have been an alternative format for organ parts, though it does not necessarily mean that the organist played exactly what was written in the solo movements. The fuller representation of the vocal parts in chorus movements that is found in the authentic organ part for *Alexander's Feast* would have had practical advantages both for the player and the singers:[67] whether such a part was written out probably depended on the time constraints before the performance and, most crucially, on who was to play the organ.

The copyist of the Aylesford parts specified Cembalo as the continuo instrument for the Utrecht and Cannons Te Deums, but this must have been

possibly have been connected with his performances of this work. The surviving fragment of the continuo part for Handel's *Oratorio* performance of 1738 in GB-Cfm MU MS 265 includes the unrealized bass line for the final 'Alleluja' of HWV 251e.

[64] See Roberts, 'The Aylesford Collection', which also gives the modern location of MSS for individual works. The part-books for the anthems and Te Deums, now at GB-Mp and US-Cu, were copied *c*.1745–50.

[65] GB-Lcm MS 224.

[66] See above, n. 63.

[67] See Cooper, 'The Organ Parts', and Burrows, 'Who does What, When?'

a mistake, arising from the copyist's own invention or from a defective source score.[68] In *As pants the hart* (HWV 251c) the same copyist followed the specification of the continuo stave from the autograph score and labelled the relevant part for 'Organo & Contrabasso'.[69] Elsewhere in the sets from the Aylesford Collection, including those for operas and oratorios, there is a remarkable absence of double bass parts. This may have been because the copyist worked rather thoughtlessly from the score and saw no need to provide a part when the double bass was not specifically named at the beginning of the movement. An alternative possibility with regard to the church music is that it may have been normal practice for the double bass player to read over the organist's shoulder from the organ part. Since the bass player had to stand higher to his instrument, this would have been a much more practical arrangement for the bassist than for the continuo cellist.[70] (Court protocol usually required all persons to stand in the presence of the monarch, and cellos used at court had holes for ropes to enable this, but some latitude may have been allowed—or taken—when the performers were obscured in a gallery.) Such an arrangement fits well with the organ/double bass combination indicated by Handel on the staves of several Chapel Royal scores.

Trumpets and Drums

Apart from the works dating from 1722–6 and the Funeral Anthem, all of Handel's Chapel Royal scores include trumpets. There was no shortage of trumpet players connected with the court. They belonged to a separate establishment of Household Trumpeters, described thus by Chamberlayne:

The Serjeant and Office of Trumpets of the King's Household There are in all Sixteen Trumpets in Ordinary, the last of which is in the Power of the Serjeant to place in whom he pleaseth, either his Servant or his Son.[71]

The Serjeant Trumpeter received £100 per annum and the rest of the Trumpeters £91.05.00 (i.e. 5/- per day).[72] Doubts as to whether the Serjeant

[68] GB-Mp MS 130 Hd4 v. 347. Continuo parts, from a set of part-books copied by S2, containing four works: Caroline and A major Te Deums correctly marked for 'Organo', Cannons and Utrecht Te Deums for 'Cembalo'. The last-named is in direct contradiction to Handel's reference to the organ in the autograph. The Aylesford scores of the Cannons and Utrecht Te Deums are, as yet, untraced.

[69] US-Cu MS 437, vol. 2, fo. 45^r.

[70] Much would have depended on the location of the organ. If the keyboard was near the centre of the performing group, the presence of a bass player might have blocked essential sight-lines. It seems unlikely that a bass player could have managed to stand behind the organist in the restricted gallery at the Chapel Royal, St James's Palace, but the Chapel's Violist and Lutenist are said to have performed there during the regular Chapel services: see Ch. 18.

[71] *Angliae Notitia*, 18th edn. (1694), 247.

[72] Ashbee, *Records*, i. 129, and similar subsequent lists.

Trumpeter was primarily a musical or ceremonial functionary have already been raised in connection with John Shore, who held the post in plurality with those of Lutenist of the Chapel Royal and Musician in Ordinary. The sixteenth trumpeter may also have been of doubtful musical value, to judge from the description of the method of his appointment.[73] The Trumpeters were even more dynastic than the Chapel Gentlemen and the Musicians, with the great families of Shore, Snow, Goodman, and, later, Abington represented in most generations. Some, possibly all, of the trumpeters also held appointments in the Guards.[74] The Trumpeters came under the general responsibility of the Lord Chamberlain, so their appointments were recorded in the same way as those of the Musicians in Ordinary.[75] Like the Chapel Royal, but unlike the Musicians, they seem to have been independent of the main run of Servants above Stairs:[76] this may have been because of their historical associations with ambassadorial and military activities, which in German courts linked trumpeters with the stables and with the equivalent of the Master of the Horse.[77] By the eighteenth century most of the English court trumpeters' work was straightforward, ceremonial, and probably not very demanding musically. No doubt the sixteen included players devoted to the craft of rough trumpet playing, which was all that was demanded by the conventional fanfares.[78]

However, some of the trumpeters took the musical aspect of their work seriously. In the 1690s the more adventurous players were trying out new techniques (and probably new instruments): a report of the 1691 St Cecilia's Day celebrations noted that the trumpeters had been taught by 'Mr Showers' (probably one of the Shore family) to play softly, and that they played some 'Flat Tunes', a feat which was 'formerly thought impossible on an Instrument designed for a Sharp Key'.[79] The development of what may be distinguished as 'art trumpeting' was already sufficiently advanced for Purcell to reward the players with responsible parts in his court odes. To the reciprocal stimulus of

[73] John Shore himself may have been appointed in this way: at the time, his uncle had been Serjeant Trumpeter since 1689.

[74] John Goodman, for example, who was an additional performer in the special Chapel Royal services 1719–21, was also a trumpeter in the Third Troop of Horse Guards (GB-Lpro LC5/157, p. 335).

[75] In the Appointments Books, GB-Lpro LC3/63–LC3/65.

[76] This is confirmed by the separate entries for the trumpeters in Chamberlayne's lists.

[77] See Altenburg, *Trumpeters' and Kettledrummers' Art*, and Menke, *History of the Trumpet*. In 18th-c. Britain the Trumpeters were administratively part of the Chamber rather than the Stables (Beattie, *The English Court*, 279–82), but these associations may still have been relevant.

[78] See the assessment of the Trumpeters' establishment in Halfpenny, 'Musicians at James II's Coronation', 106–9.

[79] *GJ*, Jan. 1691/2, 7. Concerning the instruments, see Webb, 'The Flat Trumpet in Perspective'.

players and composer was added a third factor: the magnificent silver and silver-alloy trumpets produced at this period by William Bull, and subsequently by John Harris.[80] Although the experiments of the 1690s seem to have been short-lived, Handel would have found a sophisticated tradition in London among the best trumpeters, which had previously been exploited by Purcell, Blow, and Croft.

Like his English predecessors, Handel normally scored for two orchestral trumpets. There is no evidence that these parts were played other than by soloists, and payments for additional players relating to Chapel Royal services during 1719–21 record that two court trumpeters were involved. Only in Handel's later innovative large-scale church music, the Coronation Anthems and the Dettingen Anthem and Te Deum, did he score for three trumpet parts. In the Coronation Anthems the music for Trumpet 3 is written in the treble clef, but in the Dettingen music the third trumpet part is designated 'Principal' and notated it in the soprano clef, possibly anticipating more than one player for the relatively easy fanfare part.[81] At the 1727 Coronation all of the Trumpeters in Ordinary were present in their official capacity;[82] most of them were probably ranged over the entrance to the Choir in Westminster Abbey, and thus away from the main musicians' galleries. Sandford's pictures of the 1685 ceremony show only twelve Trumpeters (with the Kettledrummer) at this station, and at least one other trumpeter is to be seen with the string players in the gallery close to the altar:[83] in 1727 the orchestral trumpet players may again have been separated from the rest, for at least part of the service.[84] On practical grounds it seems very unlikely that Handel's parts for Trumpet 1 and 2 would have been doubled by extra players, and massed trumpeters on Trumpet 3 would have dislocated the balance of the group scoring.

Handel always writes for trumpet in D in his church music and, in the context of contemporary instruments and technique, his use of the instrument is thoroughly idiomatic.[85] Apart from the opening of *Eternal source of light divine* his solo

---

[80] An oil portrait, c.1740, by Michael Dahl, shows a Trumpeter (possibly Valentine Snow) in court livery and holding a silver trumpet: see Edwards and Edwards, 'I'm almost Shore'.

[81] This might be plausible if Handel had expected his music to be performed at St Paul's Cathedral. It is unlikely that more than three trumpeters took part in the eventual Chapel Royal service.

[82] They had an important ceremonial part to play at the Coronation Banquet in Westminster Hall, as well as in the preceding service.

[83] Sandford, *A History of the Coronation*, Plates 'The Inthronization of Their Majesties' and 'A Perspective of Westminster-Abby'.

[84] The need for some trumpeters to perform both orchestral and fanfare functions may account for the lighter scoring of *Let thy hand be strengthened*, which was probably performed at a point in the service when they were needed elsewhere: see Ch. 10.

[85] See Burrows, 'Of Handel, London Trumpeters, and Trumpet Music'.

trumpet parts are less adventurous than some of Purcell's or Croft's,[86] and they pose fewer practical problems than those of his predecessors because they are more self-sufficient when the accompanying texture is not very supportive. There are extended solo passages at the start of several movements from the Chapel Royal music, usually introducing the well-tried combination of trumpet with solo alto voice; examples are to be found in the opening movement of the Utrecht Jubilate (following Purcell's model closely), 'Day by day' in the Caroline Te Deum and the first movement of *Sing unto God*. Excursions above *b″* for Trumpet 1 are rare. The opening of *Eternal source of light divine* includes a top *d‴*; a trill on *c♯‴* is demanded only once by Handel in his church music, at bar 52 of the first movement in *Sing unto God*.[87] Otherwise the topmost register of the trumpet is represented only by a single top *d‴* in the Dettingen Te Deum,[88] and in that work the first trumpet player also has to participate more than usual in the lower range, including a bottom *a* in unison with the other two parts. This note is not used for Trumpet 1 in Handel's earlier music.

Although Handel never uses the higher extremities of the range in Trumpet 2, the second parts also require more competence than could be expected from the fanfare players. The part for Trumpet 2 often crosses above Trumpet 1 in orchestral tuttis, and there are important solo passages for the two trumpets in tandem: examples range from the opening of 'Day by day' in the Utrecht Te Deum, to the duet composed thirty years later to introduce 'We believe that thou shalt come' in the Dettingen Te Deum, and the Urio-derived introduction to 'To thee cherubim' in the same work. In the Dettingen music, which makes the most extensive demands in Handel's Chapel Royal repertory, the second trumpet part needs as much stamina as the first. The upper limit of Trumpet 2 is *a″* in the earlier years and *b″* in the 1740s, and the parts require technical agility in order to encompass the melodic leaps necessary to maintain a good musical relationship with Trumpet 1, in a natural consequence of the limitations imposed by the harmonic series.[89] Trumpets are always used by Handel with a concern for sonorous spacing and for maintaining the musical interest of the individual parts, even in the densest tutti passages. The doubling

[86] As, for example, the florid trumpet part in the second movement of Croft's anthem *O give thanks unto the Lord, for he is gracious* (*c.*1719).

[87] The autograph of this movement is not extant, but the authenticity of the trill is established beyond reasonable doubt by the best sources, including the related movement in the conducting score of *Il Trionfo del Tempo* (D-Hs M C/1060).

[88] At No. 18, bar 127.

[89] See e.g. Trumpet 2 in *This is the day*, No. 1, bar 63. There is just one place in the trumpet parts for the Chapel Royal music that might have involved the modification of a natural harmonic. In the penultimate chord of the Caroline Te Deum Handel wrote a dissonant *d″* which was transmitted unaltered to all subsequent copies, including the conducting score of *This is the day*: the player may have been expected to 'lip down' this note to *c♯″*, but it is equally possible that the note in the score was a casual mistake for *e″*.

of the trumpets on the bad note *g♯″* is a solecism sufficient in itself to cast doubts on the authenticity of 'Chandos Anthem 12'.[90] The third trumpet parts in the Coronation Anthems and the Dettingen music are relatively undemanding: the range never ventures beyond *a–e″* and their music is harnessed rhythmically with the timpani.

A 'Kettledrummer' was attached to the Trumpeters in Ordinary and there was also a separate court establishment of four drummers (not necessarily playing timpani) under the Drum Major.[91] None of Handel's Chapel Royal works before the Coronation Anthems of 1727 includes drum parts, and the use of the timpani in these anthems may have been an original innovation. No comparable English church music by Purcell, Blow, or Croft has timpani parts, and nor do they appear in Greene's orchestrally accompanied church music until the later 1730s.[92] Newly composed timpani parts were probably added to Purcell's D major Te Deum and Jubilate in the mid-eighteenth century for large-scale performances such as those at the Sons of the Clergy services; by that time the Dettingen Te Deum, with its integral timpani part, was part of the repertory, and the drum parts were probably added to Purcell's music in an attempt to inflate it to a similar style.

It has sometimes been suggested, especially in connection with Purcell's canticles, that the absence of formal timpani parts in the scores does not mean that these instruments were not included in the original performances, since improvisation was a recognized part of the drummer's art,[93] but there are two reasons for doubting this suggestion. First, occasional timpani parts exist in other pre-1727 compositions: when a composer wished to use the drums and a good player was available, a written-out part could be provided, defining the nature and extent of his participation. Of Purcell's six odes whose scoring includes trumpets, two also have timpani parts,[94] and Daniel Purcell's ode for

[90] *HG* 36, p. 22, last bar, and p. 23, bar 2. On the authorship of this anthem (by Greene), see Johnstone, 'The Chandos Anthems'.

[91] Ashbee, *Records*, ii. 129, and similar subsequent lists. In the pictures of the 1685 Coronation procession the Drum Major appears to be playing a large side drum: see Halfpenny, 'Musicians at James II's Coronation'.

[92] None of Greene's earlier works for Sons of the Clergy performances at St Paul's Cathedral includes timpani parts. The first occasion on which his canticle and anthem settings included timpani was probably the service on 16 Jan. 1736/7 marking the King's return: see the comment in the letter of 18 Jan., Deutsch, *Handel*, 424. Handel's *Sing unto God* in 1736 might have been the first occasion that timpani were heard in the Chapel Royal.

[93] See e.g. Donington, *A Performers' Guide*, 102–3, and Charles Cudworth's notes to a recording of Purcell's Te Deum, ASD 2340 (1967). The drum part included in a recording of Handel's Utrecht service (DSLO 582) diminishes the distinction between this Te Deum and the Dettingen setting.

[94] *Hail, bright Cecilia* (1692) and *Come, ye sons of art* (1694). There are also timpani parts in Purcell's music for *The Fairy Queen* (1692) and *The Indian Queen* (1695).

the King's return in 1697 also has a kettledrum part.[95] Secondly, a distinction parallel to that suggested between 'basic' trumpeting and 'art' trumpeting must be borne in mind. It is clear from Handel's scoring in the Coronation Anthems and the Dettingen music that he regarded the timpani as the close relation of the Trumpet 3 or 'Principale' part. Improvisation was appropriate in the context of the music that was normally associated with these players, such as the 'Points of War' and 'Levets', but the anthems and canticles in which pairs of solo trumpeters took part, inside church buildings, were not in this category, and they were not the sort of thing on which to let loose an improvising drummer. There is no documentary evidence to support the use of drums with the trumpets in any orchestrally accompanied English church music composed before 1727, whether performed in one of the Chapels Royal, Westminster Abbey, or St Paul's Cathedral. More positively, there was a specific genre of works conceived with a scoring of trumpets and strings, originating with Purcell's D major canticles, whose aesthetic framework was rather different from that of the trumpet-and-drum style initiated by Handel's Coronation Anthems.

Although timpani parts appear in the first movements of the wedding anthems from the 1730s, there is some doubt about their inclusion in Handel's performances, and even possibly some doubt about the interpretation of the (non-autograph) musical sources in which they occur: see Chapters 12–13. For the Chapel Royal music of the 1740s there are no such doubts that Handel wrote timpani into the scores, though even then it is possible that practical difficulties in the Chapel (concerning both performing space and acoustics) may have eventually prevented their participation. The increasing use of timpani in Handel's later Chapel Royal music is on a par with the rest of his output: timpani parts are found in only five of his London operas, one of them from the year of the Coronation Anthems and three others from the period 1734–40,[96] but they are a consistent feature of his oratorios in the 1730s and 1740s.[97] Handel's increased use of the timpani may have been stimulated by the work of a particular musician, perhaps Frederick Smith, who is named on a letter from Handel in 1750 requesting the collection of the big drums from the Tower for use in his Covent Garden oratorio performances, and is also named as the timpanist for the Foundling Hospital *Messiah* performances.[98] He was

[95] GB-Lbl Add. MS 39034, fo. 94. The drum part appears to have been added after the rest of the composition had been completed.

[96] *Rinaldo* (1711), *Riccardo Primo* (1727), *Parnasso in Festa* (1734), *Atalanta* (1736), *Deidamia* (1740); the works from 1734 and 1736 were closely associated with the royal wedding celebrations in those years.

[97] See Dean, *Handel's Dramatic Oratorios*, 628. From 1732 onwards Handel regularly used timpani in his English theatre oratorios.

[98] Ibid., Plate VIIIA; Deutsch, *Handel*, 751, 800.

appointed a Trumpeter in Ordinary in 1740, and Kettledrummer four years later on the death of John Vandenand:[99] he may have been the timpanist for whom the parts in the Dettingen music were intended. What is clear, above all, is that when Handel came to composing parts for the timpani, he used the instruments with precision, to make a carefully calculated contribution to the orchestra, and to the music itself.

When timpani appear in Handel's scores they are always used with the trumpets, and since the latter are invariably pitched in D in the church music the drums are always tuned to *A* and *d*. Probably the instruments used did not differ much from the smallish drums illustrated in the pictures of the 1685 Coronation service.[100] Handel used 'tr' to indicate timpani rolls, but relatively rarely,[101] which may suggest that he regarded the roll as a special effect and used the sign as a defensive measure to ensure that rolls occurred only where he wanted them. It is not known whether Handel's timpanists were in the general habit of rolling long notes, but it would be difficult to resist the temptation to fill out the final bars of the first and last movements of the Dettingen Anthem.

No other brass or percussion instruments appear in Handel's church music.[102]

Woodwind

Oboes

After the strings, the double-reed instruments were the most essential part of Handel's regular orchestra. All of Handel's Chapel Royal scores except one require one or more oboes as part of the ensemble.[103] 'Small orchestra' works for performance in the Chapel Royal (HWV 249a, and the anthems and canticles from 1722–6) have a single oboe part, and the later Anthem on the Peace calls for one oboe and one flute together, but otherwise the Chapel Royal music normally includes two oboe parts. Even when Handel must have

---

[99] GB-Lpro LC3/65, pp. 109, 168.

[100] For the timpani of the period, see Montagu, *Timpani and Percussion*, 78–87. It is very unlikely that Handel ever employed the large 'Tower' drums in any performances of his English church music.

[101] Examples occur in the Coronation Anthem *The King shall rejoice*, No. 3, and in *This is the day*, No. 1, the latter derived from *Athalia*.

[102] *HG* 36 erroneously shows horns as well as trumpets in the score of the first movement of *This is the day*.

[103] The exception is the Caroline Te Deum, originally scored for the Purcellian orchestra of trumpets and strings: see Ch. 4. Oboes almost certainly took part in Handel's later revivals of the work and it is possible that even for the first performance the flute obbligato in No. 3 was reallocated to oboe.

expected a large body of players to be available, as in the Coronation Anthems, he never divides the oboes into more than two parts: no doubt the individual parts were doubled by several players on these occasions.[104]

It is noticeable that most of the oboe solos in the Chapel Royal music occur in the works composed before the Coronation Anthems. Of the works written in the 1730s and 1740s, only the Anthem on the Peace has a significant solo part. Handel's use of the oboe as a solo instrument in the earlier works was almost certainly inspired by the playing of John Christian Kytch. Kytch was a member of the orchestra at the opera house when Handel came to London,[105] and he was also employed by James Brydges, though Biancardi was probably the oboist during the period of the Cannons anthems.[106] In the 1720s he is named as the oboist who was employed as an extra musician for the Chapel Royal services involving an orchestra, so there can be little doubt that Handel wrote the oboe parts of the works described in Chapters 8 and 9 with him in mind. Kytch was apparently a versatile woodwind performer. He is named as a bassoon soloist on the autograph of Handel's *Rinaldo* (1711);[107] in 1719 he was advertised as playing the oboe and the 'little flute' in his own benefit concert, and he performed on the oboe and the 'german flute' for a similar occasion the next year.[108]

Handel gave Kytch at least one passage for oboe solo in every orchestrally accompanied Chapel Royal piece composed before 1727, with the exception of the first state of the Caroline Te Deum. Most of these solo passages occur in introductory ritornellos to vocal movements. The oboe melodies usually begin with the same musical motifs as the subsequent vocal material, but they do not merely anticipate the singers' themes: rather, the instrumental and vocal melodies develop along subtly different paths,[109] and sometimes the oboe part continues to develop as a complementary obbligato part after the voice has entered.[110] The melodies that Handel introduced with the solo oboe demand, first and foremost, a good lyrical style from the performer, but Kytch must also have possessed considerable technical agility to deal with the

[104] The Foundling Hospital *Messiah* accounts (Deutsch, *Handel*, 751, 800) show that four players were regularly employed on two oboe parts; the practice of doubling the woodwind in larger concerted works was probably not new in the 1750s.

[105] His name (as 'Mr. Kytes') appears in the list of the opera house instrumentalists in Jan. 1709/10, GB-Lpro LC5/155, p. 3.

[106] See Beeks, 'Handel and Music for the Earl of Carnarvon', 17; Kytch's name, in various spellings, appears in the Cannons records US-SM MSS ST 44 and 87. See also the reference in Wanley's Notebook for 15 May 1721 (Deutsch, *Handel*, 126–7), which shows that Kytch was well known at Cannons, and may suggest that he had performed in the Cannons Te Deum.

[107] GB-Cfm MU MS 254, p. 48 ('Mr. Keutcsh').

[108] *RMARC* 1, p. 106; Burney, *A General History*, ii. 994.

[109] e. g. in the A Major Te Deum, Nos. 7 and 9 (both also with bassoon).

[110] e.g. in HWV 249a, No. 1, and Utrecht Te Deum, 'When thou took'st upon thee'.

solo semiquaver figuration in the introductory Sinfonia to HWV 251c and similar passages. From the early periods there are two movements (musically related as to thematic material) in which the solo oboe, with another instrumental partner, mirrors a duet in the voices: 'Be ye sure that the Lord he is God' with solo violin from the Utrecht Te Deum, and 'O sing unto God' with solo bassoon from *Let God arise* (HWV 256b). The most impressive oboe/bassoon duet accompanies the solo alto in 'Vouchsafe, O Lord' from the A Major Te Deum. In the smaller Chapel Royal works of the early 1720s Kytch represented a complete oboe section in himself: from the payments for extra performers it appears that he was the only treble wind instrumentalist, and his music therefore combines 'Solo' and 'Tutti' functions. At the opposite extreme are large-scale works such as the Coronation Anthems, where Handel composed his oboe parts knowing that there would probably be several players to a part: in such circumstances, flexible lyrical oboe solos were out of the question. In passages for solo oboe Handel consistently uses the range $d'-b''$: this is similar to the range of his trumpet parts, and in the larger-scale pieces oboes are sometimes used with the trumpets.[111] When Handel rearranged the Utrecht Jubilate for Cannons, a single oboe took over the role of the former trumpet parts, with results so natural that the origin of the music would have been virtually undetectable if the Utrecht setting had been lost. This suggests what must have happened in the 1720s when Handel revived the Caroline Te Deum but no trumpet players were involved in the Chapel Royal performances: Kytch would have been given the Trumpet 1 part to play on the oboe. There is no direction for the transfer of the trumpet music to oboe on the autograph score, but the former trumpet part could have been used without modification. As noted in Chapter 5, at some stage the flute solo in 'When thou tookest upon thee' was allocated to oboe, but this was probably in 1714: if in the 1720s Kytch played the flute in this movement and in the new setting of 'Vouchsafe, O Lord', in addition to playing the Trumpet 1 part on the oboe, he would have been busy indeed.

The 'tutti' role for the oboes (that is, their part within the general orchestral texture) in Handel's Chapel Royal music encompasses four different functions:

1. Independent oboe parts. These are rare, and short when they do occur. They consist of the leavings of the harmony when the melodic parts have been distributed elsewhere, but nevertheless they can make a distinctive contribution. The entry of the oboes in 'Lo, thus shall the man be blessed' of *Sing unto God*, for example, enriches the harmony significantly, if also only momentarily; similarly, at bar 116 of 'His honour is great' in the Dettingen Anthem the additional decorative part for Oboe 1 fills out the texture at the approach to a structurally important cadence

---

[111] e.g. in the first movements of the Dettingen Te Deum, bars 172–7, and the Coronation Anthem *The King shall rejoice*, bars 17–18.

point. The slightly more extended independent parts at bars 19–22, 30–3, and 42–7 of 'The righteous shall be had in everlasting remembrance' in the Funeral Anthem are a rare example of Handel's use of the oboes in a continuo-style background role. Some independent parts, as in the opening bars of 'For the Lord is gracious' from the Utrecht Jubilate, are really a solo part doubled by all available oboes, matching the unison violin part.

2. Doubling another instrumental part, usually Violin 1. Sometimes Handel cued the oboes onto the Violin 1 stave, but he frequently wrote out their music in full on a separate stave, even when their music follows the violins closely. Occasionally he seems to have forgotten to put in the oboe cues, as for example in the last movement of the Utrecht Jubilate, where it is difficult to guess his precise intentions. Where the oboes do double the violin lines, Handel's approach is both artistic and practical. He silences the oboes when the violins have passages on the G string, presumably preferring the resulting drop in volume to the equally feasible alternative of doubling the violins an octave higher. In the higher register, the oboes are usually cued out when the violins go up to *d′′′*, though on some occasions again he seems to have forgotten to do this. Sometimes the oboe parts are clearly adapted to avoid the top notes, as for example at the beginning of 'And all the people rejoic'd' in *Zadok the priest* (top *d′′′* avoided) and the opening movement of *My heart is inditing* (top *c′′′* avoided by rests in bars 5–7); in the companion Coronation Anthem *The King shall rejoice*, however, Handel consistently wrote *d′′′* for Oboe 1 when this note occurred in passages doubling the Violin 1 part. On the whole he regarded notes above *a′′* as the province of violins rather than oboes, and Ex. 17.1 is typical of Handel's scoring of final cadences in its distribution of notes between violins and oboes.

3. Doubling a voice part. Very occasionally the tenor voice is doubled an octave higher, or Oboe 2 doubles an alto part,[112] but the most common procedure is for the oboe (or oboes) to double the Soprano part, a role that oboes fulfil far more frequently than the violins. Probably Handel consciously employed the oboe to fill out the tone (and possibly also the volume) of the trebles: there is a noticeable increase in his use of the oboes in the later Chapel Royal music (the Funeral Anthem, and most of the works from the 1740s), which may indicate that the treble section at that period was not as strong as it had been in earlier years.[113] The

---

[112] Examples of both occur in the Funeral Anthem, at 'All her people sigh' (No. 2), bar 43, and 'When the ear heard her' (*HHA* No. 5, *NHE* No. 4), bar 9.

[113] Compare also the use of the oboes revealed in the Foundling Hospital part-books for *Messiah*: see Watkins Shaw, *A Textual and Historical Companion*, 99–100.

Ex. 17.1. Dettingen Anthem, No. 1 (parts for tpts, timp., and voices omitted)

doubling of the trebles' part by Oboe 1 and 2 through nearly all of 'When the ear heard her' and 'They shall receive a glorious kingdom' in the Funeral Anthem supports the principle that these movements were sung chorally: from bar 87 in the latter the oboe parts divide, and the distribution of doubling between the soprano, alto, and tenor parts provides a model example of creatively derived instrumental parts. The tonal combination of treble voices and oboes, no doubt useful and effective for practical reasons, was probably also a matter of positive choice: the oboes both provided support and added a reedy edge to the boys' tone. In the A Major Te Deum the combination of an oboe and full trebles against a soft string accompaniment for the phrase 'and we worship thy Name' (No. 4, bars 41–6) is so effective in performance that we may be sorry that Handel did not use it elsewhere. On only one occasion Handel doubled a treble soloist with an oboe, at the start of 'Tears are my daily food' from *As pants the hart* (HWV 251c). This is not so effective, and it was probably the fortuitous result of rearrangement from the parallel movement of the Cannons version of the same anthem. Equally fortuitous is the doubling of the tenor soloist through nearly all of 'Strength and honour are her clothing' in *This is the day*; the *Athalia* aria from which this movement was arranged was for a soprano soloist, and the original scoring cues were retained in the anthem in spite of the change of voice.

4. Oboes, usually with bassoons, as a 'family' group. The clearest example occurs in the interludes that punctuate the alto solo in the first movement of the wedding anthem *Sing unto God*. In the 'large orchestra' anthems oboes and bassoons sometimes function as a separate group in chorus movements, alternating with passages in which they merge with strings or trumpets and drums. Good examples occur in the choruses of the

Dettingen Te Deum and Anthem, but this usage is surprisingly absent from the Coronation Anthems, where the oboes hardly have any independent solo parts and the bassoons are rarely used in direct conjunction with the oboes except in the first movement of *Zadok the Priest*. The earliest movement in which Handel laid out a separate oboe/bassoon group in the score is 'Glory be to the Father' in the Utrecht Jubilate,[114] but here the group functions with the trumpets and voices, not independently.

In the Chapel Royal music composed before 1727 Handel's oboe parts do not follow any of these four functions for extended periods: the oboe parts slip smoothly between doubling voices, doubling other instruments and following an independent path.

Flutes

Transverse flutes feature in six Chapel Royal works; there are no parts for recorders, though Handel used them in his Cannons anthems. The flute normally has a solo part: only one movement, of exceptional origin, has two flute parts.[115] The range of the parts is $e'-d'''$, with a preference for use of the higher register: when a flute is used in duet with an oboe in the Anthem on the Peace, the flute part is consistently above that for the oboe. The movements that include flute parts are in a limited range of keys (E, G, and D minors, E major), probably reflecting limitations in contemporary instruments that were more significant for flutes than for the oboes. The flute was a quiet instrument, and on every occasion Handel arranged the orchestral accompaniment to let it be heard. 'We believe that thou shalt come' in the Utrecht Te Deum is typical of Handel's 'flute' movements: the soloist's decorated cantabile melody is accompanied by simple repeated-note figures, *piano*, in the strings. Sometimes, as in 'Sing unto the Lord' from HWV 249a, the string accompaniment is also broken up by rests in order to let the flute through. Handel was careful to apply *piano* markings to the string accompaniments but not to the solo flute part. On 'When Thou tookest upon Thee' in the Caroline Te Deum he went one stage further and marked the strings staccato as well: it is clear from its position on the autograph that 'Adagio e staccato' was not intended to apply to the cantabile flute part. A curious notational point arises at the end of the same movement in the Caroline Te Deum. In the closing ritornello (bars 94–101) Handel consistently wrote the rhythm ♩ ♫ in the flute part, while giving

---

[114] Handel may have intended a similar treatment in bars 1–36 of 'The glorious company' in the Utrecht Te Deum, with bassoons alone playing the orchestral bass part; if so, this is not made sufficiently clear by his 'Soli' in the bass at bar 7.

[115] *This is the day*, No. 3, arranged from 'Through the land so lovely blooming' in *Athalia*.

dotted-note groups as ♩ ♪ ♪♫ no less consistently to the basso continuo. It is unlikely that he intended the flute solo to follow a different rhythm from that of the strings, so perhaps he expected that the flute player would make the rhythmic alteration in any case.[116]

Handel used the flute most extensively in his music from the first Chapel Royal period (1712–14). It was then still a relatively new orchestral instrument,[117] and there may have been practical difficulties in reconciling the pitch of the flute with that of the rest of the orchestra, and with that of the organ in the Chapel Royal, a matter that will be considered further in Chapter 19. This may account for the temporary reallocation of the obbligato part for 'When thou tookest upon thee' in the Caroline Te Deum to oboe. When he revived the Te Deum in the 1720s he composed a new setting of 'Vouchsafe, O Lord' which included a flute part, though not, it must be admitted, an outstandingly independent one, since the flute was mainly used to colour the violin line. More generous material is to be found in 'When thou tookest upon thee' in the A Major Te Deum from the same period, a substantial movement featuring a flute in partnership with a bassoon: their unaccompanied duet passages (bars 5–8, 39–41, 77–84) move in parallel intervals of a tenth. The Anthem on the Peace of 1749 has a part for solo flute in two movements, and the accompanying revival of the Caroline Te Deum included the two pre-existing flute movements: as noted in Chapter 14, the names of two woodwind players (Teede and Richter) appear above these movements in the autograph of the Te Deum, implying two players on the single-line part.[118]

No flautist is named among the extra players that were paid for the Chapel Royal performances of the 1720s, so it seems that the flute was played by another 'double-handed' instrumentalist, most probably the oboe player. Handel's leading oboe players are also known to have been flautists. Two relevant concert announcements relating to Kytch, the oboe soloist from the 1720s, have already been mentioned;[119] Teede, one of the flautists named *c*.1749 on the autograph of the Caroline Te Deum, was described in 1763 as a performer on 'German Flute and Hautboy'.[120] The sets of part-books from the Aylesford Collection for Chapel Royal works do not include separate books for the flute, but instead flute parts are written into the oboe partbooks, the flutes being named in the headings to relevant movements.[121] In this, the

---

[116] It may be an indication of Handel's view of the flute part that he wrote 'Verse' next to the basso continuo part at bar 94, as if a solo vocal part was involved.

[117] Flute parts are rare in orchestral scores for works in London before 1700, and Purcell showed a preference for the recorder in his odes.

[118] These pencilled names are not in Handel's hand: see Ch. 14.

[119] See n. 108.

[120] Mortimer, *The Universal Director*, in the list of 'Masters and Professors of Music', 31 et seq.

[121] GB-Mp MS 130 Hd4 v. 332, and v. 333.

copyist was probably following a normal eighteenth-century convention.[122] The Anthem on the Peace is the only Chapel Royal score to include oboe and flute parts in the same movement;[123] the flute player may have participated as a second oboe in the second and fourth movements.

The case for Handel's oboe-player also taking on the flute parts is very strong, but it is by no means proven. The convention of including the flute music in oboe part-books does not preclude the temporary participation of a different player: it would obviously have been inconvenient to have stray parts for single movements on separate sheets that could be lost or damaged. If Kytch really played all of the flute and oboe parts in the Chapel Royal music of the 1720s he would have had to make some very swift changes, putting one instrument aside, picking up the other, and adjusting his playing position and embouchure. Handel made no provision for this in the way of giving the player a few bars' rest at the end of the movements preceding a change of instrument. Inter-movement pauses would have been particularly unfortunate in the Caroline and A major Te Deums, which are constructed as a linked series of short movements, and we may also doubt whether such interruptions would have been treated with indulgence in a court performance. The absence of payments for a separate flautist for the Chapel Royal services is not in itself indicative: if Kytch did not play the flute music himself on these occasions, then the Musicians probably included a few players who could have left their violins for the occasional movement in order to cover the flute parts.[124]

Bassoons

The descriptions for Handel's 'tutti' use of the oboe can also be applied to his bassoon parts. There are occasional independent bassoon parts, and passages in

---

[122] Exceptions can be found, for example, in Greene's 1745 Te Deum (GB-Lcm MS 224) and Walsh's edition of Handel's Op. 3 Concerti, both of which have separate parts for flutes and oboes. Nevertheless, the copyist of the Aylesford parts was from Smith's circle of scribes, and is likely to have followed the conventions associated with Handel's music copyists; it is possible that, for example, the two oboe/flute parts for the Caroline Te Deum reflect the copyists' practice in the 1730s and the 1740s. As a rule the sets in the Aylesford Collection have only the minimum number of parts (including just one copy of each violin part), so there would normally have been no part-book for Ob./Fl. 2 when the music was identical to Ob./Fl. 1.

[123] In the Aylesford fl./ob. parts for the Caroline Te Deum, No. 3, bar 77 is marked 'Tutti fort', and the movement is headed 'Travers'. This may suggest that, when several wind players were available, the oboe(s) entered at bar 77, joining the flute(s)—or the cue may just have indicated the entry of the chorus voices. The movement is included in the part-books for both Ob.1 and Ob. 2 (n. 121, above).

[124] There seems nothing predictable about the combination of instruments undertaken by 'double-handed' musicians, and the flute was probably a popular alternative instrument because its uses in orchestral work were too limited to justify the employment of an extra player. For an example of trumpet/flute versatility, see Ginger, *Handel's Trumpeter*.

the large chorus movements where bassoons are used in a separate group with the oboes, but Handel's typical bassoon parts divide their time between doubling the instrumental bass and doubling an appropriate vocal line.[125] The latter is usually the chorus Bass part, but occasionally bassoons are used to strengthen a melodic thread from the Tenor part, as at the final bars of 'Day by day' in the A Major Te Deum[126] and the first Tenor entry in the Funeral Anthem. The A Major Te Deum and its companion anthem *Let God arise* (HWV 256b) include movements with extended bassoon solos. Here Handel provided his bassoonist with an interesting and demanding part which includes some agile semiquaver runs and passages that cover the whole range of the instrument (C–a'). Richard Vincent was named as the bassoonist in 1724, and Gottfried Karpa in 1726: Handel's solos would have been written for one of these, and the composition must have been influenced by the skills of a particular player.

Sometimes the bassoon is given a separate stave in Handel's scores, but frequently the path of the bassoon part has to be traced from cues that he wrote next to various vocal or instrumental lines. Except in the 'small orchestra' works, these cues regularly have the plural form 'Bassons'. In places the cues suggest that the addition of the bassoons was an afterthought: this is particularly true of the Funeral Anthem.[127] No bassoons are mentioned at all in the scores of the anthems HWV 249a, 250b, and 251c, or the Caroline Te Deum. All of these anthems, with the possible exception of HWV 250b, were originally performed without a bassoon, but bassoons were almost certainly added to the Caroline Te Deum and to HWV 251c in Handel's later revivals.[128] No bassoons are mentioned on the surviving source material for *This is the day*, but the 'large orchestra' scoring of this anthem makes it likely that they were included in the orchestral bass line. (Similarly, the regular inclusion of bassoons in Handel's theatre orchestras is only occasionally acknowledged in the scores of his operas and oratorios.) There were probably several bassoon players to a part in the Coronation Anthems,[129] but the magnificent opening movement to

---

[125] If Handel did not include the bassoon in his labels for the staves at the beginning of individual movements in a work where the instrument occurred elsewhere, the copyist nevertheless probably provided an editorial part extracted from the basso continuo, following the hints provided by the clefs and the scoring. Several examples occur in the bassoon part-books from the Aylesford Collection. This would not have applied for Handel's performances of HWV 251c, since no bassoon player was employed in 1722.

[126] As noted on p. 239, *HG* 37, p. 131 omits the essential cue 'NB les Bassons colla Parte et Violoncelli' next to the Tenor part at bar 56.

[127] Handel's cues leave some uncertainties about the details of the participation of the woodwind instruments—for the bassoons in this work, and for the oboes in the Coronation Anthem *Let thy hand be strengthened*.

[128] There are bassoon parts for both works in the Aylesford Collection.

[129] The Foundling Hospital *Messiah* accounts provide conclusive evidence that, at least by mid-century, it was common practice for the bassoon parts to be doubled when a suitably large

Zadok the priest is the only place where Handel scored for two separate bassoon parts. Having used the bassoons with remarkable and original effect here, and set their track in the last movement by cues against the vocal and orchestral bass lines, he seems to have forgotten about them in the other Coronation Anthems.[130] At the beginning of Handel's autograph of *The King shall rejoice* there is no bassoon stave where we might expect it (with the oboes) and the orchestral bass line is labelled 'Organ & 12 Viol'.[131] Double basses may have been included in the '12 Viol' (which was presumably an instruction to the copyist as to the number of parts required), but this seems to exclude the bassoons. At the chorus entry there are no cues for the bassoons with the voice parts either, but they are named in a cue next to the basso continuo line at bar 9 of 'Thou hast prevented him'. It seems a reasonable assumption that, unless there is any indication to the contrary, Handel normally expected the bassoons to double the orchestral bass part. Attempts to use his apparent carelessness over bassoon cues as an excuse for an innovative editorial bassoon part are rarely successful: the curious effect in performance of a bassoon doubling the Tenor entry at the start of *My heart is inditing* serves only to confirm that Handel knew when to leave well alone.[132]

orchestra was involved: the single bassoon part derived from the general bass line of *Messiah* was rendered by no fewer than four bassoonists.

[130] Already, at bar 51 of 'God save the King' in *Zadok the priest*, Handel probably forgot to cue the bassoons to the bass voice, in a parallel passage to bar 7.

[131] GB-Lbl RM 20.h.5, fo. 18ʳ.

[132] The doubling is included in the bassoon part of Perry's 19th-c. accompaniments to the anthem, which were still to be heard in use in the late 20th c.

18

Buildings

THE material in this chapter covers the buildings in which Handel performed his Chapel Royal music, and in addition two other relevant locations. The church of St Lawrence, Whitchurch, the site for the original performances of the Cannons anthems and canticles, is significant on account of the reworkings of the same music between the Chapel Royal and Cannons repertories that were described in Chapter 6. The Banqueting House Chapel, Whitehall, is also included because it was the venue for Handel's public rehearsals of Chapel Royal music with orchestra in 1713, 1737, and 1743; however, it is unlikely that he expected any of his music to be performed there, and so the building had little direct influence on his compositions. The Foundling Hospital Chapel and the King's Theatre, Haymarket are not included: although these venues saw the first performances of the Foundling Hospital Anthem and *As pants the hart* HWV 251e, both of which drew on music from Chapel Royal compositions, the occasions of the performances were not related to the court functions of the Chapel, and the Chapel singers were probably not central to the musical arrangements.

In consequence of their stone construction and their continued use for public worship, the original sites of Handel's English church music performances that are the subject of this chapter are still in existence today, in forms that are recognizably related to those that the composer would have known; this situation is in stark contrast to the destruction of all of the London theatres that saw his performances. The Chapels Royal at St James's Palace will be described first, and then the other sites in chronological order of the music that Handel composed for them. This chapter should be read in conjunction with the sections on 'Conditions of Performance' in the chapters of Part I, which deal with the particular arrangements in the buildings that were associated with the performances of individual works, and with the performing groups involved.

Before writing any of his English church music Handel would have known the physical properties of the building in London in which a particular piece would be performed, just as he would have known in general terms the size and the musical qualities of the performing forces that would be available, and this affected the music that he composed. The occasional miscalculation arose not because he misjudged the relationship between his music and the site of performance, but because a service took place in a different building from that which had been anticipated. The influence of the buildings on Handel's music may be summarized under two headings:

1. *Acoustic*. The 'large orchestra' and 'small orchestra' forces that were referred to in the previous chapter reflect the acoustic characteristics of different buildings. There was a dramatic difference in size between the 'large' and 'small' buildings relevant to Handel's music, as may be seen from the ground plans in Fig. 18.1. These of course do not show some other architectural features that would have affected the experience of both performers and listeners, such as the height and profile of the ceilings. All of the buildings are constructed of stone and had wooden furnishings, but reverberation times are affected by the availability of the reflective surfaces, and differences in size could have a critical effect beyond the factors that were inherent in the design of the buildings. The large interior volumes of St Paul's Cathedral and Westminster Abbey were such that a packed congregation at floor level covered only a small proportion of the reflective surfaces. In the smaller buildings, however, the presence of the congregation could make a significant difference: the combination of a capacity congregation in elaborate dress and the tapestry hangings on the walls of the French Chapel would have created a very dry acoustic for the wedding anthem in 1734.

2. *Facilities*. The arrangement of galleries and other performing areas (such as choir pews, when available) controlled the conditions of performance, by setting limitations on the number of performers who could take part, and on the layout of the performing group. For some occasions special galleries were constructed for the musicians, though their provision was almost certainly motivated by the desire to release space elsewhere, rather than by any positive concern for the comfort of the performers. The size and design of the galleries would in any case have been affected by the opportunities that were presented by different sites. When no special gallery was provided, the musicians had to make the best use of the spaces that were already available; unfortunately there little evidence on this matter for those occasions on when an orchestra was involved in the Chapel Royal itself. Musicians probably came fairly low down on the priorities at court for royal events, though a surprisingly large resource was sometimes devoted to their accommodation. The principal permanent on-site musical facility in several locations was the organ, but this could pose practical problems if it was to be used with other instruments: the substitution of a specially provided instrument probably indicates that the on-site organ took up too much space, was located in an impractical place in relation to the performers, and/or was constructed to a pitch that was incompatible with the orchestral instruments.

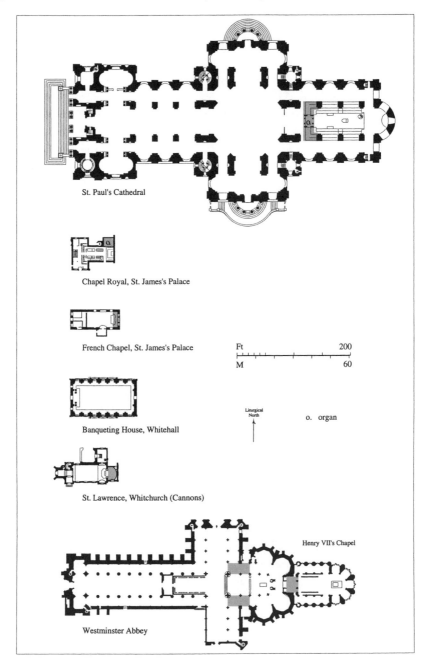

St. Paul's Cathedral

Chapel Royal, St. James's Palace

French Chapel, St. James's Palace

Ft   200

M   60

Liturgical
North

o. organ

Banqueting House, Whitehall

St. Lawrence, Whitchurch (Cannons)

Henry VII's Chapel

Westminster Abbey

Fig. 18.1. Plans of the sites for Handel's performances of his English church music. Probable performing areas are shaded. Malcolm Dickson

St James's Palace: Preliminary Note

For more than a century before 1700 there had regularly been more than one Royal Chapel in London, and indeed several were needed in order to house the various Chapel establishments that were connected with the court. However, one particular building was in personal (and public) use by the sovereign in each reign and, except under King James II, the musical establishment of the main Chapel Royal was based there. From 1703 this building was the small chapel in St James's Palace located next to the Tudor gateway to the Palace that faced the end of St James's Street. The Palace itself was the main London residence of Queen Anne, King George I, and King George II, and the monarch usually attended a service at the Chapel every Sunday morning when in residence. These services were reported in the newspapers, which gave the names of the members of the royal family who were present, the name of the priest who preached the sermon, and the name of the nobleman who had the honour of carrying the Sword of State to the Chapel before the sovereign. The royal family normally resided at St James's Palace for about two-thirds of the year, the remainder of the year (usually during the summer) being spent at Kensington, Windsor, Hampton Court or, in the case of the Georges, Hanover. Queen Anne liked to spend more time at Windsor than her successors, though she made a point of returning to St James's for special occasions such as Thanksgiving Days, and similarly George II usually returned in time for his birthday at the end of October.

The Palace of St James's included at least three buildings which were used at different times for divine worship, so the title 'Chapel Royal, St James's Palace' is potentially ambiguous. There is no doubt, however, as to the building that was in regular use by the monarch and by the Chapel Royal. Of the two other Royal Chapels in the Palace, the 'German' Chapel can be disregarded, since it did not see the performance of any English church music.[1] The remaining building, the 'French' Chapel, saw very little use between 1700 and 1760, but was put into service under exceptional circumstances during 1733–4 for the wedding of Princess Anne. It is apparent from descriptions of the court ceremonial (including the processions) that the royal weddings of 1736 and 1740 did not take place in this building, but in the regular Chapel Royal.

---

[1] The room used by the German Chapel was probably that shown on Pl. III at the top end of the courtyard, with the altar at the right-hand end. As noted in Ch. 13, John Christian Jacobi, the Keeper of the German Chapel, was responsible for a publication of German chorales, with melodies, but these were not necessarily performed at the Chapel; the texts were given in English translations. see Burrows, 'German Chorales and English Hymns'.

The relative positions of the Chapel Royal and the French Chapel within St James's Palace can be identified in Pl. III: the Chapel Royal is the T-shaped room at the bottom of the plan, to the right of the gateway, and the French Chapel is the rectangular room in the middle of the left-hand edge of the plan. Today the right-hand end of the French Chapel (as shown on the plan) is separated from the main part of the Palace by a roadway (Marlborough Road) which has been introduced since Handel's time. It will be seen that the two Chapels have a different orientation, the Chapel Royal having an unusual axis, north-west/south-east, with the altar at the northern end. Following liturgical convention, the 'altar' end of all the buildings will be described as the East End, whatever the geographical facts.

The Chapel Royal, St James's Palace

Relevant music: *As pants the hart* HWV 251a (*c.*1712); Caroline Te Deum, *O sing unto the Lord* HWV 249a (*c.*1714); *As pants the hart* HWV 251d and 251c, revival of Caroline Te Deum, *I will magnify Thee* HWV 250b, Te Deum in A Major, *Let God arise* HWV 256b (1722–6); *Sing unto God* (1736 and 1740); Dettingen Te Deum and Anthem (1743); revival of the Caroline Te Deum, and the Anthem on the Peace (1749).

Royal Chapels in London were arranged on a traditional plan, which also had parallels in continental Europe. The area used by the royal party, known as the Royal Closet (or Closets, if the area was partitioned), was always at the West end, facing the altar; the choir and the organ were located towards the opposite end, with the organ in a gallery and choir stalls on the floor below.[2] Usually, as in the two principal chapels at St James's Palace, the Royal Closet was situated on first-floor level; in the Chapel Royal this enabled the royal procession to pass from the main state apartments (which were on the first floor of the Palace) to the Closet without having to enter the main body of the Chapel. The Closet received occasional alterations to meet the changing needs of the royal family during the eighteenth century,[3] and for the royal weddings in 1736 and 1761 the main part of the Chapel was temporarily refurnished, but afterwards restored to its previous condition. It is probable

[2] This arrangement was referred to by Burney in his description of the layout at Westminster Abbey for the 1784 Handel Commemoration: 'The general idea was to produce the effect of a royal musical chapel, with the orchestra terminating one end, and accommodations for the Royal Family, the other' (Burney, *An Account*, Introduction, 5).

[3] As reported e.g. in *WEP*, 3–5 Dec. 1728, 'The Gallery in the Royal Chapel at St. James's that the King, the Queen, the Duke, and the Princesses sit in, is taking down in order to be enlarged', presumably in order to accommodate the newly arrived Prince Frederick.

that the normal state of the Chapel did not alter significantly during the eighteenth century.

The following description of the Chapel was published in 1714:

It is a most beautiful and eminent Chapel, becoming the Grandeur of her *Britannick* Majesty, and Royal Court to which it belongs, paved with black and white Marble, curiously painted in the Roof, well hung, decently Pewed, and adorned with a stately Organ, a fine Throne or Gallery for her Majesty's own Person, under a Canopy.[4]

'Well hung' probably refers to fabrics round the walls, but apart from the Royal Closet and Holbein's magnificent painted ceiling, the decoration was probably rather plain. There were some significant alterations to the Chapel interior in 1836–7, involving the removal of the organ to a new gallery halfway along the North wall, a small matching extension to the ceiling at the West end (necessitated by the creation of some modest side-galleries at the expense of some space in the Royal Closet), and the 'Gothicizing' of the furnishings, but limitations on the site have prevented major structural changes.[5]

St James's Palace had first become a Royal residence in the 1530s when King Henry VIII acquired a convent on the site, formerly the leper hospital of St James the Less, in order to create a house for Anne Boleyn. The heraldry in the Chapel ceiling reflects subsequent shifts in Henry's matrimonial career during the decade: it refers to Anne of Cleves, and one panel has the arms of Henry impaling those of Katherine Howard, showing that it was completed after Henry's divorce from Anne in July 1540. The Chapel may have been created from the hall of the former convent, thus accounting for its unusual north–south orientation. The basic 'hall space' which formed the Chapel area fixed its dimensions until the 1830s: during the eighteenth century the only expansion to the space in the Chapel was in the Royal Closet.

Unfortunately there are no eighteenth-century pictures of the Chapel interior,[6] but a sketch made by Robert Bremnell Schnebellie in 1816 (see Pl. IV) gives a view of the building, looking towards the East end, before the

---

[4] Paterson, *Pietas Londinensis*, 108.

[5] The alterations in the 1830s were designed by Robert Smirke.

[6] The picture of 'The Sacred Choire' that was published in 1716 as a frontispiece to Weldon, *Divine Harmony*, was apparently intended as a representation of a Royal Chapel viewed from the East end: the choir stalls are on the floor and an orchestra is in the first gallery. (See William C. Smith, *A Bibliography 1695–1720*, 143 and pl. 24.) The building depicted is not any Royal Chapel that was in use in 1716, and the engraving was probably based on a much earlier picture: the royal arms above the King are the pre-1689 Stuart version, with France Modern in the fourth quarter. As evidence of 18th-c. practice the picture is of very limited value: the orchestral group is an archaic combination, crudely represented, with the players' hand-holds reversed in the right-hand gallery in the interests of symmetry.

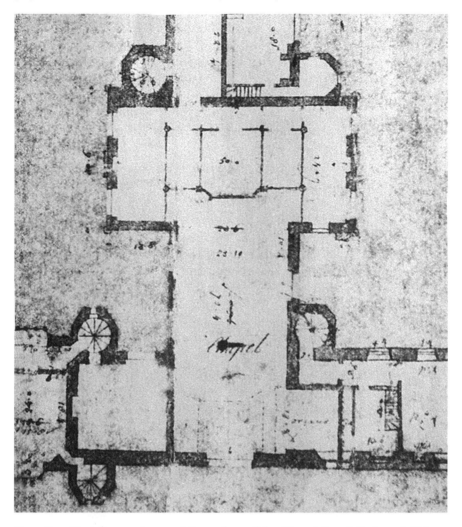

Fig. 18.2. First floor and ground floor plans of the Chapel Royal, St James's Palace; details from the survey by Henry Flitcroft in 1729. Public Record Office, Works 34/122 and Works 34/121

alterations.[7] The sketch tallies with the description of the Chapel just quoted, and also with the plans of the Chapel that were included in a survey of the Palace in 1729 (see Fig. 18.2), in which the arrangement of the pews on the

[7] The original sketch differs in some details, such as the direction of the paving, from the engraving based upon it that was published in Wilkinson, *Londina Illustrata*, ii.

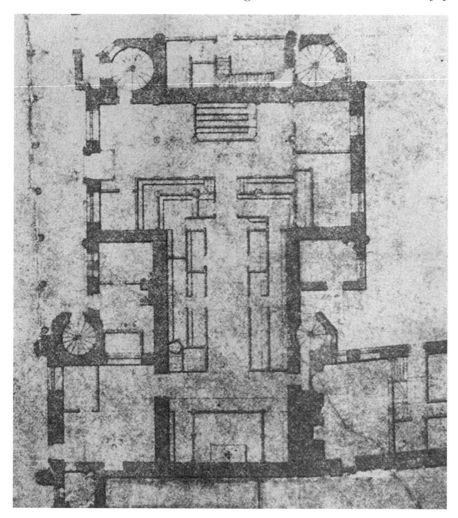

Fig. 18.2. *Cont'd*

ground-floor plan is exactly that seen in Pl. IV.[8] This, therefore, is the Chapel substantially as Handel knew it, with the organ in a gallery at the North side of the East end. As shown in the picture, the Chapel is densely furnished with tall pews,[9] and there is provision for the choir in the front pews at the centre aisle:

---

[8] The survey, prepared for the Office of Works, was the responsibility of Henry Flitcroft, who was Clerk of the Works at Whitehall, Westminster, and St James's Palaces, 1726–46.

[9] These are possibly the 'closets' supposedly provided *c.*1700 after Bishop Burnet's complaints to Princess Anne about the 'ogling and sighing' in the Chapel (Sheppard, *Memorials*, ii. 209–11).

the boys presumably stood on the ledges and used the music desks that are attached to the front pews.[10]

With one exception, all of Handel's performances in the Chapel Royal took place in the building as it stood, without any alteration to the basic furnishings: the exception was his anthem for the wedding service of the Prince of Wales in 1736, for which a temporary musicians' gallery was constructed at the East end. A similar rearrangement was made soon after Handel's death, in 1761 for the wedding of King George III, and from that event there survives a memorandum which calculated the maximum seating capacity of the Chapel.[11] The summary figures from this, with the original descriptions, are reproduced below: the Chapel area as then existing was about 70′ long, including the Royal Closet and the comparable area on the ground floor, and about 24′ wide in the nave area.

	Seats in the Chapel at St. James's against His Majesty's Wedding	
Below stairs:	On the Right Hand of the isle	102′
	On the Left Hand of the isle	<u>103′</u>
		205′
	In the Antichapel	<u>123′</u>
	164 persons at 2 feet each	328′
Up stairs:	In the King's Closet	121′
	Right Hand Closet	63′
	Left Hand Closet	<u>54′</u>
	119 persons at 2 feet each	238′
283 persons at 2 feet each:		566′

The Chapel was probably adapted to a similar capacity for the 1736 wedding, but for the other services at which Handel's music was performed it is unlikely that the building 'below stairs' could have accommodated as many as 164 people. The presence of a congregation in the elaborate dress that was required at court in the eighteenth century must have absorbed most of the building's reverberation;[12] hard wooden furnishings may have compensated a little, though it seems likely that the pew seats were upholstered and, as already noted, the description of the Chapel in 1714 as 'well hung' may refer to wall drapes that are not apparent on the 1816 picture.[13]

---

[10] Places for the boys are also shown in this position on a post-1837 plan of the Chapel in GB-Llp Fulham Papers 124. A similar arrangement can be seen in use in the picture referred to in n. 6 above.

[11] GB-Lpro LC2/29.

[12] The Chapel today has a clear but not very resonant acoustic.

[13] There were probably curtains for some of the windows, but payments for redecorating the Chapel refer mainly to whitewashing and painting, so there may not have been extensive drapes except in the Royal Closet.

The organ chamber was small, only about 14′ square (including the small gallery shown on Fig. 18.2) and 15′ high. The report on the organ in July 1706, quoted below, indicates that Bernard Smith had found it difficult to fit in an instrument of acceptable size, so the organ probably filled most of the available space, leaving a passage for access to the keyboards at the front and enough room for the organ-blower at the side. Later in the eighteenth century a 5-stop Swell department was added to Smith's original instrument, and it is possible that the additional space for the Swell was created by moving the organ forward, so that in Handel's time there was more space at the front of the gallery than is shown in the 1816 picture. The projection of the gallery into the Chapel seems to be about the same on Flitcroft's plan as in Schnebellie's drawing. In the 1750s the Chapel Royal's Serjeant of the Vestry referred to the Lutenist and Violist as 'Instrumental performers in the Organ Loft',[14] so they were presumably stationed there for the Chapel's regular services, possibly with a solo singer or two for verse anthems. The latter is implied by an order from the Chapel Royal Chapter Meeting in 1742, that 'Those who are appointed to sing the Anthem before the Royal Family, should not go the common way out of the Chapel, but go up by the Door near the Communion Table into the Organ Loft.'[15] This would have put the singers on the same level as the Royal Closet. For the purpose of accommodating an orchestra for Chapel Royal services, however, the organ loft can clearly be discounted. Most of the players must have been located in the main body of the Chapel, presumably standing within the pews or in any available aisle areas. There is just one entry in the Cheque Books referring to the arrangements for instrumentally accompanied anthems in the Chapel:

Memorandum.
concerning His Majesty's Band of Musick.

When any Instrumental Musick is to be perform'd at St. James's Chapel Royal, The Sub Dean applies himself to the Lord Chamberlain's Secretary to desire that the Royal Band of Musick may attend at the Chapel, who sends to the Master of the Band for that purpose.

When there is a Rehearsal at Chapel at Eleven o'Clock, there are no Prayers, that the Chapel may not be filled, and any Disturbance made.

On the Days of Rehearsal the Voices and Instruments were order'd to attend at the Chapel between ten & eleven o'Clock and on the Sundays to be there before twelve.

The Honourable Pew and the Back Seat were kept for the Instrumental Performers. It was order'd that no Persons should be let into the Gentlemen's Seats.[16]

---

[14] Lovegrove, *Manuscript*, p. [62]; Ashbee and Harley, ii. 58.

[15] *NCB*, pp. 109–10; Ashbee and Harley, i. 287.

[16] *NCB*, p. 136; Ashbee and Harley, i. 310; copy Royal Archives, Windsor, RA 36, p. 62. The change of tense in the third paragraph may indicate that the scribe was copying from a memorandum that recorded previous practice as a precedent.

The 'Honourable Pew' and the 'Back Seat' are not identified on any contemporary plans or descriptions.[17] Perhaps they were immediately behind the Choir stalls; another, and perhaps more likely, possibility is that the 'Back Seat' was the set of three benches shown on the ground-floor plan at the extreme West end of the Chapel below the Royal Closet, at a disturbingly large distance from the choir and organ. The memorandum was among the items that were entered into the New Cheque Book in 1742/3, by which time a routine for the services celebrating the King's return from Hanover would have been well established. Arrangements may have been more haphazard in earlier years, although it seems probable that those which had been evolved for the Thanksgiving Day services in the Chapel in 1709–10 were repeated on subsequent occasions. It is even possible that, when large numbers of performers were involved but no special galleries were provided, some of the orchestral musicians played in the side vestry to the South of the altar, with the doors open.

Handel's music for performance in the Chapel Royal, unlike that for the other venues that are the subject of this chapter, was very diverse in scoring, ranging from verse anthems accompanied by organ (possibly with lute, and in one case certainly with cello) to the Dettingen music whose style demanded the full panoply of voices and instruments associated with the Coronation Anthems, though not with so many performers to each part. His two verse anthem settings of *As pants the hart* were contributions to a long-established genre for the London choirs: the performances, if they took place, would have been within the conventions of the Chapel's daily performing practice in the first quarter of the eighteenth century. In the other works composed by Handel for services in the Chapel Royal before 1727, the orchestral scoring is well matched to the building, and to the accompaniment of the regular choir of Gentlemen in waiting and Children. At first he tried out the orchestral combination of trumpets and strings derived from Purcell's Te Deum and Jubilate in his own Caroline Te Deum, adding a flute and also, in the anthem *O sing unto the Lord* (HWV 249a), two oboes. During the 1720s he did without the trumpets, whether from choice or necessity, and developed a more intimate scoring that gave particular scope to the woodwind soloists. The later music, for the weddings in 1736 and 1740, and for the more political celebrations of 1743 and 1749, is on a much larger scale: as noted in Chapter 14, the scoring of the Dettingen music is really too large for the building. Handel reintroduced trumpets, possibly accompanied by timpani, into the Chapel in his anthem for the wedding of the Prince of Wales in 1736, the only occasion

[17] David Baldwin, the present Serjeant of the Vestry of the Chapels Royal, has confirmed this.

for which a specially constructed gallery was provided for the musicians in this Chapel. Once re-established, the trumpets remained a feature of later Chapel Royal music, including Greene's anthems celebrating the King's return from Hanover in 1737, 1740, and 1741;[18] Handel incorporated timpani as well as trumpets in his music for 1743 and 1749 but no special refurnishing of the Chapel was undertaken for these later services, so space must have been created somewhere for the drums, unless they were simply omitted at the last moment. Although Handel's Peace Anthem from 1749 includes timpani, it is not so heavily scored as the Dettingen music, and its performance was paired with a revival of one of Handel's earlier Chapel Royal works, the Caroline Te Deum.

In addition to its expansive scoring, the Dettingen music is also exceptional in Handel's repertory for this building on account of its length: the Te Deum and Anthem together take about an hour in performance, which is nearly twice as long as comparable pairings for Chapel Royal services in earlier periods, and indeed twice as long as Handel's music for the 1749 Thanksgiving. Normally the conditions of court services in the Chapel seem to have required individual works lasting about a quarter of an hour. After the Sunday morning Chapel Royal service the King usually dined in public, and the timing of this must have set a limit to the overall length of the service. George II was in the habit of standing during the performance of the anthem; by 1757 the ageing monarch was able to stand for only five minutes, but in earlier years a quarter of an hour had probably been an acceptable duration.[19] It seems likely that George II, and his father before him, paid particular attention to Handel's music at Chapel Royal services.

Handel's Chapel Royal music from the first two periods utilized the standard force of court musicians in waiting, with a few additional players: payments for the extra performers from the period 1720–6 are summarized in Appendix F. The basic performing force to which these were added, if half of the members of the relevant establishments were in waiting, was five Priests, eight Gentlemen, ten Children, the Organist, Violist, and Lutenist of the Chapel, and twelve Royal Musicians.[20] For the weddings in 1736 and 1740, and the

[18] The anthems for 1740 and 1741 were *I will give thanks* and *Rejoice in the Lord, ye righteous*: for the scoring, see the work-list under Greene in *NG II*. Comparable works by Greene for the 1733–4 wedding and the return of the King in 1735 did not include timpani. Lady Lucy Wentworth's comments on Greene's music for the King's return in Jan. 1737 (Deutsch, *Handel*, 424) indicate that the inclusion of trumpets and drums was a novelty: 'too much' music, 'as loud as an Oratoria'. See also p. 486.

[19] MS comment at the beginning of Nares's anthem *Do well, O Lord* (GB-Lbl Add. MS 19570, fo. 3ʳ): according to this, George II 'never sat during the Anthem'.

[20] Some Musicians also held places in the Chapel Royal, so perhaps twelve independent players would not have been available; if they were, the division was perhaps eight violins, two violas, two cellos.

post-Dettingen service in 1743, it is possible that the full forces of the Chapel and the Musicians (26 Gentlemen and 24 Musicians) were expected to turn out, though the complete numbers could only have been achieved if several deputies were employed.[21] A more realistic estimate is that the total group for these later services was about fifty to sixty performers, probably comparable to the numbers for the Utrecht music at St Paul's Cathedral in 1713. In a rare reference to specific numbers, a newspaper report of the Chapel Royal service marking the King's return from Hanover in January 1737, involving the performance of a Te Deum and an anthem by Greene, said that 'Thirty-three Hands of Musick of his Majesty's Band and from the Operas attended the Organ'.[22] This refers to the orchestra, and for that occasion Greene was paid for eighteen additional performers, which means that at least fifteen players came from the court establishments (Royal Musicians, and possibly Trumpeters), and there could have been a few more than that if some of the additionally paid musicians were singers.[23] It seems that orchestral provision was rather stronger for the services marking the King's return in the 1730s than for the comparable services in the previous decade for which Handel had composed: between 1733 and 1735 there is a jump from seven additional performers to fifteen (see App. H). If Greene's orchestra of thirty-three in 1737 had accompanied about eighteen to twenty singers (including the Children), the total number of performers would have been in the range fifty to fifty-five. There is no evidence that the choirs of Westminster Abbey or St Paul's participated institutionally in any of the Chapel Royal services, though individual singers who were not also members of the Chapel might have been employed as extras or deputies on some occasions.

Organ

The removal of the Chapel Royal establishment to St James's Palace early in Queen Anne's reign entailed the provision of a suitable organ for the Chapel. Bernard Smith apparently supplied a temporary instrument which was taken to Windsor and St James's as required in the first months of the reign,[24] and on

[21] The Serjeant Trumpeter (and possibly other court musicians) qualified for additional payments for the wedding of the Princess Royal, and this may have applied to other occasions as well.

[22] *DA*, 17 Jan. 1737.

[23] Another newspaper report described the performers at a rehearsal in the Chapel Royal on 11 Dec. 1736 as follows: 'the Vocal Parts by the Gentlemen of the Chapel and Mr. Beard, and the Instrumental by 34 Performers of the King's Band and from the Operas, to accompany the Organ' (*DA*, 13 Dec. 1736).

[24] GB-Lpro LC3/53, p. 75; Freeman and Rowntree, *Father Smith*, 173; Ashbee, *Records*, ii. 148.

2 July 1703 he was commanded to make 'a new small organ for St. James's'.[25] The limited space in the organ gallery at the Chapel Royal was the reason for the 'smallness' referred to in the warrant: the implied comparison is with the larger contracts that Smith already had under way at that time for the Banqueting House Chapel in Whitehall and St George's Chapel, Windsor.[26] By 3 July 1704 the organ at the Chapel Royal was nearing completion, and an inspection committee consisting of Ralph Battell (Sub-Dean of the Chapel), John Blow (the Chapel's senior Organist), and Peter Hume (Yeoman of the Removing Wardrobe) reported that they valued 'the organ at Whitehall at 1500£, that at Windsor at 990£ and that at St. James's (when completed by putting in the trumpet stop and that called Cremona and the pipes gilt) at 690£'.[27] In July 1706 the same committee reported that all three organs were 'entirely finished and completed. But the organ at St. James's being uncapable of containing the Trumpet stop and the gilding and painting of the same being performed at her Majesty's charge in the Office of her Works there is to be abated 100£ of the above sum.'[28] Smith received the final instalment of the payment for the organs in July 1707. He died in February of the following year, when his post as Organ Builder to the court passed, with the rest of his business, to his son-in-law Christopher Shrider senior.[29] It is probable that either Smith or Shrider overcame one of the deficiencies of the Chapel organ by providing a Trumpet stop in the treble register:[30] perhaps it was only 'uncapable' of containing the larger trumpet pipes.

In January 1733/4 Shrider was paid for an overhaul of the organ which included 'new gilding' the pipes,[31] but otherwise the instrument seems to have remained much in its original state until the rebuild by Hugh Russell in 1785,

---

[25] Lpro LC5/153, p. 384; Ashbee, *Records*, ii. 76.

[26] Ashbee, *Records*, ii. 63 (Whitehall organ, 1698), and Lpro LC5/153, p. 290; Ashbee, *Records*, ii. 74 (Windsor organ, 1702).

[27] Lpro T52/22, p. 232; Ashbee, *Records*, viii. 302; see also Freeman and Rowntree, *Father Smith*, 139.

[28] William A. Shaw, *Calendar 1669–1718*, xxi. 333; partly quoted in Freeman and Rowntree, *Father Smith*, 139, 186.

[29] Shrider naturally took over Smith's tuning and maintenance work, but there is no evidence to support the oft-repeated statement that he built an organ for the Chapel Royal in 1710 (Sheppard, *Memorials*, ii. 352; Freeman, 'The Organs of St. James's Palace', 194). He was engaged in building an organ for the Royal Chapel at Windsor in 1711. Shrider surrendered his court post to his son in December 1740.

[30] A short-register trumpet stop appears in Leffler's stop-list of the organ, and it may have been in the original instrument. The earlier Chapel Royal organ books from the period 1700–40 (RM. 27.a.13 and 14) do not include anthems with obbligato parts for the trumpet stop, but such parts are a feature of several of the anthems whose texts were included in the published word-books.

[31] Lpro LC5/19, p. 190.

during which the pitch was lowered and a Swell department was added.[32] It was subjected to further repair-cum-alteration in 1802; Henry Leffler recorded the specification soon afterwards and described it as 'a very good-for-nothing organ', which may have been a reflection on its condition rather than on Smith's original workmanship.[33] Within twenty years the organ was in need of further major repair. It was bought by Thomas Elliott for £200 in 1819, and found subsequent homes at the Episcopal Chapel, Long Acre (1819–67) and the Chapel of the Worshipful Company of Mercers, Cheapside (1868–84), but vanished when the Mercer's Company replaced it with a new instrument in 1884.[34] There are no pictures of the organ in its subsequent homes, so the distant view of the instrument in the background of Pl. IV is our only guide to the appearance of Smith's case. The organ that Elliott supplied in 1819 for the Chapel Royal in place of the 'Smith' organ is now at Crick, Northamptonshire.[35] It is of some value for confirming the size of organ that it was possible to accommodate in the original Chapel Royal gallery: the case front is about 10' wide and 14' 6" high.[36] The three-tower case in Schnebellie's picture was probably very similar to those of the organ cases now at Christ's College, Cambridge, and St Mary's Church, Finedon: the style of decoration on the display pipes of these organs (particularly at Finedon, which incorporates the arms of Queen Anne on the centre pipe) is also probably comparable to that of the Chapel Royal organ.

As already noted, the chamber in which Bernard Smith had to build the Chapel Royal organ was very restricted, and the relative valuations given by the inspection committee in 1704 confirm that the instrument was much smaller than Smith's other two contemporary instruments for Royal Chapels. There would hardly have been enough height to accommodate the larger pipes of the Great Diapason in the casework above the player's head. Table 18.1 presents a reconstruction of the specification of the organ as it would have been during the first 80 years of its existence, with two other contemporary organs for comparison.[37] The relevance of the Banqueting House organ needs no

[32] Sheppard, *Memorials*, ii. 352; Freeman, 'The Organs of St. James's Palace', 194; Gwynn, 'Organ Pitch', 70 and n. 47. The suggestion in Boeringer, *Organa Britannica*, iii. 231 that the Swell was developed from a previous addition by Shrider is unlikely, and is not borne out by payments to him for the maintenance and renovation of the organ.

[33] Pearce, *Notes on English Organs*, 83; Freeman, 'The Organs of St. James's Palace', 194.

[34] Freeman, ibid. 195; Imray, *The Mercers' Hall*, 121.

[35] Elliott's organ was used at the Chapel Royal until the alterations to the Chapel in 1837–8; as already noted, the organ by Hill and Davidson that replaced it was located in a different part of the Chapel.

[36] The outer towers of pipes at Crick, which appear to be later additions, have been disregarded in these measurements; alterations to the interior of the organ and to the sides of the casework render it difficult to make an accurate estimate of the original depth of the case.

[37] The sizes of the case fronts are my estimates. Some elements of all three specifications must be tentative because they necessarily rely on reconstructions from documentation of the

Table 18.1. *Three Smith/Shrider organs*

Chapel Royal, St James's Palace	St Mary's, Finedon, Northants	Banqueting House Chapel, Whitehall
B. Smith 1703–7	G. Smith or Shrider 1717, based on B. Smith (?Windsor) 1702–7	B. Smith 1699
GREAT C–c'''	GREAT C, AA, D–c'''	GREAT GG(no GG♯)–c'''
Open Diapason	Open Diapason	Open Diapason
Stopped Diapason	Stopped Diapason	Hol Flute
Principal	Principal	Principal
		Nason
Twelfth	Twelfth	Twelfth
Fifteenth	Fifteenth	Fifteenth
		Block Flute (from c♯')
Sesquialtera III	Sesquialtera (IV)	Sesquialtera III
	Cornet (V)	Cornet III (from c♯')
Trumpet (?from c')	Trumpet	Trumpet
CHAIRE C–c'''	CHAIRE C, AA, D–c'''	CHAIRE GG(no GG♯)–c'''
Stopped Diapason	Stopped Diapason	Stopped Diapason
Principal	Principal	Principal
Flute	Fifteenth	Flute (from c')
Cremona	Cremona	Cremona
		Vaux humane
	ECHO c'–c'''	ECHO g–c'''
	Open Diapason	Open Diapason
	Principal	Principal
	Cornet (?III)	Cornet II
	Trumpet	Trumpet
Organ case front 15' high, 11' 6" wide	Organ case front 21' high, 11' 6" wide	Organ case front 22' high, 10' 6" wide

further explanation: the relative values given in the 1704 report, quoted above, suggest that the Chapel Royal organ was about half the size of that for Whitehall. The Finedon organ is included because it represents an instrument built in the same style as the other two and is of an intermediate size: it may actually have been rebuilt from Smith's organ for Windsor.[38]

instruments at later periods; that for the Chapel Royal is based on my interpretation of information given by Leffler (Pearce, *Notes on English Organs, 83*), and by Hill in the letter referred to in n. 39 below.

[38] See Burrows, 'Sir John Dolben', 66: the Finedon organ was opened in May 1717, and GB-WRch Chapter Acts (VI.B.6) for 31 July include a memorandum beginning 'Whereas it appears to the Dean and Chapter that there must be a new Organ made in a short time'. The provenances of the various Windsor organs are complex (see Boeringer, *Organa Britannica*,

At the time that the former Chapel Royal organ was moved from Long Acre to Mercers' Hall in 1867–8 Thomas Hill gave a brief description of the instrument, saying that 'it is clearly a work of Father Smith's, and presents the unusual feature of having escaped any attempt at modernising. The old sound-boards of quadruple planting, the short black keys, and original stops are all preserved.'[39] It is doubtful that the organ had escaped alteration during the previous century, and in the transfers from one site to another. Hill gave the range as 'GG to D short octaves', which matches that of some other contemporary organs, but it is probable that constraints on space in the organ chamber limited the bottom of the compass to C in Smith's original instrument.[40] Otherwise Hill's specification for the Great Organ tallies exactly with that suggested in Table 18.1 (including the short-compass Trumpet stop), and the Chaire Organ differs only in Hill's description of another stop in place of the Cremona: 'a kind of dolcan to gamut G (unison), slightly wider at the top than below'.

In 1880 Alexander Ellis examined Smith's Chapel Royal organ in its later home at Cheapside.[41] Ellis measured the original pitch of the organ at A 474.1 and his inspection confirmed the change of pitch to which the organ had been subjected a century before, involving the shifting of the pipes by a semitone. Of the comparable organs, that from the Banqueting House (now at St Peter ad Vincula, Tower of London) has been subjected to successive alterations on a scale that makes it difficult to recover any reliable evidence concerning the original pitch; that at Finedon, although also altered, retains some of the original pipework, and provides some evidence of a sharp pitch.[42]

---

i. 175–88), but the gaps and ambiguities allow for the possibility that Shrider or Gerard Smith rebuilt the 'Smith' organ at Finedon. The Finedon organ is illustrated in Freeman, 'The Organ at Finedon Church', and in Bicknell, *The History of the English Organ*, pl. 35; see also the description of the surviving material from the original instrument in Bolton, *The Vicar's Gift*.

[39] Hill, 'The Chapel Royal Organ', 10.

[40] The GG extension was probably added by Russell in 1785: see Boeringer, *Organa Britannica*, iii. 231. The part-books for Organ and for Viol in the earliest sets of Chapel Royal books do not go below C, and a weakness in the bass register of the organ may have been one of the original reasons for the employment of the Violist. The opening bars of Clarke's anthem *Bow down thine ear* include a GG in the Lute book (GB-Lbl RM 27.a.12), but this note is avoided in the 'Violoncello' book RM 27.a.10; the earliest surviving Organ books do not include this anthem.

[41] Ellis and Mendel, *Studies*, 48–9.

[42] The Finedon organ has been fitted with tuning slides, but the large pipes in the case front (the lowest of which is C) do not seem to have been altered dramatically. The present tuning of the organ is about a quarter of a tone sharp to a' 440.

The French (or Queen's) Chapel, St James's Palace

Relevant music: *This is the day* (1733–4). Rehearsal of the Funeral Anthem for Queen Caroline (1737).

The building generally known as the French Chapel during the first half of the eighteenth century was constructed in 1623–6 under the direction of Inigo Jones as a chapel for the use of King Charles I's Roman Catholic wife; it was again used for Roman Catholic services from 1662 onwards for Charles II's Queen, Catherine of Braganza, who may have maintained some association with it even after the death of her husband in 1685. Catherine had acquired a lease of the site of the Friary adjoining the Chapel in 1671, which she retained until her death in 1707, after which a new lease was granted to the Duke and Duchess of Marlborough, who demolished the Friary to make way for Marlborough House. When the site was cleared, the buildings that were removed included a small domed 'choir' extension to the Chapel, essentially a separate room opening to the East end, that had been built during Catherine's occupation.[43]

On the death of King Charles II in 1685 his widow moved to Somerset House, and the use of the Queen's Chapel at St James's passed to Mary of Modena, James II's queen, but its importance was soon eclipsed by the domestic Roman Catholic chapel that James established at Whitehall Palace, in a room entirely separate from the existing Chapel Royal there. Roman Catholic services ceased in the chapel at St James's after the opening of James II's new chapel, though the building was still sometimes referred to as the Queen's Chapel.[44] Under William III and Anne the chapel became the home of the Royal Dutch and French (Protestant) Chapels, which were provided for foreign nationals who had originally come to London in William's service. A separate room was put into use at St James's Palace as a chapel for the use of German Protestants in the service of Prince George of Denmark, Queen Anne's consort, and its establishment (as the 'German Chapel') was taken over and maintained by the Hanoverians for their own German servants. In 1781 the French/Dutch and German Chapels arranged to exchange buildings,[45] so the building that was usually described as the 'French' Chapel during Handel's time was known as the 'German' Chapel in the nineteenth century.

---

[43] On the history of this chapel and its music, see Colvin, *The History of the King's Works*, v. 244–54; Sheppard, *Memorials*, ii. 227–38; MB 38 (Le Huray: *Locke*), pp. xv–xvi.

[44] Also as the Queen Dowager's Chapel; Catherine of Braganza remained in residence in London until 1692 before returning to Portugal (Boyer, *Anne (Annals)*, iv. 219).

[45] Sheppard, *Memorials*, ii. 246.

The area around the Chapel suffered as the result of a fire in 1809, but the building itself remains in essential features as it was in the seventeenth century: even the panelling survived the fire, thanks to the Chapel's substantial walls, which are 5–6 feet thick. Inigo Jones's brief for the design of the Chapel was that it had to be 'of equal bignes with that of the Princes at St. James's house'.[46] The French Chapel is, in fact, slightly longer than the Chapel Royal and, thanks to its more regular ground plan, wider through most of its length:[47] the intention behind the instruction was no doubt simply that the two Chapels should be of comparable size. An engraving by Jan Kip, of the Chapel interior viewed from the West End during its period of use for Roman Catholic services and after an elaborate redecoration in 1682–4,[48] shows a building which is structurally virtually identical to the present one: the doors, windows, and main features are in the same positions, and the extent of the panelling next to the altar confirms that the altar screen was in the same place as it is today,[49] repeating the layout of the altar area that was adorned by Grinling Gibbons's carvings in 1682. The lavish decorations of pictures (possibly tapestries) and statuary that are shown in Kip's picture were removed in the 1690s, but otherwise the empty Chapel, pewless but panelled, stood unchanged for forty years; this is confirmed by the plans in the 1729 survey (see Pl. III). The Chapel has a large gallery at the West End, again preserving the arrangement of the Royal Pew or Closet (with its original fireplace) as it was in the eighteenth century.

This gallery was not normally occupied by the monarch in the eighteenth century, since the building was not used as the principal household chapel. The demands on the Chapel by the French/Dutch establishment were light, and so it could be made available for alternative use at times when the Chapel Royal at St James's was out of commission. This happened in 1767 while the Chapel Royal was redecorated; for some reason, also, the French Chapel was used by Princesses Amelia and Caroline during the period of the King's absence abroad in 1743.[50] The underuse of the Chapel facilitated its closure for extensive refurnishing in 1733–4, in preparation for the wedding of Princess Anne. As described in Chapter 12, the marriage of King George II's eldest daughter was a special court occasion, much more lavishly treated than the other two royal weddings of the same period, and extensive temporary alterations were made to the building and its surroundings. In 1662 the windows at the East End had been filled with ornamental glass, incorporating 'a Crucifix of painted glasse':

[46] Sheppard, *Memorials*, ii. 227.   [47] The internal dimensions are about 80' × 28'.

[48] Kip's picture is reproduced in Colvin, *The History of the King's Works*, v, pl. 28. The colours on the record sleeve for Argo ZRG 855 (anthems by Locke, Blow, and Humfrey, 1977) are not present on the only known copy of the engraving.

[49] Direct comparison may be made between Pl. III and the modern photograph of the Chapel in Plumb and Weldon, *Royal Heritage*, 111.

[50] Lovegrove, Manuscript, p. [185]; Ashbee and Harley, ii. 160–1.

if these had survived, they were removed in 1733 in order to construct the musicians' galleries in the window space.

The galleries provided the opportunity for a much larger performing group than for the works that Handel had composed for the Chapel Royal in 1714–26. *This is the day* is the first work by him (or indeed by any other composer) to be performed in a Chapel Royal with an orchestra comparable in size to that for his operas and oratorios, with a full complement of oboes, bassoons, and trumpets (and possibly timpani), and presumably with a matching group of string players. Additional singers were also probably involved, supplementing those from the Chapel Royal, and this also would have been an innovation for an event in one of the Chapels, though it repeated a precedent from the 1727 coronation. Compared with Handel's previous scores for performance in the Chapel Royal, the wedding anthem looks anomalous in its application of large resources to the more intimate spaces of a Royal Chapel, but given the likely dryness of the acoustic from the circumstances inside the Chapel during the wedding ceremony, as described in Chapter 12, the result may not have been inappropriate.

Organ

The organ shown in Kip's engraving, installed in the 1660s, was given by King William III to St Anne's Church, Soho, in 1699;[51] no instrument replaced it, presumably because the French and Dutch congregations did not need one.[52] Nothing specific is known about the special organ that Knoppell provided for the 1734 wedding,[53] but the size of the payment that he received indicates that it was quite small, as it would need to be since space in the gallery was at a premium. During the wedding service it had to serve only a limited musical function. In Fig. 12.2 it is by no means clear whether the organ itself is represented by the pattern in the background on the right or the left of the second gallery. There appears to be a keyboard player (?possibly Handel) on the left, just in front of this gallery; he may be at a harpsichord, but it seems much more likely that the keyboard was connected to the organ.[54] Little is known of Knoppell: presumably he was the organ builder of that name who was responsible for alterations to the Smith organs at Canterbury Cathedral in

[51] Ashbee, *Records*, ii.64; Freeman, 'The Organs of St James's Palace', 200–1.

[52] No Organist is listed in the establishments of the French and Dutch Chapels.

[53] GB-Lpro LC5/19, p. 236: see App. I. This is the only evidence for Knoppell's involvement, so it is not known whether he had already been approached in 1733.

[54] During Handel's visit to Oxford in 1733 he may have encountered a claviorganum (Dean, *Handel's Dramatic Oratorios*, 110), but the arrangements in the musicians' galleries would have precluded the construction of anything so complicated, and Knoppell probably supplied a very simple organ.

1713 and St James's, Garlickhithe in 1718.[55] The 1734 Wedding Anthem was the only Chapel Royal work of Handel's that did not involve the use of an organ from the Smith/Shrider stable at the first performance. Shrider held the Court appointment as Organ Builder: perhaps Knoppell was a Dutchman and had some influence with the bridegroom, the Prince of Orange.

St Paul's Cathedral

Relevant music: Utrecht Te Deum and Jubilate (1713); it is also probable that Handel expected his Dettingen Te Deum and Anthem to be performed there in 1743.

The construction of Christopher Wren's new building for St Paul's Cathedral was completed in 1710, though work continued thereafter on the interior.[56] The basic structure and plan of the Cathedral has not changed to the present day, but there has been an important alteration to the furnishings. In 1860 the organ screen was removed from the entrance to the Choir, opening up the view from the Nave to the East end. The organ was at first rebuilt by William Hill, in the original case, under one of the arches on the North side of the Choir, then in 1872 the organ case was divided longitudinally, to be set up on the North and South walls of the Choir and to receive the new instrument by Henry Willis.[57] The magnificent wooden stalls and galleries lining the North and South sides of the Choir were preserved, but they were moved one bay closer to the Nave in the rearrangement of 1871–2. Plate I shows the organ gallery in its original position on the screen. Although the surrounding Cathedral is large, the original enclosed Choir was, if not intimate, at least manageable for the communication of words and music in the celebration of religious services.

In Chapter 4 Robert Trevitt's picture of the Thanksgiving Service in December 1706 was examined for the information that it provides about the disposition of the musicians, but even if it was accurate for a Thanksgiving Service in 1706, its relevance to the Utrecht Thanksgiving seven years later may nevertheless be questionable. An important piece of evidence is a manuscript plan of the seating arrangements for the Thanksgiving Services at St Paul's, now in the collection of Wren drawings at the Codrington Library,

---

[55] Freeman and Rowntree, *Father Smith*, 27; Clutton and Niland, *The British Organ*, 201.

[56] See Keene, Burns, and Saint, *St Paul's*, chs. 20–2.

[57] See Plumley and Niland, *A History of the Organs*, chs. 4–5; this book has pictures and plans of all stages in the history of the successive organs, including the Wren/Smith original. The central section from the screen, which supported the organ, is now preserved in the south transept of the Cathedral.

All Souls, Oxford.[58] The provision of additional seating for state services was the responsibility of Wren himself, as part of the duties of his public office as Surveyor of the Works. The original ink plan showed exactly the arrangement depicted in Trevitt's picture, and was subsequently subjected to some minor amendments in pencil, which mainly concerned the placing of the benches within the sanctuary rails at the East end. The lower right-hand corner of the plan is endorsed in pencil 'For July 7th 1713'. The most likely interpretation of this document is that in 1713 Wren (or one of his assistants) pulled out the plan of the seating arrangements that had been used for the previous series of Thanksgiving Services at the Cathedral and reused it, indicating in pencil the changes that were necessary for the forthcoming service. This serves to confirm that the Utrecht Thanksgiving Service was planned on the same basis as the previous services, and that the arrangements from the Thanksgivings in 1702–8 were followed again in 1713 with only minor revisions. These revisions did not include any provision for musicians in the Choir area, so they must have occupied the gallery area as before, with the same constraints on space and communication. On the evidence of Trevitt's picture, as few as four clergy (presumably including the Dean and Sub-Dean of the Chapel) may have been involved in conducting the service, so most of the Chapel Royal Priests may have been available as singers.

St Paul's Cathedral remains, as it was in Handel's time, a highly resonant building. In proportion to the reflective surfaces of the walls and roof, the seating area of the Choir is not sufficient to damp the sound to any noticeable extent. During the construction of the Cathedral the location and design of the organ had been a matter of some contention between the architect, the Dean and Chapter, and the organ builder:[59] probably at the insistence of Bernard Smith, the organ screen was eventually located well into the first bay of the Choir, as far away from the dome as practicable. The organ gallery was therefore removed from the worst of the acoustic problems posed by the dome, and the organ case probably shielded the musicians from most of the direct sound reflections from the dome area. The elevation of the musicians on the screen also helped the diffusion of sound from the barrel roof of the Choir. Within the enclosed Choir area itself the acoustics were probably quite favourable, in both resonance and clarity. If Handel had attended the Sons of the Clergy Festival Services in 1710 or 1712 he might have been able to judge the effect of his music in advance: the musicians performed from the organ gallery at these services until 1735, when they moved down onto the floor of

---

[58] GB-Oas Wren Drawing III.19; reproduced in *Publications of the Wren Society*, xiii, pl. XXVII, where the pencil amendments can just be distinguished.

[59] See Sumner, *A History and Account*, 9.

the Cathedral at the East End.[60] There is no certain evidence that Handel attended either of the services during his early years in London, or that orchestrally accompanied music was performed at them: nevertheless, he had plenty of opportunities to hear the routine services at the Cathedral, when the choir presumably performed from the stalls below.

Organ

There is no evidence that a special organ was provided for the Utrecht Thanksgiving, nor that Bernard Smith's large organ was regarded as inappropriate for use in 1713. The specification of that instrument, built during 1694–8, was as follows:[61]

GREAT CC(no CC♯)—c‴	CHAYRE FF(no FF♯ or GG♯)—c‴
Open Diapason (west front)	Quinta Dena Diapason
Open Diapason (east front)	Stop Diapason
Stop Diapason	Principall
Principall	Hol fluet
Hol fluet	Great Twelfth
Great Twelfth	Fifteenth
Fifteenth	Cimball (III)
Block Flute	Voice Humaine
Small Twelfth	Crum horne
Cornet (V—from c′)	
Mixture (III)	
Sesquialtera (IV)	
Trumpet (from FF, no FF♯ or GG♯)	

ECHOES c–c‴
Diapason
Principal
Nason
Fifteenth
Cornet (?III)
Trumpet

---

[60] See Burrows, 'Orchestras in the New Cathedral', 401–2.

[61] The organ itself was probably finished by Sept. 1698, though work continued on the case-work and fittings until 1703: see Plumley and Niland, *A History of the Organs*, 27–9. The specification of the organ as Handel found it is necessarily speculative, depending on the interpretation of Smith's contract of Dec. 1694 (Simpson, *Documents*, 161–3) in the light of Leffler's description more than a century later (see Plumley and Niland, 39–41); it is possible that in 1713 the Chayre also included the 'Quinta Dena Diapason' named in Smith's contract.

There can be little doubt about the sharp pitch of this organ. In 1800 Leffler noted the current specification with the comment 'A Fine Organ all through; Sharp pitch', and in 1802 Ohrmann and Nutt lowered the pitch by a semi-tone.[62] The dimensions of Smith's surviving pipework also support a high original pitch, which would have been sharper than a' 440, but perhaps not as high as a' 474.[63] There is no evidence for transposition of written organ parts at St Paul's, though that may have happened when an orchestra was involved.

The Parish Church of St Lawrence, Whitchurch (Cannons Park)

Relevant music: Cannons anthems and canticles HWV 246 (= Jubilate), 247–8, 249b, 250a, 251b, 253–5, 256b, and HWV 281 (Te Deum).

During the period that Handel was associated with him, James Brydges (subsequently 1st Duke of Chandos) was one of the richest men in England. The building of the large house at Cannons and the rebuilding of the adjacent parish church were displays of conspicuous consumption, but Brydges also had a genuine interest in music and the visual arts. The house at Cannons would eventually have a chapel of its own, but this was not completed until 1720. Five years previously Brydges initiated a major refurnishing and redecoration of the parish church of St Lawrence that adjoined the Cannons estate at Edgware, and this reopened for public worship on Easter Sunday 1716. The West End of the church interior was arranged to the same plan as a Chapel Royal, with first-floor closets for Brydges and his family. The church was comparable in size to the French Chapel at St James's: of similar length and breadth, but with a lower roof, and furnished with box pews. The decoration of the church is dominated by elaborate paintings in European (rather than English) Baroque styles, but the *grisaille* pictures on the North and South walls of the nave were not yet in place during the period of Handel's association with Brydges, so these walls presumably had stone surfaces at the time. The area at the East end, forming a Retro-Choir behind the altar, has a higher and flatter ceiling than the Nave: the decorative scheme and the paired Corinthian columns at the transition effectively form a proscenium arch to this area. The musicians would have been located with the organ at the East end, and would therefore have been in

---

[62] Freeman, 'The Organs of St Paul's Cathedral', 6; Plumley and Niland, *A History of the Organs*, 39, 53, 203–4.

[63] Alexander Ellis estimated that the original pitch was about a' 442 (Ellis and Mendel, *Studies*, 62). However, when Haydn in the 1790s wrote down the melody of a chant by John Jones that he heard at St Paul's, he notated it a tone higher, and this suggests a higher pitch: see Landon, *Haydn in England*, 173–4.

a separate acoustic room of their own, though opening into the Nave. In this area singers and players are able to hear each other clearly, thanks to the partial screening from the Nave, but solo singers located at the Nave end of the eastern area can be heard clearly throughout the church; there is a pleasing 'bloom' to the sound, but it dies quickly and there are no noticeable echoes. The acoustic conditions therefore favour a chamber-size performing group rather than large choral and orchestral forces, and performances of Cannons anthems in a 'cathedral' type of acoustic generally confirm that they are not suited to reverberant buildings:[64] a twofold demonstration of the match between Handel's music, his performing forces and the building.

Of the organ built by Gerard Smith (a nephew of Bernard Smith) for St Lawrence's Church in 1716, a substantial part of the original case survives, as well as pipes from two of the original ranks, which indicate that the pitch was about a' 433.[65] The compass was probably GG (short octaves)[66] to d'' and the stop-list resembled that for the Great of the Chapel Royal organ, with the addition of a (4′) flute.

Westminster Abbey (Area, Theatre, and Choir)

Relevant music: Four Coronation Anthems, HWV 258–61.

Westminster Abbey is England's coronation church: it has a layout in which the crossing (where the 'Inthronization' takes place at the coronation) is more central than usual in cathedral-style buildings, and the Choir is to the west of the crossing rather than in the normal eastern position. Around the crossing extensive temporary alterations were made for coronation services: areas were cleared, galleries were constructed, walls and screens were hung with decorative drapes. The principal duty of the Earl Marshal with regard to places for those people who had a right to attend the coronation was to see that sufficient allocation was made in prominent places for the royal family, nobility, qualifying members of the gentry, and foreign ambassadors. The Abbey singers were thus ejected from their normal performing area in the choir stalls, and no single location remained that was large enough to hold all of the singers and players, so the performers were divided between several galleries around the altar and the crossing. A reference to the exceptional expenses for the 1727

---

[64] A good demonstration of this may be heard in 'He cast forth lightnings' from HWV 255, as recorded in King's College Chapel, Cambridge, by the choir of King's College in 1968.

[65] See Gwynn, 'An Organ for St Lawrence Whitchurch', and id., *St Lawrence Whitchurch*. The organ at Gosport (Haynes, *A History*, 176 and n. 77) provides no relevant evidence, since it only has material from the instrument in the later chapel at Cannons house.

[66] Probably GG, C, AA, D in the bass.

coronation mentions 'the additionall Scaffolds and Extra preparations for the Musick',[67] but pressures on space in the Abbey would have been no less than for previous coronations, and it can be assumed that the general distribution of accommodation remained much the same.

There are no relevant authoritative pictorial representations of the coronation of King George II and Queen Caroline, nor indeed of the preceding coronations in the eighteenth century, but some idea of the physical arrangements can be gained from the pictures of the coronation of James II and his Queen in 1685 that were included in Sandford's monumental commemorative publication. While these refer to an event more than forty years earlier, it seems likely that the same general arrangements in the Abbey were followed for successive coronations; the 1727 coronation was in fact a closer parallel than the intervening ones on account of the inclusion of the coronation of a Queen consort, and also because it seems to have been the first one on a comparable scale. Furthermore, Sandford's record of the 1685 coronation is useful because he was primarily concerned with the details of the ceremonial, which involved identifying those present (as individuals and groups) and the positions that they occupied in the Abbey. The locations of the musicians can be identified from three of the pictures, read in conjunction with Sandford's ground plan of the Abbey interior.[68]

At the 1685 coronation the Westminster Abbey choir occupied a specially built gallery to the north-west of the crossing, with the Trumpeters and Kettledrummer of the Royal Household placed further west still, in the gallery over the entrance to the Choir, which, unlike that at St Paul's Cathedral, was not the site for the Abbey's organ. In the pictures the members of the Abbey choir are shown holding their music, but no choristers are visible. The Abbey choir was about 60′ to the east of the trumpeters, and a further 60′ to the east of the Abbey choir was the main body of musicians, divided between two galleries on either side of the altar, on the eastern side of the crossing. The Chapel Royal occupied the gallery on the south side, in which there was also a 'little Organ'. About 45′ separated the front row of the Chapel singers from the front row of the instrumentalists in the gallery opposite, one bay closer to the crossing. Probably some variant of this scheme formed the starting point for the arrangements in 1727. William Boyce's letter relating to the 1761 coronation, which was quoted in Chapter 10, indicates that in 1727 the musicians were again distributed in separate galleries that were sufficiently far apart to render communication difficult; it also suggests that there may have been a gallery behind the altar in substitution for, or in addition to, the earlier arrangement.

[67] GB-Lpro Works 21/1.

[68] 'A Perspective of Westminster-Abby' and 'The Inthronization' (both viewed from the west), 'A Prospect of the Inside' (viewed from the east) and 'A Ground-Plot of the Collegiate Church', in Sandford, *A History of the Coronation*.

Handel's music was designed to make the best effect with what was probably the largest professional group of singers and players yet assembled in Britain for a church service, in a large and resonant building, comparable in floor area to St Paul's Cathedral but built in a different architectural tradition, which involved a loftier roof but no dome. The West End towers which are now one of the main identifying features of the Abbey's exterior were not yet to be seen in 1727. Although planned by Wren, these additions were undertaken under Nicholas Hawksmoor and completed in 1745: they feature in Canaletto's picture of a procession leaving the Abbey in 1749.

Organ

The Abbey's own permanent organ on the north side of the choir, which had been rebuilt by Bernard Smith in 1694,[69] may have been heard at some stage during the 1727 coronation service,[70] but the instrument that was used for Handel's anthems was a specially provided second organ by Shrider. As in 1685, the 'coronation' organ was probably built in the Chapel Royal's gallery to the north of the altar. It may have had a long communicating mechanism to a keyboard at the front of the gallery, from which Handel directed the performance, but it is perhaps more likely that on this occasion the organ accompaniment was the responsibility of a separate player, presumably one of the Chapel Royal's Organists, which would explain the presence of the 'soft' and 'loud' markings at the beginning of *Zadok the priest*. The second organ would have been needed because the Abbey's instrument was too far from the performing group, and also incompatible in pitch with the orchestral instruments;[71] there may also have been an institutional issue involving a distinction in use between the 'royal' organ and that which was the property of the Abbey's Dean and Chapter. Shrider's organ was undoubtedly regarded as royal property, for in 1728 the King presented it to the Abbey,[72] and the trail of the 'coronation organ' can be followed in the newspapers:

---

[69] See Boeringer, *Organica Britannica*, iii. 257–8.

[70] It may be significant that for the 1685 coronation Sandford's plan of the Abbey describes the relevant space as 'The Great Organ and Organ Loft in which sate severall spectators'.

[71] In 1710 Shrider had been employed to lower the pitch of the organ 'half a note which will reduce it to the pitch of St. Pauls, her Majesties Chapel & all other Modern organs' (GB-Lwa Chapter Book 5, 11 May 1710), but even so the instrument would have remained sharper than the pitch of contemporary stringed and woodwind instruments. In 1718 it was also ordered that Shrider should be paid for 'cleaning the Organ after the coronation' (Chapter Book 6, 14 Apr. 1718): perhaps the coronation service for George I in 1714 had revealed inadequacies in the instrument.

[72] The fate of the previous organ is uncertain, but on 21 Oct. 1730 the Chapter directed that 'the Old Organ loft be taken down and that the Treasurer Dispose thereof' (GB-Lwa Chapter Book 8).

We hear that his Majesty has made a Present of the fine Organ that was put up for the Coronation-Day in Westminster-Abbey, to the said Church; and which is to be placed at the West End of the Choir, and to stand in the same Form as that at St. Paul's, viz. with two Fronts. Made by Mr Shrieder, the King's Organ-Builder. (*LEP*, 3–6 Feb. 1727/8)[73]

Mr Shryder, Organ-Builder to his Majesty, and Mr. Jordan, Organ-Builder of Southwark, have agreed for making a large new Organ to be set up over the Choir Doors in Westminster Abbey. (*LEP*, 25–27 June 1728)

Last week they began to put up in the Abbey-Church at Westminster, the new Organ that was play'd at the late Coronation of his Majesty; and the old organ that was up there, is to be made a Present of to the Parish of S. John the Evangelist, to be erected in their New Church. (*DPB*, 4 Aug. 1729)

This being the Anniversary of his late Majesty's Accession to the Throne, the new Organ at Westminster-Abbey being finish'd, will be play'd upon this Evening for the first Time, when a great many of the finest Voices will assist at Divine Service on that Occasion. (*SJEP*, 30 July–1 Aug. 1730)

This Day Mr. Handel, the famous Master of Musick, made Trial of the new Organ in Westminster-Abbey, upon which he played several fine Pieces of Musick, and gave his Opinion, that it is a very curious Instrument. (*SJEP*, 6–8 Aug. 1730)

Handel's trial of the organ may have been undertaken after encouragement from the court, to confirm the quality of the workmanship on the King's gift. In November 1730 the Abbey agreed that Shrider should be 'paid in full for the New Organ' (presumably the costs of installation), on receiving a report that the installation was completed.[74]

Unfortunately it is not possible to establish much useful information about the instrument itself, because every aspect of the evidence is problematic: nothing definite is known about Shrider's original organ for the coronation apart from the payment of £130 (which may have related primarily to costs associated with 'putting up' the instrument), the relationship between the contents of this instrument and the one that was finished at Westminster Abbey in 1730 is uncertain, and the fate of this organ and its case(s) to the present day is not sufficiently well documented to enable fact to be separated from myth.[75] Early in the nineteenth century Leffler recorded the current specification of the Westminster Abbey organ as follows:[76]

[73] A similar entry in *BJ*, 10 Feb. 1727/8, concluded 'It is accounted one of the best Performances of that Maker'. Lwa Chapter Minutes ordered that 'the New Organ given by his Majestie to this Church, be erected over the Entrance into the Choir' on 16 Apr. 1728, and articles of agreement with Shrider were approved on 25 May (Lwa Chapter Book 8).

[74] Lwa Chapter Minutes (Chapter Book 8), 7 Nov. 1730. An entry by George Carleton in *WA2* (p. 10) confirms that 'The New Organ by Mr Shrider and Mr Jordan was open'd on the 1st of August 1730, by Mr Robinson', and with a performance of Purcell's anthem *O give thanks*.

[75] Knight, 'The Shrider Organ', and id., 'The Organs of Westminster Abbey'.

[76] Freeman, 'The Organs of the Abbey Church', 137, from Pearce, *Notes on English Organs*, 59.

GREAT GG(no GG♯)–d‴   CHOIR GG(no GG♯)–d‴
Open Diapason [east]   Stopped diapason
Open Diapason [west]   Principal
Stopped diapason   Flute
Principal Flute   Fifteenth
Twelfth   Cremona
Fifteenth
Sesquialtera III
Mixture II
Cornet (from C♯) V
Trumpet
Clarion

SWELL g–d‴
Open diapason
Stopped diapason
Trumpet
Hautboy

Known changes to the organ during the eighteenth century include the addition of pedal pipes in the 1770s,[77] and the addition of a Cornet that was not identical to the one found by Leffler: in 1733 Shrider was paid £5 for 'altering the Organ and putting a Cornet of three Ranks into it, in Exchange of another Stop'.[78] Jordan's involvement in the construction of the Abbey organ perhaps suggests that the Swell division dated back to 1730 (but not 1727), though alternatively it may have been added in the later 1730s.[79] What does seem certain is that the specification noted above represented a rather larger instrument than that used at the Coronation.

King Henry VII's Chapel, Westminster Abbey

Relevant music: Funeral Anthem for Queen Caroline (1737).

King Henry VII's Chapel, constructed in the first decade of the sixteenth century, is a vaulted stone building at the East End of Westminster Abbey beyond Edward the Confessor's Chapel: it is a separate room, though physically linked to the main body of the church by a wide vestibule with a staircase. The Chapel is about 90′ long, but much of the space is taken up with the tomb

[77] See Boeringer, *Organica Britannica*, iii. 259.
[78] Lwa Chapter Book 8, Chapter Minutes, 31 Oct. 1733.
[79] In 1737–9 Jordan took down and cleaned the organ, and added new 'swelling stops' (Lwa Chapter Book 8, 23 Nov. 1736, and subsequent related entries in 1737, 1739), but it is not clear whether the latter were an addition to the existing Swell division.

of King Henry VII, so that the open area of floor space is comparable to that of the Chapel Royal; however, the characteristics of the room are entirely different owing to the high vaulted stone ceiling. For Queen Caroline's funeral in 1737 King Henry VII's Chapel was hung with mourning on the lower areas of the walls, probably beginning around the height of the musicians' gallery, but against the deadening effect of this must be set the height of the roof and the large remaining area of free stonework and windows, constituting more than half of the total height. The Chapel itself would therefore have remained fairly resonant, and in addition the music performed there would have been relayed, relatively unimpeded, to the vast annex of the Abbey itself. This may have resulted in some ideal musical conditions, with possibilities for good ensemble in the Chapel, yet also the benefits of the Abbey's rich acoustic enhancement by the time the sound reached the majority of the listeners. As with Handel's Coronation Anthems, the broad harmonic style of the Funeral Anthem and the concentration on choral textures would have suited these conditions, as also would the relatively slow pace of the movements. (The fastest tempo marking is Andante.) The unaccompanied voices for 'Their bodies are buried in peace' must have been striking as a contrast to the prevailing full textures for chorus and orchestra, and particularly effective in the Abbey. As described in Chapter 13, the performers were located on a specially constructed organ gallery over the entrance to the Chapel—that is, at the West End of the Chapel, in the transition to the main body of the Abbey.

Organ

The organ that was erected by Shrider on the gallery for the funeral was presumably dismantled soon afterwards. Nothing certain is known of the instrument or its casework (if any were provided), though it seems likely that Shrider or his successors would have reused the components elsewhere, and in 1737 he may even have reused the temporary organ that he had provided for the Prince of Wales's wedding the previous year. The organ that Gerard Smith the younger made for the funeral of King George II in 1760 was subsequently 'impressed' by the Dean and Chapter of Westminster, and the possibility that this also happened to Shrider's organ in 1737 cannot be ruled out. Andrew Freeman's suggestion that the organ whose case later appeared at Barnsbury Independent Chapel was the one made for the 1737 funeral is not implausible:[80] the vases on the top of the case may indicate funerary associations.

[80] See Freeman, 'The Organs of the Abbey Church', 147, but also (for an alternative provenance) Boeringer, *Organa Britannica*, ii. 234.

The Banqueting House Chapel, Whitehall

This building was the site of some of Handel's rehearsals for Utrecht Te Deum and Jubilate in 1713, the Funeral Anthem in 1737, and the Dettingen Te Deum and Anthem in 1743. In 1733 it was also the venue for the Chapel Royal's three concerts of church music, including one programme of works by Handel, in support of their Fund. The events in 1733 and 1737 both gave rise to verses that were published in the newspapers, the former mainly concerned with Handel's music and the latter referring also to Reubens's ceiling in the Chapel. The roof and ceiling saw extensive repairs and renovation from 1728 onwards:[81] some of the scaffolding was probably still in place during the 1733 concerts, and in 1737 the newly restored paintings were still a novelty. The Banqueting House was built in 1619–22, at about the same period as the French Chapel at St James's Palace and also under the direction of Inigo Jones, but as a secular building. It came into use as a chapel after the fire of 1698 destroyed the Chapel Royal in Whitehall Palace, but its significance diminished when Queen Anne removed the Chapel Royal establishment to St James's in 1703. On Easter Day 1724 it became the site for weekly sermons that had been instituted by George I in an attempt to encourage good relations with the universities: they received his patronage but not his presence. At some stage during the early eighteenth century the Chapel also became the regular site for the annual distribution of the Royal Maundy.

A colour plate showing the Banqueting House in use as a chapel was published in Ackermann's *Microcosm of London* during the first decade of the nineteenth century:[82] there is obviously an element of caricature in the persons depicted, but it gives a good general view of the heavily pewed interior and shows Bernard Smith's large organ with the 'dial' and royal arms, placed centrally on the South wall. Handel probably used the organ for his rehearsals, in which case the singers and players would presumably have been grouped as close to it as was convenient: there was only a limited amount of free floor area, at the East End, so many of the musicians probably had to stand in the pews. The building followed the normal Chapel Royal arrangement, with the royal throne or closet at the West End. On the closure of the Chapel for public worship in 1890 the organ was transferred to the Church of St Peter ad Vincula in the Tower of London, but by then the instrument had seen radical reconstructions, in 1814, 1844, and 1877: of Smith's 1699 work, only the top half of

---

[81] Colvin, *The History of the King's Works*, v. 301.
[82] In the pictures for *The Microcosm of London*, the architectural interiors were drawn by Augustus Pugin, and the human figures were added by Thomas Rowlandson.

the case front and about twenty-five wooden pipes could be identified in 1998.[83]

The size of the Banqueting House interior is close to a double cube of 60′ dimensions, much larger than the Chapel Royal at St James's—about twice as long, twice as high and twice as wide. It therefore lacks the intimacy of other Royal Chapels and is somewhat more resonant, though the flat compartmented ceiling discourages the formation of the types of echoes that are characteristic of the much larger buildings at St Paul's and Westminster Abbey, with their stone arches and vaults. Handel's rehearsals at the Whitehall Chapel seem to have attracted considerable public attention, possibly partly because the building was more accessible than the chapels within St James's Palace, and it had a larger seating capacity.

[83] Gwynn, *The Organ in the Church of St Peter ad Vincula*; also Freeman, 'Organs Built for the Royal Palace of Whitehall', and Freeman and Rowntree, *Father Smith*, 38.

19

The Chapel's Resources and Handel's Music

Voices

Trebles

FROM the Foundling Hospital accounts for Handel's *Messiah* performances in the 1750s it appears that four or six boys from the Chapel were provided by Bernard Gates for the chorus,[1] and this provides an indication of the usual number of able musicians among the trebles: of the nominal group of ten, the younger ones would have been musically inexperienced, and the reliability of the older ones would have been unpredictable on account of changing voices. With six, or even ten, trebles the chorus texture in Handel's Chapel Royal performances would not have been dominated by the top part, and the boys' voices must have blended relatively unobtrusively with the men's; his frequent practice of doubling the trebles with the oboe indicates the need to fill out their tone, though he may also have liked the combination of timbres.

The boys, though few in number, included several with considerable musical abilities. The *Esther* performances of 1732 coincided with talented group of Children, in their best voices at about the same time, and the first generation to have been trained by Gates. Many celebrated English musicians began their careers as Children of the Chapel, and some of them became important solo singers. Thomas Mountier, James Butler, Samuel Champness,[2] Samuel Howard, and, above all, John Beard later appeared as soloists in Handel's oratorios.[3] Of the singers from the Dublin cathedral choirs who sang as soloists in Handel's first performance of *Messiah*, the bass John Mason

---

[1] In 1758 and 1759 the figure of £4.14.6 appears in the *Messiah* accounts as expenses for six boys (Deutsch, *Handel*, 801, 825); the payment of £3.3.0 in 1754 (ibid. 751) was therefore presumably for four boys. See also Ch. 11 n. 32.

[2] This must have been Thomas Champness 1 (App. B, B83), who left the Chapel in Aug, 1748; identification is confirmed by an entry in the Chapel Royal Fund Receipt Book, recording payment in 1805 to the executor of 'S. T. Champness'. I have given him a place in App. B, as W13.

[3] See Dean, *Handel's Dramatic Oratorios*, app. 1, 651–61, for short biographies of these soloists.

was certainly a former Child of the Chapel Royal, and the alto William Lamb probably so.[4] Even while they were still choristers, many of the boys were soloists for Handel's London oratorio performances. Sometimes, as in *Acis and Galatea, Saul, Samson,* and *Messiah,* they sang music that had previously been taken by an adult, but for *Joseph and his Brethren, Susanna,* and *Jephtha* trebles sang solo roles at the first London performances; Handel probably composed this music for particular boys, though he identified them simply as 'The Boy' in his scores.[5]

The following treble solos occur in Handel's Chapel Royal music:

*c.*1712. The earliest version of *As pants the hart* (HWV 251a) includes a Treble/Alto duet movement for 'The Boy' and Elford. 'The Boy' may have been Thomas Gethin, for whom Croft wrote a solo anthem at this period.[6]

1713. Utrecht Te Deum. Some passages are marked 'Solo',[7] but it is by no means certain that Handel was thinking in terms of treble soloists on each occasion: several of the markings appear to be warnings to the performers of places where a treble lead receives no support from the rest of the chorus. This applies, for example, to 'When thou hadst overcome the sharpness of death', where the purpose of the 'Solo' indication might have been to draw attention to the absence of orchestral accompaniment: there is no complementary 'Tutti' marking five bars later.

*c.*1722. *As pants the hart* (HWV 251d and HWV 251c) have brief solo entries in the first chorus, where the music of HWV 251d is derived directly from HWV 251a.

*c.*1724. *I will magnify thee* (HWV 250b), No. 3. Alto, tenor, and bass parts are divided Solo/Ripieno, but there is only one treble part and this is unlabelled. It may have been sung by a soloist but, in view of the small numbers involved, possibly by all of the trebles.

[4] App. B, B46 and B53. For the Dublin *Messiah* soloists, see Watkins Shaw, *A Textual and Historical Companion,* 32–3, 109–12. John Church, one of the tenor soloists, may also have been related to Gentleman 24: see Ch. 13, in connection with the 1740 wedding anthem. John Mason, son of the Chapel Royal Gentleman of the same name (36), was recommended to Dean Swift at St Patrick's Cathedral, Dublin, by John Arbuthnot as a 'baritone voice': 'he has a pleasant mellow voice, and has sung several times in the King's Chapel [presumably as a deputy] this winter, to the satisfaction of the audience' (Aitken, *The Life and Works,* 126).

[5] See Dean, *Handel's Dramatic Oratorios,* 177, 258–62, 300, 353, 407–8, 546, 618. Handel's treble soloists would usually have been Chapel Royal Children, but the first Joas in *Athalia* was a treble from the Oxford choirs, and the 1757 *Messiah* soloist, 'Mr Savage's Boy', was presumably from St Paul's Cathedral.

[6] See above, Ex. 3.12, and Burrows, 'Thomas Gethin'.

[7] *NHE* No. 2, bars 16–23 (Treble 1 and 2); No. 4, bars 15–19 (Treble 1); No. 5, bars 8–9 (Treble 1) and 22–3 (Treble 2). Handel may have accidentally omitted 'Solo', at No. 3, bars 51–66, and No. 8, bars 17–22.

1734. *This is the day* (HWV 262), No. 3. No soloist is named in the conducting score, but this movement was certainly intended for a treble and may even have been sung by one of those who had performed in the 1732 *Esther* production. The movement was arranged from an aria in *Athalia*, and Handel's amendments to the vocal part reveal interesting differences between what he expected of a theatre-trained soprano and a Chapel-trained boy. Two extended examples are given in Ex. 19.1. The version for treble is generally simpler, though it still demands vocal agility and a good sense of line, and the range has been lowered. The normal range of Handel's Chapel Royal treble parts is e' to g''.[8] Even in chorus contexts, Handel was not confident of giving them top a'', and provided the lower octave as an alternative when the note

Ex. 19.1. Parallel passages from (*a*) *Athalia*, 'Through the land', and (*b*) *This is the day*, No. 3

---

[8] On rare occasions Handel takes them down to d': see the Caroline Te Deum, No. 6, bar 18.

occurred in the A Major Te Deum:[9] at bar 118 of the first movement of *This is the day* the lower octave was substituted when the music was transferred from *Athalia*, even though the higher note was doubled in the orchestra and the alteration distorted the melodic line.

1736. *Sing unto God* (HWV 263), No. 2. The autograph is lost, but a good text is available from secondary copies; this movement must have been intended for a treble soloist, and the Earl of Egmont's description of the performance refers to 'a boy'.[10] The movements from 1734 and 1736 were presumably revived in 1740, since the source text for Handel's 1740 wedding anthem includes the words of both treble solos (see Fig. 13.1).

1740. Dettingen Te Deum (HWV 283). At the beginning of 'To thee all Angels cry aloud' Handel wrote 'C[anto] 1 solo', but then crossed out 'solo' in favour of 'tutti', which is no doubt how it was performed: see Chapter 14. At bars 32–8 of the preceding movement the alto part is marked solo but the treble parts are not: as with parallel instances in the Utrecht Te Deum (see above) it is

[9] No. 10, bar 21.   [10] Deutsch, *Handel*, 405; see Ch. 13.

possible that the full treble section was used to balance soloists in the lower parts.

1749. *How beautiful are the feet* (HWV 266), No. 3 ('The Lord hath given strength'), solo for 'The Boy'. Unlike the treble soloist's movement in *This is the day*, the soprano aria on which this movement is based was close enough to the style associated with the Chapel trebles to be used with only minor adaptation. The boy might have been Neal Abington or Thomas Dupuis. The second movement of the anthem is derived from HWV 250b, No. 3 (see above), and once again the treble part may either have been sung by the full section or by a treble soloist. See also pp. 419–20, for the solo in HWV 267.

*c.*1751. Foundling Hospital Anthem (HWV 268). Handel's additional movements included the duet 'The people will tell of their wisdom', for '2 Boys Soprani',[11] almost certainly Chapel Royal Children (see Ch. 15). There were a number of excellent musicians among the Children who left the choir between 1751 and 1758.[12]

Gentlemen: Balance of Voices

A Chapel Royal list from 1674 shows a precisely equal division between alto, tenor, and bass voices, 6/6/6,[13] but unfortunately there is no comparably explicit source for the next hundred years and the 'voices' for many Gentlemen are unknown. Analysis of selected lists of Chapel Royal Gentlemen from the first half of the eighteenth century suggests that there was probably an approximately equal spread between alto, tenor, and bass voices, with a slight bias in favour of altos and basses;[14] this bias is increased substantially when account is taken of the fact that the best singers, whose attendance also dominated the life of the Chapel because they had 'double places', were altos and basses. Handel was well aware of the particular musical strengths of the Chapel singers. The solo movements in his Chapel Royal music are almost entirely for altos and basses, and in chorus movements he frequently divides alto and bass parts without dividing the tenors.[15] When he specified the number of voices to a part for the Coronation Anthems, he expected that the alto and bass voices would each have twice as many singers as the tenors.[16] It would be wrong to

---

[11] Described thus in Handel's pencilled cue at the end of the previous movement in his conducting score of the anthem, now in the collection of the Foundling Museum.

[12] See App. B, B89–95.

[13] Ashbee, *Records*, i. 136.

[14] See Burrows, *Dissertation*, ii. 39, n. 122, from lists relating to 1718, 1724, 1737, 1743, and 1755.

[15] This is particularly true of the repertory from the first two Chapel Royal periods: examples occur in HWV 251a, 251d, 256b, and the A Major Te Deum.

[16] GB-Lbl RM 20.h.5, fos.18, 26 (14 altos, 7 tenors, 14 basses).

infer from this that the alto and bass parts in SATB choruses necessarily sounded twice as loud as the tenor part: other factors may have been involved, and in any case a handful of tenors are able to hold their own within a large choral ensemble because of the relatively favourable carrying power of their vocal register.

The division of altos and basses into 'first' and 'second' parts was a time-honoured practice in the Chapel and provided a resource for composers: singers specialized in one area and generally maintained it consistently.[17] Bernard Gates, for example, normally took Bass 2, though the music written for him never demands the low notes around *D* for which John Gostling, the principal second bass of the previous generation, had been famous in the 1680s. The differentiation between first and second parts for altos and basses is a consistent feature of Croft's larger anthems: it is found in *Blessed be the Lord my strength* (1705) and *O clap your hands* (1706), and also in two of his anthems that were composed at the time of Handel's first contact with English church music, *O sing unto the Lord* and *Offer the sacrifice of righteousness* (November and December 1710, respectively). All of these anthems were written for special occasions such as Thanksgiving Services or the Sons of the Clergy Festival; the complete group of the best altos and basses was probably not available for the routine daily Chapel Royal services because of the alternating months of waiting. Handel clearly understood the division between 'first' and 'second' voices in the Chapel and put it to good use. As noted in Chapter 3, the disposition of the solo voices at the start of his first setting of *As pants the hart* (HWV 251a) is exactly the same as that used by Croft at the start of *O praise the Lord, all ye that fear him* (1709/10) and *This is the day* (Utrecht Thanksgiving, 1713).

Altos

The alto-clef male-voice part was normally referred to in England during the period 1700–60 as Contra Tenor or Counter Tenor. In Handel's music alto parts are clearly defined by the use of the alto clef (*c'* on the third stave-line). On solo movements he wrote the name of the soloist rather than that of the voice; in chorus movements he once wrote 'Contra Alto' early on (in HWV 249a), but otherwise he used 'A' or 'Alto' when he found it necessary to

---

[17] With the Anglican division of the choir into *cantoris* and *decani* sides, there was apparently a principle that both sides should contain both 'firsts' and 'seconds': see Ardran and Wulstan, 'The Alto or Countertenor Voice', 18. The Chapel Royal part-books show that a subtle change of practice took place during the 18th c.: although the books are still labelled 'Cantoris' or 'Decani', the significant division is between 'Chorus' and 'Verse' books, the latter containing all of the solos for the relevant voice.

provide a generic label for the part.[18] Following Handel's practice, I refer to all voice parts written in the alto clef as Alto parts, and to their performers as altos.

There is no conclusive evidence concerning the way that the Chapel Royal altos produced their tone, but Handel's music contains some hints that they were mainly falsettists. This would explain how Thomas Bell slipped from alto/tenor to bass within a short time during the 1720s: in 1720 John Perceval described him as 'an excellent base & yet Sings a high Counter-Tenor which is with all natural and not forced'.[19] Handel's specification for twice as many altos as tenors on the autograph of the Coronation Anthem *The King shall rejoice* suggests that the altos were relatively lacking in volume and carrying power.[20] The consistent use of the fifth between *d'* and *a'* as the centre of the voice for alto soloists, which Handel's Chapel Royal music shares with that by contemporary native-born Chapel composers, also suggests the extensive employment of falsetto techniques, and most of his music for alto soloists sits comfortably within the falsetto-alto voice. The chorus parts also seem well suited to falsettists: the holding notes for Alto 1 in the last movement of *Zadok the priest*, bars 35–6, for example, make effective use of falsetto tone. Handel keeps the alto parts, both solo and chorus, mainly in the higher register, avoiding the low notes which fall into an awkward mid-register position for many singers. However, the overall range of the alto parts does not provide conclusive evidence for the form of tone production that was used, and the range may in any case have been modified by differences in pitch standards from one performance site to another, an aspect that will be considered later in this chapter. The use of falsetto technique was probably not a serious aesthetic or technical issue in Handel's time: singers would have used their various registers freely in any way that produced the most effective (or vocally comfortable) result.[21]

There is the possibility that first and second altos specialized in different forms, or combinations, of tone production from each other: Hughes, a 'First Alto', may have been primarily a falsettist while Elford, a 'Second Alto', was not. Although Handel distinguishes between first and second altos in his scores, the difference in range between their parts is only about the interval of a third, less than the difference that is found in some of the music by Purcell and Croft.[22] Handel never takes Elford's part down to the regions around *d* and *e*

[18] There are examples in the Utrecht Jubilate, the Coronation Anthems, and the Dettingen Anthem.

[19] See App. C, Bell.

[20] The same considerations did not, of course, apply to the alto-register castrati soloists in Handel's theatrical companies.

[21] See the comment on Blow's *Ode on the Death of Mr Henry Purcell* in Holman, *Henry Purcell*, 35.

[22] See the ranges given for the soloists in App. C.

which are common in Croft's music for the same singer. In HWV 251a Elford's music includes c'', but this experiment was probably never repeated:[23] the area around b' to d'' was Hughes's speciality. The panegyrics for Elford should not distract from the fact that Hughes also must have been an excellent musician, as is demonstrated by the music Handel wrote for him; the contrast between the two voices seems to have been a stimulant to composers, who did not always treat Elford as the dominant partner.[24] The Chapel had a parallel pair of alto voices in the 1740s with Bayly and Mence; Bayly's was the higher voice, apparently more lyrical but less agile than Mence's. Greene distinguished clearly between them in the solo movements of his Te Deum setting composed in 1745,[25] and Handel made appropriate use of the two voices four years later in the Anthem on the Peace and the accompanying revival of the Caroline Te Deum.

Much of the best music in Handel's Chapel Royal repertory was written for the alto soloists. Their solos are more restrained than the arias given to their operatic counterparts, with shorter movements and less florid melodic decoration.[26] Yet it is not deficient in emotional range, as can be seen if, for example, Handel's settings of 'Tears are my daily food' from the Chapel Royal versions of *As pants the hart* are compared with 'The glorious company' from the Caroline Te Deum. The main constriction on the alto music in solo movements (though not in choruses) is one of pitch range, for the overall ambit is rarely much more than an octave. It is remarkable how much expression Handel (and his English predecessors) packed into so small a compass.

Basses

Constriction of range was not a feature of Handel's music for the Chapel's bass voices. A range from G to e' was taken for granted, and could be extended further at the top. In common with the practice of the native-born Chapel composers, Handel's music for the Chapel Royal bass soloists tends to lie high in the voice. Occasionally a full and equal use of the whole range is called for, especially in Handel's earlier Chapel Royal works.[27] Weely, a first bass, was the Chapel's foremost bass soloist up to 1730, though Gates was usually also given some share in the solo work, and Handel gave Baker some rather flashy solos in

[23] Whether Elford ever sang the higher notes in the Caroline Te Deum depends on the interpretation of Handel's alterations to the singers' names on the autograph: see Ch. 5.

[24] In Croft's *I will lift up mine eyes*, for example, Hughes received a greater proportion of solo music than Elford.

[25] GB-Lcm MS 224 (score and parts).

[26] The contrast between Handel's treatment of sopranos and trebles (see Ex. 19.1) is exactly paralleled by the contrast between his treatment of operatic and ecclesiastical altos.

[27] See e.g. HWV 249a, No. 3, or the section for bass solo in the Caroline Te Deum, No. 2.

the Caroline Te Deum and *O sing unto the Lord* (HWV 249a). Abbot and Wass, the former a Priest, proved worthy successors in the next generation, and Wass has a special place in Handel's association with the Chapel Royal since he was the only Gentleman to perform as a regular soloist in theatre oratorio performances under the composer.[28]

Tenors, and the Problem of Voice Definition

Tenor solos are rare in Handel's Chapel Royal music. There are only two full solo movements for this voice, both of them from the wedding anthems of the 1730s and both arranged from music that had originally been composed for a different voice. Furthermore, the soloist on the second occasion (and also possibly the first) was almost certainly John Beard, who never held a place as a Gentleman of the Chapel.[29] Presumably Handel's avoidance of tenor solos in the earlier periods is a reflection that the Chapel did not have an outstanding soloist in that voice, though no doubt it would have required a strong personality to displace the primacy of the established alto and bass soloists. In the 1720s Thomas Gethin was given some minor solos by Handel, but of no more than a few bars at a time.

The absence of substantial tenor parts in the Chapel Royal music is perhaps surprising in view of the dominance of tenors in the Cannons anthems and canticles. The middle-range parts in these works are nearly all written in the tenor clef:[30] this must have been a deliberate choice on Handel's part, since he had used both alto and tenor clefs in the conventional way in his earlier Chapel Royal music. It seems very unlikely that all of the solo tenors in London specializing in church music should have been concentrated at Cannons, and concentrated there, furthermore, only during the couple of years which saw the production of Handel's music, without spilling over into the London choral establishments. Furthermore, an examination of the wider repertory of the church music from the period reveals that composers occasionally wrote music for the same named soloist but using different clefs. This calls into question the clef convention: either the vocal distinction between 'altos' and 'tenors' was vague or the notational convention of the different clefs was loosely applied. Two high tenors are named in Handel's music for Cannons, James Blackley and Francis Rowe: Pepusch wrote for Blackley in the alto clef

---

[28] William Savage sang as a theatre soloist for Handel before gaining his Chapel Royal place in 1744, but seems to have given up his theatre career thereafter. In spite of his participation in court odes from 1744 onwards, there is no evidence that he ever sang as a soloist in Handel's Chapel Royal music.

[29] He was still on the Chapel roll as a chorister at the time of the 1734 wedding: see Ch. 12.

[30] Handel wrote alto-clef parts in only two Cannons anthems, pair II in Table 6.1.

in *Venus and Adonis*,[31] and Rowe may have been an alto soloist for Eccles's court odes in the 1730s.

Composers seem to have differed in the range that they expected of a tenor or an alto. Handel's inconsistency in the early 1720s over the clef for Bell's music may have been the result of an imperfect prior acquaintance with the singer's voice (see Ch. 8), but elsewhere the variations in the clefs associated with particular singers suggest that a certain amount of versatility of 'voice' was common in the choirs. The case of Richard Elford himself provides a good example. Before he came to London, Elford seems to have been a 'tenor': his name appears on the inside cover of a tenor part-book at Durham Cathedral.[32] His music in the Eccles's 1702/3 royal birthday ode *Inspire us, genius of the day*, composed for him soon after he had established himself in London, is partly in the alto clef and partly in the tenor clef.[33] Subsequently he normally appears as an 'alto', though there are occasional lapses: Galliard's *I am well pleased* (c.1710) includes substantial solo movements for him in the tenor clef.[34] The ranges of Elford's 'alto' and 'tenor' parts are not radically different, and no obvious scribal convenience accounts for the use of one clef rather than the other. The employment of both clefs may support the suggestion that he was not primarily a falsettist; the music for Hughes, Elford's complementary 'first alto', is never written in the tenor clef.

Although soloists specialized in one voice, the practical needs of the choirs must have demanded some versatility of the singers, especially where day-to-day numbers were low as at St Paul's Cathedral and, to a lesser extent, Westminster Abbey. If only four Lay Vicars were present at Westminster, for example, and these were two 'altos' and two 'basses', one of them would presumably have had to sing the tenor music.[35] Necessity, personal choice, and advancing years may all have played a part in persuading singers to change their 'voice'. Sometimes a complete change seems to have happened very suddenly, as in Bell's transition from alto/tenor to bass in the 1720s, which was perhaps prompted by a realization that he would not displace Hughes as the Chapel's leading alto soloist. This was, of course, a different case from the downward transition that may have followed the breaking of a boy's voice, as seems to

---

[31] GB-Lcm MS 975.

[32] GB-Drc MS C13.

[33] GB-Lbl Add. MS 31456.

[34] GB-Ob MS Mus.c.2. For details of Elford's vocal range in various works by composers other than Handel, see Burrows, *Dissertation*, app. 6.

[35] In the case of the Chapel Royal, admissions do not seem to have depended on the possession of the same 'voice' as the person replaced. Before 1714 *OCB* records the voice of the Gentleman on admission, but not afterwards; the motive for including this information in the early entries is unclear.

have happened with William Savage from St Paul's Cathedral as he performed in Handel's operas and oratorios during the 1730s.[36]

Within a single work it was not unknown for a composer to take a soloist into a different-clef part. In Blow's anthem *Blessed is the man* (*c.*1698)[37] there are a large number of short 'verse' sections. Blow wrote the music first and then added the names of the leading singers, which included four altos, and he seems to have taken pleasure in permutating his soloists in different ways. John Church, generally used as a 'tenor' in this anthem, has one low 'alto' part in an ABB interlude; on the other hand, Freeman, who has a solo movement as an alto in the anthem, is in two places deployed as the 'tenor' in short ATB sections. For Maurice Greene's D Major Te Deum composed in 1745, the original performing parts have survived with the score.[38] The section beginning 'We believe that thou shalt come to be our judge' appears in Greene's autograph score as a verse section for SATB, laid out in the appropriate clefs. The tenor-clef music does not, however, appear in the performing part for solo tenor ('Mr Loyd'): instead, it is included in the part for solo Bass 1 ('Mr Wass'). An amendment was made to one phrase, presumably in order to help Wass: it did not alter the range, but it reduced the length of the top f' (see Ex. 19.2). Handel was alert to the possibilities of using one voice to strengthen another part in concerted movements. In 'Glory and worship are before Him' from *I will magnify Thee* (HWV 250b), for example, he combines solo bass with chorus tenors, and solo tenor with chorus altos in bars 25–7; in *Let God arise* (HWV 256b) the alto and bass soloists are used to link the chorus parts for their own voices with the treble and tenor parts respectively.[39]

Ensembles

Handel combined the Chapel's alto and bass soloists in various ways for duets and larger ensembles (AA, AB, SAATBB), many of which can be related to the practice of other Chapel Royal composers. The alto-and-bass combination seems to have been a particularly favoured one. It is noticeable that Handel parted from the traditional Chapel Royal ensembles in the 1730s, but returned to them in the 1740s: this may be attributable to the circumstance that the Chapel was between generations of outstanding soloists in the 1730s, or to the particular nature of the royal weddings and funeral when compared with other Chapel Royal occasions for which he composed. In general his vocal scoring in chorus movements, and sections of movements involving chorus textures,

---

[36] Dean, *Handel's Dramatic Oratorios*, 659.
[37] Score, GB-Lsp Case B.13.
[38] GB-Lcm MS 224.
[39] In No. 1 of HWV 256b see e.g. bars 48–9 (solo Bass) and 69–70 (solo Alto).

Ex. 19.2. Greene, Te Deum: (*a*) original Tenor part; (*b*) as altered for Wass

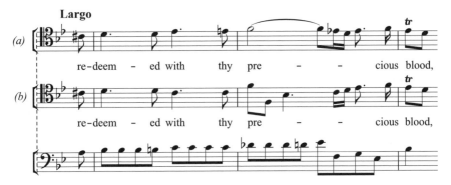

follows the normal four-part layout, with some division (often more apparent than real) in the alto and bass parts. In the Utrecht and Dettingen canticles there are two treble parts, probably following the model of the scoring from Purcell's famous D major Te Deum and Jubilate. Handel also wrote for divided treble parts in the 1737 Funeral Anthem, and one brief passage from this was carried forward into the Foundling Hospital Anthem.

The Chapel Royal and the Court Odes

Whether or not it came to performance as intended in 1713, Handel's setting of Ambrose Philips's text *Eternal source of light divine* (HWV 74) clearly falls within the genre of English court odes, and he followed established practice by writing a large proportion of the solo music for leading singers from the Chapel Royal (Elford, Hughes, Weely, and Gates), to whom were added two English women. These would not have made up the complete complement of voices, however, for at least a few additional chorus singers would have been required: the ode includes a movement for two four-part groups, and it is most probable that the extra singers would have come from the Children and Gentlemen of the Chapel Royal. The vocal ensemble for the court odes was usually provided mainly from the Chapel Royal and, as noted in Chapter 4, Handel's ode may have been one of the last of the period to include women soloists. Thereafter additional soloists, when these were involved at all, seem to have been mainly men who, though not currently holding office in the London choirs, had had some association with them: most particularly, John Beard seems to have been a regular soloist for the court odes from 1737 onwards.

The terms under which the Chapel Royal singers took part in the court odes are not known, though the management of the arrangements was probably easier from 1735 onwards when Maurice Greene succeeded as Master of the King's Musick while also continuing in his posts as Organist and Composer of the Chapel Royal. The composition and performance of the court odes was one of the primary duties of the Master of the Musick, and attendance to perform the odes was similarly one of the principal regular tasks of those Musicians in Ordinary who were in waiting at the New Year and the monarch's birthday. No such formal obligation is indicated among the conditions of service for the Chapel Royal, however. This is confirmed by an exchange of letters between the Lord Chamberlain's office and Edmund Gibson (as Dean of the Chapel) in January and February 1748. A request had come to Gibson in the following terms:

> It having been represented to my Lord Chamberlain that the Gentlemen of the Chapel are very irregular in giving their attendance on his Majesty's Birth Day and New Years Day songs, which lays the Master of His Majesty's Band of Music under great difficulties in regard to the Rehearsals, as well as Performances, His Grace desires your Lordship will be pleased to give such Orders as you think proper to prevent the like complaints for the future.[40]

To this Gibson replied:

> I do not conceive, that as I am Dean of the Chapel, it is strictly speaking, in my power, to require the Members to perform duty anywhere but in the Chapel. However, as the two Seasons are at a distance, I shall have time and opportunity to make them sensible, how rude and undutiful a part it would be to make the least difficulty of giving their best assistance at these Solemnities which are always honoured with his Majesty's presence, and in which he is more immediately concern'd.[41]

It is very unlikely that the complete roll of the Chapel's Gentlemen in waiting and Children took part in the odes: the reports in the newspapers suggest that on some occasions there may have been a small group of singers, consisting only of those who also sang the solo movements, and on other occasions the soloists were apparently supported by a few other boys and Gentlemen as chorus singers.[42] The Chapel's leading singers at particular periods can be identified from newspaper and journal reports of the rehearsals and performances of the odes, which sometimes even print the full text of the ode and name the singer for each solo movement, and from the surviving

---

[40] GB-Lpro LC5/161, p. 279 (9 Jan. 1747/8).

[41] Ibid. p. 280 (10 Feb. 1747/8); 'how difficult' deleted before 'how rude'.

[42] The newspaper reports of rehearsals and performances of the odes are vague on the matter, usually referring to the leading singers by name (including some that were not necessarily soloists on that occasion) and to Gentlemen and/or boys 'from his Majesty's Chapel' for any other singers, without any indication of names or numbers. One report, for New Year 1760, names ten Gentlemen, but this may have been an exceptional occasion.

musical scores. As we might expect, Hughes, Gates, and Weely feature prominently in the earlier period. Rowe becomes active in the 1730s as a soloist, in advance of receiving a Chapel Royal place, though he was already a member of the Westminster Abbey choir. From 1741 Bayly succeeded as the leading alto soloist, his participation in the odes coinciding with his Chapel Royal appointment, and during 1745–9 he shared the honours with Benjamin Mence. Baildon comes into the picture in 1745, and becomes the principal alto from at least 1753 onwards.[43] Abbot is a principal bass voice from 1735 to 1743, after which Savage takes over (coinciding with his Chapel Royal appointment) and continues well into the 1760s, sharing the principal role with Wass between 1748 and 1759. The termination of Mence's activity as a soloist may have had some connection with his appointment as a Minor Canon at St Paul's Cathedral in 1750, though he continued in his Chapel Royal post. In contrast to the inhibitions that applied to Priests performing in the theatre, clerical status seems to have been no bar to performing in the (secular) court odes: 'Rev. Mr. Abbot' and 'Rev. Mr. Bayly' were identified in those terms in the press coverage of the odes. There are no records of the Chapel Royal singers receiving payment for their participation in the odes during the period up to 1760, and they were presumably not included in the regular standard payments to the Master of the Musick for the composition and copying of the odes, the hire of a room for rehearsals, and the employment of 'extraordinary performers': the latter would have included not only Beard, but also the necessary additional orchestral players to supplement the string band of the Royal Musicians. Since performance at the odes was not part of the court duty for the Chapel Royal (unlike the Musicians), it is difficult to believe that a small and elite section of the choir would have performed this additional function without some reward, especially since the New Year odes fell within the Chapel's traditional 'Play Weeks'.

Pitch

The subject of pitch standards in the long ages before audio recording is a difficult one to deal with because of the nature of the evidence: the relationship between notation and and acoustic reality is uncertain, and original musical instruments (where they survive at all) have been subject to alteration and decay. Although the pitch standard for any of Handel's performances is, like his interpretation of tempo directions, largely irrecoverable, there is nevertheless a

---

[43] He is named in reports concerning the ode for New Year 1753; information from 1751–2 is limited because the odes for birthday 1751 and New Year 1752 were not performed.

certain amount of relevant factual evidence that needs to be considered. One piece of evidence that can be disregarded is that of the so-called 'Handel tuning fork':[44] even if it were authentic and unaltered by time and circumstance, it is doubtful that the pitch it supposedly represents as that used for Handel's oratorio performances in the 1750s had any relevance to his church music.

When instruments were combined with voices for his Chapel Royal music, limitations affecting pitch were principally imposed by orchestral wind instruments and permanent on-site organs. Most orchestral instruments can adjust to a certain extent to different pitches, but there is a practical upper limit, and in the case of the eighteenth-century woodwind instruments that were used in London this seems to have been about a' 430.[45] However there is ample evidence of wide differences in pitch standards in the eighteenth century, from place to place, from venue to venue, and even between different churches in the same town, as for example in the Hamburg that Handel knew.[46] Furthermore, instruments with different pitch standards might be used together: the original performing parts for J. S. Bach's cantatas and Passions reveal that at some stages he had to contend with as many as three different simultaneous pitch standards among his instruments, with organ, strings, and woodwind each having their own pitch level and the problem being resolved in practice by transposition in the written parts. Unfortunately, performing material of this sort does not survive for Handel's Chapel Royal music.[47] His scores include one transposition instruction, which will be considered below.

The best sources of evidence for the pitch standards of Handel's performances of English church music are derived from the organs. Alexander Ellis's examination of organ pitches led him to the conclusion that the organs built by Bernard Smith at St James's Palace and the Banqueting House Chapel, and Shrider's 'Coronation' organ at Westminster Abbey, were all originally constructed at a sharp pitch, approximately a' 474, and thus more than a semitone above modern concert pitch.[48] When the organs at St James's Palace, St Paul's Cathedral, and Westminster Abbey were subjected to major overhauls in the later eighteenth and early nineteenth centuries their pitch was lowered by a

[44] See Ellis and Mendel, *Studies*, 37, under 'A 442.5'.

[45] Ibid. 222 n. 79. The late Anthony Baines confirmed this with regard to surviving 18th-c. English oboes in the course a conversation with the author; pitch standards for flutes were probably even lower.

[46] Ibid. 219–20.

[47] The only surviving orchestral part-book from Handel's London theatre performances is the basso continuo part for *Alexander's Feast* (GB-Lcm MS 900); performing parts do, however, survive for some of the church music that Handel composed in Italy: see Watkins Shaw, 'Some Original Performing Material'.

[48] Ellis and Mendel, *Studies*, 48–9, 52.

semitone at least once, a circumstance that supports the other evidence for the high original pitch of these instruments. There is, furthermore, good reason to believe that the Chapel Royal routinely performed at the high pitch set by the organ. The earliest surviving set of Chapel Royal part-books from St James's Palace, compiled mainly by John Church during the first two decades of the eighteenth century,[49] includes part-books for organ, cello, and lute as well as the vocal parts. Unlike Bach's instrumental parts, these books contain no transpositions,[50] and it appears that organ, lute, cello, and voices all performed at the same notated pitch. Only in some later Chapel Royal books, dating from the period after 1750, is there occasional evidence to suggest the separate downward transposition of the organ part.[51]

The established habits of the Chapel Royal therefore seem to have involved sharp-pitch performance, and it is probable that the same applied to the other two major London choirs as well. The Chapel Royal's Lutenist and Violist might have used instruments that had been specially made for use at sharp pitch when performing with the organ in the Chapel, but problems must have arisen when an instrumental group of any size participated in the services, involving the Royal Musicians and additional players. The specially constructed temporary organs that were provided for the coronation in 1727 and for the royal weddings in the 1730s were probably at the contemporary orchestral pitch, and the impracticability of using the permanent on-site organs with a large orchestra may have been a contributory reason for their existence. However, for many of the special services at St James's Palace (including all of those up to 1726) the documentary records make no mention of an organ and it is unlikely that a special one was provided. The smaller the instrumental group, the more likely it is that the performers would have been able to find ways of matching with the sharp pitch of the Chapel Royal organ.

A look backwards to Henry Purcell's anthems is appropriate at this point. His instrumentally accompanied anthems for the Chapel Royal were performed with a small group of 'violins'. With the exception of the D major Te Deum and Jubilate, he never added any wind instruments to his church music: no woodwind instruments appear in his scores, although he used them in contemporary court odes which were performed in secular buildings where the use of a permanent organ did not arise. Even in Purcell's time there may have been a sharp 'Chapel Royal pitch', presumably related to Bernard Smith's

[49] GB-Lbl RM 27.a.1–15: see Laurie, 'The Chapel Royal Part-Books', 35–41.

[50] There is a possibility that the organist transposed his part, but it would have been more practical to transpose the parts as they were copied, or to compose the music in a more usable key, than to rely on the continued diligence of the organist.

[51] Croft's *I waited patiently*, for example, appears in G major in the Organ Book GB-Lbl RM 27.c.15: compare the original in A major in RM 27.a.13.

organ in the Whitehall Chapel, which the wind instruments were unable to match. The difference in pitch was not such an insuperable problem for the stringed instruments, and in any case a special set of instruments may have been reserved for use in the Chapel.[52] It is not known whether any such instruments survived the fire at Whitehall Palace, though during the first half of the eighteenth century special bass stringed instruments (variously described) were provided for the Chapel:[53] payments for these were made to the Sub-Dean, taking a different administrative route from the direct payments that were made to the royal Instrument Makers (John Walsh senior and junior) for the stringed instruments that were supplied to the Royal Musicians.

The ranges of the vocal bass parts in Purcell's scores seem to bear out the possibility of different pitch standards between the Chapel Royal and other venues.[54] His welcome songs from the 1680s, accompanied by strings with the occasional addition of recorders, regularly take the vocal bass parts down to *D*, but the odes from the 1690s, accompanied by an orchestra that generally included trumpets and oboes, never demanded anything below *F* of the basses. However, in his last dated anthem *The way of God is an undefiled way*, composed in 1694 and thus contemporary with the later odes, Purcell took the bass soloist down to *D*, so the absence of comparable low notes in the later odes cannot be explained by the absence of a suitable bass soloist. The addition of oboes to the orchestra may have required the adoption of a lower orchestral pitch in London during the 1690s,[55] but the Chapel Royal, tied to the sharp pitch of the organ at Whitehall and no longer involving other instrumentalists in the services, stood apart from this. Purcell's scoring of the Te Deum and Jubilate for trumpets and strings, without woodwind instruments, may have been influenced by practical necessity over pitch standards. Although the first performance of the canticles took place elsewhere, they were also performed in the Chapel Royal and (as suggested in Ch. 2) may from the first have been intended to be heard there.

[52] A pitch difference of a tone or more would have been well within the tolerance of good-quality gut strings (see Abbott and Segerman, 'Strings'), but retuning would have altered the relationship between the strings and the instruments' natural resonances. It is possible that there was a separate set of 'Chapel Violins', in just the same way that there were separate 'Chapel' instruments later on for the Lutenist and Violist.

[53] The earliest was a 'new Base to accompany the Organ' included in a payment on 27 June 1718 (GB-Lpro LC5/157, p. 134).

[54] Information in this section is based on the music texts as printed in *PS*, checked where possible against the best manuscript sources.

[55] One work from the 1680s, the welcome song *Swifter, Isis*, included oboes in the orchestra; it may be significant that the lowest vocal bass note in this work is *E*, rather than the more general *D*. If my speculations on pitch are correct, the trumpets had no difficulty in adjusting to 'sharp' pitch: see also below, n. 59.

The group of works that Handel wrote for the Chapel Royal in the early 1720s provides some internal evidence that a high 'Chapel pitch' was still in operation at St James's Palace. Each of these works includes music that was revised from earlier material, composed for performance at St Lawrence's Church, Cannons Park. In three out of four cases the music was recomposed so that the framing key was lower for the Chapel Royal:

Title	Cannons	Chapel Royal
As pants the hart	E minor	D minor[56]
I will magnify Thee	A major	A major[57]
Let God arise	B♭ major	A major
Te Deum	B♭ major	A major

The obvious implication of the transpositions is that the pitch in the Chapel was higher than at Cannons,[58] a difference that might explain the apparent absence of 'altos' in the Cannons music, and also why Thomas Gethin was a 'tenor' at the Chapel Royal but a 'counter tenor' at Cannons. The authentic pitch for performances of these Chapel Royal works may have been about the same as, or even a semitone above, modern concert pitch, though the subsequent pieces for those occasions on which a special organ was provided (the coronation in 1727, the weddings in 1734 and 1736, and the funeral in 1737) would have been performed at a lower pitch that was more agreeable to most contemporary orchestral instruments.

The orchestral musicians may have used separate instruments to accommodate the sharp pitch of the Chapel Royal for the special services there before 1727, since the string group involved was small. The trumpet players, when involved, could match the high pitch by adopting a nominal 'E flat' standard for the D trumpets.[59] Only the solo woodwind players would have had to

[56] The earliest Chapel Royal version, HWV 251a, had also been composed in D minor.

[57] Some early manuscript parts have this anthem in G major: see *HHA* III/9, p. 335, Sources C2, C3, C7, C9, and D7.

[58] When rearranging and recomposing from a Chapel Royal work to a Cannons one, Handel generally kept to the original (notated) pitch: *O sing unto the Lord* and the Utrecht Jubilate both retained their original keys for the Cannons versions. (The one transposed movement in the anthem, 'Let the whole earth', was moved upwards from D major to F major for Cannons, again suggesting a higher Chapel Royal pitch.) Practical problems that might have arisen as the result of a lower performing pitch for Cannons were, however, mainly avoided by Handel's recomposition of the vocal parts. The suggestion by Haynes (*A History*), that HWV 250a employed a transposing oboe, seems unlikely: the same player had also to accommodate much music in B flat at Cannons, and elsewhere (as for example, 'S'armi il fato' in *Teseo*) Handel did not avoid using oboes in A major.

[59] A number of different pitch levels would have been available with the use of crooks, but the highest available pitch for natural 'D' trumpets of the period was probably around E flat at *a'* 440: see Baines, 'James Talbot's Manuscript', 20, and Dahlqvist, 'Pitches of German, French and English Trumpets', 36.

make significant or difficult adjustments, and with the right reeds and a little invention the players involved may have found ways of accommodating to the situation. It is very likely that Jean Christian Kytch, the oboe-player who was employed as an additional musician for Handel's Chapel Royal music in the period 1722–6, had a special sharp-pitch oboe made, or adapted, so that he could function in the Chapel.[60] The evidence for such an instrument comes from the 'transposing oboe part' for the aria 'Su la sponda' which is found in Handel's autograph of his opera *Tamerlano*: the aria is in B flat minor, but the separately written part marked 'l'a Hautbois' is notated in A minor.[61] Handel similarly wrote an oboe part in A minor for the B flat minor aria 'Amor, nel mio penar' in *Flavio*, which was even based on the same musical theme as 'Vouchsafe, O Lord' in the A Major Te Deum.[62] The autographs of the opera arias date from 1723–4, and there are no examples from Handel's other London operas and oratorios. It is more likely that the oboe and bassoon had to conform to prevailing conditions in the Chapel Royal than that the established members of the Chapel Royal and the King's Musicians would have adopted a different pitch standard in order to accommodate a couple of woodwind players who did not even hold court offices.

The regular Chapel Royal organ was presumably used for the performances at St James's Palace prior to 1730, and on the first occasions that Handel performed music with orchestral accompaniment in the Chapel in 1714 downward transposition of the organ part may have been considered as an option for resolving the problem of pitch difference. This would account for the single statement concerning pitch in Handel's Chapel Royal autographs, the composer's annotation above the opening of the second movement of *O sing unto the Lord* (HWV 249a, *c.*1714), where he wrote 'Dieser vers wird einen thon tieffer transponiert in allen Partien. in den Orgel Part 2 thon tieffer'[63] (see Fig. 19.1). Although this implies that the organ was found to be too sharp

---

[60] I make the assumption that the same person was involved in the payments for Chapel Royal services to 'Wiliam Ketch/Keitch' (Croft, Greene, and Handel, 1720–2), John Kite (Handel, 1723/4), and Christian Kitsh (Handel, 1725/6).

[61] GB-Lbl RM 20.c.11, fo. 87^r; for the movement, see *HHA* II/15, pp. 231–3.

[62] RM 20.b.1, fos. 77–78; see *HG* 67, p. 75. Haynes (*A History*, 177, and *The Eloquent Oboe*, 347–8) suggests that the sharp oboe was played by Sammartini for the operas and that the transposition related to a general change in pitch level in the opera house at this time, but I regard this as a less convincing explanation; Kytch was one of the opera company's leading oboe players in the 1720s, when Sammartini's connection with the orchestra is uncertain.

[63] 'This movement must be transposed down one tone in all parts [but] down two tones in the organ part'. I have assumed, for the purposes of translation, that 'thon' is the same as the modern 'tone'. A semitone transposition applied separately to this movement would have produced an unlikely key sequence, as noted in Andrew Johnstone, '"As it was in the beginning"', 524 n. 32; if 'The Lord is great' were also transposed or omitted (as implied by Handel's deletion) the sequence would have been G major–E♭ minor–G major.

Fig. 19.1. A page from Handel's autograph of the Chapel Royal anthem *O sing unto the Lord*, HWV 249a, showing Handel's transposition direction and deletion for the second movement. British Library, RM 20.g.6, fo. 2ᵛ

to be used at written pitch and that a transposed organ part was required, we do not know how this related to the remainder of the anthem, and the motive for the transposition of the movement needs to be considered. Two alternative hypotheses yield rather different results:

1. The transposition may have been made for the benefit of the *singer*. No soloist's name appears on this movement. As it stands, the range of

the vocal part (*a–c′*) is appropriate for Hughes, but rather too high for Elford. If Handel had composed the movement with Hughes in mind but decided to reallocate it to Elford, then the transposition is explained and Handel's instruction can be taken at its face value. However, it is likely that the anthem was composed just before Elford's death,[64] and if he was in failing health at the time we would have expected a substitution of Hughes for Elford rather than vice versa.

2. The transposition instruction may have been the result of difficulties with the (transverse) *flute*, which has a part only in this movement of the anthem. The original key of the aria (E minor) does not, as written, present difficulties for the Baroque flute: the key indicated by Handel's transposition (D minor) is neither better nor worse in terms of technique or intonation. It may have happened that, at a rehearsal of the anthem, Handel was faced with a flautist whose instrument could not cope with the high Chapel Royal pitch.[65] In this case, the transposition instruction reflects Handel's attempt to deal with the situation by keeping the flute part at written pitch, transposing all of the string parts down, and transposing the organ part down even further.

If the second hypothesis is correct, the annotation resulted from a particular situation arising from the instrumentation of this movement. Handel crossed out the movement in his autograph: this might mean that he gave up the struggle to reconcile the pitches and cancelled the movement altogether, or it might have been his way of reminding the copyist not to transcribe the movement in the key given in the score.[66]

The transposition instruction probably reflects an experimental attempt to deal with a problem of irreconcilable pitch standards that may have arisen during the preparation of Handel's very first performance with an orchestra in the Chapel Royal, if the orchestra found it difficult to match the pitch of the organ, and the singers did not want their music shifted any lower. The plan indicated by the annotation may not have been followed through even then, and it would certainly be unwise to draw general conclusions from it, especially with regard to Handel's later Chapel Royal performances. There is no

[64] See Ch. 5, and App. C, Elford.

[65] As noted in Ch. 5, Handel replaced the solo flute by an oboe in the anthem's companion work, the Caroline Te Deum, probably also in 1714, and in response to the same pitch-difference problem.

[66] The interpretation of Handel's deletion is made difficult because he crossed out No. 3 as well as No. 2. If he really intended the removal of these movements, the resulting anthem would have been a poor thing indeed, lacking in variety and tonal contrast: if the deletions were a sign to the copyist, then it is difficult to explain the deletion of No. 3, unless it was simply a mistake on Handel's part.

other evidence of transposed organ parts for Handel's Chapel Royal music: the notated key differences between the Cannons and Chapel Royal versions of the same music indicate a difference in pitch levels between the two locations, but the evidence is inadequate for the recovery of specific pitch standards in performance. If the organ part was transposed down a semitone from a' 474, this would probably still have resulted in a higher pitch standard than that in use at Cannons;[67] it is very unlikely that organs from the Smith/Shrider school were tuned in anything resembling equal temperament, so a semitone transposition would have had uncomfortable consequences, especially when the organ was used in combination with other instruments. Most likely Handel's pre-1727 Chapel Royal music was performed at St James's at sharp pitch; as already noted, the specially provided organs would have solved any pitch-difference problems in the decade following 1727, but there is no evidence to explain what happened for Handel's Chapel Royal performances in 1740, 1743, and 1749, or the performances of Greene's orchestrally accompanied music in surrounding years. Similarly, there is at present no evidence to show how any pitch-difference problems were resolved at St Paul's Cathedral for the Utrecht music in 1713. The organ there was also at a sharp pitch, and presumably problems over pitch compatability had arisen in connection with the preceding Thanksgiving services in 1702–8: the ensemble shown in Fig. 4.3 would have involved the accommodation of a considerable number of instruments to a common pitch standard.[68]

Arrangements for Rehearsals and Performances

Orchestrally accompanied music for the Chapel Royal seems to have received two or three rehearsals. Schedules for composition and rehearsal were often unpredictable because the dates for events such as Thanksgivings and royal weddings shifted from those that were expected, or because the king's return to London was delayed. Sometimes, as with the Utrecht service, it was to Handel's advantage to be ahead of events, as the rehearsals brought him to public attention: in the case of the Dettingen music, the unexpectedly long exposure of the music prior to performance may have done something to ameliorate his

[67] See Gwynn, 'Organ Pitch', 70, and Gwynn, 'The English Organ', 32–3: in the latter Gwynn estimates the Chapel Royal organ to have been between a semitone and a tone sharp to a' 440, and the organ at Cannons (St Lawrence Whitchurch) about a semitone flat.

[68] It is possible that the performance of the canticles did not involve all of the orchestral players who were shown as being present. Haynes (*A History*, 175–6) suggests whole-tone downward transposition of the organ part, but with unsupported assumptions about 'practical pitch for the orchestra' in the performance of church music at this period.

difficulties with offended opera patrons. In 1727 (and also possibly in 1722–4) the preparation period for the performances may have been a critical time for establishing and confirming Handel's pre-eminent position as a court composer. In 1733 Maurice Greene appears to have been the loser through early preparation: his wedding anthem for Princess Anne was composed and rehearsed well in advance of the expected wedding day, only to be displaced by Handel's music. Occasionally music had to be composed and rehearsed to a very tight timetable, as happened with the Funeral Anthem in 1737.

Payment was apparently expected of the audience at a rehearsal of the Utrecht music in 1713, perhaps as a form of self-protection for the performers since at that stage Handel's music may not have achieved official acceptance from the Court.[69] In the case of his later Chapel Royal music there may have been no charge for the rehearsals: the fees for additional performers were calculated on the basis of the rehearsals that they had attended as well as the performance, and presumably attendance at rehearsals for the services was one of the routine duties for the King's Musicians. Public rehearsals were often regarded as important social events: they were reported as such by the newspapers, and Mrs Pendarves's reference to one rehearsal of Greene's music indicates that it was part of her normal round of social engagements.[70] Not all of the rehearsals for court services took place at the site of the performance. The music for the larger services—Thanksgivings, weddings, and funerals—was occasionally rehearsed elsewhere because temporary building operations put the main site out of commission, sometimes even until the day of performance. The Banqueting House Chapel, Whitehall, was a useful standby building for off-site rehearsals: Handel's first public rehearsals for the Utrecht music were held there, and so were the rehearsals for the Dettingen music in 1743. The Funeral Anthem for Queen Caroline was rehearsed in the French Chapel: Shrider was paid for the full cost of putting up an organ for the rehearsal, taking it down again and reassembling it at Westminster Abbey.[71] Not only did the rehearsals receive financial support through the Lord Chamberlain's office, but members of the royal family themselves attended some of them.[72] During the preparations for the royal weddings in 1736 and 1740, Handel's anthems were

---

[69] See Ch. 4, and in particular the reference at n. 10.

[70] Letter, Mrs Pendarves to Mrs Granville [Nov. 1729], in Llanover, The *Autobiography and Correspondence*, i. 223; at this period Mrs Pendarves seems also to have regularly attended 8 a.m. prayers at the Chapel Royal (ibid. 232). The established tradition of public rehearsals was put to good use by the Sons of the Clergy at St Paul's Cathedral, who made a collection in support of the charity at the rehearsals for their annual Festival service.

[71] GB-Lpro LC5/21, p. 5.

[72] *WEP*, 3–6 Nov. 1733; *WEP*, 13–15 Dec. 1737. Since the King did not attend the 1737 funeral, the rehearsal would have been his only opportunity to hear Handel's anthem; similarly, Princess Louisa heard a rehearsal of the Dettingen music in 1743 but not the eventual performance, because in the mean time she had left London for her marriage.

rehearsed at Bernard Gates's house in James Street, perhaps because no Royal Chapel was available, or perhaps because it was more convenient to hold at least one of the rehearsals in a more intimate venue.

There is no documentary evidence that Handel held separate rehearsals with the Chapel Royal soloists, as certainly happened with the principal singers for his operas and oratorios, and it is possible that this was not part of the routine. The demands on the Chapel Royal singers were different from those facing Handel's opera soloists: they did not have to act on stage, they probably did not have to memorize their parts, and their music was on a much shorter timescale. If necessary, the Chapel soloists could have arranged their own preliminary rehearsals with continuo players.[73] A high standard of musical literacy can in any case be assumed for the best of the Gentlemen: the nature of some of the complaints in Gibson's *Rules* for the Chapel in 1726 suggests that, in the normal course of events, the Gentlemen placed great reliance on their powers of sight-reading.

Figures 4.3 and 12.2 give a good idea of the conditions under which musicians performed at the larger court services. Fortunately, in both cases the artists seem to have provided an accurate representation of the musicians' galleries, as far as technical limitations of the engraving process would allow. One rather startling feature common to both pictures is that there is no sign of sectional arrangements among the performers: singers and instrumentalists are apparently mixed up together with no system governing the layout, and as a result people playing or singing the same part are relatively dispersed. Probably soloists and continuo players were grouped together as far as possible: in Fig. 4.3 the lute players would have been able to see the organist. No doubt the leading violinist had a conspicuous place. In Fig. 12.2, although the violinists are not all located together, they seem to be concentrated in the lower galleries: the double basses, as we would expect, are shown well to the side where they would not obscure sight-lines for other performers. It seems likely that many orchestral players would have shared music two to a part, though this is not shown on the pictures: individual parts for string players would probably have been unnecessarily cumbersome, and might have invited a challenge to the copying charges. Performers' names written on the partbooks for Boyce's anthems in 1760–1 for the funeral of King George II, and for the wedding and coronation of King George III, indicate that instrumentalists generally shared two to a part, while singers had individual copies.[74] Sight-lines must have placed particular constraints on the placing of the trebles, on account of

[73] As noted in Ch. 17, the keyboard players' part-books from the sets in the Aylesford Collection include vocal parts as well as the continuo bass line in solo movements, a format that would have been practical for separate rehearsals with the soloists.

[74] GB-Ob MS Mus.Sch.c.115a–c; MS Mus.Sch.c.117a–c; MS Mus.Sch.c.116a–c. The normal formats of the performing parts (landscape for singers and keyboard continuo, portrait for

their shorter stature; other practical considerations, such as bowing room for
the string players, would also have limited the flexibility of the arrangements.
Additionally, institutional considerations may also have influenced the layout,
with places being allocated according to seniority. The gallery dispositions for
the larger services would have made it difficult for all of the performers to see a
conductor, but evidence is lacking about the form of direction that was used,
and about any means of communication that would have enabled musical
movements to begin simultaneously and at a common speed.

Court conventions influenced some practical matters. All musicians at court
were expected to face the monarch and, with the exception of the keyboard
player shown in profile in Fig. 12.2, this is how they appear in the pictures.
Convention also forbade sitting in the presence of the monarch:[75] this probably coincided with practical needs in any case, since space was at a premium in
the crowded galleries. From Fig. 4.3, which gives better detail on this matter
than Fig. 12.2, it appears that all of the musicians are indeed standing, though
cellists and lute players may have found ways of avoiding the convention if the
front panels of the galleries gave them some cover. It would not have been
possible for the performers to memorize their music on two rehearsals, nor is
there evidence that this was demanded for court occasions. It is true that hardly
any music stands are visible in Fig. 4.3, but many of the players are looking
downwards, presumably at music which is hidden from the picture's viewing
angle by the edge of the gallery. In Fig. 12.2 the detail is so small that it is
difficult to be certain on this matter, but at least some of the singers appear to be
holding music. In neither picture, of course, can we assume that the artist was
showing the scene during performance of the music: in the case of Fig. 12.2 the
marriage ceremony itself is depicted, and this preceded the performance of the
anthem. Sandford's pictures of the 1685 coronation show all of the singers in
the Westminster Abbey choir as holding their music.

The arrangement of the performers was affected by the physical limitations
of individual sites, as described in Chapter 18. For the bigger occasions
musicians had to make the best of the space to which they were allocated:
the leading musicians and Chapel Royal authorities may have had some
influence over the arrangements within the specially constructed galleries,
and they were possibly also consulted when these galleries were designed.[76]
There must have been some tension between the limited space available and

orchestral players) may also have reflected a practice that music was shared by players but not
singers.

[75] See Harley, 'Music at the English Court', 339 n. 47.
[76] GB-Lpro LC2/32 includes several documents relating to Boyce's abortive attempt to alter
the previous arrangements for the performers in time for the 1761 Coronation, and reveals the
reluctance of those in charge of major ceremonies to make extra provision for the musicians.

the multiplication in the number of performers that was recognized as an indicator of the grandness of the occasion, especially since Handel himself seems to have promoted the trend towards larger forces from 1727 onwards. For the smaller services in the Chapel Royal, such as those marking King George I's return in the 1720s, there was no specialized accommodation for the orchestra and the instrumentalists may have been squashed into any available spaces.

Behind all other factors, however, the force of precedent applied in the physical arrangements for the performers, just as it did in all other aspects of court ceremonies. Experience gained in the arrangements for one service was naturally put to good use on subsequent occasions, and the church services in which Handel was involved were related to previous events of the same type: the Utrecht service to previous Thanksgivings, the 1727 coronation to previous coronations, and the Chapel Royal services of 1722–6 to the similar ones in the preceding years for which Croft and Greene had provided the music, which in turn probably repeated the arrangements from the services at which Handel's music was performed in 1714, and from the Thanksgiving Day services in the Chapel at which Croft's orchestrally accompanied canticles were performed in 1709–10. (There were fewer relevant precedents for the royal weddings and funeral.) Precedent controlled the availability of performing forces as well as the arrangement of those forces in the performance: if the King's Musicians were called upon to accompany the Chapel Royal on one occasion, their participation could be expected on the next similar occasion, and if additional performers were paid for one service, then this set a precedent for the future.

In those respects Handel's music for the Chapel Royal can be seen as part of a longer continuum of musical activity, contributing to church services that were a regular part of British court life. This does not, however, diminish the individuality and originality of his contribution. In some external features, such as the employment of large forces of singers and players for the 1727 coronation and the 1737 funeral, his contribution is obvious. More subtle is his success in establishing a new style for English church music involving orchestral accompaniment, in smaller-scale pieces as well as the grander works. His music gives London an important place in the history of European late Baroque sacred music, as surely as his operas and oratorios do in the history of their musical genres. To his Chapel Royal music he brought experience not only from his work in the theatre, but from liturgical music in Germany and Italy, and above all he brought the sturdiness of his own musical style. Handel's biography is a story that has primarily been told in modern times in terms of the genres of Italian opera and English oratorio, which unquestionably were the basis for most of his professional career, but his English church music is also a significant thread that runs through his creative life in London. As with his theatrical career, unforeseen events and a desire for personal advancement shaped some of the story, but there was also a match between the opportunities that arose and Handel's own creative ambitions. In that respect the Chapel Royal music provided an outlet for a side of his personality that was not fulfilled elsewhere: eventually he was able to accommodate the 'solemnity of church music' in the choruses of his oratorios, but such music also needs to be understood in relation to its original context involving the singers from London's ecclesiastical choirs who (with one exception) did not perform as soloists in the theatre oratorios. Handel's Chapel Royal music includes some of the best of English church music from any period, but also some of the best of his own music. As such it has a dual claim to our attention, as the creation of particularly interesting times and circumstances, but also as an enduring and renewing musical repertory.

APPENDICES

APPENDIX A

Handel's English Church Music

Date	Title	Scoring[a]	Place of performance
1712–13	As pants the hart (HWV 251a)	S, AA, BB; saatbb / org., ?viol/vc., ?lute	(Chapel Royal, St James's Palace)
1713	Utrecht Te Deum and Jubilate (HWV 278–9)	2S, AA, T, BB; ssaatbb / 2tpt., fl., 2ob., str., b.c., org.	St Paul's Cathedral
1714	Caroline Te Deum (HWV 280), and O sing unto the Lord (HWV 249a)	AA, T, BB; saatb / 2tpt., fl., str., b.c., org. (+2ob. HWV 249a)	Chapel Royal, St James's Palace
1717–18	Cannons anthems[b]	S, TTT, B; stttb / 2rec., ob., bn., str.(no va.), b.c., org.	St Lawrence, Whitchurch (Cannons)
	Cannons Te Deum (HWV 281)	S, TTT, B; stttb / tpt., recs., ob., bn., str.(no va.), b.c., org.	St Lawrence, Whitchurch (Cannons)
1722–6	As pants the hart (HWV 251d)	S, AA, BB; saatbb / vc., org.	(Chapel Royal, St James's Palace)
	As pants the hart (HWV 251c)	S, AA, T, BB; saatbb / ob., str., b.c., org.	(Chapel Royal, St James's Palace)
	Caroline Te Deum (revival)	AA, T, BB; saatb / ob., fl., str., b.c., org.	(Chapel Royal, St James's Palace)
	I will magnify thee (HWV 250b)	A, T, B; satb / ob., str., b.c., (org.)	(Chapel Royal, St James's Palace)
	Let God arise (HWV 256b), and A major Te Deum (HWV 282)	A, T, BB; saatbb / ob., bn., str., b.c., org. (+fl. in HWV 282)	(Chapel Royal, St James's Palace)

Cont'd

Date	Title	Scoring[a]	Place of performance
1727	Coronation Anthems (HWV 258–261)	(AA, BB semi-ch.); ssaatbb 3tpt., timp., 2ob., 2bn., str. (vns.@3), b.c, org.	Westminster Abbey
1734	*This is the day* (HWV 262)	S, A, T, B; ssaattbb 2tpt., ?timp., 2fl., 2ob., bns., str., b.c., org.	French Chapel, St James's Palace
1736	*Sing unto God* (HWV 263)	S, A, T, B; satb 2tpt., ?timp., 2ob., bns., str., b.c., org.	Chapel Royal, St James's Palace
1737	Funeral Anthem (HWV 264)	ssatb 2ob., 2bn., str., b.c., org.	Henry VII's Chapel, Westminster Abbey
1738	*As pants the hart* (HWV 251e)	S, AA, T, BB; saatbb 2cb., (bns.), str., b.c., org.	King's Theatre, Haymarket
1740	*Sing unto God*[c]	(S, A, T, B); ssaattbb 2tpt., ?timp., 2fl., 2ob., bns., str., b.c., org.	Chapel Royal, St James's Palace
1743	Dettingen Te Deum (HWV 283), and Dettingen Anthem (HWV 265)	2S, A, T, BB; ssatb 3tpt., timp., 2 ob., bns., str., b.c., org., (vns.@3 in HWV 283)	Chapel Royal, St James's Palace
1749	Anthem on the Peace (HWV 266), and Caroline Te Deum (revival)	S, AA, ?T, ?B; saatb 2tpt., timp., fl., ob., bns., str., bc., org.	Chapel Royal, St James's Palace
	Foundling Hospital Anthem (HWV 268)[d]	(2S, A, T); satb 2tpt., timp., 2ob., str., b.c., org.	Foundling Hospital Chapel

[a] Voices for principal soloists are underlined.

[b] Maximum scoring shown; most anthems have fewer vocal parts; two anthems have S, A, T, B; satb.

[c] A combination of movements from HWV 262 and 263: no independent musical source.

[d] 1749 with satb chorus only; score revised c.1751, incorporating movements for soloists; revived Apr. 1753.

APPENDIX B

Membership of the Choirs of the Chapel Royal, Westminster Abbey, and St Paul's Cathedral, 1700–1760

Arrangement

Members of the Chapel Royal are listed first, in order of admission according to the dates given in the Cheque Books. In the period 1702–14 *OCB* did not record several admissions for which there is other evidence (see Ashbee, *Records*, v. 99–103): this may have been the result of inefficient bookkeeping, but more likely indicates that for some reason the usual procedures for direct admission via the Dean or Sub-Dean were in abeyance. When these appointments finally appeared in *OCB*, they were recorded in the order of the previous admissions, except that Aspinwall overtook Laye (probably because there was a particular need for the appointment of a Priest), and William Battell's advancement was on the basis of an extraordinary place to which he had been admitted nearly twenty years previously. For this series of Gentlemen, the dates of previous known appointment are given in brackets, as are also the earliest years that the names appear in the Travelling Charges (TC); ★ indicates an appointment to an Extraordinary or Supernumerary place, which was often made at the full rate of £73 at this period.

The list includes Gentlemen, Organists, Composers, Masters of the Children, Lutenists, and Violists. Their periods of appointment to the other major London choirs are shown in accompanying columns; in these columns the dates are the earliest known ones for admission, and subsequent dates for installation are only noted if there is a special reason. Supplementary lists give the names of those members of the parallel institutions at Westminster Abbey and St Paul's Cathedral who were not also members of the Chapel Royal before 1760 (prefixes 'W' and 'SP' respectively). Many members of the London choirs also held places at St George's Chapel, Windsor; their appointments are listed in the main table, but there is no separate list for the members of the Windsor choir who did not also serve in London. Unless otherwise shown, each adult member of the choirs continued in office until his death; in practice, admissions often formalized the succession on the death of a previous incumbent of a place, and many singers served as deputies until a place became available. For earlier departures, 'res.' without further qualification means that all offices in that institution were resigned. Otherwise, resignation affected only the office named: 'res. MCh', for example, indicates that the office of Master of the Children was resigned without affecting any other concurrent appointments.

Chapel Royal Children are listed by the leaving dates given on the warrants in the Lord Chamberlain's papers. The starting point of this list is extended to 1699, in order to include William Croft. Cross-references are given in the tables for those choristers who were subsequently adult members of the choirs. Ages on dismissal are given where possible, but many of these are at present approximate or speculative.

Sources sometimes give slightly conflicting evidence on dates; in these cases, the most likely date is given. Spellings of names also vary in sources; where possible, forms from signatures are used. Gentlemen whose reference numbers are underlined have fuller entries in Appendix C.

Abbreviations used

General:	b. – before; dep. – deputizing; dis. – dismissed; h. – half place; rep. – replaced; res. – resigned; v. – place vacant by date stated
Chapel Royal:	B – Child of the Chapel Royal (Boy); C – Composer; ClCh – Clerk of the Cheque; Conf. – Confessor; MCh – Master of the Children; O – Organist; P – Priest (all entries not so modified are for Gentlemen who were not Priests, and (P) indicates a Gentleman who served as a Priest, though not so indicated in the Cheque Book at the time of admission); SD – Sub-Dean; TC – Earliest year of entry in lists of Travelling Charges
Westminster Abbey:	LV – Lay Vicar; MCo – Master of the Choristers; MC – Minor Canon; O – Organist
St Paul's Cathedral:	A/MCh – Almoner and Master of the Choristers; MC – Minor Canon; VC – Vicar Choral; VC(O) – Organist, holding Vicar Choral's place
St George's Chapel, Windsor:	LC – Lay Clerk; VMC – Vicar or Minor Canon

No.	Name	Chapel Royal	Westminster Abbey	St Paul's Cathedral	Windsor	Death	Boys
	GENTLEMEN (INCLUDING SUB-DEANS AND PRIESTS)						
1	Edward BRADDOCK	c. Aug. 1660 21–11–1688 ClCh	16–2–1661 LV 1671–1703 MCo			12–6–1708	
2	Nathaniel WATKINS	b. 23–4–1661			1640 LC	8–5–1702	
3	John GOODGROOME	b. 23–4–1661				27–6–1704	
4	Blasius [Blase] WHITE	14–3–1663/4 (P)				25–2–1699/1700	
5	Thomas RICHARDSON	11–8–1664	4–4–1666 LV			23–7–1712	
6	William TURNER	11–10–1669	1699 LV	7–2–1686/7 VC		13–1–1739/40	
7	James HART	7–11–1670 (P)				8–5–1718	
8	Andrew TREBECK	5–10–1671 (P)				19–11–1715	
9	Stephen CRESPION	13–5–1673 v. 1–4–1697 Resworn 8–5–1702	1673 MC (Chanter to 1694)			25–11–1711	
10	John BLOW	16–3–1673/4 ?14–7–1674 MCh 26–10–1676 O 2–3–1699/1700 C	1668–79 O 1695–1708 O	3–10–1687 A/Mch res. Nov. 1703		1–10–1708	
11	John GOSTLING	25–2–1678/9 (P)		15–1–1689/90 MC		17–7–1733	
12	Leonard WOODESON	15–8–1681 (P)	1697 LV		20–3–1678/9 LC 1680 VMC	14–3–1716/17	
13	Nathaniel VESTMENT	28–6–1683				23–8–1702	
14	Samuel BENTHAM	24–7–1683 (P) 9–11–1716 Conf.	1712 MC	21–2–1686/7 MC	28–6–1679 LC	27–2–1730	
15	Ralph BATTELL	b. Xmas 1689 b. 11–4–1689 SD 10–7–1699 SubAlmoner				20–3–1712/13	
16	Moses SNOW	17–12–1689	1682 LV			20–12–1702	

Cont'd

No.	Name	Chapel Royal	Westminster Abbey	St Paul's Cathedral	Windsor	Death	Boys
17	Thomas LINACRE	27–12–1689 (P)	1680 MC	1–2–1686/7 MC res. 25–10–1704		26–8–1719	
18	Alexander DAMASCENE	6–12–1690				14–7–1719	
19	John HOWELL	30–8–1691	1691 (or 1689) LV	26–11–1697 VC		15–7–1708	
20	William BATTELL	10–12–1691* (1–1–1708/9*) (P) (TC from 1709) 2–1–1710/11	1691 MC 1711 Chanter	23–2–1691/2 MC res. 13–1–1697/8		4–8–1728	
21	Daniel WILLIAMS	16–12–1692 12–6–1708 ClCh	1689 LV			12–3–1719/20	
22	Charles BARNES	10–9–1694	1694 MC 1696 Chanter	26–11–1699 MC		2–1–1710/11	
23	George HART	10–9–1694				29–2–1699/1700	
24	John CHURCH	31–1–1696/7* 1–8–1697	13–11–1696 LV 1704 MCo res. MCo 1740	7–2–1686/7 VC		6–1–1740/1	
25	Thomas JENINGS	8–11–1697	1679 LV	21–11–1698 MC		26–3–1734	
26	William WASHBOURNE	20–6–1699 (P)				15–10–1737	
27	Thomas EDWARDS	2–3–1699/1700	1709 LV (?12–6–1708)	4–1–1696/7 VC		18–8–1730	
28	John RADCLIFFE	(24–3–1696/7 Conf.) 2–3–1699/1700 (P)	1702–11 LV			29–10–1716	
29	Humphrey GRIFFITH	2–4–1700* (5–9–1702 h.) 23–12–1702	1712 MC			14–9–1708	
30	Jeremiah CLARKE	7–7–1700* 25–5–1704 h.O (1–4–1706 h.C)		6–6–1699 VC(O) 11–1–1703/4 A/MCh		1–12–1707	

No.	Name	Details	Admission	VC	LC	B I	B II
31	William CROFT	7-7-1700★ 25-5-1704 h.O (1-4-1706 h.C) 5-12-1707 O 1-10-1708 C, MCh	1709 (?1-10-1708) O			14-8-1727	
32	John FREEMAN	6-12-1700★ (5-9-1702 h.) 23-12-1702	1715 (?1692-3) LV	19-1-1701/2 VC		10-12-1736	
33	John WELDON	6-6-1701★ 1-10-1708 O (1-10-1708 C)				7-5-1736	
34	William SPALDEN	13-10-1701★ (?Did not proceed to place)					
35	Richard ELFORD	2-8-1702 ('additional place')	1712 (?1711) LV	26-3-1700 VC v. 25-3-1702	29-12-1701 LC	29-10-1714	
36	John MASON	(5-6-1704★) (TC from 1705) 12-6-1708			4-11-1706 LC	3-7-1752	
37	Bernard GATES	(1-1-1707/8★) 15-7-1708 4-9-1727 MCh (?1737 2nd place) res. MCh b. 18-3-1757	19-1-1710/11 LV Michaelmas 1740 MCo res. MCo 29-9-1757		4-11-1714 LC v. mid-1715		15-11-1773
38	Francis HUGHES	(1-7-1708★) 14-9-1708 1-10-1730 2nd place	25-1-1714/15 LV	28-9-1708 VC		16-3-1743/4	
39	Edward ASPINWALL	(1-1-1708/9★) (TC from 1709) 1-1-1711/12 (P) 20-3-1717/18 SD	(13-11-1729 Prebend)			3-8-1732	
40	George LAYE	(1-7-1708★) (TC from 1708)	19-1-1710/11 LV		6-2-1705/6 LC	6-9-1765	
41	John DOLBEN	23-7-1712 20-3-1712/13 SD v. 20-3-1717/18				(20-11-1756)	

Cont'd

No.	Name	Chapel Royal	Westminster Abbey	St Paul's Cathedral	Windsor	Death	Boys
<u>42</u>	Samuel WEELY	(1-1-1708/9★) (TC from 1709)		9-6-1710 VC		2-11-1743	B8
43	William MORLEY	29-10-1714 (1-1-1711/12★) (TC from 1712) 8-8-1715	1692 LV			29-10-1721	
44	George CARLETON	(1-7-1713★) (TC from 1713) 8-8-1715 (P) 15-8-1732 SD	13-11-1727 MC 13-6-1728 Chanter	4-12-1706 MC v. 18-3-1728/9		15-12-1746	
<u>45</u>	Thomas BAKER (sr)	(1-1-1713/14★) 8-8-1715 (P) (1743-4 acting SD)	11-10-1728 MC	5-7-1716 MC (27-3-1739 Subchanter)		10-5-1745	
46	Samuel CHITTLE	8-8-1715 (P)	29-10-1716 MC		23-3-1716/17 VMC res. 9-4-1721 25-1-1724/5 VMC	11-2-1754	
47	Luke FLINTOFT	4-12-1715 (P)	1720 (?1719) MC 1717 LV v. 1-12-1731			3-11-1727	
<u>48</u>	Thomas GETHIN	9-11-1716 dis. 3-5-1731			12-10-1716 LC v. 15-11-1717 22-2-1718/19 LC v. 24-5-1720	(emigrated Feb. 1732)	B31
49	Peter RANDALL	27-6-1717			19-4-1721 VMC 1733 LC	31-1-1745/6	
50	James CHELSUM	12-6-1718	16-12-1736 LV			3-8-1743	
51	Talbot YOUNG	8-8-1719	24-8-1730 LV			19-2-1758	
52	Thomas BLENNERHAYSETT	21-9-1719 (P) res., v. 8-5-1725		24-3-1736/7 VC		?1731 (in Dublin)	
<u>53</u>	Thomas BELL	14-3-1719/20	1-2-1719/20 LV		19-4-1721 VMC 1733 LC	7-5-1743	
54	William PERRY	1-11-1721	24-3-1743/4 LV		28-11-1727 LC	24-11-1777	B18

No.	Name					
55	Abraham SHARP	8–5–1724 P				8–9–1736
56	Edward PORDAGE	28–2–1729/30 Conf. 1–1–1727/8 P				31–10–1751
57	Lewis BLACK	23–12–1746 SD 1–10–1728 P				
<u>58</u>	John ABBOT	v. 21–9–1733 (dis.) 1–4–1730 P (?1734 2nd place) (?1737 2nd place P)	1–12–1731 LV 20–1–1738/9 MC	4–11–1730 MC		18–2–1743/4
59	David CHERITON	1–12–1731	1–4–1734 LV	11–11–1743 VC		6–1–1758
60	Richard HOWE	3–9–1732 P			12–3–1729/30 VMC	28–11–1734
61	Richard POWELL	28–7–1733 P	6–3–1729/30 MC			30–1–1738/9
62	Edward LLOYD	25–9–1733 P	8–5–1741 LV 18–2–1743/4 MC 20–12–1746 Chanter	20–12–1733 MC		9–11–1755
63	William POTTELL	13–12–1734 P		27–4–1733 MC		8–12–1740
64	John HIGGATE	8–12–1736 P, Conf.				1–8–1761
<u>65</u>	Francis ROWE	15–12–1736	1722 (?Oct. 1721) LV	24–1–1739/40 VC		27–4–1755
66	John SMITH	30–3–1739 P				18–3–1771
67	Prince GREGORY	4–4–1740			15–11–1717 LC	19–12–1755
68	William PINCKNEY	16–12–1740 P		28–2–1737/8 MC		?Dec. 1775
<u>69</u>	Anselm BAYLY	29–1–1740/1 13–3–1743/4 P b. 28–4–1764 SD res. 29–2–1792	23–12–1746 MC 10–12–1755 Chanter	20–12–1743 MC res. 22–11–1764		14–10–1794
70	William RICHARDSON	10–5–1743	18–2–1743/4 LV		24–7–1734 LC	15–6–1747
71	Nicholas LADD	15–8–1743	23–12–1746 LV		2–9–1740 LC	9–7–1783
72	Thomas VANDERNAN	12–11–1743	24–3–1743/4 LV		14–5–1739 LC	b. 28–12–1778
73	Henry EVANS	13–3–1743/4 P	17–10–1743 LV 18–5–1745 MC res. b. 23–12–1756	26–7–1739 MC v. 25–2–1758		22–8–1793
<u>74</u>	Robert WASS	13–3–1743/4	18–5–1745 LV	22–12–1743 VC		27–3–1764

Cont'd

No.	Name	Chapel Royal	Westminster Abbey	St Paul's Cathedral	Windsor	Death	Boys
75	Benjamin MENCE	14–4–1744 res. b. 8–1–1753		16–1–1749/50 MC res. 21–5–1767		19–12–1796	
76	William SAVAGE	14–4–1744		5–4–1748 VC, A/MCh res. 5–4–1777		27–7–1789	
77	Thomas BAKER (jr)	24–5–1745 P	10–12–1755 LV 23–12–1756 MC			24–5–1779	
78	Thomas BARROW	31–3–1746	3–12–1763 LV			12–8–1789	B68
79	William FITZHERBERT	26–12–1746 P	21–1–1750/1 LV 19–2–1754 MC res. b. 4–4–1778	24–3–1743/4 MC 20–4–1778 Subchanter		2–10–1797	
80	Robert DENHAM	16–10–1747	9–8–1747 LV		13–5–1746 LC v. June 1765	7–12–1782	B70
81	Fifield ALLEN	2–12–1751 SD				26–4–1764	
82	Thomas BAILDON	3–8–1752	?29–4–1755 LV	31–3–1744 VC	14–11–1745 LC v. 27–3–1750	1–10–1762	
83	Moses WIGHT	8–1–1753 22–2–1754 P	19–2–1754 LV 10–12–1755 MC res. b. 9–10–1758	13–6–1745 MC		5–1–1795	
84	John BUSWELL	26–2–1754	2–6–1762 LV		16–3–1756	14–11–1763	B84
85	Hugh COX	30–4–1755	24–1–1758 LV			16–12–1763	B80
86	Benjamin PEARCE	16–12–1755 P		22–3–1737/8 MC		19–1–1771	
87	William COSTER	24–12–1755			16–7–1743 LC	b. 28–10–1767	
88	Ralph COWPER	12–1–1758	1–11–1762 LV	14–1–1758 VC	2–2–1759 LC Supernumerary, to Oct. 1762 only	27–12–1771	
89	Robert HUDSON	4–3–1758		22–11–1755 VC 1777 A/MCh res. 1793		19–12–1815	

CHAPEL ROYAL

PERSONS LISTED OCCASIONALLY WITH THE GENTLEMEN, THOUGH PROBABLY NOT APPOINTED AS SUCH

	Name	Notes	Date	
100	Jonathan SMITH	4-4-1720 ClCh (office previously held by Gentleman 21)	Feb. 1752	
101	John BOMAN (?Bowman)	11-10-1727 Gentleman Extraordinary, in Coronation lists only		
102	John BOWACK	In TC lists with the Gentlemen 1711–13, 1718. Probably schoolmaster for the Children and supplier of books.		

ORGANISTS

	Name	Notes	Start	End	B
O1	John BLOW (= 10)	26-10-1676	1-10-1708		
O2	Francis PIGGOTT	(?Dec. 1695) 24-3-1696/7 ('Organist in Ordinary')	15-5-1704		
O3	Jeremiah CLARKE (= 30)	7-7-1700, Gentleman extraordinary, to succeed as Organist 25-5-1704, jointly with Croft (O4)	1-12-1707		
O4	William CROFT (= 31)	7-7-1700, Gentleman extraordinary, to succeed as Organist 25-5-1704, jointly with Clarke (O3); 5-11-1707 (full place)	14-8-1727		B1
O5	John WELDON (= 33)	1-10-1708	7-5-1736		
O6	Maurice GREENE (=SP17)	4-9-1727	1-12-1755		
O7	William BOYCE	21-6-1736 Composer, to perform one third duty of Organist; 23-6-1758 (full place)	7-2-1779		
O8	Jonathan MARTIN	21-6-1736 Organist, to do part of Composer's duties	4-4-1737		B58
O9	John TRAVERS	10-5-1737	11-6-1758		
O10	James NARES	13-1-1756; 1768-77 Violist's place annexed, 1777-80 Lutenist's place annexed, probably to increase value of MCh	10-2-1783		B61

COMPOSERS

	Name	Notes	Start	End
C1	John BLOW (= 10)	2-3-1699/1700	1-10-1708	
C2	Jeremiah CLARKE (= 30)	(1-4-1706, jointly with Croft C3)	1-12-1707	
C3	William CROFT (= 31)	(1-4-1706, jointly with Clarke C2) (1-1-1707/8 full place) 1-10-1708 (18-10-1708, probably from 1-10-1708) 8-8-1715	14-8-1727	
C4	John WELDON (= 33)	25-2-1722/3	7-5-1736	
C5	George HANDEL		14-4-1759	
C6	Maurice GREENE (= O6)	4-9-1727	1-12-1755	
C7	William BOYCE (= O7)	21-6-1736	7-2-1779	
C8	Jonathan MARTIN (= O8)	21-6-1736 Appointed as Organist, to perform part of Composer's duties	2-4-1737	
C9	James NARES (= O10)	13-1-1756	10-2-1783	

MASTERS OF THE CHILDREN

	Name	Notes	Start	End
MCh1	John BLOW (=10)	21-7-1674	1-10-1708	
MCh2	William CROFT (= 31)	1-10-1708 (from 1-7-1708)	14-8-1727	

Cont'd

		Chapel Royal	Westminster Abbey	St Paul's Cathedral	Windsor	Death	Boys

(CHAPEL ROYAL)

No.	Name	Chapel Royal				Death	
MCh3	Bernard GATES (= 37)	4-9-1727; res. b. 18-3-1757				(15-11-1773)	
MCh4	James NARES (= O10)	18-3-1757; res. b. 1-6-1780				(10-2-1783)	

LUTENISTS

L1	John SHORE	(TC from 1705); (1-4-1706★); 8-8-1715				20-11-1752	
L2	John IMMYNS	13-12-1752				15-4-1764	

VIOLISTS

V1	Francisco GOODSENS	(1-10-1711); (TC from 1712); 8-8-1715				b. 18-11-1741	
V2	Peter GILLIER	18-1-1741/2				b. 22-10-1767	

No.	Name	Chapel Royal	Westminster Abbey	St Paul's Cathedral	Windsor	Death	Boys

SUPPLEMENTARY LISTS: MEMBERS OF THE OTHER LONDON CHOIRS 1700–1760 WHO DID NOT HOLD CHAPEL ROYAL OFFICES DURING THE SAME PERIOD

WESTMINSTER ABBEY

No.	Name	Chapel Royal	Westminster Abbey	St Paul's Cathedral	Windsor	Death	Boys
W1	Litleton TAYLOR		1693 LV			10-11-1701	
W2	Josia BOUCHER		1699 LV			1714	
W3	John BOWYER		1702(?Nov.1701) LV 1703 MC			1709	
W4	Joseph HALLETT		1709 (?1708) LV			b. 25-11-1710	
W5	Humphrey PERSEHOWSE		1710 MC			26-1-1762	
W6	John ROBINSON		30-9-1727 O			30-4-1762	
W7	James RICHARDS		26-2-1738/9 LV ?deputizing as MC			b. 8-5-1741	B13
W8	John HADLOW		17-1-1739/40 LV			20-4-1755	
W9	David JONES		8-5-1743 LV ?deputizing as MC			4-1-1750/1	
W10	Mayo TIMS		10-8-1743 LV			17-10-1743	
W11	David Walter MORGAN	17-9-1761 P Confessor	23-12-1756 LV	14-3-1740/1 MC		12-3-1795	
W12	Benjamin COOKE	29-9-1757 MCo 27-1-1758 LV res. LV 1-7-1762	9-10-1758 MC			14-9-1793	

W13 John GIBBONS (sr)	1–7–1762 O (from 1–5–1762) (1762 dep. P) 28–4–1764 P	9–10–1758 LV 3–2–1762 MC res. 1–12–1778	25–2–1758 MC 1767–71 Sacrist		b. 1–7–1783	
W14 Thomas CHAMPNESS		(4–5–1763 dep. MC) 4–4–1778 LV	22–12–1764 MC	24– 4–1781 VMC	17– 5–1782	?B91
W15 Samuel CHAMPNESS	30–11–1789	23–6–1779 MC July 1783 LV			Jan. 1803	B83
ST PAUL'S CATHEDRAL						
SP1 John SPICER			7–2–1686/7 VC 7–2–1686/7 MC v. 8–4–1703		b. June 1710	
SP2 Charles GREENE						
SP3 Samson ESTWICK			22–12–1691 MC 1698–1702 Sacrist 1715 Succentor		16–2–1738/9	
SP4 Charles BADHAM			1–6–1698 MC res. 5–6–1716			
SP5 Henry JACKSON			12–2–1698/9 MC		5–11–1727	
SP6 Henry GOSTLING			28–12–1698/9 MC 1712 Sacrist		29–10–1730	
SP7 Everingham CRESSY			June 1700 ?MC (to Dec. 1703)	7–12–1703 LC	b. 22–12–1714	
SP8 Richard FYSON			31–10–1700 MC v. 26–2–1701/2			
SP9 Edward DeCHAIR			26–2–1701/2 MC		1–12–1749	
SP10 Francis Le SAU			11–9–1704 MC v. 4–12–1706			
SP11 Charles KING			Dec. 1704 (MC) 1708 or before A/MCh 31–10–1730 VC		17–3–1747/8	

Cont'd

No.	Name	Chapel Royal	Westminster Abbey	St Paul's Cathedral	Windsor	Death	Boys
SP12	Grent JONES			5-4-1705 MC v. 20-5-1706	6-2-1705/6 VMC v. May 1717		
SP13	John HUSBAND			20-5-1706 MC		6-2-1737/8	
SP14	Richard BRIND			4-3-1707/8 VC/O			
SP15	John WILLIS			23-3-1710/11 MC v. 27-11-1711		14-3-1717/18	
SP16	Benjamin GOODWIN			27-11-1711 MC res. 23-8-1723			
SP17	Maurice GREENE (= Chapel Royal O6)			20-3-1717/18 VC/O		1-12-1755	
SP18	William REYNER			23-8-1723 MC		10-3-1764	
SP19	William WARNEFORD (1)			8-12-1727 MC v. 27-4-1733			
SP20	Christopher MORRISON			17-3-1728/9 MC 1730 Sacrist res. 7-5-1739		8-1-1751	
SP21	Francis COOKE			25-3-1729/30 MC		b. 19-12-1765	
SP22	Thomas HILLMAN			4-11-1730 MC 9-12-1755 Subchanter		20-9-1765	
SP23	Henry BOUGHTON			14-11-1739 MC v. 1-10-1740	5-7-1725 VMC res. b. July 1728		
SP24	William WARNEFORD (2) (see SP18)			1-10-1740 MC v. 23-5-1760			
SP25	John JONES			23-1-1756 VC/O		7-1-1796	
SP26	William TASWELL			19-10-1758 MC res. b. 22-12-1764			
SP27	Weldon CHAMPNESS		10-4-1762 LV (17-3-1766 dep. MC) 4-4-1778 MC 1794-1808 Chanter	23-5-1760 MC	1778 VMC	26-10-1810	

CHAPEL ROYAL CHILDREN (BOYS)

No.	Name	Date	Other refs.	Age
B1	William CROFT	24–4–1699	31	20
B2	William ROBERT	24–4–1699		
B3	John READING	22–12–1699		?22
B4	Anthony YOUNG	25–3–1700		
B5	Thomas CLARK	16–7–1700		
B6	James SWEET	14–12–1700		?19
B7	Michael MARSHALL	30–4–1701		?19
B8	Samuel WEELY	5–2–1701/2	42	?17
B9	Henry REEVE	10–11–1702		
B10	Henry SILVESTER	6–4–1703		?18
B11	Bernard GATES	9–3–1704/5	37	18
B12	Matthew BENSON	27–4–1705		
B13	John ROBINSON	12–5–1705	W6	23
B14	Josiah PRIEST	17–1–1705/6		
B15	Nathaniel PRIEST	18–1–1705/6		
B16	William GWATKIN	14–5–1706		16
B17	Samuel SMITH	14–2–1706/7		
B18	William PERRY	19–12–1707	54	
B19	James HESELTINE	19–12–1707		?16
B20	Gervase DEAN	22–6–1708	(Funeral Charges)	
B21	George HENDERSON	3–7–1708		?15
B22	Joseph FORSTER	23–11–1709		
B23	Thomas MOUNTIER	23–11–1709		17
B24	Thomas BRIGNELL	28–12–1710		
B25	Edmund BAKER	28–12–1710		
B26	John WILLIAMS	29–2–1711/12		
B27	Henry FRANKS	30–5–1713		
B28	Benjamin JACKSON	30–5–1713		
B29	William PAYNE	21–12–1714		
B30	Joseph CENTLIVRE	19–5–1715		

Cont'd

CHAPEL ROYAL CHILDREN (BOYS) cont'd

No.	Name	Date	Other refs.	Age
B31	Thomas GETHIN	24–3–1715/16	48	19
B32	John DUNCOMBE	24–3–1715/16		?18
B33	James KENT	30–3–1717		17
B34	Edmund WOODESON	28–5–1718		16
B35	Thomas POWELL	28–5–1718		?17
B36	Stephen KAY	27–5–1720		17
B37	Charles PEACH	27–5–1720		
B38	Roger GETHIN	8–7–1721		18
B39	Thomas ELLIS	8–7–1721		?19
B40	Benjamin GODIN	12–2–1722		?20
B41	Joseph DEAN	1–6–1723		17
B42	Samuel SHACKLETON	1–6–1723		
B43	William JONES	1–6–1723		
B44	Charles STROUD	26–5–1724		19
B45	John BARKER	26–5–1724		19
B46	John MASON	29–5–1725		16
B47	Hildibrand HINCHLY	24–6–1725		
B48	John BARRETT	24–6–1725		?19
B49	Henry LLOYD	9–6–1727		?15
B50	Charles DEGARD	30–6–1727		
B51	Manly MORGAN	30–6–1727		
B52	Luke COLTMAN	30–6–1727		
B53	William LAMB	30–6–1727		?19
B54	Henry BROWN	10–3–1728/9		
B55	Thomas SKELTON	10–3–1728/9		?18
B56	Thomas WELDON	31–3–1729		
B57	Carleton WHITE	6–3–1729/30		
B58	Jonathan MARTIN	6–3–1729/30	O8	15
B59	John POTTER	4–12–1730		
B60	James CLEAVELY	30–7–1731		17
B61	James NARES	30–7–1731	O10	16

B62	Samuel HOWARD	12-6-1733		?23
B63	Price CLEAVELY	2-7-1734		?19
B64	John BEARD	29-10-1734		17
B65	John RANDALL	1-5-1735		18
B66	John MOORE	2-9-1735		?16
B67	James ALLEN	7-2-1736/7		15
B68	Thomas BARROW	7-2-1736/7	78	15
B69	James BUTLER	7-2-1736/7		?18
B70	Robert DENHAM	12-6-1737	80	c.14
B71	Thomas MORLAND	c. 1738		
B72	John WYNN	18-5-1739		
B73	Edward Henry PURCELL	19-7-1739		17
B74	William BARROW	12-12-1739	19	?17
B75	Thomas DIPPER	29-4-1740		
B76	Elias ISAAC	27-7-1742		17
B77	Thomas LUCAS	1-2-1743/4		?17
B78	William RANDALL	10-6-1744		
B79	Lewis CAPPEL	28-5-1747		16
B80	Hugh COX	3-2-1747/8	85	17
B81	William SHALLER	3-2-1747/8		
B82	William SPRAGG	3-2-1747/8		21
B83	Thomas CHAMPNESS (1)	30-8-1748	(= Samuel W15)	17
B84	John BUSWELL	21-3-1748/9	84	c.16
B85	Thomas HOUGHTON	12-2-1749/50		
B86	Neal James ABINGTON	12-2-1749/50		15
B87	Thomas Saunders DUPUIS	19-2-1751		17
B88	Joseph WALKER	c. 1751		
B89	Richard RANDALL	18-4-1751		
B90	William MONK	18-4-1751		18
B91	Thomas CHAMPNESS (2)	20-7-1753	(= Thomas W14)	15
B92	George MEDLEY	1-8-1755		?15
B93	Nicholas STEELE	21-7-1755		
B94	John REYNOLDS	18-8-1757		
B95	Samuel ARNOLD	21-8-1758		18
B96	Peter VALTON	16-4-1760		

APPENDIX C

Handel's Chapel Royal Soloists

This Appendix gives biographical details of all the soloists (listed alphabetically) who are named by Handel on his autographs of English church music, with more extensive entries for the Chapel Royal singers. Further biographical information on some soloists can be found in *NG II*, in Ashbee and Lasocki, *A Biographical Dictionary*, and Highfill, Burnim, and Langhans, *A Biographical Dictionary*. Vocal ranges for the soloists' music in Handel's works are recorded on the basis of notated pitches. The listing of Handel's music for each singer is followed by selected references to sources of music by other composers that also name the same soloist; for more comprehensive lists relating to the pre-1727 soloists, see Burrows, *Dissertation*, ii. app. 6.

John Abbot

Born *c*.1706. Admitted to Westminster School August 1715; King's Scholar 1721; left 1723. Matriculated New College, Oxford, 15–2–1725/6, age 20, son of Thomas Abbott of Christ Church, London. (The singer's signature has the spelling 'Abbot' in GB-Cfm MU MS 1011, but 'Abbott' in *WA2*; he regularly used the first form elsewhere.)

Chapel Royal: Admitted Priest 1–4–1730 ('Revd. Mr. John Abbot'); second place, probably as Gentleman from April 1734 (*vice* Jenings, 25), then as Priest from November 1737 (*vice* Washbourne, 26), but not recorded in the Cheque Books.

Westminster Abbey: Lay Vicar, 'to officiate as Priest', 1–12–1731; Minor Canon 20–1–1738/9.

St Paul's Cathedral: Minor Canon, 5th Prebend, probation 4–11–1730, collated 20–11–1731.

Member of the Academy of Vocal Music from 1730. Soloist in Court odes, 1735–43. Subscriber to Greene, *Forty Select Anthems* (1743), and Boyce, *Solomon* (1743).

Died 18–2–1743/4 'in 39th year'; buried 23–2–1743/4, Westminster Abbey. Gratuity of 5 guineas to his mother from the Dean and Chapter of Westminster, 2–6–1744.

Handel's Chapel Royal music
Named on *This is the day* (1734); Dettingen Te Deum and Dettingen Anthem (1743). *Voice*: Bass, range *B–e'*.

Other sources
GB-Ob MS Mus.Sch.d.267c. Boyce, *David's lamentation over Saul and Jonathan* (1736), Tenor solo part.

GB-Ob MS Mus.Sch.c.110b. Boyce, *The charms of Harmony display* (*c*.1738), Bass solo part.

Thomas Baker

Born *c.*1686 or *c.*1689. Chorister, Christ Church, Oxford, 1700–5; Head Chorister from 1703; Lay Clerk, Sept. 1707–11; Chaplain 1712–16 (left after six weeks of the third quarter). Matriculated Christ Church, Oxford, 6–4–1704, age 15, son of William Baker, cleric, of Lichfield; BA 1708, MA 15–1–1710/11. Member of the Oxford Music Club 1712–14. Incorporated MA Cantab. 1714. Sub-Preceptor to the Royal Princesses, appointed Nov. 1714 (see *EP*, 18–20 Nov.).

Chapel Royal: Supernumerary place, 1–1–1713/14, with full salary; admitted Gentleman, 8–8–1715 (Travelling Charges from 1716); probably Priest from March 1716/17; he acted for Sub-Dean in 1743–4, but died before a vacancy occurred in that office. Attended Vestry meeting 23–4–1720 (signature).

Westminster Abbey: Minor Canon 11–10–1728, installed 17–10–1728. Before 1737, refused to be steward for the Annual Feast.

St Paul's Cathedral: Minor Canon, 7th Prebend, probation 5–7–1716, collated 4–7–1717; 6th Prebend, collated 27–3–1739, and admitted Sub-Chanter.

Vicar of Mucking, Essex, 30–6–1714, vacant by 16–4–1736. Rector of Nailstone, Leics., from 1735/6 to death. Founder-member of Academy of Vocal Music, 1725/6–7.

Died at home, Park Prospect, Westminster, 10–5–1745 'age 59'; buried 13–5–1745, Westminster Abbey. (Notice of death *DA*, 11 May). He was succeeded in his Chapel Royal place by his son Thomas (77), who also administered his estate. His daughters included Ann (died 1764) and Elizabeth, who married Henry Evans (73).

Another Thomas Baker was a contemporary professional musician, named as timpanist in Galliard's *Merlin* (GB-Drc MS E30), and an early member of the Society of Musicians.

Handel's Chapel Royal music
Named on the Caroline Te Deum ('Beker') (1714); *O sing unto the Lord* ('Baker') (*c.*1714); *As pants the hart* (HWV 251c, *c.*1722). *Voice*: Bass (2nd Bass), range E–e′.
Other sources
GB-Lcm MS 2043. Weldon, Service in D major (*c.*1715–17).
GB-Lcm MS 995. Croft, *Come all ye tunefull sisters* (1720).

Anselm Bayly

Baptized 10–4–1719. Exeter College, Oxford, matriculated 4–11–1740, age 21, son of Anselm Bayly of Haresfield, Gloucs; B.C.L. (Christ Church) 12–6–1749; D.C.L. 10–7–1764. Incorporated Ll.B. Cantab. 1749. Lay Clerk, Christ Church, Oxford: Singing-man 4–11–1740, Serviter 20–2–1740/1; paid from 1741 (6 weeks into first quarter) to the end of 1743.

Chapel Royal: Gentleman 29–1–1740/1; Priest (resigned Gentleman's place, the first recorded in this way) 13–3–1743/4; Sub-Dean before 28–4–1764. Resigned as Priest and Sub-Dean 29–2–1792.

Westminster Abbey: Lay Vicar 22–1–1740/1; Minor Canon 23–12–1746; Chanter 10–12–1755; replaced before 5–11–1794.

St Paul's Cathedral: Minor Canon, 4th Prebend, probation 20–12–1743, collated 12–2–1744/5; 12th Prebend, collated 28–5–1745; resigned 22–11–1764.

Vicar of Tottenham, Middx., 1751; Vicar of Langdon Hills, Essex, 1753; Vicar of Holy Trinity, Westminster, 1760–74.

Soloist in court odes from Birthday 1741 to New Year 1750. Subscriber to Greene, *Forty Select Anthems* (1743) and Boyce, *Cathedral Music*, vol. 2 (1768). Bayly wrote the preface to *A Collection of Anthems used in his Majesty's Chapel Royal* (1769), and his publications included two treatises on music, one of which specifically concerns singing (*The Sacred Singer*, 1771, republished as *A Practical Treatise on Singing and Playing*) but gives no hint of his own early career as a performer under Handel and Greene. In 1787 he patented an elastic girdle or bandage.

Married Jennet Yates 3–6–1746; she died 15–11–1775 and was buried at Westminster Abbey, 21–11–1775; two days later he married Rebecca Moore. Children by his first wife died in 1749, 1751, 1754, and 1782; a daughter by his second wife died in 1778.

Died 14–10–1794. Obituary (*GM*, Nov. 1794 and others), 'Lately, in Bedlam, where he had been confined 49 years, 11 months and one day, Rev. Mr. Bayly'. This may be a conflation of two separate obituaries, or possibly Bayly was minister of Bedlam. He signed entries in *NCB* for admissions to the Chapels Royal up to July 1791.

Handel's Chapel Royal music
Named on the Anthem on the Peace and revival of the Caroline Te Deum (1749). *Voice*: Alto (Alto 1), range *a–d''*.

Other sources
GB-Lcm MS 224. Greene, Te Deum in D major (1745), 'Contratenor' part.

GB-Lcm XXl. c.10. Greene, *Florimel*, word-book for performance at the Apollo Society: Bayly sang the title role.

Ob MS Mus.Sch.c.115b. Boyce, *The souls of the righteous* (Funeral of King George II, 1760), 'Alto/Contratenor' part.

Ob MS Mus.Sch.d.277. Boyce, Coronation Anthems for King George III (1761), 'First Contratenor/Decani' part.

John Beard

Born *c*.1717. As a Child of the Chapel Royal, Beard sang the role of Priest of the Israelites in Gates's production of Handel's *Esther* in February 1732. He left the choir on 29–10–1734 and did not proceed to an adult place in any of the London choirs, but followed a stage career, singing for Handel in operas (from 1735) and then in oratorios, where he became Handel's leading tenor soloist. He also regularly performed as a soloist in the court odes from (at least) New Year 1736 onwards. (The portrait of him by Hudson may possibly show him in court dress.) Although not named on Handel's Chapel Royal autographs, he sang the tenor solo music in *Sing unto God* for the wedding of the Prince of Wales in 1736, and was probably among the additional performers for Handel's subsequent Chapel Royal music, though this repertory has no movements for a tenor soloist. At the wedding of Princess Anne in 1734 he was probably a soloist in *This is the day*, though it is uncertain whether as a treble or a tenor.

In 1739 he married Lady Henrietta Herbert (d. 1753), and then in 1759 Charlotte Rich, daughter of John Rich, whom he eventually succeeded as owner-manager of Covent Garden Theatre. Died 5–2–1791; his monument in the church at Hampton carries the opening bars of the vocal part of 'When thou tookest upon Thee to deliver man' from the Dettingen Te Deum as a musical quotation, though Handel designated this movement for the bass John Abbot in 1743.

Thomas Bell

Chapel Royal: Gentleman 14–3–1719/20, from Bristol Cathedral. Attended Vestry meeting 23–4–1720 (signature).

Westminster Abbey: Lay Vicar 1–2–1719/20, though he also signed for a salary at the Abbey in 1719; part of his income was shared with Thomas Gethin (48) during the 1720s.

Cannons: His name is included in lists and account books from 1–6–1720 to New Year 1720/1, but absent from the list for New Year 1721/2. Place as 'Counter Tenor' shared with Thomas Gethin (48).

St George's Chapel, Windsor: Elected 19–4–1721 to Minor Canon's place, sworn 29–7–1722. He was not ordained, and complaints by the other Minor Canons that he was improperly appointed led to a court case, as a result of which was removed to Lay Clerk, before 5–9–1733. (GB-WRch Chapter Acts VI B 6 records the events leading up to the hearing before the Lord Chancellor, but not the result.) Money was paid from a fund at Windsor for his sons' apprenticeships in 1730 and 1749, the latter to Elizabeth Bell.

In view of the considerable attention that Bell received at the time of his appointment to the Chapel Royal (see below), it is remarkable that he is rarely named as a singer for the court odes; he is mentioned only for the birthday ode in 1736 (*DA*, 29 Oct.). It is curious, also, that he did not perform as expected in Greene's music at the Chapel Royal service on 9 July 1721 (see App. E).

Wife Elizabeth; children included sons James (b. 1725), Herbert (Thomas Bell's executor), and two daughters who died in infancy.

Died 7–5–1743, at Windsor (*LEP*, 7–10 May).

Other references

Letter from Arbuthnot to Swift, 11 Dec. 1718 (Swift, *Correspondence*, ii. 304–5): 'It is mighty hard to get such a sort of Voice. There is an excellent one in the King's Chappell [presumably Francis Hughes] but he will not go [to Dublin]. The top one of the world is in the Bristol Quire & I believe might be manag'd.'

WJSP, 5 Dec. 1719: 'The Gentlemen belonging to the King's Chapel at St. James's, having been informed, that one Mr. Bell, of Bristol, performed in an extraordinary Manner, and had an inimitable Voice in singing, they sent for him to Town, and, on Sunday se'nnight, he performed at the Royal Chapel with such Applause, that he has had a Supernumerary Place given him in the Chapel, of 70£ per Annum.'

WEP, 28 Nov.– 5 Dec. 1719: 'The famous Singer, lately come from Bristol, 'tis said, meets with good Encouragement here, being very much admir'd; and such intercession is making for him, that 'tis believed that he will be admitted as a Gentleman-Singer in the Chapel-Royal.'

Letter from John Perceval to his brother, London, 2 Feb. 1719/20 (GB-Lbl Add. MS 47029, fo. 8ᵛ): 'I was told lately by one of the Kings Quire, that one Bell who is in pursieut of a place in the Chappel was offred a hundred a year if he would go to Ireland to Sing in the Cathedrals of Dublin. Pray write me if it be trew. It seems there is no vacancy here at this time, and he finds it difficult to obtain a Supernumary place, which is what he aims at. There is not such another voice in the Kingdom, for he has an excellent base & yet sings a high Counter-Tenor which is withall natural & not forced. His Manner for a Quire is also good, and his Voice Sweet & mellow. If I knew the utmost wou'd be done for him in Ireland, and had proper Authority I would send him & propose his going.'

AOWJ, 26 Mar. 1720: 'The famous Mr. Bell, who was lately sent for from Bristol, and was entertain'd in his Majesty's Chapel as a Supernumary for his extraordinary Qualifications in Singing, is now put into the Place of Mr. Williams, deceas'd, late one of the Singing men there.'

Handel's Chapel Royal music

Named, variously Alto, Tenor, and Bass, as follows: *As pants the hart* (HWV 251d, *c*.1722), Alto (Alto 2), range *g–b♭′*; *As pants the hart* (HWV 251c, *c*.1722), Alto 2, Chorus Tenor, and Tenor (changed from alto clef), range *d–g″*; A major Te Deum (*c*.1724–6), Alto 2 (music deleted and transferred to Hughes, Alto 1), range *e♯′–g♯″*; Coronation Anthems (1727), Bass semi-chorus, range *d–e′*.

Other sources

GB-Lbl Add. MS 17861. Croft, *Give the King thy judgments* (1727, Bass voice).

GB-Ob MS Mus.d.36. Greene, *Descend ye nine, descend and sing* (1730, Bass voice, higher than Gates).

James Blackley

Not a Chapel Royal singer, but Tenor 1 at Cannons (anthems, and *Acis and Galatea*), range *f–a′*. Also a soloist in Pepusch, *Venus and Adonis* (Drury Lane Theatre, 1715).

John Church

Born ?Eton/Windsor *c.*1675/6. ?Chorister, St John's College, Oxford. Richard Church (1699–1776, Organist of New College and Christ Church, Clerk of Magdalene College, Oxford, from 1732) was probably his cousin; John Church (a member of the Dublin cathedral choirs and soloist in the first performance of *Messiah*) was also possibly related.

Chapel Royal: Gentleman extraordinary 31–1–1696/7; full place 1–8–1697. Attended Vestry meeting 23–4–1720 (signature).

Westminster Abbey: Lay Vicar 13–11–1696; Master of the Choristers 1704; resigned Mastership at Michaelmas 1740.

Principal music copyist for the Chapel Royal partbooks (RM.27.a.1 et seq.), *c.*1705–32. In charge of the account books for the Chapel Royal Fund and Westminster Abbey 'Tombs Money': later entries suggest that there was some friction between him and Cheriton (50), who succeeded him. Probable compiler of *Divine Harmony* (published word-book of anthems, 1712); author of *An Introduction to Psalmody* (1723). Supplied items for Thomas Tudway's MS collection of church music, *c.*1716; Tudway's letters also show that he performed at Sons of Clergy Festival services (GB-Lbl Harl. MS 3782, f. 88). Subscriber to Croft, *Musica Sacra* (1724). Admitted to the Society of Musicians 6–4–1740.

Wife Elizabeth died 19–12–1732, buried Westminster Abbey, where several of their children were also baptized and buried.

Died 6(or 5)–1–1740/1; buried 10–1–1740/1, Westminster Abbey; surviving children included John (d. 1785) and Ralph (d. 1787, editor of Spenser's *Faerie Queene*).

Handel's Chapel Royal music

Named as chorus leader on *The King shall rejoice* (Coronation Anthem, 1727). *Voice*: Tenor, range $f\sharp$–g'.

Other sources:

Named in at least eight sources for anthems and canticles by Blow, Croft, and Weldon, 1695–1713, including:

GB-Lcm MS 840. Croft, Te Deum in D major (1708/9).

GB-Lcm MS 839. Croft, *This is the day* (Thanksgiving, 1713).

Sang a duet by Purcell with Freeman (32) in *The Indian Queen* (1695): see Baldwin and Wilson, 'Purcell's Stage Singers', 279. Sang, with other Chapel Royal Gentlemen, in a concert of music by Purcell and Croft at Inner Temple Hall, 2–2–1725/6.

Thomas Edwards

Born *c.*1659. Possibly related to the Chapel Royal chorister of the same name, who left 12–8–1664.

Chapel Royal: Epistler 2–3–1699/1700. No record of date of admission to full place, but probably before 1700; included in the general readmission of Gentlemen in 1702 for Queen Anne's reign (Ashbee, *Records*, v. 97). Attended Vestry meeting, 23–4–1720 (signature).

Westminster Abbey: Lay Vicar by 1709, probably from June or July 1708.

St Paul's Cathedral: Vicar Choral, probation 4–1–1696/7, admitted 21–10–1698.

Subscriber to Croft, *Musica Sacra* (1724). Member of Academy of Vocal Music, November 1726.

Died 18–8–1730; buried 22–8–1730, Westminster Abbey, in 71st year. His son Thomas was executor for his estate; other children included Mary, 1700–41. Griffith Edwards, Bishop's Boy at Westminster Abbey in 1748, was possibly his grandson. Wife Mary died 26–6–1738, age 67; buried 30–6–1738, Westminster Abbey. She had probably moved to Greenwich after her husband's death.

Handel's Chapel Royal music

Named on *As pants the hart* (HWV 251c, *c*.1722). *Voice*: Chorus Bass (Bass 2), range *c–d'*.

Other sources

GB-Ob MS Mus.c.26, GB-Lbl Add. MS 31453. Purcell, *Hail, bright Cecilia* (composed 1692, further performance *c*.1699?).

GB-Lbl RM 24.e.4. Purcell, *Celebrate this festival* (1693).

US-AUS 'Gostling' MS. Blow: *O sing unto the Lord* (1702).

He also sang a duet by Purcell, with Freeman (32), in *Bonduca* (1695): see Baldwin and Wilson, 'Purcell's Stage Singers', 279.

Richard Elford

Baptized Lincoln 3–1–1676/7; chorister, Lincoln Cathedral. Singing man, Durham Cathedral, 1695–9; his name is written in a Tenor partbook from the period at GB-Drc. He may have had a short career on the London stage, though no roles are documented: 'His person being awkward and clumsy, and his action disgusting, he quitted the theatre' (Hawkins, *A General History*, ii. 718). Songs composed by him were sung by Mrs Hodgson in plays at Lincoln's Inn Fields around the year 1700.

St Paul's Cathedral: Vicar Choral, probation 26–3–1700. Collected money until December 1701, but not thereafter; probably did not advance to a full place.

St George's Chapel, Windsor: Admitted Lay Clerk 29–12–1701, 'having been recommended by the Princess [Anne], and to have augmentation of £18 p.a.'; 3–11–1709 'Clerk's place to be left void during Mr. Elford's receiving £40 p.a.' (GB-WRch Chapter Acts V B 5, pp. 177, 238). He continued to be paid until his death in 1714, but the extent of his service with the choir is uncertain: as a Chapel Royal Gentleman he was paid Travelling Charges for those periods when the Chapel attended the Queen at Windsor. On his death in 1714 he was succeeded as Lay Clerk by Thomas Elford, who may have been a relative, and may also have been the Verger of the same name.

Chapel Royal: Not included in the list of the Chapel Royal for Queen Anne's coronation, April 1702. Admitted Gentleman, 'in an Additional place to be added to the Establishment', 2–8–1702: his appointment restored the Chapel Royal to former numbers, so it was not strictly additional, though it was not in immediate succession to another Gentleman. He was the only Gentleman to receive Travelling Charges to Bath, 17 Aug.–19 Oct. 1703 (GB-Lpro LC5/153, p. 451). In 1706 he petitioned for, and was granted, and 'additional allowance' of £100 per annum (Ashbee, *Records*, vii. 307), but it is uncertain for how long this continued.

Westminster Abbey: Lay Vicar 1712 (probably from Jan 1710/11).

Elford performed, presumably as the principal Alto soloist, in Croft's odes at the Oxford Act on 10 July 1713 (*BM*, 15 July), and in Cambridge for a similar event the following year: 'At the Commencement at Cambridge, the Vice-Chancellor and Heads of Houses made large Presents to Mr. Elford, and others of her Majesty's Musick for their fine Performance of the Te Deum of the later Mr. Purcell' (*WP*, 10–17 July 1714). The title page to *Divine Harmony* (1716), a music edition of anthems by John Weldon, 'Organist of his Majestys Chappel Royal', said that the anthems had been 'there Performed by the late Famous Mr: Richard Elford'.

Married Catherine London, 10–12–1706 at Westminster Abbey; she was buried there 15–12–1715, age 26. Her brother-in-law was guardian for her minor children Anne and Bridget, following her husband's death. The dancer 'Mrs Elford' who performed at the London theatres in 1700–6 may have been related to Richard.

Died 29–10–1714, 'in 38th year'; buried 1–11–1714, Westminster Abbey.

Newspaper obituary, *PB*, 30 Oct. 1714: 'On Friday last about Two in the After-noon, the justly celebrated Mr. Richard Elford died of a Fever at his House in Queen-Street, Westminster, in the 38th Year of his Age, and was buried last Night in the Abby Cloisters; his Corps being attended by the Gentlemen of his Majesty's Chapel and the Choir of Westminster. He was bred a Chorister at Lincoln; after which he serv'd in the Church of Durham; and apon his coming to London, he was (within a little while) received into the Choir of St. Paul's, from whence he was invited to the Choir of Windsor and Eaton; and being recommended to Her late Majesty, She was pleased to make him one of the Gentlemen of her Chapel, and distinguished him by a particular Mark of her Royal Favour, with an additional Pension of 100l. per Ann. The Places he last enjoy'd, were those in the *Chapel Royal* and the Choirs of Westminster and Windsor. His voice had all the Advantages Man could wish for, or Nature bestow, which, together with his excellent Acquirements of Manner and Judgement, render'd him the most complete and agreeable Performer produced in this Age, whether among his own Countrymen or Foreigners. His singular Humanity, Plainness and Good-Nature, made him universally belov'd; and his Musical Qualifications rarely found so consummate in one Person; and having as yet no apparent View of being equall'd, renders his loss as universally lamented.

Other references

William Croft: Preface to *Musica Sacra*, i (1724): 'I must acknowledge the great Advantages the several *Anthems* here published have received from the great Skill and fine Voices with which they have been performed, *Mr. Elford*'s Name upon this

Occasion must not be forgotten, who was a bright Example of this Kind, excelling all (so far as is known) that ever went before him, and fit to be imitated by all that come after him, he being in a peculiar Manner eminent for giving such a due Energy and proper Emphasis to the *Words* of his *Musick*, as rendered it serviceable to the great end of its Institution.'

Handel's Chapel Royal music

Named on *As pants the hart* (HWV 251a, *c*.1712, 'Eilfurt'); Utrecht Jubilate (1713, 'Elfurt'); Caroline Te Deum (1714, 'Eilfort'); *O sing unto the Lord* (HWV 249a, *c*.1714, 'Eilfort'); also court ode *Eternal Source of Light divine* (1713, 'Eilfurt' and 'Eilfort'). *Voice*: Alto (Alto 2), range *f–c''*

Other sources

Named in surviving music for more than twenty-five anthems and odes by other composers, usually as Alto, very occasionally as Tenor but of similar range. They include the following sources that relate to Thanksgiving Services during Queen Anne's reign:

GB-Bu Barber MS 5009, GB-Ob MS Tenbury 1031. Croft, *O clap your hands* (June 1706).

GB-Ob MS Tenbury 798. Croft, *The Lord is my light* (Dec. 1706).

GB-Lcm MS 840, GB-Bu Barber MS 5007a/b. Croft, *Te Deum and Jubilate in D major* (Feb. 1708/9).

GB-Ob MS Mus. Sch.b.7. Croft, *Sing unto the Lord* (Feb. 1708/9).

GB-Lbl Add. MS 41847. Weldon, *Rejoice in the Lord* (Feb. 1708/9).

GB-Lcm MS 839. Croft, *O praise the Lord, all ye that fear him* (Nov. 1709).

GB-Ob MS Mus.c.2. Galliard, *I am well pleased* (?Nov. 1710).

GB-Lcm MS 839. Croft, *This is the day* (July 1713).

John Freeman

Born *c*.1666.

Chapel Royal: Gentleman extraordinary 6–12–1700; joint place with Humphrey Griffith 5–9–1702; full place 23–12–1702. Attended Vestry meeting, 23–4–1720 (signature).

St Paul's Cathedral: Vicar Choral, probation 19–1–1701/2; admitted 2–3/1702/3.

Westminster Abbey: Lay Vicar 1715, probably from mid-1714, on death of Boucher (W2). Possibly also Lay Vicar 1692–3.

Subscriber to Croft, *Musica Sacra* (1724); founder member of the Academy of Vocal Music, 1725/6. Sang at the Sons of the Clergy Festival service, 1723, and for the court odes for the New Year and Birthday, 1736.

Married Avis Wallet at Charterhouse Chapel, 13–10–1692. She died 30–10–1732, age 60; buried 6–11–36, Westminster Abbey.

Died 9 (?or 10)–12–1736, age 70; buried 14–12–1736, Westminster Abbey. His daughter Elizabeth administered his estate; she subsequently married James Kent (B33)

Handel's Chapel Royal music

Named on Coronation Anthem *The King shall rejoice* (1727). *Voice*: Alto (Chorus leader); range *a–b'*

Other sources

Named as a soloist on at least twenty anthems, canticles, and odes by other composers, 1695–1730, sometimes as an Alto in the early years, but generally as a Tenor later; the latest is GB-Ob MS Mus.d.36, Greene, *Descend ye nine, descend and sing* (1730). He was also a soloist in Purcell's odes and stage works, 1690–5: see Baldwin and Wilson, 'Purcell's Stage Singers', 279–80.

Bernard Gates

Born at The Hague, 23–4–1686, second son of Bernard Gates.

Chapel Royal: Child of the Chapel Royal by 1697, left 9–3–1704/5 (B11). Appointed Gentleman 17–4–1708, on full salary from 1–1–1707/8, 'until a full place is provided for him' (Ashbee, *Records*, v. 100); admitted to full place 15–7–1708. He was also appointed Tuner of the Regals and Organs on 21–8–1727: this was not strictly a Chapel Royal appointment, and so was not recorded in the Cheque Books, but was of relevance when a special organ was needed for services in which the Chapel was involved. Master of the Children, 4–9–1727. Second Gentleman's place, probably from Nov. 1737, as a place fell vacant when Abbot moved to Priest. Resigned Master of the Children before 18–3–1757; retired to North Aston, Oxon., but retained his places as Gentleman. Attended the Chapel's Vestry meetings in April 1720 (signature) and May 1756.

Westminster Abbey: Lay Vicar 19–1–1710/11, sharing a place with George Laye; probably full place from August 1712. Master of the Choristers Michaelmas 1740. Resigned Master of the Choristers (only) by 29–9–1757.

Windsor: Chosen (Lay) Clerk 4–11–1714, sworn 8–12–1714; paid for *c*.7 months. Not in the list for 1715–16, so presumably did not continue.

Lived in James Street, Westminster, from 1728, where he gave occasional concerts, and probably a performance of Handel's *Esther* with the Chapel choristers in 1732. His house was also used for rehearsals of Handel's anthems for the royal weddings in 1736 and 1740. GB-Lbl RM 27.a.14, an organ book from the Chapel Royal partbooks, includes Gates's anthem *Rejoice in the Lord* with a section in his autograph, and directions for alternative treatment of the basso continuo part depending on whether the organ was accompanied by the lute.

Performed in William Croft's Odes at the Oxford Act on 10 July 1713 (*BM*, 15 July); regular soloist in performances of court odes, 1719–45, and still named (probably as a chorus singer) in 1754, 1756. Subscriber to Croft, *Musica Sacra* (1724), and to publications of Handel's *Alexander's Feast* and operas (1736–8). Founder member, Academy of Vocal Music, 1725/6; the Children of the Chapel Royal were also included in the Academy membership later in 1726. Named to examine music-copyists' bills, May

1731; his withdrawal of the Chapel boys in 1734 encouraged the Academy's move towards 'Ancient' music. Founder member of the Society of Musicians, 28–8–1739. Subscriber to Greene, *Forty Select Anthems* (1743), and Boyce, *Cathedral Music* i (1760) and iii (1773—'late Mr. Bernard Gates').

Wife Elizabeth died 10–3–1736/7, age 48; buried 10–3–1736/7, Westminster Abbey. She had been brought up by Mrs Atkinson, Bodylaundress to Queen Anne, from whom she inherited in 1726. Two children died in infancy (buried 1717, 1719), a daughter Atkinson Gates lived 1718–36; all three buried at Westminster Abbey.

Died at North Aston, Oxon., 15–11–1773; buried 23–11–1773, Westminster Abbey, 'age 88'. He left his property to a nephew, with provision for his former choristers Dupuis and Arnold if he should have no issue; Dupuis paid for a memorial tablet in North Aston church.

Obituary in *PA*, 20 Nov. 1773. According to this, Gates's father came to England at the Revolution in 1688–9 and was Page of the Back Stairs to King William III; he was probably, nevertheless, an Englishman, and continued to receive an annual pension of £40 into George I's reign. The obituary also states that Bernard Gates junior, the singer, held a supernumerary place at St Paul's Cathedral from *c.*1715 until receiving a second Chapel Royal place in 1734, but this is not supported by surviving records of the St Paul's choir.

Handel's Chapel Royal music

Named on *As pants the hart* (HWV 251a, *c.*1712, 'Gates'); Utrecht Jubilate (1713, 'Geatz'); Caroline Te Deum (1714, 'Gaitz'; also revival *c.*1722, 'Gates'); *As pants the hart* (HWV 251c, *c.*1722, 'Gates'); Te Deum in A Major (*c.*1724–6); *The King shall rejoice* (Coronation Anthem 1727) as chorus leader for Bass 2, Weely and Bell being the semi-chorus soloists in other anthems. Also named on the court ode *Eternal source of light divine* (1713, 'Gates'). Probably also a leading singer in *This is the day* (1733–4), though Handel named Abbot for the bass aria. *Voice*: Bass (Bass 2), range G–e'.

Other sources

Named on at least fifteen anthems, canticles, and odes by other composers between 1708 and 1730, including:

GB-Lbl Add. MS 17847. Croft, *I will alway give thanks* (Thanksgiving, 1708).

GB-Bu Barber MS 5007a/b. Croft, *Te Deum and Jubilate in D* (1708/9).

GB-Lcm MS 839. Croft, *O praise the Lord, all ye that fear him* (Thanksgiving, 1709).

GB-Lcm Ms 839. Croft, *This is the day* (Thanksgiving, 1713).

GB-Ob. MS.Mus.d.45. Greene, *The Lord is our light* (Sons of the Clergy, 1720 and 1722).

GB-Ob. MS.Mus.d.36. Greene, *Descend ye nine, descend and sing* (1730).

Thomas Gethin

Baptized Bridewell Chapel 30–12–1696, eldest of four surviving sons of Roger and Mary Gethin (née Gartrill); his father was Clerk at Bridewell Chapel. Younger brother

Roger baptized 6–3–1702/3, Child of the Chapel Royal (B38, left 8–7–1721). There were also two other younger brothers, Nicholas and Peter.

Chapel Royal: Child of the Chapel Royal, left 23–3–1715/16. Gentleman 9–11–1716 (scribal error 'John' in *OCB*). Attended Vestry meeting 23–4–1720 (signature). Dismissed at Chapter meeting 3–5–1731.

Westminster Abbey: Lay Vicar from (March) 1717. Resigned 1–12–1731 'going abroad to the West Indies'.

Windsor: Lay Clerk, admitted (probation) 12–10–1716. Never proceeded to place: succeeded by Prince Gregory 15–11–1717. Readmitted Lay Clerk 22–1–1718/9, with a house (at Windsor) 'to be repaired and a cellar made'. Again did not proceed to place: his name is not included by 24–5–1720.

Cannons: In lists and account books, 20 April 1720 to New Year 1720/1; absent from list, New Year 1721/2. Place as 'Counter Tenor' shared with Bell (53).

Married Elizabeth Lloyd (born *c*.1690), 21–12–1718, at St Bride's, Fleet Street. Daughter Elizabeth died 5–6–1721, age 5 days; buried 15–6–1721, Westminster Abbey. There was possibly another daughter, Mary (*c*.1722–41). Wife died 10–10–1725, 'in 35th year', buried Westminster Abbey 13–10–1725.

According to a newspaper report in *LEP*, 16–18 Feb. 1731, he had recently been 'voted in' to Royal Academy of Music: this may have been an error for the Academy of Vocal Music, though his name does not appear in GB-Lbl Add. MS 11732. The terms of his dismissal from the Chapel Royal suggests some unreliability prior to 1731; he left London for Barbados 26–2–1732, and nothing further is known of him. He was probably the 'Mr Gethin' who is mentioned as a visitor in the prison diary of the trumpeter John Grano in 1729: see Ginger, *Handel's Trumpeter*.

Other references

'Gething' (sometimes 'Getting jr') was advertised as 'Singing in Italian and English' at Drury Lane theatre in the 1724–5 season, and at a concert at Stationer's Hall in May 1725: this may have been Roger, or possibly Thomas.

See also Burrows, 'Thomas Gethin'.

Handel's Chapel Royal music

Named on *As pants the hart* (HWV 251c, *c*.1722, 'Getting'); Te Deum in A Major (*c*.1724–6, 'Mr Gething'); *I will magnify thee* (HWV 250a, 'Mr Getting'). *Voice*: Tenor; range *g–a'*.

Other sources

GB-Lbl Add. MS 17847. Croft, *I waited patiently* (*c*.1712, composed for Gethin as a treble at the Chapel Royal).

Gaetano Guadagni

Never a member of the Chapel Royal or the London choirs. Alto castrato singer, who performed in Handel's oratorios from 1750 onwards. Handel added music for him, including a solo aria, in his revision to the Foundling Hospital Anthem, probably *c*. July 1751. Range *a–e♭''*.

Francis Hughes

Year of birth uncertain, possibly *c.*1666 or *c.*1680. Appeared at Drury Lane theatre and in London concerts from 1700 onwards. At Drury Lane he sang roles in Clayton's *Arsinoe* (January 1705) and the Haym/Bononcini *Camilla* (March 1706); in *Thomyris* (April–May 1707) he alternated a role with the castrato Valentini. Left the stage in 1708, probably under pressure of competition from castrati and Italian opera in London.

Chapel Royal: Appointed Gentleman on full salary from 1–7–1708, 'until a full place is provided for him' (Ashbee, *Records*, v. 100); full place 14–9–1708; second place 1–10–1730, a privilege granted for his 'extraordinary skill in singing', and obliging him to be in waiting all twelve months of the year thereafter. Attended Vestry meeting, 23–4–1720 (signature).

St Paul's Cathedral: Vicar Choral, probation 28–9–1708; admitted 9–6–1710.

Westminster Abbey: Lay Vicar 25–1–1714/15.

Performed in Croft's odes at the Oxford Act in July 1713 (*BM*, 15 July). Soloist in court odes 1719–31, 1734. Subscriber to Croft, *Musica Sacra* (1724). Founder member, Academy of Vocal Music 1726–30.

He was frequently named as a soloist for concerts in London, and was the Chapel's leading alto soloist after Elford's death. The latest reference to Hughes as a performer in the court odes was for New Year 1733/4, by which time Rowe (65) was probably taking over as an alto soloist. By February 1742/3 he was excused Chapel Royal attendance on account of the state of his health; in October 1743 an entry in the account books at St Paul's Cathedral stated that he was 'in the Country'.

Died 16–3–1743/4 at his lodgings in Hammersmith; buried 21–3–1743/4, Westminster Abbey ('age 77'). His legatees included his sister and Maurice Greene.

Handel's Chapel Royal music

Named (always spelt 'Hughs') on the following: *As pants the hart* (HWV. 251a, *c.*1712); Utrecht Jubilate (1713); Caroline Te Deum (1714); *As pants the hart* (HWV 251c, *c.*1722); *Te Deum in A Major* (*c.*1724–6); *Let God arise* (HWV 256a, *c.*1724–6); *I will magnify thee* (HWV 250b, *c.*1724–6); *The King shall rejoice* and *My heart is inditing* (Coronation Anthems, 1727, semi-chorus and chorus leader). Also court ode *Eternal source of light divine* (1713). In ensemble movements Hughes was regularly paired with Weely (Bass), Elford (Alto 2, to 1714) and Bell (Alto 2/Tenor, after 1714). *Voice*: Alto (Alto 1), range g–d''.

Other musical sources

Named on at least twenty sources for anthems, canticles, and odes by other composers, including:

GB-Lcm MS 840, GB-Lbl Add. MS 17845. Croft, Te Deum and Jubilate (1708/9 and 1715).

GB-Ob MSMus.Sch.b.7. Croft, *O sing unto the Lord* (Thanksgiving, 1709).

GB-Lcm MS 839. Croft, *O praise the Lord, all ye that fear him* (Thanksgiving, 1709).

GB-Lcm MS 839, Lbl Add.MS 31405. Croft, *This is the day* (Thanksgiving, 1713).

GB-Lcm MS 1065. Croft, *O give thanks unto the Lord, and call* (Thanksgiving, 1715).

GB-Ob MS Mus.d.45. Greene, *The Lord is our light* (Sons of the Clergy, 1720, 1722).

GB-Ob MS Mus.d.36. Greene, *Descend ye nine, descend and sing* (1730).

Probably the same singer as 'Hews' named on Daniel Purcell, *Again the welcome morn* (ode for Princess Anne's birthday 1699/1700, GB-Lbl Add. MS 30934).

George Laye

Born 27–2–1684/5, baptized Windsor 12–3–1684/5; son of Thomas Laye, Lay Clerk of Windsor.

Windsor: Admitted to whole Chorister's place 13–7–1696 ('George Lee'); left 24–11–1703, to have £5 'as usual'. (His brother Thomas was dismissed 26–12–1705, with £5 to Croft to buy him a spinet as a leaving present.) 6–2–1705/6, 'To wear a surplice in the Choir and to have the profits of a Clerk's place until the General Chapter when, with the consent of the rest of the Canons, he may be admitted if they think fit'. 23–7–1709, sworn into place as Lay Clerk and allowed seniority over John Mason. 12–2–1755, given 10 gns. in consideration of his age and constant attendance in his duty.

Chapel Royal: 31–8–1708, appointed Gentleman on full salary from 1–7–1708, 'until a full place is provided for him' (Ashbee, *Records*, v. 100). Travelling Charges from 1708. Admitted to full place as Gentleman on or after 23 July 1712, 'a Countra Tenor from Windsor': at latest 2–10–1712, see Ashbee, *Records*, v. 102. Attended Vestry meeting 23–4–1720 (signature).

Westminster Abbey: Lay Vicar 19–1–1710/11; half place for the first year, shared with Bernard Gates.

Founder member of the Society of Musicians, 28–8–1739.

Married Elizabeth Demarin, 2–5–1709; she died 25–11–1731, age 55; buried 28–11–1731, at Windsor. At least four children, three of whom died in infancy.

Died 5–9–1765, buried 12–9–1765 at Windsor. Ann Laye (his sister) is named as executor in the Chapel Royal Fund Receipt Book.

Handel's Chapel Royal music

Named on *My heart is inditing* (Coronation Anthem, 1727, 'Mr Lee'), semi-chorus; Caroline Te Deum (revival, 1749 or later, 'Mr Leigh'). *Voice*: Alto (Alto 1). Range: a–b', possibly a–d'' if he took over all of Bayly's music in the Caroline Te Deum.

Other sources

Named in sources for anthems, canticles, and odes (Croft, Weldon, Greene), including:

GB-Lcm MS 840, GB-Bu Barber MS 5007b. Croft, Te Deum and Jubilate (1708/9). Bu MS is Laye's original performing part; he sang Alto 1 in the section for four alto soloists.

GB-Ob MS Mus.d.45. Greene, *The Lord is our light* (Sons of the Clergy Festival, 1720, 1722).

GB-Ob MS.Mus.d.36. Greene, *Descend ye nine, descend and sing* (1730, 'Lee').

Edward Lloyd

Not named on Handel's autographs of Chapel Royal music, but mentioned as a leading singer in a report of a rehearsal of the version of *Sing unto God* for the royal wedding in 1740. He performed in court odes ('Rev. Mr. Lloyd'), from New Year 1735 to birthday 1743: he had been admitted to the Chapel Royal as a Priest on 25–9–1733. In GB-Ob MS Mus.Sch.d.267c (Boyce, *David's lamentation over Saul and Jonathan*, 1736), he is named on a part for Alto chorus and solo, but in GB-Lcm MS 224 (Greene, Te Deum, 1745) he is named on a Tenor part. A word-book for a performance of Greene's *Florimel* at the Apollo Society in the 1740s (GB-Lcm XXI.c.10) names Lloyd for the role of Cupid. He died in 1755, leaving a wife and daughter.

Thomas Lowe

Not a member of the Chapel Royal or other London choirs. He was a theatre singer, and a tenor soloist in Handel's oratorio performances. Handel added an aria for him to the Foundling Hospital Anthem, *c.* July 1751. *Voice*: Tenor; range *d–g'*.

Benjamin Mence

Baptized 13–2–1723/4, St Helen's Church, Worcester. Matriculated Magdalen Hall, Oxford 6–3–1739/40, age 16, son of Benjamin Mence. B.A. Merton College, Oxford, 1746; incorporated M.A. King's College, Cambridge, 1752.

Chapel Royal: Admitted as Gentleman 14–4–1744; resigned before 8–1–1753.

St Paul's Cathedral: 2nd Minor Canon (Senior Cardinal), probation 16–1–1749/50, collated 13–2–1750/1; resigned 21–5–1767.

Soloist in court odes, 1745–9. Soloist in *Messiah* at the Three Choirs Festival in 1759, unless this was his son. Rector of Harrington, Worcs. 1749–50; Vicar of St Pancras, 1750; Rector of All Hallows, London-Wall, 1758.

Son Samuel born *c.*1743, Chapel Royal Gentleman 20–11–1762, died 1786. Benjamin may have married Sarah Henderson (?2nd wife), 20–3–1745/6 at St George's, Mayfair. Died 19–12–1796. Obituary *GM*, Dec. 1796: 'At Worcester, in his 74th. year the Rev. Joseph [*sic*] Mence, late of Kentish-Town, Middlesex, Vicar of St. Pancras and All Hallows, London Wall; in whom the musical world have lost a scientific genius whose vocal powers (as an English singer) remain unrivalled.' Mence's father may have been a Lay Clerk of Worcester Cathedral, and Mence himself may have held a similar position there from the 1760s onwards.

Handel's Chapel Royal music

Named ('Mr Menz') on the Anthem on the Peace and the Caroline Te Deum (revival), 1749. *Voice*: Alto (Alto 2), range $g–b'$, possibly $g–c''$ in the Te Deum.

Other sources

GB-Lcm MS. 224. Greene, Te Deum in D major (1745), solo 'Countertenor'.

GB-Lcm XXI.c.10. Word-book for performance of Greene's *Florimel* at the Apollo Society; Mence is named for the role of Myrtillo.

He was named as a singer in newspaper reports of King George III's wedding (1761), but is not named on any surviving partbook for Boyce's anthem *The King shall rejoice* (GB-Ob MS Mus.Sch.c.117b).

Francis Rowe

Born *c*.1689.

Westminster Abbey: Lay Vicar 1722, probably from October or November 1721.

Chapel Royal: Gentleman 15–12–1736.

St Paul's Cathedral: Vicar Choral, probation 24–1–1739/40; admitted 7–3–1740/1.

Subscriber to Croft, *Musica Sacra* (1724), and Boyce, *Solomon* (1743), and possibly to Handel, *Atalanta* (1736). Performed music by Purcell and Croft (with five other Chapel Royal Gentlemen, Charles King, and three trebles) at the Inner Temple Hall, 2–2–1725/6. Member of Academy of Vocal Music from 2nd subscription (1726); founder member, the Society of Musicians, 28–8–1739. Named as soloist for court odes 1732–3, 1735, 1737–8, 1742: at this period he may also have been one of the principal soloists in the Chapel Royal, probably as an alto and coming to prominence as Hughes became less active.

Wife Elizabeth died 4–2–1755; buried 6–2–1755, Westminster Abbey.

Died 27–4–1755; buried 1–5–1755, Westminster Abbey ('age 66'). In his will (changed just before wife's death) he was 'of Smith Square, Westminster.' He left his estate, including lands in Simondsbury, Dorset, to Richard Buck of Lincoln's Inn, and also £50 each to the Westminster Infirmary and the Foundling Hospital; the only relative named was his sister-in-law Jane.

Not named on Handel's Chapel Royal music, but (as 'Mr Row') on his autographs of the Cannons Te Deum and *Acis and Galatea* (Cannons, 1718), and also possibly on the Cannons anthem HWV 253. His name does not appear in any of the surviving receipt books from Cannons. *Voice*: Tenor 2, range $a–a'$ (Te Deum). GB-Ob MS Mus.Sch.110c (Boyce, *The charms of Harmony display*, *c*.1738) has the name 'Mr Row' on the part for Alto 2 solo.

Robert Wass

St Paul's Cathedral: Chorister under Charles King (Arnold, *Cathedral Music*, 1790, i. 101). Vicar Choral, probation 22–12–1743; admitted to full place 26–3–1763 (the procedure for promotion seems to have lapsed in the 1740s).

Chapel Royal: Admitted Gentleman 13–3–1743/4.

Westminster Abbey: Lay Vicar, half place 18–5–1745; full place 2–7–1747.

Regular soloist for court odes 1745–59. Admitted to the Society of Musicians, 3–4–1748. Principal bass soloist for Handel's London oratorio performances 1752–6, after which Wass led the chorus basses. Oratorio soloist at Oxford (Commemoration of Benefactors) 1754, 1759, and at the Three Choirs Festival 1756, 1757, 1759.

Died 3 a.m. 27–3–1764. His wife had probably died previously; his estate was administered by Ann Paterson. His children were given £1 for Christmas 1764 from St Paul's Cathedral.

Handel's Chapel Royal music

Named ('Mr Wase') on the Caroline Te Deum for the revival in 1749. *Voice*: Bass; range d–d' in the opening movement, G–e' for the solo in 'Thou art the King of Glory, O Christ' (Wass not named). Wass's name was also written on the lost conducting score of the Anthem on the Peace.

Other sources

GB-Lcm MS.224. Greene, Te Deum in D major (1745), bass partbook, incorporating a short section of the 'Tenor' solo.

GB-Ob MS Mus.Sch.c.112b. Boyce, *Gentle lyre, begin the strain* (?1749), Bass solo part.

Samuel Weely

Chapel Royal: Child of the Chapel, left 5–2–1701/2. Appointed 29–6–1709 as Gentleman on full salary from 1–1–1708/9 (Ashbee, *Records*, 101), and Travelling Charges from 1709, but no record of admission as Gentleman in *OCB* until 29–10–1714 ('a base from St Paul's'). Attended Vestry meeting on 23–4–1720 (signature).

St Paul's Cathedral: Vicar Choral, probation 9–6–1710; admitted 20–3–1717/18. His nephew, also Samuel Weely, occasionally collected money on his behalf, 1733–40.

Named as a soloist in London concerts from 1708, and also as a singing teacher (*RMARC* I, pp. 71, 84). In July 1713 he was one of the soloists for the performances of Croft's odes at the Oxford Act. The latest reference to him as a soloist at the Chapel Royal is in connection with Greene's anthem celebrating the King's return, 2–11–1735, and the last reference for the court odes is for the Birthday Ode in October 1740.

Subscriber to Croft, *Musica Sacra* (1724), Greene, *Forty Select Anthems* (1743), and Boyce, *Solomon* (1743). Founder Member, Academy of Vocal Music 1725/6.

Died 2–11–1743; in an account book at St Paul's Cathedral he was reported as being 'in the Country' during October 1743.

Other references

Weely is mentioned in Hawkins, *A General History* (ii. 743, 784, 852) in connection with anecdotes about Blow, Jeremiah Clarke, and Handel. Hawkins may just have received these stories from Weely himself; see also *MT* 78 (1937), 1027.

Obituaries: 'Last Week died Mr. Samuel Weely Sen. one of the oldest Gentlemen belonging to his Majesty's Chapel Royal; as also the Choirs of St. Paul's and West-minster-Abbey. A few Years ago a Gentleman, who was of his Name, left him an Estate of several Hundred Pounds per Annum' (*DA*, 8 Nov. 1743). 'Mr. Weeley, a Gentleman late of the three Choirs, died at Weely-Hall (his Seat) in Essex. He had distinguish'd himself, by his great skill in Choir-Musick, of which he was a perfect Master. When 'tis affirm'd that he was a most agreeable Companion, a true Friend, and inspired with an universal Benevolence towards Mankind, his numerous Acquaintance will bear Witness to the Truth of this Character' (*DA*, 9 Nov. 1743).

Samuel Weely, presumably his nephew, appears in the subscription list to William Hayes, *Cathedral Music in Score* (1795) as 'Samuel Weely Esq., Weely Hall, near Colchester'; he also subscribed to Boyce's *Fifteen Anthems* (1780) and *A Collection of Anthems* (1790).

Handel's Chapel Royal music

Named on *As pants the hart* (HWV 251a, *c.*1712, 'Mr Whely'); Utrecht Jubilate (1713, 'Mr Whale'); Caroline Te Deum (*c.*1714, 'Whely'); *As pants the hart* (HWV 251d, *c.*1722 'Mr Whely', 'Mr. Wheely'); *As pants the hart* (HWV 251c, *c.*1722 'Mr Whely'); Te Deum in A Major (*c.*1724–6, 'Mr Wheely'); *Let God arise* (HWV 256b, *c.*1724–6, 'Mr Wheely'); *I will magnify thee* (HWV 250b, *c.*1724–6, 'Mr Wheely', 'Mr. Whely'); *The King shall rejoice, My heart is inditing, Let thy hand be strengthened* (Coronation Anthems, 1727, semi-chorus and chorus leader, 'Wheely'); also on court ode, *Eternal source of Light divine* (1713, 'Mr. Whaly', 'Whely'). *Voice*: Bass (Bass 1), range A–f♯'.

In all the duet movements for Alto and Bass in these works, Weely was partnered by Francis Hughes (38).

Other sources

Named as Bass soloist on at least seventeen sources for works by other composers, including:

GB-Lcm MS 840, GB-Bu MS 5007a/b. Croft, Te Deum and Jubilate in D major (1708/9).

GB-Ob MS Mus.Sch.b.7. Croft, *O sing unto the Lord* (Thanksgiving, 1709).

GB-Lcm MS 839. Croft, *O praise the Lord, all ye that fear him* (Thanksgiving, 1709).

GB-Lcm Ms 839, GB-Lbl Add. MS 31405. Croft, *This is the day* (Thanksgiving, 1713).

GB-Lcm MS 1064. Croft, *O give thanks unto the Lord, and call* (Thanksgiving, 1715).

Appendix C

GB–Ob MS Mus.d.45. Greene, *The Lord is our light* (Sons of the Clergy, 1720 and 1722)

GB–Ob MS.Mus.d.36. Greene, *Descend ye nine, descend and sing* (1730)

GB–Ob MS Mus.Sch.d.267c. Boyce, *David's lamentation over Saul and Jonathan* (1736), partbook with Tenor solos, but Bass in choruses.

GB–Ob MS Mus.Sch.c.112b. Boyce, *Gentle Lyre, begin the strain* (1740/1), Bass solo part.

APPENDIX D

The British Royal Family, 1702–1760

This appendix includes only the immediate family circle of the British monarchs. The symbol ★ indicates that the person named was not born in England.

Queen Anne's Family

Queen Anne, born 6–2–1664/5. Reigned 8–3–1701/2 until death 1–8–1714.

Married *George, Prince of Denmark*★ (1653–1708) in 1683, by whom fourteen children (including nine stillborn); longest surviving issue, William Duke of Gloucester, 1689–1700.

Anne's father, James II of England, was cousin to Sophia, wife of Ernst August of Hanover and mother of King George I.

King George I's Family

King George I★ (Georg Ludwig), born 28–5–1660. Reigned 1–8–1714 until death 11–6–1727. Visited England 1680–1. Arrived in Britain, as King of Great Britain, in September 1714; thereafter settled in London, but visited Hanover in 1716–17, 1719, 1723–4, and 1725–6. Died at Osnabrück on journey to Hanover in 1727.

Married Sophia Dorothea, daughter of Georg Wilhelm, Duke of Celle, in 1682. Marriage dissolved 1694; Sophia Dorothea was never Queen of Great Britain.

Two children:

(1) *George August*★, King George II of Great Britain, born 1683—see below.

(2) *Sophia Dorothea*★, born 1687. Married Friedrich Wilhelm I (King in Prussia from 1713) in 1706, by whom nine children, including Friedrich II ('The Great'), King of Prussia from 1740.

King George II's Family

King George II★ (Georg August), born 30–10–1683. Accompanied King George I to London in 1714, and created Prince of Wales soon after arrival. Reigned 11–6–1727 until his death, 25–10–1760. Settled in London from 1714, but visited Hanover twelve times between 1729 and 1755. Handel's anthems HWV 258–61 were composed for his coronation (with Queen Caroline), 11–10–1727.

Married *Wilhelmine Caroline★* (born 1–3–1682/3), daughter of Johann, Margrave of Brandenburg-Anspach, in 1705. Caroline followed her husband to London, arriving in October 1714, as Princess of Wales. Queen of Great Britain from 1727 until her death, 20–11–1737. Handel's anthem HWV 264 was composed for her funeral, 17–12–1737.

There were nine children of King George II and Queen Caroline:

Children born in Germany, before 1714

(1) *Frederick Louis★*, born 20–1–1706/7. Created Duke of Gloucester in 1716 and Prince of Wales in 1728. Came to England in December 1728, where he remained until his death, 20–3–1750/1. Since he died before his father, Frederick never became King of Great Britain. His eldest son and second child, George (born 4–6–1738), succeeded as King George III in 1760. Frederick married Augusta, daughter of Frederick II Duke of Saxe-Gotha, 27–4–1736 at the Chapel Royal; for that occasion Handel composed *Sing unto God*, HWV 263.

(2) *Anne★*, born 2–11–1709. Came to London with her mother, October 1714. Princess Royal. Married Willem, Prince of Orange-Nassau, 14–3–1733/4 at the French Chapel, St James's Palace; for that occasion Handel composed *This is the day*, HWV 262. Died in the Netherlands, 12–1–1759.

(3) *Amelia★* (Amalie), born 10–7–1711. Came to London with her mother, October 1714. Died 31–10–1786.

(4) *Caroline Elizabeth★*, born 10–6–1713. Too young to accompany her mother to England in 1714: brought over from Hanover, May 1715. Died 28–12–1757.

The three daughters above were retained at St James's Palace in December 1717 by King George I, and remained with the King for the period during which their parents were refused residence at the Palace. Handel was appointed Musick Master to these three Princesses, probably *c*.1723; the appointment was renewed in 1727 at the beginning of the reign of King George II, and he retained the post (to a gradually diminishing number of Princesses) until his death. Handel's duties may not have extended officially to the other royal children, whose Musick Master is named as 'Weber' or 'Webber'.

Children born in England, after 1714

(5) One stillborn son, 9–11–1716.

(6) *George William*, born 2–11–1717, died 6–2–1717/18. An incident at his christening precipitated the separation between King George I and George, Prince of Wales.

(7) *William Augustus*, born 15–4–1721. Duke of Cumberland. Died 31–10–1765.

(8) *Mary*, born 22–2–1722/3. Married Friedrich of Hesse-Cassel in 1740, who succeeded as Landgrave Friedrich II in 1760. Betrothal service, bridegroom by

proxy, at the Chapel Royal, 8–5–1740; for that occasion Handel produced a wedding anthem comprising movements from HWV 262 and 263. Died 14–1–1772.

(9) *Louisa*, born 7–12–1724. In 1743 married Frederick, King of Denmark from 1746. (Betrothal in Hanover, marriage in Christiansborg.) Died 8–12–1751. Handel's Suites HWV 447 and 452 may have been composed for her, *c*.1739.

APPENDIX E

Thanksgiving Services during Queen Anne's Reign

Date	Occasion	Location of royal service	Psalms and canticles[a]	Music[b]
12–11–1702	Signal successes of Her Majesty's Forces	St Paul's Cathedral	Pss. 33, 98, 145 Te Deum and Jubilate	Purcell, Te Deum and Jubilate in D 'several other anthems'
7–9–1704	Victory at Blenheim	St Paul's Cathedral	Pss. 75, 76, 144 Te Deum and Jubilate	[?Purcell] Te Deum [and Jubilate], 'perform'd by her Majesty's Choir and Musick' Blow, *Awake, awake, utter a song* Blow, *Blessed be the Lord my strength* Blow, *Let the righteous be glad*
23–8–1705	Forcing of the Enemies' Lines	St Paul's Cathedral	Pss. 9, 47, 92 Te Deum and Jubilate	'Musick, both vocal and instrumental' [?Purcell, Te Deum and Jubilate] Clarke, *I will love Thee*
27–6–1706	Victory at Brabant [Ramillies]	St Paul's Cathedral	Pss. 33, 52, 149 Te Deum and Jubilate	Purcell, Te Deum [and Jubilate] Croft, *O clap your hands* Clarke, *The Lord is my strength* ?Blow, *Blessed is the man*
31–12–1706	Successes of the year	St Paul's Cathedral	Pss. 21, 47, 62 Te Deum and Cantate Domino	Purcell, Te Deum Croft, *The Lord is my light*
1–5–1707	Union of England and Scotland	St Paul's Cathedral	Pss. 122, 133; Te Deum & Cantate Domino	[?Purcell] 'Te Deum, sung'; Blow, Clarke, and Croft, *Behold how good and Joyful*
19–8–1708	Success against the Pretender's invasion, and victory at Oudenarde	St Paul's Cathedral	Pss. 33, 76 Te Deum and Jubilate	Purcell, Te Deum [and Jubilate] Croft, *I will alway give thanks*

Date	Occasion	Location	Psalms / Canticles	Music
17–2–1708/9	Protection from enemies, and successes of the campaign	St James's Palace (Chapel Royal)	Pss. 92, 144 / Te Deum and Jubilate	Croft, Te Deum and Jubilate in D; Weldon, *Rejoice in the Lord*; Croft, *Sing unto the Lord*
22–11–1709	Victory at Blaregnies, near Mons	St James's Palace	Pss. 44, 75 / Te Deum and Jubilate	[?Croft, Te Deum]; Weldon, *O give thanks unto the Lord*; Croft, *O praise the Lord, all ye that fear him*
7–11–1710	Success of campaign, and victories in Spain	St James's Palace	Pss. 47, 118 / Te Deum and Jubilate	[Croft] 'Te Deum [and Jubilate] was sung to excellent Musick'; Croft, *O sing unto the Lord*; ?Galliard, *I am well pleased*
7–7–1713[c]	Conclusion of Peace with France	(St Paul's Cathedral)[d]	Pss. 85, 122, 145 / Te Deum and Jubilate	Handel, Utrecht Te Deum and Jubilate; Croft, *This is the day*
OTHER SERVICES				
23–4–1702	Coronation of Queen Anne	Westminster Abbey		Piggott, *I was glad*; Turner, *The Queen shall rejoice*; [—], *Zadok the Priest*; Blow, *Behold, O God our defender*; Clarke, *Praise the Lord, O Jerusalem*; Blow, *The Lord God is a sun*; Croft, *The souls of the righteous*
24–8–1714	Funeral of Queen Anne	King Henry VII's Chapel, Westminster Abbey		

[a] From the published liturgies (*A Form of Prayer and Thanksgiving . . .*); the Psalms and Canticles are those specified for Morning Prayer.
[b] Information on the music is derived from newspapers, journals, anthem word-books, and annotations on printed and manuscript music. Attributions to dates or occasions on anthem manuscripts are sometimes ambiguous or inaccurate, and only the most convincing ones have been followed: see Burrows, *Dissertation*, i. 46–8.
[c] Published liturgy dated 16–6–1713, the originally intended day for the Thanksgiving.
[d] The State Thanksgiving was held at St Paul's Cathedral, but at short notice the Queen went privately to the Chapel Royal.

APPENDIX F

Special Services during the Reign of King George I

INFORMATION FROM DOCUMENTARY SOURCES

All services except nos. 3 and 4 took place at the Chapel Royal St James's Palace; all services except nos. 3, 4, and 5 took place on Sundays.

No.	Date	GB-Lpro references	Newspaper references	Commentary
1.	26–9–1714	—	See Ch. 5 (Handel Te Deum)	First Sunday after the King's arrival
2.	17–10–1714	—	See Ch. 5 (Handel Te Deum)	First Sunday after the arrival of Princess Caroline
3.	20–10–1714	£18 paid to Croft for 'pricking and fair writing of Musick for Voices and Instruments' LC5/156, p. 134; also AO/319 and LC3/53, p. 139.	'The Te Deums and other Hymns and Anthems were sung by the Gentlemen of his Majesty's Chappel and the Choire of Westminster'. (DC, 21 Oct.)	Coronation, Westminster Abbey
4.	20–1–1714/15	£24 paid to Croft for 'pricking and fair writing' LC5/156, p. 134; also AO/319 ('for the Te Deum Jubilate and Anthems at St. Paul's') and LC3/53, p. 139.	Croft Te Deum and Jubilate rehearsed 13 Jan. (St. James's Palace) and 15 Jan. about noon (?St. Paul's). (BWM, 12–15 Jan.; Dawks, 15 Jan.) Reports of service in Dawks, 20 and 22 Jan.; PB and EP, 18–20 and 20–2 Jan.; also Boyer, The Political State, ix. 59.	Thanksgiving, St Paul's Cathedral See Ch. 6.
5.	7–6–1716	—	'His Majesty did not go this Day . . . to St. Paul's Cathedral'. (EP, 5–7 June) 'This being the Thanksgiving Day for Suppressing the late unnatural Rebellion, His Majesty, the Prince and the Princess were at St. James's Chapel.' (Dawks, 7 June) No reports of music.	Thanksgiving. The King had been expected to go to St Paul's, but went to the Chapel Royal. See Ch. 6.
6.	20–1–1716/17	—	'On Sunday His Majesty went to the Royal Chappel and both before and after, received the Compliments of a vast	The King arrived at St James's from Hanover on 19 January

Number of Persons of Quality Ec ... There was the greatest Appearance at Court that has been known.' (*SJEP*, 19–22 Jan.) No reports of music.

No.	Date	Performers / payment	Description	Remarks
7.	15–11–1719	£11 paid for extra performers: Mr Abingdon, Mr Goodman (Trumpets), Mr David (Double Bass). 2 Practices of the Te Deum and performance before his Majesty at St. James's. LC5/157, p. 295.	'There have been Rehearsals made of Dr. Croft's Te Deum and Anthem at the Chapel Royal at St. James's, the last being made yesterday: It is to be performed before the King the first Sunday after his Majesty's Arrival.' (*WJSP*, 14 Nov.) '...was sung before the King, Dr. Croft's *Te Deum*, also a new Anthem with Instruments compos'd by him; which was admirably well peform'd by his Majesty's Choir and Instrumental Musick'. [*WM*, 14–21 Nov.) '[after the Sermon] Dr. Croft's Te Deum and Anthem were sung, plaid to by the Organs, but the Jubilate being too long, and tedious was omitted'. (*WJSP*, 21 Nov.)	The King arrived at St James's from Hanover on 14 November. Newspapers say that there was a 'numerous Appearance of Nobility and Persons of Distinction' on 15 November to compliment the King on his arrival.
8.	1–1–1719/20	—	'In the Forenoon the King went to the Royal Chapel...Prayers and an Anthem'. (*SJP*, 1–4 Jan.) 'Dr. Croft's famous *Te Deum* was sung at the King's Chapel at St. James's...There was no Sermon, but a great deal of Musick.' (*WJSP*, 9 Jan.)	New Year's Day (Friday). In the afternoon Chapel Royal soloists and the King's Musicians joined, as usual, in the Ode.
9.	15–5–1720	—	[Thursday, 12 May] 'was a Rehearsal of a New anthem composed by Mr. Clayton, in the Chapel Royal at St. James's, with other Musick, which is to be performed on Sunday next before his Majesty'. (*WJSP*, 14 May) 'Tomorrow,....a new Anthem, compos'd by Mr. Clayton, will be perform'd before his Majesty at the Chappel Royal at St. James's'. (*WEP*, 12–14 May.)	Soon after the reconciliation between the King and the Prince of Wales.
10.	13–11–1720	£15 paid for extra performers: Joseph Abingdon and John Goodman (Trumpets), William Ketch (Hautebois), and Pysenwolt David (Double Bass). 2 practices of the Te Deum and performance before his Majesty at St. James's. LC5/157, p. 396.	Croft, Te Deum and New Anthem. References given in full in App. G.	The King arrived at St James's from Hanover on 11 November.

Cont'd

No.	Date	GB-Lpro references	Newspaper references	Commentary
11.	9–7–1721	£15 paid for extra performers: Joseph Abingdon and John Goodman (Trumpets), Wm. Keitch (Hautebois), Pessenwolt David (Double Base). 2 practices of the Te Deum and performance before his Majesty at St. James's. LC5/158, p. 14.	Greene, Te Deum and Anthem References given in full in App. G.	Sermon preached by John Hoadly. Although the connection with the Spanish Peace was denied, the Spanish Ambassador also heard a Te Deum in his private Chapel on the same day. (*SJEP*, 13–15 July)
12.	7–10–1722	£7.11.6 paid for extra performers: William Keitch (Hautebois), Pessenwolt David, and Henry Rosha (Double Base). 1 practice of the Te Deum and performance before his Majesty at St. James's. LC5/158, p. 140: see App. F.	'Last Sunday the Reverend Dr. Leng preach'd before the King, and his Royal Highness the Prince of Wales, at the Royal Chappel at St. James's, where an Anthem was sung to Musick.' (*PM*, 6–9 Oct.) Also *SJEP*, 6–9 Oct. and *WJBG*, 13 Oct.	The King and court returned to reside at St James's on 5 October, following the summer season at Kensington.
13.	5–1–1723/4	£25.4.0 paid for extra performers: John Kite (Hautboi), George Angels, and David Williwald (Double Bases), Richard Vincent (Bason) and Christopher Smith (Tenor, i.e. Viola) 3 practices of the Te Deum and performance before his Majesty at St. James's. £3.18.6 paid to Handel for 'Writing the Anthem'. LC5/158, pp. 247–8: see App. F.	'Yesterday being the First Sunday after his Majesty's safe Arrival at St. James's, *Te Deum* and a fine New Anthem composed by the famous M. Handel, were performed both vocally and instrumentally at the Royal Chapel there by the greatest masters, before his Majesty and their Royal Highnesses.' (*DP*, 6 Jan.) See also *PM* and *EP*, 4–7 Jan., *WJBG* and *LJ*, 11 Jan., *UJ*, 8 Jan., and Boyer, *The Political State*, xxvii. 68.	The King arrived at St James's from Hanover on December 30.
14.	?16–1–1725/6	£18.18.0 paid for extra performers: Christian Kitsh (Hautboi), Godfried Karpa (Bason), David Beswilliwald, and George Angel (Double Bases) and Christopher Smith (Tenor). 2 practices of the Te Deum and performance before his Majesty at St. James's. £8.13.0 paid to Mr Smith for scores and parts in the Te Deum performed before his Majesty at St. James's. LC5/158, pp. 426, 435: see App. F.	'On Sunday last there was a great Appearance in the Royal Chapple at St. James's.' (*EP*, 15–18 Jan.) 'On Sunday last the Rev. Mr. Burnet . . . preached before his Majesty and their Royal Highnesses at St. James's Chapel' (*EP*, 15–18 Jan.) Similar reports appear in other newspapers, none of them referring to any music.	The King arrived at St James's from Hanover, after a bad North Sea crossing, at 10 p.m. on Sunday, 9 January.

MUSIC PERFORMED AT SERVICES 1–11

Date	Music, and scoring of orchestral accompaniment[a]
1. 26-9-1714	Handel, Te Deum ?Handel, anthem
2. 17-10-1714	Handel, Caroline Te Deum (2 tpts., str.) Handel, ?O sing unto the Lord (HWV 249a) (2 tpts., ob., str.)
3. 20-10-1714	Croft, *The Lord is a sun and a shield* (2 tpts., str.)
4. 20-1-1714/15	Croft, Te Deum and Jubilate in D (2 tpts., ob., str.) Croft, *O give thanks unto the Lord, and call* (str.)
5. 7-6-1716	?Croft, *O give thanks unto the Lord, and call* (str.)[b]
6. 20-1-1716/17	No music known[b]
7. 15-11-1719	Croft, Te Deum in D (2 tpts., ?ob., str.)[c] Croft, *O give thanks unto the Lord, for he* (tpt., str.)
8. 1-1-1719/20	Croft, Te Deum[d]
9. 15-5-1720	Clayton, an anthem
10. 13-11-1720	Croft, Te Deum in D (2 tpts., ob., str.) Croft, *Rejoice in the Lord, O ye righteous* (ob., str.)
11. 9-7-1721	Greene, Te Deum and Jubilate[e] Greene, a new anthem[e]

[a] For fuller details of the sources and attributions for the music, see Burrows, *Dissertation*, i. 250–3.

[b] Weldon's Te Deum in D major (without orchestra, GB-Lcm MS 2043) was composed at this period, and may have been performed at one of these services.

[c] No additional oboe player is recorded in GB-Lpro payments for this service: the oboe obbligato in No. 13 may have been given to violin.

[d] If the canticles were not orchestrally accompanied, it is probable that Croft's setting in E flat (GB-Lbl Add. MS 38668, composed Mar. 1718/19) was performed.

[e] Of Greene's surviving settings of the Te Deum, two seem to have originated at about this period, now GB-Ob MS Mus.d.50/Lbl Add. MS 17854 and US-Wc ML. 96 G.796 case. Both of them demand slightly larger orchestras than are allowed by Lpro payments for this service, though that at US-Wc is nearly correct. The newspaper references for the service, and for the related Sons of the Clergy performance on 14-12-1721, leave a slight doubt as to whether Greene composed the Te Deum as well as the Anthem.

APPENDIX G

Newspaper Reports Relating to Chapel Royal Services in 1720 and 1721

13 November 1720 (App. F, Service 10)

Yesterday, and this Day, Te Deum, together with the New Anthem compos'd by Dr. Cross, was rehears'd at the Chapel Royal at St. James's, on Account of the King's safe Arrival and Deliverance from his Enemies; and will be perform'd on Sunday next before His Majesty. (*WEP*, 10–12 Nov. 1720)

This week two Rehearsals were made of Doctor Croft's Te Deum in the Chapel-Royal at St. James's, which is to be performed before his Majesty the next Sunday, in Case he arrives this Week; if not, it will be deferred till the Sunday following. (*WJSP*, 12 Nov.)

Yesterday there was a numerous Court at St. James's; His Majesty and their Royal Highnesses the Prince and Princess, went to the Royal Chapel (the Lord Viscount Falmouth carrying the Sword of State) where Te Deum, Compos'd by Dr. Crofts was perform'd with a Melodius consort of Musick. The Anthem, peculiarly adapted to the Day, was also sung in Concert with the same Musick. (*SJP*, 11–14 Nov.)

On Sunday there was a numerous Court at St. James's. His Majesty and their Royal Highnesses the Prince and Princess went to the Royal Chappel together; the Lord Viscount Falmouth carried the Sword of State; *Te Deum* composed by Dr. Crofts, and an Anthem adapted to the Occasion, were both performed with a Consort of fine Musick. (*WEP*, 12–15 Nov.)

On Sunday his Majesty, with their Royal Highnesses the Prince and Princess and a great Number of the Nobility, went to the Royal Chapel at St. James's; the Sword of State was carried by the Viscount Falmouth, and the Sermon preached by Dr. Trimnel, Brother to the Bishop of Norwich; on which Occasion was performed the celebrated Te Deum, composed by the ingenious Dr. Crofts. (*WJSP*, 19 Nov.)

9 July 1721 (App. F, Service 11)

To Morrow there is to be an excellent new Anthem performed before his Majesty in the Royal Chappel at St. James's by some of the best Masters, with above 30 Instruments, and the Reverend Dr John Hoadley, Brother to the Lord Bishop of Bangor, is to preach the Sermon. (*PM*, 6–8 July)

To morrow the new Te Deum (which was lately rehears'd at Sion College) composed by the famous Mr. Green Organist of St. Paul's, will be perform'd at the Chapel-Royal at St. James's. (*WJSP*, 8 July)

To Morrow, on Occasion of the Peace with Spain, *Te Deum* will be perform'd at the Royal Chapel at St. James's; and a fine Anthem, compos'd by Mr. Green, will be sung by Mr. Whaley, Mr. Hughes, Mr. Chelsam and Mr. Bell. (*DP*, 8 July)

Yesterday his Majesty, accompany'd by their Royal Highnesses the Prince and Princess of Wales, went to the Royal Chapel at St. James's, where *Te Deum* with a fine Concert of Instrumental Musick was perform'd, and a new Anthem composed by the ingenious Mr. Green, Organist at St. Paul's, was sung by some of the best Voices; but the Solemnity was not on any publick Account, as was reported. The Lord Effingham Howard carry'd the Sword of State before his Majesty, and Dr. Hoadly preach'd the Sermon. (*DP*, 10 July)

Last Sunday the King and the Prince, and Princess [of] Wales came sooner than usual to the Royal Chapel at St. James's, where the Singing of the Te Deum, and the Performance of the Instrumental Musick took up a considerable Time. (*PM*, 8–11 July)

On Sunday last Mr. Green's Te Deum was vocally and instrumentally performed before his Majesty and their Royal Highnesses, at the Royal Chapel at St. James's, by the following Persons, Mr. Hughes, Mr. Wheeley, and Mr. Chelsam, but not on Account of the Peace with Spain, as has been publish'd. Mr Bell did not perform any part. (*WJSP*, 15 July)

APPENDIX H

Chapel Royal Services Involving Orchestral Accompaniment during the Reign of King George II

All services except those marked ★ took place on Sundays. In the years marked † the King had been to Hanover.

Date	Place	Occasion	GB-Lpro references	Music
11-10-1727★	Westminster Abbey	Coronation of King George II and Queen Caroline	LC5/18, pp. 15–16, 37: see App. I. Copying charges, extra performers and organ	Handel, Coronation Anthems (HWV 258–261)
2-11-1729	Chapel Royal, St James's Palace	Return of King to St James's†	LC5/18, p. 189; 6–3–1729/30. £5.16.4 + fees for writing the Te Deum (98 sheets); £18.18.0 + fees for 'oboes and bassoon' (5 names)[a]	Greene, Te Deum and 'new' anthem
29-10-1732	Chapel Royal	Return of King to St James's†	LC5/19, p. 64; 4–1–1732/3. £5.7.0 + fees for writing 'the Vocal and Instrumental Musick'; £18.18.0 + fees for 'oboes and bassoons' (6 names)[b]	Greene, Te Deum and anthem
14-3-1733/4★	French Chapel, St James's Palace	Wedding of Anne, Princess Royal	LC5/19, pp. 233, 235–6; see App. I. Copying charges, extra performers, and organ; also payment to Greene for anthem not performed	Handel, This is the day (HWV 262)
2-11-1735	Chapel Royal	Return of King from Hanover	LC5/20, p. 68; 5–11–1735. £67.4.8 for copying charges (Te Deum and anthem, 200 sheets) and 13 extra performers	Greene, Te Deum, and anthem Blessed is the man whose strength
27-4-1736★	Chapel Royal	Wedding of Frederick, Prince of Wales	LC5/20, pp. 134, 182, 239; see App. I. Copying charges, extra performers, organ, and arrangement of gallery	Handel, Sing unto God (HWV 263)
16-1-1736/7	Chapel Royal	Return of King from Hanover	LC5/20, p. 195; 31–3–1737. £59.10.0 for vocal and instrumental parts of Te Deum and anthem (102 sheets) and 18 extra performers	Greene, Te Deum and anthem

Date	Location	Occasion	Reference / charges	Music
17-12-1737★	King Henry VII's Chapel, Westminster Abbey	Funeral of Queen Caroline	LC5/20, pp. 308–9; LC5/21, p. 5; see App. I. Copying charges, extra performers, organ for rehearsal and performances	Handel, *The ways of Zion do mourn* (HWV 264)
8-5-1740★	Chapel Royal	Marriage of Princess Mary	LC5/21, p. 149; see App. I. Copying charges, extra performers	Handel, *Sing unto God* (see Ch. 13)
19-10-1740	Chapel Royal	Return of King from Hanover	LC5/21, p. 180; 19-11-1740. £61.10.0 for writing the several parts of the anthem and Te Deum, and extra performers	Greene, Te Deum, and anthem *I will give thanks*
25-10-1741	Chapel Royal	Return of King from Hanover	LC5/21, p. 294; 18-12-1741. £61.13.0 for writing the usual parts of the anthem and Te Deum, and extra performers	Greene, Te Deum, and anthem *Rejoice in the Lord, O ye righteous*
27-11-1743	Chapel Royal	Return of King from Hanover	LC5/22, p. 30; see App. I. Copying charges, extra performers	Handel, Dettingen Te Deum and Anthem (HWV 283, 265)
20-10-1745	Chapel Royal	Return of King to St James's[b][c]	LC5/22, p. 216; 22-7-1746. £64.10.0 for the usual parts of the anthem and Te Deum, and extra performers	Greene, Te Deum (GB-Lcm MS 224), and anthem
27-4-1746	Chapel Royal	Duke of Cumberland's success in Scotland	LC5/22, p. 217; 22-7-1746. £64.10.0 for writing the anthem and Te Deum, and extra performers	Greene, Te Deum and anthem
27-11-1748	Chapel Royal	Return of King from Hanover	LC5/23, p. 91; 21-6-1749. £60.6.0 for writing compositions for the Te Deum and anthem, and extra performers	Greene, Te Deum and anthem
25-4-1749★	Chapel Royal	Thanksgiving for Peace of Aix-la-Chapelle	LC5/23, p. 98; see App. I. Copying charges, extra performers	Handel, Caroline Te Deum (HWV 280) and *How beautiful are the feet* (HWV 266)

No further orchestrally accompanied services until the funeral of King George II, 11-11-1760.

[a] John Christian Keitch, Charles Wideman, Charles Hudson, Christian Dietrich, and Ephram Levegot Kelner, 'Hautboys and Bassoon', but probably including one or two double bass players and accidentally omitting one name. Two rehearsals and performance.

[b] Charles Wiedman, George Angel, Christian Dieterich, Richard Collet, Samuel King, John Richter, 'Hautboys and Bassons', but probably including double basses. Two rehearsals and performance.

[c] LC5/22 says 'on his Majesty's return from abroad in 1745'. The King returned from Hanover on 31-8-45, and proceeded to Kensington; Greene's music was performed on the first Sunday after his removal from Kensington to St James's: see *DA*, 19 Oct.

APPENDIX I

Documents from the Lord Chamberlain's Records Relating to Handel and the Chapel Royal

All documents are from GB-Lpro; the 'annext' bills and lists mentioned in several warrants do not survive. In these transcriptions the scribes' various forms of '&c' (for 'et cetera') have been regularized, superscripts have been lowered, and some contractions (including 'ye' for 'the') have been expanded. Some scribes also indicated an abbreviation on 'sum', presumably for 'summa': these have been disregarded. Original spellings and punctuation have been retained, though in some cases it is uncertain whether initial letters were intended as capitals.

Chapel Royal Services in the 1720s

Warrant Book LC5/158, p. 140

These are to Pray and require You to Pay or Cause to be paid to Mr: William Keitch Hautboi, Mr: Pessenwolt David and Henry Rosha Double Base the sum of sev'n Pounds Eleven Shillings and Six Pence for their attending one Practice of the Te Deum and performing in the same before his Maj[es]ty at St. James's, And for so doing this shall be your Warr[an]t. Given under my hand this 12th day of Feb[rua]ry 1722/3 in the Ninth Year of His Majesty's Reign.
To Charles Stanhope Esq. &c.   Holles Newcastle
Marginal entry: Hauteboi & Double Base for performing in the Te Deum at St James's
   £7.11.6

Appointments Book LC3/63, p. 282 (see Fig. 7.1)

These are to require You to Swear and Admit Mr: George Hendall into the place and quality of Composer of Musick for his Majesty's Chappel Royal To have hold Exercise, and Enjoy the said place together with all rights, Profitts, Privileges, and Advantages thereunto belonging; And for so doing this shall be Your Warrant Given &c. this 25th day of Feb[rua]ry 1722/3 in the Ninth Year of his Majesty's Reign.
To His Majesty's Gent[lemen] Ushers &c.   Holles Newcastle
Marginal entry: Mr. Geo: Hendall to be sworn Composer of Musick for his Maj[es]ty's Chap[el] Roy[al].

Warrant Book LC5/158, pp. 247–8

These are &c. to Mr. John Kite Hautboi, Mr. George Angels and David Williwald Double Bases Richard Vincent Bason and Christopher Smith Tenor the sum of Twenty Five Pounds Four Shillings for attending three Practices of the Te Deum and performing in the same before His Majesty at St: Jame's Also to pay them the sum of Three Pounds two Shillings and Sixpence for Office Fees Amounting in all to the Sum of Twenty Eight Pounds Six Shillings and Six Pence. And &c. Given &c. this 1st Day of April 1724. in the Tenth Year of His Majesty's Reign.

To Charles Stanhope Esq. &c.   Holles Newcastle

Marginal entry: Hautboy and Double Base &c. for p[er]forming in the Te Deum at St Jame's.

£28.6.6.

These are &ca to Mr. George Frederice Handle the sum of Three Pounds Eighteen Shillings and Sixpence for Writing the Anthem which was P[er]form'd at St. Jame's before His Maj[es]ty And &c. Given &c. this 1st day of April 1724. in the Tenth year of His Ma[jes]ty's Reign.

To Charles Stanhope Esq. &c.   Holles Newcastle

Marginal entry: Mr. Handle for writing the Anthem which was P[er]formed before his Ma[jes]ty

£3.18.6d.

Warrant Book LC5/158, pp. 426, 435

These are &c. to Mr: Christian Kitsh Hautboi Mr. Godfried Karpa Bason Mr. David Beswillibald and Mr. George Angel Double Basses, and Mr. Christopher Smith Tenor the sum of Eighteen pounds Eighteen Shillings for attending two Practices of the Te Deum and P[er]forming in the same before His Ma[jes]ty at St. James's. Also to pay them the sum of One Pound Nineteen Shillings for Office Fees Amounting in all to the Sum of Twenty Pounds Seventeen Shillings. And &c. given &c. this 1st Day of March 1725/6 in the Twelfth year of His Majesty's Reign.

To Charl[es] Stanhope Esq., &c.   Grafton

Marginal entry: Hautboys and double Base &c. for P[er]forming in the Te Deum at St. James's.

£20.17s

These are &c. to Mr. [space] Smith the Sum of Eight Pounds Thirteen Shillings for Scores and parts &c. in the Te Deum performed before His Majesty at St. James's Also to pay him the Sum of Eleven Shillings for Office Fees. Amounting in all to the sum of Nine Pounds four Shillings and &c. given &c. this 6th. Day of April 1726. in the Twelfth Year of His Majesty's Reign.

To Ch[arles] Stanhope Esq. &c.   Grafton

Marginal entry: Mr. Smith for Scores &c. in the Te Deum perform'd at St. James's

£9:4–

The 1727 Coronation

Warrant Book LC5/18, pp. 15–16, 37

These are to pray and require you to pay or Cause to be paid to Mr. Christopher Smith the sum of Thirty Pounds Ten Shillings for Copying the Anthems composed by Mr. Handel for His Majesty's Coronation, Also to pay him the sum of Three pounds two Shillings and Six pence for Office Fees. Amount[in]g in all to the sum of Thirty Three Pounds Twelve Shillings & Sixpence. And for so doing this shall be your Warrant Given under my hand this 27th. Day of Feb[rua]ry 1727/8 In the first Year of His Majesty's Reign.

To the Hon[oura]ble S[i]r John Hobart Bart. &c.   Grafton

Marginal entry: Mr: Smith for Copying Anthems Composed for His Majesty's Coronation

      s d

£33:12:6

These are to pray and require you to pay of Cause to be paid to Mr Barn[ar]d Gates for the several persons in the Annext List for two Rehearsals and P[er]forming the Anthems at his Majesty's Coronation the several Sums opposite to their Names. Amounting to the Sum of Forty four pounds two Shillings as Certifyed by the Sub Dean of His Majesty's Chapel. Also to pay them the sum of Four pounds Ten Shillings and Sixpence for Office Fees Amounting in all to the sum of Forty Eight Pounds Twelve Shillings and Six pence. And for so doing this shall be your Warrant Given under my hand this 27th Day of Feb[rua]ry 1727/8. in the first Year of His Majesty's Reign.

To the Hon[our]ble S[i]r John Hobart Bart. &c.   Grafton

Marginal entry: Vocal Musick for p[er]forming at His Ma[jes]t[y]'s Coronation.

      s d

£48:12:6

These are to pray and require you to pay, or Cause to be paid to Mr: Christopher Smith for the Fifty Seven Supernumery P[er]formers of Musick at His Majesty's Coronation each the sum of Three pounds three Shillings, and for the use of the Instrum[en]ts and other expences the sum of Fifteen Pounds Fifteen Shillings as appears by the Annext Bill Certifyed by Mr. Handal. Also to pay them sum of Twenty Pounds and four pence for Office Fees Amounting in all to the sum of Two Hundred Fifteen pounds Six Shillings and four pence. And for so doing this shall be your Warrant. Given under my hand this 27th day of Feb[rua]ry 1727/8. In the first Year of His Majesty's Reign.

To the Hon[oura]ble S[i]r John Hobart Bart. &c.   Grafton

Marginal entry: Instum[en]t[a]l Musick for p[er]forming at His Majesty's Coronation

      s d

£215:6:4

These are to pray and require your Lordship to pay or Cause to be paid to Mr: Christopher Shrider the sum of One Hundred and Thirty Pounds for putting up a large Organ in Westminster Abbey for the P[er]formance of Mr: Handals Vocal and Instrumental Musick on the Coronation of His Majesty and the Queen as Appears by the Annext Bill Certifyed by Mr. Barnard Gates Tuner of the Regals and Organs. And for so doing this shall be your Lord[shi]p's Warrant. Given under my hand this 8th Day of June 1728. In the first Year of His Majesty's Reign.

To the R[igh]t Hon[oura]ble the L[or]d Hobart Bart. &c.   Grafton

Marginal entry: Mr Shrider for provide[in]g an Organ for His Majesty's Coronation

£130

Wedding of Princess Anne, 1734

Warrant Book LC5/19, pp. 233, 235–6

These are &c. to Mr: Christop[her] Smith the sum of One hundred and Four Pounds Eight Shillings and Six pence for extraordinary performers of Musick & for Copys of the Anthem for the Marriage of Her Royal Highness the Princess Royal and the Prince of Orange, as appears by the annext Bill, Also to pay him the sum of Fourteen Pounds and Five Pence for Office Fees. Amounting in all to the sum of One hundred and Eighteen pounds Eight Shillings and Eleven pence. And &c. Given &c. this 20[th] Day of June 1734, in the Eighth Year of His Majesty's Reign.

To the L[or]d Hobart &c.   Grafton

Marginal entry: Mr: Smith for Extr[aordinar]y Performers of Musick for the Marriage of the Princess Roy[a]l and the Prince of Orange.

s d

£118:8:11

These are &c. to Dr Green Organist to His Majesty the sum of Twelve pounds for an Anthem prepared for the Marriage of Her Royal Highness the Princess Royal and the Prince of Orange as appears in the annext Bill, Also to pay him the sum of One Pounds Twelve Shillings and three pence in Office Fees, Amounting in all to the sum of Thirteen Pounds Twelve Shillings and three pence And &c. given this 20th Day of June 1734. in the Eighth Year of His Majesty's Reign.

To the Lord Hobart &c.   Grafton

Marginal entry: Dr Green for an Anthem prepared for the Marriage of the Princess Roy[a]l

s d

£13:12:3

These are &c. to Mr: Bernard Gates Tuner of the Organs &c. to His Majesty, the sum of Seven Pounds Seventeen Shillings and Six Pence for attending at the French Chapel to give Orders for fixing the Organs for the Marriage of the Princess Royal with the

Prince of Orange, as appears in the annext Bill, And &c. Given &c. this 20th Day of June 1734. In the Eighth Year of His Majesty's Reign.

To the L[or]d Hobart &c.   Grafton

Marginal entry: Mr. Bernard Gates Tuner of the Organs for attending to give Orders to fix the Organs at the French Chapel for the Marriage

 £7:17:6

These are &c. to Mr: John Knoppel Organ-maker the sum of Thirty two Pounds for setting up the Organs in the French Chapel at St: James's for the Marriage of the Princess Royal with the Prince of Orange, Also to pay him the sum of Four Pounds six Shillings for Office Fees, Amounting in all to the sum of Thirty Six Pounds Six Shillings. And &c. Given &c. this 20th: Day of June 1734. In the Eighth year of his Majesty's Reign.

To the L[or]d Hobart &c.   Grafton

Marginal entry: Mr: Jno: Knoppell for setting up the Organs in the French Chapel for the Marriage of the Princess Royal

  s
 £36.6.–

Wedding of the Prince of Wales, 1736

Warrant Book LC5/20, pp. 134, 182, 239

These are &c. to Mr: Christopher Smith the summ of Eighty Six Pounds Two Shillings and six Pence Office Fees incl[uded], for extraordinary performers of Musick and for writing the Anthem for the Marriage of His Royal Highness the Prince of Wales, as appears in the annext Bills And for so doing this shall be your Lordsh[i]p's Warrant. Given under my hand this 7th Day of July 1736 in the Tenth Year of His Majesty's Reign.

To the Lord Hobart &c.   Grafton

Marginal entry: Mr: Smith for Extraordinary P[er]formers of Musick for the Prince of Wales's Marriage

 £76: 6:10
  9:15: 8 Fees
  86: 2: 6

These are &c. to Mr: Christop[her] Shrider Organ Maker in Ordinary to His Majesty the Summ of One Hundred Sixty Three Pounds for taking down the great Organ in St. James's Chapel and for provid[in]g a new Organ and placeing the same over the Altar for the Marriage of the Prince of Wales; Also for mending and repairing the old Organ and putting it up again after the Marriage and taking down the new One, as appears by a Bill of particulars hereunto annexed Certifyed by Mr: Bern[ar]d Gates Tuner of the Regals. And &c. Given &c. this 7th: Day of Feb[rua]ry 1736/7. in the Tenth Year of His Maj[es]ty's Reign.

To the Lord Hobart &c.   Grafton

Marginal entry: Mr: Shrider for the Use of an Organ for the Marriage of the Prince of Wales & for mending and repairing the Old One

   s d

£163:0:0

These are &c. to pay or cause to be paid to Mr: Barnard Gates Tuner of his Ma[jes]ty's Regals and Organs the Sum of Five Pounds for his ext[raordina]ry Attend[an]ce at the Chapel Royal at St: James's and giving Directions for fixing the Organ in the Musick Gallery there, on Account of the Nuptials of his Royal Highness the Prince of Wales and his attendance at several Rehearsals of Musick And &c. Given &c. this 2d. Day of Sep[tembe]r 1737. in the Eleventh Year of his Majesty's Reign.

To the L[or]d Hobart &c.   Grafton.

Marginal entry: Mr: Gates, Tuner of the Organs &c. for Ex[traordina]ry Disburse-m[en]ts & Attend[an]ce on acco[un]t of the Nuptials of the Prince of Wales.

£5.

Funeral of Queen Caroline, 1737

Warrant Book LC5/20, pp. 308–9

These are &c. to Mr: Christian Smith the Summ of Two Hundred and Thirty Four Pounds Thirteen Shillings and Seven pence, Office Fees inc[lude]d, for the hire of Instrumental and Vocal Performers of Music for the Anthem Composed for the Funeral of Her late Majesty according to the Annex[e]d List, certified by Mr. Handel. And &c. Given &c. this 2d Day of February 1737[/8] in the Eleventh Year of His Majesty's Reign.

To the Lord Hobart &c.   Grafton

Marginal entry: Mr Christian Smith for the hire of P[er]formers of Music for the Anthem at the Funeral of her late Majesty.

£207:18:0

  26:15:7

 234:13:7

These are &c. to Mr Christian Smith the Summ of Forty Pounds Twelve Shillings and Six pence, Office Fees inc[lude]d, being money Disburst by him for Copying the Anthem composed by Mr. Handel for the Funeral of Her late Majesty in the Several Scores of Musick for the Performers and for Royal paper and Binding and other Expences, as appears by the Bill here unto annext. And &c. Given &c. this 2 Day of Feb[rua]ry 1737[/8] the Eleventh Year of His Majesty's Reign.

To the Lord Hobart &c.   Grafton

Marginal entry: Mr Christian Smith money Disburst for copying Anthems &c.

£36: 2:0

  4:10:6

 40:12:6

These are &c. to the Reverend Mr George Carleton Sub Dean of His Majesty's Chapel the Summ of Fifteen Pounds Eighteen Shillings and three pence, Office Fees incl[ude]d, being money disburst by him for fair writing Anthems and for printing a Great number of the Same for the Funeral of her Late Majesty as appears by a Bill of Particulars hereunto Annext And &c. Given &c. this 2d Day of February 1737[/8] in the Eleventh year of His Majesty's Reign

To the Lord Hobart. &c.   Grafton

Marginal entry: The Revd: Mr G. Carleton Sub Dean of His Maj[esty]'s Chapel for copying Anthems &c.

   £14. 2.0
     1.16.3
    15:18:3

Warrant Book LC5/21, p. 5

These are &c. to Mr Christopher Shrider Organ Maker in Ordinary to His Majesty the Summ of Seventy Eight Pounds Ten Shillings for providing puting up and pulling down an Organ in the French Chapel at St James's for rehearsals and for putting up in King Henry the Seventh's Chapel in Westminster Abby for the practice and performance of the Funeral Anthem for her late Majesty as appears by the Annext Bill certified by Mr. Bernard Gates Tuner of the Regals and Organs. And &c. Given &c. this 17th Day of October 1738 in the Twelfth Year of His Majesty's Reign.

To the Lord Hobart,   Grafton

Marginal entry: Chris[topher] Shrider, for provided an Organ &c. for the Funeral Anthem for Her late Majesty,

   £78.10.0

Wedding of Princess Mary, 1740

Warrant Book LC5/21, p. 149

These are &c. to Mr Christopher Smith the Summ of Ninety Six Pounds Fifteen Shillings & Ten Pence halfpenny, Office Fees inc[lude]d, for Ext[raordinar]y p[er]formers of Music, and for Writing the Anthem for the Marriage of Her Royal Highness the Princess Mary, as appears by the Anext Bill. And &c. Given &c. this 2d of June 1740 in the Thirteenth Year of His Majesty's Reign.

To the L[or]d Hobart   Grafton

Marginal entry: Mr. C. Smith for Ext[raordina]ry P[er]formers & for writing the Anthem for the Marriage of P[rince]ss Mary

   £[sum not entered]

Dettingen Te Deum and Anthem, 1743

Warrant Book LC5/22, p. 30

These are &c. to Mr. Christian Smith the Sum of Twenty five pounds four shillings & five pence / Office Fees incl[uded] being money disburst for writing in scores and parts for the different Performers the New Te Deum and Anthem composed by Mr Handel on His Ma[jes]ty's safe Arrival from beyond Sea in November 1743 as appears by the annext Bill attested by Mr Handel. And &c. Given &c. this 17th Day of Jan[ua]ry 1743/4 in the Seventeenth Year of His Ma[jes]ty's Reign
To the Lord Hobart &c.   Grafton
Marginal entry: Mr Christian Smith for writing the scores & parts of the Te Deum &c.upon his Ma[jes]ty's safe arrival from abroad

s
£22. 7. 6d
<u>2.16.11</u>
<u>25. 4. 5</u>

These are &c. to Mr. Christian Smith the Sum of Ninety one pounds four shillings & six pence / office fees inc[lude]d / being mony disburst for the Hire of ext[rordina]ry Performers for the New Te Deum and Anthem composed by Mr Handel on His Ma[jest]ty's safe Arrival from beyond Sea in November 1743 according to the annext List attested by Mr Handel. And &c. Given &c. this 17th Day of Jan[ua]ry 1743/4 in the Seventeenth Year of His Ma[jes]tys Reign
To the Lord Hobart &c.   Grafton
Marginal entry: Mr. Christian Smith for the Hire of ext[raordina]ry Performers for the Te Deum &c. &c.

s d
£80.17.0
<u>10.17.6</u>
<u>91. 4.6</u>

Peace of Aix-la-Chapelle, 1749

Warrant Book LC5/23, p. 98

These are &c. to Mr. Christ[opher] Smith the Sum of Fifty eight pounds one shill[ing] / Office fees incl[uded] / being mony disburst for writing in Scores & parts for the different performers, for the New Te Deum & Anthem composed by Mr Geo. Fred. Handell for the Thanksgiving Day 1749 also for the Hire of ext[raordinar]y Performers for the said Te Deum & Anthem as appears by the annext List certifyed by Mr Handell

And &c. Given &c. this 21st day of June 1749 in the Twenty third Year of His M[ajes]ty's Reign.

To R[ichar]d Arundell Esq &c.   Grafton

Marginal entry: Mr. Christ[opher] Smith for writing in Scores Mr Handels Te Deum &c. 1749

£58.1.0

£. s. d.
52: 0: 6
 6: 0: 6
58: 1: 0

BIBLIOGRAPHY

The bibliography includes details of the principal documentary manuscript sources and printed literature (including musical editions) that are referred to in the book, but not the following:

(i) Class references to documentary manuscript sources, for which individual references are given in footnotes.

(ii) Manuscript musical sources and less significant printed musical sources, for which individual references are given in footnotes.

(iii) Special liturgies for Thanksgivings and Fasts, as described in Chapter 2. These have been consulted from the collections at GB-Lbl (where they are catalogued under 'Church of England, Liturgies'), GB-Ob, and GB-Llp.

(iv) London newspapers. Extracts are quoted from newspapers in the collections at GB-Lbl (Burney Newspapers) and GB-Ob (Nichols Newspapers), and the run of *The Daily Advertiser* at the Library of Congress, Washington, DC. Many newspapers repeated the same or similar news items; I have generally referred only to one version, usually the earliest or most informative text.

Detailed references for manuscript documentary materials, printed liturgies, and musical sources are to be found in the bibliography, and the notes to the tables (i. 46–8, 250–3), in Burrows, *Dissertation*. Included here are a few relevant post-1981 publications to which no direct reference is made in the book.

Editions of Handel's Music

References to volumes from the *HHA* edition are given in the form III/3 (= Serie III, Band 4). The following volumes of Handel's English church music have been published in Serie III of the *HHA* edition:

3 Utrecht Te Deum and Jubilate (HWV 278, 279), ed. Gerald Hendrie
4 Anthems for Cannons I (HWV 246, 247, 248, 249b), ed. Gerald Hendrie
5 Anthems for Cannons II (HWV 250a, 251b, 252, 253), ed. Gerald Hendrie
6 Anthems for Cannons III (HWV 254, 255, 256a), ed. Gerald Hendrie
9 Anthems for the Chapel Royal (HWV 249a, 250b, 251a, 251c, 251d, 251e, 256b), ed. Gerald Hendrie
12 Funeral Anthem for Queen Caroline (HWV 264), ed. Annette Landgraf

Also of relevance to the Chapel Royal is I/6, the Birthday Ode for Queen Anne (HWV 74), ed. Walther Siegmund-Schultze. Other *HHA* volumes referred to are I/7, *Passion nach Barthold Heinrich Brockes*, ed. Felix Schroeder; I/8, *Esther*, ed. Howard Serwer; I/14.2, *Israel in Egypt*, ed. Annette Landgraf; I/17, *Messiah*, ed. John Tobin;

II/4.1, *Rinaldo*, ed. David Kimbell; II/13, *Flavio, Re de' Longobardi*, ed. J. Merrill Knapp. All volumes have extensive prefaces and critical commentaries; the commentary for the ode is published separately, and that for the Cannons anthems is included in Band 6.

Scores of all the Chapel Royal works that are not yet published in *HHA* are included in *HG*, ed. Friedrich Chrysander, apart from the Anthem on the Peace. The volumes of English church music in the *HG* series are:

11 Funeral Anthem for Queen Caroline (HWV 264)
14 Coronation Anthems (HWV 258–61)
25 Dettingen Te Deum (HWV 283)
31 Utrecht Te Deum and Jubilate (HWV 278–9)
34 Anthems I (HWV 246, 247, 248, 249b, 250a, 250b, 251b, 251c/e)
35 Anthems II (HWV 252–5, 256a, 256b)
36 Anthems III (HWV 257 [by Greene], 262–3, 265, 268, 249a, 251d)
37 Three Te Deums (HWV 280–2)

Reference is also made to vols. 20, *The Triumph of Time and Truth*; 24, *Il trionfo del Tempo* (HWV 46a); 32, Italian Duets and Trios (2nd edn., 1890); 38, Latin Church Music; 54, *[Il] Parnasso in Festa*. For works by Stradella and Urio that were published in supplementary volumes to the edition, and to sections of the Anthem on the Peace that were included in a facsimile publication of *Messiah*, see the entries for *HG* (p. xviii), and Chrysander, *Das Autograph* (p. 623). *HG* volumes have no critical commentaries, and Chrysander's prefaces are limited in scope.

The following editions of individual Chapel Royal works (mainly available in vocal score) include information about musical sources and about the original performances:

As pants the hart (HWV 251a), ed. Donald Burrows (*NHE*, forthcoming)
Utrecht Te Deum (HWV 278), ed. Watkins Shaw (Sevenoaks, 1969)
Utrecht Jubilate (HWV 279), ed. Watkins Shaw (*NHE*, 1994)
As pants the hart (HWV 251c, 251e), ed. Donald Burrows (*NHE*, 1988)
I will magnify Thee (HWV 250b), ed. Donald Burrows (Croydon, 1984)
Four Coronation Anthems (HWV 258–61), ed. Donald Burrows and Damian Cranmer (*NHE*, 2002); ed. Clifford Bartlett (Oxford, vocal score 1988, full score 1990)
This is the day (HWV 262), ed. Donald Burrows (*NHE*, forthcoming)
Sing unto God (HWV 263), ed. Paul Steinitz and Donald Burrows (Oxford, 1994)
The ways of Zion do mourn (Funeral Anthem, HWV 264), ed. Watkins Shaw (*NHE*, 1979)
Dettingen Te Deum (HWV 265), ed. Walter Emery (London, 1962)
The Anthem on the Peace (HWV 266), ed. Donald Burrows (*NHE*, 1981)
Foundling Hospital Anthem (HWV 268), ed. Donald Burrows (London, vocal score and full score, 1983)

There have also been various individual editions of the Cannons anthems; HWV 254 and 256a are included in *NHE*. For the Cannons Te Deum there is an edition by Joseph Barnby (London, before 1895), published under the title *The Chandos Te Deum*.

Handel's Latin psalm settings are included in *HG* 38, without the 'Gloria Patri' to *Nisi Dominus*. For his church music composed in Rome during 1707–8, which forms a background to his subsequent English church music, the *HG* volume needs to be supplemented by *Dixit Dominus*, ed. Watkins Shaw (*NHE*, 1979); *Laudate Pueri Dominum*, ed. Watkins Shaw (*NHE*, 1988); *Nisi Dominus*, ed. Watkins Shaw (*NHE*, 1985); and *Three Antiphons and a Motet for Vespers*, ed. Graham Dixon and Watkins Shaw (*NHE*, 1990).

General Bibliography

ABBOTT, DJILDA, and SEGERMAN, EPHRAIM, 'Strings in the 16th and 17th Centuries', *GSJ* 7 (1974), 48–73.

ABRAHAM, GERALD (ed.), *Handel: A Symposium* (London, 1954).

ACKERMANN, RUDOLPH [publisher], *The Microcosm of London*, 3 vols. (London, 1808–10).

AITKEN, GEORGE A., *The Life and Works of John Arbuthnot* (Oxford, 1892; repr. New York, 1968).

ALFORD, MARMADUKE, Manuscript Register of weddings etc. in the Royal Chapels, and general common-place book recording the rules and customs governing the life of the Chapel Royal, kept by Alford, Yeoman of the Vestry 1675–1714/15 and Serjeant of the Vestry 1715. GB-Lpro RG8/10. Printed edition in Ashbee and Harley, *Cheque Books*, ii.

ALTENBURG, JOHANN ERNST, *Trumpeters' and Kettledrummers' Art*, trans. Edward H. Tarr (Nashville, Tenn., 1974). See also the review by Eric Halfpenny in *ML* 56 (1975), 399–401.

ARDRAN, G. M., and WULSTAN, DAVID, 'The Alto or Countertenor Voice', *ML* 48 (1967), 17–22.

ARKWRIGHT, G. E. P., *Catalogue of Music in the Library of Christ Church, Oxford. Part 1: Works of Ascertained Authorship* (London, 1915, repr. 1971).

—— 'Purcell's Church Music', *Musical Antiquary*, I (1909–10), 63–72, 234–48.

ARNOLD, SAMUEL (ed.), *Cathedral Music; being a Collection in Score of the most valuable & useful Compositions for that Service by the several English Masters of the last two hundred years*, 4 vols. (London, 1790). Includes short biographies of Chapel Royal musicians.

ASHBEE, ANDREW, *Records of English Court Music*, 9 vols. (Snodland and Aldershot, 1986–96).

—— and HARLEY, JOHN, *The Cheque Books of the Chapel Royal*, 2 vols. (Aldershot, 2000).

—— and LASOCKI, DAVID, *A Biographical Dictionary of English Court Musicians, 1485–1714*, 2 vols. (Aldershot, 1998).

BAINES, ANTHONY, 'James Talbot's Manuscript', *GSJ* I (1948), 9–26.

BAKER, C. H. COLLINS, and BAKER, MURIEL I., *The Life and Circumstances of James Brydges, First Duke of Chandos* (Oxford, 1949).

BAKER-SMITH, VERONICA, 'The Daughters of George II: Marriage and Dynastic Politics', in Clarissa Campbell Orr (ed.), *Queenship in Britain* (Manchester, 2002), 193–206.

BALDWIN, DAVID, *The Chapel Royal: Ancient and Modern* (London, 1990).

BALDWIN, OLIVE, and WILSON, THELMA, 'Purcell's Stage Singers', in Michael Burden (ed.), *Performing the Music of Henry Purcell* (Oxford, 1996), 105–29, 275–85.

BATTELL, RALPH, *The Lawfulness and Expediency of Church-Musick asserted in a Sermon Preached at St. Bride's-Church, Upon the 22nd of November, 1693* (London, 1694).

BAYLY, ANSELM, *A Practical Treatise on Singing and Playing with Just Expression and Real Elegance* (London, 1771).

BEATTIE, JOHN M., *The English Court in the Reign of George I* (Cambridge, 1967).

BECKER, HEINZ, 'Die frühe Hamburgische Tagespresse als musikgeschichtliche Quelle', *Beiträge zur Hamburgischen Musikgeschichte*, 1 (1956), 22–45.

BEEKS, GRAYDON, 'The Chandos Anthems and the Te Deum of George Frideric Handel (1685–1759)', 2 vols. with continuous pagination (Ph.D. diss., University of California, Berkeley, 1981).

—— '"A Club of Composers": Handel, Pepusch and Arbuthnot at Cannons', in Stanley Sadie and Anthony Hicks (eds.), *Handel Tercentenary Collection* (London, 1987), 209–21.

—— 'Handel's Chandos Anthems: The "Extra" Movements', *MT* 119 (1978), 621–3.

—— 'Handel's Chandos Anthems: More "Extra" Movements', *ML* 62 (1981), 155–61.

—— 'Handel and Music for the Earl of Carnarvon', in Peter Williams (ed.), *Bach, Handel, Scarlatti: Tercentenary Essays* (Cambridge, 1985), 1–20.

—— 'Handel and Queen Anne', *Newsletter of the American Handel Society*, 10/3 (Dec. 1995), 1, 6.

—— 'William Boyce's Adaptations of Handel's Works for Use in the English Chapel Royal', *Händel-Jahrbuch*, 39 (1993), 42–59.

BICKNELL, STEPHEN, *The History of the English Organ* (Cambridge, 1996).

BISSE, THOMAS, *Musick the Delight of the Sons of Men. A Sermon preached at the Cathedral Church of Hereford, at the Anniversary Meeting of the Three Choirs. Gloucester, Worcester and Hereford, September 7th, 1726* (London, 1726).

BLOW, JOHN, *Amphion Anglius. A Work of many Compositions* (London, 1700, repr. Farnborough, 1965).

—— *[Anthems I] Coronation Anthems and Three Anthems with Strings*, ed. Anthony Lewis and H. Watkins Shaw (*MB* 7; 2nd edn., London, 1969).

—— *Anthems II (Anthems with Orchestra)*, ed. Bruce Wood (*MB* 50; London, 1984).

—— *Anthems III (Anthems with Strings)*, ed. Bruce Wood (*MB* 64; London, 1993).

—— *Anthems IV (Anthems with Instruments)*, ed. Bruce Wood (*MB* 79; London, 2002).

BOERINGER, JAMES, *Organa Britannica: Organs in Great Britain 1660–1860*, 3 vols. (Cranbury, NJ, London, and Mississauga, Ont., 1983–9). Based on the Sperling notebooks, with additional commentary.

BOLTON, JOHN L. M., *The Vicar's Gift: The Organ Attributed to Christopher Shrider in the Parish Church of St. Mary the Virgin, Finedon, Northamptonshire* (Kettering, 1993).

BONONCINI, GIOVANNI, *When Saul was King*, ed. Anthony Ford (Sevenoaks, 1982).

BOYCE, WILLIAM (ed.), *Cathedral Music, being a Collection in Score of the most Valuable and Useful Compositions*, 3 vols. (London, 1760, 1768, 1773). Includes biographies of Chapel Royal musicians.

—— *Fifteen Anthems, together with a Te Deum and Jubilate in Score . . . Composed for the Royal Chapels*, ed. Philip Hayes (London, 1790).

BOYDELL, BARRA (ed.), *Music at Christ Church before 1800: Documents and Selected Anthems* (Dublin, 1999).

BOYDELL, BRIAN, *A Dublin Musical Calendar 1700–1760* (Blackrock, 1988).

BOYER, ABEL, *The History of King William the Third in III Parts*, 3 vols. (London, 1702–3).

—— *The History of the Life and Reign of Queen Anne* (London, 1722).

—— *The History of the Life of Queen Anne Digested into Annals*, vols. 1–11 for 1702–12 (London, 1703–13).

—— *The Political State of Great Britain. Being an impartial account of the most material occurrences ecclesiastical, civil, and military. In a monthly newsletter to a friend in Holland*, 60 vols. (London, 1711–40). Vols. 1–6 (1711–13) are entitled *Quadriennium Annum Postremum or the Political State of Great Britain*: these vols. were republished in a 2nd edn., 1718. Boyer was the nominal author/editor of the series until October 1729.

BRISCO, FREDERICK, A., ' "The King shall rejoice" (HWV 265) by George Frideric Handel: a Critical Edition and Commentary', (D.M.A. diss., University of Maryland, 1987).

BUMPUS, JOHN S., *A History of English Cathedral Music, 1549–1889* (London, 1908; repr. with intro. by Watkins Shaw, 1972).

BURNEY, CHARLES, *An Account of the Musical Performances in Westminster-Abbey, and the Pantheon . . . in Commemoration of Handel* (London, 1785, facs. repr. Amsterdam, 1964). The main body of the book has two independent series of page numbers: 'Sketch' identifies the first set of page numbers, including the 'Sketch of the Life of Handel' and the accompanying List of Handel's Works, and references from the second set are given as 'First Performance' (etc.).

—— *A General History of Music, from the Earliest Ages to the Present*, 4 vols. (London 1776–89); references are to the repr., ed. Frank Mercer, in 2 vols. (London 1935; repr. New York 1957).

BURROWS, DONALD, 'The Autographs and Early Copies of *Messiah*: Some Further Thoughts', *ML* 66 (1985), 201–19.

—— 'German Chorales and English Hymns: The Work of Three Germans in London (Jacobi, Lampe and Handel)', *Händel-Jahrbuch*, 51 (2005), forthcoming.

—— *Handel* (Oxford, 2001).

BURROWS, DONALD, 'Handel and Hanover', in Peter Williams (ed.), *Bach, Handel, Scarlatti; Tercentenary Essays* (Cambridge, 1985), 35–59.

—— 'Handel and the English Chapel Royal during the Reigns of Queen Anne and King George I', (Ph.D. diss., The Open University, 1981).

—— *Handel and the English Chapel Royal*, Church Music Society Lecture (London, [1984]).

—— 'Handel and the Foundling Hospital', *ML* 58 (1977), 269–84.

—— 'Handel and the London Opera Companies in the 1730s: Venues, Programmes, Patronage and Performers', *Göttinger Händel-Beiträge*, 10 (2004), 149–65.

—— 'Handel and the 1727 Coronation', *MT* 118 (1977), 469–73 (see also p. 725).

—— 'Handel, Stuarts and Hanovenians: Handel's English church music and the image of the British Monarchy', *Händel-Jahrbuch*, 49 (2003), 95–103.

—— 'Handel's "As pants the Hart"', *MT* 126 (1985), 113–16.

—— 'Handel's Dublin Performances', *Irish Musical Studies*, 4 (Blackrock, 1996), 46–70.

—— 'Handel's Peace Anthem', *MT* 114 (1973), 1230–2.

—— 'Handel's Performances of *Messiah*: The Evidence of the Conducting Score', *ML* 56 (1975), 319–34.

—— 'Handel's 1735 (London) Version of *Athalia*', in David Wyn Jones (ed.), *Music in Eighteenth-century Britain* (Aldershot, 2000).

—— 'Handel's 1738 *Oratorio*: A Benefit Pasticcio', in Klaus Hortschansky and Konstanze Musketa (eds.), *Georg Friedrich Händel—ein Lebensinhalt: Gedenkschrift fur Bernd Baselt* (Halle an der Saale, 1995), 11–38.

—— 'Handel's Teaching Exercises', in Thomas J. Mathiesen and Benito V. Rivera (eds.), *Festa Musicologica: Essays in Honor of George J. Buelow* (Stuyvesant, NY, 1995).

—— 'Orchestras in the New Cathedral', in Keene, Burns, and Saint, *St Paul's*, 399–402.

—— 'Of Handel, London Trumpeters, and Trumpet Music', *Historic Brass Society Journal*, 11 (1999), 1–9.

—— 'Sir John Dolben, Musical Patron; Sir John Dolben's Music Collection', *MT* 120 (1979), 65–7, 149–51.

—— 'Some Misattributed Eighteenth-Century Anthems', *MT* 121 (1980), 521–3.

—— 'Sources for Oxford Handel Performances in the First Half of the Eighteenth Century', *ML* 61 (1980), 177–85.

—— 'Thomas Gethin: A Handel Tenor', *MT* 116 (1975), 1003–6; see also *MT* 117 (1976), 34–5.

—— 'Who does What, When? On the Instrumentation of the *Basso continuo* and the Use of the Organ in Handel's English Oratorios', paper given at the American Handel Society Conference, College Park, Md., May 2001.

—— and RONISH, MARTHA, *A Catalogue of Handel's Musical Autographs* (Oxford, 1994).

—— and DUNHILL, ROSEMARY, *Music and Theatre in Handel's World: The Family Papers of James Harris 1732–1780* (Oxford, 2002).

CALDARA, ANTONIO, *Kirchenwerke*, ed. Eusebius Mandyczewski (Denkmäler der Tonkunst in Österreich, 26, Jg. xiii/1; Vienna, 1906).

CECI, JOSEPH E., 'Handel and Walpole in Caricature', *MT* 92 (1951), 17–20, 80.

CHAMBERLAYNE, JOHN, *Magnae Britanniae Notitia; or, The Present State of Great Britain*. Series commenced as *Angliae Notitia* by Edward Chamberlayne in 1668, continued by John (his son), and title changed after the Union with Scotland in 1707. All editions from 1694 (18th edn.) to 1755 (38th edn.) have been consulted. (Published in London.)

CHAPEL ROYAL, St JAMES'S PALACE. Minute Book of the Chapel Royal Fund. MS entries 1730–1837, with signatures.

—— 'New' Cheque Book [*NCB*]. Manuscript volume, with entries overlapping with and continuing from *OCB* 1721–1867. Printed edition in Ashbee and Harley, i; films of both Cheque Books, GB-Lpro PRO 28/1. *NCB* has a slightly larger format (*c*.18¼ × 12½ in.) than *OCB* (*c*.16¼ × 10½ in.).

—— 'Old' Cheque Book [*OCB*]. Manuscript volume, with entries 1561–1744. Maintained principally by successive Clerks of the Cheque of the Chapel. Printed editions in Ashbee and Harley, i, and Rimbault, *The Old Cheque-Book*. The entry for Blow's appointment as Composer transcribed in Ashbee and Harley, i, p. 45 should be dated 'March 2d 1699' (i.e. 1699/1700).

—— Receipt Book for the Chapel Fund. MS entries 1736–1810.

—— Rules and Orders of the Friendly Society of the Chapel Fund, instituted 1729, as revised 1809. MS dated 7 Jan. 1810.

—— See also Lovegrove, William.

CHARPENTIER, MARC-ANTOINE, *Te Deum Laudamus*, ed. Lionel Sawkins (London, 1996).

CHRYSANDER, FRIEDRICH, *G. F. Händel*, 3 vols. (Leipzig, 1858; repr. Hildesheim, 1966).

—— *Das Autograph des Oratoriums 'Messias' von G. F. Handel* (Hamburg, 1892; repr. New York, 1969).

—— 'Der Bestand der Königlichen Privatmusik und Kirchenkapelle in London von 1710 bis 1755', *Vierteljahrsschrift für Musikwissenschaft*, 8 (Leipzig, 1892), 514–31.

CLARK, GEORGE, *The Later Stuarts, 1660–1714* (Oxford, 1955).

CLAUSEN, HANS DIETER, *Händels Direktionspartituren ('Handexemplare')* = *Hamburger Beiträge zur Musikwissenschaft*, 7 (Hamburg, 1972).

CLIFFORD, JAMES, *The Divine Services and Anthems usually Sung in His Majesties Chappell, and in all Cathedrals and Collegiate Choires in England and Ireland* (London, 1663; 2nd edn., 1664).

CLUTTON, CECIL, and NILAND, AUSTIN, *The British Organ* (London, 1963).

A Collection of Anthems, As the Same are now Performed in his Majesty's Chapels Royal Ec. Published by the Direction of the Reverend the Sub-Dean of his Majesty's Chapels Royal (London, 1724). Anthem word-book.

A Collection of Anthems, As the Same are now performed in his Majesty's Chapels Royal Ec. Published by the Direction of the Reverend the Sub-Dean of his Majesty's said Chapels Royal (London, 1736). Anthem word-book.

A Collection of Anthems, As the same are now performed in his Majesty's Chapels Royal Ec. Published by the Direction of the Reverend the Sub-Dean of his Majesty's said Chapels Royal (London, 1749). Anthem word-book.

A Collection of Anthems used in his Majesty's Chapel Royal (London, 1769). Anthem word-book, with preface by Anselm Bayly, Sub-Dean.

COLVIN, H. M. (general ed.), *The History of the King's Works*, iv/2 (London, 1982); v (London, 1976).

A Complete Account of the Ceremonies Observed in the Coronation of the Kings and Queens of England (London, 1727).

COOPER, BARRY, 'The Organ Parts to Handel's *Alexander's Feast*', *ML* 59 (1978), 159–79.

[COXE, WILLIAM], *Anecdotes of George Frederick Handel and John Christopher Smith* (1799; facs. repr. New York, 1979).

CROFT, WILLIAM, *Musica Sacra*, 2 vols. (London, 1724–6).

—— *Te Deum*, ed. Watkins Shaw (Oxford, 1979).

CROSBY, BRIAN, *A Catalogue of Durham Cathedral Music Manuscripts* (Oxford, 1986).

CRUDEN, ALEXANDER, *A Complete Concordance to the Holy Scriptures . . . To which is added a Concordance to the books, called Apocrypha* (London, 1737)

CRUM, MARGARET, 'An Oxford Music Club, 1690–1719', *Bodleian Library Record*, 9/2 (1974), 83–99.

DAHLQVIST, REINE, 'Pitches of German, French, and English Trumpets in the 17th and 18th Centuries', *Historic Brass Society Journal*, 5 (1993), 29–41.

DANIEL, RALPH T., and LE HURAY, PETER, *The Sources of English Church Music 1549–1660*, 2 vols. (London, 1972).

DAUB, PEGGY ELLEN, 'Music at the Court of George II (r. 1727–1760)' (Ph.D. diss., Cornell University, 1985).

DAVIES, WALFORD, and LEY, HENRY G. (eds.), *The Church Anthem Book* (Oxford, 1933).

DAWE, DONOVAN, *Organists of the City of London 1666–1850* (Padstow, 1983).

DEAN, WINTON, 'Charles Jennens's Marginalia to Mainwaring's Life of Handel', *ML* 53 (1972), 160–4.

—— *Handel's Dramatic Oratorios and Masques* (London, 1959).

—— 'Handel's Early London Copyists', in Winton Dean, *Essays on Opera* (Oxford, 1990), 8–21.

—— and KNAPP, JOHN MERRILL, *Handel's Operas 1704–1726* (Oxford, 1987).

DEUTSCH, OTTO ERICH, *Handel: A Documentary Biography* (London, 1955).

DEXTER, KERI, *'A good Quire of Voices'. The provision of choral music at St George's Chapel, Windsor Castle, and Eton College, c.1640–1733* (Aldershot, 2002).

Divine Harmony; or a New Collection of Select Anthems, us'd in Her Majesty's Chapels Royal, Westminster Abby, St Paul's Cathedral, Windsor, both Universities, Eaton and most Cathedrals. Publish'd with the Approbation of the Sub-Dean of Her Majesty's Chapel Royal and of several of the Greatest Masters [probably compiled by John Church] (London, 1712).

DONINGTON, ROBERT, *A Performer's Guide to Baroque Music* (London, 1973).

EDWARDS, DAVID, and EDWARDS, JULIE, 'I'm almost Shore it's Snow!', *Historic Brass Society Newsletter*, 5 (Summer 1993), 13–14.

E[DWARDS], F. G., 'Handel's Coronation Anthems', *MT* 43 (1902), 153–5.

[EDWARDS, F. G.], 'Three Royal Funeral Anthems', *MT* 42 (1901), 169.

ELLIOTT, KENNETH (ed.), *Music of Scotland* (MB 15; 3rd edn., London, 1975).

ELLIS, ALEXANDER J., and MENDEL, ARTHUR, *Studies in the History of Musical Pitch* (Amsterdam, 1968). Includes reprints of articles by Ellis from 1880–1.

ESTWICK, S., *The Usefulness of Church-Musick. A Sermon . . . Preach'd at Christ-Church, Novemb. 27. 1696. Upon Occasion of the Anniversary-Meeting of the Lovers of Musick, On St. Cæcilia's Day* (London, 1696).

EVELYN, JOHN, *The Diary of John Evelyn*, ed. E. S. De Beer, 6 vols. (Oxford, 1955).

FELLOWES, EDMUND H., *Memoirs of an Amateur Musician* (London, 1946).

—— *The Vicars or Minor Canons of His Majesty's Free Chapel of St George in Windsor Castle* (Windsor, 1945).

FISKE, ROGER, *English Theatre Music in the Eighteenth Century* (London, 1973).

The Form and Order of the Service that is to be Performed in the Coronation of Their Majesties, King George II and Queen Caroline, . . . in the Abby Church of St. Peter, Westminster on Wednesday the 11th of October 1727 (London, 1727).

FREEMAN, ANDREW, 'The Handel Organ at Gosport', *Organ*, 7, no. 25 (1927), 52–4.

—— 'The Organ at Finedon Church, Northants', *Organ*, 6, no. 21 (July 1926), 33–5.

—— 'Organs Built for the Royal Palace of Whitehall', *MT* 52 (1911), 521–3, 585–7, 720–1.

—— 'The Organs of St James's Palace', *Organ*, 4, no. 16 (Apr. 1925), 193–202.

—— 'The Organs of St Paul's Cathedral', *Organ*, 2, no. 5 (July 1922), 1–15; supplemented by subsequent articles in 2, no. 6, 105–8 (Somers Clarke), 10, no. 38, 65–8 (W. L. Sumner).

—— 'The Organs of the Abbey Church at Westminster', *Organ*, 2, no. 7 (1923), 129–48.

—— and ROWNTREE, JOHN, *Father Smith* (Oxford, 1977); a republication of Freeman's original book (London, 1926), with new supplementary material.

FREEMAN, WILLIAM, *A Compleat List of the Stewards, Presidents, Vice-Presidents . . . belonging to the Royal Corporation for the Relief of the Poor Widows, and Children of Clergymen, from the time their Charter was granted, by King Charles II* (London, 1733).

FRITZ, PAUL S., *The English Ministers and Jacobitism between the Rebellions of 1715 and 1745* (Toronto, 1975).

FRITZ, PAUL S., 'From "Public" to "Private": The Royal Funerals in England, 1500–1830', in Joachim Whaley (ed.), *Mirrors of Mortality: Studies in the Social History of Death* (London, 1981), 61–79.

GERRARD, CHRISTINE, 'Queens-in-Waiting: Caroline of Anspach and Augusta of Saxe-Gotha as Princesses of Wales', in Clarissa Campbell Orr (ed.), *Queenship in Britain 1660–1837* (Manchester, 2002), 143–61.

GINGER, JOHN (ed.), *Handel's Trumpeter: The Diary of John Grano* (Stuyvesant, NY, 1998).

GREGG, EDWARD, *Queen Anne* (London, 1980).

GWYNN, DOMINIC, 'The English Organ in Purcell's Lifetime', in Michael Burden (ed.), *Performing the Music of Henry Purcell* (Oxford, 1996), 20–38.

—— 'An Organ for St Lawrence Whitchurch', *Choir and Organ*, 3/1 (1995), 30–4.

—— 'Organ Pitch in Seventeenth-Century England', *BIOS Journal*, 9 (1985), 65–78.

—— 'The ?1704 ?Bernard Smith organ at St. Mary, Finedon, Northamptonshire', paper given at BIOS study day, Finedon, 1996.

—— *St Lawrence Whitchurch, Little Stanmore, Middlesex: Organ by Gerard Smith, c.1716*, The Harley Foundation, Technical Report No. 17 (1995).

—— (comp.), *The Organ in the Church of St Peter ad Vincula in the Tower of London* (Welbeck, 1998).

HALFPENNY, ERIC, 'Musicians at James II's Coronation', *ML* 32 (1951), 103–14.

HARLEY, JOHN, 'Music at the English Court in the Eighteenth and Nineteenth Centuries', *ML* 50 (1969), 332–51.

HARRIS, ELLEN T., *The Librettos of Handel's Operas*, 13 vols. (New York and London, 1989).

[HARRISON, DOUGLAS], *The First and Second Prayer Books of King Edward VI*, with an introduction by Douglas Harrison (London, 1968).

HATTON, RAGNHILD, *George I, Elector and King* (London, 1978; 2nd edn., New Haven, 2001).

HAWKINS, JOHN, *A General History of the Science and Practice of Music*, 5 vols. (London, 1776); references are to edn. in 2 vols., ed. J. Alfred Novello (London, 1853; repr. New York, 1963).

[HAWKINS, JOHN], *An Account of . . . the Academy of Ancient Music by a Member* (London, 1770).

HAYNES, BRUCE, *The Eloquent Oboe: A History of the Hautboy 1640–1760* (Oxford, 2001).

—— *A History of Performing Pitch: The Story of 'A'* (Lanham, Md., 2002).

HERBAGE, JULIAN, 'The Oratorios', in Gerald Abraham (ed.), *Handel: A Symposium* (London, 1954).

HERISSONE, REBECCA, ' "To fill, forbear, or adorne": The Realization of Organ Parts in Restoration Sacred Music', paper given at the 11th Biennial International Conference on Baroque Music, Manchester, July 2004.

HIBBERT, CHRISTOPHER, *The Marlboroughs: John and Sarah Churchill 1650–1744* (London, 2001).

HICKS, ANTHONY, 'Handel, Jennens and *Saul*: Aspects of a Collaboration', in Nigel Fortune (ed.), *Music and Theatre: Essays in honour of Winton Dean* (Cambridge, 1987), 203–27.

—— 'Handel's Early Musical Development', *Proceedings of the Royal Musical Association*, 103 (1977), 80–9.

HIGHFILL, PHILIP H., Jr., BURNIM, KALMAN, A., and LANGHANS, EDWARD, A. (eds), *A Biographical Dictionary of Actors, Actresses, Musicians, Dancers, Managers and Other Stage Personnel in London, 1660–1800*, 16 vols. (Carbondale and Edwardsville, Ill., 1973–93).

HILL, THOMAS, 'The Chapel Royal Organ', letter with accompanying specification and commentary, *Church Choirmaster*, 1/1 (Jan. 1867), 10–11.

HOGWOOD, CHRISTOPHER, 'Thomas Tudway's History of Music', in Christopher Hogwood and Richard Luckett (eds.), *Music in Eighteenth-Century England: Essays in Memory of Charles Cudworth* (Cambridge, 1983), 19–47.

HOLMAN, PETER, *Four and Twenty Fiddlers: The Violin at the English Court 1540–1690* (Oxford, 1993).

—— *Henry Purcell* (Oxford, 1994).

—— 'Purcell's Orchestra', *MT* 139 (1996), 17–23.

HOWARD, PATRICIA, *Gluck: An Eighteenth-Century Portrait in Letters and Documents* (Oxford, 1995).

HUNTER, DAVID, 'Patronizing Handel, Inventing Audiences: The Intersections of Class, Money, Music and History', *EM* 28 (2001), 32–49.

—— 'Royal Patronage of Handel in Britain: The Rewards of Pension and Office', paper given at the Handel Institute Conference, London, November 2002.

HURLEY, DAVID ROSS, ' "The Summer of 1743": Some Handelian Self-borrowings', *Göttinger Händel-Beiträge*, 4 (1991), 174–93.

HUSK, W. H., *An Account of the Musical Celebrations on St. Cecilia's Day* (London, 1857).

HYDE, RALPH, 'Images of St Paul's', in Keene, Burns, and Saint, *St Paul's*, 317–34.

IMRAY, JEAN, *The Mercers' Hall* (London, 1991).

JACOBI, JOHN CHRISTIAN, *Psalmodia Germanica; or, The German Psalmody. Translated from the High Dutch. Together with their Proper Tunes and Thorough Bass.* 2nd edn., with dedication to the Prince of Wales and the Princess Royal (London, 1732). An enlarged version of the 1st edn. (London, 1722, with dedication to Prince Frederick), which was revised from *A Collection of Divine Hymns* (London, 1720).

JOHNSTONE, ANDREW, ' "As it was in the beginning": Organ and Choir Pitch in Early Anglican Church Music', *EM* 31 (2003), 507–24.

JOHNSTONE, H. DIACK, 'Handel and his Bellows-Blower (Maurice Greene)', *Göttinger Händel-Beiträge*, 7 (1998), 208–17.

—— 'Handel at Oxford in 1733', *EM* 31 (2003), 249–60.

JOHNSTONE, H. DIACK, 'Music and Drama at the Oxford Act of 1713', in Susan Wollenberg and Simon McVeigh (eds.), *Concert Life in Eighteenth-Century Britain*, (Aldershot, 2004), 199–218.

—— 'The Chandos Anthems: The Authorship of No. 12', *MT* 117 (1976), 601–3, 998; also *MT* 129 (1982), 613.

KEENE, DEREK, BURNS, ARTHUR, and SAINT, ANDREW, *St Paul's: The Cathedral Church of London 604–2004* (New Haven and London, 2004).

KENYON, J. P., *The Stuarts* (London, 1958).

KING, RICHARD, G., 'Anne of Hanover and Orange (1707–59) as Patron and Practitioner of the Arts', in Clarissa Campbell Orr (ed.), *Queenship in Britain 1660–1837* (Manchester, 2002), 162–92.

—— 'Handel's Travels in the Netherlands in 1750', *ML* 72 (1991), 372–86.

—— 'On Princess Anne's Lessons with Handel', *Newsletter of the American Handel Society*, 7/2 (Aug. 1992), 1, 4–5.

—— 'On Princess Anne's Patronage of the Second Academy', *Newsletter of the American Handel Society*, 14/2 (Aug. 1999), 1, 6.

KIRKENDALE, URSULA, *Antonio Caldara: Sein Leben und seine venezianisch-römischen Oratorien* (Graz and Cologne, 1966).

KNIGHT, DAVID STANLEY, 'The Organs of Westminster Abbey and their Music, 1240–1908' (Ph.D. thesis, King's College, University of London, 2001).

—— 'Resources for Musicologists in Lambeth Palace Library', *A Handbook for Studies in 18th-Century Music*, 14 (2003), 1–15.

—— 'The Shrider Organ from Westminster Abbey: Lord Thynne, Organ Donor?', *BIOS Journal*, 22 (1998), 40–51.

KRIEGER, J., MURSCHHAUSER, F. X., and KRIEGER, J. P., *Gesammelte Werke für Klavier und Orgel*, ed. Max Schneider (Denkmäler der Tonkunst in Bayern, 30, Jg. xviii; Leipzig, 1917).

KUHNAU, JOHANN, *Frische Clavier Früchte* (Leipzig, 1696).

LAFONTAINE, HENRY CART DE, *The King's Musick, a Transcript of Records Relating to Music and Musicians, 1460–1700* (London, 1909; repr. New York, 1973).

LANDGRAF, ANNETTE, 'Aachen und Burtscheid zu Händels Zeit', *Händel-Jahrbuch*, 50 (2004), 375–94.

—— 'Die Begräbniszeremonie für Queen Caroline', *Händel-Jahrbuch*, 49 (2003), 115–25.

LANDON, H. C. ROBBINS, *Haydn: Chronicle and Works*, iii: *Haydn in England 1791–1795* (London, 1976).

LARSEN, JENS PETER, *Handel's 'Messiah': Origins, Composition, Sources* (London, 1957; 2nd edn. New York, 1972).

LAURENCE, DAN, H. (ed.), *Shaw's Music: The Complete Music Criticism*, 3 vols. (London, 1981).

LAURIE, MARGARET, 'The Chapel Royal Part-Books', in Oliver Neighbour (ed.), *Music and Bibliography: Essays in Honour of Alec Hyatt King* (London, 1980), 25–50.

LE HURAY, PETER, *Music and the Reformation in England, 1549–1660* (London, 1967).

LEGG, L. G. WICKHAM, *English Coronation Records* (London, 1901).

LEWIS, ANTHONY, 'English Church Music: Purcell', in Anthony Lewis and Nigel Fortune (eds.), *Opera and Church Music 1630–1750* (New Oxford History of Music, 5; Oxford, 1975), 526–37.

LIESENFELD, VINCENT, J., *The Licensing Act of 1737* (Madison, Wis., 1984).

LINDGREN, LOWELL, 'The Three Great Noises Fatal to the Interests of Bononcini', *MQ* 61 (1975), 560–83.

LLANOVER, LADY (ed.), *The Autobiography and Correspondence of Mary Granville, Mrs Delany*, 6 vols. (London, 1861–2).

LOCKE, MATTHEW, *Anthems and Motets*, ed. Peter le Huray (*MB* 38; London, 1976).

The London Stage, 1660–1800, 5 pts. in 11 vols. (Carbondale, Ill., 1960–8); Part 2 (1700–1729), ed. Emmett. L. Avery; Part 3 (1729–1747), ed. Arthur H. Scouten; Part 4 (1747–1776), ed. George Winchester Stone, Jr.

LOVEGROVE, WILLIAM, Manuscript volume of memoranda kept by the Serjeant of the Vestry of the Chapel Royal, initiated in 1752 by William Lovegrove, Serjeant 1752–77. Chapel Royal, St James's Palace. Includes transcriptions from *OCB* and *NCB*, but also additional material. Published transcription in Ashbee and Harley, ii. 1–273.

LULLY, JEAN-BAPTISTE, *Te Deum Laudamus*, ed. H. Prunières, in *Œuvres Completes de J-B. Lully*, Les Motets, Tome II/ii (Paris, 1935).

LUTTRELL, NARCISSUS, *A Brief Historical Relation of State Affairs from September 1708 to April 1714*, 6 vols. (Oxford, 1857).

McGUINNESS, ROSAMOND, *English Court Odes 1660–1820* (Oxford, 1971).

[MAINWARING, JOHN], *Memoirs of the Life of the late George Frederick Handel* (London, 1760; facs. repr. Amsterdam, 1964).

MATTHESON, JOHANN, *Grundlage einer Ehren-Pforte* (Hamburg, 1740).

MATTHEWS, BETTY, 'Unpublished Letters Concerning Handel', ML 40 (1959), 261–8.

MATTHEWS, W. R., and ATKINS, W. M., *A History of St Paul's Cathedral* (London, 1964).

MEE, JOHN, H., *The Oldest Music Room in Europe: A Record of Eighteenth-Century Musical Enterprise in Oxford* (Oxford, 1911).

MENKE, WERNER, *History of the Trumpet of Bach and Handel*, trans. G. Abraham (Nashville, Tenn., 1972).

MIES, PAUL, 'Das Anthem So wie der Hirsch schreit und seine Fassungen', *Händel-Jahrbuch*, 4 (1931), 1–14.

MONTAGU, JEREMY, *Timpani and Percussion* (New Haven and London, 2002).

MOREHEN, JOHN, 'The English Anthem Text, 1549–1660', *Journal of the Royal Musical Association*, 117 (1992), 62–85.

MORTIMER, Mr, *The Universal Director* (London, 1763).

MOSS, CHARLES, *A Sermon preached at the Anniversary Meeting of the Sons of the Clergy, in the Cathedral Church of St Paul, on Thursday, May 9, 1799* (London, [1799]).

The Oxford Act, A. D. 1733, Being a particular and exact Account of that Solemnity . . . in a Letter to a Friend in Town (London, 1735).

PATERSON, JAMES, *Pietas Londinensis: Or, the Present Ecclesiastical State of London* (London, 1714).

PEARCE, CHARLES, W., *Notes on English Organs of the Period 1800–1810* (London, 1912). Includes material from J. H. Leffler's notebook.

PEARCE, ERNEST HAROLD, *The Sons of the Clergy: Some Records of Two Hundred and Seventy Five Years* (2nd edn., London, 1928).

A Performance of Musick, For the benefit of The Hospital for the Maintenance and Education of Exposed and Deserted young Children, On Thursday the 25th of May, 1749. The Musick compos'd by Mr. Handel (London, 1749). Word-book for Handel's concert, which took place on 27 May.

PLANCHÉ, J. R., *Regal Records* (London, 1838).

PLUMB, J. H., *The First Four Georges* (London, 1956).

—— *Sir Robert Walpole*, 2 vols. (London, 1956, 1960).

—— and WELDON, HUW, *Royal Heritage: The Story of Britain's Royal Builders and Collectors* (London, 1977).

PLUMLEY, NICHOLAS, and NILAND, AUSTIN, *A History of the Organs in St Paul's Cathedral* (Oxford, 2001).

PROUT, EBENEZER, 'Graun's *Passion Oratorio*, and Handel's Knowledge of It', *Monthly Musical Record*, 24 (1894), 97–9, 121–3.

PURCELL, HENRY, *Ode for St Cecilia's Day, 1692*, ed. Peter Dennison (*PS* 8; London, 1978).

—— *Sacred Music, Part 1: Nine Anthems with Orchestral Accompaniment*, ed. Peter Dennison (*PS* 13; London, 1988). [Includes anthems with strings Z. 3, 28]

—— *Sacred Music, Part II*, ed. Peter Dennison (*PS* 14; London, 1973). [Anthems with strings Z. 1, 16, 18, 19, 29, 42, 47, 49, 55]

—— *Sacred Music, Part III: Seven Anthems with Strings*, ed. H. E. Wooldridge and G. E. P. Arkwright, rev. Nigel Fortune (*PS* 17; London, 1964). [Anthems Z. 20, 30, 44, 46, 48, 63, 65]

—— *Services*, ed. Alan Gray (*PS* 23; London, 1923). [Includes Te Deum and Jubilate in D major]

—— *Sacred Music, Part IV: Anthems*, ed. Anthony Lewis and Nigel Fortune (*PS* 28; London, 1959). [Anthems with strings Z. 2, 5, 21]

—— *Sacred Music, Part V: Anthems*, ed. Anthony Lewis and Nigel Fortune (*PS* 29; London, 1960). [Anthems with strings Z. 31, 38]

—— *Sacred Music, Part VII: Anthems and Miscellaneous Church Music*, ed. Anthony Lewis and Nigel Fortune (*PS* 32; London, 1962). [Anthems with strings Z. 57, 60; also Funeral Sentence Z. 58C]

—— *Sonnata's of III Parts* (London, 1683; facs. repr. Cambridge, 1975).

PUTTICK and SIMPSON, *Catalogue of the very important and interesting musical collection of a distinguished amateur . . . to which are added the well known and very important series of Handel's works written . . . for his friend and patron Bernard Granville Esq . . . and (from another collection) a Gloria also in Handel's autograph etc. Friday January 29st* [sic] *1858 and the following day* (London, 1858).

REDINGTON, JOSEPH (prepared by), *Calendar of Treasury Papers, 1556/7–1728*, 6 vols. (London, 1868–89) (series continued by W. A. Shaw; see below).

REID, DOUGLAS J. [assisted by Brian Pritchard], 'Some Festival Performances of the Eighteenth and Nineteenth Centuries. 1. Salisbury and Winchester', *RMARC* 5, pp. 51–79; Addenda and Corrigidenda by Arthur D. Walker, *RMARC* 6, p. 23, and by Betty Matthews, *RMARC* 8, pp. 23–33.

RIMBAULT, EDWARD, F. (ed.), *The Old Cheque-Book or Book of Remembrance of The Chapel Royal from 1561 to 1744* (London, 1872; facs. repr. New York, 1966).

ROBERTS, JOHN, H., 'The Aylesford Collection', in Terence Best (ed.), *Handel Collections and their History* (Oxford, 1993), 39–85.

—— 'German Chorales in Handel's English Works' *Händel-Jahrbuch*, 42–3 (1996–7), 77–100.

—— 'Handel's Borrowings from Telemann: An Inventory', *Göttinger Händel-Beiträge*, 1 (1984), 147–71.

—— (ed.), *Handel Sources: Materials for the Study of Handel's Borrowing*, 9 vols. (New York and London, 1986).

ROBINSON, PERCY, *Handel and his Orbit* (London, 1908).

ROGERS, PATRICK, 'Dating Acis and Galatea', *MT* 114 (1973), 792.

SADIE, STANLEY, (ed.), *The New Grove Dictionary of Opera*, 4 vols. (London, 1992).

SANDFORD, FRANCIS, *The History of the Coronation of the Most High, Most Mighty and Most Excellent Monarch, James II . . . and of His Royal Consort Queen Mary: Solemnised in the Collegiate Church of St. Peter in the City of Westminster on Thursday the 23d of April, . . . in the Year of Our Lord 1685* (London, 1687).

SCANDRETT, ROBERT, L., 'The Anthems of William Croft (1678–1727)' (Ph.D. diss., University of Washington, 1961).

SCHAZMANN, PAUL-EMILE, *The Bentincks: The History of a European Family*, trans. Steve Cox (London, 1976).

SCHERING, ARNOLD, 'Händel und der protestantische Choral', *Händel-Jahrbuch*, 1 (1928), 27–40.

SCHOELCHER, VICTOR, *The Life of Handel* (London, 1857).

SEDGWICK, ROMNEY, (ed.), *Some Materials towards Memoirs of the Reign of King George II by John, Lord Hervey*, 3 vols. with continuous pagination (London, 1931).

See and Seem Blind: Or, A Critical Dissertation on the Publick Diversions, &c. (London, [1732]).

SHAPIRO, ALEXANDER HERMAN, ' "Drama of an Infinitely Superior Nature": Handel's Early English Oratorios and the Religious Sublime', *ML* 74 (May 1993), 214–45.

SHAPIRO, ALEXANDER HERMAN, 'Drama of an Infinitely Superior Nature: Handel's First English Oratorios to Eighteenth-Century Sacred Music Theory and Practice' (M.Litt. diss., University of Cambridge, 1988).

SHAW, H. WATKINS, *A Textual and Historical Companion to Handel's 'Messiah'* (London, 1965).

—— 'Some Original Performing Material for Handel's Latin Church Music', *Göttinger Händel-Beiträge*, 2 (1986), 226–33.

—— *The Succession of Organists of the Chapel Royal and the Cathedrals of England and Wales from c.1538* (Oxford, 1991).

—— *The Three Choirs Festival* (Worcester and London, 1954).

—— and DIXON, GRAHAM, 'Handel's Vesper Music', *MT* 126 (1985), 392–7.

SHAW, WILLIAM, A. (prepared by), *Calendar of Treasury Books, 1669–1718*, 32 vols. (London, 1904–57). Vols. 16–32 cover the years 1700–18.

—— (prepared by), *Calendar of Treasury Books and Papers, 1729–45*, 5 vols. (London, 1897–1902). Series continued from Redington; see above.

SHEPPARD, EDGAR, *Memorials of St. James's Palace*, 2 vols. (London, 1894).

SIMON, JACOB (ed.), *Handel: A Celebration of his Life and Times* (London, 1985).

SIMPSON, W. SPARROW (ed.), *Documents Illustrating the History of S. Paul's Cathedral* (Camden Society, 24; 1880).

SMALLMAN, BASIL, *The Background of Passion Music: J. S. Bach and his Predecessors* (2nd edn., London, 1970).

SMITH, GREGORY, (ed.), *The Spectator*, 4 vols. (rev. edn., London, 1945).

SMITH, RUTH, *Handel's Oratorios and Eighteenth-Century Thought* (Cambridge, 1995).

—— 'The Argument and Contexts of Dryden's *Alexander's Feast*', *Studies in English Literature*, 18 (1978), 465–90.

SMITH, WILLIAM, C., *A Bibliography of the Musical Works Published by John Walsh during the Years 1695–1720* (London, 1968).

—— *Concerning Handel, his Life and Works* (London, 1948).

—— 'George III, Handel and Mainwaring', *MT* 65 (1924), 789–95.

—— assisted by Charles Humphries, *Handel: A Descriptive Catalogue of the Early Editions* (2nd edn. with supp.; Oxford, 1970).

SMITHERS, DON, L., *The Music and History of the Baroque Trumpet before 1721* (2nd edn., Carbondale and Edwardsville, Ill., 1988).

SPINK, IAN, *Restoration Cathedral Music 1660–1714* (Oxford, 1995).

Stanley, Arthur Penrhyn, *Historical Memorials of Westminster Abbey* (6th edn., London, 1886).

Sumner, W. L., *A History and Account of the Organs of St Paul's Cathedral, London* (London, 1931).

Swift, Jonathan, *The Correspondence of Jonathan Swift*, ed. Harold Williams, 4 vols. (Oxford, 1963).

Sykes, Norman, *Church and State in England in the Eighteenth Century* (Cambridge, 1934).

—— *Edmund Gibson, Bishop of London, 1669–1748* (London, 1926).

—— *William Wake, Archbishop of Canterbury, 1657–1737* (Cambridge, 1957).

Taylor, Carole, 'Handel and Frederick, Prince of Wales', *MT* 125 (1984), 89–92.

—— 'Italian Opera-going in London, 1700–1745' (Ph.D. diss, Syracuse University, 1991).

Taylor, Thomas, F., *Thematic Catalog of the Works of Jeremiah Clarke* (Detroit, 1977).

Timms, Colin, 'Handel and Steffani', *MT* 114 (1973), 374–7.

—— *Polymath of the Baroque: Agostino Steffani and his Music* (Oxford, 2003).

Wallbrecht, Rosenmarie Elisabeth, *Das Theater des Barockzeitalters an den welfischen Höfen Hannover und Celle* (Quellen und Darstellungen, 83; Hildesheim, 1974).

Walsh, John, Haydon, Colin, and Taylor, Stephen, (eds.), *The Church of England c.1689–c.1833: From Toleration to Tractarianism* (Cambridge, 1993).

Webb, John, 'The Flat Trumpet in Perspective', *GSJ* 46 (1993), 154–60.

Weedon, Cavendish, *The Oration and Poem Spoken at the Entertainment of Divine Music Perform'd at Stationer's-Hall on Tuesday the 6th of Jan. 1702.* (London, 1702).

—— *The Oration, Anthems & Poems, Spoken and Sung at the Performance of Divine Musick at Stationers-Hall, for the Month of May, 1702. Undertaken by Cavendish Weedon, Esq.* (London, 1702).

—— *The Oration, Anthems and Poems, Spoken and Sung at the Performance of Divine Musick. For the Entertainment of the Lords Spiritual & Temporal, And the Honourable House of Commons. At Stationers-Hall, January the 31st 1701* [i.e. 1700/1] *Undertaken by Cavendish Weedon Esq.* (London, 1602 [*recte* 1702]).

Weldon, John, *Divine Harmony*[.] *Six Select Anthems for a Voice alone with a Thorow Bass for the Organ, Harpsicord or Arch-Lute Compos'd on several Occasions by Mr. Jno Weldon Organist of his majesty's Chappell Royal and there Performed by the late Famous Mr. Richard Elford* (London, 1716). Included a frontispiece 'The Sacred Choire', possibly representing a Chapel Royal in the previous century. A second collection 'Compos'd by Several Eminent Masters' followed in 1717. These musical publications were distinct from *Divine Harmony* (1712), a word-book of anthems.

Wilkinson, Robert (publisher), *Londina Illustrata. Graphic and historic memorials of monasteries, churches, chapels . . . in the cities of London and Westminster*, 2 vols. (London, 1819).

Bibliography

WILLIAMS, E. NEVILLE, *The Eighteenth-Century Constitution, 1688–1815: Documents and Commentary* (Cambridge, 1960).

WILLIAMS, NEVILLE, *Elizabeth, Queen of England* (London, 1967).

WILSON, JOHN, *Roger North on Music* (London, 1959).

WOOD, BRUCE, 'John Blow's Anthems with Orchestra' (Ph.D. diss., University of Cambridge, 1977).

[WREN, CHRISTOPHER] *Publications of the Wren Society*, 20 vols. (Oxford, 1924–32). Vols. i, ii, xiii, xiv, xvi include material relating to St Paul's Cathedral; vol. vii includes some on St James's Palace.

YOUNG, PERCY, M., 'The First Hundred Years', in Barry Still (ed.), *Two Hundred and Fifty Years of the Three Choirs Festival* (Gloucester, 1977), 9–15.

ZACHOW [ZACHAU], FRIEDRICH WILHELM, *Gesammelte Werke*, ed. Max Seiffert, rev. Hans Joachim Moser (Denkmäler deutscher Tonkunst, 1, Folge 21–2, reissued in 1 vol.; Wiesbaden, 1958).

ZIMMERMAN, FRANKLIN, B., 'Anthems of Purcell and Contemporaries in a Newly Rediscovered Gostling Manuscript', *Acta musicologica*, 41 (1969), 55–70.

—— *Henry Purcell, 1659–1695, an Analytical Catalogue of his Music* (London, 1963).

INDEX OF HANDEL'S WORKS

INDEX

This includes all personal names from the Appendices. Unless stated otherwise, all royal names and titles are English/British, and all ecclesiastical offices (e.g. Sub-Dean) refer to the Chapel Royal; alternative titles are given if they appear in the book. Office-holders are indexed under the forms that they appear in the text. Numbers in brackets refer to the lists in Appendix B.